John Osborne

JOHN OSBORNE

'Anger is not about ...'

PETER WHITEBROOK

First published in 2015 by Oberon Books Ltd
521 Caledonian Road, London N7 9RH
Tel: +44 (0) 20 7607 3637 / Fax: +44 (0) 20 7607 3629
e-mail: info@oberonbooks.com
www.oberonbooks.com

A catalogue record for this book is available from the British Library.

HB ISBN: 978-1-78319-877-1
E ISBN: 978-1-78319-876-4

Visit www.oberonbooks.com to read more about all our books and to buy them.
You will also find features, author interviews and news of any author events,
and you can sign up for e-newsletters so that you're always first to hear about our
new releases.

Cover photo by Nobby Clark
Cover design by James Illman
Text designed and typeset by Caroline Waldron, Wirral, Cheshire
Printed, bound and converted by CPI Group (UK) Ltd, Croydon, CR0 4YY.

Contents

List of Illustrations   vii

PART 1: BEGINNINGS   1

1   A New Start   3
2   A Sense of Loss   12
3   Charity's Child   17
4   The Journalist   30
5   The Actor   40
6   Bridgwater Bound   51
7   Repertory   61
8   Doomed in Derby   72
9   Creation   82
10 Royal Court   93
11 The Year of the Angry Young Man   108

PART 2: EXTRAVAGANCE   125

12 The King at the Court   127
13 Transatlantic   144
14 Black and White   154
15 The Battle of Cambridge Circus   162
16 Betrayal   172
17 Protest   190
18 Other Englands   200
19 A Sixties Millionaire   210
20 Of Mother, Money, Marriage and Manners   224
21 The Baron Who Went Too Far   233

PART 3: RESILIENCE   247

22 Love and Loss   249
23 The Cavalry and the Law   262
24 Fearing the Future   268
25 Detachment   277
26 Despair   289
27 Desolation   301
28 Retrenching   306
29 Defiance   323
30 Redemption   340
31 Afterlife   352

    Bibliography   363
    Notes   369
    Acknowledgements   401
    Index   403

List of Illustrations

1.)   John Osborne aged three, 1933. (Estate of John Osborne)

2.)   John Osborne and Tom Godfrey, early 1930s. (Estate of John Osborne)

3.)   John Osborne as a teenager with Nellie Beatrice, later 1940s. (Estate of John Osborne)

4.)   Nellie Beatrice behind the bar. (Estate of John Osborne)

5.)   John Osborne and Pamela Lane (left) at Derby Playhouse, 1954. (Raymonds News Agency)

6.)   Pamela Lane.

7.)   Programmes from the Kidderminster Playhouse 1952 and the Royal Court Theatre, 1956 and 1958.

8.)   John Osborne aboard the houseboat, River Thames 1956. (Frank Pocklington/ Getty)

9.)   John Osborne at the Royal Court Theatre, 1957. (Bob Willoughby)

10.) George Devine. (Ida Kar)

11.) Tony Richardson. (Sandra Lousada)

12.) Harold Hobson.

13.) Kenneth Tynan. (Elsbeth R. Juda/V&A Images)

14.) Kenneth Haigh (*left*) and John Osborne outside the Royal Court Theatre, 1956.

15.) Jimmy Porter (Kenneth Haigh, *left*), Cliff (Alan Bates, *centre*) and Alison (Mary Ure, right) in the first production of *Look Back in Anger*, 1956. (Picture Post)

16.) The poster for the film of *Look Back in Anger*, 1959. (Getty)

17.)   The opening scene of the film of *Look Back in Anger*. Cliff (Gary Raymond) and Sally (Bernice Swanson) look on as Jimmy Porter (Richard Burton) plays the trumpet. (AE Archive/Alamy)

18.)   John Osborne Mary Ure, Vivien Leigh and Laurence Olivier, 1957.

19.)   Laurence Olivier as Archie Rice, 1957. (John Franks/Getty)

20.)   The press reports John Osborne and Mary Ure's romance.

21.)   John Osborne and Mary Ure in Times Square, New York, 1957. (Joseph Scherschel/Getty)

22.)   John Osborne in a quandary directing *The World of Paul Slickey*, 1959. (Pictorial Press/Alamy)

23.)   Kenneth Macmillan, John Osborne, Dennis Lotis and Jocelyn Rickards in rehearsals for *The World of Paul Slickey*, 1959.

24.)   John Osborne backstage with Albert Finney: the first night of *Luther* 1961. (Evening Standard/Getty)

25.)   John Osborne and Mary Ure campaign for nuclear disarmament: Whitehall, London 1961. (Keystone/Getty)

26.)   Press coverage of renovations at The Old Water Mill, 1961.

27.)   John Osborne, Vanessa Redgrave and Doris Lessing in Trafalgar Square, September 1961. (Mirrorpix/Alamy)

28.)   John Osborne at home in Belgravia, 1960s. (Mark Gerson/NPG)

29.)   Penelope Gilliatt.

30.)   John Osborne and Jill Bennett looking fashionable strolling in Chelsea Square, 1968. (David Cairns/Getty)

31.)   John Osborne and Jill Bennett at their wedding, 1968. (Mike McLaren/Getty)

32.)   John Osborne and Jill Bennett Looking pensive a year later. (Evening Standard/Getty)

33.)   Michael Caine (*right*, as Jack) and John Osborne (*left* as Kinnear) in Get Carter, 1971.

34.)   The Hurst, John Osborne's home in Shropshire.

35.)   John Osborne and Helen Osborne at The Hurst, late 1980s.

36.)   Peter Egan as JP in *Déjàvu*, London 1992. (Mike Hollist/Associated News)

37.)   A country gentleman. (Jane Bown)

For Eva,
and for William,
always

PART 1

Beginnings

CHAPTER 1

A New Start

LATE AT NIGHT ON 22 September 1961, a three-vehicle convoy consisting of two cars and a furniture removal van turned off the main London to Eastbourne road and drove quietly into the Sussex village of Hellingly. It was a leafy, peaceful place, comprising a manor house, a few houses and cottages, a fourteenth-century church incorporating stained glass by William Morris and, on the outskirts of the village, an extensive mental hospital. But the occupants of the vehicles were less interested in village history than its potential as a refuge from the scandal whirling about them in London. Theirs was a clandestine flight, elaborate precautions having been taken to elude newspaper reporters and photographers galvanised by the white heat of pursuit. And as they nosed into the lane leading to their destination, it appeared that the operation had successfully gone unnoticed. Before them, standing silhouetted in the moonlight and surrounded by an overgrown and densely entangled garden, stood The Old Water Mill, a deserted seventeenth-century house and couple of outbuildings including the disused eleventh-century mill that gave the property its name.

But as the vehicles advanced, sudden movement disturbed the hedgerows and bushes. Dark figures sprang forward, bringing the procession to a jolting halt. Voices, urgent and demanding, pierced the silence and flashlights punctured the still night air as jostling journalists and cameramen identified the second car as that carrying their quarry. John Osborne, a thirty-one-year-old Londoner celebrated on both sides of the Atlantic as 'Britain's most provocative playwright', and one of the most photographed and written-about figures of the day, had been ambushed and his cover comprehensively blown.[1]

The popular press both loved and loathed Osborne in equal measure. This was a time in England, as Philip Larkin observed, midway 'between the end of the *Chatterley* ban and the Beatles' first LP', and the air was full of unsettling social change, like the tangy scent of a new season.[2] It had brought with it a growing moral liberalism and a new spirit of pruriently inquisitive journalism, spearheaded by the ruthlessly competitive gossip columnists of the popular

daily newspapers and the editorial demand for progressively intrusive photographs to accompany their stories. John Osborne was discovering that in
contrast to previous years, it was no longer possible for a public figure to expect
to lead a private life.

Although the memory of world war was still so vivid that the majority of
people just wanted a quiet, ordered existence, Britain was beginning to change
and, depending upon who you were, you either welcomed it or not. And symbolic
of that change was John Osborne, the young man now peering into reporters'
cameras from a car window in a secluded Sussex lane. He presented a curious
face to the nation. Although immensely articulate, courteous and well spoken, his
'belligerent asides' on the governing Conservative Party, the H-Bomb, journalists, the theatre, critics, the monarchy, women, athletes, gardeners and anyone
and anything else that took his fancy had made him notorious.[3] Again, depending upon your point of view, he was either exhilaratingly outspoken and was
saying what desperately needed to be said, or intensely irritating. John Osborne,
it appeared, was making a career of being confrontational and it had already
made him enviably wealthy. His current earnings were estimated at a stupendous
£20,000 a year (about £394,000 at 2015 values) or, it was reproachfully pointed
out, 'twice the nation's rate for the prime minister.'[4]

His journey from anonymity and penury to professional success, prominence
and wealth, had been dazzlingly rapid; one month, he was unknown, but by
the next you couldn't get away from him. The turning point had come five
years earlier in 1956 with his writing Look Back in Anger, an unheralded play
produced at a small London theatre. Until then, Osborne had been an obscure
and unreliable regional repertory actor, but the play changed everything. Co-
starring Mary Ure, his second wife, it was a portrait of a venomous marital
struggle that had astonished, invigorated and appalled critics and audiences.
Both the play and its author immediately attracted the attention of journalists
who, on the lookout for something to brighten up the grey tedium of the mid-
1950s, identified Jimmy Porter, the play's raging, vividly expressive hero, and
John Osborne, his equally combative, eloquent creator, as representative of a
new and shocking social type. The 'Angry Young Man', well mannered but
appallingly uncouth, had arrived. In the whistling slipstream of Look Back in Anger
had come a flurry of plays, novels and films brimming with social 'fury and
disgust'.[5] While cultural commentators debated quite what the Angry Young
Man was angry about, if anything, the popular press gleefully recorded the
outrageous and frequently ludicrous examples of 'anger' and 'angry' activities
and opinions that John Osborne, conveniently neither a reticent nor a discreet
man, both wittingly and unwittingly provided.

Already, Osborne's exploits that summer of 1961 had included his joining
the widespread protests against the H-Bomb by publishing an open 'letter to my
fellow countrymen' in a left-wing weekly paper. This recklessly inflammatory
tirade, composed 'in sincere and utter hatred' of the government, culminated
in the intimidating cry of 'Damn you, England.'[6] For several weeks after-

wards, newspaper columns had been clogged with the clamour of approval and rebuke, with politicians, clergymen, trade unionists, writers and the general public all pitching in to have their say. That the 'letter of hate' had been written and dispatched when its author was lounging on a sun bed at a luxury villa on the French Riviera had naturally fanned the flames of controversy still higher. The unrepentant playwright had returned to England only to be arrested at a Ban the Bomb demonstration in Trafalgar Square. These adventures, though, merely added piquancy to the main Osborne story running that summer, that of his very public liaison with a married woman prominent in London's cultural circles and with vague connections to the Royal Family, while his wife, Mary Ure, was giving birth to a baby whom the press assumed to be his at an expensive London nursing home.

The 'other woman' in the case was sitting beside Osborne in the car that night in Sussex. Penelope Gilliatt was a vivacious, twenty-nine-year-old *Vogue* journalist and film critic for the *Observer*. She was also the wife of Dr Roger Gilliatt, an eminent and socially well-connected neurologist who had been best man at Anthony Armstrong-Jones's wedding to Princess Margaret the previous year. Both she and Osborne looked equally startled to find themselves the targets of a shouted volley of reporters' questions. What exactly were Osborne and Penelope up to, they wanted to know. Did he not have a wife in London who had just given birth to a baby? Whose was the furniture in the removal van? Why had they left London? Osborne's recent purchase of The Old Water Mill, a rural piece of the England he claimed to loathe, had been widely reported in the press. Were he and Penelope proposing to live together? What did they have to hide? What did they have to say? By now, Osborne was wise enough to the ways of daily newspaper journalism to say nothing. Instead, jumping out of the car and with Penelope at his side, he darted across the garden, closely followed by their accomplices, his friend Anthony Creighton, his secretary, Sonia McGuinness and her husband, Frank. Once inside the house, he slammed and bolted the door behind them.

Osborne's dash to Sussex turned out to be one of the most extravagantly publicised of all his escapades that year. To an eager press, the story promised a wealth of such entertaining gossip that journalists immediately set up camp outside The Old Water Mill. Over the next few days both the *Daily Express* and the *Daily Mail* reported more details of the errant dramatist's moonlit manoeuvres. The *Sunday Pictorial* splashed the 'John Osborne and Friend in Midnight Mystery Move' story on its front page, flanked on one side by a picture of Osborne and Mary Ure, and on the other by a snap of Penelope and Roger Gilliatt.[7] At first, Osborne retaliated to the barrage of questions at the kitchen window with a salvo of 'No comment's. But a day later, having cornered 'the Angry Young Man in one of his better moods', the *Daily Telegraph* enlivened its centre page with an extensive interview, even though the Angry Young Man himself was being uncharacteristically and disappointingly evasive.[8] All he wanted, Osborne repeated, was a bit of peace and quiet.

Although this was highly unlikely in the short term at least, the need for a new beginning was something preoccupying not only Osborne himself but, had he thought about it, was something that had run like a thread through several generations of his family.

*   *   *

His fourth wife, the actress Jill Bennett, once described him as a Welsh Fulham Upstart – in other words, a lower-middle-class provincial who had got above himself. A description calculated to taunt, it was one he accepted without rancour and even sported with some truculent affection. Fulham he certainly was, having been born there, the son of a lower-middle-class father with artistic inclinations and a working-class mother whose grievances seemed to encompass the world. And if a mark of being an upstart is to be possessed of a fierce drive to achieve despite the social odds, then he was that as well. Yet his Osborne forebears were only glancingly connected with Wales. During the 1970s, when he was in his forties and writing the first volume of his autobiography, the professional gene-alogists he asked to delve into his family history confirmed that in the male line only his father, grandfather and great-grandfather had Welsh blood. His mother, her forebears and his remaining Osborne ancestors, for many generations at least, were thoroughly English. This news gratified him immensely, since over the years he had gone to considerable lengths to rise above what he considered lowly beginnings, and was then well on his way to becoming an English gentleman, complete with a rambling country estate, dogs lolloping at his heels, and a distant view of hills. As he wryly confided to a notebook, forgetting for the moment that he was half-Welsh: 'Whatever else, I have been blessed with God's two greatest gifts: to be born English and heterosexual.'[9]

The name Osborne derives from the Old English Osbern, which in turn derives from Old Norse or Old Danish. The family may therefore have been Nordic in origin, although by the seventeenth century they had become estab-lished in and around the village of North Tawton in Devon, making their living as carpenters and bakers. During the early years of the nineteenth century, as the Napoleonic Wars rumbled and thundered overseas, Philip Osborne, John Osborne's great-great grandfather and a carpenter in the family tradition, crossed the Bristol Channel with Martha, his wife, and settled in Newport, a thriving town on the Monmouthshire coast. There, they joined swarms of English incomers seeking work in the mines, the ironworks and new indus-tries transforming the southern Welsh valleys into a mighty, coke-consuming furnace, a place the dour Scottish sage Thomas Carlyle would liken to a 'vision of hell'.[10] It was here that Lord Nelson, his redheaded mistress Emma Hamilton, and her husband, Sir William, a former ambassador to Naples and authority on volcanoes, had arrived in the summer of 1802 to inspect the cannons being forged for the Navy and that would eventually outgun the French at Trafalgar.

If Philip and Martha Osborne had indeed arrived in Newport in search of a new start, they would have taken particular pride in the progress of Henry, their first son, born in 1839. Henry became a domestic servant at the King's Arms, a public house on a corner of Commercial Road near the docks, busy with stevedores and a first and last port of call for sailors. When he was thirty, Henry made a judicious marriage to Louisa Thomas, a determined, practical girl whose father, Griffith Thomas, like Philip Osborne, was a carpenter. By now, Henry was the landlord of the King's Arms and was able to make a home for his family in rooms above the bar. He and Louisa had three children, the eldest, Henry junior, being born a year after the marriage in 1870 and Thomas following two years later. James, the youngest, who would become John Osborne's grandfather, arrived on 10 April 1873. Determined to insulate the boys as much as possible from the working-class spoor of the pub and thrust them up the social ladder, Henry and Louisa dispatched the children as boarders to a school in Cambridge. Unfortunately, all three proved academically negligible. Reluctantly, Henry and Louisa conceded that their plans for their sons' social advancement would have to be modified in favour of the more mundane paths of Newport trade. Consequently, Henry junior found work in an ironmonger's shop and Thomas in a draper's. James became an apprentice to a jeweller.

By 1890, Henry senior had died and Louisa was left to preside over her sons' futures alone. But both husband and wife had saved assiduously, and Louisa was not the kind of woman to allow widowhood to disrupt her ambition for her boys. Nobody, she thought, ever got anywhere by working for someone else. She had only to emerge from her sitting-room, descend the stairs and peer into the public bar of the King's Arms to recognise that, in good times or bad and whatever its virtues and evils, drink was in constant demand and that pushing pints across a bar put money in your pocket and food on the family table. Therefore, she saw to it that Henry abandoned the ironmonger's and become the landlord of a local free house, while Thomas was lifted out of the draper's to take over the King's Arms. James was provided not with a pub, but the lease of a small jewellery shop nearby.

But on 16 September 1897, when he was twenty-four, James (known as Jim) set out not for the shop but for St Mark's Church. There he married Anne (known as Annie) Prosser, a girl two years his younger whom he had been courting for several months. Doubtless Louisa Osborne approved the match, for Jim was following the example of his brothers before him and making a 'good' marriage. Like Louisa, Annie's mother was a widow. However, her husband had been a successful ironmaster who owned a 'rather grand' house and on his death had left his wife and four children well provided for.[11] Like Louisa, Annie, a conventional, rather reproving woman, had high hopes for her family.

But while beer was a bestseller and Henry and Thomas and their families cruised along contentedly on the profits, the same, alas, could not be said for either jewellery or Jim. His business presented an imposing enough face to the world. His shop window displayed trays of rings, necklaces and brooches, while his advertisements in the local press promised prospective customers a 'Grand Selection of Gold and Diamond Goods from the finest Manufacturers in the trade', and assured the owners of failed watches and broken pendants that repairs would be 'executed by experienced London Workmen.'[12] But Jim, who had inherited neither his father's perseverance nor his mother's entrepreneurial flair, also remained impervious to his wife's ambitions. Far more interested in sport than in jewellery, Jim followed rugby in the winter and, unusually for a Welshman, cricket in the summer. Leaving the shop in the charge of an assistant, he ambled off to local matches, content as long as the business generated sufficient money to provide for Annie and pay the wages of the cook and the maid they employed at the house they had bought at 16 Bryngwyn Road. His income, though, was soon stretched almost to breaking point by the birth of their two children. Their first, Thomas Godfrey, who became John Osborne's father, was born on 8 May 1899. Nancy, their second child, arrived three years later in 1902.

Somehow, the shop kept the family's heads above water throughout the First World War. In the early 1920s, Nancy fleetingly joined her father in the business but quickly abandoned him to his rugby and cricket and made good her escape by getting married. Her husband, William Henry (known as Harry) Porter, was a local man and, as a manager for a company with extensive interests in Nigeria, divided his time between eighteen months in Lagos and three months' leave in Britain. It was on one of his visits to relatives in Newport that he met the jeweller's daughter. As soon as Nancy left home as Mrs Porter, Jim's floundering business rapidly sank and he put up the 'Closed' sign for the last time. At Bryngwyn Road, the cook and the maid were dispensed with and the Osbornes resorted to fending for themselves. But while Henry and Thomas and their families continued to prosper, Jim and Annie and Thomas Godfrey, who was still living at home, were struggling. Jim was reduced to borrowing money and inheriting his brothers' cast-off suits, privations he acknowledged with the stoical resignation with which he accepted everything else. Annie's lips, however, thinned in resentment. The family, or their part of it, was rapidly going down in the world. Perhaps it was at her instigation, then, that the Osbornes upped sticks and moved to London in the hope of another new start.

It failed to work, and so did Jim. The family arrived at 68 Ellerdine Road in Hounslow, then on the western outskirts of the capital, where they subsisted mostly on money sent home from Lagos by Harry and Nancy, and by borrowing from relatives. Thomas Godfrey (known variously as Tom Godfrey, Godfrey and the matier Geoff – all the Osbornes were known by diminutives) had been a sickly child and was now a slender, pale young man in his early twenties and suffering from tuberculosis. Having an aptitude for drawing and painting, he had left school at fourteen and embarked upon a correspondence course in commercial illustration, the fees for which were met from the proceeds of a small trust fund Louisa had founded for her grandchildren, her last act of thoughtful provision before her death. The Osbornes may therefore have moved to London for Tom Godfrey's sake, hoping that he would find better treatment for his illness and brighter prospects of a job. Not that there was

much likelihood of his father suddenly becoming employable. While his brothers eventually sold their pubs to breweries and retired comfortably to Surrey
on the proceeds, Jim was left to make occasional and dismal forays to the local
Labour Exchange. He came away with intermittent gardening work, but there
was little prospect of a former jeweller in his fifties finding a permanent occupation, and nor did he seem to want it.

But at least Tom Godfrey struck lucky and was able to contribute to the
beleaguered family exchequer. Having qualified as a commercial artist, he travelled into town to work in the advertising agencies clustered about Shoe Lane
and Fleet Street, providing illustrations for advertisements in newspapers and
magazines. Yet all was not happy at home. Jim had become silent and withdrawn and Annie bitter. In this 'oppressive' atmosphere, Tom Godfrey became
increasingly restless and frequently 'broke away', sometimes staying out all
night or all weekend, on drinking sessions, it was suspected, or on jaunts with
young women.[13] It may have been after one of these that he returned home one
day to announce to a bewildered household that he was engaged to be married
to a barmaid. In his mother's eyes, the family had suddenly fallen even lower
in the world.

*   *   *

Nellie Beatrice Grove was six years older than her prospective husband, having
been born in South London on 5 January 1893. Having left school at twelve,
she had begun her working life cleaning at a foundling hospital before leaving
the world of mops and buckets to become a waitress in a café and then a
barmaid in the pubs at the further end of the Strand. Her regulars included men
from the nearby newspaper and advertising agency offices and it was there that
she encountered Tom Godfrey. Lonely in London, he was drawn to the warmth
and undemanding companionship of pubs. And Nellie Beatrice, cheerful, easy-
going and gregarious, was a good talker and the kind of barmaid to make any
lonely soul believe he had found an undemanding, understanding ally.

Alcohol flowed through the veins of both the Osbornes and the Groves,
for like Tom Godfrey's uncles and grandfather, Nellie Beatrice's parents were
publicans and she herself had been born in rooms above the Bermondsey pub
where her father was the landlord. William Crawford Grove, a raffish, expansive
figure who embodied much of the jovial optimism of the Edwardian age, had
since become the manager of the Duncannon in Duncannon Street, a turning
off Trafalgar Square. Renowned among his regulars as the 'smartest publican
in London', he liked a night at the theatre, and the pub could hardly be better
placed for the theatres in Shaftesbury Avenue, the Strand and Covent Garden.[14]
Shows such as No! No! Nanette! and its pervasive song, 'Tea for Two', were all
the rage, as were the Bing Boys revues, from which young men emerged murmuring the lyrics of 'If You Were the Only Girl in the World' into the ears of
their female companions. William Crawford Grove revelled in it all, possessing

a jaunty, pubby effervescence and a liking for the music hall that his daughter inherited. It was through them and Tom Godfrey that John Osborne came to love the breezy theatricality of the music hall and its simple, sentimental songs.

A spirited London clan of several branches, the Groves had a pugnacious zest for life the more cautious Welsh Osbornes entirely lacked. When William Crawford Grove retired from the Duncannon, waving goodbye to the bright lights and the chorus girls, the booze and gossip, he and his wife Adaline (known as Ada) decamped to a rented house at 113 Harbord Street in Fulham. Once a rather comfortable area, Fulham had become much shabbier over the years, a patchwork of streets where stucco peeled from the terraces, a world of second-hand clothes shops, launderettes and rented rooms, a bolt-hole for those scraping by in hard times. The Groves' new home was in a small Victorian terrace in a narrow street with a room at the front, a parlour at the back, two rooms above and a tiny patch of front garden, for which they paid eight shillings a week in rent. If its interior was typical of the period, it would have been rather dingy, decorated in the murky colours and furnished with the heavy dark furniture fashionable before the First World War and still common afterwards. The family would have lived mostly in the back room, where there was a gas fire fed by a shilling-in-the-slot meter, the front room being used only on family occasions of the utmost ceremony, its windows veiled with near-impenetrable net curtains and perhaps further screened by an aspidistra, the indestructible symbol of the working and lower-middle classes. In *A Better Class of Person*, an autobiographical television play broadcast in 1985, Osborne portrays a family Christmas at Harbord Street in the mid-1930s, loud with feuding relatives and brimming with garrulous gossip over the lunchtime chicken, the King's voice delivering the annual Christmas Speech leaking from the nearby wireless. On the face of it, the Groves seemed an astounding choice of in-laws for the reticent, softly-spoken Tom Godfrey.

It was probably to the bewilderment of both families, therefore, that Tom Godfrey and Nellie Beatrice were married at Hammersmith Register Office on 4 June 1925. Jim Osborne rather ostentatiously entered his profession in the register as jeweller (master), while William Crawford Grove described himself as a licensed victualler (retired). Tom Godfrey, then twenty-six, declared himself to be an advertising copywriter and artist while the bride elected not to enter a profession but preferred instead to trim three years from her age, claiming a decorous twenty-nine rather than her actual thirty-two. There seems little evidence that the Osbornes and the Groves saw much of each other before or after the wedding, for apart from never having signed up to the temperance movement, they had absolutely nothing in common. Yet the Groves could be furiously tenacious. Years later, when he was wealthy, John Osborne would be badgered by suburban relations appealing for financial assistance against the random fates that left them out of pocket. In response, he reluctantly dispatched generous cheques supplemented by bulging food hampers at Christmas. In 1968, though, he exacted revenge by recalling them in *The Hotel in Amsterdam*, a play in which Laurie, a disenchanted writer, remembers his relatives as: 'retired rotten, grafting publicans, shop assistants, ex-waitresses. They live on and on. Having hernias and arthritic hips and strokes. But they go on: writing poisonous letters to one another. Complaining and wheedling and paying off the same old scores . . . calculating, greedy, stupid . . .'[15]

This was the orbit into which the newly married Tom Godfrey and Nellie Beatrice moved, lodging in rooms at 366 Fulham Palace Road, within easy walking distance of the Groves at Harbord Street. After Faith, their first child, was born on 24 April 1928, they moved again, this time renting rooms at 86 Langthorne Street nearby. It was from there that Nellie Beatrice went into the Crookham Nursing Home, a terraced house of three floors and a basement at 2 Crookham Road, for the birth of their second child. A boy, he came howling into the world at fifteen minutes past midnight on 12 December 1929. Bearing him triumphantly back to Langthorne Street, the proud parents named him John James Osborne. His birth chart, compiled many years later by an astrologer who knew his identity and his reputation as a playwright, established that Mercury ruled his horoscope, indicating an 'argumentative and rebellious' nature. He possessed, declared this planetary interpreter, a love of language and learning; he was 'industrious, highly critical and not easy to please . . . a perfectionist.' Moreover, his career would rise 'like a bright comet into the sky'; impulsive, he would be married more than once, and always to 'rather out-of-the-ordinary type of women.'[16] All, as it turned out, true enough.

CHAPTER 2

A Sense of Loss

OSBORNE WAS BORN midway between two world wars, in the year that *Bitter Sweet*, Noël Coward's musical comedy, opened in London to be greeted, observed its author, then at the summit of his success, by reviews 'almost incoherent' with praise.[1] It was also the beginning of what the historian Eric Hobsbawm, for reasons nothing to do with Coward, called 'the Age of Catastrophe'.[2] These were years of despondency, and even though memories of the catastrophic slaughter of the First World War were still vibrant, in Europe the warning bells were tolling again.

In May 1929, seven months before Osborne's birth, Britain had elected a Labour government for only the second time. Lacking an overall majority in the House of Commons, the Prime Minister, Ramsay MacDonald, depended for his authority upon the support of the Liberal Party, but within months this fragile coalition was quickly falling apart. Declining industrial production in the United States precipitated the calamitous collapse of the American stock market in October, and with the vaccine of foreign lending suddenly withdrawn, the virus of economic recession rapidly spread to Europe. Germany sagged into crisis while in Britain manufacturing faltered, exports tumbled and factories began to close. As weeks stretched into months, the padlocks rusted on the gates, and the numbers out of work, especially in the north, quickly increased. In January 1930, a month after Osborne's birth, over 1.5 million people were registered unemployed. A desperate MacDonald called a General Election the following year and was returned as the head of a National government in which most of the leading figures were Conservatives. But like the old administration, the new government proved impotent in the face of such an inexorable economic collapse. By the end of 1932, over 2.8 million people had no work and an estimated one-sixth of Britain's population of 45 million was left with no income other than government welfare. Poverty and despair bit deeply into the life of the nation.

In Fulham, the Osbornes suffered their own share of misfortunes and tragedy. Although only in his early thirties, Tom Godfrey's tuberculosis, regularly treated at Brompton Hospital with subsequent periods of convalescence at Colindale Sanatorium in north London, meant that he was able to work only sporadically and the family finances suffered badly. Ill-health had given him a prematurely elderly appearance. He moved slowly and deliberately, and his hair had already turned white. As tuberculosis is infectious, the family feared not only destitution but that the children would contract their father's illness. And indeed Faith succumbed to an early death of tuberculosis and meningitis at Westminster Hospital on 12 March 1930, when she was twenty-two months old and John barely three months.[3]

'I was born with a sense of loss,' recalled Osborne many years later.[4] Although he was not referring directly either to the death of his sister or his father's inability to work consistently, a sense of loss, a conviction of having been denied, was something that Osborne carried with him throughout his life. It is one of the great impulses of his writing, underlying the restless discontent of Jimmy Porter in Look Back in Anger and permeating many of the characters Osborne created afterwards. Certainly, he was a child who from his very earliest days lived in the presence of illness, dispossession and death. It would return ten years later when his father died, an event that profoundly marked Osborne's adolescence, as the death of Jimmy Porter's father marked his. Osborne, like Jimmy Porter, would be convinced that these childhood and youthful experiences had contributed to his sensitivities being far more acute than other people's. Dubbed an Angry Young Man, he would be asked throughout his life what he was angry 'about'. He never really attempted to explain, but: 'Anger is not hatred', he cautioned in a notebook many years later when he came to write his final stage play.[5] In some ways, it was the condition into which, as a highly intelligent, rawly emotional man, he was born. But although he later recalled his parents and wider family speaking of his sister as an 'exquisite prodigy', and the fact of her death 'lovingly and medically described' by his mother, he grew up having no image of her in his mind at all.[6] Faith was an absence rather than a presence, like the outline of dust on wallpaper left by a picture that has been taken down.

While coping with the loss of their daughter, Tom Godfrey and Nellie Beatrice were obliged to escort their son at three-monthly intervals to Brompton Hospital, where nurses monitored the child's chest for any signs of tuberculosis leaving its mark. These austere inspections, Osborne remembered, were ordeals rather like waiting for a jury to bring in its verdict. At home, grief and apprehension resulted in Tom Godfrey and Nellie Beatrice arguing, and sometimes their arguments became violent. Crockery was thrown and broken. Sometimes mother and son were left on their own as Tom Godfrey went off by himself to live apart from the family in rented rooms. Perhaps this was the result of the rows, or perhaps he believed that periodically leaving the family home was the best way of protecting his son from the contagion of his illness. Perhaps he had resorted to drinking bouts, or perhaps, believing that he had brought nothing other than burden and heartbreak to his family, he felt a sense of humiliation and guilt. It may be that the reasons for his absences from home were a mixture of all of these. His son must have felt both isolated and helpless and, not surprisingly, Osborne looked back upon his Fulham childhood without much affection. It was, he wrote, 'not so much unhappy as devoid of happiness'.[7] He was a small boy alone in a world of adults, the clamorous, fractious Groves and the subdued, timorous Osbornes. From each family, however, he absorbed qualities that would seep deeply into his own character. From the Groves it was a sense of invective and battle, a conviction that life was a cruel business but that one must overcome the obstacles, while from his father he learned a sense of suffering, dignity and independence. A deep, hard resilience, though, was a quality both families shared, and this too he inherited.

By this time, although the doctors had pronounced him delicate, John was attending the nearby Finlay Street Infants' School, a short walk through the dismal Fulham streets. He was not there for long, because by 1936, when he was six years old, his father's health had improved sufficiently for him to apply himself to a concerted stint of work for an advertising agency in the City. The family fortunes therefore glowing a little brighter, the Osbornes moved again, this time withdrawing from Fulham and its enclave of Groves to suburban Surrey. It would be another new start.

Twelve miles south of Waterloo, Stoneleigh, like many of the London suburbs, had been built in a feverish rash of speculation. There were ranks of semi-detached houses, some blasted with pebbledash and others embellished with laid-in creosoted beams. There were shopping parades, schools, churches, a 'fashionable mock-Tudor style superpub' and a 'supercinema'.[8] This was the Rembrandt in Kingston Road, built in artificial stone with fifteen-hundred seats in a rose-pink auditorium, a monumental chapel to black-and-white films and the screen stars of the day, Humphrey Bogart and Edward G. Robinson, Barbara Stanwyk and Merle Oberon, Charles Laughton and Norma Shearer. Stoneleigh was a brand-new symbol of lower-middle-class material security. This was also an age of burgeoning bureaucracy, and here slept the bank clerks and local government workers, the junior managers, the secretaries and the telephonists; foot soldiers in the expanding army of office workers who left for London by train each morning and returned, clutching their newspapers, each evening.

Stoneleigh was small, conventional and self-contained. It was safe. It was what people wanted. Here, the wider world had little meaning. In Spain, a civil war was being fought between the newly elected Republican government and the rebel fascist forces led by General Franco, the struggle against fascism attracting poets and novelists, idealists and romantics. In 1956, in Look Back in Anger, Jimmy Porter would recount that his father had fought for the Republicans and, soon after his return to England, had died as a result of the wounds he had suffered. George Orwell, another tuberculosis sufferer and a writer Osborne would come to admire very much, had also fought for the Republicans and, returning to England, discovered the suburban middle-class largely indifferent to the conflict. The suburbs and London itself, reflected Orwell, were still sleeping 'the deep, deep sleep of England, from which I sometimes fear we shall never wake till we are jerked out of it by the roar of bombs.'[9]

The bombs were indeed on their way and four years later would be falling upon London. The seeds of fascism, nourished by economic collapse, unemployment and social distress, were producing thirstily malevolent shoots in the parched political soil of Europe. The Osbornes kept track of these sombre events mainly by listening to a large Elko radio portentously stationed in the living-room. Otherwise, there was the News of the World and the Daily Express, the most popular newspapers of the day. In Italy, Benito Mussolini had been in power since 1922, while in Germany, Adolf Hitler had become Chancellor in 1933. In Britain, Oswald Mosley, a former Labour Minister who had resigned from MacDonald's cabinet to create the New Party in 1931, re-emerged a year later as leader of the British Union of Fascists. But if suburbia slept, government and opposition ministers were alert to the possible prospect of war. In 1932, the Conservative, Stanley Baldwin, had warned in the House of Commons that: 'I think it is well for the man in the street to know that there is no power on earth that can protect him from being bombed . . . The only defence is offence . . .'[10] Rearmament began three years later and by 1938 had created a million jobs, mostly in the ailing steel, coal and engineering industries in the work-hungry north.

In the midst of all this, Tom Godfrey, Nellie Beatrice and young John arrived in slumbering Stoneleigh to be greeted by the elder Osbornes. The largely impecunious Jim and Annie Osborne had been recently installed by their daughter and son-in-law in a new, pebble-dashed house at 17 Clandon Close. Harry and Nancy Porter, who were still spending much of their time in Lagos, now had a son, Anthony, born a few months after John, in 1930. As the Porters were paying the rent for Clandon Close, they felt entitled to leave their infant son in the charge of his grandparents each time they flew back to join the expatriate community in Nigeria, and so when Tom Godfrey and his family moved into 68 Stoneleigh Park Road not far away, the two families began to see rather more of each other.

John, though, enjoyed spending most of his time with his father, whom he grew to idolise. Although wearied by ill health, he struggled on as best he could, and to his son his optimism seemed heroic. They went on long Sunday walks together, Osborne remembering being left on the doorstep of the various pubs Tom Godfrey visited on the way. At home, he entertained John by drawing pictures for him and portraits of him. One of the advertising campaigns on which he was employed was for Virol, a malt extract drink the manufacturers claimed to be beneficial for anaemic children and for which Tom Godfrey used his pale, dark-haired son as the model for his illustrations. While Tom Godfrey drew, John would read his comics. He was an avid reader of the Gem and the Magnet, each week's issue being eagerly awaited. Long established but still enormously popular, their highlights were stories of life at public school, the Gem featuring the adventures of Arthur Augustus at St Jim's and the Magnet those of Harry Wharton and Co. at Greyfriars, a company which included the bespectacled Billy Bunter, the 'fat Owl of the Remove'. Osborne continued to read the Gem and Magnet even as an adolescent, buying back-numbers from market stalls. Both comics, George Orwell noted, recalled in tone and ethos an idealised, conservative, Edwardian England in which 'everything is safe, solid and unquestionable', and in which 'the clock has stopped at 1910. Britannia rules the waves, and no one has heard of slumps, booms, unemployment, dictatorships, purges . . .'[11]

Reading provides a means – and at that time, almost the only means – whereby a solitary, introspective child can slip away from domestic reality and immerse himself in the world of the imagination. Reading also strengthened the bond between father and son, for they would often read aloud to each other, particularly the stories of Rudyard Kipling and Robert Louis Stevenson. Apart from walking and reading and the comfort of silence as Tom Godfrey drew and John read, there were visits to music halls to hear from the stage songs that would afterwards be sung round the upright piano at the Osbornes' in Stoneleigh and the Groves' in Fulham. These excursions were Osborne's introduction to the theatre.

Like the Groves, Tom Godfrey loved sentimental songs, but his taste in music was wide and inherited by his son. The first records Osborne bought as a boy were by artists as diverse as Fats Waller and Handel. They also listened to orchestral concerts on the radio. 'The BBC was our sole music mentor,' recorded Osborne.[12] In this way, he first heard Elgar and Vaughan Williams, the latter becoming one of John Osborne's and Jimmy Porter's favourite composers, his music representing 'something strong, something simple, something English.'[13] While the reality of Osborne's childhood therefore was one of loss and financial struggle against the backdrop of national austerity, much of his boyhood imagination was rooted in an England fading or already long gone, a romanticised England of Empire and adventure recreated in the stories in his comics and by nineteenth- and early-twentieth-century authors, by the boisterous sentimentality of the music hall and by the great works of English music. It triggered the idealising of the past later embedded in both his plays and his journalism, and that grew deeper the older he became.

But by 1938, tuberculosis had so weakened Tom Godfrey that he was forced to give up work altogether. His employers at the agency presented him with a parting cheque and wished him well, but without his being able to work, the family's financial position once again became acute. There was now no alternative than to do full-time what they had done only occasionally before, and rely on charity.

CHAPTER 3

Charity's Child

THE NATIONAL ADVERTISING Benevolent Society, an insurance organisation for advertising industry employees and their dependants, had offices in St Paul's Churchyard, near the cathedral. Whenever he could, Tom Godfrey paid premiums to the Society and the Society in turn was generous in support. For the past six years, since shortly after John's birth and whenever Tom Godfrey had been too ill to work, the General Secretary, a Mrs Ure (no relation to the actress Mary Ure), had authorised the payment to the family of an occasional weekly maintenance cheque averaging £2 5s.[1] Now the Benevolent Society stepped in again, directing payments not to 68 Stoneleigh Park Road, but to Corner House Parade, in Ewell. The Osbornes were in flight yet again, and had moved a few miles deeper into suburbia.

Like Stoneleigh, Ewell was a dormitory for London. Corner House Parade was not much to look at: a terrace of shops with flats above, their front windows overlooking the street, their back doors leading on to a walkway protected by iron railings and with steps down to a yard below. The Osbornes rented Flat 3. Below them, a twopenny library was wedged between a wool shop and a butcher's. Ewell was older than Stoneleigh, more established, and consequently thought itself marginally grander. Whereas Stoneleigh was lower-middle class, Ewell was middle-middle, a fine, but to many of those who lived there, crucial distinction.[2] Those who took the train each day to work in London were a notch or two higher up the bureaucratic ladder than those in Stoneleigh and owned their own semi-detached houses in one of the rural-sounding Avenues, Drives, Ways and Closes. Several families sent their children to one of the nearby independent schools and some even boasted a housemaid, often a live-in northern girl paid very little money to open the front door to visitors and tradesmen and do the cleaning.

The Osbornes, who had no hope of buying a home, let alone employing a maid, were quickly noticed by the more critical of their neighbours. Tom Godfrey's inability to work marked them out, and rumours circulated that the family were forced to scrimp and tended to slide into arrears with the rent.

There were whispers, gossip and fluttering curtains. Nellie Beatrice was even
suspected of slipping out early in the morning to filch the occasional bottle of
milk from a nearby doorstep. And there was worse. The more reproving residents took a dim view of a married woman in her forties whose husband was
incapacitated 'dolling herself up in yellows and browns, wearing high heels
that she couldn't walk in properly, dying her hair a dreadful, unnatural black
and wearing loads of make-up.' They thought her brash and 'not quite of the
right class'. They did not approve the way she sometimes 'disappeared' on an
early train to London, leaving her husband alone, and catching the last one
back at night. There was a 'coarseness' about her. 'She squabbled with people,
and once she started, she could shout like God knows what,' remembered a
neighbour, resorting to language they believed best suited, like Nellie Beatrice
herself, to the less salubrious of public bars.[3]

In Stoneleigh, there had been sufficient money remaining from Louisa
Osborne's trust fund to send both John and his cousin, Anthony Porter, to a
private school, the Blue Gates, run by two elderly spinsters, but the money
for such reckless aspiration had now run out. Instead, John, now eight, was
enrolled at Ewell Boys' School, the local state-run Church of England elemen-
tary school housed in a forbiddingly cold and damp building. It was at Ewell
Boys' School, however, that he made his first real friend in Michael (known
as Mickey) Wall, whose father, typically for the area, was a junior government official in Whitehall and whose mother, equally typically, worked at a
local newsagent's. John often visited their house, which, unlike the Osborne
household, kept furiously scrubbed to pristine cleanliness in Nellie Beatrice's
daily battle against invading germs that could so easily infect her vulnerable
family, was refreshingly cluttered and, considering the dirty plates that seemed
a permanent fixture in the sink, probably freely contaminated by a multitude of
malignant microbes in search of a home.

What the rather withdrawn John admired about the much more forthright
Mickey was his cheek, his self-assured spontaneity and bravado. Wall probably enjoyed the sensation of leadership. They united in a playground gang of
two, The Viper Gang Club, which specialised in sending postcards to teachers,
parents and fellow pupils, bearing the warning that 'The Viper Gang is Watching You'. It was a childish, hit-and-run exercise in power insulated by the
reassurance of anonymity. During the 1970s, Osborne would take up the idea
again in the creation of The British Playwrights' Mafia, an association of dramatists equipping themselves with bogus military credentials and whose purpose
was to expose the critics and producers they believed had blighted their careers.
But by then he was signing his efforts, which to their recipients lent them an
attractive collectors' value.

Mickey Wall's bracing lack of self-consciousness began to liberate John's
own. Wall liked to style himself M. Geoffrey Wall, and John emulated this by
adorning his school books with the name of J. James Osborne. A little later,
when he began to try his hand at writing short stories and poems, an activity

very much encouraged by his father, he decided to drop the 'boring, common-place' name of John altogether, opting instead for his more 'forthright, and adult-sounding' second name, James.[4]

Yet his precarious health caused his attendance at Ewell Boys' School to be sporadic and liable to be suspended altogether during the winter months, either by genuine illness or his mother's assertion that his chest was too delicate to withstand the whipping winds or percolating damp, and that on no account must he venture from the house. To the various Schools Attendance Officers who knocked on the Osbornes' front door to remonstrate, Nellie Beatrice's reply was unvarying: John was a sensitive boy whose health, like that of his father, was being closely monitored by no less an authority than Brompton Hospital. He must not, therefore, be unnecessarily exposed to whatever germs might be hovering in the atmosphere.

Meanwhile, the National Advertising Benevolent Society had reached similar conclusions regarding Tom Godfrey, whose health was continuing to decline. Instead of enduring another hazardous winter in England, it was decreed that he should be transferred to the warmer, restorative air of the continent. Therefore, on 3 November 1938, at the Society's expense, he climbed aboard a train at Victoria Station that would take him to the south of France and a sanatorium at Menton, near the Italian border. As soon as he arrived, however, a specialist concluded that he would make better progress at Vence. Once there, another specialist shunted him on to Plateau d'Assy, where he spent Christmas and New Year before, like a parcel nobody wanted to claim, he was handed on yet again, this time to doctors at Gervais. From each stop, Tom Godfrey dispatched optimistic bulletins of his progress to Nellie Beatrice and to John, who spent a glum ninth birthday at Ewell and a morose Christmas with the loudly feuding Groves at Harbord Street.

His condition little improved, Tom Godfrey returned in April from a politic-ally jittery continent where the clouds of war were massing. In Britain, the National government, now led by the Conservative Neville Chamberlain, was keeping a wary eye on mainland Europe while simultaneously hoping to repel the old bugbear of unemployment at home. But although the nation's eco-nomic fortunes had improved, the number out of work had never fallen below 1.5 million. Even if Tom Godfrey had been able to reduce the number by one, he would have been very lucky to have found a job. That the government seemed undecided about what to do was reflected in the increased support both for the Labour Party and the Communist Party, the latter in 1938 proudly claiming a membership of almost 18,000. More ominously, Oswald Mos-ley's British Union of Fascists also claimed unprecedented numbers endorsing their leader's views. Although neither Communism nor Fascism looked like becoming anything more than an irritant to mainstream politics, the govern-ment was nevertheless sufficiently agitated to impose counter-measures against them. The Incitement of Disaffection Act of 1934 was designed to forestall the Communist Party, while the Public Order Act of two years later was intended to curtail British Union of Fascist rallies and marches through the poorer and predominantly Jewish areas of the East End of London. 'True to our traditions', noted Stanley Baldwin, as he surveyed the darkening skies of mainland Europe, 'we have avoided all extremes. We have steered clear of fascism, communism, dictatorship . . .'[5]

Much of the press and the majority of Conservative Members of Parliament were supporting Chamberlain's policy of appeasement with Germany, hoping to avert a conflict for which Britain was woefully unprepared and sharing his view that it was Soviet Communism rather than Nazi Germany that represented the real long-term threat to European democracy. During the summer and autumn of 1938, the Daily Express, the country's most widely read newspaper and owned by the rich, right-wing Canadian entrepreneur and government ally, Lord Beaverbrook, optimistically reassured its readers that Britain would not be involved in a European war either that year, or the next. Not for the first time, many were dubious about what they read in newspapers.

At the end of September, and in an effort to avoid at all costs what seemed an increasingly inevitable conflict, the seventy-year-old Chamberlain, a thin, Edwardian figure, a prominent Adam's apple throbbing above a stiff winged collar, ventured aboard an aircraft for the first time in his life and flew to Munich to meet Hitler, Mussolini and the French leader, Eduoard Deladier. Hitler had already annexed Austria into Germany and was now eyeing Czecho-slovakia, whose government was hopeful of British support against possible invasion. Once in Munich, however, Chamberlain, outmanoeuvring Deladier, agreed a settlement agreeing to Hitler's demands. 'PEACE!' cried the headline in the Daily Express on 30 September, in the largest capital letters ever used in a British newspaper. Chamberlain arrived home the following day to stand on the steps of No.10 Downing Street and confirm to cheering crowds that: 'I believe it is peace for our time.'[6]

It was a futile pronouncement. Even before Tom Godfrey left for France seven weeks later, the government was completing the distribution of 38 million gas masks, the Osbornes being among the recipients. 'Fitting on these grotesque combinations of pig-snout and death's-head,' wrote the historian Angus Calder, 'sniffing the gas-like odour of rubber and disinfectant inside them, millions imagined the dangers ahead more clearly.'[7] In March 1939, a few weeks before the Osbornes were reunited at Ewell, Hitler's troops marched on from occupied Sudetenland into Prague and swiftly annexed the whole of Czechoslovakia. A humiliated Chamberlain, clinging to the disintegrating raft of appeasement and the absurd Munich agreement, declared that if Germany continued onward and invaded Poland, then Britain would retaliate. In August, the trappings of war wrapped themselves ever more tightly around ordinary Londoners. Air Raid Precaution officers were briefed and plans drawn up for the evacuation of children and women from the capital and the larger regional cities consid-ered vulnerable to enemy bombardment. Meanwhile, Hitler made a pact of non-aggression with the Soviet Union and, on 1 September, Germany invaded

Poland. Two days later, at 11 o'clock on a sunny Sunday morning, the Prime Minister who twelve months previously had assured the nation that 'everything's fixed up now', announced on the wireless with as much statesmanship as he could muster, that Britain was indeed at war with Germany.

At sunset that night, the nocturnal blackout began. Diligently following regulations, the Osbornes, like millions of others, draped black material across their windows in order to ensure that not a chink of light was visible either to the enemy or anyone else, the effect scrutinised by Air Raid Precaution Wardens patrolling the streets. By day, the country mobilised. The National Service (Armed Forces) Act required all fit men between the ages of eighteen and forty-five to present themselves for conscription into the armed services. Thousands more volunteered. Tom Godfrey, though, was pronounced to be too ill to fight. And as nothing of consequence happened during the following few weeks, it seemed that the crisis might indeed be over by Christmas. But people still kept their gas masks nearby, just in case, and everyone had been issued with an identity card and number. John's was EPHA 64 3. At Ewell Boys' School, just to be on the safe side, lessons were punctuated by air raid practices, the children pulling on their masks and heading for the safety of the nearest shelter.

Meanwhile, at the National Advertising Benevolent Society, Mrs Ure had already mobilised her own forces. She and Hubert Oughton, a Society official who had taken an interest in the Osbornes' welfare, decided that for the second winter in succession Tom Godfrey, who was spending increasingly more time ailing in bed, must be stationed abroad. Another posting to France, vulnerable to a German advance, was clearly unwise. Instead, both he and his family would be transported to the comparative safety of the Isle of Wight, its balmy Channel air long renowned for its recuperative properties. A cottage, Mon Abri, was rented near Ventnor on the southern coast and travelling and removal expenses paid. Consequently, on 28 September, a large Daimler ambulance nosed its way into the alleyway behind the shops of Corner House Parade. Curious neighbours looked on as it stopped, its doors opened, and stretcher-bearers ascended the iron steps and disappeared into Number 3. A few moments later, Tom Godfrey, thin and spectral, was manoeuvred carefully down the steps on the stretcher and into the rear of the ambulance. Nellie Beatrice and John followed, climbed inside to sit beside the patient and the doors closed on them. The vehicle moved off as slowly as it had arrived, as though anxious not to damage its fragile cargo. Although his departure from Ewell was orchestrated by the National Advertising Benevolent Society rather than the London County Council, John Osborne became one of many thousand child evacuees.

Mon Abri turned out to be a small house surrounded by an overgrown garden wandering almost to the cliff's edge. From his bedroom window, John had an uninterrupted view of the Channel, and in the days to come would watch naval convoys making their way slowly out to sea. Sometimes, he heard far-off gunfire. Turning his bedroom into a small boy's briefing room, he followed the uncertain progress of the war with the aid of the newspaper and a radio, pinning flags at strategic points on the large map of Europe he pinned to a wall. The Osbornes' seclusion, though, was soon invaded by enemy forces in the shape of School Attendance Officers, who, despite Nellie Beatrice's protestations of her son's frailty, ordered that he be enrolled at the nearby St Boniface's School, from where, probably with his mother's connivance, he often played truant, wandering the cliffs or reading books and newspapers with his now mostly bedridden father.

The milder air did little to revive Tom Godfrey. Within weeks his condition deteriorated still further and he was ferried to Ventnor and the National Cottage Hospital for Consumption and Diseases of the Chest, where on good days patients lay propped up on their beds on the veranda, staring out over the English Channel. But after having undergone a series of examinations, he was sorrowfully returned to Mon Abri, the doctors confiding to Nellie Beatrice that he had only about another six weeks to live. Far from home and the familiarity of Fulham, the support of the Groves and the distraction of her beloved pubs, Nellie Beatrice probably did her best to cope. But she was on her own in desperate circumstances and seems to have been unable to hide her anxiety and exasperation from her son, who, at nine years old, interpreted both as self-pity and meanness of spirit. It seemed to the young Osborne that his mother saw herself as trapped by a malign and unfair fate, that she identified his father's dependence upon her as an almost intolerable burden blighting her life. She endured, but not in silence, her frustration and complaints drilling into Osborne's heart. His birthday and Christmas that year were as miserable as the previous year's, although John's presents included the *Boys Own Annual* for 1940, inscribed to 'Skipper', his father's nickname for him. Tom Godfrey had asked for one of three paperback books: *Ariel* by Andre Maurois, *A Safety Match* by Ian Hay, and *Death of a Hero* by Richard Aldington. Having diligently saved his pocket money, John bought all three.

Tom Godfrey's decline was rapid and remorseless. It must have been terrifying for a small, lonely boy to witness. In *A Better Class of Person*, his autobiographical play, Osborne dramatises an incident that apparently happened one day during the third week of January 1940, when he and Nellie Beatrice saw what appeared to be an apparition at the top of the stairs. It was Tom Godfrey standing naked on the landing, his body spectrally pale in the watery winter light. Swaying, he attempted to descend, lost his footing and plummeted down the stairs to land, groaning with pain, at their feet. He had gone blind. Some infection must have further damaged the optic nerves and extinguished his already weakened sight. Somehow, mother and son got him back up the stairs and to bed. Once downstairs again, Nellie Beatrice anxiously dispatched urgent telegrams to the family and to the Benevolent Society, which promptly arranged for a nurse to visit and paid for Jim Osborne to make the journey from Stoneleigh to the Isle of Wight to see his son for what turned out to be the last time. A couple of days later, on 27 January 1940, Tom Godfrey died. He was forty, his wife forty-six and his son ten.

It was the second death in the family in a decade, halving their number from four to two, but crucially, it was this, the seemingly needlessly cruel death of his beloved father, that ignited Osborne's lifelong loathing of his mother, whom he now saw as wishing Tom Godfrey's end upon him. At least, this is the explanation Osborne himself gave, yet perhaps it is not quite as simple as that. The death of Osborne's father certainly added to his sense of loss, of being randomly, cruelly deprived, and his 'anger' may have been compounded by his loss and what he perceived as his mother's shortcomings, but it may have been that his own feelings of helplessness and impotence played as great a part. Perhaps it was partly a case of his projecting his own inadequacies on to her. But from this moment onwards, he kept a flame of resentment against her burning in his heart, writing and talking about her constantly. Thirteen years later, in a notebook, he recalled the: 'three hours after he died, when I was dragged back from the corpse, the hatred between us . . .'[8]

Very quickly, the young Osborne identified the essential differences between his mother and his beloved father as being those of manners and sensibility that came with social class. Quite simply, Tom Godfrey was a better class of person. He was sensitive, creative, sophisticated; a man whose life was ruled by illness but who endured with integrity, courage and love for his son. In John's universe, Tom Godfrey became a revered, near saintly figure. The memory of their shared affection, expressed through their reading together, their talks, their Sunday walks and the awkwardly cheery postcards Tom Godfrey dispatched from sanatoriums abroad, would remain infinitely precious to him, all the more so as they became mementos snatched from the maw of sickness and of untimely death. Nellie Beatrice, on the other hand, according to Osborne, had no such redeeming qualities. In later years, he freely admitted to friends and wives the abhorrence he felt for her, what he saw as her working-class vulgarity, her pubby coarseness, her petty malice and, when he was a boy, her mockery of his juvenile gawkiness and timidity. In a strikingly autobiographical passage in Look Back in Anger, which Osborne dedicated to Tom Godfrey, Jimmy Porter recalls that he was ten years old when his father died, and that his mother believed herself hampered by a man whom providence never treated kindly. 'Perhaps she pitied him. I suppose she was capable of that. But I was the only one who cared!' Convinced that he, rather than his mother, had felt real affection and sympathy, Jimmy declares that it was at his father's death that for the first time he felt a burning, unquenchable helplessness and anger. 'You see – I learned at an early age what it was to be angry – angry and helpless. And I can never forget it.'[9]

Jimmy Porter articulates Osborne's response to his father's death. Yet from the recollections of some of those who encountered Nellie Beatrice during these years, it seems that while recognising the inevitability of her husband's death, she cared for him and their son, given her circumstances, as best as she could. To her son, though, it seemed the opposite. 'He blamed her for "killing his father",' explained a close friend many years later. 'She would nag his father so much that it eventually destroyed him . . . He willed himself to die and that's why John couldn't stand her.'[10] Many years later, Osborne still remembered that 'I felt something I hadn't felt with anybody else and rarely felt since . . . a malign feeling . . . I've always felt hard about her. Disliked her intensely. Still do . . . my mother was a very dislikeable woman.'[11]

*   *   *

In Southampton, on 31 January 1940, Nellie Beatrice and John followed Tom Godfrey's coffin into the cemetery chapel. Later, they transported his ashes to London, across the wintry English landscape seemingly more still and silent than ever, for burial beside the remains of Faith in the sprawling cemetery at Fulham Palace Road. These were the uneasy, anxious months of the 'phoney war' in which, although Britain was supposedly at war, nothing of military consequence appeared to be happening.

In this uncertain atmosphere Nellie Beatrice, now a single mother, and John, an only child, returned not to Ewell, but to Stoneleigh. As the family had given up 3 Corner House Parade when they left for the Isle of Wight, mother and son lodged temporarily with Jim and Annie Osborne at Clandon Close. This was now a house of double bereavement, for the elder Osbornes had recently lost both of their children, Tom Godfrey's sister Nancy having died, also of tuberculosis, in 1938, when she was thirty-six. During 1940, death extended its grasp to the Groves when William Crawford Grove, Nellie Beatrice's father, having lived a boisterous life, expired aged seventy-four. The following year, Jim Osborne, Tom Godfrey's father, as if corroded by a lifetime of dependency upon others and by the deaths of his children, died aged sixty-seven. The Osbornes and the Groves, depleted of their men, became families dominated by long-living, long-suffering widows: Ada, Annie and Nellie Beatrice. John was now a bereaved boy in a family governed by a regiment of women.

Tom Godfrey had little more than memories to bequeath to his wife and son. John had his books and his collection of postcards mailed from continental sanatoria. A single letter from Tom Godfrey to his mother less than a month before his death, survives. 'Everything's got very melancholy and cheerless for us these last few years', he had written.[12] The money from an insurance policy, Tom Godfrey's sole financial legacy, went not to his wife, but to his mother. The final demands upon her husband's life Nellie Beatrice directed towards the National Advertising Benevolent Society, who settled the outstanding domestic accounts from the Isle of Wight, and paid the undertaker's bill of £31 4s 6d. Thereafter, Mrs Ure and Hubert Oughton transferred their vigilance from Tom Godfrey to his dependants, the Society's maintenance cheques following them wherever they went for the subsequent seven years, supplementing Nellie Beatrice's income while she was working, and supporting her entirely when she was not.

And so, mother and son set out from Clandon Close on yet another new start, this time to look for rooms to rent. This became the dispiriting pattern

of John Osborne's adolescence, although in wartime the search for accommodation was simple enough, as many newsagents' and tobacconists' shops had
notice-boards in their windows on which women whose husbands were fighting abroad or had been killed, advertised for lodgers. Tracking the Osbornes'
moves though, is a near-futile exercise as sometimes they stayed at an address
for only a few weeks before moving on, pursued by rumours of unpaid rent
and rows between Nellie Beatrice and exasperated landladies. Soon they were
back in Stoneleigh and a room in Worcester Park Road, from where John went
each day to Stoneleigh East School in Chadacre Road.

Wherever he went, John, like everyone else, took his gas mask in its card-
board box, for now the phoney war of waiting was over and British troops
found themselves in serious conflict for the first time. At home, more men
were being mobilised, more women and children evacuated and everywhere
the nocturnal blackout was scrupulously enforced. During the hours of darkness, civilian drivers used masked headlights, while pedestrians groped their
way about using torches directed at the pavement before them. Sandbags,
intended to absorb the damage from flying glass and masonry shattered during
the probable bombing raids to come, lined the pavements in front of shops and
public buildings, and barrage balloons hovered over the capital in the hope of
discouraging low-level attacks. In May, Chamberlain resigned as Prime Minister, having lost the confidence of the House of Commons, to be succeeded by
Winston Churchill. During the subsequent long, hot summer, stringent food
rationing was introduced, and within weeks the roar of bombs, as Orwell had
prophesied, jolted southern England at last. The blitz had begun.

On the afternoon of 'Black Saturday', 7 September, bombs fell upon Wool-
wich Arsenal, the Victoria and Albert, the East India and Surrey Commercial
Docks, setting ablaze the piers, the wharves and the warehouses of paint, alcohol,
spices and paper lining the Thames. The bombing continued for seventy-
six nights and then intermittently until the following spring. Hundreds were
killed and thousands more injured and made homeless, and swathes of London
were reduced to rubble. In *A Better Class of Person*, Osborne dramatises an incident
during a raid when, instead of running to the outdoor shelter, mother and son
bolt into a cupboard beneath the stairs. After a while, Nellie Beatrice ventures
up the stairs to the lavatory. Moments later, a bomb explodes nearby. As John
emerges from his under-stair hideaway to confront the wreckage, he glimpses
his mother looming through the swirling, choking dust, her clothes in disarray, stumbling from the lavatory, its open door rocking from its hinges. Seeing
her distress, he bursts into uncontrollable, delighted laughter. Did this incident
actually happen? It may well have done, as German aircraft frequently jettisoned
surplus bombs in the area before flying homeward across the Channel. But it is
equally likely that Osborne invented it, his talent being the expression of feeling
rather than the retailing of hard fact, and the story has the atmosphere of wish-
fulfilment about it. Yet it may have been as a result of bomb damage that the
Osbornes were obliged to move again.

They were not the easiest of lodgers. One former wartime landlady conceded that while Nellie Beatrice – and this runs entirely contrary to what her son later professed to have thought of her – 'obviously doted on John and did everything she could for him', her attentiveness to his needs could be enormously taxing for others.[13] Insisting that her son's delicate health merited special consideration, she demanded that the lion's share of strictly rationed meat and eggs be reserved for him, so that he might build up his strength and stamina. Sometimes a piece of meat that seemed to have eluded rationing might appear, to be cooked especially for John's nourishing evening meal. It was widely assumed, correctly, that Nellie Beatrice had Black Market connections and was able to find supplies of food, not to mention nylon stockings, that were otherwise stringently rationed. Her contact, a man named Eric, was a former Berwick Street market trader and one of her regulars at the pub. And it was not at all uncommon for a landlady to enter her bathroom to discover that Nellie Beatrice had tied the bath taps securely with stout string to prevent anyone else drawing the precious hot water that she had reserved for John's invigorating bath.

But once her son returned to school, Nellie Beatrice was free to return to work, gratefully resuming her old life as a barmaid, this time at the 'superpub', the Stoneleigh Hotel, where she quickly became a favourite with the regulars who knew her as 'Bobby'. Both the Osbornes and the Groves were particularly fond of family nicknames and contractions, but quite why Nellie Beatrice became Bobby, nobody now seems able to recall. To her Grove family she was known, bewilderingly, as Dolly. Both mother and son, however, became easily recognised local figures, the thin, quiet boy with the small black patch sewn to his sleeve in memory of his father, eliciting the sympathy of neighbours as he trudged to and from school.

Several neighbours took pity on John, who seemed always to be on his own, including Betty Edenborough's mother, who would invite him to join them for an evening meal. Betty was the same age as John, and they would sometimes go cycling together. 'He taught me how to play Monopoly,' she remembered, 'and we'd play for hours on end. His mother worked all hours. But she was proud when he became famous.' Over fifty years later, she recalled that 'we never saw him after he left Ewell, but I used to say to my husband. That John Osborne. He was my first boyfriend.'[14]

At night, when his mother was working, John would often bed down in an air raid shelter, reading by torchlight. Otherwise, by day and reunited with Mickey Wall, he would lie in the fields and watch the planes overhead, identifying the British and German fighters, as the Battle of Britain unfolded in the skies over southern England, 'the most thrilling spectacular we could ever have imagined.'[15]

One evening in February 1942, Nellie Beatrice went off to the pub, leaving her twelve-year-old son at home. When she returned, she found him waiting anxiously, complaining that his legs seemed paralysed. A doctor was summoned, who listened to the boy's chest and who sent for a specialist, who listened to the rhythm of his heart, prodded his back and legs and diagnosed rheumatic fever. John, they ordered, must rest in bed and lie as still as possible. Alerting the Benevolent Society, who paid the medical expenses yet again, Nellie Beatrice stopped working in order to care for her son. He remained bedbound for nine months and, having little else to do, launched himself upon a programme of intensive reading, ploughing his way through a multi-volume children's encyclopaedia and novels lent to him by a sympathetic neighbour, and following the daily events of the war on the radio. As well as the news bulletins, he listened to popular comedy programmes such as ITMA (It's That Man Again). He also succumbed to a correspondence course in writing. The British Institute of Fiction Writing Science, its name suggesting that the mysteries of art might be explained only by a few fail-safe principles, issued its correspondents with a series of tutorials, promised impartial criticism of whatever they wrote and offered advice on what to attempt next. Too timid to send in his own stories, Osborne submitted two of his father's, which were extravagantly praised. Having gained confidence by proxy, he submitted some he had written himself, whereupon the Institute's response became instantly 'reproachful, impatient, and eventually ill-used and sorrowful'. Disheartened, he gave up. 'I was already aiming too high to effect a sale,' he concluded.[16]

Eventually, in November, the Society paid for a wheelchair into which Nellie Beatrice lifted her son's thin body in order to take him on expeditions into suburbia, once venturing into the fug of the Rembrandt Cinema to see Gone with the Wind, while Mrs Ure and Hubert Oughton arranged for professionally supervised convalescence. According to Benevolent Society records, he was 'omitted' to a convalescent home for children at Shaftesbury on 22 December 1942, a few days after his thirteenth birthday, the Society paying his travelling expenses and a £1 weekly subsistence.[17]

After six weeks of physical exercise and exposure to bracing Dorsetshire air, he was pronounced if not fighting fit, then at least fit enough to return to Stoneleigh and the school at Chadacre Road. Nellie Beatrice, meanwhile, had retreated to work behind the bar while the watchful Mrs Ure and Hubert Oughton had been poring over John's educational records. His lack of progress, they concluded, was not the result of an absence of academic spark but of his appallingly disrupted domestic circumstances. But everything might still be rectified by sending him away to boarding school. Accordingly, after 'considerable discussions in regard to the future care and education of John', Nellie Beatrice agreed that he would be sent to school in Devon.[18]

At the beginning of the summer term of 1943, therefore, John left Stoneleigh and Nellie Beatrice for a new career at Belmont College, the Society paying his annual fees of £72. The school (which no longer exists) was housed in an imposing Georgian manor house standing in private grounds near the village of Bickington, its playing fields overlooking the estuary of the Rivers Torridge and Taw. But if John hoped to assimilate quickly and smoothly into boarding-school life, he was only partially successful. Having grown up in a world of adults, he was self-contained and ill-equipped, at least at first, to deal with youthful communal life. Belmont was a boys' school, although a dozen or so girls had been billeted there during the war, and many years later, one recalled him as 'a tall, slender boy with curly hair, studious but silent. He seemed unhappy.'[19]

Osborne was always dismissive of Belmont College (which in his autobiography he called St Michael's), claiming that while masquerading as a public school, it provided only a meagre, slovenly second-rate education. And yet, some of his contemporaries recalled a rather different story. It appears that after an awkward beginning, he quickly began to make his mark, 'gravitating naturally to the company of older boys and becoming one of the stars of the school, doing well in the social side of things, and particularly in singing and drama.'[20] His abilities were quickly recognised by two teachers, a man named Prentiss, elderly and stooping, who taught English literature, and Miss Tunks, small and fat, who taught music and ran the school choir. The Prentiss educational strategy was to read aloud from well-thumbed copies of the classics and, from a near recumbent position behind his desk, ruminate on literature and life in general. If any of his pupils wished to contribute to these pleasant meanderings, they were very welcome to do so. This was a method to which John instinctively responded, for it reminded him of his father. Prentiss encouraged an already well-read boy in further literary explorations into the works of Tennyson, Henry Fielding and Matthew Arnold.

    Seated commandingly at an upright piano, like an admiral on the bridge of a battleship, the maternal Miss Tunks enticed her pupil to sing well enough to give solos at the school concerts, rousing juvenile affairs comprised of patriotic songs and sketches. He was particularly admired for his rendition, in 'a light baritone voice', of 'The Cobbler's Song' from Chu-Chin-Chow.[21] He made his acting debut in short one-act plays, appearing as Lord Bunstead in The Stoic, and the Gardener in The Hare's Scut, performances earning the congratulations of his fellow cast. Offstage, he edited the school magazine and Prentiss awarded him a literature prize, a large, intimidating book on the Austro–Hungarian Empire which, twenty years later, he would dip into while researching the background for a play, A Patriot for Me. During the summer of 1945, when he was fifteen, John travelled to Bideford to sit the School Certificate Examination and passed. Nellie Beatrice was thrilled and the Benevolent Society delighted. Everything seemed to be going so well. And so it was, before he was expelled.

    In his various memoirs, Osborne records that he was expelled from Belmont College after an incident in which he punched his headmaster, Eric Heffer, whose dark suits and obsessive, lower-middle-class neatness some of his snootier pupils dismissed as being more fitting for a bank clerk. According to Osborne's accounts, the boys were drinking their nightly cups of cocoa one evening, crowded around the wireless listening to Frank Sinatra, when Heffer, incensed by the music, switched off the wireless and, catching sight of Osborne's expression of insolent defiance, struck him across the face. Osborne records that he then punched his headmaster in retaliation, whereupon Heffer sprawled backwards, cocoa flooding the table and dripping to the floor. However, a former pupil recollected things rather differently. It was the custom for one of the older boys to escort a junior female teacher to her home in the nearby village of Sticklepath after her invigilation of the evening preparation hour. There was, 'naturally', fervent competition for this honour, and considerable resentment among his rivals when John seemed to be rewarded more frequently than most. One evening an argument between John and some of the less favoured boys escalated into a fight, into which Heffer intervened. 'John hesitated for a moment, as if unable to decide whether to continue punching those he had been fighting or whether to lash out at Heffer. He was clearly thinking about it but before he could act, Heffer ordered him out of the room. And he went.'[22]

Whichever version is the most accurate, the incident indeed resulted in the star of the school's patriotic concerts being expelled. Yet something other than spontaneous impulse may have sparked his antagonism against Heffer, for at some point in his school career, he had expressed hopes of going to university, and sitting the examinations for Oxford or Cambridge. For some reason he had been dissuaded. Whether or not it was Heffer who curbed his academic ambitions is unclear. In any event, twenty-five years later, Osborne would exact a small revenge upon his former headmaster by appropriating his name for the self-possessed, priggish public school boy in The Right Prospectus, a television play.

His leaving of Belmont College under the cloud of expulsion would mark the beginning of a decade of sackings and hurried departures. But when he returned to Stoneleigh and to Nellie Beatrice, it was to a London at peace for the first time in six years. In 1944, the tide of war had turned against Germany, and early the following year the allied armies had invaded Berlin. On 30 April 1945, Hitler and Eva Braun, the German leader's lover, had committed suicide and on 2 May, Soviet troops rolled into the German capital, consolidating the allied occupation. Within a week, Germany had surrendered. On 8 May, VE Day, celebrating Victory in Europe, Winston Churchill appeared with the King and Queen on the balcony of Buckingham Palace, while beyond the Palace gates, a vast and swaying crowd sang Land of Hope and Glory. Had he lived, Tom Godfrey would also have been celebrating his forty-sixth birthday.

CHAPTER 4

The Journalist

'YOUNG PEOPLE OF my generation were full of hope, and in 1945, after the fears and hardships of the war, we believed we really could change society,' recorded Tony Benn, then a young man of twenty who would later become a distinguished and long-serving Labour Member of Parliament.[1] Immediately following VE Day, they had the chance. Churchill called a General Election for 5 July and the young idealists of Benn's generation, voting for the first time, joined those of an older generation determined there would be no return to the dole queues and the grim inequalities of the 1930s. After a long and debilitating war, in which 360,000 British nationals had died, thousands of lives affected and swathes of urban landscape destroyed by bombing, they were united by the conviction that not only was there much to be rebuilt but that society must be rebuilt on entirely different foundations. The sense of common purpose that had carried the country through the war would surely now be harnessed to winning a lasting, prosperous peace and a new equality in which more people would have more opportunities. Such was the dream.

In the eyes of many voters, the Labour and Conservative Parties offered a clear alternative: on the one hand, decisive change or, on the other, a reversal to what things were like before being so rudely interrupted by war: a country unjustifiably divided by social class and money. Against a Labour Party aiming to establish 'the Socialist Commonwealth of Great Britain' by nationalising the utilities and implementing a utopian programme of welfare reform, the Conservatives clung obstinately to the principles of the free market, resolutely opposing state intervention.[2] The bravura egotism and authority that had served Churchill so well in the war and popularised him as the saviour both of his country and of Europe, did not, however, make him a credible party politician. Although, like the Labour Party, the Conservatives envisaged a comprehensive welfare programme – and, like Clement Attlee, the Labour leader, Churchill proposed a national insurance scheme serving everyone 'from the cradle to the grave' – the Prime Minister fought a campaign concentrating not upon social reform but on attacking Labour.[3] Cranking up the defiance of his wartime oratory, he seemed to suggest in a disastrously ill-judged radio broadcast on 4 June that voting for Labour would be comparable to voting for the forces the nation had just overcome. 'No Socialist government . . .' he warned, 'could afford to allow free, sharp or violently worded expressions of public discontent. They would have to fall back on some form of Gestapo, no doubt very humanely directed in the first instance.'[4]

Supposedly intended to warn voters of the dangers of excessive state power, the speech backfired badly, resulting in the great war leader looking suddenly out of touch with an electorate who, far from fearing state intervention, very much approved of the state assuming responsibility for the general good. Early opinion polls predicted a Labour win, but as the results were declared on 25 July, it was clear that the scale of Labour's victory would be beyond anything imagined. This was history in the making. At Labour Headquarters, Tony Benn monitored the results, watching Conservative Members of Parliament 'falling like ninepins' and the political map of Britain turning from blue to red.[5] Not far away, dejection engulfed Churchill as the tide of losses flooded into the leader's wartime bunker. His housekeeper, reverting to the traditional British remedy in times of trouble, rapidly retreated to the kitchen. 'I don't know what the world's coming to,' she declared, 'but I thought I might make some tea.'[6]

By the end of the night, Attlee's Labour Party had galloped to power with a total of 393 MPs and an astonishing majority of 146 seats in the House of Commons. Kingsley Amis's short story, I Spy Strangers, written several years later, neatly encapsulates popular attitudes to Labour's victory. While Corporal Archer anticipates a socialist England 'full of girls and drinks and jazz and books and decent houses and decent jobs and being your own boss', the upper-middle-class Major Raleigh gloomily anticipates 'something hostile to his accent and his taste in clothes and modest directorship and ambitions for his sons and redbrick house at Purley with its back-garden tennis court.'[7] Yet Attlee's would become the first majority Labour government not only to run its full term of office but also win a second General Election.

This, therefore, was the landscape of Osborne's adolescence: a Labour government promising a New Jerusalem; the Soviet Union, a former enemy who had become an ally during the war becoming an enemy again as it withdrew behind what Churchill memorably described as an Iron Curtain of Communism; a mainland Europe radically realigning as the continent carved itself into blocs of opposing powers and influence, and the pervasive influence of the United States. American money and the inferno of American firepower had proved crucial to the allies winning the war, while American atomic bombs laying waste the Japanese cities of Hiroshima and Nagasaki in August had brought the war in the Pacific to an abrupt and terrifying end. The United States and the Soviet Union now faced each other as emergent superpowers, and Britain discovered itself to be somewhere it had never been before. From having been accustomed to being top dog, or somewhere near it internationally, its political clout in a new world order now looked unceretain.

At home, the new administration immediately launched its nationalisation programme, beginning with the Bank of England and the coal industry. The National Insurance Act of 1946 created the first full system of social welfare, providing benefits during unemployment, ill health and retirement. The Education Act provided the hope of secondary education for all. These were the foundation stones of a new Welfare State, the effects of which were both immediate and lasting, providing fair chances for, and changing the expectations of, millions.

*   *   *

Luckily, Osborne's expulsion from Belmont College had failed to deter the National Advertising Benevolent Society from doing their best to give him his own fair chance. His choices of career were challenging: 'I thought I'd be a newspaper editor, an opera singer or a priest,' he remembered. But: '[I thought] whatever I did do, I'd do it better than anybody else.' Perhaps encouraged by Prentiss, and taking a more realistic decision that 'the only thing I could do was write', Osborne decided upon becoming a journalist.[8] The inexhaustible Hubert Oughton arranged for him to attend a shorthand and typing course, the Society writing a cheque for £12 to cover his tuition fees for six months. So that he might continue to build up his physical strength, the Society also bought him a bicycle and splashed out more money on a mackintosh and a protective cape and leggings. Thus attired, Osborne pedalled daily from Stoneleigh to Clark's Secretarial College in Surbiton, where he found himself almost the only male in a class of neat young women preparing to swell the army of post-war bureaucracy by becoming typists, telephonists and receptionists. Yet he had not entirely given up his academic hopes, and in May 1946 wrote to Mrs Ure, proposing that if he could pass the necessary examinations, the Benevolent Society might pay his fees at Oxford. For the first time, the Society prevaricated. If he managed to win a scholarship, they conceded, then they might 'consider in what manner they could help'.[9]

As far as Osborne was concerned – and this would always be the case – even the slightest equivocation implied outright rejection. Abandoning his hopes for Oxford, he therefore resigned himself to his shorthand and typing, while in his time off scribbling stories and poems and nurturing a dream that journalism might one day lead to his becoming a writer. None of Osborne's youthful efforts appear to survive, but he was confident enough to show some of his poetry to Hugh Berrington, a friend from Ewell who also knew Mickey Wall. Berrington had struck up conversation with Osborne when he noticed him on a bus clutching a bundle of *Gem* and *Magnet* comics, which he enjoyed reading himself. Osborne's prose style, he thought, bore 'a close affinity' to D. H. Lawrence. It seems too that Osborne may have hankered after the existential. One story ended with one character informing another that he was about to embark on a journey. Where was he going? '"To reality," he replied'.[10] Existentialism was something with which Osborne was currently wrestling as part of his continuing programme of self-education. It was 'the macrobiotic food of the day,' he wrote, 'and Mickey Wall and I were "into" the impenetrable brown rice of Heidegger, Kierkegaard, Jaspers and, of course, Sartre.'[11] Even though he professed to detest his mother, Osborne evidently showed his work to Nellie Beatrice as well, for she mentioned it to Berrington, 'and said how good it was.' According to Berrington, 'she was very encouraging to him.'[12]

Meanwhile, Oughton began notifying the editors of various local news-papers of his protégé's abilities in the hope that someone might take him on as a trainee reporter. But the *Sutton and Cheam Herald* did not want a trainee. The *Croydon Advertiser* did, but a sudden appendicitis in July prevented Osborne from attending the interview. Uncomplainingly, the Benevolent Society paid the £24 fees for his appendectomy at Epsom Cottage Hospital and the cost of a convalescent holiday for the patient and his mother in Penzance. Returning home, they discovered that Oughton had come up trumps again. The chairman of the Benevolent Society was also the chairman of Benn Brothers, a company that published a series of trade journals, and a bit of string-pulling landed Osborne a post as a junior reporter at a wage of 45 shillings a week. He duly began working for *Gas World* on 18 November 1946, a few weeks before his seventeenth birthday. Although very much on the back burner of journalism, *Gas World* at least had its offices in Bouverie Street, off Fleet Street, then the hub of the newspaper industry. The area was also familiar Osborne stamping ground, for Bouverie Street was close by the advertising agencies where Tom Godfrey had worked, and the pubs where, twenty years earlier, Nellie Beatrice had pulled perfect pints of beer.

Osborne had a depressing daily journey from the suburbs to central London, crossing a city disfigured by bomb damage. He passed rows of houses punctu ated by dilapidated gaps, and skirted bomb craters marking the places where families had once lived. In Oxford Street, department stores had been hit and water mains ruptured, and in Regent Street, the Strand and Westminster, build-ings stood roofless and windowless, their broken, jagged walls propped up by timber to prevent them collapsing. Once arrived at the dingy *Gas World* office, Osborne embarked upon his first job, prospecting for nuggets of gas-related news in the daily papers that he carefully polished for the benefit of his readers. Sometimes, he attended press conferences given by Emmanuel Shinwell who, as Attlee's Minister of Fuel and Power, proudly proclaimed the wonders of nation-alisation. Otherwise, he compiled notes on new models of gas cookers for 'On the Selling Side', a column he wrote under the pseudonym of 'Commentator'.

Yet beyond his office window, the hopes of 1945 were rapidly withering as the creation of a New Jerusalem proved a far more arduous enterprise than its advocates envisaged. Britain had ended the war in debt, bailed out by America, yet no sooner had the government introduced its rebuilding programme and

welfare reforms than the Americans cut its fiscal lifeline and precipitated the
administration's first economic crisis. The coal industry, spectacularly mis-
managed, was falling apart and while yet another American loan was being
frantically secured, the government admitted that there might be insufficient
coal – the source of over ninety per cent of Britain's energy supplies – to last the
winter. Emergency measures were hastily implemented but industry stagnated
and disaffection kindled. By the end of the year, the northern cotton mills had
closed and much of the industrial midlands was planning a four-day week to
conserve dwindling fuel supplies. At the beginning of 1947, lack of coal forced
steel works to shut down and because of a transport strike in London, the army
was drafted in to help distribute food. Wartime food rationing, though, was
still continuing and would do for another five years or more. Constant rain had
virtually ruined the wheat crop, and bread, seldom in short supply during the
war, now joined the list of rationed foods.

As the cultural historian Robert Hewison has noted, 1947 became 'the year
when optimism finally disappeared'.[13] In January, the economic emergency that
might conceivably have been avoided was compounded by a second and very
British catastrophe that could not: bad weather. Britain found itself engulfed
by the worst winter conditions for over a century. Temperatures plunged to
minus 16 degrees Fahrenheit and heavy snowstorms created fifteen-foot drifts
in the countryside, disrupting transport. In March, a thaw created widespread
flooding, presenting Osborne with an opportunity at last for a bit of intrepid
newsgathering.

Dispatched to Windsor to investigate the battle against the floodwater at
the local gasworks, he paddled through the flooded streets in a hired boat,
navigated his way into the company yard and conducted an inquisition of the
works manager who told him proudly that by hiring divers, they had managed
to guarantee supplies to Windsor by connecting its piping system with that of
neighbouring Slough. Osborne's story, 'WINDSOR GASWORKS FLOODED',
emblazoned with the flattering byline of 'Our Special Correspondent', appeared
in a prominent position in the *Gas World* of 22 March. He celebrated by buying
a second-hand typewriter at a shop in Fleet Street, an essential requirement in
his ambition to become a journalist of substance, and hoped his story might
be picked up by the daily press. Disappointingly, however, it seemed that
his exclusive had passed unnoticed at Fleet Street news desks and no editor
appeared interested in identifying the boating newshound and welcoming him
to the full flame of investigative journalism.

In April, the snow returned and the government prohibited the domestic use
of coal and gas fires until September. Power supplies broke down, traffic lights
failed, office workers persevered at their desks by candlelight. As people began
complaining that conditions were even worse than during the war, a plethora
of government slogans appeared, exhorting them to bear up and get on with it.
An export drive went forward under the terrifying banner of 'Export or Die',
while factory workers were harangued with the cry that: 'We're up against

it! We Work or Want'. This was Austerity Britain, a nation of ration books, coupons, queues and a thriving black market, a peacetime akin to wartime, in which the benefits administered by the new welfare schemes were curtailed, improvements in housing, health and education were far less than anticipated and confidence in the national new start seeped away far quicker than the receding floodwaters.

This, too, was a formative influence for a young writer. Austerity resulted in disillusionment, a feeling that while Labour's promises had sounded bracingly optimistic, in practice they were nothing more than words. Economically dependent upon America, it seemed the country could not even decide its own destiny any more and as a result, its people, victors in Europe, were woefully reduced. '. . . most of us are not men or women,' grumbled the portly aesthete-critic Cyril Connolly, a Labour Party supporter and the editor of the literary magazine, Horizon, 'but members of a vast, seedy, overworked, over-legislated neuter class, with our drab clothes, our ration books . . . And the symbol of this mood is London, now the largest, saddest and dirtiest of great cities, with its miles of unpainted, half-inhabited houses . . . its shops full of junk . . . its crowds mooning around the stained glass wicker of the cafeterias . . .'[14] This is the atmosphere George Orwell recreated in 1984, a novel that Osborne read and greatly admired. The great novel of the Attlee years, 1984 portrays a London of bomb-sites and shored-up housing and creates a world of limitless production drives, fearsome state ministries, decrepit proletarian sectors and the futility of personal rebellion.

Osborne, though, was preoccupied with other things. Making a lateral move within Benn Brothers, he left Gas World and joined The Miller, the trade paper of the flour industry. But while the world of gas journalism was hardly one of high pressure, he discovered there was even less urgency in milling. Compiling the 'Grain and Flour Trades Review' column under the pseudonym of 'Cereal' was enough to convince him that by working at Benn Brothers, he would take a very long time going nowhere. Therefore, he began making alternative plans. He would become an actor.

*   *   *

A legacy of his mismatched parents was his love of the theatre and music hall. 'I have been stage-struck since I was eighteen, probably before,' he told an interviewer in 1981.[15] It was something intricately bound up with his memories of his father, who had first provided his young son with a glimpse into the world of the stage. Places such as The Granville, a music hall at Walham Green, were a world far removed from his everyday experience: boisterous, irreverent and good-hearted. While he was writing The Entertainer, a play partly about the music hall, in 1956, one of the actors at the Royal Court Theatre played him some recordings of music hall songs, including 'Give My Regards to Leicester Square', sung by Victoria Monks. 'Listening to that is like seeing a photograph of yourself as a small child,' Osborne observed. 'It might be unrecognisable at first, but nevertheless that is what you were. That is where we come from.'[16]

After the war, he had begun going to the West End theatre more frequently. During 1946, Rattigan's The Winslow Boy and J. B. Priestley's An Inspector Calls opened, although whether Osborne saw either at the time is uncertain. He could also have seen Ronald Duncan's adaptation of Cocteau's The Eagle Has Two Heads, the beginning of a vogue for French drama that would continue until his own debut at the Royal Court in ten years' time. But most of Osborne's earlier theatre-going was in the company of Nellie Beatrice whose tastes were firmly geared towards the wispily romantic, Ruritanian musicals by Ivor Novello: Perchance to Dream, Dancing Years and King's Rhapsody, which they sat through entranced on their journeys together 'up west', rounding things off with tea at a department store.

Another inducement to the theatrical life was provided by the cinema. One of Osborne's most vivid childhood memories was having seen the Walt Disney cartoon film of Pinocchio, which features a splendidly raffish fox that captivated him with his song, 'Hi-diddle-de-dee, An Actor's Life for Me'. Here was an invitation to jump ship, to abandon the treadmill of routine and lower-middle-class conformity and clamber on to a raft of breezy, bohemian independence. Whether it was Rattigan or Priestley, Ivor Novello, a high-kicking line of long-legged chorus girls, music hall chumminess or a cartoon fox, the theatre offered an irresistible chance of escape into another world, somewhere homely or exotic, a place of costume and tinsel and charged imagination.

And so, during his year at Benn Brothers, he reinvented himself, securing the attributes appropriate for a life in the theatre, both as an actor and a writer. In a sense, acquiring a suitable character was something every actor and dramatist was required to do, for the conventional public image of the theatrical profession was still that which had been established during the 1920s and even earlier. The most successful West End playwrights, such as Terence Rattigan and William Douglas-Home, were either upper-middle class or if they were not – such as Noël Coward – carefully assumed upper-middle-class manners and, in order to secure theatrical production, wrote about the upper-middle class. Their plays, set in the better houses in the better parts of London or the Home Counties, dealt with well-bred and mostly well-behaved characters and were cast accordingly. There was no room either onstage or off for slovenliness in appearance or speech. Therefore Osborne applied himself for another new start by enrolling for an intensive course of elocution and dancing lessons at the ambitiously entitled Gaycroft School of Music, Dancing, Speech Elocution and Drama. This was in North Cheam, not too far from where he was still living with his mother in rooms in Stoneleigh, and which boasted among its successes several members of the Tiller Girls dance troupe.

A converted shop with its windows plastered with photographs of Gaycroft graduates in evening dress executing the intricacies of the paso doble and the rumba, the school was run by Audrey Garnett, a woman in her late fifties, and

Betty, her daughter, a dark, lissom woman in her mid-thirties. While Audrey fiercely beat out the tempo of choral enunciation in her elocution classes, Betty supervised mass dance instruction. In the company of young men and women intoxicated by the glamour of Ivor Novello's Ruritanian fantasies and determined to banish austerity for an evening, Osborne submitted himself to the mysteries of the samba and the quickstep. He was now a tall youth of seventeen, with a long face, prominent cheekbones, wary eyes, a high forehead and dark, gently waving hair. It surprised the few friends he told that he had once been ill for almost a year with rheumatic fever, for there was little sign of frailty about him as he cantered energetically down the Gaycroft ballroom in full foxtrot. It was on the Gaycroft dance floor, if Osborne's memoirs are to be believed, that he whirled past his first girlfriend.

This was Renee Shippard, 'a quiet but open, affectionate girl' of his own age, who worked for the Halifax Building Society in the Strand and whose father disappeared each morning through the doors of the Chase Manhattan Bank further down the street.[17] Within weeks, their quickstep had progressed as far as a marriage proposal, the purchase of a cheap ring, again at a shop in the Strand and for which Nellie Beatrice lent her son the money, gazing into the windows of furniture shops and deliberating over the accoutrements of a future marital home. 'I was at once titillated and alarmed by the pattern of events I had so blithely set in train,' he wrote later. However, perhaps while gazing at a three-piece suite or a coffee table, he blinked twice and realised that 'I was standing at a crucially Existential crossroads.'[18] In one direction lay suburban predictability and perhaps contentment of a sort, but in the other lay Art and independence. Osborne chose the latter. The engagement had lasted three months. Meanwhile, Audrey Garnett, who assured him he looked just like Leslie Howard, the suave star of The Scarlet Pimpernel, and told him to go into films, was hard at work cleansing his voice of any broad London vowels he might have acquired from Nellie Beatrice and the Groves. They did a good job, for after several months' tuition, he emerged 'a very good dancer' and equipped with a 'precise, dry, slightly nasal articulation' that betrayed little of his lower-middle-class origins.[19]

Maintaining his programme of intensive self-education, he was keeping up with the political news and reading prodigiously and widely. He sped through 'books about the General Strike, the Jarrow March and, of course, every available word of Orwell . . . Strachey's The Theory and Practice of Socialism', and 'chortled over Quentin Hogg's book The Case for Conservatism.'[20] Moving from fairy stories by the brothers Grimm and Oscar Wilde, he plunged into Wilde's complete works, the prose as well as the plays, 'Edgar Allen Poe, Dumas, Hugo, Stevenson, Kipling, Belloc for some reason . . . politics, histories of the world by Wells . . . Gulliver's Travels, Rape of the Lock . . . The Fairie Queen . . . Alice in Wonderland . . . Everyman editions of Tacitus and Suetonius . . .'[21] He bought books whenever he could, and some of the editions he read as he grew up remained in his possession for many years.

Hugh Berrington was the first person of his own age to whom he could talk seriously about literature, or indeed anything else. Osborne's interests at this time, recalled Berrington, were 'literary and philosophical', whereas his own were 'primarily political, historical and religious', but they dovetailed neatly and Berrington quickly realised his friend was 'really very well read indeed. He was able to talk well about Bernard Shaw, D. H. Lawrence, Conrad, and he introduced me to Plato.' He noticed that Osborne had developed a fondness for Keats, being very impressed by the line, 'A thing of beauty is a joy for ever', from Endymion. 'Of the three of us, Osborne, Mickey Wall and me,' Berrington recalled, 'it was certainly John who made the intellectual running. He was self-educated in the best sense, and an exceptionally talented young man.'[22]

It was Berrington who persuaded the vaguely socialist Osborne who had swallowed Strachey 'and many another Gollanz orange-covered edition' to join the local branch of the Labour Party, of which he was a dedicated member.[23] Osborne, though, had little aptitude for the discipline of Party politics and found the firebrand speeches of the chairman, a Mr Freeman, diverting for all the wrong reasons. Impeded by an inability to distinguish between a hard and soft 'g', Freeman would work himself up to a climactic piece of oratory at the height of which he would inevitably cry that: 'The real gist of the issue is . . .', pronouncing gist in the same way as gust, which Osborne, to Berrington's irritation, thought enormously funny.[24]

By this time, Osborne and Nellie Beatrice were living in rooms at a modern semi-detached house at 105 Briarwood Road in Stoneleigh, where the landlady was Hugh Berrington's elder, married sister Hilda. Both she and her brother liked 'Bobby' very much and noticed that Osborne, who talked expansively about his plans to leave Benn Brothers for the stage, 'was very eager to make something of himself.'[25] But although Osborne was happy to talk about himself, and about books, the theatre and the cinema, there were other aspects of his life he did not mention. 'We never knew anything about his extended family,' remarked Berrington, 'and he never spoke about his father. It was always John and Bobby: always a duo.'[26]

Berrington also detected a more disturbing facet of his friend's character. 'One of the things I clearly sensed about him at the time and which became much clearer later on, was his dismissiveness of other people. I found that aspect of him, which resulted in his attacks upon his mother, extremely distasteful.' His sister noted that he would very quickly dismiss others as 'stupid'. Both discerned a ruthlessness in him that others would also notice in later years. 'He was filled with self-concern,' observed Berrington. 'He could be very exploitative of others. There was a narcissism there, a hedonism almost.'[27]

Meanwhile, Osborne's plans were given a further boost in October 1947 when, having submitted himself to a medical inspection at Kingston upon Thames, he was pronounced unfit for National Service. Unlike most young men of his age, he would not be obliged to endure a year of compulsory conscription into the armed forces. No matter what emergencies might befall his country, Britain would not be calling upon John Osborne for active assistance. He was free to do as he pleased.

At the Gaycroft, Audrey and Betty Garnett were urging him to audition for acting roles, sending him out to demonstrate his newly acquired vocal and terp-sichorean skills whenever something came along that looked as though it might be promising. When he returned empty-handed, the Garnetts simply turned him around and pushed him off again until he found himself in front of Michael Hamilton, a director specialising in touring recast versions of popular West End stage successes around the provinces. This time, Osborne struck lucky and was hired as assistant stage manager for a twelve months tour of No Room at the Inn at a wage of £4 a week. Consequently, the gas cooker and Windsor floodwaters veteran handed in his notice at Benn Brothers, accepted the congratulations of the Gaycroft dancers who waved him on his way, and on 5 January 1948, aged eighteen, began his first day's work in the professional theatre.

CHAPTER 5

The Actor

INSPIRED BY A real-life evacuation scandal, *No Room at the Inn* was a wartime melodrama in which five young London evacuees arrive in the home of a woman in a provincial town who turns out to be an alcoholic who relentlessly mistreats them. A canvas tightly stretched on the frame of sentiment, sensationalism and social concern, the play, 'a timely and full-blooded war drama', had opened in the West End in May 1946 and become an immediate success.[1] Its author was Joan Temple, a middle-aged woman who lived in Cheltenham and, having dashed off the play in a fortnight, secured not only a London production but a subsequent film contract, the play being adapted for the screen by none other than the poet and celebrated drinker, Dylan Thomas. Both play and film were noted for a powerful, uncompromising, almost documentary feel unusual at the time: 'A work of cruelty which has no parallel on British screens,' claimed one reviewer.[2] As Hamilton's touring stage production cantered around Britain, it was greeted by enthusiastic audiences and approving reviews. In Edinburgh, where it docked at the Royal Lyceum Theatre, the *Scotsman* critic noted appreciatively that 'realism [has] returned to the stage in no uncertain measure'. Miss Temple, he added, 'crusades as hotly as Dickens crusaded against the evils of his day'.[3]

And so Osborne launched himself upon the relentless slog of touring Britain's municipal theatres, arriving in one town one week and another the next, living in digs and out of a suitcase. *No Room at the Inn* had no room for the pleasures of the paso doble or the flash of his newly-acquired foxtrot: instead, as assistant stage manager, his days and weeks were governed by a series of 'calls'. Like most other touring companies, the *No Room at the Inn* cast assembled each Sunday for the 'train call' at the local railway station, where they embarked on the journey to the next stop on their schedule. Once there, he assisted at the 'get in', transporting the props and scenery into the theatre and erecting them on the stage. In the minutes before the curtain went up each evening, he alerted the actors required for the first scene on the stage and, retreating to a corner in

40

the wings, became the prompter, following the script in case anyone forgot a line. At the end of each week, he lined up for 'treasury call' to collect his wages, almost half of which he spent on his digs, and after the final performance each Saturday, helped at the 'get out', dismantling scenery, gathering props and packing costumes in readiness for their transportation to the following week's venue. In addition, he understudied for one of the leading actors and, despite having no teaching experience or qualifications whatsoever, acted as tutor to the evacuee children of a boy and four girls.

Having joined the company after New Year for a fortnight's scrambled rehearsal, Osborne assisted at the first performance of the tour on 19 January 1948 at the Prince of Wales Theatre in Cardiff. This marked the beginning of what would become six years of touring and of weekly repertory. A week later, the company set off for Southport, and then to Cambridge, Lewisham and Wimbledon before turning north to Sunderland and Huddersfield, darting south again to Bristol and doubling back to Wolverhampton, travelling by the newly nationalised railways and living in digs under the watchful, sometimes tyrannical, often affectionate but seemingly always suspicious eyes of Britain's army of theatrical landladies.

Travelling in itself was a new experience, for Osborne had previously not ventured much further north than an outpost of his mother's relatives in Tottenham, and now as the company hurtled north, south, east and west, he heard accents that he had previously encountered only on the wireless and his visits to variety shows. On his mornings and afternoons off, he explored provincial libraries and sat in the smoky darkness of cinemas. As the No Room at the Inn tour ploughed on, crossing and re-crossing its own path as it ticked off West Hartlepool, Leeds, Manchester and Liverpool, Newcastle, Aberdeen and Edinburgh, and Norwich, Peterborough and Plymouth, they found themselves either just ahead of, or just behind Charley's Aunt and No Orchids for Miss Blandish, warhorse productions that seemed doomed to be forever trudging around the provinces. Increasingly, touring revues hurtled across their bows, shows hoping to entice audiences already more than halfway to the cinema by fielding a cast of light comedians and leggy chorus girls. As Don't Blush, Girls appeared from one direction, its counterpart, Don't Blush, Boys disappeared in another while Giggles and Girls sped by on its sniggering way north and Naughty Girls of 1948 scampered south in a hectic confusion of cosmetics and nylon stockings.

While Osborne had agreed to endure a full year of No Room at the Inn, those more hopeful of finding other work had taken the precaution of signing contracts for only six months. One of several actors shoe-horned into the show for the final half of its twelve-month trail across Britain was a tall, sturdy, red-haired woman named Stella Linden. Ten years older than Osborne, she was the daughter of a family who owned a string of sweet-shops in Birmingham, striking to look at, self-assured and ambitious. She was also on to her second marriage. Having divorced her first husband, she had allied herself to Terence Duff, a bubblingly confident homosexual whose black hair shone with oil and

whose teeth seemed permanently clamped around a half-cigar. Having served
in the Royal Air Force during the war, he had assumed the name of Patrick
Desmond and flung himself upon a career as a theatrical Jack of all trades. He
popped up as an actor in weekly repertory; he did stints as an actors' agent and
could turn his hand to providing instant dialogue for plays that needed perking
up a bit; all this to set the scene for his grand appearance as a director and
theatrical impresario. Yet although his unswerving faith in himself was endorsed
to the hilt by his wife, no theatre manager had yet been convinced to let him
loose on a resident company.

But the Desmonds were two of life's eternal optimists, always ready to bet
on a chance, slender as it might seem, and, as *No Room at the Inn* circled the
outer fringes of London before plodding on to Wales, it seemed that a golden
opportunity had just fallen into their hands. Mesmerized by Stella, Osborne had
revealed that he had hopes of becoming a dramatist and that for several weeks
had actually been working on a play. This was *Resting Deep*. He had begun writing
during the first week of March 1948, when *No Room at the Inn* had parked itself
at the Empire Theatre, Sunderland, and completed the first draft a month later
in Leeds. Partly, it was for something to do, as assistant stage managing and
understudying small roles left him with time to kill, and partly because, having
watched *No Room at the Inn* each evening for several months from his prompter's
position in the wings, he had developed a healthy contempt for it and had
decided he could do far better himself.

Set in a remote Welsh village, *Resting Deep* told the story of a young poet
running up against local prejudice. Stella persuaded him to read her what
he had written so far and when he did, she saw the enticing glimmer of a
potentially bright prospect. Alerting her husband, who was negotiating various
deals in London, she informed him that the assistant stage manager 'looked
like a Greek god and wrote marvellous poetry.' This was enough to intrigue
Desmond, who arrived at the *No Room* theatre full of curiosity but was disappointed to find Osborne not to be quite as gilded as Stella had claimed. He was
less a Greek god than 'a willowy, good looking young man of eighteen', he
thought, and having read the play, he concluded that it was 'very interesting,
but useless.'[4]

But it was only useless, countered Stella, in that it had no dramatic structure,
and this could easily be rectified. In fact, she and Osborne would collaborate
and revise the play together, this time following the principles of stagecraft
and storytelling established in the nineteenth-century well-made play and
used without fail ever since. She was a one-woman British Institute of Fiction
Writing Science. Pinero's *The Second Mrs Tanqueray*, she explained, would be the
perfect model for them to follow. That Osborne had never heard of it, she
assured him, was of absolutely no impediment at all. Desmond concurred and
returned to London, from where he announced that he was poised to take over
the management of the Granville Theatre in Walham Green, coincidentally very
close to Osborne's childhood haunts in Fulham. His appeal to the owners, he

declared, would be strengthened enormously if he presented himself as part of a package deal. If, as a director, he could immediately call upon not only a leading lady but also a new young dramatist with a play ready to go, no owner in his right mind could turn him down. Why didn't the three of them, therefore, join forces?

While Desmond negotiated, Osborne industriously re-wrote while Stella suggested improvements in script conferences revealing she still saw her collaborator as a Greek god. A relationship that would have been considered scandalous outside the easy-going world of the theatre marginally enlivened the tour's crawl through the kiss-me-quick, squeeze-me-slow indolence of the southern seaside resorts and provided amused, speculative gossip among their fellow actors: 'He was attracted to women who could take him over, and Stella could devour a man,' explained another actress in the company. 'Age didn't matter at all to her.'[5]

A few weeks later, Osborne achieved a rather different breakthrough, emerging from his prompter's box at last and into the dazzle of the stage lights. At the Empire Theatre, Sheffield, during the week of 20 September 1948, nine months after the No Room at the Inn tour began, he made his professional acting debut. Standing on stage for the first time since his first forays into acting at Belmont College three years earlier, he understudied for a couple of evenings as Mr Burrells, the billeting officer.

As autumn faded into winter and the long last lap of the tour passed through Grimsby, Nottingham, Torquay, Exeter, Cambridge and Scunthorpe, Desmond reported that sadly, the Walham Green deal had fallen through. But not to worry, he cried, the hunt for a theatre would continue, his day would come and success would soon be theirs. And that was the last Osborne heard of Desmond for several weeks. On 18 December, at the Empire, Wood Green, the No Room at the Inn company gave their final, exhausted performance and Osborne assisted in consigning their now battered and threadbare scenery into the awaiting lorries for the last time. After spending Christmas with Nellie Beatrice, and with no other work in prospect, he joined Stella in Brighton, where they moved into a basement flat leased by the Desmonds at 7a Arundel Terrace. This was a terrace of still impressive but then rather shoddy white stuccoed properties in the Kemp Town area, only a few minutes' walk from the promenade, the amusement arcades, the shingle beach and the sea.

Osborne loved Brighton, and always would, partly in memory of the carefree love he shared there with Stella, and partly for the place itself. With its peeling cream-and-white stucco terraces, its piers and its holiday season fortune tellers, it was a town that even in winter retained something of the jaunty charm of a briny summer. It was also the home of a small theatrical community. Terence Rattigan 'was around the corner, and the stars were above and around us,' Osborne recalled.[6] Other residents included Max Miller, a breezy-to-blue music hall comedian whom Osborne admired tremendously, Hugh 'Binkie' Beaumont, producer of many of Shaftesbury Avenue's star-encrusted drawing-room dramas and who produced Rattigan and Noël Coward, and T. C. Worsley, the drama critic of the *New Statesman*. Patrick Desmond did not object in the slightest to the seaside cohabitation between Osborne and his wife, but remained in London, from where he pelted the collaborators with assurances that it was only a matter of time before a manager offered him a job as a resident director. As soon as this happened, he promised, he would produce *Resting Deep*, now retitled *The Devil Inside Him*, and they would all be in clover.

It is impossible to distinguish from the finished script which passages represent Osborne's work and which Stella's, although the plot, never Osborne's strong point, and the appearance of a semi-comic cleaning lady, a figure familiar to repertory theatre audiences, might have been Stella's input, while its theme of youthful disillusionment is one that audiences would later associate with Osborne. Otherwise, *The Devil Inside Him* is a traditional three-act melodrama, similar in technique to most of the West End and repertory successes of the day. Despite Stella's restructuring, it is also frequently verbose, something for which in later years Osborne would be berated by his critics. Set in a South Wales boarding house owned by the Prosser family (the name taken from Osborne's paternal mother's family and later reused in his 1976 play, *Watch it Come Down*), the protagonist is Huw, a romantic young man reviled by his friends and pitied by his parents because he writes poetry. If he is wholly or mostly Osborne's creation, as is probable, Huw represents his first attempt at creating an anti-hero, even an existentialist one. A prototype Angry Young Man, an embryonic Jimmy Porter, Huw, like his successor, is given to the simmering, self-pitying rhetoric that would later be identified as an Osborne trademark. Dilys, a manipulative girl dismayed to discover herself pregnant by a former lodger, taunts him in the hope of provoking an assault, intending to claim that Huw has raped her. Huw indeed responds by attacking her, but it culminates not in rape but in his strangling her, after which, rather like Raskolnikov in Dostoyevsky's *Crime and Punishment*, a book that Osborne had read, he experiences a spiritual and moral liberation. The play ends with Huw condemned by his family, the church and the law, and convinced, like Jimmy Porter after him, that the world is set wholeheartedly against him.

Desmond's promise that he would direct *The Devil Inside Him* as soon as he had a theatre was encouraging but of no immediate use to the collaborators, whose finances were by now woefully strained. Osborne appeared as a pirate in *Treasure Island*, one of the local pantomimes, over Christmas, but no other work was forthcoming. As their National Assistance (unemployment) benefit did not stretch very far, Stella took a job as a waitress at a restaurant near the Palace Pier, while Osborne travelled to nearby Rottingdean to wash up in the kitchens of the Elizabethan Court Hotel. In between shifts, they began collaborating on another play, *Happy Birthday*, the leading character of which was based upon Stella's mother and at least some of which Osborne wrote in verse. He had recently seen *The Lady's Not For Burning*, Christopher Fry's verse play, and had emerged from the theatre in a blaze of enthusiasm, convinced that verse drama was something he might be good at himself. He was also inspired by seeing Peter Brook's production of *Dark of the Moon*, a 'legend with music' by Howard Richardson and William Berney at the Ambassadors Theatre in London. Set in the Appalachian Mountains, the leading character is John, a witch-boy who endeavours to become human after falling in love with a young girl. It represented, thought Osborne, 'a blessed change from the drawing room' productions so prevalent elsewhere in London.[7]

But both Stella and Desmond emphatically dismissed Osborne's new-found enthusiasms, reaffirming their whole-hearted allegiance to Pinero. *Happy Birthday* did not survive the impasse. The script was never finished and has not survived. The end of their playwriting partnership coincided with the end of the summer of 1949 and the end of their relationship. Stella left to join a theatre at Kendal in the Lake District. Perhaps she was disappointed; perhaps it was just time to move on. Osborne might have been abandoned by Stella, but not by the ebullient Patrick Desmond, who came sweeping down from London to his rescue. He had struck lucky at last and become a director of the Saxon Players at the Theatre Royal, a weekly repertory theatre in Leicester. Unfortunately, he could not redeem his pledge about *The Devil Inside Him* as he was not permitted to choose the repertoire. But it was a start in the right direction and why didn't Osborne join him there as stage manager? Having nothing else to do, he agreed.

*   *   *

Privately owned, regional repertory theatres operated a hectic schedule, a continuous cycle of presenting a play twice nightly for a week while at the same time rehearsing the following week's play that would replace it. Most had their own resident companies of actors, some of whom spent their entire working lives in one place. Weekly rep is something almost forgotten now, consigned to theatrical and social history. Its demise came during the 1950s, partly because of the rising popularity of the cinema, and later television, which put many local theatres out of business, and partly because of the introduction of state subsidy, which meant that many weekly reps were no longer wholly dependent upon box office takings for their income and could therefore afford a less frantic rate of production. But in the years immediately following the war, there were still over a hundred regional repertory theatres in Britain, many of them the last outpost of the sometimes engagingly amateur, often eccentric actor-manager. Their survival depended entirely upon their pleasing the public, which generally meant serving up a continuous stream of light comedies, farces, detective thrillers and the occasional judiciously selected drama.

Richard and Margaret Stephenson, the managers of the Saxon Players, knew a lot about giving customers what they wanted. Their Dewsbury laundry and dry-cleaning business was doing well enough for Richard Stephenson to indulge his wife's theatrical pretensions and consequently he operated a modest circuit of theatres in Dewsbury, Barrow-in-Furness and Leicester, where his wife energetically fostered a family atmosphere between the company and their audiences who came back, week after week, for more of the same. Ticket sales were buoyant and despite the continuing privations of rationing, grateful audiences often bestowed gifts of chocolates, home-made cakes and even hand-knitted socks upon their favourite actors.

The company was led by Adele Strong, lauded in the programmes as an 'extremely versatile character artiste', and by Peter Storme, 'a master of high-speed farce'.[8] In the little orchestra pit in front of the stage sat Cliff and Clarrie, two elderly pianists, one small with sunken cheeks and the other fat and fond of light ale, who not only tinkled away at their keyboards during the intervals and between performances, but also played the entire score when the Players made their sporadic forays into musical comedy. As new arrivals, Desmond and Osborne were eyed warily by this Saxon old guard. Desmond aroused distrust on account of his vegetarianism, a diet then considered by many to be distinctly cranky, if not actually perverse. That he was scruffily dressed was thought needlessly provocative, his habit of kicking off his shoes and conducting rehearsals in his socks considered unhygienic, and his noxious cigars were a nuisance. The new stage manager, on the other hand, seemed all right. Although Osborne had also become a vegetarian, partly through financial necessity and partly a result of Stella refusing to cook meat, his tweed jackets and corduroy trousers were conventional enough for him to pass muster. As stage manager, Osborne had gone up in the world from the days of No Room at the Inn, and he could now delegate some of his former responsibilities, such as prompting, to his assistant. This he often did, disappearing once the show had begun into the Green Room with paper and pen, inviting speculation that he was writing a play of his own. This time, however, nobody was shown the result of his labours.

Not that Osborne had too much time for writing, there being two performances a night, at 6 and 8.15, and daytime rehearsals for the show the following week. It was both time-consuming and arduous. 'Nervous breakdowns among the actors were not unknown,' recalled one of Osborne's assistants.[9] Osborne successfully avoided a breakdown, but not boredom. After little more than a couple of months and with no hope of The Devil Inside Him or anything else he might write being taken up by the Saxon Players, he lost interest in the company and decided to engineer his escape. This was easy enough. As one of Margaret Stephenson's rules was that profanity was expressly forbidden within her hearing, his calculated and profligate swearing goaded her so successfully that she rewarded him with the sack.

He returned to Stoneleigh and Nellie Beatrice and to ferreting out another job from the classified advertisements in The Stage, the weekly theatrical newspaper that relayed the news and reviews from the West End, and from repertory theatres from Aberdeen to Penzance. In its columns of classified advertisements, landladies trumpeted the advantages of their accommodation, managers appealed for comedians to fill the lower rungs of variety bills, retiring or defeated actors offered their evening suits for sale and actresses their ball gowns, pensionable magicians attempted to rid themselves of trunk escape mechanisms and adagio dancers desperately sought new partners. Anxious pleas for young actors to join repertory companies that always seemed disconcertingly far from London were couched in a stark shorthand: 'Juv char. male, good wardrobe, study, wkly rep, state lowest, photo, SAE'.[10] Decoded, this meant that a weekly repertory company required a juvenile character actor owning his own basic stage wardrobe of lounge suit and other formal wear. He was also required to be able to learn lines quickly and have a recent head-and-shoulders photograph ready to send with his application, not forgetting to enclose a stamped, addressed envelope for their reply. In addition, the applicant, probably already disheartened by penury, was almost invariably instructed to 'state lowest', in other words, suggest the minimum wage for which he was prepared to work.

Scanning the advertisements, Osborne came across The Saga Repertory Group, a travelling theatre company in Devon. It offered no salary whatsoever, but instead dangled the doubtful carrot of a share in any profits that might be made. The company was clearly impoverished, but nevertheless Osborne dispatched one of his portrait photographs and an artfully embroidered account of his experience to an address at Ilfracombe. Almost by return of post a letter whizzed back, begging him to join the company as soon as possible. Not only was The Saga obviously broke, it was evidently desperate for recruits. Rattling down to the West Country by steam train, Osborne found the company in residence at the Gaiety, a tiny theatre on Ilfracombe's windblown seafront, lashed by out-of-season rain and sea spray. It was there that he met Anthony Creighton, a man who was to play a more significant part in his life than anyone he had met so far.

*   *   *

The innocent ambition that Osborne detected in The Saga's advertisement glowed like a beacon in its twenty-seven-year-old director. A short, cheerful-looking man, his dark curly hair already quickly receding, Anthony Creighton had founded The Saga earlier that year, in the summer of 1949. Born in Toronto in 1922, he was seven years older than Osborne. His parents having separated while he was very young, he had arrived with his mother for a new life in England. Like the similarly itinerant Osbornes, Elsie and the young Tony had suffered financial difficulties and done their share of moving from one address to another before settling in a village near Saffron Walden in Essex. There, Elsie Creighton had 'developed an eye for furniture' and created a profitable small business by buying antique furniture at East Anglian auction rooms and selling it on to metropolitan dealers.[11]

In 1934, when he was twelve, Tony had been taken to London to see John Gielgud in Hamlet, at the New Theatre, an experience that proved to be a Road to Damascus conversion. Inspired by Gielgud's lyrical delivery, he decided

that he too must become an actor and began giving solo recitals from Shakespeare outside a local pub, timing his performances to begin as the lunchtime
sessions closed, thereby hoping to attract a generous audience of sufficiently
mellowed farmers. At the outbreak of the war, he had joined the RAF, serving
as a navigator on bomber aircraft and was awarded the Distinguished Flying
Cross after saving the lives of fellow Halifax crew members during a raid over
Hamburg. He also found a ready niche for his theatrical ambitions by performing in entertainments for servicemen at RAF ground stations, where he met
Terence Rattigan, then a wireless operator and gunner. They appeared together
in at least one concert, entitled Boys in Blue or, Things in Wings, which featured a
chorus line of RAF personnel in drag. Having survived both this and the war
unscathed, Creighton completed a course at the Royal Academy of Dramatic
Art in London and subsequently joined the John Gay Players at Barnstaple in
Devon. But convinced that he possessed the feline grace that he had detected in
Gielgud and impatient to display his talents to a wider audience, he accepted a
£200 gift from his mother, and with three other actors from Barnstaple, formed
his own travelling company. 'We were all absolutely fired with ambition,' he
remembered, 'all desperately wanting to get on.'[12]

'For the first time in many years, north Devon has a company of strolling
players', approved The Stage on 16 June 1949. 'They are The Saga Repertory
Group, and they are taking their plays from village to village in a converted
ambulance.' As company manager, however, Creighton had both advantages
and disadvantages. He was 'kind, gentle, enthusiastic, and a lot of fun, [with]
a great sense of humour,' recalled one of the actors who worked with him.
But although admired as a director, his administrative skills were erratic and as
an actor he was very far from what The Stage would call a quick study. 'Tony as
usual doesn't know a word,' became a familiar cry of despair.[13]

Being unable to drive, Creighton entrusted the company's transport arrangements to the man he optimistically described as his business partner. This was
the corpulent Clive St George, who booked the venues where they were due to
perform and took to the wheel of their decommissioned ambulance to convey
cast and props from one village to the next, swerving along single-track roads
where high hedges protected the fields on either side. Each evening, they put
up their fraying scenery in a village hall, plugged in their few lights and performed their play – Emlyn Williams's 1936 thriller, Night Must Fall, in which
the leading character is a psychopathic murderer, was a favourite – before
whomsoever Clive's frantic publicity campaigns had induced to turn up. Afterwards, they would unplug the lights, dismantle the scenery and, if no one had
offered accommodation for the night, sleep in the back of the ambulance. But
although The Saga operated a profit-sharing policy, its actors soon found that,
once necessities had been paid for, there were seldom any profits to share. 'We
had no money,' recalled Creighton contentedly. 'But it didn't matter. You could
live on almost nothing in those days. We were happy. We were doing what
we wanted to do.'[14]

Yet such bucolic living was susceptible to the hazards of an English autumn and by the time Osborne was on his way to Leicester, The Saga had abandoned rural touring and retreated indoors, taking up residence at the Manor Theatre in Sidmouth. There they ambitiously expanded their repertoire, Creighton having secured the local rights to Rattigan's *Flare Path*, set among a group of civilians at an RAF base awaiting the squadron's return from a night raid. Perhaps rashly, considering The Saga's permanent financial plight, Creighton increased the acting company to seven, the new recruits including Lynne Reid Banks, then twenty and fresh from drama school, and later to become a respected and prolific novelist. By November, the Sidmouth gamble had proved a financial catastrophe, as Saga ventures usually did, and the company had shifted operations to Ilfracombe, where they arrived after a terrifyingly rainswept journey in the ambulance. Moving into their digs at the Collingwood Hotel, where Osborne joined them, they bravely announced their programme of thrillers, comedies and dramas at the Gaiety Theatre. While Osborne, 'tall and thin, with a grey overcoat and a scarf', applied himself to learning the lines for his first performance, the company took the opportunity to observe their new recruit. His photograph had given the impression of a handsome, even debonair young man, and the reality did not disappoint. 'Quite a good looking chap. Not bad,' approved one Saga actress.[15] A homosexual, Creighton also found Osborne 'very attractive' and after a few weeks of wondering whether the newcomer might be receptive to an advance, made a tentative approach. 'I said a couple of things,' he remembered many years later, 'but John was baffled. He seemed not to know about homosexuality.'[16]

And so while Creighton withdrew and admired silently, Osborne threw himself into the work of The Saga. 'He was a very quick learner,' approved Creighton, 'a very good actor and always helping. He'd paint the scenery and help load and unload it. He was very keen.'[17] According to Banks, however, Osborne's acting 'left a lot to be desired', especially if he was unsympathetic to the play they were performing.[18] Among Osborne's first ventures at Ilfracombe was Mary Hayley Bell's *Duet for Two Hands*, a ludicrous melodrama in which a malevolent surgeon grafts the hands of a murderer on to the severed wrists of an innocent young pianist, as a result of which he develops an irresistible urge to throttle everyone he meets. Having grappled his way through this unenviable role for a week, Osborne found his share of the profits to be a depressing ten shillings.

However, The Saga was a much happier company than those he had experienced so far. He also had time for some writing, and would sometimes make a late-night appearance in the Collingwood Hotel's guests' lounge, where the actors gathered after the show, bearing 'a scene from some play he was writing and insist, in his languid way, on our listening while he read to us.'[19] Their content, though, seems to have been unmemorable. At the Gaiety, the company were largely reliant on trade from summer holidaymakers and as autumn slouched past in overcast grey, their audiences rapidly dwindled until

all that was left was a small winter residue of elderly women protecting themselves against the performances and the lack of heating in the auditorium by
wrapping themselves in travelling rugs. Faced by rows of empty seats and
diminishing cash, the Gaiety was abandoned and the company quickly reduced.
Osborne chose to stay but several others, including Banks, gratefully took the
opportunity to leave. Eleven years later, she would adapt some of her Saga experiences in the 'flashback' scenes of her first novel, The L-Shaped Room, in which
the twenty-seven-year-old Jane Graham gives up attempting to establish herself
as an actress in the north of England, arrives in London and rents a top-floor
room in Fulham.

Yet despite 'facing thousands of difficulties', the ever-resilient Creighton
decided that rather than waving the white flag, he would retaliate with an
aggressive, last-ditch business plan.[20] The Saga would resume small-scale
touring, but this time abandon village halls in Devon in favour of those within
striking distance of London. The closer they were to the capital, Creighton
assured the remaining company members, the more likely it was that theatrical agents would see them and, as a result, they might even be offered paid
work. They would travel not in the ambulance, which they would sell, but in
Clive's somewhat unreliable car, hauling their equipment on a trailer hitched
to the back. It would be a final, cut-price stand in the name of their art. It
failed dismally. Night Must Fall attracted only half a dozen people at Hartley
Whitney, their first stop, while the residents of East Grinstead, alerted perhaps
by some warning jungle telegraph, remained resolutely at home and ignored
their arrival altogether. Even Creighton surrendered in the face of so fiery a
dragon of rejection. It was unequivocally the end for The Saga Repertory Group.
They must go their separate ways.

CHAPTER 6

Bridgwater Bound

CREIGHTON AND OSBORNE arrived back in London at the end of the year. Creighton set about planning his next moves from his basement flat in Hammersmith, while Osborne returned to Nellie Beatrice and Stoneleigh to hear surprising news. Not only had Patrick Desmond and Stella Linden reunited, but they had realised their managerial ambitions by inaugurating the grandly-named Patrick Desmond Players. Its venue, though, the Theatre Royal at Huddersfield, a market town in Yorkshire, was both distinctly unglamorous and a long way from London. Like Creighton, however, Desmond remained effervescently confident in his own abilities, promising to attract 'leading artists of the stage and screen' to star in his productions.[1] Moreover, he informed Osborne, *The Devil Inside Him* would now be blessed with the Desmond touch. Presented as a collaboration between John Osborne and Stella Linden, the play would open on 29 May 1950 and run for one week. Stella would be directing, while Huw Prosser would be played by Reginald Barratt, a short and somewhat short-sighted man who, although not yet a star either of stage or screen, an actor, Desmond assured Osborne, who would nevertheless be giving a remarkable performance.

Arriving in Huddersfield for the few rehearsals Desmond had allocated for the momentous world premiere, Osborne appeared to the cast 'a shy and rather awkward young man' whose 'slightly startled expression' as he watched the actors go through lines he now barely recognised, gave some the impression he wished he, and not Stella, were in charge of things.[2] More likely, he was as nervous as any novice playwright when seeing something he had written – or at least partially written – being rehearsed for the first time, and the lapse of time between writing and production had probably made the defects of the play all the more apparent to him. For her part, Stella's 'film-starry appearance' in slacks and the tails of her blouse tied in a knot below her breasts to expose her midriff, provoked gasps of astonishment and admiration among the Players. 'People thought her very daring,' remarked one actress, who noticed that Osborne was 'clearly mesmerised' by her, although there was no revival of their earlier relationship.[3]

Advance bookings were thin, but Desmond cheerily predicted that since the play was opening on Whit Monday and therefore a national holiday, most of the first-night tickets would be bought last-minute at the door. Although the logic of this sounded dubious, he was nonetheless correct and it was in a gratifyingly full house that the twenty-year-old author took his seat for the first night of his first play. After only two-and-a-half years in the professional theatre, he was watching a play on which he had collaborated being performed by a professional company before a paying audience. If the performance was less than a triumph, the audience did not seem to mind and the applause at the end was friendly enough for Barratt to be thrust before the curtain by one of the actors, who pronounced that a new star had been discovered. The critic of the *Huddersfield Daily Examiner* was more circumspect but conceded that there was 'real dramatic instinct behind the play'.[4] It was not enough, however, to induce either Desmond or anyone else to enquire whether the collaborators had anything else tucked away in their desk drawers.

At the end of the week, Osborne discovered that his first week's earnings as a professional dramatist were £9 10 shillings, which was at least an improvement on The Saga.[5] He stayed on to appear as a gendarme in Desmond's next project, a touring stage version of *The Blue Angel*, the 1930 film starring Marlene Dietrich as Lola, a cabaret singer with whom a repressed teacher becomes disastrously infatuated. Adapted by Edgar K. Bruce, a florid character actor of the old declamatory school whom Desmond agreed could play the teacher on condition that he paid the production costs, the show started its tour badly and went remorselessly downhill, tottering on as far as the Brighton Aquarium where it was declared bankrupt and unceremoniously ditched. The company gratefully dispersed and, with Desmond and Stella both signalling that they owed him no further favours, Osborne was free to return to London. Far from fainthearted, Desmond went back to repertory acting, his impresario ambitions still burning brightly. Stella evidently felt more disenchanted, for she left both her husband and Britain soon afterwards, bewitched by the prospect of fame in Hollywood. Stardom, however, proved more elusive than she imagined and, unable to find work, she eventually moved to Mexico.[6]

*   *   *

But in the six months since The Saga had been scuppered, Anthony Creighton had not forgotten Osborne, and once his friend returned to London he proudly notified him that, fully repaired and refitted, The Saga was ready to take to the theatrical high seas once more. This time it would set sail before a full wind in the shape of a substantial £1,000 investment he had managed to gather from friends. With Clive St George now out of the picture, Creighton had already used part of his capital in leasing the Victoria Theatre at Hayling Island and invited Osborne to join him there as co-director. Although Hayling Island, connected by a causeway to the Hampshire coast, was more remote backwater than high seas, a stack of impressively headed notepaper was ordered, proclaiming Anthony Creighton and John J. Osborne [sic] as co-directors of the re-formed Saga Repertory Group. With the novelty of money in the bank, the partners engaged a company of five actors at a wage of £4 a week each, and set off for Hayling Island.

The Victoria Theatre turned out not to be quite as imposing as its name implied, but a slightly dilapidated hall used for dances and private parties and standing adjacent to the Victoria Hotel: 'H & C in all rooms, two minutes sea, from £5 5s weekly'.[7] But more encouraging for their purposes were the five holiday camps within easy reach that would hopefully provide their audiences. In those days before cheap foreign travel, holiday camps were enormously popular, giving many working families a seaside holiday at a reasonable cost. Inaugurated by Billy Butlin, a fairground entrepreneur who pulled off the trick of reproducing over ground the classless camaraderie of the subterranean wartime air raid shelter, visitors were accommodated in wooden chalets and chivvied into a regimen of bonny baby competitions, bathing belle contests, sing-along concerts and plain but nourishing food. Hoping to coax the same holidaymakers twice within the same week, Osborne and Creighton decided to run their performances not from Monday to Saturday but from Wednesday to Tuesday. It worked. Opening in July with their old standby of Night Must Fall, the co-directors were soon celebrating a sight unprecedented in the short history of The Saga, that of queues at the rickety table that served as their box office. On many evenings that summer the 'House Full' signs were proudly set outside the door of the Victoria Theatre. 'It was', recollected Creighton, 'all terribly exciting.'[8]

Such feverish summer success prompted greater ambitions. The London theatre, they agreed, was moribund, relying largely on the kind of drawing-room drama prevalent before the war, and desperately needed fresh energy. Recent London successes included Emlyn Williams's Accolade, Rattigan's The Browning Version, William Douglas-Home's Now Barabbas, and a slew of verse dramas including T. S. Eliot's The Cocktail Party and Christopher Fry's Ring Around the Moon. Despite Osborne's liking for verse drama, they agreed that the theatre needed modernising to reflect the new, post-war age, and that they were the people to do it. 'We talked all the time about how boring the theatre was, and how we were going to change it,' remembered Creighton. 'So many plays in London were comfortable upper-middle-class dramas, and John and I had tremendous ideas of writing and of producing something much more radical and starting something really new.'[9] Consequently, they decided to transform the company from an anonymous seaside weekly repertory group into a creative hothouse of progressive ideas. The name of The Saga would henceforth be synonymous with daring theatrical innovation. But in this they immediately came a cropper. The advertisement for new plays they placed in The Stage, promoting The Saga as a fulcrum of dramatic experiment and promising that 'all mss [manuscripts] of

plays showing a healthy reaction to prevalent tradition will be promptly read',
drew a disappointingly paltry response.[10] It seemed that either there were few
dramatists interested in reacting against anything, or that Hayling Island was
not thought of as the place to do it.

Chastened, the directors retreated from the parapet of the avant-garde and
fell back upon Plan B, that of lashing themselves to the mast of Hamlet. Not only
would he adapt the play for their company of seven, announced Osborne, but he
would also play the Prince while Creighton would direct and appear as Claudius.
Quickly filleting the domestic meat from its political bones, Osborne slashed the
play by well over half, reducing it to less than two hours of stage time.

Hamlet: My father – methinks I see my father.
Horatio: Where my lord?
Hamlet: In my mind's eye, Horatio.[11]

Whether Osborne thought of his own father in Hamlet's tragedy is unknown.
But in his programme notes to the production, Osborne explained that Hamlet
was a man too powerfully provoked by passion. His indecision, cowardice,
brutality and apparent madness were nothing less than the flames of greatness
burning so intently that they consumed him. In other words, Hamlet, the moral
centre of a corrupt society, was an anti-hero, and, like Huw Prosser, another
prototype Angry Young Man. Creighton was enormously impressed with both
the adaptation and his friend's performance and delighted in the bravado of
it all, although Osborne liked to deprecate it in later years as a youthful folly.
Nellie Beatrice travelled down from London to see it and was proud, and one of
The Saga's regular local patrons remembered the performance as 'very powerful', although, clad in black tights and body-hugging black sweater, conceded
that the Osborne Hamlet uncannily resembled a life-sized burnt runner bean.[12]
However, Osborne thought enough of the enterprise, or his part in it, to keep
the copy of the play he had used for the adaptation for the rest of his life.

Yet Hayling Island, like Ilfracombe, was dependent upon summer visitors,
and as the leaves fell from the trees and a chill autumnal wind gusted along
the empty beach, the 'House Full' signs were consigned to storage. Its sails
sagging, its supplies depleted, The Saga drifted into December and onto the
dangerous rocks of pantomime. Their Aladdin, a desperately makeshift affair into
which, in the hope of guaranteeing a sympathetic audience of fond mothers
and well-wishers, Osborne and Creighton had drafted a chorus of children from
the Hayling Island School of Dancing, proved an emphatic failure. Osborne
appeared as both Abanaza and the Dame, while Creighton played Wishee-
Washee, and together they muddled their way through as much slapstick and
music-hall patter as they could remember. It was a performance that would be
echoed six years later in Look Back in Anger, in which Jimmy and Cliff entertain the
visiting Helena with a mock knockabout double-act, but it left Hayling Island
cold. The Saga was wrecked.

Almost incredibly, however, the company had survived for six months. But now, with their £1,000 capital all but gone, and in the face of such awkward matters as unpaid Entertainment Tax – ten per cent of the gross profits – and a local shopkeeper who had declined to extend his credit any further and was anxious for his money, The Saga did what it did best, hurriedly disbanding and vanishing into the night. Osborne and Creighton arrived in London early one morning as the winter sun began to bleach the cold suburban sky and devoted themselves once again to scouring the classified advertisements in The Stage. Creighton was unsuccessful and eventually took employment at a café, but Osborne's seemingly reliable luck turned up trumps once more, and at the end of March 1951, he boarded a train back to the West Country to begin a season appearing with the Roc Players at Bridgwater, a small market town in Somerset. He would last only just over three months, but it would be a momentous few weeks nonetheless.

*   *   *

Like the Saxon Players in Leicester, the Roc Players were managed by a married couple and, like the Stephensons, Michael Goodwin and Rae Allan served up the usual 'desperately hackneyed' weekly diet of light comedy, farces and detective thrillers at the local Town Hall.[13] According to The Stage, this thin gruel had succeeded in making the Players 'the most popular entertainment' in Bridgwater and a company of sufficient local standing to attract increasing audiences from nearby villages.[14]

Both the Goodwins and Bridgwater immediately roused Osborne's newly emerging lively sense of antipathy, borne probably of impatience, and relayed in regular letters to Creighton in London. This correspondence comprises the beginning of a substantial series of letters Osborne wrote to his friend, extending over the following decade. (Most of those from Creighton to Osborne seem to be lost.) Both were highly intelligent men interested in politics, the world around them, in literature and the discovery and discussion of books and plays. In his letters from Bridgwater, Osborne delivers his opinion on politics (still as hazy as he was in Ewell but broadly pro-Labour in that he was anti-Tory), on books (a continuing enthusiasm for George Orwell and 1984 in particular), on music (still preferably English and especially Vaughan Williams), and on plays (a growing admiration for the Elizabethan and Jacobean dramatists and a fervour for Arthur Miller and Tennessee Williams, then relatively unknown in England, otherwise a general all-round exasperation). Osborne's over-riding preoccupation, though, in the Bridgwater letters, is the progress of his relationship with Pamela Lane, the Players actress who would become his first wife.

The letters provide a remarkable insight into his private thoughts and feelings. Osborne withheld little and appears to have used letter writing not only as a means of relaying information, but as a dramatic exercise, and as such, they are the most consistent early examples of Osborne's gift for extravagant, free-flowing invective. Here in the letters from Bridgwater is the beginning of a writing style and a tone of voice that would later be recognised as uniquely his, familiar to those who saw his plays and read his journalism. Here is the true early and embattled voice of Jimmy Porter.

'Well, here I am,' Osborne reported on his arrival in Bridgwater, 'entrenched in the bloody Roc Players – right in the enemy's lines . . . I feel very much in the wilderness. There is no soul to touch mine here, but that's no new experience . . .'[15] Bridgwater, he advised, was infested with the conservative, middle-class values he had come to loathe, a place full of smug, self-serving people, devoid of imagination or feeling and implacably opposed to such ambitious, imaginative, revolutionary spirits as his own.

Certainly, he considered joining the Players an infuriating professional setback. At twenty-two, and as a former company manager and performed play-wright, he did little in Bridgwater to counter the impression that he thought himself above the likes of an amiable country rep. Not surprisingly, Osborne's arrogance did not endear him either to the Goodwins or their company. But having worked off his initial resentment in a missive to Creighton, he set about rehearsing for his first appearance. The play was My Wife's Family, an innocuous romantic comedy set in the 1920s in the country house of Jack and Stella Gay, but, considering what was to follow, an uncannily prescient choice. As the curtain rose on 13 April 1951, the script directed that Osborne, in the role of Willie Nagg, Stella's brother and a penniless aspiring writer, be revealed entangled in an enthusiastic embrace with Sally, the Gays' housemaid, to whom he is secretly married. She was played by Pamela Lane.

*   *   *

Five months Osborne's junior, Pamela was a local girl, tall, energetic and good looking, with red hair (like Stella Linden) and blue eyes. Osborne fell for her immediately, sensing a kindred, rebellious spirit, as indeed she was. Her parents, though, were conservative enough: her father was a former First World War flying officer, while her mother was descended from rural gentry, and together they ran the town's drapery shop. Her brothers played rugby for the local team. All had been astounded when Pamela announced she had won a place at the Royal Academy of Dramatic Art in London where, coincidentally, she had been a contemporary of Lynne Reid Banks. But although she was now living at the family home, she did not fit easily into the modest middle-class Bridgwater fold. Having led 'a dashing life' in London for three years, she missed the capital, believed that a bright career was ahead of her there and was impatient to go back and achieve it.[16] In Osborne's eyes, this fiery resolve was an encouraging sign of independence and mutiny against the Goodwins and Bridgwater itself.

As far as Pamela was concerned, Osborne presented an exhilarating, raffish figure consumed by a vivid fervour and passion for living and who brought with him a refreshing gust of modern, metropolitan sensibility. He was brimming with ideas, incandescently invigorating and she was swept along by him, loving him as much as he loved her. His appearance, too, was unusually flamboyant. Having long since abandoned his Gaycroft fancy that he resembled the young Leslie Howard, Osborne had adopted a more bohemian look. He had allowed his naturally curly hair to grow longer – these were the days when the standard hairstyle for men was a well-trimmed and neatly-combed short back and sides well clear of the ears and collar – and this, he imagined, lent him a mysterious, romantic quality rather reminiscent of Keats. Together with a deliberately languid manner and an assumed expression of insolent indifference, it further antagonised the Goodwins, who expected their actors to be as neatly turned out and their behaviour as well modulated as any members of the business and shopkeeping community they served. They demanded that he have his hair cut and blend in. Osborne refused. Blending in, he had decided, was not his style.

The Goodwins may have been provoked by Osborne, but on the other hand, they recognised his usefulness in that he was a competent, if unremarkable actor, and if they had thought of dismissal, they decided against it. At the same time as appearing in what was optimistically billed as the 'hilarious complications' of Kenneth Horne's *A Lady Mislaid*, Osborne kept Creighton up to date with hostilities against the Goodwins and the dramatic effect it was having on himself.[17] 'I feel, wrongly I suppose – that I have been giving so much of myself to other people for years. I feel shattered and worn out. My nerves are all to pieces . . .'[18] Yet all would be rectified by Pamela. She was his 'security', he explained, and essential to all his dreams for the future. Life was impossible without his being able to gaze into her eyes. At the same time, he assured Creighton, his relationship with Pamela presented no threat to their old allegiance and 'my love for you . . .'[19]

The assurances of his 'love' for Creighton are a constant refrain in Osborne's letters from Bridgwater. Certainly, there was an extraordinary intimacy between the two men. Osborne often addresses Creighton as 'mouse', or 'mousie', and frequently signs his letters with 'my love, always, forever, Johnny', a contraction of his name that none of his other associates used. (Although it would later be used by his third wife, Penelope Gilliatt.) But while Creighton found Osborne sexually attractive, there is no evidence in the letters, despite the flowery extravagance of his writing, that Osborne reciprocated this interest. He was, nonetheless, very much attached to, even dependent upon, Creighton. There were aspects of him, such as his immense consideration for Osborne, his enthusiasm, encouragement and loyalty that, before he met Pamela, he had seen consistently only in his father, and, to a lesser extent, Hugh Berrington in Ewell.

These were qualities that the always emotionally vulnerable and needy Osborne searched for in others throughout his life. An intense and forgiving loyalty from those around him was enormously important. Therefore, Osborne expended a lot of energy and space in his letters and his regular telephone calls to securing Creighton's allegiance, promising his friend that because Pamela had now entered the picture, Creighton would not be cast out of it. Their alliance would remain intact, but extended by a third musketeer. From now on, it would be the three of them united in what several times in his letters Osborne called 'my scheme of things'. 'I am passionately in love,' he told Creighton, but 'I feel that there is no need to say to you at this time that your place in my scheme of things is in no way usurped, or even remotely threatened . . . And this above all: knowing your animal hatred of women, your natural distrust and suspicion, you will never have anything to fear from her.' [20] Everything, he declared, would work out all right in the end.

Within a few weeks of his meeting Pamela, Osborne proposed they marry and Pamela immediately accepted. 'Don't for God's sake, let this horrify you,' he wrote to Creighton. 'I know only too well that the word "marriage" probably seems to spell . . . the end of everything to a very lonely and cut-off – for the moment – Mouse. Your place in my heart has never been so real, secure or assured, or your place in my life and my scheme of things . . . It may seem a strange paradox to you that I have my security in Pam & you may not even believe it. Nevertheless it is the truth.'[21]

Yet if Creighton was mystified by these whirlwind developments, the Lanes were appalled. What was the meaning of it all? And who exactly was this John Osborne? It was known among the Players that he had been the director of a failed theatre company and a young man who had great plans for the future, and it was also understood that Pamela stood to inherit a £2,000 legacy when she was twenty-five. Was he, therefore, more interested in her money than in Pamela herself? These doubts were thwarted, he reported to Creighton, by the simple expediency of his ensuring that Pamela signed the money over to her parents.

Yet there was also something else, even more alarming than his possible angling for money. Anthony Creighton had not been the only one over the past two years to wonder whether Osborne's clipped, nasal speech mingled with a lazy charm, indicated that he was homosexual. Several of his fellow actors at Hayling Island and Bridgwater had reached a similar provisional conclusion. Why else would he have stayed with The Saga, they reasoned, which was clearly destined for failure, if he and Creighton were not bound together by something more intimate than a merely professional comradeship? Yet all this remained only rumour and conjecture. The relationship between Osborne and Creighton was, at its heart, an alliance, as each saw in the other a man whose enthusiasms mirrored his own. Osborne stayed with The Saga because he felt a considerable affinity with Creighton, who, apart from the Desmonds, who came and went with the wind, had become his first real collaborator in the theatre. Their careers were at a similar stage, both were ambitious, and they shared a sense of theatrical adventure and a conviction that English drama must somehow be wrenched into the contemporary world. Already, they were considering joining forces in writing plays that were new and different, aligned to the changing post-war world.

Osborne's somewhat ambiguous manner was an effect he deliberately assumed, partly to provoke, and partly to conceal the remnants of his lower-class past and the taint of Nellie Beatrice. But Pamela's mother was in no doubt whatsoever. Mrs Lane responded to her daughter's announcement that she intended to marry an apparently arrogant, penniless young actor with horrified disbelief. William and Elizabeth Lane prided themselves upon the lustre of their civic reputation as shopkeepers. Yet, suddenly and inexplicably, Pamela was intent upon marrying a man who in their eyes was not only highly unsuitable but also, possibly morally degenerate. Elizabeth Lane was not a passionate admirer of the Keats look. She was aghast, both at what she saw in Osborne and what she imagined she saw. 'The big gun she brings up against me,' reported Osborne, 'is that I am QUEER (Yes!) Or as she puts it: a NANCY BOY . . . I'll confess it all made me feel a little sick and ill.'[22] The Lanes' unequivocal dislike confirmed them in Osborne's eyes as field marshals of lower-middle-class priggishness. They were 'natural born fascists,' he cried, '. . . blind, intolerant and stupid.'[23]

Mrs Lane was, he informed Creighton, 'even worse' than his own mother: 'selfish, indulgent to the point of every kind of mental horror, dishonest to a degree, joyless, calculating, blackmailing, completely without scruple . . .'[24] Towards Mr Lane on the other hand, he remained sympathetic, representing him as largely ineffective, marginalised and beleaguered by a fearsomely overbearing wife. In later years, Osborne would often be suspicious of women married to men he liked or admired. The Lanes form part of the background to *Look Back in Anger*, in which Colonel Redfern, Jimmy Porter's father-in-law, is portrayed in much the same way as Osborne felt about William Lane, while Alison's unseen mother is a representation of Mrs Lane.

Reading the blow-by-blow accounts of the manoeuvres of his friend and the Lanes in the letters that dropped regularly through the letterbox of his Hammersmith flat, Creighton derived the impression of Osborne casting himself in a battle royal against the combined forces of provincial lower-middle-class convention, and deriving considerable delight from it. In recreating Elizabeth Lane as a dragon to be vanquished, he was limbering up for a lifelong battle against Nellie Beatrice, who, behind her bar in Stoneleigh remained entirely ignorant of her son's wedding plans. Like Huw Prosser and his version of Hamlet, Osborne had arrived at the view that those who were not with him were against him, and it was vital to his fragile self-esteem that those who were ranged against him, in this case the Goodwins and the Lanes, be defeated. For the Lanes, on the other hand, protecting their daughter from what would surely be humiliation and disaster was a simple moral obligation.

Meanwhile, work with the Players continued, and in E. D. Tidmarsh's 'festival of fun' *Is Your Honeymoon Really Necessary?* Osborne appeared as a man who, having just married his second wife, discovers that his first, whom he presumed has died while travelling abroad, is very much alive and has decided to return home.[25] But as far as the Lanes were concerned, a honeymoon involving Osborne and their daughter was something to be prevented at all possible cost.

Stepping up their campaign to prevent the marriage, they summoned him to a summit conference one afternoon at their home. There were appeals to his better nature, threats and denials, culminating in a verbal skirmish ending in both sides remaining as diametrically opposed as when it began. 'They tried abuse, cajolery, remorse, tears, appeals to my better nature – the lot,' Osborne reported to Creighton in a long and detailed dispatch from the front. 'I knew just how to deal with it. I stamped on it. I told them frankly that I knew they hated me . . . and I hated them.'[26]

In subsequent bulletins, Creighton learned that the Lanes had notched up their offensive by monitoring their daughter's movements, watching for any letters that might be delivered to her and pricking up their ears each time she took a telephone call in an effort to track the frequency of her contact with her fiancé. To Osborne's dismay, they recruited reinforcements in the form of Pamela's old friend, Lynne Reid Banks, whom they hoped might convince her of his ineligibility as a husband. She failed. Pamela was 'quite determined' to marry.[27] 'I love you more and more through all this and always shall,' she assured him. 'Pray God that gives you the courage and strength to deal with whatever comes along. I'm with you and closer to you than ever.'[28] Osborne, meanwhile, was appearing in the 'the high-speed comedy' of Austin Melford's *It's A Boy*, in which a newly married man attempts to conceal from his young wife that he already has a grown-up son.[29]

In a desperate last-ditch attempt to divert the marriage, the Lanes hired a private detective to shadow Osborne in the hope, although they could hardly bear it, that some indiscretion might prove his unworthiness as a husband. They were disappointed. Meanwhile, Osborne and Pamela agreed that the only way to outflank her vigilant family would be a clandestine wedding. Rejecting the notion of a register office ceremony as the local registrar was a close friend of the Lanes and would surely alert them, they scurried off to nearby Wells where, for £4, they obtained a special licence granting their marriage within three days. Hoping that the matrimonial equivalent of an early-morning raid would rout the Lanes, they arranged for the wedding to take place at 9.30 a.m. on 23 June at St Mary's Church in Bridgwater, a time when Pamela's parents would surely be occupied at the draper's shop. Two of their allies in the company agreed to act as best man and witness. Absolute secrecy was insisted upon and promised. Pamela did not demur when Osborne explained that since he disliked his mother intensely, he would not be sending her an invitation. She loved him and accepted his decision.

Yet on the big day, it transpired they had been unwise to assume that any wedding in a small market town could remain under wraps. Somehow, the Lanes had been tipped-off and they scrambled down from the shop to arrive breathlessly at St Mary's, where they sat, bewildered and desolate, as their daughter joined her fiancé at the altar rail and John James Osborne, twenty-one years old, bachelor, was pronounced the lawful wedded husband of Pamela Elizabeth Lane, twenty-one, spinster of this parish.

CHAPTER 7

Repertory

IMMEDIATELY AFTER THEIR WEDDING, Osborne and Pamela handed their notices to the Goodwins, began a week of appearances in *Grumpy*, a farce written by Horace Hughes and the exotically named T. Wigney Percival, and on Sunday 1 July 1951, the morning after the production ended, boarded a train to Paddington. Before they did so, perhaps mindful of William Lane's distress, Osborne wrote him a letter assuring him that he would forever love and look after his daughter. Once in London, husband and wife moved into one of the many small private hotels in Cromwell Road, South Kensington. Creighton, meanwhile, was wondering what effect Pamela's arrival would have on their friendship. But, as Osborne had predicted, they took to each other straight away. 'She was a marvellous girl and we became very good friends,' he recalled.[1]

Obliged to spin out what little money they had as far as possible, the Osbornes had hardly settled into their hotel before they moved out and into a cheaper lodging house nearby. From there, they set out for the West End and the tramp from one theatrical agents' office to another in the hope of being offered work. But as the agents shook their heads and apologetically spread their hands, their money rapidly dwindled. Even though they had their National Assistance benefit, they seemed to be teetering permanently on the brink of poverty. And yet Osborne appeared to have a knack of attracting luck when it was most needed, and within a few weeks he found acting work at the Camberwell Palace, a theatre in Denmark Hill in south London.

The city had not changed much in the few months he had been away. The result of the General Election in February the previous year had merely proved what many assumed: if Labour had failed, not enough people were convinced the Conservatives could do any better. Attlee had been returned to power but grudgingly so, his 1945 majority of 146 slashed to five. Socialism, or the British version of it that had once seemed so inviting, was turning out to be ruinously expensive. Already the National Health Service was costing an alarming £356 million a year and becoming a more insatiably cash-devouring beast than even many of its supporters had either predicted or wanted. Moreover, several trade unions were defying Attlee's appeal to moderate their demands for increased wages, and industrial disaffection rankled. The government's difficulties were compounded by squabbles within the Party, many on the left arguing that economic dependence upon the United States had simply rendered Britain subservient to American political and military will. Their case appeared incontrovertible when charges were imposed for the first time on false teeth and spectacles provided by the National Health Service. Controversially, the resulting revenue was destined for the arms industry, for the government had agreed to support the United States in its military defence of South Korea against Communist incursion from the North. As Party morale sank to low ebb, Attlee retreated into hospital suffering from a painful duodenal ulcer, a human metaphor for an enfeebled government.

The conviction that things were adrift was unintentionally epitomised by the government-sponsored Festival of Britain. Supposedly a morale-boosting celebration of national culture and scientific advances, it spectacularly failed to enthuse a nation still burdened by food rationing and the carrying of identity cards. Osborne and Pamela had arrived in London in time to spend a day at the £11 million extravaganza, transforming the South Bank of the Thames from a bomb-torn wasteland into a theme park of hopeful post-war renaissance. The Festival Hall, a new concert hall, rose above temporary pavilions displaying various exhibits, each intended to provide a vision of a nation reborn in splendour and with its eyes set purposefully upon the future. Visitors were invited to eat at the Regatta Restaurant, consider the gargantuan bronze sculptures by Henry Moore and Barbara Hepworth, ride on Roland Emmett's crazy railway and marvel at the technological wonders exhibited in the Dome of Discovery. Over it all hovered Skylon, a steel-and-aluminium needle 300 feet high, an exclamation mark of confidence and pride seemingly suspended in space though tethered by lightweight steel cables. Created as 'something jolly . . . something to give the nation a lift', the Festival only emphasised the parlous state in which the nation found itself.[2] Once securely anchored, it now, like Skylon, appeared to have no visible means of support.

Neither did Attlee, who was forced to declare another election in October. This time, the voters declined to give the Labour Party the benefit of the doubt, and as Osborne started work at the Camberwell Palace, Churchill's Conservatives were returned to power with a slim majority of seventeen. Acknowledging that this was at best only reluctant approval, and perhaps also mindful of his disastrous 1945 campaigning style, Churchill wisely conceded the achievement of Labour's social reforms in his first speech in the Commons after the election. The country, he announced, required 'several years of quiet steady administration, if only to allow socialist legislation to reach its full fruition.'[3]

The precariousness of the country was mirrored in miniature at the small and shabby Camberwell Palace, which was built on drained marshland, and on days of torrential rain, brackish water flooded into the little orchestra pit.

By now, Osborne was doing little to conceal his aversion to weekly repertory. Not even the surprise Keystone Kops diversion of the theatre door crashing open one day and gesticulating policemen disrupting rehearsals as they chased a check-suited bookie's runner across the stage alleviated his listlessness. To his fellow actors he appeared 'tired, untidy and unhappy', while Harry Hanson, the Palace's 'waspish, fastidious and intensely house-proud' manager, was aghast at the indolence with which Osborne treated the theatre's stock of costumes – the best, he cried, that the finest theatrical costumiers in London could provide.[4] Hearing echoes of the Stephensons and the Goodwins, and having negligently played Charley in Brandon Thomas's *Charley's Aunt*, Osborne succeeded in pro- voking Hanson into confrontation and left Camberwell, as he had Leicester, by being given the sack.

The daily trek to and from agents' offices in search of work now began not from the Osbornes' lodgings, but from Hammersmith. Creighton had come to their assistance by offering them a room in his flat at 53 Caithness Road, recently vacated by a previous lodger. For thirty shillings a week, they had a bedroom and shared the kitchen and living-room with Creighton and his pet dachshund. Every so often, Osborne took time from job-hunting and hurried down to Stoneleigh to see his mother, his aversion to her not preventing his collecting the food parcels she prepared for him, possibly supplemented by Eric and the black market, and returning laden to Hammersmith to share them with Creighton and Pamela. Not that Nellie Beatrice knew that Pamela existed, let alone that her son was married. In the eyes of the Lanes, though, their daughter's marriage was a calamity that continued to torment them, and one day they advanced from Somerset and laid siege to Caithness Road in a final attempt to persuade her to return home. It was not a success. Elizabeth Lane appealed to Pamela, harangued Osborne, interrogated Creighton and, catching sight of his dog, seized upon its enquir- ing presence as clinching evidence of the homosexuality of the male occupants of the flat. Only homosexuals, she cried, owned dachshunds. No further proof of Osborne's iniquity was required. Her son-in-law's lover was clearly this man Creighton. Incensed, Creighton demanded the Lanes leave, and while Pamela resolutely stood her ground and Osborne, Creighton and the dachshund stood theirs, the Lanes admitted defeat at last and withdrew to Somerset.

*   *   *

Osborne and Pamela had agreed that they would accept work wherever they could find it, even if it meant their separation. In the event, they stayed together at Caithness Road for five months before Pamela joined a touring production of Noël Coward's *Present Laughter* at the beginning of 1952, leaving her husband to continue his search alone. Eventually he too found work, accepting a sea- son's contract with the Repertory Players at Kidderminster, in the midlands. Creighton continued his search alone while working part-time at a telephone exchange.

Arriving in the second week of April, Osborne found the Playhouse Theatre to be a small and ostentatious auditorium fitted out in red plush seating and locally woven carpets. In Robert Gaston, the company director, he discovered a man whose theatrical tastes were rather more adventurous than those of the Stephensons and the Goodwins. Yet Gaston took care not to be too highbrow for too long, only slipping the occasional Shaw, Shakespeare, and even, daringly, Tennessee Williams, between several weeks of the usual light comedies and whimsical romances. Osborne had arrived in Kidderminster as a character actor, but luck soon came his way again when one of the leading actors suddenly left and he was asked to take his place at a wage of £8 a week. With the incentive of playing leading roles, Osborne quickly settled down and survived a full season of twenty-four plays without being sacked. Apart from his time with The Saga, his six months at Kidderminster Playhouse turned out to be his longest continuous stint of weekly repertory. The season opened at the end of April 1952, with Michael Clayton Dulton's The Happy Family, followed by Tennessee Williams's A Streetcar Named Desire, one of Gaston's brief excursions into more demanding terrain and in which Osborne played Stanley Kowalski. Meanwhile, he learned his lines for another American play, John Steinbeck's Of Mice and Men.

He had perked up considerably since leaving London. Gone was the scruffy, dejected, pallid young man who had moped about the Camberwell Palace. Instead, according to Brenda Kaye, who frequently appeared opposite him on stage, the John Osborne who marched purposefully into the Playhouse each day, wearing flannel trousers and a tweed jacket, had 'the air of a public schoolboy. He was alert, intelligent, witty, and confident, a very attractive young man' who proved himself to be 'a talented and versatile actor, a good light comedian and a very good farceur.'[5] Osborne was clearly at ease and enjoying himself, partly because having discarded the arrogance that had gained the upper hand in Bridgwater and Camberwell, he discovered himself to be well liked and appreciated, and partly because he had successfully lobbied for Anthony Creighton to join the Players as an actor and stage manager. They shared digs, as many company members did, and although some speculated idly as to whether or not their association was more than close friendship, the Players was a harmonious group and the two men became popular members of it. They first appeared together in May in Of Mice and Men, an amiable tale of the loyalty of two brothers and set among the itinerant workers on a Californian ranch, Osborne playing Curly, the ranch-owner, and the dapper Creighton the kindly ranch-hand, George. During the following months, they would appear together in ten plays and, when confined to his duties as stage manager, Creighton admiringly watched his friend on stage from the wings. Although still on tour with Present Laughter, Pamela managed to visit occasionally and observed her husband's performances rather more shrewdly. Nellie Beatrice also arrived once or twice, huffing and puffing from the exertions of the journey from Stoneleigh, and pronouncing herself enormously impressed.

Playing leading roles resulted in Osborne finding his name cropping up
regularly in reviews, both in *The Stage* and the local press. But while *The Stage*
reviewer preserved a critical detachment, the dexterity of Osborne's performances quite turned the head of the man from the *Kidderminster Shuttle*. Reviewing
Sheridan's *The Rivals*, he declared that 'John Osborne's Faulkland, balanced on
the agate edge of amorous indecision, was made from the moment the fop
flung his first bow in the approved period style', and in Shaw's *Arms and the Man*,
he gave 'his best performance to date' as Bluntschli, the Serbian artillery officer,
wearing his uniform 'with careless bravado'.[6] By the time the season ended in
October, Osborne had appeared in sentimental comedies and headlong farces,
Edwardian family dramas and contemporary American realism. He had played
the title role in Bram Stoker's *Dracula*, a part in which he 'really went to town',
Maxim de Winter in Daphne du Maurier's *Rebecca*, and Malvolio in *Twelfth Night*,
in which the diminutive Creighton played the diminutive role of Fabian.[7] The
Kidderminster season boosted Osborne's self-confidence and consolidated his
experiences of stagecraft and of plays that would be of enormous value in his
subsequent writing; yet while it had been diverting, it was, in the end, disappointing. When Osborne, Creighton and Pamela returned to Caithness Road in
December, it was to unemployment again. None of them had been spotted,
as they hoped they might, either by a London agent or by a director from
one of the more prominent repertory companies. Instead, Osborne resorted to
working at the Post Office in nearby Blythe Road, which took on casual staff
to speed the distribution of the seasonal mail. Creighton joined a firm of debt
collectors in Oxford Street.

In January 1953, things looked up again when Pamela joined another tour,
but Osborne and Creighton toured only as far as the local Labour Exchange.
Unemployment was briefly punctuated by the unexpected arrival of Patrick
Desmond, who had lost none of his optimism and claimed Osborne for the
part of a sailor in a threadbare tour of *Rain*, a play by Somerset Maugham in
which a clergyman is corrupted by a prostitute. Although Desmond still persisted that great things were only just ahead of them, *Rain*'s business, never
steady, quickly diminished to a meagre drizzle that took only a few weeks to
peter out altogether. At a loose end again, Osborne joined the Under Thirty
Group, a summer company run by the actor Oscar Quitak at a makeshift
theatre at Frinton-on-Sea, a small and very middle-class town on the Essex
coast. Despite his Kidderminster experience, he was awarded only minor roles,
one in an Agatha Christie play and another in Philip King's farce, *See How They
Run*, a wartime comedy of mistaken identity. Peter Nichols, a fellow Frinton
actor and later a successful dramatist, recalled that Osborne's character was
billed as The Intruder, 'which his future career in art and life would show to be
very good casting.' His 'uncommonly scathing, sneering manner', however,
which Nichols thought made Osborne 'very watchable', did not accord with
the management's opinion and, to his relief, Osborne was once again sacked.[8]
A weekly wage was not worth it, he explained to Creighton, if one was

appearing in plays one disliked in front of audiences one disliked and in a place
one disliked as well.

*   *   *

While Osborne languished in Frinton, a new Queen was being crowned at
Westminster Abbey. At least 27 million people gathered in pubs and front
rooms across the nation to watch the Coronation on one of the fascinating
new television sets, peering at the flickering, black-and-white images of the
ceremony relayed from the Abbey, while outside their streets were festooned
with red, white and blue. Although rationing would not finally end for another year, the Age of Austerity was beginning to be replaced by an era of
mass media, in which the immediacy of pictures broadcast to a family sitting
in its front room brought a thrilling sense of one's armchair overlooking the
world. On Coronation Day, 2 June 1953, it was as if everyone was able to
take a place in the Abbey. Such a magnificent technological wonder as live
television was as much cause for national pride as the Coronation itself. 'Let
us have done with unworthy murmurs that we, with our great past and great
traditions, are now a second-class power,' chided the writer Violet Markham.[9]
And for a day, few people doubted her, or at least not publicly. The Coronation and the festivities that surrounded it signalled that while Britain might
have shed great chunks of its Empire and might not be the economic power
it once was, it was nevertheless still – surely – a historical and moral force
to be reckoned with. The Coronation, 'an elaborate piece of romantic theatre
that managed to be both a celebration of hierarchy and empire, and a family
affair', succeeded where the Festival of Britain had dismally failed.[10] It suggested that Britain remained a society whose strength lay in consensus, the
threads of the social pecking order running from the aristocracy to the working class still interwoven with those of traditional, conservative values into
one seamless fabric.

   Yet the pomp and circumstance of Westminster Abbey and the buns and
bunting of street parties could not conceal a sense in some quarters of national
unease. Not only the political and the social, but also the cultural landscape of
Britain had been altered by the war and its aftermath, and its new alignments
were not yet fixed. There was still not a lot of money about. Several political
and cultural commentators were pointing out that the United States was asserting a new and immensely powerful imperial influence, not only politically
and economically, but also culturally in films, popular music, fashion and the
theatre. Up and down the land, glamorous Hollywood movies played upon the
daydreams of millions in the murky darkness of cinemas; in the larger cities,
the sounds of American jazz floated from subterranean clubs and American big
band music from dancehalls, and everywhere women read magazines lavish
with pictures of American film stars and articles on the latest American trends
in hairstyles and hem lengths. London's West End was not immune and was
suddenly loud with big, brash American musicals. The open-air optimism of

Oklahoma! had created an enormous impact in 1947, and was quickly followed by *Carousel*, *Kiss Me Kate*, *South Pacific* and, in Coronation year, the urban, sassy, dice-rolling *Guys and Dolls*. The American musical cared nothing for national insecurities, the sloth of the rebuilding programme, food rationing or drudgery: 'youthful, and irresponsible', it brimmed with 'flamboyance, colour, energy and spirit'.[11] The confidence and expansiveness of America was enormously invigorating and powerfully seductive, and proved a force to which many happily, even gratefully submitted.

By contrast, the most significant events in British culture in the few years since the end of the war were the incessant lamentations of its decline. Osborne was eleven when Virginia Woolf's death in 1941 had signalled the end of pre-war Bloomsbury and its intellectual, gossiping pacifists, south of England country houses and intricate love affairs; and twenty-one in 1950, when George Orwell, the novelist, pamphleteer and journalist who instinctively sided with the underdog but understood the enormous attractions of being top dog, expired of tuberculosis in London. During the same year, Bernard Shaw died at his home in Hertfordshire, thereby creating 'an extraordinary outpouring of memories and obituaries' and theatre lights on Broadway to be briefly dimmed in tribute.[12] Their deaths seemed to create a vacuum. The critic Cyril Connolly was among those who first set the ball of pessimism rolling, bemoaning in successive articles in *Horizon* that on the cultural front, absolutely nothing was happening. '. . . From now on,' he prophesied despondently in 1949, 'an artist will be judged only by the resonance of his solitude or the quality of his despair.'[13] As the curtain went up on *The King and I* at Drury Lane and Gene Kelly splashed exultantly down the street in *Singin' in the Rain* at the nation's cinemas, *The Times Literary Supplement*, the *Observer* and others joined Connolly's chorus of doom, complaining that so far, the peace had produced no writers of any note. Not that Drury Lane or cinema audiences minded, but to cultural mandarins like Connolly, the crisis was cataclysmic. The end of the novel was deemed to be nigh, as it so often is, and the British theatre had apparently expired unnoticed. 'There are still no signs of any literary revival,' reported T. C. Worsley, the theatre critic of the *New Statesman* in 1950; 'no movements are discernible, no trends.'[14]

British, as opposed to American, literature and theatre indeed seemed becalmed. Evelyn Waugh, the former chronicler of the Bright Young Things of the 1920s and who had now become so crustily right wing that he was done to a turn, looked upon Britain not with the hope that Tony Benn and many others had shared in 1945, but with loathing. 'England as a great power is done for,' he grunted into his diary in 1946.[15] The previous year, Waugh had saturated his novel *Brideshead Revisited* in nostalgia for the pre-war age of aristocracy, of the English country house, of lifelong friendships to be made between young men at Oxford and of the expensive meals and pretty girls on which they might guzzle without any niggling worries about money or social ethics. It was a world away from Orwell's political satires of Soviet Communism and

English Socialism. Yet such politically opposed novelists as Waugh and Orwell shared something that the critic D. J. Taylor identified as dominating serious fiction of the immediate post-war years: that of decline. This was something the newspaper-reading Osborne was well aware of, and it would become a vitally important theme in his own writing.

As for the English theatre, Osborne had arrived at the same conclusion as many others, that in content and production style it seemed largely to be frozen in the pre-war years. The West End of London was still dominated, as it had been during the 1930s, by star-laden, well-made plays set in the Home Counties produced by Hugh 'Binkie' Beaumont, who ran the H. M. Tennent production empire from his eyrie at the top of the Globe Theatre on Shaftesbury Avenue, reached by a geriatric lift. But despite its opulent upholstery and star performances, the Binkie style was looking increasingly remote. Cut-glass drawing-room dramas and genially undemanding comedies set among the upper-crust in Belgravia and in country houses were slipping badly on the cogwheels of time. Binkie's stable of playwrights such as Noël Coward and William Douglas-Home appeared increasingly to be mailing their work from a former world. In Coward's *Relative Values*, in 1951, one character complains that the trouble with contemporary English life is that so many of one's friends must work for a living, while the play ends with the butler casting a backward glance to Attlee's socialism and proposing a toast to 'the final inglorious disintegration of the most unlikely dream that has ever troubled the foolish heart of man, that of social equality.'[16]

For younger dramatists such as Osborne and Creighton, however, there was some flicker of encouragement to be gained from Rattigan, one of Binkie's strongest cards, who, with *The Winslow Boy* and *The Browning Version* had established himself as a master of the well-made play. But in *The Deep Blue Sea*, first produced in 1952, he had also revealed himself as bracingly alert to a post-war sense of political and social disillusion. The story of Hester Collyer, who, in quest of emotional and sexual fulfilment, turns her back on her loveless marriage to a judge and – scandalously – moves into a dingy room rented by Freddie Page, a volatile former fighter pilot unable to adapt to the inaction of peace, had won tremendous critical acclaim. However, the following year, Rattigan blotted his copybook with the theatrical progressives who had detected in *The Deep Blue Sea* the refreshing sensibility of post-war uncertainty. His *Collected Plays* were published in two volumes, each with a light-hearted preface by the author, in the second of which he described a typical member of his audience. She was, he wrote, 'a nice, respectable, middle-class maiden lady, with time on her hands and the money to help her pass it. She enjoys pictures, books, music and the theatre, and though to none of these . . . does she bring much knowledge or discernment, at least she . . . "does know what she likes". Let us call her Aunt Edna.'[17]

The implication that no English dramatist could survive without Aunt Edna's benediction became the Aunt Sally of those, such as Osborne and Creighton, determined to reinvigorate the theatre. In a testy letter to the *New Statesman* just before leaving for Kidderminster, Osborne complained that the tyrannical figure of Aunt Edna represented the reason why British plays and audiences had remained largely unchanged for twenty years. Over the years, Osborne would frequently fire off letters to the press, in later life becoming a regular correspondent to *The Times*. To the writer and critic Richard Findlater, he declared angrily that the almost supreme power held by Tennent had resulted in contemporary theatre being 'corrupt and complacent. It is the jolly playground of free enterprise and the burial ground of art and integrity . . .'[18]

As he and Creighton had discovered when they advertised for contemporary new plays at Hayling Island, experimental writers just did not seem to be attracted by the stage. In fact, there were few outlets for new plays. Although the Arts Council, only four years old, had £570,000 to play with in grants and interest-free loans, most of the money was channelled towards music and opera and concentrated upon London. The Old Vic became the happy recipient of £26,000 but produced no new drama, embarking instead upon an ambitious five-year plan to produce all the Shakespearian plays. Elsewhere, both in London and the regions, theatre managers dependent upon their box offices fought shy both of Shakespeare and of new writing and relied instead upon the dramatists and the plays that had proved reliable in the past. Regional repertory in particular faced a crisis. Due partly to the attraction of the cinema, supported by powerful American distribution networks, the theatre's popularity was falling rapidly. Provincial repertory managers, touting their familiar war chest of thrillers and comedies, took to hovering in the foyer before the evening's performance, watching sorrowfully as increasing numbers of their once faithful public deserted them for the nearby silver screen. By the early 1950s, there were over 4,500 cinemas in Britain, and of a population of 50 million, over 30 million were regular film-goers, attracted not only by American features and British comedies, but by the Pathé and Movietone newsreels which, in the days before every home had a television, brought national and international events to audiences far more vividly than the newspapers or the wireless. The mass desertion of their audiences resulted in many regional repertory theatres over the following decade being transformed into cinemas, bingo halls or carpet warehouses before being bulldozed into submission and replaced by municipal car parks. Each week, as theatre closures spread, *The Stage* mournfully listed the casualties. In Leicester, the Theatre Royal, the home of the Saxon Players, was sold to an insurance company. 'You've got to make brass,' was Richard Stephenson's none-too-regretful verdict.[19]

*   *   *

The production of *The Devil Inside Him* had given Osborne the impetus to get down to writing again and by the time of the Coronation he had completed two new plays. While living in Brighton with Stella, he had been sufficiently intrigued by Christopher Fry's *The Lady's Not for Burning* to try his hand at his own verse play. Nothing had come of it, but the West End vogue for verse plays, created both by Fry, a former schoolmaster, and T. S. Eliot, whose modernist masterpiece The Waste Land Osborne very much admired, encouraged him to have another go. The Great Bear; or Minette, and The King is Dead, both exercises in blank verse and dealing with historical subjects, were the result. An early and partial draft of the first play survives, revealing that Osborne conceived of it as a kind of Gaelic romance in three acts featuring Owen, a Keatsian poet (Osborne was still evidently interested in Keats), in love with Cordelia, and who deserts her for Dawn. There is little of note in the play other than the basic plot of a love triangle anticipates Look Back in Anger and, more significantly, that it employs for the first time the 'bear and squirrel' motif (Osborne and Pamela's pet names for each other) subsequently used to far greater effect in the later play. Osborne sent a completed version to several managements, all of whom returned it. When he showed it to Pamela, he discovered why. It was, she said, not only written in a 'sub-Eliot style', it was also 'dull and boring'. He accepted her judgment and 'jettisoned' the script, the contraction, 'd and b', meanwhile, becoming a private shorthand between them to be applied to anything they thought a waste of time.[20] It was an expression they continued to use until his death.

She awarded much the same unflinching verdict to The King is Dead, which Osborne completed in January 1953, and which appears to have been very much influenced by his continuing admiration of Elizabethan and Jacobean playwrights. He was immersing himself in Shakespeare, in the savagery and rhetoric of Christopher Marlowe, the author of Tamburlaine and Doctor Faustus, and in John Webster, the author of The Duchess of Malfi. Osborne admired the Elizabethans and particularly the Jacobeans principally for the architecture of their language, its extravagance, virility and vividness. The Jacobean world, the historian Peter Ackroyd has written, 'signifies melancholy, morbidity, restlessness, brooding anger, impatience, disdain and resentment; it represents the horror of life', the characters 'possessed by a will and desire rather than belief . . . this is a world from which God seems to have departed.'[21] This would have struck a particularly responsive chord in the young Osborne, highly intelligent, hungry for intellectual sustenance, still vulnerable from the death of his father, trailing his sense of loss and grievance, alert to the immense possibilities of words and image and impatient to make a contribution. Language and rhetoric used for the sheer flamboyant love of it signalled intensity of passion and as such, would always remain for Osborne something to be celebrated. The recurring Jacobean character of the malcontent, the dissatisfied outsider at odds with both the social structure in which he finds himself and the world of the other characters in the play, and who frequently comments on the action, was also of tremendous interest to him. Hamlet would hold a life-long fascination for Osborne, and he would also have noticed Bosola, the enigmatic, amoral servant in The Duchess of Malfi as a resonant prototype.

Although no script of The King is Dead seems to survive, it appears to have been influenced less by Eliot than by Webster, perhaps a dynastic story of revenge modelled on one of his plays. Undeterred this time by Pamela's doubts, however, Osborne sent it to a new correspondent, the young writer and critic Richard Findlater. 'I really wonder. Am I wasting my own and other people's time?' Osborne asked.[22] Findlater assured him he was not. Encouraged, Osborne sent a script to the Edinburgh Festival but met with no success before sending it to Dame Sybil Thorndike, who, whether she read it or not, bestowed her blessing, and to Kenneth Rose, the owner of the Kidderminster Playhouse. 'You out-Webster Webster,' Rose acknowledged, 'but times have changed. People no longer lap up these horrors with avidity.'[23] He had also, he added dryly, read several plays recently, all of which had arrived with the warning light of Dame Sybil's liberally-awarded seal of approval.

Like Stella before them, both Creighton and Pamela insisted that verse drama was simply not what Osborne was good at. Disappointed, Osborne seems to have conceded that they were right. 'I kept telling him many times', remembered Creighton, 'to drop all the romantic Welsh melodrama and poetry and write prose, and prose about contemporary ideas and situations. I went on and on about this being the only way forward. In that sense, Personal Enemy was the real beginning.'[24]

CHAPTER 8

Doomed in Derby

DURING THE EARLY autumn of 1953, Osborne returned from Frinton to Caithness Road to find that Creighton had already begun a revolutionary assault upon Aunt Edna and the theatrical repertoire. Sitting hunched over a typewriter, he was busily tapping away at a play that he promised would be 'a tremendous breakthrough'.[1] Not only was it in prose, but it bulged with 'contemporary ideas', taking advantage of the current fascination with things American by being set in the United States during the recent Korean War. This had ended only a few weeks earlier in what Sylvia Plath later memorialised as 'that queer sultry summer they electrocuted the Rosenbergs', two American citizens convicted of passing secret information on the development of the atomic bomb to the Soviet Union.[2]

While the Rosenbergs are not mentioned in the play, the atmosphere of *Personal Enemy* draws upon the currents of suspicion and retribution they symbolised. Creighton had been sketching ideas for the play while at Kidderminster, and now urged Osborne to collaborate in the writing. Indeed, for its time, the play appeared startlingly radical in its use of Senator Joe McCarthy's crusade against suspected Communist infiltration of the American establishment as a means of protesting against the widespread social vilification of homosexuals. This was a cause close to Creighton's heart. In America, the prosecutions of suspected homosexuals in the Federal Government were running concurrently with the tracking down of suspected Communists, the so-called 'Lavender Scare' being synonymous in many minds with that of the 'Red Scare'. In Britain, sexual activity between males was still illegal, and homosexuality, or the fear of homosexuality, was also attracting considerable, and disagreeable, newspaper coverage. In the early autumn, the arrest of John Gielgud, an actor as renowned as Laurence Olivier, on a charge of importuning males at a Westminster public convenience, was extensively reported, as was his subsequent conviction and fine. So, early the following year, were the trials of Lord Montagu of Beaulieu and Peter Wildeblood, a diplomatic correspondent of the *Daily Mail*, who were

accused of gross indecency with two RAF servicemen. These and other more
serious stories, some revealing the abuse of adolescents in care, were supplemented by lurid warnings by newspaper columnists and grave pronouncements
by churchmen.

The mainspring of Personal Enemy is the disappearance of Don Constant, a
much-loved elder son and a local hero in his home town of Langley Springs,
who is believed to have been killed while serving in the Korean War. But when
Federal Bureau of Investigation agents reveal that, instead of being killed in
action, he has defected to the Chinese Communists, the family implodes in
shame and recrimination. Don's political conversion appears to have been influenced by his friend Ward Perry, a local librarian, a suspected Communist and
homosexual who, since Don left for Korea, has turned his attention to Arnie,
the Constants' younger, seventeen-year-old son. The ensuing scandal results
in Arnie drowning himself, and his father resorting to drink. The point of the
play, explained Creighton, was to demonstrate not only that homosexuality
was as bogus a threat as Communism, but also to dramatise the dreadful con-
sequences of a persecution-mania.[3]

While the structure of the play is largely Creighton's, some of the writing
is clearly Osborne's. But while the play was extremely topical and within its
limits of domestic melodrama, competently written, the considerable barrier
of official state censorship remained to be overcome before it could be produced. While the Director of Public Prosecutions had the powers to prosecute
the publishers of a novel held to be seditious, blasphemous, defamatory or
obscene, and publishers had the right of defence, the theatre was governed
by a much less publicly accountable form of state-imposed supervision. The
typescripts of all new plays, and new additions to old ones, were required to
be submitted in advance of production, with a payment of one guinea for a
one-act piece and two guineas for a play of two acts or more, to the Lord
Chamberlain's office at Stable Yard, in the grounds of St James's Palace. There,
the Lord Chamberlain, currently the Earl of Scarborough, a former politician
and colonial governor, would distribute each script to his panel of Examiners,
comprising mostly career civil servants or retired military officers, whose duty
it was to scrutinise them for indecency, offensiveness, violence and anything
which might incite public subversion or impair a friendly relationship with a
foreign power.

If pronounced clear on all fronts, the play would then be awarded a licence
for public performance. If not, the coveted licence would be withheld until
the material had been thoroughly cleansed of the offending impurities. The Devil
Inside Him had survived official perusal in 1950, but as the representation of a
homosexual character and reference to homosexuality was still considered to
fall within the province of offensive material, Osborne doubted whether any
producer would be foolhardy enough to submit to Stable Yard so evidently a
lost cause as Personal Enemy. Yet Creighton assured him that while the homosexual theme in the play was not so muffled that it would elude an attentive

audience, it was sufficiently shrouded by the Communist veil to satisfy the censor. *Personal Enemy*, he insisted, would re-launch both their careers.

Osborne's instinct was correct. As one producer after another rejected the play, a disappointed Osborne decided to leave London for Derby, city of industry and porcelain, where Pamela had joined the local Playhouse company as a leading actress. She had already been there for several weeks, renting a room in a lodging house at 32 Ashbourne Road, for which she paid £3 10s from her weekly wage of £10. Proclaiming her faith in the collaborative venture in Hammersmith, and maintaining their arrangement that if one was working and the other not, then the former would help support the latter, she had sent Osborne £3 a week to supplement his National Assistance payments. But although she budgeted stringently, helping her husband meant that occasionally she had to fall back on pawning some of the jewellery given to her by her family. However, she remained buoyant, her letters bristling with encouragement and 'Bear' and 'Squirrel' affection. At the same time, she urged Leslie Twelvetrees, the Playhouse's tall, ascetic director, to give her husband a helping hand similar to that which Osborne had extended to Creighton from Kidderminster, and find him a place in the Derby company. 'Trying to get old Bears work in Derby,' she wrote encouragingly.[4] Anxious to accommodate his leading lady, who had already impressed with her performance of Lady Bracknell in *The Importance of Being Earnest*, Twelvetrees acquiesced, and at the end of January 1954, Osborne left London and joined his wife at Ashbourne Road. In their two-and-a-half years of marriage, it was the first time they had lived behind their own front door and in a room of their own.

At first, all went well and they seemed happy enough. Another actor in the company remembered Osborne as 'a good-looking, charming young man, obviously very intelligent. He could be delightful to talk to, full of ideas, very knowledgeable about the theatre and very emphatic about which playwrights he liked and which he didn't.'[5] Most Saturday mornings, both Osborne and Pamela would turn up at Ramsden's, a coffee shop behind a bakery in the town centre, to join a group of Playhouse actors who would meet to discuss 'literature, the theatre, politics and philosophy – we took ourselves very seriously,' remembered one of the regulars.[6] On Sunday afternoons, Osborne could frequently be seen sitting alone at the nearby Gainsborough Restaurant, reading and writing.

Yet Osborne's talking, planning and generally putting the world to rights at Ramsden's was one thing; applying himself to the daily grind of weekly repertory another, and Twelvetrees soon discovered that Osborne's acting abilities were not quite what he had been led to believe either from Pamela or the lavish endorsements of the *Kidderminster Shuttle*. Consequently, he again found himself playing only minor roles in the kind of plays in which he had appeared before. The continuing doleful reports from Hammersmith about the fate of *Personal Enemy* did nothing to lift his spirits. Yet a sudden and unexpected beam of hope provided by the American actor, Sam Wanamaker, whose Communist sympathies had resulted in his being blacklisted in the United States and his deciding to resume his career in Britain, caused great anticipation. Having received a script from Creighton, Wanamaker invited the collaborators to a meeting. 'This is the moment for P[ersonal] E[nemy],' signalled Osborne exultantly from Derby.[7] But while Wanamaker told them that he thought the play had considerable merit, he doubted it would be produced as the Stable Yard Examiners and theatre managers would think it anti-American. Creighton's 'tremendous breakthrough' was likely to remain wishful thinking. Osborne's precarious Kidderminster confidence began to ebb away.

His rapidly increasingly despondency was in stark contrast to his wife, who was sparkling with determined self-confidence. Sitting in their frayed armchair at Ashbourne Road and watching Pamela cook their frugal meals, or learning her lines for the following week while he read or listened to the wireless, he felt the difference between them becoming increasingly apparent. The star quality that he romantically saw in her at Bridgwater was not just something of his own romantic imagination; it was really there. Not only was she popular in the company and with audiences, she was also a very good actress, the local critics particularly admiring her portrayals of the emotionally fraught Paula in Pinero's *The Second Mrs Tanqueray*, the anguished Hester Collyer in Rattigan's *The Deep Blue Sea*, and in the title role of Ibsen's *Hedda Gabler*. There was speculation that a London management might soon come calling. Hers was a talent that Osborne recognised he just did not have. She was ambitious and becoming successful while he felt increasingly becalmed. He became known in the company as 'Mr Lane'. This rankled. Osborne became moody and withdrawn.

In his notebook, he jotted down random thoughts: lines that would later reappear in *Look Back in Anger*, terse reflections on his sense of deprivation and isolation and of being overlooked and undervalued. Dispirited, he reasoned that Pamela must be exasperated by him as well and doubting whether she still loved him. She seemed to be detaching herself from him. 'You see, ever since I have been up here, she seems to have gone deliberately out of her way to treat me like a stranger,' he explained in one of another series of letters to Creighton explaining his predicament. 'She has given me *nothing* . . . . She has very little to say except this: *I had to realise she was very different when she was working!* . . . I couldn't believe my ears . . .'[8]

As Osborne became increasingly exasperated, time began to drag. '. . . My life has no direction, no shape,' he wrote plaintively.[9] He and Pamela were arguing regularly, the trigger frequently being their lack of money, about which she worried continually. Twice, she had announced she was pregnant; the first ended in a miscarriage, and the second time, they agreed they were too poor to bring a child into the world and the pregnancy was terminated. There seemed barely enough money for their own requirements and Osborne indignantly resented her asking him to contribute equally to their weekly household expenses. This was partly because some of his money was being channelled elsewhere, which he kept secret from his wife. Although he claimed to loathe his mother, he sent her money when he could afford it and also dispatched a regular remittance to the still unemployed Creighton. '£4 in the P[ost] O[ffice Savings Bank] £2 to you, 7/6 to my mother, repairs to my bike . . .' more or less left him destitute, he reported, and subsisting mainly on a daily salad and wholemeal bread. '. . . do you know what I do?' he asked Creighton. 'I steal (yes steal) pieces of bread, hide them in my trunk and eat them when she's out. At twenty-four, I'm an eccentric . . .'[10] The rapid deterioration in the relationship between Osborne and Pamela was quickly noticed in the company. He began to treat her 'in a somewhat cavalier fashion', remembered one of the actors they joined at Ramsden's for earnest Saturday morning conversations, 'which could be embarrassing, as she seemed to worship the ground he walked on. He was extremely dismissive of her views, although at the same time listening to other people's.'[11]

One of those to whose views he listened was John Rees, a fellow Playhouse actor who rented a room below theirs in the same house. A shrewd, wide-eyed Welshman, a 'kind, gentle person who would do anything for anyone', Rees often climbed the stairs to the top floor, where he helped dispel Osborne's Sunday evening dejection by arguing good-naturedly with him over the newspapers and by talking to Pamela, whom he regarded with easy-going, sympathetic affection.[12] Osborne also found diversion in the scintillating presence of John Dexter. Ostentatious, garrulous and, daringly for the time, openly homosexual, Dexter was the son of a local railway worker who had completed National Service in Egypt before becoming an occasional actor at the Playhouse. Always aflame with news and views of the theatre in London and of music, literature and life in general, Dexter radiated energy and a galvanising sense of optimism. These were qualities that, together with absolute loyalty, Osborne valued above all else, qualities that he shared with Creighton and had once shared, or imagined he shared, with Pamela. 'I can only think she's the biggest PHONEY ever to walk,' he told Creighton. 'I feel ill and dazed.'[13] They were arguing more frequently now, and some of their quarrels became physically violent. 'She doesn't even have a twinge of regret,' cried Osborne, 'not an ounce of remorse, absolutely no inkling of compassion . . . I hate and loathe the very sight of her.'[14] 'So much had changed,' recalled Creighton. 'He was disheartened and restless and when he looked at Pamela, he felt a great loss.'[15]

Here is the beginning of *Look Back in Anger*. Osborne had lost a sister, a childhood and his father and was now, it seemed, losing a wife. He felt as though he was suffocating, he told Creighton, for the room at Ashbourne Road was not only physically cramped but had become emotionally oppressive as well as Pamela became the unfortunate target of his disappointments and frustration. Stockpiling his suspicions and resentment, he began to suspect that her family was renewing its appeals that she leave him and that her friends were advising much the same. When a friend of Pamela's came to stay for the weekend, Osborne imagined a conspiracy being hatched against him. '. . . you've no idea how <u>sinister</u> it all is,' he confided to Creighton. 'The atmosphere is really one of popish intrigue . . .'[16] Feverishly searching for evidence of plots being hatched against him, he scrutinised Pamela's mail when she was out, searched through drawers and suitcases and interrogated her on her return as to whether she had discussed their predicament with others. Every move, each detail he related to Creighton, both by letter and telephone. '. . . I had her trapped,' he exulted, reporting the progress of one of their furious arguments. 'I brought out that trump card I've kept all this time: the letter she wrote to Mummy all those months ago. Was she *shaken!* . . . I knew I'd got her up against the ropes, and I was enjoying every moment of it. A few more blows smashed home and it was a knockout. She was sobbing her heart out and I was obliged to try and comfort her . . . The fact is that it was a very real triumph for me. I was able to break her like a stick in my hands and every moment was a joy . . .'[17]

This is the correspondence of an enormously articulate young man torn by bitterness and incomprehension, and emotionally out of his depth. Written with hardly any revision but with an extraordinary lucidity, sharpness and fluency, his letters from Derby, like those written from Bridgwater, uncannily anticipate the rages of Jimmy Porter. 'I rushed home from the theatre last night to hear Vaughan Williams' 6th. Just caught the beginning and sat down . . . stupendous. For a while I was lifted right out of Derby. Madam . . . then decided to start washing a jumper — splash, splash, bang, crash. She couldn't even wait for the finish. I hit the ceiling . . .'[18] This incident, like many others, is transposed almost verbatim into Look Back in Anger.

Pouring his energies into devising new insults to hurl at her, he recorded accounts of their clashes with such malicious vitality it is as if writing them down gave him the opportunity of savouring language. 'He was elated by his discovery of the word pusillanimous in a dictionary,' remembered Creighton. 'He exulted in it. He said the definition fitted Pamela exactly.'[19] Osborne would also use this in Look Back in Anger. And when Pamela, a remarkably resilient woman, accused him of selfishness, Osborne protested innocence: he had given her his love, he declared, and that was surely the most selfless act of all.

Meanwhile, each found respite in brief and initially secret affairs, Osborne with an actress in the company and Pamela with a local dentist who was also a member of the Playhouse board of directors. As if fates were at work, Osborne's first role at Derby had been that of Valentine, the dentist in Shaw's You Never Can Tell; a performance in which 'more crispness and polish' was required, according to the Derby Evening Telegraph.[20] In Osborne's eyes, Pamela's unfaithfulness (he seems not to have counted his own) was the ultimate treachery. 'She must have been BORN with disloyalty in her heart . . .' he snarled.[21]

In some of his letters, when he paused for reflection, Osborne conceded that he was ruthless, heartless and bullying. The recognition of his own shortcomings both then and in later years is a distinctive, perhaps redeeming quality in Osborne, but at twenty-four he appeared self-centred and unable to rationalise or control his feelings. Eventually, declaring themselves exhausted by the conflict between them, he and Pamela agreed to separate, at least for a time. It was summer. Pamela's contract at the Playhouse was renewed for the autumn season; Osborne's was not. Alone and defeated, he turned away from Pamela, Rees, Dexter and the Ramsden regulars and headed south once more to London, to Caithness Road and Creighton. 'When he arrived back in London,' said Creighton, 'he told me that it all been a terrible waste.'[22]

*   *   *

Creighton did his best to jolt his friend out of his lassitude by suggesting that even though Personal Enemy had so far failed to find a producer, 'the old firm of Creighton and Osborne' should get 'back to business' and begin another play.[23] This would become Epitaph for George Dillon, 'the most conventional and easily assimilated of all my plays,' reflected Osborne, dealing with the misfortunes of a young, idealistic but unsuccessful actor-dramatist.[24] The play was finished within weeks. Working with Creighton was, he noted, at least a more straight-forward matter than working with Stella Linden, since it was 'undisturbed by sexual emotions, at least on my part.'[25]

While the impetus of the play is Creighton's, its tone, its theme of com-promised ideals and the character of Dillon himself, a dissatisfied but aspiring playwright all too aware of his talents and shortcomings, are a remarkable reflection of Osborne and the confusion of his feelings at the time. George Dillon, the protagonist, whose name Osborne borrowed from an actor he had known in Brighton, has left his successful actress wife, whom he accuses of having betrayed him, and lodges with the Elliots, a recreation of the kind of lower-middle-class family the collaborators had encountered in the suburbs and provinces and whom Dillon privately despises. Again, the idea and much of the writing was Creighton's, although Osborne supplied the crucial scene in which Mrs Elliot's sister Ruth, the family rebel who has recently cast off both a lover and Communism as being unworthy, demands that instead of continuing to harangue the world for ignoring his talents, Dillon buckle down to prove himself as a writer.

Mired in doubt and despondency, he concedes defeat. Reluctantly agree-ing to marry Ruth's niece, Josie, who is pregnant by him, he accepts the advice of Barney Evans, a seedily opportunist producer of third-rate touring plays loosely modelled upon Patrick Desmond (something that Osborne denied when Desmond protested), to abandon his literary ambitions and instead dash off sexually suggestive potboilers for a mass audience. 'This play of yours,' advises Evans. 'It's got possibilities but it needs re-writing . . . cut out all the highbrow stuff, give it pace. You know – dirty it up a bit . . . Get someone in the family way in the Third Act, you're halfway there. I suppose you saw I Was A Drug Fiend? . . . We were playing to three or four thousand a week on the twice-nightly circuit with that. That's the sort of money you want to play to.'[26] And so Dillon writes Telephone Tart, which, produced by Evans, achieves the dubious distinction of becoming a hit in Llandrindod Wells, a small town in Wales. Thrilled by the news of his success, the Elliots present him with a new typewriter and Dillon's humiliation is complete.

In October, while Creighton continued typing, Osborne left for Wales, the land of his fathers, having been cast as the vacuous Freddy Eynsford-Hill in a production of Shaw's Pygmalion, touring the halls and miners' institutes of the Rhondda Valley. Returning to Caithness Road, he discovered Creighton full of news, not of Epitaph for George Dillon, but of Personal Enemy. Almost unbelievably, Patrick Desmond had surfaced once again, announcing that he had moved his operations from Huddersfield to the nearby spa town of Harrogate and become the director of the White Rose Players at the Opera House, an ornate auditorium of red velvet and swirling gilt. With Barney Evans-like zeal, he fell upon Personal Enemy as an 'adult' drama that would create an invigorating flurry of controversy in the resolutely genteel, scone-and-teacake society of Harrogate. While Creighton was thrilled that the play might at last be produced, Osborne, given Desmond's involvement, was dubious. Even in the unlikely event of Personal Enemy being granted a public performance licence, he doubted it would cause much concerned rattling of the Harrogate teacups. Besides, he was absorbed in thoughts of writing another new play of his own.

At the Lord Chamberlain's office in Stable Yard, the script fell into the hands of the Assistant Examiner, Lieutenant-Colonel St Vincent Troubridge, whose eyebrows, as Osborne predicted, immediately shot up in alarm before descending in fury. Personal Enemy, he decreed, could not possibly be put before an audience until it had been thoroughly purged of all suggestions of 'sexual perversity'.[27] But as Desmond had already scheduled the production and was rehearsing the cast, the authors had no choice but to comply, and in 'two frantic days of re-organisation' diverted the play from the perilous steeplechase of theatrical controversy to the gently rolling pastures of a melodrama on the corrupting influence of Communism.[28] This thoroughly expurgated version opened for a week's run under Desmond's direction on 1 March 1955, the authors travelling to Yorkshire for the first performance. Hoping to cash in on the fashion for things American, Desmond had recklessly advertised it as 'the European premiere of the sensational American drama.'[29] The performance was enlivened, according to Osborne, by the startling appearance of the actor playing Arnie, clad only in jeans and sneakers, the upper part of his body sponged with make-up intended to simulate an authentic American suntan. Unfortunately, Desmond had allocated no time for the effect to be tested beneath the stage lights, with the result that Arnie's torso appeared bright orange, reminding Osborne of nothing less than a large bottle of Haliborange cough medicine. Although the critic of the Harrogate Advertiser diplomatically overlooked this and suggested that the actors 'very nearly succeeded in making sense of the piece', the outcome was predictable.[30] At the end of the week the play closed, having comprehensively failed to achieve either the breakthrough

for which Creighton had hoped or the controversy that Desmond had anticipated.

Ironically, it was not Osborne or Creighton or Desmond, but Binkie Beaumont, purveyor of country house dramas to the West End, who had successfully
created a breakthrough of sorts and a huge controversy into the bargain, this
time with an authentically American play. Six years earlier, in 1949, Tennent
productions had used a loophole in the law to turn itself into a non-profit-
making charity in order to stage the British premiere of Tennessee Williams's
A Streetcar Named Desire at the Aldwych Theatre in the West End, directed by
Laurence Olivier and starring his wife, Vivien Leigh, as Blanche Dubois. The
prospect of the theatrical Royal couple and an apparently shocking American
play proved an enormous draw, with the theatre receiving over ten thousand
postal applications for tickets. Such was the frenzy of anticipation that fights
broke out in the first night queue at the box office, generating more valuable
publicity that increased still further after opening night. Critical reaction was
sharply divided, while the Reverend Colin Cuttell, priest-Vicar of Southwark,
wondered whether there was not a 'statesman in high places who will speak
out from other than political and economic motives and tell the United States
to keep the sewage?'[31]

In October 1956, over a year after *Personal Enemy* was produced in Harrogate,
Tennent again successfully evaded the Lord Chamberlain, who had refused a
licence to produce another American play, Arthur Miller's *A View from the Bridge*,
on account of its mild reference to homosexuality. This time, Tennent chose the
Comedy Theatre in the West End, having first taken the precaution of converting
the theatre into a private members' club to avoid legal retribution. Membership was obtainable merely on application. This was an old dodge, and one
that had been used during the 1880s in order to smuggle the plays of Bernard
Shaw and Ibsen on to the stage. It would be used in the future as well. *A View
from the Bridge* played to enthusiastic audiences: Osborne attended the opening
on 11 October; also present were Miller himself and his then wife, Marilyn
Monroe, wearing 'a scarlet satin gown so tight around the knees that walking
was an achievement.'[32] Writing in *The Sunday Times*, Harold Hobson acclaimed
the play as 'a masterpiece', an assessment with which Osborne, considering his
admiration of Miller, probably agreed.[33] The production caused a kerfuffle in
the press, some journalists wondering whether the Lord Chamberlain's powers
should be curtailed or even dispensed with altogether. But although Beaumont
had fired a damaging shot across the bows of state censorship, its sinking would
take several more years to achieve.

In 1955, though, Osborne and Creighton were sufficiently encouraged by
their Harrogate excursion to try *Epitaph for George Dillon* on Desmond. This time,
however, even Desmond was momentarily defeated, and he declined. Out it
went again, but after several rejections the dispiriting process of chasing producers was overtaken by other events and the play was consigned to the desk
drawer. In the early summer, and after many years of ferrying the antiques of

East Anglia to London salesrooms, Creighton's mother had died and left him a small legacy. Having long fancied the idea of living on the river, Creighton suggested that he and Osborne move out of Caithness Road and live on a houseboat on the Thames. It would be far cheaper, he reasoned, and much more fun. When Osborne agreed, Creighton happily began leafing through the classified advertisements in the evening papers in search of a suitable vessel for sale, one on which he could stride about the deck, polishing up the brass as they made their way, like George, Harris and J in *Three Men in a Boat*, leisurely down the river from one mooring to the next. Osborne, meanwhile, was anxious to finish his new play. Set in a one-room attic flat, the home of Jimmy and Alison Porter, it was his sixth completed play, and the third (after *The Great Bear or, Minette*, and *The King is Dead*) that he had written entirely unaided.

This time he was writing as he had never written before. Nothing was contrived, nothing was worked on. He was writing compulsively, furiously, hardly keeping up with his thoughts as the play surged almost fully formed from his subconscious. It became the vessel into which he poured all the love and confusion, rage and resentment he had felt, and many of the events he had experienced, over the last couple of years and more. A good deal of the play is inspired by Osborne's perception of his marriage, while the leading character of Jimmy Porter, with all his talents and faults, is an astonishingly candid portrayal of himself. Alison, good-natured, pragmatic, heroically patient, is modelled upon Pamela, although the fictional character differs in several respects, one being that the social position of Alison's parents is entirely different from that of the shop keeping Lanes. By the time it was complete, he had considered several working titles: *My Blood is a Mile High*; *Bargain From Strength or, Close the Cage Behind You*; *Farewell to Anger*; and *Man in a Rage*. All of these he eventually ditched in favour of his final choice: *Look Back in Anger*.

He began typing the final draft on 4 May 1955 and completed the first of the three acts two days later. Writing was briefly interrupted by a dash to Morecambe for a week on 23 May to appear in a local repertory production of Hugh Hastings's farce, *Seagulls over Sorrento*, and while there, he put the finishing touches to Act 2. By 3 June, the third and final act was complete and a week later he had a fair copy neatly typed on the portable Olympia typewriter that Pamela had given him as a wedding present. Creighton, meanwhile, had discovered his houseboat, a Rhine barge named the *Egret* and moored beneath overhanging trees at the Cubitt Yacht Basin near Chiswick Bridge. Without bothering to arrange for a professional inspection, he made the transaction with the owner on the spot, and on 1 July the two men became river-dwellers. While Creighton took the chance of good weather to devote himself to repairing and painting, Osborne began the business of bundling up copies of *Look Back in Anger* and sending them to theatres and agents.

CHAPTER 9

Creation

PARTLY AS A RESULT of articulate and quotable commentators such as Cyril Connolly complaining of shivering in the bleak winds of cultural despair, the artistic and social landscape of the mid-1950s is conventionally portrayed as being a gloomy prelude to the extravagant, dancing sunlight of the 1960s. But in fact, the sun was already rising; it was just that for people such as Connolly, who found the season not to their liking, there was far more chill than warmth in the air.

Beyond the distracted concerns of London cultural commentators, though, life went on much the same as before, which for most people meant a steady and welcome improvement. At the General Election of 1955, the Conservative Party, sailing under the effective if uninspiring flags of caution and moderation, coasted to a satisfying victory with a majority of sixty, the patrician Sir Anthony Eden, the former Foreign Secretary, succeeding Churchill as Prime Minister. The post-war hopes of a social and political consensus were at last being realised, and that the nation was on the right course was evident in the employment figures. In dramatic contrast to pre-war England, the 1950s was a decade of record low unemployment. In the year of the election, 215,000 people were out of work, a mere 1% of the working population, and during the entire decade, unemployment never rose above a million. There was never a feeling of full employment, but theoretically, it was not far off. Money was still in short supply and jobs hard to come by, yet there was a growing optimism about and Osborne was never particularly worried about being out of work for long. Although the regional theatre was enduring difficult times, television and the wireless were offering new opportunities to actors, and National Assistance Benefit was there as a backup.

Yet despite Eden's reassuring authority, these were politically uncertain times as the Cold War between Britain and the United States on the one side, and Communist Eastern Europe on the other, began to intensify under the threat of developing atomic weaponry. A hundred Cambridge University scientists had appealed to the government in 1950 not to follow the lead of the United States by developing a hydrogen bomb, and four years later a million signatures appeared on a petition handed to 10 Downing Street calling for a unilateral disarmament conference. Whether Osborne signed it is unknown, but he and Creighton were avidly following the debate which, as the government pressed ahead with the creation of 'the bomb', would culminate in the creation in 1958 of the Campaign for Nuclear Disarmament, the first organised mass movement of the post-war years. Elsewhere, there were the first moves towards reforms anticipating the more liberal social changes of the following decade. The Wolfenden Committee met in 1954 to deliberate the laws regarding homosexuality, which three years later resulted in homosexual acts between consenting adults in private no longer being considered a criminal matter. Meanwhile, the first steps were taken on the road to the abolition of capital punishment.

While the nation was still being rebuilt and life still had a drabness about it, for the first time in a very long time, more young people, especially among the lower-middle and working classes in the larger cities, had money in their pockets to spend on themselves. As a result, towards the end of the decade, a distinctive youth culture was emerging in clothes, music and films that not only proclaimed young people as being different from their parents, but from each other as well. The London 'Teddy boys', wrote the social historian Jonathan Green, began 'the whole teenager epic.'[1] So called because of their preference for clothes inspired by the Edwardian era, including tapered trousers, richly ornamented waistcoats and long jackets with narrow lapels, the young, working-class Teddy Boys became associated in the public mind with a disturbing rise in youthful gang violence. Other young people adopted an 'Italian' look by wearing neat and dapper shiny suits, while 'ton-up boys' crowded the streets on motorcycles and met for leather-jacketed conferences at transport cafés. Teenagers and young adults were also becoming associated with a new kind of predominantly American music. There was jazz, seen as the preserve of intellectuals, and there was rock and roll, an exciting new sound exemplified by Bill Haley and the Comets, Little Richard, Chuck Berry and Elvis Presley. Fashion and popular music spearheaded a new consumer market during the mid- to late-fifties that would see a tremendous expansion over the following few years.

There were encouraging signs of rejuvenation elsewhere in the arts. A group of new writers including Philip Larkin, Kingsley Amis and Thom Gunn were credited with establishing a new form of poetry. The down-to-earth, realistic, documentary style of the so-called 'Movement' was intended to be a dynamic contrast to the airy, romantic-symbolism of the pre-war years. There was a similar renaissance in painting. At the This Is Tomorrow exhibition at the Whitechapel Art Gallery, the astonishingly vibrant colours and collages of pop art, including Richard Hamilton's Just what is it that makes today's homes so different, so appealing? could be seen for the first time. Many young writers and artists were beginning to feel a palpable sense of energy being renewed. The aspiring artist and designer Jim Downer was sharing a lodging house in Bloomsbury at the time, where his fellow tenants included Ted Hughes, preparing his first volume of poems for publication, and the actors Albert Finney and Peter O'Toole, then students at Pamela Lane's former training school, the Royal Academy of Dramatic Art. 'Art and design were very much "in the air",' wrote Downer later, 'the country was full of a new sense of excitement . . . Suddenly anything and everything seemed possible . . . We were certain that Britain was going forward with increasing speed and we were all worried we would be left behind.'[2]

Even those heavyweight commentators predicting the end of the novel had done so too soon, as the mid-fifties turned out to be a particularly good time for new novelists. However, they were not the kind favoured by the old guard of literary critics. First-time novelists such as John Wain, Kingsley Amis and Iris Murdoch, and poets such as Ted Hughes and Philip Larkin were middle and lower-middle class, suburban and provincial, the sons and daughters of bureaucrats, local government officials and clerks, and reflected a new, post-war sensibility. Many of them were enthusiastic supporters of the Labour Party.

This new, post-war Welfare State generation was the first to benefit from the dramatic expansion of opportunities offered by the 1944 Education Act, which enabled many who might otherwise not have gone on to higher education to do so. State-supported scholarships meant that the sons and daughters of poorer families would not find the doors of universities and, crucially as far as the theatre was concerned, drama schools, closed to them. Higher education suddenly ceased to be the preserve of the economically and socially privileged and became available to people such as Jimmy Porter, one of the first generation of graduates from the new 'white tile' universities.[3] The voices now beginning to make themselves heard in music, design, painting and literature were suburban and regional, often speaking in accents unfamiliar to Londoners, and with a wariness of things metropolitan and hostile towards the upper-middle-classes and above. This was the birth of a new meritocracy.

However, the older universities, particularly Oxford and Cambridge, remained dominant influences in British cultural and political life. Wain, Amis and Larkin were Oxford graduates and Hughes had studied at Cambridge, yet their awareness remained resolutely egalitarian and non-metropolitan. In 1953, John Wain published *Hurry On Down*, in which Charles Lumley, fresh from university and in flight from conformity, sidesteps the conventional graduate destiny of Whitehall, the BBC, journalism or academia. Relying not on a private income but a haphazard kind of self-help, he becomes by turn a window-cleaner, unwitting drug-runner, hospital orderly and chauffeur before ending up as a radio gag-writer and with the girl of his dreams. The following year three more exceptional first novels appeared, reflecting distinctly post-war sensibilities. There was William Golding's *Lord of the Flies*, a chilling fable of social disintegration, and Iris Murdoch's picaresque *Under the Net*, in which Jake Donoghue pursues a down-but-not-quite-out existence in both London and Paris, and Kingsley Amis's *Lucky Jim*, a spiky romantic comedy dealing with the troubles of Jim Dixon, a youthful history lecturer at a provincial university.

Walter Allen, a critic at the *New Statesman* who had welcomed the arrival of Charles Lumley, immediately responded to Jim Dixon. 'A new hero has risen among us,' he proclaimed in his review of the novel on 30 January 1954. 'Is he the intellectual tough or the tough intellectual? He is consciously, even conscientiously graceless. His face, when not dead-pan, is set in a snarl of exasperation . . . it is to the phoney to which his nerve-ends are tremblingly exposed, and at the least suspicion of the phoney, he gets tough. He is at odds with his conventional university education . . . he has seen through the university racket as he sees through all the others. A racket is phoniness organised, and in contact with phoniness he turns red . . . In life he has been with us for some little time . . . In fiction I think he first arrived last year, as the central character of Mr John Wain's novel, *Hurry on Down*. He turns up again in Mr Amis's *Lucky Jim*.'

'Phoney' was a word then very much in vogue and part of Osborne's vocabulary, his having used it liberally in connection with Pamela Lane and several others. It seemed that T. C. Worsley's longed-for literary revival was showing signs of actually emerging as a new generation of novelists began chronicling the adventures of a new social type. He (and it was always a he) was more likely to be found in the provinces than in London, although both Charles Lumley and Jim Dixon end up in the capital, having landed not only new jobs but also the women they have pursued. He was lower-middle class and although he had a university education, he rejected the expectations of preceding generations and relied instead on his own resources. The construction of his own moral framework, though, was both a confusing and exasperating process. Although the new social type was unsure of quite what he stood for, he was much more certain of what he rejected. He appreciated culture but not 'high culture', drank beer rather than wine, preferred jazz to madrigals or rock and roll, wore shabby clothes, did not own a car but possibly possessed a bicycle. He both loved and loathed England and the English, but was intensely suspicious of 'abroad', especially of France.

France and things French were making an enormous impact in London's cultural circles. Several critics and commentators, especially Cyril Connolly, pined for Paris, convinced that Britain should lift itself out of its torpor by looking for renewed inspiration across the Channel. There, in the boulevard cafes, such writers as Jean-Paul Sartre, Simone de Beauvoir and Marguerite Duras were leading a country awakening from four years of occupation and resistance into a glistening literary and philosophic recovery. In 1953, Osborne, still a keen existentialist, fell into the pattern of things by reading *The Age of Reason*, the first volume of Sartre's post-war *Roads to Freedom* trilogy, scribbling notes to himself in a journal as he went: 'I can't help feeling that those existentialists for all their raffishness have got something . . . We really do seem to be dominated by chance, don't we?'[4] From its writers to its wine, its philosophy to its sunshine, France was considered the thinking person's antithesis to damp, decaying Britain. As if in tribute, French expressions and phrases appeared like badges in the commentary columns of the better newspapers. By contrast, Jim Dixon derides Professor Welch's sons, 'the effeminate writing Michel and the pacifist painting Bertrand' because their French names imply all the affectation to which he is resolutely opposed.[5] Two years later, in 1956, the French influence was still powerful enough for Jimmy Porter to throw aside his Sunday newspaper in disgust having given up the book review he is reading because 'half of it's in French.'[6]

The theatre, too, succumbed to the fashion for France, and in the West End translations of French plays jostled for attention alongside American musicals and English drawing-room comedies. Jean Anouilh had seven plays in London between 1950 and 1954 and, despairing of finding outlets for their own work, British dramatists fell back upon reworking plays by Giraudoux, Genet and Ionescu. The trend continued for much of the decade.

The sense of gloom and tedium felt by many during the early to mid-1950s was not because nothing was happening, but because what was happening was not happening fast enough. The metropolitan younger generation felt politically and culturally stifled, their way blocked by a pre-war old guard who largely dominated opinion. Yet Osborne and those who agreed with him were lucky to have allies in the press as impatient as they were. One such was Kenneth Tynan. A vaultingly ambitious, fearlessly outspoken and outrageously young theatre critic on the *Observer*, Tynan, like Osborne, was infuriated by Aunt Edna, appalled by the tendril-like tenacity of the country house play and equally anxious to make his mark. 'If you seek a tombstone,' he cried in 1954, 'look about you . . .' The setting of most successful plays, he complained, 'is a country house in what used to be called Loamshire but is now, as a heroic tribute to realism, sometimes called Berkshire. Except when someone must sneeze or be murdered, the sun invariably shines. The inhabitants belong to a social class derived partly from romantic novels and partly from the playwright's vision of the leisured life he will lead after the play is a success – this being the only effort of imagination he is called upon to make.'[7] The post-war theatre, he concluded, was simply devoid of life. It was more than appalling; it was a national catastrophe. Beside the achievements of Paris and New York, London seemed insular and diminished.

Over the following twenty years, Kenneth Tynan was to become a vitally important figure in the theatre. Born in Birmingham in 1927, he was two years older than Osborne and had started 'serious metropolitan theatre going' in 1943, when he was sixteen.[8] Highly articulate, he had blazed his way through Oxford where his mannered flamboyance and liking for gold-lamé suits had given him a dazzling social reputation that camouflaged his enviable capacity for hard work. Bewitched by the theatre and by stardom, he had descended upon London in 1952, landing at the *Evening Standard* where he quickly established himself as the most audacious journalistic stylist and most perceptive and waspish critic in the country. Two years later, when he was twenty-six, he joined the *Observer* as its theatre critic, settling in by pinning a notice above his desk instructing himself to: 'Rouse tempers, goad and lacerate, raise whirl-winds.'[9]

By this time, he had seen, and was seeing, a phenomenal number of plays, both in London and abroad. Returning from New York in the spring of 1954, he bemoaned the fact that the English theatre had barely heard of Tennessee Williams or Arthur Miller. Although he loved American musicals, praising the London production of *Guys and Dolls* and confessing himself 'ready to . . . drop on my knees before Frank Loesser, who writes the music and lyrics', English plays were another matter entirely and were hardly worth talking about.[10] Apart from the Shakespearian productions at the Old Vic, presided over by one of his early heroes, Laurence Olivier, London was a virtual wasteland. That season, he noted grimly, of the twenty-six plays on offer, twenty-four were about the upper or upper-middle classes and the remaining four were broad farces. This meant that at the parties Tynan delighted in giving and loved to attend, he felt himself embarrassingly stumped for conversation. Opera and ballet were talking points, he agreed, and Italian films the buzz of the moment. But 'apart from revivals and imports, there is nothing in the London theatre that one dares discuss with an intelligent man for more than five minutes.'[11]

The following year, and flying gloriously in the face of critical consensus, Tynan saluted the first English language production of Samuel Beckett's *Waiting for Godot*, tucked away at the tiny Arts Theatre. Osborne saw the play on 6 October, although he did not record his impressions, but as far as Tynan was concerned, it 'forced me to re-examine the rules which have hitherto governed the drama and having done so, pronounce them not elastic enough.' Never mind what Aunt Edna would have thought: 'It is validly new and hence I declare myself, as the Spanish would say, *godotista*.'[12] While continuing to scorn what he perceived as second-rate, Tynan fiercely banged the drum for a new kind of drama. 'We need plays about cabmen and demigods, plays about warriors, politicians and grocers,' he cried. '. . . I counsel aggression because, as a critic, I had rather be a war correspondent than a necrologist.'[13] Something, he declared, must surely happen soon. And it did. But *Look Back in Anger* did not emerge out of nowhere. Given the context of the times, keen eyes such as Tynan's were on the lookout for it. It was the right play at the right time. The question was, who would produce it? It was in the answer to this question that John Osborne was about to have his greatest stroke of luck yet and a spectacular new start.

*   *   *

With *Look Back in Anger* Osborne hit his stride as a writer, finding both a theme that would broadly preoccupy him for the rest of his career and the means with which to express it. The theme was essentially himself and his own experiences, and throughout his career the best of Osborne's writing represents a remarkably honest self-examination that almost uncannily appears to match something of the wider public sensibility, while the worst sinks into maudlin self-pity. The means was a magnificent use and control of language. At its best it is expansive, poetic, precise and remarkably vivid and distinctive, at its worst it lapses into arrogance, sneering and cheap jibes.

Look Back in Anger, though, represents some of the best of Osborne. While he had been making notes for the play for several months, writing lines and speeches in a series of notebooks, the resulting manuscript version, now kept at the Harry Ransom Humanities Research Center in Texas, reveals astonishingly few revisions. It lends credence to Osborne's contention that once he began the actual writing, his plays somehow welled-up already fully formed from within. An intensely autobiographical play that coincidentally distils the political and social frustration that many young people were feeling, Look Back in Anger is also a remarkably mature performance for a young man of twenty-five. Although audiences were ignorant of Osborne's personal story, those who kept up with what was happening politically and culturally recognised both the situation in which Jimmy and Alison Porter found themselves and Jimmy's feverish hostil-ity to what he identifies as contemporary complacency. A modern melancholic, his sensibility had already been hinted at in Hurry On Down and Lucky Jim, but Jimmy Porter was a far more vital creation than either Charles Lumley or Jim Dixon, and a wholly new figure in post-war theatre.

*   *   *

Like Hurry On Down and Lucky Jim, Look Back in Anger is set in the provinces, which in the theatre was highly unusual. After Osborne had left Derby, Pamela had moved from Ashbourne Road into a large attic room at 114 Green Lane, nearer the Playhouse Theatre. Osborne had visited her there 'once or twice' while he was formulating the play in his mind and it was the Green Lane room that became the model for the drab, one-room attic flat inhabited by Jimmy and Alison Porter. Although its location in the stage directions is given only as the midlands, according to Pamela Lane, Osborne 'remembered the place [Derby and her room] rather accurately when we talked about it in later years and hinted that he had it in mind' for the play.[14]

Again like that of Hurry On Down and Lucky Jim, the narrative of Look Back in Anger is the very English one of love across the class divide, in this case that of a well-educated but lower-middle-class young man in love with an upper-middle-class girl. But whereas Hurry On Down and Lucky Jim deal with pursuit, Jimmy Porter has already pursued and married before the play opens. A blaz-ingly articulate graduate, Jimmy, like his creator, was ten when he lost his father and still mourns his death. Having been wounded in the Spanish Civil War, Jimmy's father had returned home to die, watched over by his son and nursed by a wife who sounds very much like Osborne's perception of Nellie Beatrice in that she believed she had 'allied herself to a man who seemed to be on the wrong side in all things.'[15] Like Osborne, Jimmy is aware that the depth and rawness of feelings created by his father's death render him vulnerable, and fears that the giving of love means disappointment and betrayal. He also believes that his experiences have given him an insight and understanding others lack. 'I knew more about – love . . . betrayal . . . and death', he declares, 'when I was ten years old than you will probably know in all your life.'[16]

Jimmy and Alison Porter have been married for three years, as were Osborne and Pamela by the time of their separation in Derby. Alison is the daughter of a retired government official who has returned from serving in India. It emerges that she and Jimmy met (perhaps a little implausibly) at a party, Jimmy arriving in a dinner jacket stained with bicycle oil and seeming to Alison so vigorously alive, so different from the other guests that she felt that she had no choice but to devote herself to him. 'The old story of the knight in shining armour,' admits Alison, 'except that his armour didn't really shine very much.'[17] She had no idea of whether he loved her or not, only that he had made up his mind to appropriate and marry her and, intoxicated by the potency of his will, she acquiesced to it. Not that he could support her in the manner to which her upbringing might have led her to expect, but then that was part of the attraction.

But Jimmy has graduated not into a society to which he feels he can contribute, but one from which he feels excluded. He has therefore resorted to running a market sweet-stall with his friend Cliff Lewis, who lodges in the same house as the Porters. With the return of the Conservatives, it is as if the ideals of 1945 never existed, and consequently: 'There aren't any good, brave causes left.'[18] Cheated socially, Jimmy Porter is also embittered emotionally, and much of the play comprises Jimmy's invective against the absence of sensitivity, passion and real beliefs, both in others and in society as a whole, his principal target being Alison, whom he attempts to goad into a response as fervent as his own. Jimmy both withdraws into himself and proclaims his presence by playing jazz melodies on his trumpet, and many of the play's early audiences would have instantly recognized the cultural significance of this: here was a thoroughly contemporary young man, and one of restless, brooding independent intelligence. 'Jazz', remembered Osborne, 'was a special voice that we all latched on to, because it was exotic and it was powerful, and it was completely different from the kind of life we knew at the time.'[19]

Helena, an actress friend of Alison's, comes to stay with them and persuades Alison, who confides that she is pregnant, that she must leave Jimmy. She does so when Colonel Redfern, her father, arrives to collect her. Helena then takes Alison's place in Jimmy's bed and at the ironing board behind which Alison has been standing for much of the first act, until she returns, having suffered a miscarriage. Alison's experience of pain and loss means that she can now share some of Jimmy's and perhaps they can love each other on an equal footing. The play ends with the couple in a tight embrace, consoling each other in their private world of 'Bears and Squirrels'. The likelihood of their remaining together or not is left for the audience to decide.

Look Back in Anger is the first play Osborne had written that was drawn directly and wholly from his own experience and it is the one with which, throughout his career, he would become most identified. It would also pay the mortgage for many years to come. Much of Jimmy's slashing, bilious invective against Alison and the world echoes Osborne's letters and telephone calls to Creighton. For the most part, however, Alison's defence is silence, which Jimmy interprets alternately as either disinterest or stinging cruelty: 'That girl there can twist your arm off with her silence.'[20] Yet Alison's reticence is her defence. From Jimmy's position on the opposing line of battle it appears cruel, because he recognises that she knows that her silence weakens him and thereby he perceives her deployment of it as a strategy to exhaust and humiliate him. Few things are more diminishing to a frail male ego than female implacability, and for much of the time, Jimmy's verbal grenades are either deflected or fall impotently to the ground. 'I pretended not to be listening,' says Alison to Cliff, 'because I knew that would hurt him.'[21] And it does: while Jimmy's assertion that 'there aren't any good, brave causes left' is frequently quoted, less so is the conclusion of the speech in which he suggests that 'there's nothing left for it . . . but to let yourself be butchered by the women.'[20] Similar sentiments throughout the play suggest that Jimmy's principal fear is the natural female power of his wife, alternately erotic and merciless, and its ability to undermine his rickety self-assurance.

Of the other characters who appear in the play, Cliff, the Porters' Welsh friend who arbitrates between them and is first seen at the beginning of the play reading the Sunday newspapers with Jimmy, is based upon John Rees, the Osbornes' friend – also a Welshman – who often joined them in their attic flat on Sunday evenings. Much of their banter is taken from those occasions, although Creighton's nickname of 'Mouse' and the friendship between Osborne and Creighton is evoked when Cliff performs a comic dance while piping a series of 'eeks', the mouse-like sounds which sometimes concluded Osborne and Creighton's telephone conversations. Helena Charles, Alison's friend, and Colonel Redfern, her father, are both loosely-defined 'types' from an upper-middle-class background. Helena, an amalgamation of some of Pamela's friends, is assertive, manipulative, and both appalled and fascinated by Jimmy, while Colonel Redfern, who bears some resemblance to William Lane, Pamela's father, is a perplexed emissary from an earlier age. Having left England with his wife for service in India in 1914, Redfern has returned after thirty-two years and two World Wars to discover an England he no longer recognizes. Jimmy understands this, and although they never meet in the play, he has a sympathy and respect for his father-in-law similar to that which Osborne had for Pamela's father. As Alison says to her father in one of the play's most important lines: 'You're hurt because everything is changed. Jimmy's hurt because everything is the same.'[22] A representative of an idealised Edwardian England of order, ease and Empire that Osborne remembered from his boyhood reading, Redfern is a figure whom Osborne instinctively understood, and a character that he would develop in later plays.

The shadows of some of Osborne's other friends and acquaintances appear in some of the many characters referred to but never seen on stage. Stella Linden is suggested by Madeleine, a girl whom Jimmy knew when he was nineteen, while the flamboyant John Dexter – and perhaps also Anthony Creighton – are recalled in Jimmy's friend Webster, a man with 'bite, edge, drive . . . enthusiasm.'[23] Is it fanciful to suggest that he may have been named after the author of The Duchess of Malfi, a play Osborne admired tremendously? Mrs Tanner, who gave Jimmy the money to set up his sweet-stall, may have been named after an elderly neighbour in Ewell, while her son, Jimmy's old friend Hugh, may conceivably have been named after Hugh Berrington. In the early notes for the play, Jimmy's surname is Brown, that of Porter being awarded to Cliff before being transferred to Jimmy. Osborne borrowed the name from his cousin, Anthony Porter, the son of William Porter and Osborne's Aunt Nancy, with whom he used to play occasionally as a boy in the London suburbs.[24]

Jimmy's courtship of Alison, his dislike of her mother, the doubts of some of her friends, her family's horror at the news of their engagement, their hiring of a private detective to stalk him, his descriptions of their wedding and the current state of their marriage, are all taken from Osborne's Bridgwater experiences, while the note which Alison leaves for Jimmy after she leaves, admitting that she will 'always have a deep loving need of you', closely resembles a similar letter that Osborne received from Pamela after their separation.[25] And, like the Osbornes, the Porters reach out to each other for comfort and mutual protection in their private game of 'Bears and Squirrels', a motif that recurs throughout the play.

Osborne also stuffed Look Back in Anger with the fruits of his reading. Jimmy Porter's close observation of those around him, and his tirades of rage and self-revelation, clearly echo that of the Jacobean melancholic. Elsewhere, there are passing references to Oscar Wilde, Bernard Shaw, Rudyard Kipling, Orwell, Genet and several other authors. The Cess Pool, the title of a song that Jimmy composes, is perhaps a joke on The Waste Land. Later in the play, Jimmy and Cliff perform an impromptu music-hall song-and-dance sequence, not unlike Osborne and Creighton's pantomime routine at Hayling Island, calling themselves T. S. Eliot and Pam, which may be an oblique joke upon Osborne and Pamela and her 'd and b' verdict on his attempt at writing dramatic verse.

Most of all, Look Back in Anger represents a huge linguistic advance on anything Osborne had written before. He had been inching towards it for some time, both Creighton and Pamela having urged him to jettison poetry and concentrate upon writing that was spare, vibrant and direct. He had begun to do this in the second act of Epitaph for George Dillon, and in Look Back in Anger he sustained it dazzlingly for an entire play. The language has none of the artificial elegance that was expected in the theatre at the time, none of the understated refinement or the concealed emotion of Rattigan or Coward, but is instead uncluttered, explicit and combative, lucid and full of imagery: 'a language', wrote Osborne, 'in which it is possible only to tell the truth.'[26]

Jimmy Porter is a superior version of Huw Prosser, the misunderstood poet in The Devil Inside Him and of George Dillon, the failed dramatist of Epitaph for George Dillon; he is a Charles Lumley and a Jim Dixon taken to spectacular extreme. Yet if Jimmy is a representation of Walter Allen's 'new hero', he is also a self-portrait of his creator, a young man floundering emotionally and convinced that the authenticity of his feelings is largely unrecognised. However, Osborne was not the first contemporary dramatist to choose a disaffected young man as his principal character. He had already appeared in the guise of the drug-taking Nicky Lancaster in Noël Coward's The Vortex in 1924, while his post-war version had emerged as Freddie Page in Terence Rattigan's The Deep Blue Sea. But Osborne had done something very different: he had moved him to the centre of the stage. Like Hamlet, Jimmy Porter is at the very centre of the play.

*   *   *

By now, in the summer of 1955, Osborne and Pamela had been separated for almost a year. While Creighton continued to potter about their houseboat, painting and polishing, rejected copies of Look Back in Anger began arriving from the agents and theatres to which Osborne had sent it in the hope of a produc-tion. Patrick Desmond turned it down, as did Leslie Twelvetrees at Derby, the Tennent organisation and several other London managers. 'But we were very happy on the houseboat,' remembered Creighton. 'It was a lovely summer, and living was cheap. We were both vegetarians. We'd make soup from the nettles on the river bank. We would write and read and have long talks about Look Back in Anger, and look for acting work together.' Sometimes their search was success-ful. Osborne at least found intermittent television work. In 1952, he had played Wingate, a prefect, in two episodes of Billy Bunter of Greyfriars School and a year later appeared in a small part in Robin Hood. As he packed up his copies of Look Back in Anger, he made fleeting appearances as a military recruit in The Makepeace Story, a serial set in a Lancashire mill town during the eighteenth century. 'It was a wonderful time,' recalled Creighton, 'the happiest of times, one of the happiest of my life.'[27]

Both men searched the advertisements in The Stage each week and, at the end of July, Osborne read of the plans of the newly-formed English Stage Company, which had taken up residence at the Royal Court Theatre in Sloane Square. George Devine, the director, was appealing for new plays from 'good writers who have not yet written for the theatre'.[28] Thrusting a copy of Look Back in Anger into a fresh envelope, Osborne dispatched it immediately. Within a couple of days a letter arrived from Devine. They must meet, he said, as soon as possible.

CHAPTER 10

Royal Court

OSBORNE'S MEETING WITH Devine on board the *Egret* marked the beginning of a remarkable partnership. Not only would they lead the front-line troops reinvigorating the English theatre, they would form a close friendship that would last until Devine's death in 1966. George Devine became the single most influential figure in Osborne's entire professional life, a man upon whom he would look with undivided loyalty as the one who had faith in him from the first, who nurtured his work and who became in the process a mentor and father-figure to him.

With his brusque manner, white hair, dark-framed spectacles and a pipe frequently wedged between his teeth, Devine looked older than his forty-four years. Born in Hendon, he was an only child and, like Osborne, the son of a reticent father and an overpowering mother with whom he had an uneasy relationship. Short and fat, George Devine senior was a clerk in a branch of Martin's Bank with a passion for collecting butterflies and playing long-distance chess. Family legend had it that Ruth Cassady, a Canadian whom he married early in 1910, had permitted him only one conjugal encounter, reluctantly conceded on the night of their wedding. Whether this was true or not, the birth of George junior on 20 November that year seems to have disoriented Ruth entirely, for while the boy was still an infant, she bolted, taking him with her. Today, her condition might be understood as a severe post-natal depression but then it was widely regarded as lunacy. Eventually, mother and son were traced to an isolated cottage in the New Forest from where they were induced to return home to her husband who, in the meantime, had acquired a new house in the semi-rural surroundings of Hampstead Garden Suburb.

Even when he was an adult, there was little communication between mother and son, and Devine seldom spoke about her. After her husband's death, she left Hampstead Garden Suburb and, although far from impoverished, lived reclusively in a bed-sitting room in Finchley, where she obsessively hoarded stacks of yellowing newspapers. Sometimes, during the 1950s, she would dismay her son and his family by appearing uninvited at their home, invariably enveloped in a shapeless tweed coat and a beret pulled down over her skull, from beneath which straggled wisps of grey hair. Whenever Ruth descended on one of her random visits, Devine would rapidly retreat to his study, lock the door and refuse to emerge until she had gone. Eventually, the family arranged for her to be taken into a nursing home. After her death, it emerged that she had regularly drawn large sums of money from her bank, but how she spent it remained a mystery. It was assumed that she had given it away.

Devine's schooling was consistent but bizarre. From the age of eight, he attended Clayesmore, a private boarding school in Hampshire haphazardly run by his uncle, Alexander Devine, who seems to have been something of a William Crawford Grove figure. Whereas George senior was the model of conventional propriety, Alexander was a dashing, reckless figure, a newspaper correspondent in the First World War and a passionate advocate of Montenegrin independence. Despite having comparatively little money, he was careful to choose the finer things in life, insisting upon smoking only the best cigars and drinking the most expensive brandy, and spending each Thursday night at Claridge's Hotel in London where he claimed to fraternise with the wealthy and the famous. Something of his passion for gentlemanly style was inherited by his nephew, who in turn would instruct Osborne, himself eager to acquire the manners and accoutrements of a sophisticated man-about-town. By the time Devine went up to Oxford in 1929, the year of John Osborne's birth, and inspired perhaps by Alexander's vivid imagination, he was developing a fascination for the theatre. As a student at Wadham College, where he read History, he joined the Oxford University Dramatic Society, in which his contemporaries included Terence Rattigan.

Having become president of OUDS, Devine played Mercutio in a society production of *Romeo and Juliet* directed by John Gielgud, which transferred to London and provided him with a launching pad into the profession. Over the following years, Devine became a good actor, rarely out of work, and a proficient lighting designer and director. His real talent, though, again perhaps inspired by Alexander, was as a teacher. For three years from 1936, Devine taught young actors at the London Theatre Studio, housed in a converted Methodist Chapel in Islington. Both at the Studio and subsequently, Devine was noted as being meticulous in his preparation. 'The homework would always have been done, and the rehearsal etiquette strictly observed,' wrote his biographer, Irving Wardle.[1]

In 1940, and now well known in London theatrical circles, Devine married Sophie Harris, ten years his elder, a stage and costume designer and one of a successful trio of women designers working under the professional name of Motley. Their only child, Harriet, was born two years later, shortly after Devine had left England to serve with the army in India and Burma. On his return, he assisted in running the Old Vic School and the Young Vic Theatre while simultaneously hurling himself into a demanding freelance career, directing opera at Sadler's Wells and Shakespeare at Stratford. But by 1955, something extraordinary had happened: gone was the familiar tubby, jolly old George and in his place stood someone altogether slimmer. He had, he informed a friend, lost the equivalent of a suitcase full of books in weight. He had also become more reserved, even abrupt in his manner.

The reasons for this astounding change were both personal and professional. The family had recently moved to a house at 9 Lower Mall, close by Hammersmith Bridge and overlooking one of the calmer reaches of the Thames, which made them close neighbours of Jocelyn Herbert. She was seven years younger than Devine and a daughter of A. P. Herbert, a contributor to *Punch* and the lyricist for Vivien Ellis's operetta, *Bless the Bride*. A former design student at the London Theatre Studio, she was now married to Anthony Lousada, a lawyer. Devine and Jocelyn fell in love; his marriage to Sophie was unhappy and a distance had grown between him and Harriet. The relationship between Devine and Jocelyn would be lifelong and nourishing but, since he could not bring himself to abandon his family and Jocelyn was similarly unable to leave hers, they remained apart for a further five years, their affair sustained by letters and snatched meetings. At the same time, Devine's already busy professional life was becoming even more hectic, for he had plunged into negotiations to become artistic director of the fledgling English Stage Company.

For several months, Devine had been planning the creation of his own writers' theatre, producing new and contemporary plays reflecting the uneasy, speculative, post-war age in which they lived. His confederate in this venture was Tony Richardson. Tall and gangling, with a strident voice that rose to snap at words he wished to emphasise as though snatching at insects, energetic and, on occasion, ruthless, Richardson was eighteen years younger than Devine. Born in Shipley, a small, grey stone town in Yorkshire, in 1928, he was the son of Clarence Richardson, a pharmacist, and his wife Elsie. The family lived above the shop. Clarence and Elsie christened their son Cecil Antonio in recognition of a slave owned by a nineteenth-century ancestor, a wanderer and adventurer who had ended up in Argentina where he managed several estates and employed a small army of slaves. After the general emancipation, one, Antonio, had remained loyal to his master, rather in the manner of Firs in Chekhov's *The Cherry Orchard*. It had therefore become a Richardson tradition that faithful old Antonio be remembered by his name being inherited by sons of the family.

Like Osborne, little Cecil Antonio (quickly abbreviated to Tony), had been diagnosed a 'delicate' child, cosseted not only by his mother but also his widowed grandmothers and a spinster aunt, all of whom lurked in dark rooms in the upper reaches of the family home. Like Devine and Osborne, Richardson was also educated at a minor public school, in his case at Ashville College in Harrogate. Like Osborne, he was exempted from National Service because of his frail health and, like Devine, went up to Wadham College, Oxford, where he in his turn became a president of OUDS. Irving Wardle, a contemporary, recalled Richardson as being in 'a tremendous hurry' at Oxford, 'plugged into some source of energy denied to the common herd.'[2] When he first contacted

Devine in London one day in 1952, Richardson was a twenty-four-year-old television director hoping to cast him in an adaptation of *Curtain Down*, a short story by Chekhov. Devine promptly refused, objecting that the project sounded tedious, but when Richardson persisted, Devine eventually relented. It was the beginning, he said, of a 'great friendship'.[3]

Devine was captivated by the younger man's energy, his quicksilver intelligence and his seemingly immense knowledge of American and continental playwrights, many of whose names, as yet, were unfamiliar in England. Richardson, on the other hand, respected Devine as an experienced man of the theatre, yet one who retained an essential liberalism and was brimming with ideas he was burning to put into practice. He was particularly adamant that the theatre must be reinvigorated by new young writers and a new young audience. When Richardson enthusiastically agreed, they began planning a company in earnest, busily writing memoranda, drawing up budgets, debating artistic policy and repertoire.

At the same time, unknown to Devine and Richardson, plans were afoot elsewhere, many miles from London, deep in the Devon countryside. This was the home territory of Ronald Duncan, a high-church author of verse plays, and in 1946 the librettist of Benjamin Britten's *The Rape of Lucretia*. In 1953, Duncan had founded the Taw and Torridge Festival, not far from Belmont College, John Osborne's old school. His confederates in this rural enterprise included Britten, J. Edward Blacksell, the headmaster of a school in Barnstaple, and the Earl of Harewood, a musicologist and a cousin of the Queen. Already they had lured small operatic groups and musical ensembles to give performances, but their great coup so far had been to stage the first but not very good production in England of Bertolt Brecht's *Mother Courage*. But as it proved almost impossible to persuade theatre managers to fund performances for only the few days their festival required, Duncan decided to form his own English Stage Company to produce and tour non-commercial work, including his own. The Taw and Torridge organisers, therefore, set to work in rustling up the necessary backing money. Blacksell the schoolmaster turned to Neville Blond, a former RAF contact and a supremely wealthy Mancunian textile manufacturer who was also chief government adviser on transatlantic trade. For his part, Duncan appealed to Greville Poke, an old Cambridge friend and keen amateur actor, and together they met Blond over lunch when he agreed to join them as chairman. He had only three conditions, one being to set up a managing Council, the second to engage an artistic director, and the third to lease a London theatre. This was beyond anything that either Duncan or Poke had envisaged, but Blond breezily waved all doubts aside. Leaving his hosts 'flabbergasted', he promised to find both director and theatre.[4]

News that Blond was looking for both a theatre and an artistic director on behalf of the English Stage Company quickly reached the alert ears of Oscar Lewenstein. A Communist in his mid-thirties and former business manager of Unity, a left-wing theatre company based in Holborn, Lewenstein was now the general manager at the Royal Court Theatre in Sloane Square. As he knew Devine, whom privately he thought 'a bit of a snob', he engineered a lunch of his own between Duncan and Devine to see what might transpire.[5] Over the meal, Devine outlined his plans. Although he detested verse plays and especially the kind written by Duncan, Devine nevertheless saw the opportunity before him and gave the other man the impression of being wholly in sympathy with his ideas, with the result that by the coffee stage, he had been invited to become artistic director of the English Stage Company at a salary of £1,560 a year. He accepted, provided that Tony Richardson became his assistant. Over two lunches, therefore, Duncan's scheme had been effectively hijacked and the aims of the English Stage Company redirected 'from a provincial festival service to a continuous metropolitan management.'[6]

The company's quest for a theatre finally ended, perhaps predictably, given Lewenstein's involvement, at the steps of the Royal Court. '. . . more than a building,' wrote Richard Findlater several years later, 'it is an attitude, a discipline, an inheritance . . .'[7] Next to the Underground station on the eastern side of Sloane Square, the theatre had the advantage of being in Chelsea, which still retained something of a Bohemian reputation, and in late 1955, when Devine pushed open the doors and stood in the cramped, dusty foyer, he recognised that he was walking into a place where history had indeed already been made. It was here in 1904 that Harley Granville Barker opened an ambitious repertory season of serious plays dealing with contemporary social issues, a daring gamble in which he had been supported by Bernard Shaw and William Archer, the progressive theatre critic of The World. But since those heady pioneering days, when Barker produced a dozen Shaw premieres as well as plays by himself and other, lesser-known dramatists, the theatre had lost much of its lustre. Having been extensively bomb damaged during the war, the building had been hastily patched together but not fully restored. And although Chelsea had social cachet, it had the disadvantage of being well off the beaten track of most theatre-goers heading for the West End and Shaftesbury Avenue. The Royal Court had fallen into the hands of Alfred Esdaile, a retired music-hall comedian, pioneer of non-stop variety and the inventor of a nifty mechanism enabling a microphone located beneath the front edge of the stage to rise up to the height the performer required. The theatre was languishing, but when he reported to Blond, Devine was emphatic. 'It's perfect, Neville,' he told him. 'Let's take it.'[8]

Esdaile chirpily sold the remaining thirty-five years of his lease for £25,000, and in February 1956 the Royal Court Theatre passed into the hands of the English Stage Company and its hastily assembled Council started looking for funds to cover the months ahead. Blond donated £8,000, covering the annual rent of £5,000, rates and insurance, and other Council members chipped in with what they could afford, or perhaps what they were willing to lose. An application was made to the Arts Council who, when Duncan had approached them with his proposal of an 'English Stage Society' touring new plays to regional arts festivals, had indicated they should not hold their hopes too high.

But imposingly drawn-up plans involving a London theatre, an artistic director and the prospect of a repertory season were something else entirely and the Council promptly turned round with the offer of a £2,500 production grant and a £7,000 subsidy for the first year of their operation. This might have been negligible by the standards of mainland Europe, but in Britain at the time it constituted both a sizeable financial investment and a significant act of faith.

Although theatre historians have made much of the radicalism of the English Stage Company's repertoire, its championship of such playwrights as Osborne, John Arden and Arnold Wesker, and the pugnacity of Devine's progressive views, he was just the sort of person whom the Arts Council in 1955 saw as a safe pair of hands. He was, after all, an Oxford man, as was his assistant, a highly regarded teacher and an actor and director with an impressive track record. As such, he was an established figure in the London arts world, an 'insider' noted Lewenstein, and part of 'the central magic circle'.[9] There were few people in London better qualified to run a new theatre company and his involvement appears to have made the crucial difference to the Arts Council who, as one historian has written, with Devine on board 'clearly' saw the English Stage Company as 'a pivot of Arts Council funding strategy.'[10] Moreover, the ESC Council, stuffed with formidable names and topped off with an impressive scattering of titles, boasted not only considerable business expertise but also influential social connections: 'such an odd job lot', mused Devine, 'that the company's bound to succeed.'[11] Devine was a canny operator. He recognised that the English way of changing things or doing something new is often best achieved by working within the recognised order, rather than without. The best way of challenging the Establishment (a term first coined in *The Spectator* in 1955) was to allow oneself to be embraced by it.

Meanwhile, the new company was being aggressively publicised. 'Of the 900,000 people in Greater London, Mr Devine is convinced there are sufficient enthusiastic playgoers who would keep the Court open,' reported the *Theatre World*. His intention was to quickly 'build up a public who would *always* go to the Court.'[12] What this faithful audience would be going to see, however, was rather more difficult to say. When Devine had appealed the previous summer in *The Stage* for suitable plays, he had been rewarded with a postbag of 750 scripts. This was considerably more than The Saga had received at Hayling Island after their advertisement for plays showing 'a healthy reaction to prevalent tradition', but in terms of quality it yielded, with a single exception, a similar, dismal result. Almost all the scripts that thudded onto Devine's desk were examples of the West End fare he particularly wanted to avoid, either domestic dramas that Binkie Beaumont had possibly rejected, or verse plays in the style of Eliot and Fry. The sole exception was *Look Back in Anger*. Once Devine read it, he gave it to Richardson, whose verdict was immediate. 'By the time I was through the first act,' he recalled, 'I knew, whatever the battles to come, we'd win the war.'[13]

*   *   *

And so, having arranged to meet Osborne at his houseboat, Devine made his way to Cubitt Yacht Basin. 'John was thrilled,' recalled Creighton. 'We both were.'[14] Unfortunately, when Devine got there the tide was in, and the Egret, surrounded by water, was cut off from the riverbank. It seemed as if Devine would have to bellow his negotiations to the playwright, who was wearing a trim blazer and tie that he had bought in Derby and warily watching him from the deck, until he noticed another young man in a small boat sploshing his way towards him, gesticulating as he did so. This was Anthony Creighton. Having been ferried to the barge, Devine scrambled on board, introduced himself, glanced at his surroundings, quickly secured an option to produce Look Back in Anger for £25 and set about interviewing his new playwright. Osborne remembered Devine from having seen his performance as George Tesman in Hedda Gabler a few months previously. But 'what I had not anticipated about him', he recorded, 'was that he was driven by that most blessed of human virtues, abiding and open curiosity. That, and unfeigned hope . . .'[15]

Back at the Royal Court, Devine and Richardson busily supervised the revamping of the Royal Court auditorium for the first season, now scheduled to begin in April 1956. The theatre roof was repaired, the electricity supply made safe and the walls repainted. Actors were auditioned, including Osborne, who became part of the company acting pool of twenty-two engaged to play as cast in whichever productions they were needed, at a wage of £12 a week. To paper over the absence of any unknown new dramatists apart from Osborne, Devine and Richardson had been obliged to fill out their first season as best they could with recognisable names, alighting first on Angus Wilson, whose new novel, Anglo-Saxon Attitudes, a denunciation of English hypocrisy and an analysis of England over forty years, would be published in May. A bird-like man of exotic plumage, a former Bletchley Park code-breaker and deputy supervisor of the British Museum Reading Room, Wilson was a sharp satirist and, although a novelist, was also the author of a play, The Mulberry Bush. A cautious, sub-Chekhovian piece about the high-principled Padley family whose dogmatism and fearsome benevolence tends to ruin lives rather than enhance them, it had been well received at the Bristol Old Vic the previous year but it was not, as Richardson noted, 'a particularly exciting' effort with which to launch a company supposedly closely in touch with the youthful post-war spirit.[16] Indeed, the best that might be said about it was that it was new to London, while Devine reasoned that Wilson's name might bring the Court some useful publicity. To this end, he wheeled in a star actress, Gwen Ffrangcon-Davies, to play the central role of Rose Padley, whom Wilson had modelled on the pioneering socialist, Beatrice Webb.

The Mulberry Bush, therefore, would open the company account, quickly followed by something more adventurous, the British premiere of Arthur Miller's The Crucible. Devine would direct both productions. A week later, it would be Richardson's turn with Look Back in Anger, after which Devine would honour an agreement with Ronald Duncan to produce a double-bill of Duncan's Don Juan and The Death of Satan, verse plays which Devine was already editing with the intention, some surmised, of getting the evening over and done with as quickly as possible. Altogether, *Look Back in Anger* was scheduled for twelve performances in repertory until the end of June, when *Cards of Identity*, which Nigel Dennis was adapting from his own novel, and directed by Tony Richardson, would close the first season. The plays would then run in repertory until October, when the second season would open with Devine directing Brecht's *The Good Woman of Setzuan*, followed by William Wycherley's rowdy Restoration comedy, *The Country Wife*. Promising that the English Stage Company would create a new style in acting and production, this rather jumbled menu was flourished before the press, whose response, according to Richardson, was both 'superior and grudging.'[17] Yet T. C. Worsley, who a few years earlier had despaired of 'any kind of literary revival', pronounced in the *New Statesman* that the season appeared to be 'one of the most exciting and important events in the British theatre for a great many years', adding that there were high hopes for the work of a new playwright, one 'Paul [sic] Osborne.'[18] Surprisingly, the *Observer's* Kenneth Tynan was more sceptical. Glancing down the list of plays, he paused momentarily at *Look Back in Anger*. The title, he said, would never do. 'Tell the author to change it.'[19]

But Osborne was loath to change anything, let alone the title. With the play scheduled for production, he and Creighton whiled away the winter months as best they could, Osborne tinkering with a new play, *Love in a Myth or, An Artificial Comedy*, a pastiche of the sentimental domestic comedy genre. It was touch-and-go financially, even though their expenses on the *Egret* were minimal. Osborne gratefully spent several evenings at Devine's house at Lower Mall, where good food was available and where he encountered several of the director's friends and colleagues. Angus Wilson and Nigel Dennis dropped in, as did dramatists from abroad, including Eugène Ionescu and Samuel Beckett, the two writers with whom the Francophile Devine felt most wholly at ease.

At some of these Lower Mall conferences, Richardson gently suggested cuts and improvements to the script of *Look Back in Anger* but, although Osborne begrudgingly adjusted a few lines, Richardson quickly realised that whatever the strength of Osborne's talents, re-writing was not one of them. 'What came out was what you got,' he concluded, 'and it was up to you [the director] to make the best of it.'[20] For his part, though, Osborne discovered that he was being taken very seriously as a writer. It was immensely encouraging. Advising him to acquire an agent, Devine directed him to Margery Vosper, a middle-aged woman and sister of the actor Frank Vosper, famed for his portrayal of urbane villains. Operating from three cramped and cluttered upper-floor rooms at 32 Shaftesbury Avenue, Margery's clients included Ronald Duncan and Emlyn Williams, in whose plays Osborne had appeared in repertory. A fund of theatrical gossip, Osborne liked her immediately and stayed with her for almost twenty years.

*   *   *

On 2 April 1956, the curtain rose on The Mulberry Bush, and the atmosphere of Oxford wafted across the stalls of the Royal Court Theatre. Like the new novels, the English Stage Company was dominated by Matthew Arnold's dreaming spires. Here was a play by an Oxford-educated author about an Oxford family staged by an Oxford director who had an Oxford assistant. That it was a safe, unassuming choice was confirmed by Binkie Beaumont, who, after the performance, congratulated Wilson upon 'a wonderful evening' of 'real theatre.'[21] The playwright himself, on the other hand, thought the production a 'disaster', while the critics were nonplussed.[22] Wilson was not an English Chekhov, and neither was The Mulberry Bush the stimulatingly energetic new writing which Devine and Richardson had confidently told them to expect. The reviews were tepid, audiences sporadic and business poor. From his desk at the Observer, Kenneth Tynan ended his review by firing a warning shot in the direction of the English Stage Company: 'I wish their enterprise too well to embarrass it with further criticism.'[23] Things picked up a little with The Crucible, yet Devine's production, according to an anxiously watchful Richardson, lacked passion and failed to convince. 'Again,' he concluded, 'it was either a draw, or a scrape through on points.'[24] Everything now rested upon Look Back in Anger, an unknown play by an entirely unknown writer who had once hoped of going up to Oxford but never did.

*   *   *

Casting had begun at the beginning of the year. Devine and Richardson had made a point of recruiting actors unfamiliar to London audiences and over the following years a post-war generation of actors, often with regional accents and from unassuming backgrounds, made their first appearances at the Royal Court. For Look Back in Anger, Kenneth Haigh, dark-haired and wiry and from Yorkshire, fitted the bill for Jimmy Porter, while Alan Bates, twenty-two and from Derby, was cast as Cliff; Helena Hughes, half-Irish, whose composer father had been a friend of James Joyce, as Helena; and John Welsh, originally from Ireland, as Colonel Redfern. All were from the company's acting pool and had appeared in the first two ESC productions. Casting Alison, though, proved trickier. When nobody in the resident company seemed quite right, Richardson urged Osborne to consider Mary Ure, a young blonde actress from Glasgow, who had recently given a notable performance in Anouilh's Time Remembered at the Lyric, Hammersmith.

The granddaughter of a Lord Provost of Glasgow and the daughter of Colin McGregor Ure, a wealthy civil engineer, and his wife Edith, Mary had been born in one of Glasgow's more prosperous suburbs in 1933. Carefully shielded from the city's meaner streets of slums and razor-wielding gangs, she had been dispatched to the Mount School at York, run by the Quaker religious organisation, and from there she had foraged further south to the Central School of Speech and Drama in London. Now aged twenty-three, she was of medium height with fine features, sensual and fragile, 'like glass' people said, and her star was in the ascendant.[25] In *Time Remembered*, she had appeared opposite Paul Scofield, to whose Hamlet at Stratford she had subsequently played an impressively deranged Ophelia in an austere production directed by Peter Brook, another rapidly emerging talent. She was, remembered Scofield, 'an enchanting girl, pretty and sometimes beautiful . . . imaginative and intelligent with a vague, removed quality, a drifting away as if she were no longer there . . .'[26] One of her later directors more prosaically attributed this less to an ethereal spirit than to her short-sightedness. But she would, declared Richardson, be the perfect Alison, and Mary was cast.

In March, Charles Heriot, one of the Lord Chamberlain's cadre of hawk-eyed play Examiners, completed his reading of *Look Back in Anger*, noted that it was both 'impressive and depressing' and fired off a list of deletions and alterations required before the necessary public performance licence could be issued.[27] However, these were surprisingly few and Osborne was spared a repetition of the scrambled night of rewriting he had endured with *Personal Enemy*. Heriot decreed that Jimmy could not accuse Alison's mother of being 'as tough as a night in a Bombay brothel and as hairy as a gorilla's behind', although he conceded it was permissible to describe her as being 'as rough as a night in a Bombay brothel and as tough as a matelot's arm.' Heriot also insisted that other passages be 'considerably toned down', while phrases such as 'short-arsed' could not possibly be uttered on the English stage.[28] With changes made and the necessary licence extracted from the censorial grasp, rehearsals began on 19 April at a church hall just behind the Peter Jones department store on the opposite side of Sloane Square from the theatre. Richardson, whose experience was restricted to television, had never directed a stage play before. 'Rehearsals were terse and a bit glum,' he recalled. 'I hadn't got a lot of personal confidence – only confidence in the play.'[29]

On Monday 7 May, there was a preview. As the curtain rose on the Porters' dishevelled room, with its double bed, gas stove, food cupboard, strewn clothes, ironing board and bookshelf, items – apart from the books – not usually seen on the London stage, the audience, comprised largely of young people, rippled with laughter; perhaps uneasily, perhaps from recognition. At the beginning of Act 3, ironic cheering greeted the reappearance from Act 1 of the Porters' ironing board, this time with Helena rather than Alison, wielding the iron over one of Jimmy's shirts. 'There was a lot of laughter throughout the first week,' confirmed Kenneth Haigh. 'Which was only right. The play is very comic, almost Shavian in a way.'[30]

The following evening, 8 May 1956, the official first night, the fifty-seventh anniversary of Tom Godfrey's birth and the eleventh anniversary of VE Day, was mild and spring-like. The theatre was only partly filled, the audience scattered across the stalls and dress circle like confetti left after a wedding. The English Stage Company Council was out in force and Anthony Creighton was there, but not Pamela Lane, who was appearing in repertory in York. Nellie Beatrice was booked in for the following evening. Binkie Beaumont arrived with his guests, Terence Rattigan and the actress Margaret Leighton, who were photographed as they entered the theatre, looking noticeably apprehensive. So were Osborne, Devine and Richardson as they watched the critics file in: Philip Hope-Wallace of the *Manchester Guardian* and John Barber of the *Daily Express*, Milton Shulman from the *Evening Standard*, Patrick Gibbs from *The Daily Telegraph*, J. C. Trewin from the *Birmingham Post*, Harold Hobson from the *Sunday Times* and the tall, ostentatious figure of Kenneth Tynan, the self-styled war correspondent from the *Observer*. Osborne took his place beside Oscar Lewenstein in the front row of a disappointingly half-filled dress circle, grateful that Kenneth Haigh was not only in good spirits but also in good health and safely ensconced in Jimmy Porter's armchair on stage, waiting for the curtain to go up. Osborne was Haigh's understudy and even though he had written the play, he was none too sure of Jimmy Porter's lines. 'For God's sake,' he had warned Haigh earlier, 'don't be off tonight. I don't really know the part.'[31]

Once the curtain fell on the first act, there was a hurried review of progress so far. In contrast to the previous evening, there had been very little laughter. The audience seemed disconcerted. Osborne was unaware that Beaumont was tersely announcing to his party that as the play was evidently worthless, he was leaving the theatre in a bid to retrieve the remainder of a wasted evening. Nor did he realise that a similar escape by Rattigan was foiled by T. C. Worsley, who appealed to the author of *The Deep Blue Sea* that a play by a first-time dramatist should at least be seen through until the end. After the final curtain, as Rattigan began to make his getaway at last, another figure loomed up to block his path. It was a reporter from the *Daily Express*. His readers, he said, would be interested to hear Rattigan's impression of this curious first play. What did he think Osborne was trying to say? 'Look Ma, I'm not Terence Rattigan,' abruptly replied the creator of Aunt Edna.[32] The critics, pushing past him in the aisle, armed with their notebooks and pens and in flight for their deadlines, agreed. Whoever John Osborne was, he was certainly not Terence Rattigan.

*   *   *

It is ironic that *Look Back in Anger* and some of the plays that followed at the Royal Court should have had the effect of relegating Rattigan to the ranks of the old-fashioned, a perception that persisted until a revival of his work during the 1980s began to restore his reputation. There are parallels between the work of both playwrights that were overlooked at the time, both by Osborne and Rattigan and by the critics. Jimmy Porter not only has some affinity with Freddie Page, the disaffected former pilot in *The Deep Blue Sea*, but there is also an echo of the plight of Hester Collyer, the play's sad heroine whom Osborne had seen Pamela play at Derby, and who, like Jimmy, is unable to find in others a passion and depth of feeling to match her own. And in *Table by the Window*, the first of the plays comprising the double-bill of Rattigan's *Separate Tables*

produced at the St James's Theatre in 1954, sharply attentive playgoers might
have seen other glancing similarities. John Malcolm, the central character, is
a man from the working class whose political career is ruined after he is convicted of assaulting his Kensington-born wife. Since his release, and corroded
by rancour and self-contempt, Malcolm has sought the sanctuary of an unobtrusive private hotel from where he contributes bitter and anonymous articles
to left-wing journals. Those who saw both *Table by the Window* and *Look Back in
Anger* might have noted that both deal in their different ways with marriages in
which the violence of the husband has resulted in separation, yet the emotional
demands of both partners bring them, for better or for worse and however
temporarily, together again.

But if anyone was thinking of Rattigan that night, it was of the contrast rather
than the similarities with Osborne, for where he differed from Rattigan and
everyone else was in his creation of an anti-hero who was not only terrifyingly
articulate but who remorselessly dominates the centre of the stage throughout
the three acts of the play. People just did not know what to make of him. But
Kenneth Tynan did. He later recalled that as he emerged from the theatre with
the rest of the audience, he found himself 'surrounded by disgruntled middle-
aged faces', which made him even more euphoric than he was already. For
Tynan, 'something very heart-warming had happened and . . . one was just
dying to be on the street with the news.'[33] Finally, he had found a flag to wave
in his crusade for an invigorated English theatre and at last he had something
to talk about at parties.

Although Tony Richardson remembered the first-night audience response
being encouraging, the reviews the following morning were divided. The
consensus was that nobody liked Jimmy Porter or could fathom why Alison
tolerated him. He was both a boor and a bore: a 'boorish oaf', 'an egomaniac',
'a spoilt neurotic bore who badly needed the attention of an analyst', and 'a
character who should have gone to a psychiatrist rather than have come to a
dramatist'. Why did Alison, his 'wretched little wife' put up with it all and
stay with this ghastly person and in that terrible flat? Surely, reasoned Robert
Wraight in the *Star*, in real life she would have left him long ago. In the *Birmingham Post*, J. C. Trewin was still simmering at the memory. 'I look back in
anger upon a night misconceived and misspent,' he wrote. 'I wonder only, in
helpless distaste, that this is a play to be done in a season that began with hope
so eager.'[34]

Yet if they found the characters distasteful and their motives bewildering,
most critics acknowledged that Osborne was clearly a writer with something to
say if only anyone, including the author, could work out what it was. It was an
'interesting' play, announced the *News Chronicle* warily, and although 'less than
successful' it was 'at least noteworthy for trying to say *something* about contemporary life.' It was 'not a masterpiece' agreed Cecil Wilson in the *Daily Mail*, yet
the English Stage Company had 'discovered a dramatist of outstanding promise,
a man who can write with searing passion.' T. C. Worsley complained that

Osborne 'has written all the soliloquies for his Wolverhampton [sic] Hamlet and virtually left out all the other characters and all the action', but affirmed that 'in these soliloquies you can hear the authentic new tone of the Nineteen-Fifties, desperate, savage, resentful and, at times, very funny. This', he announced, 'is the kind of play which, for all its imperfections, the English Stage Company ought to be doing . . .' And Derek Granger in the *Financial Times* was even more upbeat, enthusing that *Look Back in Anger* was 'arresting, painful and sometimes astonishing . . . a play of extraordinary importance . . . and its influence should go far, far beyond such an eccentric and contorted one-man turn as the controversial *Waiting for Godot*.'[35]

Written mostly by middle-aged men apprehensively aware that the post-war spirit, the bewildering mainland European absurdism of Beckett and the dangerous American realism of Arthur Miller and Tennessee Williams threatened the foundations of English country house drama, the reviews were much better than might have been expected. Indeed, several pronounced that *Look Back in Anger*'s strength was that it authentically represented the younger generation. Jimmy Porter 'is like thousands of young Londoners today,' argued John Barber in the *Daily Express*, adding that the play was 'intense, angry, feverish, undisciplined. It is even crazy. But it is young, young, young.' T. C. Worsley agreed. 'If you are young, it will speak for you. If you are middle-aged, it will tell you what the young are feeling.'[36]

Meanwhile, Nellie Beatrice went along to the following night's performance with Hugh Berrington's stepmother and declared it 'all very exciting', while Pamela Lane came down with a friend from Yorkshire and, having recognised both herself and her estranged husband in the figures of Alison and Jimmy, emerged from the Royal Court 'with mixed feelings.'[37] She had found the evening both perturbing and exhilarating, at one point after a remark of Alison's, turning to her companion and whispering: 'Oh, I never said that!'[38] At the same time, she recognised that in *Look Back in Anger* her husband had written a play that might make his name, 'something John and I always hoped might happen', yet the 'personal side' had nevertheless 'loomed rather large. I had a hunch,' she recollected many years later, 'that both John and I would be associated with the characters, that I would be seen as the model for Alison, and that if the play was a success, that association might haunt me down the years.'[39]

On Sunday, Harold Hobson and Kenneth Tynan pronounced. In the *Sunday Times*, Hobson warned that Osborne 'is a writer who at present does not know what he is doing', but he was nevertheless a dramatist 'of outstanding promise.'[40] While Osborne had concentrated mainly upon Jimmy Porter, he, Hobson, had found himself much more interested in Alison. Other critics saw her as merely a silent target for Jimmy's rage but for Hobson it was her endurance, the futility of her attempt to escape and her final breakdown which had been the most moving and ultimately uplifting part of the evening. A practising Christian, Hobson detected a redemptive, almost spiritual dimension to the play that others had overlooked. It was significant that it was Alison, he noted perceptively, 'when she makes her heartbroken, grovelling, yet peace-securing submission, to whom the final big speech is given . . . It is peace that she gets at the end, as Raskolnikov gets it when he ceases to maintain himself innocent.'[41]

Tynan, on the other hand, having denounced Loamshire and cried out for plays about demi-gods, had discovered that someone had apparently heard him. Look Back in Anger had been written instinctively and Tynan responded to it in much the same manner. After all, this was a man who, two years earlier in a Picture Post article entitled 'What Men Hate Most About Women', had advised his readers that 'A love affair nowadays is a tableau of two wild animals, each with its teeth sunk in the other's neck, each scared to let go in case it bleeds to death.' Women, added Tynan, wanted men to 'surrender all [their] secrets.'[42] Sitting in the stalls that night, he immediately recognised that his personal and profes-sional convictions were being played out on the stage before him. Delighting in the play's youthfulness and passion, he hailed Osborne as a dramatist who had brought off 'that rarest of dramatic phenomena, the act of original crea-tion.' The play and its protagonist were much more than merely exhilarating; they were incandescent. Look Back in Anger, he cried in his review on 13 May, portrayed post-war youth as it really was: 'All the qualities are there, qualities one had despaired of ever seeing on the stage – the drift towards anarchy, the instinctive leftishness, the automatic rejection of "official" attitudes, the surreal sense of humour . . . the casual promiscuity, the sense of lacking a crusade worth fighting for, and, underlying all these, the determination that no one who dies shall go unmourned.'[43]

Look Back in Anger, he admitted, was likely to remain a strictly minority taste. But 'what matters, however, is the size of that minority. I estimate it at roughly 6,733,000, which is the number of people in this country between the ages of twenty and thirty. And this figure will doubtlessly be swelled by refugees from other age groups who are curious to know what the contemporary young pup is thinking and feeling.' In what has since become one of Tynan's most famous pronouncements, he rapturously exclaimed that: 'I doubt if I could love anyone who did not wish to see Look Back in Anger. It is the best young play of its decade.'[44]

This was what he had been looking for in the English theatre. But it had also been an evening of self-recognition. The qualities Tynan had seen on the stage, were very much the kind of qualities he liked to see in himself. In many ways, he and Osborne were strikingly similar. Tynan was a man of whom his wife, in the guise of his biographer, afterwards remarked that: 'Throughout his life he refused to be moderate or even reasonable', an assessment that later in his life some might have argued suited Osborne himself.[45] Tynan's reviews could be wildly enthusiastic, even adulatory, but they were also 'provocative, scornful, compelling', all epithets that would be applied to Osborne.[46] Both Osborne and Tynan valued enthusiasm and loyalty and believed they possessed a depth of feeling that they frequently despaired finding in others.

There was another similarity between them. Like Osborne and George Devine, Tynan had a complex and distant relationship with his mother. Letitia Rose Tynan, a working-class woman of Irish origin, had never married Peter Peacock, the man with whom she lived in Birmingham, for the simple reason that he was married already. A draper in Birmingham and the owner of Peacock Stores, he travelled north by chauffeur-driven car to Warrington once a week, where he slipped into the other half of his carefully managed double life as Sir Peter Peacock, six-times elected Mayor, a justice of the peace and successful businessman, the father of five children and husband to a wife who refused to divorce him. Kenneth Tynan was illegitimate and claimed not to have discovered this until his father's death in 1948, when Tynan was twenty-one and at Oxford, and he was informed of the fact by the family solicitor. He never forgave his parents for their deception of him, and Rose subsequently became 'a tolerated rather than a loved figure' whose sensibilities and opinions were often 'an embarrassment' to him.[47] Given their resemblances, Osborne and Tynan might easily have become professional allies and personal friends, but in the event, perhaps because of their similarities, perhaps because Osborne may have rather envied the other man's Oxford credentials and social ease, their association would always be circumspect and frequently, from Osborne's side, hostile.

CHAPTER 11

The Year of the
Angry Young Man

AND SO BEGAN A YEAR in which John Osborne was celebrated as an Angry Young Man, the year in which he was catapulted from obscurity to fame and acclaim, in which critics and pundits pored over his play and debated what it might mean and in which journalists clamoured for Osborne's views on everything from the theatre and politics to fashion, food and women. The most pressing question, though, was what, exactly, did Jimmy Porter and his creator stand for?

'What are you angry *about*?' an interviewer asked Osborne, four days after the premiere of *Look Back in Anger*. It would become a familiar question. Was it 'social class or a set of moral values you think are invalid?' 'Both these things and other things as well,' replied Osborne helpfully. 'It's anger about the present state of personal relationships between men and women which seem to be in a very interesting and complex condition at the moment.'[1] Like Jimmy Porter, he was also angry that nobody seemed to feel passionately about anything anymore. Questioned by Malcolm Muggeridge on BBC television on 9 July, he declared that: 'We have a Welfare State but nothing else. Our culture is poverty-stricken.'[2]

In the public imagination, John Osborne and Jimmy Porter very quickly became one and the same person. Osborne 'has created the angry young Jimmy Porter in his own image' noted Robert Muller in *Picture Post*. Jimmy Porter 'rants, among other things, against public apathy, *News of the World* morality, Bishops who praise H-Bombs, English Sundays, J. B. Priestley, the entire English middle class and its prejudices, American evangelists, homosexuals, church bells and anything remotely "posh" or "phoney".'[3] Here was Walter Allen's 'new hero' brought to life, a man who 'at the least suspicion of the "phoney" . . . gets tough.' And Osborne amiably agreed that he did indeed share much of Jimmy Porter's indignation. 'But perhaps I'll mellow by the autumn,' he warned, 'and become less of an angry man – a bit grumpy perhaps, but less angry. But I doubt it.'[4]

Yet correspondents who tracked down the author fearful of encountering a splenetic Jimmy Porter, were reassured to discover a well-spoken, hesitant, even rather shy young man. John Osborne is 'gentle-voiced, courteous, something of a dandy,' *The Sunday Times* assured its readers, 'a friendly, serious, bony young man who thinks before he speaks, worries about being lazy, smiles often' and who 'writes about what he has experienced himself.'[5] He was photographed by Cecil Beaton, photographer of Royalty and fashion, who declared that the Angry Young Man had the face of an elegant camel. Osborne 'describes himself as vaguely Welsh and has a houseboat in Chiswick', reported Robert Muller. The Angry Young Man was also estimated to have made an astonishing £20,000 from *Look Back in Anger* by the end of the year. But 'will success spoil John Osborne?' wondered Muller; a question to which it would be unlikely that any interviewee would reply in the affirmative. 'According to him, no. "Success," he says, in the clipped and scornful, naïve-sophisticated manner of Jimmy Porter, "success pays the electricity bills".'[6] A reporter from the *Empire News* tracked down the Angry Young Man's mother to the Spring Hotel in Ewell, eager for the reaction of the 'charming lady' who was happily working behind the bar. 'I never did stand in John's way,' she affirmed. 'He was never a strong boy – he survived double pneumonia, double hernia, double this and double that. But I never thought he'd end up a down and out. I thought he might be a barrister or something.'[7]

*　　　*　　　*

There are several versions of how the phrase Angry Young Man came about, although it had already been anticipated by Robert Tee in his review of *Look Back in Anger* in the *Daily Mirror* on 9 May 1956, in which he announced that: 'An angry play by an angry young author made its first appearance at the Royal Court last night.' In his memoirs, however, Osborne records that George Fearon, the Royal Court Theatre's press officer, wondering how best to promote a desperately ailing production, for not even the combined weight of Hobson and Tynan had done much to increase ticket sales, told him that he disliked the play and hazarded that he, Osborne, must be a very angry young man. Osborne cautiously assented. On the other hand, Fearon's widow contended that her husband first used the phrase while attempting to describe Osborne to J. W. (Jack) Lambert, Hobson's deputy at *The Sunday Times*.[8] Others noted that Leslie Allen Paul, a religious philosopher who had founded a youth movement alternative to Baden's Powell's khaki-clad boy scouts called the Woodcraft Folk who presented themselves 'uniformed in the green of nature', had in 1951 published an autobiography entitled *Angry Young Man*, in which he recorded his conversion from youthful Marxism to Christianity.[9]

However the phrase emerged, it immediately seized the imagination of journalists who launched themselves upon a summer of speculation as to the nature of Osborne as an Angry Young Man and the new social type he represented.

Articles began to appear everywhere, in the heavyweight Sunday newspapers, in the dailies and in magazines, and in the cultural and gossip columns. There were earnest talks and discussions on television and the wireless. Word began to filter across the Atlantic and American correspondents picked up the theme.

Yet the idea of Anger and the Angry Young Man as a social phenomenon to watch (and probably be very indignant about) was largely popularised by the right-wing mass-market newspapers, particularly the Daily Mail and the Daily Express, which seemed to be permanently engaged in a never-ending circulation battle. Several daily papers, including the Mail and the Express, were fighting competition from television news by publishing more sensational stories and gossip about the rich, the well-known and the controversial, accompanied by large photo-spreads. The newly assertive popular press of the 1950s liked to see itself as morally unimpeachable, frequently claiming to thoroughly disapprove of much of what it published while simultaneously arguing that doing so was acting in the public interest. This was the beginning of a new era of more intrusive and unforgiving journalism. As far as the popular press was concerned, John Osborne, Anger and the emerging youth culture represented something deliberately provocative, possibly subversive, something, like American rock and roll and Teddy Boys, that had to be grappled with, explained and, if it all went too far, denounced. Whatever Osborne said or did, therefore, became enormously interesting. Reporters, gossip columnists and photographers watched and waited.

More serious cultural columnists were equally curious to know who this new social type, the Angry Young Man, was. In his profile of Osborne, published in Picture Post under the title of 'Angry Young Men', Robert Muller explained that Jimmy Porter was similar to the youthfully rebellious character created by the American film star, James Dean. He was 'a Rebel Without a Cause' (this being the title of Dean's most successful film). According to T. C. Worsley in the New Statesman, he was 'a self-destructive, teddy boy intellectual'. Although he was far more voluble, several critics sought to establish a connection between Osborne's Jimmy Porter, John Wain's Charles Lumley and Kingsley Amis's Jim Dixon. Look Back in Anger, suggested Worsley, 'is set on the seamy side of the Kingsley Amis world.'[10]

The previous year, Amis had published That Uncertain Feeling, his second novel, set in the fictional Welsh industrial town of Aberdarcy. John Lewis, its central character, a librarian resentful of social privilege but nevertheless ensnared in adultery with the Anglicised Elizabeth Gruffyd-Williams, was seen as very much in the Jim Dixon, and therefore the Jimmy Porter, mould. After all, Jimmy Porter, Jim Dixon and John Lewis had lower-middle-class backgrounds, held vaguely left-wing opinions and scorned social privilege. Look Back in Anger, wrote Harold Hobson, 'put on to the stage the outlook of That Uncertain Feeling.'[11]

Very quickly, Osborne found himself the focal point of what was becoming an emerging group of Angry Young Men, to which John Wain and Kingsley Amis had been tentatively recruited. Commentators anxiously searching for other candidates to swell their numbers soon alighted upon the rather incongruous figure of the twenty-four-year-old Colin Wilson, whose first book, *The Outsider*, appeared within weeks of *Look Back in Anger*.

If Osborne represented truculent dissent and Wain and Amis intellectual wit, Wilson presented an astonishing image of the Angry Young Man as metaphysical thinker. Having trawled through the works of Albert Camus, Hermann Hesse and T. E. Lawrence, and a good deal of Nietzsche, Dostoyevsky and Sartre, he had cobbled together a lengthy and hazily existentialist speculation on the alienation afflicting men of genius, the absence of genuine feeling in modern man, and the meaning of life in general. It behoved great men, he asserted, not merely to shake off the shackles of conventional law and morality, but to project themselves beyond philosophy into a quasi-religious transcendental state defined not by Christian love but the power of the Will. Although none of this was very original and neither was it very clear, Wilson's success was immediate. He was celebrated as a philosopher, and an Angry one at that. *The Outsider* had the most venerable critics rocking on their heels in amazement. 'Extraordinary,' gasped Cyril Connolly in *The Sunday Times*, 'one of the most remarkable first books I have read for a long time.'[12] It was 'an exhaustive and luminous study of a representative theme of our time,' echoed Philip Toynbee in the *Observer*.[13]

Connolly and Toynbee did for Wilson what Hobson and Tynan had so far failed to do for Osborne. The day after these breathless effusions were published, *The Outsider* sold out its initial 5,000 print-run and within three weeks, as the acclamations continued to pile up, the book was in its third impression. Within six months it had sold 20,000 copies, earned Wilson almost £4,000 in royalties and both figures were increasing daily. His publisher, Victor Gollancz, who also published Kingsley Amis, claimed that he had lost count of the number of impressions printed. Was it eight? Was it nine? No matter: as literary luminaries elbowed each other aside to offer their praises, the presses rattled on, churning out more books. The short story writer V. S. Pritchett clapped a hand to his forehead and pronounced *The Outsider* 'dashing, learned and exact', the novelist Elizabeth Bowen gasped that she was 'thunderstruck' by the young philosopher's erudition, and Kenneth Walker in the *Listener* declared it the 'most remarkable book on which the reviewer has ever had to pass judgment.'[14]

Convinced of his own genius, Wilson agreed wholeheartedly, but other reviewers were more dubious. The logical-positivist philosopher A. J. Ayer worried about the Nietzschean influence, while the Marxist cultural commentator Raymond Williams was troubled that in his concern for the genius-Outsider, Wilson appeared dismissive of the great toiling mass of 'insiders'. The supposedly Angry Young Men whom Wilson had apparently joined were equally sceptical. Kingsley Amis acidly noted in the *Spectator* that: 'One of the prime indications of the sickness of mankind in the mid-twentieth century is that so much excited attention is paid to books about the sickness of mankind in the mid-twentieth century', while Osborne sniffily informed the *Daily Express* that:

'I really must read it. I'm told it's a very good reference work – such a wealth of bibliography.'[15]

But who, wondered the press, was Colin Wilson? Gratifyingly, Wilson was only too ready to let people know. Promising 'The Inside Story of the Outsider', the London *Evening News* revealed that Wilson had been born in 1931, the son of working-class parents from Leicester. The young existentialist had left school at sixteen, worked in various factories, moved to London and embarked upon a deeply labyrinthine programme of self-education. Having snatched time off to marry and then father a son, he had gone to Paris where he had imbibed the bohemian atmosphere of the Left Bank. Back in London, he had worked intermittently at a plastics factory before abandoning employment altogether, whereupon his wife had abandoned him, escaping with their son to Leicester. Wilson, meanwhile, sat himself down at the British Museum Reading Room to compose what he knew would be his great work. In order to avoid unnecessary expense on rent, he had slept out on Hampstead Heath during the summer before retreating to a flat for the winter.

Wilson's bizarre existential thinking and his nights beneath the stars added up to his being presented in the press as both a mastermind and a rebel. Journalists were avid for interviews and Wilson eagerly complied. Emerging from an audience with the philosopher, Daniel Farson proclaimed: 'I have just met my first genius.'[16] One of several journalists hoping to consolidate their own reputations by scrambling aboard the bandwagon of the Angry Young Men, Farson, a Soho habitué and renowned drinker, provided the *Daily Mail* with a torrent of Angry stories over the following months. The man who would achieve the distinction of being 'often unable to tell the truth or the difference between it and fiction' enthused that Wilson's 'clear, clean vision' was so piercing that this 'rare person' was able to bang away on his typewriter 'rapidly without corrections'.[17]

The *Daily Express*, on the other hand, was fascinated by his diet. Wilson confided that he lived almost entirely off canned foods and biscuits. A great deal of comment was being made about John Osborne's houseboat; Wilson posed philosophically for the camera, cooking at a primus stove in his *Look Back in Anger*-like Notting Hill flat, his workroom overlooking a garden throttled with weeds. This, vouchsafed the *Express*, was what 'a classic rebel in a classic setting' looked like.[18] In America, *Time* magazine glowed that *The Outsider* was 'causing a run on critical superlatives in highbrow London', while Wilson genially obliged *Life* magazine by trudging back to the Heath, zipping himself into his sleeping-bag and staring up at the sky for the benefit of a photocall. The resulting snap adorned a feature recounting all the '*Fuss over English Egg-head*'.[19]

With his duffel coat, horn-rimmed glasses, turtle-neck sweater, corduroy trousers and sandals, Wilson indeed epitomised what was then the image of a bohemian intellectual. But no sooner had readers finished (or abandoned) *The Outsider*, than they were presented with yet another and even younger Angry Young Man. This was Michael Hastings, an eighteen-year-old tailor's apprentice who lived in 'a four-room flat in Brixton with his widowed mother', and whose first play, *Don't Destroy Me*, was produced at the New Lindsay Theatre in Notting Hill in July.[20] 'The ultimate in James Deanery', the play dealt with a sixteen-year-old who spoke 'entirely in groans and moans', whose father drank and whose mother carried on an affair with a neighbour.[21]

The ranks of Angry Young Men were filling out rapidly. Alongside Wain's class warrior, Amis's reluctant historian and Osborne's ragingly articulate graduate, Wilson offered the pensive philosopher and Hastings the wounded adolescent. Wain and Amis and Osborne set him in lodging houses in the provinces; Wilson set him anywhere in bed-sitterland and Hastings in a Brixton boarding house. It was all very new and all very different. 'A bright, brash, and astonishingly bitter new crop of Angry Young Men has pushed up into the London scene this year,' noted the *Daily Express*, 'writing plays and books bristling with fresh if feverish opinions.'[22] In the *Daily Mail*, the relentless Daniel Farson confirmed that 'the post-war generation' had arrived and were here to stay. 'A number of remarkable young men have appeared on the scene', he announced, adding portentously that 'I have met them.'[23]

Yet quite what Osborne, or Jimmy Porter, or the Angry Young Men stood for remained infuriatingly difficult to define. Were they rebels without a cause as Robert Muller suggested, or merely rebels without a reason? In the *Daily Express*, John Barber used the centenary of Bernard Shaw's birth to announce that Osborne, Hastings, Amis and Wain, 'four laughing, urgent, angry young men', had 'a dab' of Shaw's 'genius'. 'He was a rebel. And before he was done his blazing anger had woken up Britain . . . The new young men are also rebels', and John Osborne, he declared, 'stands for a thing that meant much to Shaw – getting a crowd to share your anger about the way life hits and hurts.'[24]

That the subjects of all this agitated commentary neither knew each other nor were particularly sympathetic to each other's work, did not seem to matter to the likes of Daniel Farson. Although Wain and Amis had been acquainted since university and each had read the other's novels, neither knew the non-university graduates, Osborne, Wilson or Hastings. They in their turn did not know the other members of what was rapidly becoming a journalistically-created group. By 1957, Osborne had met Amis only once, and briefly, and had encountered Wilson and Hastings only at a disastrous party organised by the inevitable Daniel Farson. Amis pointed out to enquiring journalists that he was not at all angry, did not like the theatre and did not want to see *Look Back in Anger*. Colin Wilson, whom Farson had cajoled into seeing the play, declared that he 'hated' it and dismissed Osborne as a writer of mere political and social realism.[25]

*   *   *

However, like the authors themselves, cultural historians have traditionally dis-missed the Angry Young Men as merely the creation of a press with little else to do during the summer months, when parliament is in recess and news usually at low ebb. But many people – including some of the seven million people between the ages of twenty and thirty identified by Kenneth Tynan as *Look Back in Anger's* natural audience – *were* exasperated with the social, political and cultural climate of the mid-fifties. There *was* a conviction that after the war things should have changed for the better but had not, and it was this that Wain, Amis, Osborne and their protagonists articulated in their different ways, and to which their readers and audiences responded. There was no Angry 'movement' as such, but so-called Angry works, and especially *Look Back in Anger*, were different from what went before in that their lower-middle-class sensibility and their intense suspicion of the current social order identified them as those of a new, post-war generation. His play was a success, Osborne told the *Daily Mail*, precisely because 'it is about real people'.[26]

In 1984, and looking back from a distance of almost thirty years, the stage and film director Lindsay Anderson agreed that the Angry Young Man was 'a most extraordinary journalistic invention', but sagely added that: 'I don't mean there was no basis in reality.'[27] By the autumn of 1956, he was already explaining what that reality was, writing in the film magazine, *Sight and Sound*, that 'the young people who respond so unmistakably to *Look Back in Anger* are responding to its outspoken attacks on certain venerable sacred cows, and also to its bitter impatience with the moral vacuum in which they feel public life, and cultural life, is today being conducted. Class resentment', he added, 'is only part of it.'[28]

According to Anderson, Anger was a symptom not only of the resentment of one social class of another, but also of a widespread disappointment among the Left that the bravely egalitarian ideals of 1945 had been largely abandoned, and a demoralised Labour Party, now led by Hugh Gaitskell, seemed both bereft of ideals or hope. 'If there "aren't any good, brave causes left" (or if that is the feeling in the air),' noted Anderson, 'the fault is not so much that of the Right, the Tory element in politics and art, as of the Left, the progressives, the Liberals in the best sense of that long-suffering word.'[29]

One of the generation that celebrated the 1945 Labour Party victory as the beginning of the building of a new Jerusalem, Anderson gazed mordantly about him and saw dreariness everywhere. 'It isn't just the food, the sauce bottles on the café tables, the chips with everything', he wrote sadly. The immediate impression upon returning to Britain from visiting the far more cosmopolitan continent was 'like going back to the Nursery . . . Nanny lights the fire, and sits herself down with a nice cup of tea and yesterday's *Daily Express* but she keeps half an eye on us too.'[30]

Being looked after by a nanny in a nursery would not have been the experience of many of his readers, but they would have known what he meant. Too much of Britain seemed a monotonous, gloomy kind of place, still dominated by pre-war ways of doing things. This was the age of the rise and sprawl of the middle classes, natural Conservative voters who deferred to the old Tory ways of doing things, which, despite the Welfare State, were still firmly in place. Like almost everything else, parliamentary politics, despite the party divide, was still very much the preserve of public school and Oxbridge men. Attlee retained the ethics he had learned at Haileybury and Oxford, and Churchill held similar principles instilled by Harrow and Sandhurst, while Hugh Gaitskell and Sir Anthony Eden, their successors as Party leaders, were both public school and Oxford men with backgrounds in colonial administration and the landed gentry. The BBC, the law, medicine, the Church and journalism were also largely the provinces of the more privileged social strata and the old universities, and by failing to change this after the war, according to the historian Anthony Howard, the Attlee governments oversaw 'the greatest restoration of traditional values since 1660.'[31]

But at the same time, the will for change was in the air and England was slowly becoming a more transitional place. It was this that Colonel Redfern and many like him found increasingly difficult to fathom. Many of the old social structures were still in place, but they were weakening. The shell remained but much of the substance was rotting away. The annual tradition of young debutantes, for instance, being escorted to Buckingham Palace by their rich and titled aristocratic parents and being presented to the monarch, still continued. 'If in possession, swords should be worn', was the dress advice to gentlemen.[32] This archaic ritual marked the beginning of the 'Season', an enormously expensive six-month summer jamboree of glamorous dances, upper crust match-making, getting your name in the Jennifer's Diary column in *Tatler* and generally trying to keep up with the aristocratic Joneses. Not Jimmy Porter's world at all.

But in 1958, the ritual of being presented at the Palace would end, officially rendered obsolete by changing times. Many of the increasingly cash-strapped aristocracy, burdened by the mounting costs of maintaining a large house and grounds, simply could not afford it any more. At the same time, more of those who had no claim to social pedigree but had a lot of money to pay for social pretensions could afford it, with the result that of those gaining access to the Queen 'the wheat was no longer distinguished from the chaff.'[33] This is incidental in itself, perhaps, but it was emblematic of a much wider social transformation. Much of what Colonel Redfern had once recognised now seemed to be in danger of being contemptuously brushed aside. Fiona MacCarthy, the future cultural historian and herself born into an atmosphere of wealth and privilege, was sixteen when she saw *Look Back in Anger*, two years before she became one of the last debutantes to curtsey before the Queen. '. . . my heart bled for Colonel Redfern,' she wrote later. 'In the course of the Season I met many Colonel Redferns, bemused and vaguely disappointed, looking for a role again . . . These were the lost heroes . . .'[34]

There was some reassurance to be had, however. In 1953, the country had celebrated a Coronation, the conquest of Everest, and England regained the Ashes from Australia after twenty years of defeat. The following year, wartime food rationing was declared officially over. There was even an element of old-fashioned comfort to be extracted from the long-running saga, eagerly exploited by the popular press, of the affair between Princess Margaret, the Queen's sister, and Group Captain Peter Townsend, a divorced war hero sixteen years her elder. It was widely assumed that the couple wanted to marry; but could the Princess marry a divorced man? What was the official position of the Church of England? When the romance was called off in 1955, with the Princess announcing her renewed commitment to the Commonwealth, and Townsend murmuring about duty, his reticence and discretion earned him considerable public sympathy and were seen as evidence that these honourable qualities of Britishness still remained. Surely, this was a nation that had a right to be proud of itself.

Yet young people like Jimmy Porter appeared bewilderingly dissatisfied. Many of Colonel Redfern's contemporaries were nonplussed by the music they liked: the skiffle and pop and most alarmingly, the rock and roll that began blaring from the new record shops by day and dance halls by night. In 1956, Elvis Presley recorded 'Heartbreak Hotel' and suddenly became the most popular singer in the world. Bill Haley and the Comets sang 'Rock Around the Clock', and Colonel Redfern would have been appalled to read newspaper stories over breakfast testifying to young people not merely dancing wildly in the aisles of cinemas showing the film in which the song featured, but vandalizing seats, and afterwards engaging in pitched battles against police in the streets. This was not how their elders had behaved. According to the *Daily Mail* the trouble with rock and roll was symptomatic of something far more insidious: 'It's deplorable. It's tribal. And it's from America.'[35]

The political power and cultural influence of the United States was a crucial part of a general mid-twentieth-century English crisis of identity. Socially and culturally, there was an assumption that whatever happened in America today would recur in Britain tomorrow, that most of it was for the worse, and that in the process the somehow indefinable Britishness of Britain would be eradicated. 'I must say it's pretty dreary living in the American Age – unless you're an American of course,' muses Jimmy Porter. 'Perhaps all our children will be Americans. That's a thought, isn't it?'[36] Concern about the Americanization of English culture, especially through movies, musicals and music, was something on which Jimmy Porter could have called upon influential academic support. Richard Hoggart's *The Uses of Literacy*, one of the most significant – and widely read – books of the time, was published in 1957, and echoed Jimmy Porter's suspicions of American cultural imperialism. An English lecturer at the adult education department of Hull University, Hoggart evoked an elegiac vision of traditional northern working-class life, full of hardships, but one in which families were bound together by a shared decency, honesty and faith. This was something authentically English, but it was quickly being eroded by a mass consumer culture emanating from the United States, 'full of corrupt brightness, of improper appeals and moral evasions' and promising 'the cheap glitter of affluence.'[37]

Hoggart warned that the more mass the market, the cheaper would be the goods on offer, and that this trend would seep into every aspect of life. Staple working-class pastimes, including reading and the communal life of the family, the pub and the variety theatre, would be swept aside by cheap, garish entertainment and anemic popular music. Already, in the American influenced coffee bars, with their jukeboxes and tubular plastic furniture, he observed northern working-class youth 'living to a large extent in a myth-world compounded of a few simple elements which they take to be the American dream . . . they have no aim, no ambition, no protection, no belief.'[38]

Although Osborne had no desire whatever to live a northern working-class life, and arguably neither did many who did, Hoggart's apocalyptic vision was one that he recognised. Shortly after *The Uses of Literacy* was published, he nominated it as 'the book that had recently most appealed' to him.[39] An idealised past, and the dramatically contrasting contemporary erosion of culture, values, manners and language become principal themes of Osborne's writing from *Look Back in Anger* onwards: they are there in *The Entertainer*, recur in different forms in *Luther*, *Inadmissible Evidence* and *A Patriot for Me*, and are central to two of his plays of the early 1970s: *West of Suez* and *Watch It Come Down*, by which time his vision had become very bleak indeed.

At its core, then, the Britain of the late 1950s was still a deeply conservative nation, but change was beginning to be felt, whether it was the Angry Young Man, the youth market, the tower blocks arising in city landscapes, the hydrogen bomb, rock and roll, the juvenile delinquent, the influence of the United States or talk of the 'Establishment'. Change was in the air, but whether or not it had the clear breath of new life depended upon your age and point of view. Anger, that essentially post-war, irreverent, mocking, youthful phenomenon that so caught the unease of its time, did not, therefore, emerge out of the blue but was symptomatic of the disquiet of a generation coming of age in an era in which they might have expected to contribute and receive much, but discovering instead that the country was still locked in the past. Anger was not so much a new beginning as a new movement in the symphony of political disappointment and social disaffection that had begun several years previously, during those opening months of 1947, when, epitomised by appalling weather, everything seemed to start going wrong.

*   *   *

Disturbing changes at home; disquieting news from abroad. By the end of 1956, it was emphatically clear that the Britain that had led Europe during the war was not only a much diminished power, it was also arguably far less principled. The Suez fiasco in particular would have far-reaching repercussions upon Britain's sense of itself. Relations between Britain and Egypt had been deteriorating for some time, fuelled by British concern over Colonel Gamal Nasser, the Egyptian President, encouraging a resurgence of Arab nationalism after the creation by allied authorities in 1947 of Israel as a homeland for the Jewish people. Britain regarded the Middle East as being of tremendous strate-

gic importance to its interests and saw the Suez Canal, the majority shares in
which were owned by the British and French governments, as a vital international waterway. But as Nasser's continued overtures to the Soviet Union and
the Communist bloc alerted Britain to the possibility of losing its influence, the
already fraying relationship between Britain and Egypt snapped like old shoe-
laces. When Britain and the USA attempted to check Nasser's pro-Soviet drift
by cancelling the promised financial assistance for the building of the Aswan
High Dam on the River Nile, Nasser retaliated by nationalising the Suez Canal
Company, thereby imperilling the flow of Middle Eastern oil, which was crucial
to the petrol-swilling British economy.

The Prime Minister, Sir Anthony Eden, convinced that what he perceived as
Egyptian expansionism must be stopped and that Nasser, to whom he had developed a considerable personal antipathy, must be toppled, desperately began
casting about for a knock-out response. The security service, MI6, suggested
assassinating the Egyptian President by the use of nerve gas, but Eden preferred
a military option and, although the legality was questionable, instructed that
armed intervention be prepared, in secret, in league with French and Israeli
government officials. For Eden and the British government, the defeat of Nasser
was the ultimate objective. 'If Nasser wins or even appears to win,' the British
Colonial Secretary informed Eden, 'we might as well as a government (and
indeed as a country) go out of business.'[40]

On 5 November, British and French troops landed in Port Said, an operation denounced as foolhardy by a formidable diplomatic alliance led by the
United Nations and the USA. Denied essential political and military support,
and divided between its public interest, that of retaking the Canal and establishing it once more as an open and secure waterway, and its covert mission
of replacing Nasser with a president more amenable to London, Britain found
itself wrong-footed and isolated, and in the unfamiliar position of having its
moral intentions called into question. International pressure resulted in the
Anglo-French strategy being halted two days later on 7 November, and troops
being replaced by a United Nations peace-keeping force. It was a political, a
military, and for Eden, a personal humiliation.

Almost simultaneously, Soviet tanks rolled into Hungary. Since 1949, the
country had been a 'people's republic' under an imposed Soviet-style constitu-
tion. But a poor harvest and increasing fuel shortages resulted in students and
workers uniting in widespread demonstrations against Soviet domination, and
on 4 November, the day before the invasion of Egypt, Soviet infantry entered
Budapest and quashed the insurrection. Failure to adequately support Hungary,
or even exert any influence upon events, represented a further diplomatic
embarrassment for Britain, now exposed as being as powerless as a shrimp
before a shark. Suez and Hungary became emblems of ignominy and defeat,
evidence that the British way of doing things nowadays either ended in chaos
or, worse still, had no tangible effect at all.

*   *   *

At the same time, the Royal Court Theatre had been quietly, almost furtively, getting on with its repertoire of new productions. Ronald Duncan's *Don Juan* and *The Death of Satan*, 'the pound of flesh that had to be paid for putting on the season', had opened on 15 May.[41] Duncan, who had watched *Look Back in Anger* 'with a malevolent eye', was now obliged to watch his own plays, which Devine had savagely condensed, feeling 'like a holed barge being towed out to be torpedoed.'[42] Probably equally irritating for Duncan was the sight of one of the torpedoes, John Osborne, appearing on the Royal Court stage for the first time as an actor, playing Antonio in the first play and Lionel in the second. Coming directly after *Look Back in Anger*, verse plays seemed an astonishing back-track, and neither critics nor audiences could quite decipher the message the English Stage Company was broadcasting. Was the Royal Court intent upon producing a new kind of drama or not? Transmission seemed oddly scrambled.

The productions were disastrous and after four nights swiftly bundled into the wings, never to re-emerge. The snub to verse drama seemed emphatic and the message to audiences clear when *Look Back in Anger* briefly returned before Osborne appeared on stage again on 26 June, this time ludicrously sporting a bald wig and protruding teeth in his role as Dr Scavenger in Nigel Dennis's *Cards of Identity*. A novelist in his forties, Dennis was 'not in any sense "angry", either in temperament . . . or his work' noted the journalist Kenneth Allsop, although his writing was 'intensely involved in the cultural revolt'.[43] Dennis's novel and the play he adapted from it, is set in a country house taken over by the Identity Club, whose members adopt new names and backgrounds, and act out their new roles. But although 'the basic joke never got properly under way,' recalled Irving Wardle, Richardson's staging was successful enough to paper over the play's weaknesses and allow 'a win on points' on the critical scoring card.[44]

With Fearon's press campaign and newspaper attention frenetically fanning interest in John Osborne, *Look Back in Anger* returned for a longer, eleven-week run, but even then did not sell out. It was not until BBC television screened an eighteen-minute extract on 16 October, something normally done only when a play was doing so well that nothing could harm it or so badly that any publicity might do it good, that the telephone and cash tills at the Royal Court suddenly started to ring and weekly takings rose from £950 to £1,700. 'A completely new audience arrived,' recalled Michael Halifax, the theatre manager. 'Just what we were trying to find.'[45] But within days, the production closed to make way for the opening of *The Good Woman of Setzuan* on 31 October, in which Osborne played Lin To, a Chinese peasant. A jauntily Marxist play by an author who had gratefully made his home behind the Iron Curtain but kept most of his money in the West, its timing, as the Soviet Union invaded Hungary to suppress a democratic uprising, was catastrophic. It proved an honourable failure.

Yet *Look Back in Anger* had taken flight. A live performance of the entire play was broadcast by Granada Television, one of the new independent television companies, a few weeks later on 28 November, and seen by an estimated 4,387,400 viewers. The *Manchester Guardian* estimated this to be 'equivalent to a run of 25 years if six performances a week plus a matinee were given in a theatre holding 500.'[46] It was a startling indication of the power of television. By this time, a stage revival of the play had opened, at the Lyric, Hammersmith, and sold out for its three-week run, transforming the financial fortunes of the English Stage Company. The first year's accounts reveal that the season's productions had cost £75,747, while box office income and grants had totalled £74,185, leaving a modest deficit of £1,562. The 151 performances of Look Back in Anger had taken £23,089, far more than any other production.

But more importantly, the English Stage Company and the Royal Court now had a clear identity and in John Osborne a mast on which other new playwrights might hoist their colours. At last, Look Back in Anger had become a play that everyone who aspired to be anyone had to see. Philip French, later to become an eminent film critic of the Observer, saw Osborne, whom he did not know, during the interval of a performance at the Royal Court, grasped his hand and told him that he had become the spokesman for their generation.[47] Michael Billington, then a schoolboy of fifteen and later to become a highly respected and long-standing theatre critic for the Guardian, made 'a pilgrimage' from his home in Leamington Spa to see the play. 'The excitement of Look Back in Anger was that it was about real people and real issues,' he remembered. 'It did indeed become a declaration for a generation.'[48] Fiona MacCarthy had felt much the same: '. . . the play seemed alarming and amazingly exciting in its fierce iconoclasm,' she later wrote, 'its hints of sadomasochistic sexual relationships, its glorification of real life and raw emotion in contrast to pernicious conventionality . . . It was one of those works of art that shaped a generation.'[49]

*   *   *

So the Angry Young Man became the man of the moment. He was here, there and everywhere. The Observer canvassed his views on a newly published collection of plays by Tennessee Williams. 'To ignore these plays', he wrote, 'is to ignore the world we live in. Every serious British dramatist is indebted to them . . .'[50] Williams's 'sheer professional skill staggers me sometimes.'[51] The Daily Express, on the other hand, asked 'the Theatre's Bright Boy' to list 'the things I wish I could do.' 'Every winter,' he twittered, 'I am appalled by the number of things I need to do to make my life fuller, more interesting, more accomplished, more gracious. These are things like reading Proust and Tristram Shandy, which I have started three times in the last ten years.' Opera was something else he wanted to catch up on, and ballet needed his perseverance, but it was art, and especially painting, that provided the Angry Young Man with his most pressing problem. 'If only I could learn how to respond to it.'[52]

This was a candid admission, as Osborne, almost entirely self-educated in cultural matters, now found himself among people at the Royal Court and elsewhere accustomed to different art forms and entirely at ease in discussing them. Osborne knew about the theatre and the music hall, was confident in literature and had a limited knowledge of classical music in that he knew what he liked, but he remained largely unacquainted with opera, dance and art and felt the gaps in his knowledge and understanding deeply. Anxious lest an unwitting chance remark betray his ignorance, he worked hard to rectify his lack of acquaintance with art forms with which he was not familiar. Very much wanting to appear assured and sophisticated, he also took great care over his clothes and manners so as to blend in with the Oxford-educated group at the Royal Court and the culturally aware people he met. Consequently, features journalists enquired as to his fashion choices, and views on blazers and Norfolk jackets. Meticulously, he set aside time for reading and contemplation. His 'morning bath', he revealed, was reserved for his 'morning think'; perhaps about art.[53]

Meanwhile, gossip columnists sniffed and photographers watched and soon Osborne was being snapped out on the town with Mary Ure, the actress playing Alison in Look Back in Anger and who was then living in a basement flat in Southwell Gardens in Kensington. She found him immensely attractive, was convinced that he was a great writer and loved the embrace of success that was enfolding them both. Osborne found her intriguing and her effervescence refreshing, and after the theatre or a late supper they were sometimes tracked by shadowy press observers as far as the door of Southwell Gardens or the deck of the Egret.

Within weeks, the Angry playwright and the bewitching blonde actress were acknowledged by the popular press as London's fashionably Golden Couple, celebrities in the modern sense. The pleasure of their company was requested at parties and dinners where they met the influential, the established and the up-and-coming. Here they were at dinner with Peter Hall, the Cambridge-educated young director of Waiting for Godot, and his wife, Leslie Caron, the French actress and star of the film An American in Paris. There they were, dining with Richard and Sybil Burton at Emlyn Williams's house in Pelham Crescent, where they were admitted by an intimidating butler into the presence of the man in whose plays Osborne had appeared with The Saga Repertory Group. Here they were again, eating interesting meals at fashionable Chelsea restaurants. 'I care enormously about food,' he informed a hovering reporter. 'This seems odd to many people as I am a vegetarian . . . I find', he added mysteriously, 'people are far more intolerant about food than they are about sex and plays.'[54] He had come a very long way in the short time since he had admitted to Creighton that he stole bread to eat in Derby. Daringly, for unmarried couples did not usually do such things, he and Mary took a holiday in Spain, the first time he had ventured beyond British shores. This was a highly newsworthy event in those days before package holidays and budget flights, when international travel remained well beyond the reach of most. Yet he remained, he claimed, firmly patriotic with no wish, after his first excursion overseas, to leave the country permanently. By the end of the year, he and Mary had moved into a small, nineteenth-century mews house at 15 Woodfall Street, a cul-de-sac off the King's Road in Chelsea, within walking distance of the Royal Court and which Mary had bought with a loan from her father.

From his cabin on board the *Egret*, Anthony Creighton watched Osborne's sudden glittering success and his developing relationship with Mary with mixed feelings. Admiring his friend intensely, Creighton was thrilled by his achievement and 'never begrudged him anything.' [55] But at the same time he recognised that Osborne no longer had any need of a collaborator and that, unless he were able to strike out on his own, he, Creighton, would fade into the perimeter shadows as the glow of Osborne's newfound radiance increased. There was not much likelihood of his emergence as a dramatist in his own right, as he was the kind of writer who wrote best in partnership with someone else. He continued to search for acting work, would occasionally play small roles at the Royal Court and on television, but more frequently he was obliged to resort to part-time jobs to make ends meet. He did another stint as a night operator in a telephone exchange; he worked in a café, and returned to the Oxford Street debt collectors. From Woodfall Street, Osborne continued to reassure him, as he had in the past, that neither his success nor his relationships would alter the fact that they were old friends and allies.

Amid all the hullaballoo of the Osborne phenomenon, only Harold Hobson, the Francophile theatre critic of the *Sunday Times*, had taken the time during recent months for a little more serious reflection. Osborne, he asserted, was a very promising writer and one to watch, but surely he was not yet half as rebellious as Hobson's critical colleagues were suggesting. Jean Anouilh, the French dramatist twenty years Osborne's elder, he declared, was 'France's angry middle-aged man.' His version of *Antigone*, widely seen as an allegory of wartime Nazi occupiers and French collaborationists, had provoked genuine controversy, while *Pauvre Bitos*, which had opened in Paris in 1956, in which a group of aristocrats dress as leading figures of the Revolution in order to humiliate one of their number, succeeded yet again in incensing both the political Left and Right. Hobson identified parallels with more recent times and contended that the play 'kicks in the stomach . . . the Liberation and more particularly the men of the left wing Resistance.' Anouilh was daring and thought-provoking: a genuine maverick. Conceding that 'the rasp and ache and torture of [Osborne's] dialogue cannot be matched in England', Hobson contended that otherwise the Angry Young Man was playing it very safe indeed. That Osborne was 'angry with snobbery, with the relics of Anglo-Indian supremacy, with the churches' and much else besides, was clear enough, but the point was this: 'Mr Osborne attacks only what it is permitted to attack. M. Anouilh assaults the best established idols . . . Mr Osborne has not got to this brand of nonconformity yet. He is content to say with incomparable pungency what everyone else is thinking . . . one wonders whether in twenty years' time, Mr Osborne will have retained Anouilh's fire, or indeed his courage.'[56]

But elsewhere, there were no such scruples. Osborne was awarded the *Evening Standard* Most Promising Playwright of the Year Award for *Look Back in Anger*, and in December the paper elected him as one of 'the top ten of 1956', a distinction he shared with Diana Dors, the film star and 'eye-filling, gasp-provoking blonde bombshell.'[57] Writing in the *London Magazine*, and deploying an infuriating, confusing but fashionable scattering of the French idiom that Jimmy Porter abhors, Derek Granger observed that 'Osborne alone' had 'captured the young imagination and with it the fisher-sweatered noctambules from Espresso-land, the *jeunes-mariés* from Knightsbridge, the bed-sitter *avant-garde* from Bayswater and Notting Hill.'[58] The more plain-speaking *Daily Mail* agreed, proclaiming on 13 December that 1956 was, without doubt, 'The Year of The Angry Young Men.'[59]

PART 2

Extravagance

CHAPTER 12

The King at the Court

VICTOR SEAFORTH SPECIALISED in impersonations. A one-man hall of fame, he recreated comedians, singers and especially film actors playing their best-known roles, all in their moments of glory. His stage was the music hall, beloved of John Osborne, his father, Tom Godfrey and his maternal grandfather, William Crawford Grove and millions like them entranced by the dust swirling beneath the stage lights and the banter between performer and audience. Billed as 'The Man of a Hundred Voices', Seaforth had perfected his twelve-minute turn of 'song, comedy and pathos' for over twenty-six years, clawing his way up from the wilderness of far-flung provincial halls to the number one circuit and appearances with the post-war star entertainers, Max Miller, Vic Oliver and Jack Radcliffe among them.[1]

A perfectionist, Seaforth prided himself on the meticulous accuracy of his impersonations and the near-instant changes from one to another with the aid of only a few props and dramatic switches of carefully arranged lighting. Quickly waxing his moustache, he raised an eyebrow, clapped a boater on his head and twirled around as Maurice Chevalier. Popping on a false nose, pince-nez, top hat and cape, he fell to his knees and shuffled forward as Toulouse-Lautrec. But the impression he cherished as his most authentic was that of Charles Laughton playing Quasimodo in the film, *The Hunchback of Notre Dame*. Standing beneath a white spotlight and with his back to the audience, he flung over his shoulders a cape with a hump concealed in the lining, shoved bicycle clips around his trouser turn-ups, tousled his hair and contorted his face into an approximation of Quasimodo's contorted features. As he swung around, spluttering and croaking, the stage lights flicked from white to a dim, Gothic green, and there he was: Quasimodo, crying 'Sanctuary! Sanctuary!'

In the summer of 1956, when Seaforth was on the bill at the Chelsea Palace, a variety theatre in the King's Road, a few minutes' walk from the Royal Court Theatre, Osborne wandered along to see the show. He seldom missed a chance to visit a music hall or a variety theatre and since boyhood had watched a

legion of comics, singers and acrobats, dancers, animal acts and impression-
ists, sitting attentively through the great and the dreadful, noting their sense
of timing, how they played their audiences and how they overcame – or not –
the indifferent, the restive and the rebellious. Over the years he acquired
an encyclopaedic knowledge of music-hall history that would surprise and
impress his friends, and already he could reel off a comprehensive list of the
stars he had seen. There was Max Miller, of course, the Cheeky Chappie in his
outrageous suits, especially the baggy blue one with daisies splashed across it,
coming on stage as the band played 'Mary from the Dairy', and bringing with
him the briny air of Brighton, the seafront and the racecourse, celebrating an
extravagance and a raffishness that Osborne adored. There was the 'incomparable' Sid Field, 'Monsewer' Eddie Gray, Flanagan and Allen, Old Mother
Riley and her Daughter Kitty, Vesta Tilley . . . and so it went on. Most of their
songs he knew by heart.

The music hall was unique, essentially a theatre for the working class, local
and intimate, combative on behalf of its audiences, chiding them sometimes
but never patronising them. For Osborne it both transported him back to his
childhood and represented the epitome of something essentially English: a
harsh, sometimes cruel yet essentially compassionate communal spirit. Yet by
the mid-1950s, only a few music halls remained, the war years having consigned them to the past, and the cinema and television depriving them of their
audiences. Within months of Osborne's being there that night in the summer of
1956, the Chelsea Palace itself would be turned into a television studio before
being demolished to make way for a department store. But as he watched Victor
Seaforth's preparation for Quasimodo, as 'a smoky green light swirled over the
stage and an awesome banality prevailed for some theatrical seconds', Osborne
saw something unique: 'the drama and poetry, the belt and braces of music-hall
holding up epic.'[2] '. . . I knew then that I had to write a play.'[3]

He began writing in the autumn of 1956 and continued over the winter.
Written in thirteen 'numbers' in the form of a music-hall programme, The Entertainer is set partly on the stage of the variety theatre in which the embittered,
down-at-heel comedian Archie Rice glumly wades through his act, and partly
in the sitting-room of the Rice family's digs, the former scenes being interspersed between the latter. Osborne contrasted Archie's world of contemporary
decay with Billy Rice, Archie's retired show business father, whose fastidious-
ness, prejudices and memories of Edwardian finesse Osborne imagined evoked
the England of former years. Aged 'about fifty', Archie has fallen from music-
hall grace, reduced to appearing in Rock'n'Roll New'd Look, a tawdry, twice-nightly
revue in which he has invested borrowed money, recycling worn-out jokes
and singing cynical songs before a bored nude girl posing indifferently as
Britannia.[4] Etched with the fissures of professional and moral failure, Archie's
contempt both for himself and the show is projected into his resentment of
Billy, his scorn for Phoebe, his wife, and deep unease with Jean, his twenty-
two-year-old daughter, and Frank, the son who remains at home while Mick,

his brother, serves with the forces in Suez. In choosing the last days of the music hall as the subject for his new play, Osborne created a vividly poignant metaphor for England, a nation once grand but now inexorably disintegrating. Suez gave it a bitingly contemporary topicality, for 'the effect of Suez on the national psyche was profound', the historian Peter Hennessey has written. 'The realisation of lost power was brutal and lasting . . . we never saw ourselves, or the world, in the same light again . . .'[5]

While Look Back in Anger had been written instinctively and the characters more or less transferred from life to the stage, The Entertainer, its title taken from a ragtime tune made famous by the trumpeter Bunk Johnson, was much more considered in its planning. From the image of the defeated and failing performer, Osborne developed a broad theme of the dereliction of England. As a result, the characters are more fully imagined and realised than those of Look Back in Anger. There are still autobiographical echoes: the family bickering at the Rice digs is reminiscent of life at the Groves' in Harbord Street; there is more than a hint of William Crawford Grove, Nellie Beatrice's celebrated publican father, in Billy Rice, another version of Colonel Redfern, and a suggestion of Nellie Beatrice herself in the gin-loving Phoebe. And Archie's daughter, Jean, an art teacher and advocate of the peace movement, has clear affinities to Ruth in Epitaph for George Dillon. But although Victor Seaforth provided the vital nudge towards the creation of Archie Rice, he is not at all like him. Seaforth was a hard-working, reliable and popular entertainer, while Archie Rice, disillusioned and side-lined to the ramshackle world of touring revues and provincial digs, lacks even the dignity of self-respect. No audience applauds his entrance on stage; nobody sings along with him or laughs at his jokes. Instead, Archie Rice stands alone, staring into half-empty theatres and facing audience apathy at best, hostility at worst. 'Don't clap too hard,' he sighs, 'it's a very old building. Well, I have a go, don't I? I do. I 'ave a go.'[6]

While Jimmy Porter is not yet ready to submit to disillusion and his emotions remain electrically alive, Archie's tragedy is that he is aware that he has failed as a husband, a father and a performer and that he has few real feelings left: 'I'm dead behind these eyes.'[7] Only the report of Mick's death in Egypt, one of the very few Suez deaths, pierces his self-obsession to provoke the bile of real feeling. A substantial development from Jimmy Porter, Archie is the first version of what would become a dominating Osborne character, that of a man confronting the terrible realisation of his own flaws and failure. He would return most notably as Bill Maitland, the self-loathing lawyer in Inadmissible Evidence, as Alfred Redl in A Patriot for Me and as Wyatt Gillman in West of Suez. The anatomy of human failure – and particularly male failure – would from now on become one of Osborne's great dramatic themes. Matched with an almost Jacobean facility with language, it could have a tremendous theatrical effect.

*   *   *

Osborne's absorption into the English Stage Company had conferred upon him something he had never experienced before: the feeling of security within a 'family' where he was not only taken very seriously but seen as its prize asset. 'It's difficult to believe,' he told Richard Findlater, '[but] for the first time in my life I have a "home" in the theatre, and it's wonderful.'[8] He still retained many of his repertory theatre and houseboat habits, including carefully entering his income and expenses in his Post Office Savings Book, but now he was staring in wonderment as the balance increased instead of decreased. The German language rights alone of Look Back in Anger had earned him £300, an enormous amount of money at the time, enough to buy a complete set of the Encyclopædia Britannica with plenty left over. As a result of living for so long in cramped and temporary spaces, he still kept his possessions neatly in order and remained an obsessive list maker: of things he had done and still had to do, of books he had read and intended to read.

But although there were moments of doubt when he was convinced he might never write another word and his achievement so far would be blown away like leaves in the wind, such fears were masked by a growing air of professional and personal confidence. Here he was, only in his late twenties, the much talked-about author of one of the most talked-about plays of recent years and his next much anticipated, living in Chelsea and with money falling into his newly opened bank account. And the new play, he knew, would command attention. 'This one's really going to shake them up,' he told Creighton.[9] His optimism was partly that the play was politically topical, and partly the result of a seemingly astonishing decision by Laurence Olivier to play the leading role of Archie Rice.

One of Britain's most lauded Shakespearean actors, Olivier was recognised as 'the undisputed king of British theatre', and as Tony Richardson, who would once again be directing, admitted, for 'the Court to have the king join us on our own terms was a great triumph.'[10] Yet Olivier arguably needed the Royal Court Theatre more than the Royal Court needed him. At forty-nine, admired equally in London and New York and exalted by Kenneth Tynan for his portrayal of a succession of Shakespearian martial heroes, Olivier had led both the Stratford and Old Vic companies, and was a veteran of tours to Europe, Australia and New Zealand. He was an established Hollywood film star, having played Heathcliff in Wuthering Heights and Maxim de Winter in Rebecca, and when he was not in front of the camera he was often behind it, directing himself in a hugely patriotic wartime Henry V, as a deeply brooding Hamlet and a limping, sneeringly malevolent Richard III. The previous year, he had also appeared as Malvolio, Macbeth and Titus Andronicus at Stratford, playing opposite his wife, Vivien Leigh.

Glamorous and admired, the Oliviers were established theatrical royalty. In Notley Abbey, their twelfth-century manor house in Buckinghamshire, they had acquired a slice of appropriately regal history, the house in its time having been frequented both by Henry VIII and Cardinal Wolsey. Having meticulously restored it, and furnished it in a suffocating splendour of antiques and country-house paintings, the Oliviers received their friends, the aristocracy of acting, the Redgraves, the Millses, the Nivens and the Fairbankses at bounteous summer weekend parties. There were picnics and games of croquet on the magnificently spreading lawns. Guests arriving in the evening would see the lights of Notley, 'like those of Manderley' beckoning them onward, and be greeted in the music room by Noël Coward or Danny Kaye playing the piano.[11] Yet although they were extravagant hosts, Olivier and Vivien were dismally unhappy. A woman of entrancing beauty who had become an international film star by playing Scarlett O'Hara in Gone with the Wind but knew that she could never be her husband's equal on stage, Vivien had become the victim of debilitating manic depression, suffering spells of hysteria, tantrums and moodiness only barely contained by the electro-convulsive therapy she endured. Her husband, meanwhile, had spent the summer of 1956 in London, filming Rattigan's The Prince and the Showgirl with the notoriously unpunctual and emotionally semi-stable Marilyn Monroe, and meditating, while waiting for Monroe to appear on set, on the chasm between his public image and private dejection. Knighted and feted, acclaimed as an ambassador both for his profession and his country, Olivier had become something of a national monument while at the same time confronting stupendous personal and professional doubts. 'My career', he reflected, 'was becoming predictable, solid and rather dull.'[12]

He remained, however, fiercely competitive, and the controversy over Look Back in Anger had him sitting up like a squirrel, his professional whiskers quivering in curiosity. Attracted by the title, Monroe had suggested that she and her then husband, Arthur Miller, who was visiting London, see the play and that Olivier accompany them. After the performance, and despite being in the pit of a marital crisis himself, Olivier tersely announced that the play was nothing but 'a lot of bitter rattling on' about nothing very much.[13] But when Miller protested that in the context of a British theatre 'hermetically sealed from reality', it represented something vigorous and new, Olivier stopped and took note.[14] Insisting that the play was far from the 'travesty on England' that Olivier alleged, Miller enthused over its 'roughness and self-indulgences' and 'its flinging high into the air so many pomposities of Britishism, its unbridled irritation with life, and its verbal energy.'[15] Deciding that if this was the way the wind was blowing, then he would be blown with it, Olivier discreetly contacted George Devine in a bid to read whatever it was that Osborne happened to be writing at the moment. Devine sent him a copy of The Entertainer. Having read it, Olivier concluded that 'John Osborne had put the whole of contemporary England on stage with one amazing sweep of his brush.'[16] And Olivier was intent upon dominating contemporary England. Moreover, he was happy to accept the Royal Court's derisory – for him – weekly wage of £60 in order to do it.

*   *   *

But 'the whole play,' protested St Vincent Troubridge, the Lord Chamberlain's Examiner on to whose desk the typescript of the play landed on 13 March 1957, 'is impregnated with sex, sexy references and half references and general lavatory dirt, which I think must be debited to the bad taste account.' Sixteen instances of 'verbal dirt and Smart Alec lines' must be deleted.[18] So distinguished an actor as Sir Laurence Olivier could not possibly announce a song entitled 'The old church bells won't ring tonight 'cos the vicar's got the clappers', and nor could the play contain such outrageous expressions as 'ass-upwards'. The terrible words 'pouf' (twice), 'rogered' (twice), 'camp' and 'balls' must be instantly removed. He also noted that Archie Rice sang 'Thank God We're Normal', a song mocking the England of Empire before a Britannia who was clearly naked.[17] The Royal Court was primly instructed to provide a series of photographs of the nude in order that the Examiners might deliberate upon a permissible pose.

Letters shuttled back and forth between Tony Richardson and Troubridge, the director appealing and cajoling, the Examiner digging in his heels. Three photographs of the nude Britannia were dispatched to Stable Yard for official scrutiny. The first showed her in profile, wearing nothing but her helmet and a rather miffed expression, gripping her trident and sitting upon a stuffed and aggrieved-looking bulldog. The second, also in profile, showed her standing, one leg raised and a foot resting upon the dog's back, and the third, kneeling, facing the camera, wearing a hat and with her hands demurely folded across her lap and the dog nowhere to be seen. 'The positions will be taken behind a gauze,' soothed Richardson.[18] This assurance and perhaps the seaside postcard insolence of the model seemed to pacify the censors, who ball-penned 'Yes' upon her thigh on the first two pictures, but 'No' on the third. As her breasts were partially exposed, the Examiners instructed that 'she must sit more side-ways or something.'[19]

The prospect of The Entertainer also prompted a similar fluttering in the dove-cote of the English Stage Company Council, the company's governing body, who protested the Royal Court could not produce a play in which Olivier, so long the embodiment of the nation's values, so openly disparaged them. As Richardson negotiated compromises with Troubridge, who reluctantly awarded The Entertainer a public performance licence while still maintaining the 'aver-sion and disgust' of 'an angry middle-aged man', Neville Blond, again using the tactic of an extravagantly generous lunch, mollified a querulous Council.[20] It was then that Olivier sprang his own surprise, by proposing that Vivien Leigh should play Phoebe, Archie's wife. Although this was a role to which both Osborne and Richardson thought Vivien was 'hopelessly unsuited', they were hesitant to say so outright for fear of jeopardising their relationship with Olivier.[21] Hoping that flattery might succeed where blunt honesty might not, they suggested that surely Vivien was too young and too beautiful. Immediately recognising either the logic or the cunning of this, Olivier agreed, but, sensing an opportunity to deploy his beloved range of stage make-up and disguises, suggested that her youth and undoubted good looks be obscured by a rubber mask, elaborately etched with wrinkles and emblazoned with warts. It 'took several meetings' recalled Richardson, before Olivier agreed this was unfeasible and the part should instead be awarded to the less well-known but far more appropriate Brenda de Banzie.[22]

As rehearsals began, Olivier and Osborne visited several of London's surviving music halls, including the Chelsea Palace, the Metropolitan in the Edgware Road and Collins's in Islington, where Olivier chatted with chorus girls and a plaque was raised to commemorate his visit, only to be lost when the theatre closed the following year. At the same time, he decided upon Archie's costume of check suit with spongebag trousers slightly too short; a bow tie, white socks and grey bowler hat. Then came the clipped, short back-and-sides hair; the heavily pencilled eyebrows; the gap marked between the front teeth; the accent striving for refinement; the leer; the loud, vulgar laugh and the lifeless eyes. 'I see him', recorded Olivier, 'as an intelligent man aware of his failure, pushing it under the carpet under a haze of gin. He knew where he was and what he'd become and the only way to cope with it was to abdicate all responsibility.'[23]

Osborne appeared at rehearsals, 'a charming man who spoke like a sixth-former from Eton,' thought Stanley Meadows, who was cast as Olivier's understudy. 'He was obviously thrilled that Olivier was appearing in his play.' They watched as Olivier learned to sing and – despite intermittent whispers of gout – dance well, in order, as Archie does, to perform badly.[24] 'He was a prima donna, but a genius in his way,' concluded Meadows. 'He had tremendous stamina and magnificent technique. There was probably nothing he couldn't do.'[25] Aware that the cast might find his knighthood and reputation intimidating, Olivier made strenuous efforts to be one of the boys, freely distributing the cigarettes he endorsed in advertisements, inviting the company to drinks at Lowndes Cottage, the house he had rented nearby and instructing them to 'just call me Larry, darling heart.'[26] But despite his meticulous amenability, Richardson still found him daunting. 'How do you interrupt him during a scene? How do you direct him?' he whispered anxiously to Colin Clark, the assistant stage manager.[27] Olivier diplomatically solved this, observed Meadows, by 'more or less directing himself as well as doing some tactful directing of the other actors – "How about trying it like this, dear heart?" – but always so that Tony wouldn't notice.'[28]

Each day, after rehearsals, Osborne walked back to Woodfall Street and Mary. She was still rather an enigma to him, as she was to many of those who encountered her. At the same time, he had begun to mull over his relationship with Pamela, who was still playing in repertory in York. 'I had no idea of what pain I had inflicted on Pamela and reflected on it daily,' he admitted.[29] The only resolution seemed to be divorce, and in such a manner as would cause as little acrimony as possible.

It was while he was turning this over in his mind one afternoon in March 1957, that the journalist Robert Hancock knocked on Osborne's front door. Having arranged to interview the playwright for The Spectator, Hancock, who evidently disapproved of the Angry Young Man, had done a little research into the Chelsea property market. As houses in Woodfall Street, he informed his readers, were fetching a pricey £7,000 these days, Osborne was obviously doing very well for himself. Taking a seat in the living-room, he took in his surroundings. That there was no ironing board or washing in evidence was, noted Hancock, 'unsurprising', but then the 'striped regency wallpaper' and Osborne's 'gaily-coloured' Finnish slippers hardly featured in the *Look Back in Anger* world either. The slippers were 'beautifully warm', explained the creator of Jimmy Porter. 'I really have the most terrible cold feet.' Hancock went on to the playwright's 'Paisley-pattern bow tie' and 'smart single-breasted suit'; these, Osborne explained, were in anticipation of a dinner engagement later that evening. As Hancock noted this riveting snippet of information, another young man appeared, bearing unappetizing 'tea with condensed milk', and promptly disappeared into a back room. This was Anthony Creighton, who Osborne claimed to be a kind of general factotum 'who just comes in to make me a cup of tea.' Looking quizzically about him, Hancock detected other domestic details of interest, which he duly inscribed in his notebook.

A few days later, on 5 April, Hancock's readers learned that while Osborne's marriage to Pamela Lane was now 'in the hands of the lawyers', 'a woman's fur coat' hung conspicuously over the banister at Woodfall Street. Moreover, a 'demand note in red from the Income Tax for Miss Mary Ure' stood propped upon the mantelpiece, her press cuttings were 'scattered about the room' and 'parcels addressed to her [lay] on top of a pile of women's shoes.' Although Mary did not appear to be actually in the house at the time of his interview, wrote Hancock, she 'is seldom out of Mr Osborne's mind.' This was malicious, for although Osborne's forthcoming divorce and his liaison with Mary were well publicized in the press, the implication they were cohabiting while Osborne was still legally married amounted to a calculated reproach to their – and particularly Mary's – public reputation. It prompted a swift retaliatory letter of protest from Osborne, published the following week, followed by a flurry of supportive messages from readers protesting against a 'vicious and vulgar attack on John Osborne.'[30]

Although more young couples were cohabiting before marriage those days, it still remained a defiant social gesture. Hancock's article appeared at a tricky moment for Osborne as it might have influenced his divorce case scheduled for only four days later and which would certainly be covered by reporters closely following the progress of his private life. During the late 1950s, according to surveys, only two out of every thousand married couples sought a divorce, and it was not something that could be accomplished either quietly or easily. Although Osborne and Pamela had lived apart for over two years and had mutually agreed to go their separate ways, this was considered insufficient grounds for divorce until 1973, when the matrimonial laws were adapted to accommodate 'breakdown of marriage'. As the law stood until then, one spouse was required to be found guilty in court either of desertion, adultery or cruelty. Lawyers must be hired, evidence marshalled and presented and the names of co-respondents were required to be provided. If there were none, then couples frequently resorted to hiring a private detective, whose 'evidence', in the form of a photograph of a supposedly compromising scene in a seaside hotel bedroom (Brighton being a favourite venue), would be solemnly presented before the presiding judge. Realising that the press reports of his divorce would alert his mother to the fact of his marriage, Osborne quickly nipped down to Stoneleigh and at last informed Nellie Beatrice that for the past four years he had had a wife whom he was now planning to exchange for another, an 'astonishing revelation' that she had no choice but to accept with 'as much good grace as she could muster.'[31]

On the morning of 9 April, therefore, and freshly attired in an Aquascutum suit bought for the occasion, Osborne arrived at the Divorce Court in the Strand flanked by his newly acquired and savvily protective lawyer. This was Oscar Beuselinck: thirty-six, stocky, ebullient, artful, and one of the most brilliant negotiators in the business who would go on to represent Osborne for almost thirty years, navigating him over the hurdles of four divorces and through labyrinthine financial and legal hazards.

One of the most flamboyant characters Osborne would encounter, Beuselinck was born in Bloomsbury, the son of a Belgian Catholic father who worked as a chef on the Union Castle Line, and a formidable Cockney mother known locally as Fighting Win. Unable to take up the scholarship he had won to a grammar school because his father was not British, he had become a messenger boy for a legal firm, studying law by night. During the war, he briefly joined MI6 and finally became a qualified lawyer in 1951. Since then he had dedicated himself to building an enviable show business client list that in time included Tony Richardson, Kenneth Tynan, Sean Connery, The Rolling Stones and many more. It was a list of which the vigorously egalitarian Beuselinck was justly proud. 'He wanted to be the Number One client,' he remarked of Osborne many years later. 'But he wasn't. There were others. Lots of them.'[32] Just as he made a virtue of his impoverished background, claiming that 'I never had a proper bath until I was fourteen', and that the family home had consisted of 'one room and mice by the thousand', Beuselinck liked to project himself as a man entirely devoid of social pretension, even social nicety.[33] He accomplished this by assaulting his clients with banter of such pugnacious vulgarity, frequently featuring what he claimed to be his own sexual exploits, that it often disconcerted even those who were accustomed to him. But this, he maintained, was merely his way of being down-to-earth and straightforward. Clients, after all, liked a straight talker. It was the method he had deployed when Osborne was first shown into his Ludgate Hill office a few months earlier. 'I spoke to him in a language I thought he'd understand, to put him at his ease.'[34] It worked. Osborne liked him immediately. They then got down to the serious business of arranging a divorce.

Over the previous few weeks Osborne had made several trips to York, and together he and Pamela had worked out a strategy without their resorting to the humiliating farce of the services of a fictitious lover, a seaside hotel and a private detective. Osborne would bring a suit against Pamela, while John Rees, their old friend from Derby, agreed to act the purely fictional role of co-respondent, after which Osborne would admit to his own adultery. It was a fabrication that protected Mary's name as much as possible. 'I certainly didn't cross-question my client on his co-respondent,' declared Beuselinck forty years later. 'That would have been highly improper. We had a written confession and that was enough. We went to court on that.'[35]

Obliged to wait for most of the day while several divorce petitions were heard, a procedure, noticed an observing journalist, which seemed 'strong meat even for a playwright who does not mince words over the facts of life',[36] Osborne, 'a tall, lean figure in a black suit, [his] wavy hair worn long and ending with sideburns on the cheeks rather Valentino-style', eventually took his place in the witness box.[37] Having given the oath 'in a loud, firm voice', he volunteered his evidence before Mr Justice Barrington and, after written sub-missions from Pamela Lane and Rees, was duly granted a decree nisi without costs.[38] Emerging a single man once more, he dodged a waiting gaggle of cam-eramen and photographers and fled back to Woodfall Street.

The following morning, 10 April, newspapers published the story of the Osborne divorce, and that night the reporters were after him again, this time hoping for a few words at the steps of the Royal Court before the premiere performance of The Entertainer, 'the most eagerly awaited first night of the year'.[39] In contrast to the first night of Look Back in Anger, the expectations raised by Osborne's second play and Olivier's presence in it created the glamorous atmosphere of a social and cultural event of some importance. It was a combin-ation that Osborne would never quite repeat. Independent Television News was there, filming the arrivals, Anthony Creighton among them, many glanc-ing at the cameras, perhaps in the hope of being recognised and stopped for a comment or two. Nattily clad in evening dress, Osborne gave an interview to the news crew, jauntily agreeing that his new play might 'make some people angry.' Was that his intention? 'Oh no,' he replied. 'The intention is to make [people] more conscious. More conscious of life and what's going on. More conscious of themselves.'[40]

But while first night critics applauded Osborne the next morning for attempt-ing to present a snapshot of the nation, there were reservations about his camerawork. In The Daily Telegraph, W. A. Darlington voiced the consensus by declaring that Osborne appeared 'torn between the desire to write a play and the temptation to make Archie a star part.'[41] Kenneth Tynan agreed. While com-mending the many 'miracles' of Olivier's performance in 'one of the great acting parts of our age', and Osborne's 'big and brilliant notion of putting the whole of contemporary England on to one and the same stage', the play, he argued, remained unconvincing. As in Look Back in Anger, Osborne had relied upon creat-ing dramatic impact through a single character and, as a result, 'something was still missing.' Although successfully portraying Archie's 'desperation', which was 'a hard dramatic achievement', Osborne had failed to fully explain and account for the depths of such anguish. 'And that', concluded Tynan, 'is the task to which I would now direct this dazzling, self-bound writer.'[42]

Several critics commented on the staging. The technique during the music-hall scenes whereby notices were held up at the side of the stage announcing Archie Rice's next appearance and a gauze curtain descending behind him to provide a backcloth and obscure the set of the family digs, was surely exciting evidence of Osborne having absorbed the kind of Spartan staging effects used by Bertolt Brecht and his company, the Berliner Ensemble, which had recently been seen in London. Osborne countered by protesting that he had never read Brecht. He had, though, seen a production of Mother Courage given by the Berliner Ensemble shortly after Look Back in Anger was produced, and acted in The Good Woman of Setzuan at the Royal Court, both of which, he felt, had given him enough understanding of Brecht to dismiss his theatrical theories as a 'horseless carriage.'[43] The techniques he had used in The Entertainer, Osborne pointed out, might look Brechtian to an audience that had never ventured beyond the West End, but they had been used up and down the land in the music hall and pantomime for many years.

While The Entertainer has little to do with Brecht, it has affinities with the American dramas Osborne admired, particularly Arthur Miller's Death of a Salesman, and Eugene O'Neill's great family saga Long Day's Journey into Night, completed in 1942. Although not performed in Britain until 1958, the play was published in 1956 and Osborne may have come across it while writing The Entertainer. O'Neill's themes of guilt, fury and despair and the need for understanding, penitence and forgiveness are echoed in much of Osborne.

*　　　*　　　*

Meanwhile, the press, watchful for the emergence of more Angry Young Men, had alighted upon a thirty-five-year-old Yorkshireman brandishing a first novel that, according to the Evening Standard put its author 'right up beside Kingsley Amis and John Osborne as a leading member of the new school of young writers.'[44]

This was John Braine. The son of a council sewage works supervisor and his wife, Braine had abandoned a failing career as a journalist in London before being admitted to Grassington Sanatorium in the Lake District, where he spent eighteen months recovering from tuberculosis and working on Room at the Top before returning to his hometown of Bingley and employment in the local library. Set in the fictional Yorkshire towns of Warley (Bingley) and Leddesford (Bradford), during the early years of Attlee's Labour government, Room at the Top was the first Angry work to offer in its anti-hero, Joe Lampton, an uncompromisingly right-wing central character.

Realising that he presents a dismal figure in his 'light grey suit . . . plain tie, plain grey socks and brown shoes', a 'badly wrinkled' trench coat and a hat 'discoloured with hair oil', Joe Lampton has no time for Attlee's ethics of compassionate socialism.[45] Intent upon jettisoning his lowly Town Hall job as soon as possible and driven by rampant self-interest, sexual confidence and an unshakable conviction there is room at the top, Joe determines to scramble to the summit and clap his hands upon his share of material and sexual goodies: 'I wanted an Aston-Martin, I wanted a three-guinea linen shirt, I wanted a girl with a Riviera suntan – these were my rights, I felt, a signed and sealed legacy.'[46]

Like *Hurry on Down* and *Lucky Jim*, the novel portrays a young, lower-class man in pursuit of a woman apparently socially beyond him; or, in Joe's case, two, for he plans his entrapment of Susan Brown, the innocent daughter of a local businessman, while simultaneously continuing an affair with the married Alice Aisgill. But if Charles Lumley and Jim Dixon are hesitant figures who ultimately value their girls above their careers, Joe Lampton scorns such delicate, high-flown sensibilities. Susan Brown might be unsophisticated, even socially embarrassing, but she is an available route to higher things, especially the money and power represented by her father. As a wealthy industrialist and an influential member of the town's Conservative Club, Mr Brown is very much worth knowing and exploiting. While *Room at the Top* embodies the perennial Angry theme of hostility against a social hierarchy still gauged by class and manners, the acquisition of cash and status, according to Joe, overcomes all constraints. Having therefore ensured that Susan qualified for the 'grade' financially as well as sexually, he sets her squarely in his sights.[47]

Braine's chip-on-the-shoulder novel had, as far as London was concerned, an authentic northern tang of gasworks, canals, factories and pubs and, more tantalisingly as far as the popular press were concerned, a hero galvanised by a buoyantly aggressive desire for sex and money while conveniently lacking moral sensibility. Critics fell upon it like day trippers to a seaside amusement arcade. 'If you want to know the sort of way in which the young products of the Welfare State are feeling and reacting, it will tell you,' enthused the *Evening Standard*.[48] 'It's a long time since we heard the hunger of youth really snarling,' advised the *Daily Express*, 'and it's a good sound to hear again . . . Joe will set a new fashion in heroes: brash, innocent, cynical – wide and wide-eyed . . .'[49] The *Express* enthusiastically published extracts, draped with enticing banner headlines: 'Ambition and Women: Right to the end it was to be explosive stuff!'[50] A bestseller was created.

In succession to John Osborne and Colin Wilson, Braine relayed accounts of his Cinderella struggle to journalists eager to jot down his catalogue of jobs in a furniture shop and a piston-making factory, his sudden success and subsequent resignation from the library service, his hostility to London and determination to stay in Yorkshire. He had written in praise of money, and within a year, according to the *Express*, he was positively rolling in it: 'It's cash, cash, cash all the time for the man at the top.'[51]

*   *   *

Back in London, and largely because of Olivier's presence, The Entertainer transferred to the Palace Theatre on 10 September, thereby becoming the first
Osborne play to reach the West End. Osborne himself returned to the Royal
Court to appear in The Making of Moo, a play by Nigel Dennis set somewhere
in the further reaches of the colonies and which claimed at some length that
God was generally not a good thing. Osborne played Donald Blake, an unlikely
composer of modern hymns, and managed to secure Anthony Creighton an
inconspicuous role as Second Native.

At the same time, he was writing his way towards another skirmish with the
Establishment by putting the final touches to his contribution to Declaration, an
opportunist book of essays edited by Tom Maschler. A young and enterprising
publisher at MacGibbon and Kee, Maschler had cajoled eight of the 'young and
widely opposed writers [who] have burst upon the scene' to set out their stalls
in the market square of a slim volume.[52] Although Maschler in his introduction denounced 'the lower level of journalism' which had produced the phrase
'Angry Young Man', the book was nevertheless widely perceived as a guide to
what the Angry Young Men were supposed to be thinking, even though one of
their number, the novelist Doris Lessing, was a woman and not quite as young
as the others.[53] Apart from Osborne and Lessing, the contributors included
the usual suspects of Kenneth Tynan, Lindsay Anderson, John Wain and Colin
Wilson. Making up the numbers were Bill Hopkins and Stuart Holroyd, two
writers whom Wilson was strenuously promoting as dazzlingly original think-
ers and of whom nothing much was ever heard again.

Kingsley Amis declined to contribute, protesting that he disliked 'twittering
about the "state of our civilisation"' and suspected anyone 'who wants to buttonhole me about my "role in society".'[54] In effect, he was again signalling his
resignation from a group he had never considered joining, a group that had
never considered itself a group and persisted that it did not represent a movement. Those who complied, however, saw their articles flagged with fulsome
potted biographies and flattering portrait photographs. Lindsay Anderson wrote
combatively of his exasperation with the class system and called for a new
political commitment, while Lessing described her loathing of British xenopho-
bia. Kenneth Tynan demanded a reinvigorated international theatre, which, if
sufficiently interesting, would surely lean naturally leftwards but not be wholly
socialist. Strictly socialist plays, he explained, were unfortunately not much fun.
A soft-left theatre, he suggested, might pull off the trick of being both radical
and entertaining.

In his own article, 'They Call It Cricket', Osborne recalled his family, the
Osbornes and the Groves, and put forward his manifesto as a playwright. He
dealt, he declared, with 'the texture of ordinary despair', and his primary
aim was to provoke an emotional response. 'I want to make people feel, to
give them lessons in feeling. They can think afterwards. In some countries
this could be a dangerous approach, but there seems little danger of people
feeling too much — at least not in England as I am writing . . . Shakespeare

didn't describe symptoms or offer explanations. Neither did Chekhov. Neither do I . . .'[55]

It was a succinct summary of something that preoccupied him deeply. In general, he believed, people did not really listen either to the demands of their own hearts or to each other, and neither did they acknowledge that one's primary responsibility was to oneself. In this sense, very few people were absolutely emotionally honest. This was something to which he returned, both professionally and privately, throughout his life. Often combatively critical of others, he could be equally harsh on himself. The leading characters in his plays are men who, in confronting their failure, do so with unforgiving candour.

That said, he turned his attention to sounding off, as he frequently did elsewhere, about Britain in general: the hydrogen bomb, daily journalism, political and moral sloth and the clergy being favourite bugbears. But it was what he saw as the decrepit state of the upper classes, and in particular the monarchy, that agitated him the most. Like the end of the music hall, it represented something of the British decline. 'Are we going to continue to be fooled by a class of inept deceivers,' he wondered, 'are we going to go on being ruled by them?' In the intrusive, voyeuristic age of television and the popular press, Osborne contended, the Royal Family was no longer a remote and powerful symbol of unchanging values, but had been reduced to a family much like any other, a 'substitute for values'. The crowds gathering outside St Peter's Church in Rome, he explained, were 'taking part in a moral system, however detestable it may be', but when 'the mobs rush forward in the Mall they are taking part in the last circus of a civilisation that has lost faith in itself . . . My objection to the Royal symbol is that it is dead; it is the gold filling in a mouthful of decay.'[56]

The book, and particularly Osborne's view of the monarchy, received considerable unmerited attention. His attack upon Royalty was denounced as deliberately ill-mannered at a time when Britain had in Elizabeth II a new young Queen who enjoyed the goodwill of her people. The English Stage Company Council, membership of which included in Lord Harewood a cousin of the Queen, reacted as if their collective finger had been thrust into a live electric light socket. 'Members are shocked at the John Osborne piece,' explained a clearly rattled George Devine, and 'in particular' his allusion to the Royal Family.[57] A launch party for the book at the Royal Court Theatre was hastily cancelled. The Entertainer, with its anti-Suez, anti-government sentiments then regaling Shaftesbury Avenue, was provocative enough, but the theatre holding a celebratory cocktail party for Declaration would seem to endorse the Angry Young Man's republican sentiments and place Harewood especially in an invidious position. The Council therefore 'wish to be disassociated from the book in every way,' emphasised Devine.[58] The guests, who included Aneurin Bevan, the veteran Labour politician and shadow Foreign Secretary, were informed that the book's launch upon a suspecting world would now take place at the Pheasantry, a Chelsea restaurant. Such publicity giving a furious last-minute polish to its subversive credentials, Declaration sold an astonishing 25,000 copies within three months.

But reviewers confident of reading a guidebook to the Angry Young Men found only contradiction where they hoped to discover consistency. Not only did Declaration lack coherence, it also lacked almost everything else. The almost uniform worthiness – only Anderson and Osborne's contributions had touches of levity – wallpapered over an embarrassing naivety, leading Angus Wilson in the Observer to dismiss the book as 'trivial'.[59] But Osborne at least, found exhilarating support from the News Chronicle. 'Give 'em hell, Mr Osborne!' cried James Cameron. 'If John Osborne can make his customers feel, good luck to him, because if they feel enough it may stimulate their curiosity and when they start investigating the roots of their dilemma they will in all probability be angrier than he'.[60]

Osborne might have won the approval of the News Chronicle and along with Lessing, Tynan and Anderson survive the critical mud hurled at the book, but Colin Wilson of Outsider fame was not so fortunate. He had already fallen foul of a succession of unfortunate, almost slapstick, embarrassments. At the end of 1956, the Daily Express recorded that in a speech given to a spiritualist society, Wilson had made the astonishing confession that The Outsider was 'a fraud'.[61] He protested that he had not intended to suggest the book was a hoax, merely that he had presented as an objective analysis what was in reality a personal vision. The following day, the Sunday Pictorial reported that the man 'widely hailed as the greatest literary genius of the century' had caused his estranged wife and child hardship as a result of his withholding maintenance money.[62] Wilson retaliated, claiming he sent her £25 a month. A few days later, a letter in the Times Literary Supplement alleged that in a sample of 249 lines of quotations used by Wilson in The Outsider, there were 82 'major' and 203 'minor' errors.[63] And in February 1957, there was the preposterous story of the diary, the artichoke dinner and the horsewhip.

By now, Wilson had a new girlfriend, a 'slim blond girl' called Joy Stewart, the daughter of a Bedford accountant and his wife who, like the Lanes before them, thoroughly disapproved of her liaison with an Angry Young Man.[64] When Joy's sister discovered a journal of Wilson's in which he had recorded the activities of sex criminals, the Stewarts launched a desperate rescue mission. Taking the train to London, they invaded the couple's flat, a place of 'startling squalor' decorated with 'a portrait of Nietzsche'.[65] There, they discovered Wilson and Joy eating artichokes, the first course of a dinner to which they had invited the writer Gerald Hamilton, 'an ageing roué' and reportedly the original of Christopher Isherwood's sexually unorthodox, blackmailing Mr Norris in the novel Mr Norris Changes Trains.[66] As Mrs Stewart swung into action and 'belaboured' Wilson 'over his head with her umbrella', her husband, in the manner of an outraged Victorian patriarch, apparently uttered the words: 'Aha, Wilson, the game is up!'[67] Even more: he brandished a horsewhip and threatened to use it upon the man he claimed as the ultimate outsider. As the Stewarts attempted to fend off Wilson while dragging their daughter past the empty wine bottles, the camp bed, inflatable mattress and the bicycle cluttering the room and manoeuvre her to safety, Hamilton nipped off to a public telephone box and spilled the beans to the newspapers. Reporters hurried to the scene to hear John Stewart proclaim Wilson to be 'no genius – just plain mad'.[68] Yet Joy, like Pamela Lane, resisted parental blandishments, proclaimed her love and refused to be hustled away. The arrival of the police brought a temporary, smouldering truce.

All this was entertaining enough: but there was even more to come. On the urging of Wilson's agent, the couple fled to Devon, Wilson ill-advisedly alerting the press to their flight, who joined in the fun by relaying reports of Wilson's increasingly bizarre domestic affairs. Wilson, however, remained in deadly earnest throughout, loftily announcing that he had 'hidden' Joy because 'I cannot risk another kidnapping attempt by her family.'[69] At the same time, he foolishly handed over some of the diaries discovered by Joy's sister to Daily Mail journalists, who couldn't believe their luck and splashed long extracts over the newspaper's centre pages. Readers therefore, had the pleasure of discovering that Wilson was convinced that 'the day must come when I'm hailed as a major prophet.' His estimation of himself appeared to go beyond the messianic and touch the mythological: 'I am the major literary genius of our century,' he reassured himself. 'I've always wanted to be worshipped.'[70]

Wilson not only appeared to lack any sense of the ridiculous, he seemed actively to attract it. When he submitted a play, The Death of God, to the Royal Court, he let it be known that he had Olivier in mind for a leading role. When the Court turned it down, Wilson published an outraged response in, yet again, the Daily Mail. And when Declaration was followed within a week by the appearance of Religion and the Rebel, the fuzzily Nietzschean successor to The Outsider, Wilson found himself in the invidious position of watching his literary reputation collapse. Philip Toynbee began his Observer review of the book by retracting his admiration of Wilson's first opus, which he now considered 'clumsily written and still more clumsily composed', before pronouncing its successor 'deplorable'. Toynbee, however, was the only critic courageous enough to recant in public, although the experience, he admitted, was 'unpleasant'.[71] The New Statesman agreed that it was all 'highly embarrassing', while the Daily Mail, the newspaper that had lampooned Wilson the most, selected him as one of the 'Comics of 1957'.[72] American criticism was equally withering, Time magazine captioning Wilson's photograph with the unequivocal legend: 'Egghead, Scrambled'.[73]

Although Wilson had arguably invited much of the critical opprobrium, it was still remarkable how abruptly and viciously journalists turned against him. Yet the Wilson saga was symptomatic of the popular press's general disenchantment with the idea of the Angry Young Man. Having done much to manufacture it in the first place, the press was now losing interest and neutralising the Angry image by the simple British expedient of making it a target of mockery and derision. A satire appeared in the Daily Mail in which Flook, the popular comic cartoon character, acquired an 'angry' friend by the name of Len Bloggs, a skiffle musician who lurks in provincial digs, pours scorn on the

Sunday newspapers and his wife, and whose career is thwarted by the popularity of an Eskimo calypso singer. Simultaneously, the *Daily Telegraph* ran a series of columns by the 'angry' writer, 'Eric Lard'. While the Bloggs storyline had been inspired by *Look Back in Anger*, Lard was based much more upon Osborne himself, the character firing volleys of ire at anything that caught his imagination. Omitted from *Declaration*, Lard announces a rival volume, *Proclamation*, in which, Osborne having appropriated almost every other target from gardening to the Royal Family, Lard contents himself with deriding the National Playing Fields Association.

Only a few months previously, the press had cast the Angry Young Man as a rebel; now he was being transformed into a figure of fun. It seemed as though everyone had had enough. The year of the Angry Young Man was over. In *Books and Bookmen*, Daniel Farson apocalyptically declared that *Declaration* represented nothing other than 'the death of the "Angry" epoch.'[74] Others agreed. 'From now on,' wrote the literary editor of the *News Chronicle*, 'the phrase Angry Young Man will not be used on this page in any context whatsoever.'[75]

CHAPTER 13

Transatlantic

ON 11 AUGUST 1957, four months after his divorce from Pamela Lane and the premiere of The Entertainer, Osborne turned up at Chelsea Register Office for his marriage to Mary Ure, a bridegroom for the second time at the age of twenty-seven. His mood was uneasy rather than confident. He had loved Pamela – still did in many ways – and his first wedding had been conducted in a spirit of conspiratorial defiance. But this time, he admitted, 'I was not in love', and he presented himself before the Chelsea Registrar as a reluctant partner in a ceremony he felt unable with any decency to avoid.[1]

According to Osborne's memoirs, which are often inaccurate while bracingly candid on the subject of his own feelings and failures, it was Mary who was determined upon marriage and had assumed charge of the arrangements. Osborne allowed himself to be bowled along, half hoping something might happen that would avert the inevitability of a wedding. 'A ready complaisance took me over as it sometimes does when I decide to concede to a helpless position and retreat until the ingenuity of time or delayed inspiration will rescue me.'[2]

But time was neither ingenious enough, nor was inspiration forthcoming. They married on a Sunday, when they hoped they might elude the most persistent of the press. In this, they failed. John Osborne was far too fascinating a fox for news and gossip journalists, and his wedding worthy of a front page splash. Photographers were waiting for their arrival at the Register Office, where Mary arrived emblazoned in eye-scorching pink dress, hat and shoes. After the 'civic mateyness' of the ceremony, reporters pursued the Golden Couple to a reception at Au Père de Nico, a Chelsea restaurant.[3] 'Angry Young Man Weds Star', ran a headline the following morning.[4] Despite Mary Ure being Scottish, the Evening Standard enjoyed itself analysing the alliance between an 'English rose' and a 'stinging nettle'.[5] Guests from the Royal Court Theatre, Mary's family from Scotland, Anthony Creighton and Nellie Beatrice, to whom Osborne this time had given advance notice of his wedding, looked on as the newlyweds were presented with a preposterous piece of pottery in the shape of a bear embracing a honey jar and a squirrel clutching nuts, a whimsical reminder of their having met during Look Back in Anger. Nellie Beatrice, however, thoroughly approved of Mary. Being beautiful, well known and clearly adoring of her new husband, she was powerfully emblematic of his success, a phenomenon that seemed to Nellie Beatrice almost beyond belief, yet one in which she took tremendous maternal satisfaction. 'Nellie Beatrice', observed Osborne's old friend Hugh Berrington, 'was always extremely proud of him and spoke of him most affectionately. And she liked Mary very much.' Within weeks, elaborately framed photographs of Osborne and Mary adorned the fastidiously tidy side tables of her flat in Stoneleigh, to be proudly shown off to visitors.[6]

Later that afternoon, photographers having seen through the newlyweds' ruse of booking tickets under false names, stationed themselves at Heathrow Airport to snap them as they boarded a flight to Nice. They spent two nights at the Martinez Hotel, much favoured by the wealthy and those intent upon being noticed, before flying back to London where Mary was working on a film.

A honeymoon, even for only a couple of nights, in the exotic south of France still held a dizzying aura of film-star glamour, but by now, Osborne was quickly becoming accustomed to airport lounges, boarding passes and customs checks. A fortnight earlier he had visited Moscow, at the heart of a vast and intimidating Soviet Union, where the English Stage Company was presenting Look Back in Anger at the Arts Theatre as part of a cumbersome socialist enterprise called the Sixth World Festival of Youth. But while TASS, the Russian news agency, extravagantly praised the play, declaring that 'one of its most attractive features is its faith in everything that is good and radiant in the soul', Osborne found little that was good and radiant in Moscow itself.[7] Despite grand claims of socialist efficiency, nothing worked. The company hotel was shoddy and their interpreter surly and morose, while the Festival itself appeared to be administered by unsmiling bureaucrats proficient only at being hugely inefficient. Slogans fluttering from the roofs of buildings, and massive statues of muscular young men and buxom young women thrusting hammers and sickles triumphantly into the air, proclaimed a socialist paradise where patently none existed. Peering around him at the coldly-monumental, neo-classicist Stalinist architecture, the grey austerity of the streets and the dismal, empty shops, Osborne concluded that Moscow resembled a cross between a vast replica of a forgotten wedding cake and the dingier recesses of the seedier English provincial towns familiar to Archie Rice.

Having returned from Moscow, married in London and honeymooned in France, Osborne embarked upon a hectic international schedule, flying on to New York, where Look Back in Anger was due to open at the Lyceum Theater on Broadway on 1 October. Tony Richardson was once again directing Kenneth Haigh and Mary in the leading roles. Checking in at the Algonquin Hotel on West 44th Street, an old-fashioned, easeful place where, during the 1920s,

Robert Benchley and Dorothy Parker had presided wittily over things literary, Osborne discovered his reputation had preceded him. He was 'a most angry fella', cautioned The New York Times, who spoke in 'a kind of neutral English – somewhere between Cockney and BBC – with a gentle, almost tired inflection.' The people on whose behalf he spoke, the newspaper explained, were the British 'working-class intellectuals, men who are given new teeth and free education but nowhere to go.'[8]

But despite the reputation of the play in London, hopes in New York were not high. Its producer, David Merrick, a ruthless operator and master publicist later known alternatively as 'Mr Broadway' and 'The Abominable Showman', had struggled to find investors. By Broadway standards, Look Back in Anger, with its single set and five characters, was a low budget affair, costing about 40,000 dollars to produce. But even this proved difficult to find, a quarter of it eventually being rustled up from a first-time investor in Indiana who had previously never heard of John Osborne. Few people in Manhattan were willing to predict a Broadway triumph for a British play set in a dilapidated attic flat in the English Midlands, inhabited by an aggressively unsympathetic protagonist and his disenchanted wife and played by an entirely unknown cast. At most, Merrick was hoping for a succès d'estime. On the first night, the response was similar to that in London. The audience was patient, mystified but, prepared perhaps by The New York Times, intrigued by what British 'working-class intellectuals' were watching these days. After the performance, Merrick shunted off the author, director and cast to Sardi's restaurant on 45th Street, to await the all-important critics' decisions. The strategic advantage of Sardi's was that it was adjacent to The New York Times building where Brooks Atkinson, the paper's theatre critic and probably the most powerful judgmental voice in town, was even then putting the finishing touches to his review. His verdict, relayed by messenger to the anxious producer and cast was magnanimous. 'An October bonfire opened last night and lit a blaze on Broadway . . .'[9]

Atkinson and others did for the play in New York what the combined forces of Tynan, Hobson and the BBC had done in London, transforming doubt into certainty, caution into enthusiasm and Look Back in Anger into a play that had to be seen. As a result, John Osborne became an author who had to be seen as well. Once the critics had given the green light, Osborne quickly discovered that in New York, nothing succeeds like success. Welcomed aboard a frenzied professional and social carousel, he found himself deluged with requests for interviews, while discussions with agents tumbled over invitations to lunches, dinners and parties, parties, parties. 'Everyone' suddenly wanted to meet the young man from Fulham who had written such an excitingly original play. 'Already Osborne is a success here on a big-time scale', wired the American correspondent of the Daily Express, while Osborne relayed the heady thrill of it all in jubilant letters home to Creighton.[10] 'The play is the SMASH OF THE SEASON,' he cried. The box office at the Lyceum was 'jammed' and 'success here is irresistible.'[11] Dizzy with acclaim, 'full of excitement', he walked streets he had previously seen only in films fifteen years ago at the Rembrandt in Stoneleigh, and later in provincial Odeons.[12] He explored avenues of soaring buildings, where subway vapours seeped from grilles in the roads, as if some leviathan was slumbering beneath and might suddenly burst upwards through the tarmac. Here it all was: the teeming office workers by day, the beckoning streetwalkers by night and yellow cabs swerving to the sidewalk at the flick of a finger; a city of bagels and pizzas, sandwiches named after film stars, bars selling fluorescent cocktails and where pianos idly tinkled; an endlessly beguiling city of many ethnicities, of record shops selling records unobtainable in England and bookshops laden with titles he had never seen before; a city that seemingly never slept and, most dazzling of all, blazed forth his own name in lights. He made a flying visit to Hollywood, mythological home of the stars, and another to Las Vegas, home of the rattling, flashing slot machine. How different from London it was. It was wonderful; he was *alive*. '. . . this is big success,' he crowed. 'I feel abuzz with enthusiasm.'[13]

At the same time, Marjory Vosper, his London agent, breathlessly kept him abreast of his multiplying fortunes in Britain and elsewhere. *The Entertainer* was still going strong at the Palace, *Look Back in Anger* was being revived yet again in the provinces, an Arts Council tour of the play was well under way and a new production was about to open in Warsaw. The whole world wanted the English Angry Young Man. And so did Harry Saltzman, a chubby, Quebec-born American in his early forties, whose expensive grooming, bespoke suits and highly polished shoes proclaimed assurance and style, and who advanced upon Osborne offering dreams of movies and money.

Saltzman was a born wheeler-dealer. He had worked in vaudeville and in advertising; he had once managed a circus and, during the Second World War, when he had been attached to the supply depot of the Royal Canadian Air Force, he had allegedly smuggled jukeboxes inside crates of Red Cross bandages in order to sell them in Europe. He was now, he claimed, 'in films', which was true enough. Harry had hovered about the film world a lot, waiting to pounce, and done a bit of talent scouting, but his actual credentials so far amounted to collaborating on *The Iron Petticoat*, a Cold War comedy starring Bob Hope and Katherine Hepburn, and which Hope later successfully suppressed. Nevertheless, Saltzman was nothing if not supremely confident. To those, like Oscar Beuselinck, who were less enchanted by him than some, he seemed a parody of the popular image of a film producer. 'D'ya wanna make a movie,' Beuselinck would mimic, spreading his arms wide, 'or d'ya wanna make a movie?'[14] Saltzman whisked Osborne off on a tour of Manhattan nightlife and the places 'everyone' went, pouring the elixir of movies into his ears. *Look Back in Anger*, he cried, must be filmed, and Osborne must write the screenplay. Then he must write another one. He, Harry, would produce anything Osborne wrote. Meanwhile, they slipped into hit shows, dropped into chic restaurants and finished up at smoky subterranean jazz clubs, Saltzman the Showman all the while introducing, talking, persuading, promoting. '. . . at 5am, we went

down to Harlem,' Osborne reported to Creighton, and 'saw a Negro Vaudeville show which was the GREATEST.'[15] They caught Thelonious Monk playing
at the Five Spot, looked in at the Apollo in Harlem, where Wednesday night
was Amateur Night, and went along to Birdland, on Broadway and 52nd,
and where the list of performers comprised a jazz world Who's Who. In tiny
improvisation theatres, would-be comedians tried their luck: 'I think I laughed
all night.'[16] And all the while, like Patrick Desmond before him, Harry promised unimaginably wonderful things to come. All they had to do was make
some pictures together.

Osborne loved New York and New York loved him in return. 'I think one
reason for this is that he fits into the exaggerated pattern the Americans love
more than anything,' explained the Daily Express, 'the boy who rises from rags to
riches.'[17] This was the very stuff of American mythology. These were the days
before widespread mass communication, instant celebrity and the celebration
of youth. Television, football, fashion, rock music and films, all of which would
soon make a lot of young people a lot of money, were still largely local, at
most national endeavours; that they could become a cornucopia of international
fame and fantastic wealth was only dimly conceived. A global economy was
something that as yet only economists thought about, and in the theatre, plays
and musicals were created primarily to be produced locally, and then nationally. The kind of trans-Atlantic success lavished upon Osborne was at the time
something conferred upon only the very few, and for a young man of twenty-
eight it was extraordinary.

As for Creighton, sitting in his cabin on the Egret, Osborne's reports from
New York, with their ecstatic underlinings and waterfalls of double exclamation marks, came as if from another world. Yet while Osborne loved being
courted and feted, he was not wholly seduced, resisting the requests of Harold
Freedman, his newly acquired American agent, to write a Hollywood film
screenplay. It was not, he thought, something he could yet manage. With Harry
Saltzman too, he prevaricated. A film of Look Back in Anger might be a good idea,
or it might not. Mary, however, was not nearly so guarded. Already, there were
rumours that both the play and her performance would be nominated for Tony
Awards, and instructing her agent to convey the news of her Broadway acclaim
as quickly as possible to the golden groves of Hollywood, she stood poised in
the hope that a contract might wing its way quickly back.

A startlingly pragmatic woman, Mary's ambitions were professional and
maternal and, for her husband, professional and sartorial. Convinced as soon
as she had read the script of Look Back in Anger that he was going to be a great
playwright, she had set about remodelling his appearance according to her idea
of what an important writer looked like. Jettisoning his tweed jackets, nauti-
cal blazers and boyish v-necked sweaters, she steered him into Savile Row and
emerged with him wearing one of several newly acquired handmade suits.
Dumping his pipe, assumed in repertory days, she replaced it with Cuban cigars
and black Russian Sobranie cigarettes. In New York, she rearranged his smile,

dispatching him to a dentist to have his teeth capped. She was also intent upon motherhood.

Such dedicated zeal disconcerted Osborne. He neither expected nor liked such meticulous planning. 'I like women to be friendly and pretty and gay and chatty,' he plaintively informed the Daily Express at the time.[18] But this was not Mary, or not entirely, and this he discovered in New York. He had not expected her to be so resolutely ambitious. It implied competition, and was a quality in women, or women close to him, that he distrusted and frequently resented. Like Pamela Lane before her, Mary possessed an elusiveness that from afar he found enormously attractive, but at close quarters bewildered him. There was something in her that he could neither understand nor govern. Although passionately committed to his writing, he had not mapped out a career for himself. Having been lucky enough to have been discovered, he was now allowing himself to be whirled along by a current going his way. Mary's rigorous planning of their life together exposed his indecisiveness. Rather than face up to her resolve, he gratefully snatched at the thin straw of opportunity to bolt back to England offered by the news in November that Anthony Creighton had been involved in an accident on his scooter.

Since Osborne's move to Woodfall Street, Creighton had subsisted as best he could but had frequently relied on a regular £20 weekly handout Osborne had arranged through his bank. Although Osborne could afford to be more generous these days, he steadfastly concealed from his wife not only Creighton's subsidies, but also a similar amount paid to Nellie Beatrice and the occasional cheque written in response to appeals from various Grove relatives. Mary did not trust Creighton, warning her husband that he was jealous of his success and could easily become a burden, an idea Osborne dismissed. Once in London, he was reassured to discover that Creighton was more or less unscathed. Hardly a confident driver at the best of times, even of a Lambretta, a machine with little more power than a motor-mower, Creighton had contrived to collide with a lorry parked in St Martin's Lane. Both driver and scooter had been conveyed back to the Egret, where both lay slightly battered, awaiting attention. Osborne prescribed recuperation in the form of a motoring holiday. Having recently taken driving lessons, he had acquired an Austin saloon car, a conservative choice – 'a grocer's car' snorted George Devine – but one which bore the ostentatious licence plate number of AYM [Angry Young Man] 1.[19] And so, one morning, they locked the cabin doors of the Egret and, with Creighton installed in the passenger seat, set off on a motoring tour of Wales, Osborne pursued by agitated cables from Mary in New York, where Merrick had further boosted the notoriety and the box-office takings of Look Back in Anger by arranging – for a fee of $250 – for a supposedly irate woman to interrupt a performance by striking Kenneth Haigh in apparent protest against Jimmy's treatment of Alison.

Osborne had promised to go back to New York, but, reluctant to return to Mary's preoccupation with Hollywood fame and a child, he allowed Harry Saltzman, still talking money and movies, to take him off to Paris for Christmas instead. Ensconced in a room at the Hotel Napoleon near the Champs-Elysées, and from where he sent Mary an insolent telegram: 'We love Paris, Paris, Paris!', he enjoyed himself immensely before flying back to New York and a reception from Mary understandably as freezing as the January streets outside their hotel.[20] He was grateful that an ally had returned in the shape of Tony Richardson, who was now rehearsing the Broadway production of The Entertainer.

In London, Look Back in Anger had opened on the fifty-seventh anniversary of Tom Godfrey's birth. The American production of The Entertainer opened in Boston on 27 January 1958, the eighteenth anniversary of his death. With Olivier still in the leading role, the production arrived in New York a fort-night later and opened at the Royale Theater on 12 February, next door to the Lyceum where Look Back in Anger was still running. Osborne's fame and Olivier's name had ensured that The Entertainer's twelve-week run was already sold out and that tickets were changing hands at inflated prices. But this time there was no bonfire lit on the Great White Way. Audiences who had paid to see a great English Shakespearian actor were perplexed and disappointed. Why were they confronted with a tawdry vaudeville show interspersed with long stretches of obscure domestic dialogue? Who were these people? What were they complaining about? This time, the critics had no answer, no reas-surances to give.

Yet Olivier's name kept the show alive and interest in Osborne himself was undiminished. Requests for interviews and invitations to parties continued unabated, while each evening the House Full notices, reminiscent of The Saga's sojourn at Hayling Island, were placed outside the Lyceum and the Royale. With two plays running side by side and his name in lights, Osborne was at once celebrated and, as he tactlessly informed the impoverished Creighton, contemplating undreamt-of wealth. There was so much that he wanted to do, he added, so many plays that he wanted to write and places he wanted to see and it would surely all be so much easier now that he was 'RICH'. At this rate, 'I'll be able to buy cars for everyone soon!'[21] Once more, he allowed himself to be absorbed into the Never-Land of Harry Saltzman, partly as a way of evading Mary, for whom both the call from Hollywood and conception were proving frustratingly elusive.

By this time, however, he had concluded that Mary's theatrical and cinematic ambition far outstripped her abilities. She was, he conceded, a good enough actress, but her voice had a harsh edge to it and her range was limited. She could never aspire to a Lady Macbeth or a Cleopatra, and if the call from Hol-lywood ever came, he suspected it would only be to play the amiable British blonde that she was. Once again, he resorted to 'the ingenuity of time or delayed inspiration', and once again, along came a chance. Saltzman springing the idea of a great celebratory trip to Montego Bay along with Tony Richard-son, provided just the avoidance strategy Osborne was seeking. Explaining to the baffled playwright that Montego Bay was in Jamaica, Harry-the-munificent promised to make all the arrangements. But a few days later, the producer

1.) *top left*: John Osborne aged three, 1933. 2.) *top right*: John Osborne and Tom Godfrey, early 1930s.
3.) *bottom left*: John Osborne as a teenager with Nellie Beatrice, later 1940s.
4.) *bottom right*: Nellie Beatrice behind the bar.

5.) *above*: John Osborne and Pamela Lane (left) at Derby Playhouse, 1954.
6.) *Below*: Pamela Lane.

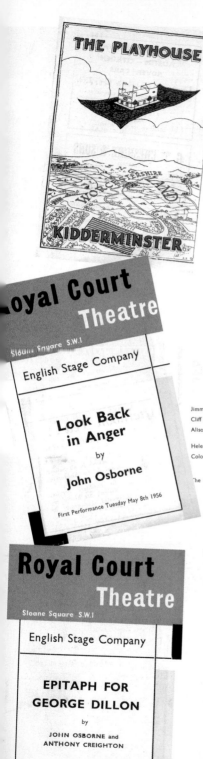

Phone 3760

The Playhouse
Phone 3760

KIDDERMINSTER

(In association with the Arts Council of Great Britain)

Director .... KENNETH ROSE

Manager and Licensee .... MICHAEL P. HULME

MONDAY, AUGUST 11th, 1952 .... And all the Week.

Evenings at 7.30.

Saturday 5.15 and 8 p.m.

THE PLAYHOUSE

Presents

THE REPERTORY PLAYERS

in

"REBECCA"

by Daphne Du Maurier.

Cast in order of appearance :—

Frith	ERIC JONES
Beatrice Lacy	BRENDA KAYE
Giles Lacy	JOHN STYLES
Frank Crawley	PAUL ANSTEE
Maxim De Winter	JOHN OSBORNE
Mrs De Winter	BRENDA VERNON
Mrs. Danvers	BARBARA KEOGH
Robert	JACK ROBINSON
Jack Favell	WILLIAM MOORE
First Maid	ROSEMARY TOWLER
Second Maid	JULIA BEDDOES
Mrs. Fortescue	ELEANOR GREET
Colonel Julyan	DAVID SAXBY
William Tabb	ANTHONY CREIGHTON

Look Back in Anger

by

John Osborne

Cast in order of appearance :

Jimmy Porter	Kenneth Haigh
Cliff Lewis	Alan Bates
Alison Porter	Mary Ure
	by Courtesy of Tennent Productions Ltd. and London Film Productions Ltd.
Helena Charles	Helena Hughes
Colonel Redfern	John Welsh

The action of the play takes place in the Porter's one-room flat in a large Midland town.

ACT I
Early evening one Sunday in April.

ACT II
Scene 1 : Evening, two weeks later.
Scene 2 : The following evening.

ACT III
Scene 1 : Sunday evening, several months later.
Scene 2 : A few minutes later.

There will be two 12 minute intervals.

Act II by Worth & Riley, Ltd. Miss Hughes' has In Act II by Denlos, the Lady Newborough. Additional costumes made in the Company's workroom by Sydney Adams. Lighter by Ronson. Stockings by Kayser. Photographs by Julie Hamilton. Sound Equipment by Stagesound (London) Ltd. Electrical Installations by Strand Electric & Engineering Co. Ltd. Virginia Cigarettes by Abdulla.

Permanent Surround by Motley

The English Stage Company receives financial assistance from the Arts Council of Great Britain

General Manager		G. Hamilton Gay
Business Manager	For	M. Michaels
Stage Director	The	Michael Halifax
Stage Managers	English	Jeremy Hare
	Stage	Jean Wilkinson
Wardrobe	Company	Stephen Doncaster
Properties		Clare Jeffery

Press Representative .... George Fearon (GER 3169)

Box Office (Mr. Bruns), open from 10 a.m. to 8 p.m. .... SLO 1745

The management reserve the right to refuse admission and to make any change in the cast necessitated by illness or other unavoidable causes.

Also in present repertoire

from 2nd April   First Performance in London

The Mulberry Bush by Angus Wilson

from 9th April   First Performance in London

The Crucible by Arthur Miller

from 15th May   First Performance in London

Don Juan and The Death of Satan by Ronald Duncan

from 26th June   World Premiere

Cards of Identity by Nigel Dennis

For Performance Dates   See Over

Anthony Creighton

ANTHONY CREIGHTON was born in Toronto thirty-five years ago. He came to England at the outbreak of war and joined the R.A.F. After being demobilised he studied for two years at the Royal Academy of Dramatic Art and then spent some time in repertory before forming his own company at Ilfracombe. It was here that he first met John Osborne when the latter joined the company as an actor.

From Ilfracombe he came to London where he worked in Television and with various Repertory Companies.

It was about four years ago when he and John Osborne started to work together on "Epitaph for George Dillon".

Anthony Creighton joined the English Stage Company as an actor in "The Apollo de Bellac" and "The Making of Moo". He is shortly to direct a new play for the English Stage Society.

7.) Programmes from the Kidderminster Playhouse 1952 and the Royal Court Theatre, 1956 and 1958.

8.) *above:* John Osborne aboard the houseboat, River Thames 1956.
9.) *below:* John Osborne at the Royal Court Theatre, 1957.

10.) *Top left:* George Devine. 11.) *top right:* Tony Richardson.
12.) *bottom left:* Harold Hobson. 13.) *bottom right:* Kenneth Tynan.

14.) *above:* Kenneth Haigh (left) and John Osborne outside the Royal Court Theatre, 1956.
15.) *below:* Jimmy Porter (Kenneth Haigh, left), Cliff (Alan Bates, centre) and Alison (Mary Ure, right) in the first production of *Look Back in Anger*, 1956.

16.) *above:* The poster for the film of *Look Back in Anger*, 1959.

17.) *below:* The opening scene of the film of *Look Back in Anger*: Cliff (Gary Raymond) and Sally (Bernice Swanson) look on as Jimmy Porter (Richard Burton) plays the trumpet.

18.) *above*: John Osborne Mary Ure, Vivien Leigh and Laurence Olivier, 1957.
19.) *below*: Laurence Olivier as Archie Rice, 1957.

confessed there had been a last-minute hitch. Something had come up and Osborne would have to go ahead while he and Richardson would follow later. Meanwhile, he presented Osborne with two air tickets to Jamaica, one of which was for himself. The other, he said, was for Francine.

*   *   *

Osborne had first encountered Francine Brandt at one of Saltzman's parties. She was tall, dark, self-confident and beautiful, her smoky Swiss-French accent sounding silkily glamorous amid the harsh Manhattan timbre. In order to enhance her exotic appeal, she carefully clouded much of her past in mystery. It seemed she had once been married to a Persian and had arrived in New York in pursuit of vague show-business ambitions. But having fleetingly appeared in a television series, *Captain Gallant of the Foreign Legion*, opposite the Olympic swimming gold medallist-turned-actor, Buster Crabbe, and in which she played the daughter of a sheik, she had devoted herself to becoming a presence in the circles of the rich and famous. She knew the film director Roger Vadim and his young wife, Brigitte Bardot; she had stepped aboard the *Christina O*, the fabulously expensive 'superyacht' owned by Aristotle Onassis, the absurdly rich Greek shipping tycoon whose guests included the likes of former Prime Minister Winston Churchill, Richard Burton and Elizabeth Taylor, Grace Kelly, Frank Sinatra and Maria Callas. Francine was well known but always referred to discreetly. 'Francine Brandt was a courtesan,' recalled Elaine Anderson, a young woman who, having been photographed dancing to the Duke Ellington Orchestra at the 1956 Newport Jazz Festival, had found herself propelled into the orbit of New York show business. 'I would call her the most expensive call-girl in the world.'[22] From a bungalow apartment decorated in strident primary colours in Beverley Hills, Francine the spider spun a web of allure within which Osborne the fly was soon tightly enmeshed.

Having landed at Montego Bay and installed themselves at the Half Moon Hotel overlooking the water, Osborne whiled away his days sunbathing, reading and eating al fresco meals with his new lover. In the evenings, he summoned up his Gaycroft dancing experience to execute an energetic hokey-cokey to the rhythm of a steel band. Mary, meanwhile, remained in wintry New York where she was still appearing in *Look Back in Anger*, and where, Osborne reported to Creighton, she was possibly having an affair with an American television actor. If so, he reasoned, then surely it mitigated his own infidelity. But 'for the first time, I'm having a deep sense of guilt,' he confessed, although he did not let it divert him from the calypso of romance with Francine.[23] The thing was, he told Creighton, he believed he was actually falling in love with her. Not that he divulged her profession to his old friend in London or that their relationship depended upon cheques unobtrusively dispatched to an address in Geneva. How would it all end, he wondered? No doubt, he concluded, everything would work itself out in time. It was a convenient course to take. It avoided confrontation and responsibility, and relied again on 'the ingenuity of time or delayed inspiration.' Meanwhile, he was enjoying himself no end.

*   *   *

Before Osborne had left for New York, George Devine had tackled him about a new play. Having nothing else, Osborne had given him the script of Epitaph for George Dillon, the second play he had written in collaboration with Creighton and completed prior to his typing of Look Back in Anger. It had already been produced the previous year by the Experimental Theatre Club in Oxford, whose director, Don Taylor, had simply written to the author of Look Back in Anger enquiring whether he might have an unperformed piece they could give an airing. Tynan had written an encouraging report in the Observer, and Devine, having read the script, bowled it in the direction of William Gaskill. A recent arrival at the Royal Court, Bill Gaskill was from the same Yorkshire village as Richardson and, like Devine and Richardson, an Oxford graduate. With Robert Stephens playing the title role, for which he emulated many of Osborne's mannerisms and vocal inflections, the production opened on 11 February 1958, while Osborne was cavorting in Jamaica. To the collaborators' surprise, it transferred to the Comedy Theatre in the West End on 29 May, where, apprehensive that audiences might be deterred by the funereal whiff of Epitaph, the producer Donald Albery insisted that the title be truncated to George Dillon.

Since the production represented a welcome recovery in his fortunes, Creighton was delighted but Osborne, who returned to London to see it, felt as removed from it as he had at the openings of The Devil Inside Him and Personal Enemy. So much had happened in the intervening three years since he and Creighton had beaten out the play on the typewriter at Caithness Road, that he had wholly lost touch with it. The character of George Dillon, the thwarted actor-dramatist, was loosely representative of Osborne at the time of writing but since the bright lights of Sloane Square and Broadway had been turned upon him, confirming that he was aflame with talent and success, he had become almost indifferent to the fate of a piece which had been written, it seemed, in a previous life.

As Kenneth Tynan noted when he saw the play again, Epitaph for George Dillon has the zest of truth while being curiously unresolved. 'If George is seriously intended to be a persecuted genius,' he wrote, 'then the whole play, not just the hero, is paranoid to the point of hysteria. If, on the other hand, he is a mediocre writer forced at length to accept his own mediocrity it is a play of astounding courage and strength.'[24] Perhaps this equivocation was felt by audiences generally, for the play lasted only six weeks at the Comedy Theatre. But it was long enough for Merrick to agree to produce it on Broadway in the autumn. Yet Osborne missed by several weeks the chance of being able to claim a trio of plays running simultaneously in New York. Despite being nominated for a

Tony Award for Outstanding Play, *Look Back in Anger* had failed to survive the sti-fling heat of a Manhattan summer and *The Entertainer* had also closed by the time *George Dillon* arrived at the John Golden Theater on 4 November 1959. It proved to be a brief visit. The water flung upon the dying embers of the previous year's October bonfire, the production closed within a month. With Christmas approaching and the lights fading on his marriage, so Osborne's name faded over Broadway and he returned to London and Woodfall Street.

Once they were home, Mary adopted a line of resistance similar to that of Alison Porter, whom she had played for almost three years, culminating in her being nominated for a Tony Award for Best Actress. According to an Ameri-can critic: as 'the tormented wife, Mary Ure succeeds in retaining the pride of an intelligent young woman by filling her silences with unspoken vitality.'[25] Although crushed that Hollywood had not called, aware that her husband now cared little for her and did nothing to conceal his betrayal with Francine, Mary nevertheless managed to preserve an outward stoicism. Perhaps Osborne was right, and she was also having an affair of her own; perhaps it was a defence to conceal her emotional fragility. Yet at the same time, her faith in his writing remained unshaken and she continued to stoke the fire of his self-confidence by assuring him that one day he would be recognised as one the great English dramatists of the century.

There was no concealing, though, the frequent and furious quarrels between them. The writer Doris Lessing was present when Mary was reduced to tears beneath one of her husband's verbal assaults in a London bistro. 'I was there with somebody else and we attempted to diffuse the situation, but he never let up for a second. He flayed her, quite like Jimmy Porter,' she remembered.[26] In her distress, Mary had also begun drinking excessively, which would further fuel the arguments between them. These would often begin, or resume, at breakfast and might culminate in Mary hurling their newly acquired Spode china at her husband as he attempted to eat his meal. The Angry Young Man would then be ignominiously obliged to change out of clothes bespattered by soaking tea leaves before emerging from his front door, refreshed and spruce in one of his twelve Savile Row suits, perhaps the 'charcoal grey' with a 'soft white shirt with collar attached' and 'a tightly knotted grey tie', to face a new day.[27]

CHAPTER 14

Black and White

BESIDES ATTENDING TO HIS dry cleaning, Osborne was now busy maintaining the apparatus of his professional success. Not too long ago, as a sometime actor and fitful dramatist, he had returned an income tax declaration to the Inland Revenue with the blunt assertion of: 'No income: no tax.'[1] Now, everything had changed and it was estimated that Osborne was earning up to an astonishing £20,000 a year.

'Of course I enjoy money,' he declared. 'Anyone who says he doesn't is a fool. I like expensive clothes and the other things it brings.'[2] But with wealth and public and professional prominence came the urge to continue reinventing himself, shaking off what he regarded as the cultural encumbrance of lower-middle-class inheritance and assuming an air of self-made cosmopolitan assurance. In his late teens, he had learned how to dance and had overhauled his accent in order to reinvent himself as an actor. Now, as he entered his thirties, and beginning under Mary's guidance, he refurbished his wardrobe in order to remodel himself further and emerge as a snappily dressed metropolitan playwright. He had his hair cut at a fashionable Chelsea hairdresser's. In addition to his bespoke suits, Norfolk jackets, crisp shirts and a rack of silk ties, he had now acquired a small fleet of handmade shoes. 'He had a real sense of style,' observed a close friend. 'He was almost aristocratic in his bearing.'[3]

Nowadays, he was looking more like the pivot of a small but immensely successful corporate enterprise. Not only did he have in Margery Vosper and Harold Freedman a British and an American agent, but David Higham, a prominent London literary agent, was now negotiating his publishing contracts with Faber and Faber. The company of which T. S. Eliot was still a director had approached Osborne about publishing his plays soon after his debut at the Royal Court. This had both surprised and flattered him for it was a rather unorthodox move for a house with an austere reputation of highbrow literary and intellectual endeavour. Yet beginning with *Look Back in Anger*, Faber would continue to publish everything he wrote. Eliot himself, however, seems to have recorded no comments on Osborne's writing, although Valerie Eliot, his widow, recollected that while in New York, they had seen The Entertainer, after which the Nobel laureate had concluded that 'as nothing happens, the play proved you could get good theatre without action.'⁴

Elsewhere in London, the pugnaciously ebullient Oscar Beuselinck continued to preside over Osborne's increasingly complex legal affairs while the Mayfair accountants Bryce, Hamner, Isherwood and Company, whose clients would soon include The Beatles, welcomed him as a valued name. Spreading before him meticulous columns of figures representing his income and expenditure, they advocated the financial advantages of planned investment and of dividing himself into separate companies, each dealing with a specific aspect of his output. John Osborne Productions (co-directors J. Osborne and O. Beuselinck), therefore, now supervised the productions of his plays, while Dillon Productions Ltd (co-directors J. Osborne and A. Creighton) stood ready to exploit the opportunities created by Epitaph for George Dillon. Already, they were hearing encouraging noises, including proposals for a film version of the play to be scripted by Keith Waterhouse and Willis Hall and possibly starring Dirk Bogarde. But interest dwindled, the film was never made, the play was rarely revived and any money in the company was slowly siphoned off in subsidising the intermittently impecunious Creighton.

Osborne had now, also at the direction of his accountants, become an employer. A secretary arrived daily at Woodfall Street who diligently typed his scripts, answered the telephone and organised his correspondence. This was Helen Henderson, a frail Scottish Communist in her early fifties. Mary approved of Helen, who lived a reclusive life with a sister in north London and whose age and temperament offered no temptation to her husband and whose mild gentility and lilting voice brought a sentimental reminder of her own Scottish childhood. There was also a chauffeur, Jimmy Gardner, an aspiring actor who drove the Golden Couple to their various meetings and evenings at the theatre. Despite the urging of his accountants, however, Osborne was initially at least a reluctant employer. He conceded to the secretary and the chauffeur, but resisted for the moment the suggestion of a cook and emphatically drew the line at employing a valet to assist with his wardrobe. The introduction of a Jeeves figure into Woodfall Street was distinctly unappealing.

When Osborne had boasted to Creighton that if the bright blaze of his success continued, he would soon be able to buy cars not only for himself but also his friends, he was not being entirely disingenuous. Now that he had money, Osborne much preferred spending to investing. Following Devine's acerbic dismissal of the unassuming Austin saloon as a 'grocer's car', Osborne traded it in and acquired instead something far more redolent of Hollywood glamour: a magnificent American Buick Sapphire. This was again far from the image of an Angry Young Man created three years earlier, but as the theatre magazine Encore observed, 'It is hard, of course, to be angry on fifteen thousand a year.'⁵ If he spent freely on himself, materially at least, he was also extremely generous to others. Throughout her life, he would support Nellie Beatrice, buy random gifts for his wives, remember his employees at birthdays and Christmas and unobtrusively help many others in need. And for the time being, he agreed to subsidise Creighton.

Pedestrians sufficiently impressed by the sight of a chauffeur-driven Buick Sapphire gliding through the West End of London to take the trouble to notice the figure in the back seat, would have discerned John Osborne scrutinizing the plans of his newest business venture. Woodfall Films was very much Harry Saltzman's creation. Having materialised in London and installed himself at Lowndes Cottage in Chelsea, recently vacated by Laurence Olivier, Saltzman breezily installed a platoon of secretaries, a chauffeur and a cook and carried on from where he had left off in New York, talking about the magic of movies, of filming Look Back in Anger, and of all the films to come. Richardson was as intrigued as Osborne, but, if films were going to be made, warned the ever-vigilant Oscar Beuselinck, reaching for his law books, then everything must be legally binding. Osborne must recast himself as a company director, and the company must have a name. As Osborne lived in Woodfall Street, it was decided to call the new company Woodfall Films. With Richardson and Beuselinck joining Osborne and Saltzman as directors, the company nestled itself in offices at 11a Curzon Street in Mayfair, as close to the seat of the Establishment as Jimmy Porter's attic is to the clanging cathedral bells. Richardson stationed himself directorially behind a desk on which three telephones, one black, one white and one red, stood presidentially arranged. Look Back in Anger would be their first project.

*   *   *

Like the theatre, the immediate post-war British cinema had generally fought shy of anything other than a reassuring, idealised portrayal of life. The most consistently popular of British films were those produced by Ealing Studios, where Michael Balcon presided over the creation of a steady stream of amiable, mildly anarchic comedies. In Passport to Pimlico, for example, an ancient document is discovered suggesting that the London borough of Pimlico once belonged to the kingdom of Burgundy and is therefore independent of the British Parliament. Released in 1949, it was followed two years later by The Lavender Hill Mob, celebrating the misfortunes of an inept gang of bank robbers. These films and many like them offered a view of England that Kenneth Tynan scorned as 'patriotic neo-realism', but it was one that many wanted to see.[6] Ealing presented the image of a united nation of affable small shopkeepers, chummy publicans, good-natured policemen and criminals who cheerfully submitted to fair cop; a nation tolerant both of eccentricity among its aristocrats and of minor misdemeanours among its lower orders, provided that the supposed British virtues of fair play, justice and community spirit were upheld in the end.

It was a fantasy, and vulnerable at that. As American distributors became more powerful and Hollywood films became ever more plentiful, Ealing began to suffer. Even the appearance of a delinquent, as opposed to an Angry, young man in *The Blue Lamp*, a comparatively shocking thriller that Ealing released in 1950, in which affable PC George Dixon is shot and killed by the neurotic Tom Riley, failed to revive Ealing's flagging fortunes. Neither could *The Cruel Sea*, a stirring saga of adventure upon the high seas, salvage a studio overburdened by debt and torpedoed by American competition. The end came in 1955, when Ealing's studios were sold to BBC Television, which successfully resurrected PC Dixon as the homely central character of the long-running *Dixon of Dock Green* police series.

Yet almost surreptitiously, the British cinematic rejuvenation had already begun elsewhere under the assertively democratic banner of Free Cinema. This was devised by two young film-makers, Lindsay Anderson and Karel Reisz. Prickly, self-reliant, a man who seemingly thrived on struggle and invariably wore a red shirt, Anderson was born of Scottish stock in India in 1923. Like George Devine and Tony Richardson, he was a graduate of Wadham College, Oxford, where he had co-founded *Sequence*, a magazine intended to create waves in what he was convinced was the stagnant pool of British film-making. Reisz was three years younger, a Czechoslovakian educated at a Quaker boarding school, and Emmanuel College, Cambridge, from where he had mailed his own contributions to *Sequence*. By 1956 he was working, conveniently, as programming officer at the National Film Theatre on London's South Bank where the first flowering of Free Cinema burst forth in a programme of short films shown in February. And so 1956, that memorable year in which the Angry Young Man came into being, that witnessed the debacle of Suez, the disaster of Hungary, the rise of Elvis Presley and the beginnings of a new youth culture, also saw the emergence of a new style of film-making.

Anderson had devised the banner title of 'Free Cinema' both to indicate their independence from the established studios and the demands of the marketplace, but also in the hope that critics would write not only about the films but also about the robustly austere ethics of their making. In case they were uncertain as to what these were, the Free Cinema-makers provided a handy manifesto. 'As film-makers', it read, 'we believe that:

No film can be too personal.
The image speaks. Sound amplifies and comments. Size is irrelevant.
Perfection is not an aim.
An attitude means style. A style means an attitude.'[7]

As a set of principles, they were unlikely to be opposed by anyone aligning themselves to progressiveness in the arts. On the other hand, they were so vague as to be almost meaningless and so elastic that they could be stretched to encompass almost anything the Free Cinema-makers cared to do. As the English

Stage Company set itself in opposition to Binkie Beaumont's West End, so the
Free Cinema-makers took up arms against the studio-made films of the day.
A fan of such films as The Grapes of Wrath and All Quiet on the Western Front, which
he claimed would be culturally impossible to make in Britain, Anderson established himself as the movement's most vocal polemicist. With Ealing firmly
in mind, he derided the prevailing 'Southern English' cinema as 'snobbish,
anti-intelligent, emotionally inhibited, wilfully blind to the conditions and
problems of the present, [and] dedicated to an out-of-date, exhausted national
ideal.'[8] By contrast, Free Cinema claimed that film-making should be both a
poetic and a humanist activity: poetic in the sense that a film should tell a story,
and humanist in that it should depict 'real' characters, unencumbered by what
Anderson described as the usual characteristics of social class whereby aristocrats were portrayed 'though respectfully, as a fine old figure of fun', while the
working classes were comic, villainous or a combination of both. Cinema, he
pronounced, must take up a position in which it was 'imaginatively in touch
with the present: vital, illuminating, personal and refreshing.'[9]

The first Free Cinema programme included screenings of Anderson's
O Dreamland, a study of a down-at-heel funfair designed to suggest that trivial
culture trivialises human nature, something that Richard Hoggart and many
others would have recognised, and Momma Don't Allow, a twenty-two-minute
documentary film made by Tony Richardson and featuring Chris Barber's jazz
band performing at the Wood Green jazz club. During the five subsequent Free
Cinema programmes over the following three years, the directors attempted to
promote their poetic and humanist ideals in such films as Anderson's Every Day
Except Christmas, a documentary on the Covent Garden fruit and vegetable market
hopefully evoking 'the poetry of everyday life', and Reisz's We Are the Lambeth
Boys, about a London youth club.[10] But although the Free Cinema 'manifesto'
may have implied a radical perspective, the films themselves were celebratory
rather than critical, peering at work and workers from a romantic viewpoint,
mostly because the film-makers had only a vague idea of what working lives
in the poorer parts of London, let alone the Midlands or the north of England,
might really be like.

But although Every Day Except Christmas won a Grand Prix at the Venice Film
Festival in 1958, no commercial studio darted forward to offer Anderson
work. Instead, he joined Devine and Richardson in directing plays at the Royal
Court before making his debut feature film, an adaptation of David Storey's
This Sporting Life in 1963. For his part, Reisz turned to making advertisements
for Independent Television before moving on to full-length films with Saturday Night and Sunday Morning in 1960. After three years, the great Free Cinema
experiment had run its course and in March 1959 commemorated its own
demise with another fuzzily-defined manifesto. Like the first, it was couched
in tones of uppity defiance: 'In making and presenting these programmes, we
have tried to make a stand for independent, creative film-making in a world
where the pressures of conformism and commercialism are becoming more

personal every day. We will not abandon these convictions, nor the attempt to put them into action.'[11]

Yet the movement, if not its ethics, fizzled out partly because mainstream cinema had recognised the market potential of the new post-war writing. The film version of Kingsley Amis's *Lucky Jim*, however, premiered amid trumpeting publicity at the Edinburgh Festival in August 1957, proved an embarrassingly false start. Amis had little to do with the film, which was produced by the Boulting Brothers whose past successes included a faithful transference to the screen of *Brighton Rock*, Graham Greene's darkly atmospheric tale of a teenage delinquent and the murky underworld of the south coast seaside resort. But *Lucky Jim*, adapted by the humorist Patrick Campbell in the style of a conventional light-hearted romp and starring a miscast Ian Carmichael, was generally considered, and certainly by Amis himself, a momentous failure.

Instead, the first indications of cinematic renewal came in *Room at the Top*, an adaptation of John Braine's novel produced by the Romulus studio, directed by Jack Clayton and starring Laurence Harvey as Joe Lampton and the French actress, Simone Signoret, as Joe's lover, Alice. Breathlessly advertised as 'a savage story of lust and ambition', it opened on 22 January 1959, a few weeks in advance of Free Cinema's demise and marched into the nation's cinemas brandishing an enticing X certificate.[12] This was a rating awarded by the British Board of Film Censors prohibiting those under sixteen years old from witnessing what was unblushingly trailed as the 'unblushingly frank' sexual activity on the screen.[12] Once again, Anger became notorious and, according to the critic and film historian Alexander Walker, *Room at the Top* became 'the first important *and successful* film to have as its hero a youth from the post-war working class.'[13]

The northern provincial setting, a central character motivated by financial and physical greed, the use of sex as a means of social advancement, and the sexual explicitness – though demure by later standards – were new and provocative, while Susan's evident pleasure after she and Joe make love on a river bank: 'Oh, Joe, wasn't it super, wasn't it simply super!' marked the first time, according to Walker, that a woman in a British film had referred to the sexual act so candidly.[14] That *Room at the Top* portrayed a society and a morality wholly alien to some metropolitan critics is evident from the anonymous review in *The Times*, which asserted that Joe Lampton was 'more of a cad than a card' and rebuked Leddesford's 'upper set, or whatever they call themselves' for displaying 'the most deplorable manners . . .' 'Still,' added the reviewer with evident distaste, 'perhaps such people exist . . .'[15] Other newspapers, such as the *Evening Standard*, made the most of the film's quickening reputation as a potent cocktail of money and sex. *Room at the Top*, advised the paper, was a sensational story of 'brass and brassières'.[16] Penelope Houston, on the other hand, in the more discriminating *Sight and Sound*, the magazine of the British Film Institute, declared that 'it has the impact of genuine innovation: a new subject, a new setting, a new talent.'[17] This was a view with which many of the American critics, who shared little of *The Times*' dislike of the characters, concurred. *The Saturday Review*

observed that they 'connive, commit adultery like recognizable (and not altogether unlikable) human beings. And the effect is startling. One feels a whole
new chapter is about to be written in motion-picture history.'[18]

This prelude to 'a whole new chapter' had cost £280,000 to make. Simone
Signoret's performance and Neil Paterson's screenplay won American Academy
Awards in 1959, and the film's success augured well for the film version of *Look
Back in Anger*, which opened four months later on 28 May 1959. Filmed, like
Lucky Jim and *Room at the Top* in black-and-white, it was both Tony Richardson's
first feature and Woodfall's first production.

The omens certainly looked favourable when Richard Burton agreed to play
Jimmy Porter. Dark-haired and handsome, Burton was then thirty-two, three
years older than Osborne, and his dashing performances as Prince Hal and
Henry V at Stratford and as Hamlet and Coriolanus at the Old Vic, had established him as one of the star actors of the moment. Opposite Burton, Mary
Ure was contracted to recreate the role of Alison, while Claire Bloom was
cast as Helena. Mostly as a result of Burton's involvement, Saltzman managed
to squeeze £250,000 out of the American Warner Brothers corporation and
Associated British-Pathé, a British company in which Warners owned a part
interest, a surprisingly high production budget for a film that Warners privately
regarded as having little commercial potential.

At Curzon Street, Richardson launched himself into the enterprise determined to put Free Cinema principles into action and create something
specifically for the screen instead of simply filming a stage performance. This
necessitated Osborne's original script being extensively rewritten to include
outside locations and additional characters. Wary of the technicalities of film,
Osborne was reluctant to write the screenplay and Richardson turned instead
to Nigel Kneale. It was a propitious choice, as *The Quatermass Experiment*, Kneale's
science-fiction thriller for BBC Television, was widely considered one of the
finest small-screen dramas yet made. Armed with Kneale's screenplay (with
'additional dialogue by John Osborne'), Richardson took the cameras outside
the Porters' attic flat and into a provincial townscape of morose faces, hard
work, run-down pubs and pouring rain. Following an opening sequence
that echoes *Momma Don't Allow*, in which Jimmy plays the trumpet with Chris
Barber's Band at a jazz club, Richardson filmed scenes at the market at which
Jimmy has his sweet stall, and where he defends an Asian stallholder, the
victim of racial prejudice. This allowed Jimmy a social conscience and would
have been highly topical to an audience watching the film in the aftermath of
the race riots in Nottingham and Notting Hill during the summer of 1958.
Matching the bleakness of the Porters' attic with the dreariness of the urban
Welfare State, Alison awaits news of her pregnancy at a dismal National
Health Service surgery while Jimmy maintains a lone vigil at the hospital
bedside of Mrs Tanner. The outside locations, comprising establishing shots
in Derby, the market scenes at Deptford Market and other scenes at Dalston
Junction, give a rough-and-ready edge to a film that capitalises far more than

the stage version on contemporary life: youth, jazz, the generation gap and the increasing awareness of racial tension.

It was while *Look Back in Anger* was shooting in 1958, a year after his marriage to Mary Ure and while he was continuing an intermittent affair with Francine Brandt, that Osborne encountered Jocelyn Rickards, who was designing the film's costumes. Small and dark, with wide, clear green eyes, she was an Australian, the daughter of Albert, a businessman, and Gertrude, his wife, known perhaps inevitably to their friends as Bert and Gert. Having studied at art school in Sydney, she had arrived in London to become a painter and a designer. When she met Osborne, she was thirty-four and inhabited a world of intellectuals and artists, a world of bohemian ease centred upon her flat in Eaton Square and which Osborne found a comforting contrast to the emotional combat zone of Woodfall Street. She could also name some influential lovers, including the philosopher A. J. 'Freddie' Ayer, the novelist Graham Greene, and a fellow Australian, the fashion photographer Alec Murray. It was a roll-call that, as Mary began rehearsals for *Othello* at Stratford, playing a 'disconcertingly argumentative' Desdemona opposite Paul Robeson, Osborne lost little time in joining.[19] According to Rickards, he did so as the last London 'peasouper' fog shrouded the streets beyond her Belgravia windows.[20]

CHAPTER 15

The Battle of Cambridge Circus

WHILE SITTING BENEATH the sun at Montego Bay in February 1958, Osborne had picked up the script of *Love in a Myth or, An Artificial Comedy*, the play he had begun on the *Egret* while waiting for *Look Back in Anger* to be produced. Working to the sound of the steel band drifting from the beach, he turned it into a musical.

This was a mistake. The original script appears not to survive, but, doodling away on the houseboat, two years previously, he had imagined *Love in a Myth* as a light comedy of manners, a glance, perhaps, towards the kind of drawing-room comedy in which he had appeared many times as a repertory actor, which implies a delicacy of touch Osborne did not then possess. In transforming it into *The World of Paul Slickey*, he concocted instead a theatrical strip-cartoon with songs, a not particularly stylish and often petulant satire of the world of the newspaper gossip columnist.

By now, Osborne had learned to treat the press with considerable circumspection. While he was still courted by editors for his contributions on matters topical and literary, the persistent interest of diarists and gossip-columnists, particularly those writing in the *Daily Mail* and the *Daily Express*, in his personal affairs increasingly irked him. His divorce from Pamela, relationship with Mary, his changes of address and his estimated earnings, even the colour of his ties and the cut of his suits, were the subject of front-page news. While his long-distance affair with Francine Brandt and his closer-to-home relationship with Jocelyn Rickards would continue for some months yet, both were liaisons the Angry Young Man did not want to see featured in the press. The *Spectator* episode had signalled a disturbing new spirit of intrusiveness, while a remark by a *Daily Mail* diarist in which he was bizarrely described as 'the original teddy boy' had piqued him to the extent of his threatening court action before the paper published an apology.[1]

It was with tremendous relish, therefore, that he set about impaling gossip columnists on the point of his pen. The central character of *The World of Paul Slickey* is Jack Oakham, the editor of the *Paul Slickey* diary column in the *Daily*

Racket. Writing in *Queen* magazine, then known as 'the Bible of the Chelsea Set', Penelope Gilliatt revealed that Slickey's name was a crude amalgamation of *Paul Tanfield,* the *Daily Mail* gossip column edited by Alan Gardner, 'a florid little man whose professional colleagues follow his activities with feelings of awe, disgust and envy', and of *William Hickey,* the *Daily Express* diary edited by Peter Baker, whose jaw had reputedly once been broken by a man irate at being featured in his column. Tanfield and Hickey were each served by an undercover army of informers prowling London society parties and the more expensive foreign holiday resorts, earning up to £40 a week by reporting the antics of minor royalty and the privileged, the wealthy, the eccentric and the adulterous. 'What Hickey likes more than anything else', explained Gilliatt, 'is the sight of the rich at play; to pick his way among the oily limbs on a beach in the south of France arouses him to ecstasy.' Tanfield, on the other hand, 'has an insatiable appetite for marriages going wrong, jobs being lost, children behaving callously to their declining parents and second-rate stars having rows with film directors. If Hickey ever wrote a book, it would be called *Success;* Tanfield's would be called *Failure.*'[2]

Osborne sketched out a convoluted plot in which Oakham is dispatched to Mortlake Hall, where his father-in-law, the elderly Lord Mortlake (who does not realise that Oakham is Slickey), is apparently dangerously ill. Under the terms of his trust, the old man must live for a further two years if his family are to escape death duties and his children safely inherit his money. The *Daily Racket,* however, suspects that Mortlake is already dead and that the family are concealing this from the tax authorities. Meanwhile, Oakham's marriage to Lesley is disintegrating and he is conducting affairs not only with his secretary but also with Deirdre, his sister-in-law, who is married to Michael Rawley, a Member of Parliament who is himself involved in an affair with Lesley. All four agree that the only way to escape this marital confusion is to undergo a sex-change operation. Into this complicated scenario Osborne wedged Gillian Giltedge-Whyte, a debutante; Terry Maroon, a pop singer; and Father Evilgreene, a reprobate priest whose eccentric conducting of Mortlake's eventual funeral service is accompanied by jiving dancers singing 'You Can't Get Away with It'.

Happily discharging volleys of grapeshot at any target that happened to come within range, Osborne attacked hypocrisy and material ambition, sniped at organised religion, scorned the wealthy who complained that income tax was too high, derided the supporters of hunting and anti-ban-the-bomb demonstrators, and in 'Bring Back the Axe', composed a satirical song in support of capital punishment. This, at least, was topical, for although it was highly controversial, death by hanging was still the sentence for murder, and the debate over whether or not to retain it was being ferociously contested in the Conservative Party, the only political party not to unanimously call for its abolition. The death penalty remained in force until 1965. The show was all good fun, Osborne breezily announced to the press, a story about modern people in a modern, mad world.

Even so, it was just a little early in the century for satire. At the end of the 1950s, Britain still remained a largely deferential country, its contentment nourished by slowly increasing prosperity, like a greenhouse marrow warming in the sun. Salaries and consumer spending had not been so buoyant for many years, and with everything pointing towards an economic boom, Harold Macmillan, the Conservative Prime Minister who had succeeded Sir Anthony Eden in 1957, felt confident enough to assert: 'Most of our people have never had it so good.'[3]

Although more people could look forward to owning a telephone, a television and a washing machine, Britain remained a country largely ordered by social class, accent, education and wealth. In the theatre, on television and the wireless, comedy was an amiable business that did not seek to prick the national conscience. The sabre of satire would not flash its blade until 1960, when four Oxbridge undergraduates, Jonathan Miller, Alan Bennett, Peter Cook and Dudley Moore, took their Beyond the Fringe revue to the Edinburgh Festival and subsequently to the West End. The satirical journal, Private Eye, amateurishly printed, did not appear until a year later and the BBC had yet to launch the topical revue That Was the Week that Was. Yet satire is frequently an Establishment business. Being a member of a club legitimises one's right to mock it. Many of the Sixties satirists emerged from public schools and the old universities and were in close proximity to the people and the institutions they ridiculed. Seen in this light, John Osborne was an outsider, and in the 1950s these things still mattered. The World of Paul Slickey was critically and publicly disparaged because it was not very good, but perhaps also because it was written by an author who was not a natural member of the Establishment it sought to satirise.

The first scent of foreboding came when Devine refused to stage the play. Neither did Richardson think much of it. Shocked and hurt at the hand that had fed him being so peremptorily withdrawn, Osborne decided to take The World of Paul Slickey elsewhere and turned to Donald Albery, who had produced George Dillon in the West End, who promised a theatre and a budget, and engaged Christopher Whelan, a virtually unknown composer recommended by Margery Vosper, to write the score. Whelan promised a lively mix of jazz, jive and pop, the music of the moment that was tentatively making its way from espresso bars, dance halls and clubs and on to the West End stage. Wolf Mankowitz's Expresso Bongo, a limp British pop musical charting the rise to stardom of a bongo player, and Leonard Bernstein's sassier, sturdier West Side Story, with its vibrant jazz-influenced score, had just opened in London and both were doing well. Musicals in general were perennially popular: arriving from New York almost on the same ship as West Side Story, Lerner and Loewe's more orthodox My Fair Lady, with Julie Andrews and Rex Harrison heading the cast, was currently packing them in at Drury Lane. However, Albery had taken on a considerable gamble in that The World of Paul Slickey was a satire, albeit by the foremost Angry Young Man, that its composer was unknown and that in the absence of Tony Richardson, Osborne was directing the show himself.

This uncertain combination, however, did not deter actors' agents, who bombarded Osborne with recommendations of their clients' vocal talents and ingenious footwork. Actors who Osborne had encountered in the past called to remind him of how well they had got on, while others, admitting their entire lack of musical experience, assured him they were even now learning to sing and dance. Anxious queues formed at his auditions: among them, and singing for the title role, was a then-unknown Sean Connery, whom Osborne turned down. Yet in the light of what would happen over the following few weeks, not being in The World of Paul Slickey might arguably have been seen as a more judicious career move. Osborne eventually settled in favour of Dennis Lotis for the central role, a thirty-two-year-old South African and a former electrical engineer who had arrived in Britain nine years previously to try his luck as a singer. 'Sinatra-sized but Perry Como-styled,' Lotis had won a loyal following by singing with the Ted Heath Orchestra, and two years earlier, in 1957, had been voted Britain's favourite male singer by the annual poll of Melody Maker readers.[4]

Arriving for rehearsals on 9 March 1959, Lotis encountered actors from the Royal Court and elsewhere, as well as a venerable couple from the Edwardian theatrical heyday returning, like Colonel Redfern and his wife, to a new and bewildering world. Marie Lohr, whose stage career had begun in 1894 when she was four years old and who had appeared with such august actor-managers as the Kendals and Beerbohm Tree, had claimed the role of Lady Mortlake, while Harry Welchman, a veteran musical comedy star, had agreed to play her questionably deceased husband. This was something of a coup in itself, but Osborne had also assembled a remarkably impressive production team. Kenneth McMillan, a former dancer quickly gaining a reputation as an inventive choreographer at the Royal Ballet, was supervising the dancing; Jocelyn Rickards, fresh from the film of Look Back in Anger, was overseeing the wardrobe, and Hugh Casson, the celebrated architect and Professor of Interior Design at the Royal College of Art, was busily designing the stage sets.

But almost immediately, Osborne became bogged down in a quagmire of his own making, struggling to master the art of direction and maintain the momentum of rehearsals while at the same time watching over the choreography and the music. Progress became so erratic that Albery took fright and withdrew from the production altogether. Suddenly landed with neither a producer, nor the budget and the theatre that came with him, Osborne desperately searched elsewhere until, with the good luck that often seemed to come his way when he most needed it, he ran into David Pelham, a former assistant of David Merrick. Eager to make a name for himself in London, Pelham agreed to take on the show and, with the passion of the converted, industriously set about promoting it as 'a frothy, delicious soufflé'.[5] Leaping to the telephone with Saltzman-like fervour, he recruited an improbable team of three investors to re-inflate the production to the tune of £28,000. There was Leon Hepner, a furniture manufacturer whom Pelham persuaded to make his first excursion into show business; Cedric Levitt, a man with an indifferent entrepreneurial record in films, and Gilda Dahlberg, the jewellery-bedraped widow of an American industrialist with money to burn and who installed herself in a suite at the Dorchester from where she regularly summoned the author to give him the benefit of her theatrical advice. Osborne prudently decided not to invest any money of his own, having resolved never to back any of his own horses.

'What's Osborne up to behind those closed doors?' wondered the Daily Mail. 'Is fresh triumph in store for the author of Look Back in Anger? Or . . . will he stumble in the pitfalls of musical comedy and become a spectacular cropper?'[6] Indeed, several of the actors, fearful of exactly that, were petitioning the author for cuts and re-writes. So was the Lord Chamberlain. Osborne refused the former and attempted to placate the latter while pressing ahead in the feverish faith that conviction and effort would overcome all. In this, he was encouraged by the resilient optimism of Jocelyn Rickards, with whom, after rehearsals had finished for the day, he regularly reviewed progress, and by Pelham's battle-plan of a West End opening in May after an experimental three-week warm-up tour in Bournemouth, Brighton and Leeds.

In April, therefore, the Slickey company arrived at their first stop in Bourne-mouth. A south coast resort famed for its ageing population of retired colonels and their wives, palm court orchestras and family hotels, the natural home of Agatha Christie detective plays and whist drives, Bournemouth bristled with Conservatism. Osborne installed himself in his suite at the Royal Bath Hotel on the seafront, with Jocelyn in a room on the floor above, and was later snapped by a trailing press photographer, lying lankily on a deckchair in the municipal gardens, an open newspaper covering his face against the sun. The World of Paul Slickey, the paper informed him, was 'not just another show. Its fate affects a theatrical phenomenon of the 'fifties, the Osborne legend.'[7] Two days later at the Pavilion Theatre, the theatrical phenomenon, with Jocelyn at his side, looked about him at the audience who had scurried through the rain for the first night.

'Bournemouth gasped as it saw them,' noted David Nathan of the Daily Herald. The collective sharp intake of breath by Bournemouth's great and good was provoked not by the notorious, and married, Angry Young Man appearing in public with his latest mistress, but a love scene on the stage. In an era during which stage passion was conventionally conveyed by a fully clothed couple briefly clasping each other while remaining standing and preferably well away from the furniture, the spectacle of Deirdre Rowley 'dressed in a slip and riding breeches and [Jack Oakham] in trousers and a singlet – lying in an embrace on a bed' was provocative indeed, the kind of steamy stuff that Tennessee Williams or films such as Room at the Top went in for.[8] It was also a flagrant contravention of the demands issued only the previous day by the Stable Yard censors, who insisted that Oakham and Deirdre must sit, not lie, on the bed, remain 'fully clothed . . . and Deirdre's slip must be in her breeches.'[9]

As the performance progressed, added Nathan approvingly, 'angry old Tories sat shocked' as 'angry young man John Osborne toppled their institutions and idols.'[10] Unfortunately, the audience appeared unaware of Osborne's intended satire, the song calling for the return of the executioner's axe being greeted with enthusiastically approving cries of 'Hear! Hear!' from the more reactionary elements entrenched in the stalls.[11] There had been hopeful speculation among the local press that the sight of Father Evilgreene jiving his way through Lord Mortlake's requiem might incite audience revolt; a performance the critic from *Dancing Times* would later describe as 'a nightmare ritual taking the form of a rowdy alcoholic rock'n'roll orgy' led by a 'cigar smoking clergyman [wearing] a garment more like a tutu than a surplice.'[12] But despite 'regular first nighter' Lady Cobham pronouncing that 'Mr Osborne's attitude to the church is tantamount to blasphemy', a thorough search after the curtain failed to locate a churchman prepared to comment upon the 'controversial coffin scene' with 'cavorting bearers' and a 'pervert priest'.[13] With Fleet Street alacrity, however, the man from the *Star* had positioned himself in the foyer and was eagerly filling his notepad with the condemnation of 'respectable citizens' filing out of the theatre. 'I thought the whole thing was dreadful,' cried one. 'Give me the potted palms of Bournemouth to these angry young men.'[14]

A few nights later, Oscar Beuselinck turned up to inspect his client's latest theatrical venture and took the opportunity to observe at close quarters the arctic relationship between Osborne and Mary Ure, who had joined her husband at the Royal Bath Hotel, and Jocelyn Rickards. At the hotel after the performance, the party of four entered the lift. When it reached the Osbornes' floor, the doors opened. Nobody moved. After a few tense, silent moments, during which Osborne stared into the middle distance, Mary got out and the doors closed. The lift continued upwards to the floor where Jocelyn had her own room and where Osborne also got out and wished Beuselinck goodnight. The lawyer was 'astonished. John Osborne could be very cruel, but that was one of the cruellest things I ever saw him do,' he remembered, marvelling at Mary's 'dignity'; 'she had done nothing to deserve being treated like that.'[15]

*   *   *

Osborne's week in Bournemouth proved to be the opening round of what was to be a progressively more bruising experience. During the following two weeks on tour to Brighton and Leeds, he was assailed by local critical disdain, pelted with audience derision, implored for re-writes from the cast and deluged with letters from theatre-goers especially incensed by the sight of the 'jiving priest'. 'I can only hope that the funeral of someone close to you is conducted in the same disgraceful manner', wrote one infuriated correspondent.[16] But 'if you are shocked by *The World of Paul Slickey* you are shocked by life', countered Kenneth Robinson in the *Church of England Newspaper*, which surprisingly emerged as Osborne's first ally. The production presented 'a series of honest pictures of the world we live in,' Robinson added, 'and one of [its] best characters is the jiving clergyman . . . I don't know why so many people have been offended by this.'[17] Other well-wishers emerged from *Slickey's* audiences, offering tips against an otherwise certain London catastrophe. All the show required, advised one, was total re-writing. Everything should go and be replaced with 'a broad, simple story line and fewer characters.'[18] But: 'Mr Osborne's latest startler is far from being the horror it is painted', argued a theatre-goer from Worthing. The World of Paul Slickey had been widely 'calumnied, castigated and near-crucified', she wrote, but 'Expresso Bongo was much worse.'[19] Yet, like an intensively besieged military commander, Osborne grimly hung on to his dugout position: 'I believe in this show', he cried, 'as I believe in everything I do.'[20]

Even though publicity was the one thing that The World of Paul Slickey did not lack, Pelham had arranged for the London opening at the Palace Theatre in Cambridge Circus, where The Entertainer had played eighteen months previously, to be well advertised in advance. Moreover, a long list of eminent names had been invited to the first night on 5 May, many of whom, either impervious to or intrigued by the provincial warnings, actually turned up. Looking around the stalls, Osborne and Pelham noticed Noël Coward, John Gielgud, Cecil Beaton, Michael Foot, the editor of Tribune, Aneurin Bevan, and John Profumo, the Conservative Secretary of State for War, soon to be embroiled in his own difficulties with gossip columnists fascinated by his liaison with a nightclub hostess linked to a Soviet Naval Attaché. George Devine was there, as well as a phalanx of critics and journalists. High in the balcony sat an intimidating gathering of Gallery First Nighters, a band of theatre enthusiasts who attended most West End premieres, queuing for the cheaper seats and led by a large, late middle-aged and irritable Cockney known as Sophie, the mere mention of whose name struck terror into the hearts of many playwrights. In the tradition of Rattigan's Aunt Edna, the First Nighters 'knew what they liked' and their loudly voiced approval or censure during the performance could set the tone of the evening.

Within minutes of the curtain going up, it was from the balcony and from Sophie's wreath of supporters that the first growls of irritation came, like a wind whipping up before a storm. By the second act the squall was gusting alarmingly through the circle to the stalls. As the cast sang of axes falling, as dancers jived and a priest shimmied, as adultery was celebrated and sex-changes contemplated, gales of protest from the audience almost equalled the sound from the stage. The clack-clack of seats tilting back as loudly complaining ticket-holders began pushing their way out of the theatre, added to the chaos. At the final curtain, the National Anthem, re-orchestrated to include a loud, defiant raspberry played on the trombone, provoked howls of derision while the cast took their curtain call to a fusillade of boos and contemptuous whistling, 'the most raucous note of displeasure', observed the critic Milton Shulman, 'heard in the West End since the war.'[21]

Sitting in the stalls, Aneurin Bevan 'bowed his head and put his hands over his ears' as pandemonium erupted around him and from the stage the actress playing Lesley Oakham retaliated by mouthing 'four naughty words' towards the balcony. 'The forward rows of the Debrett and show business audience heard them,' chided the Daily Mail. 'Noël Coward, the Duke of Bedford, Aneurin

Bevan could have heard . . .'[22] Coward, however, did not flinch. Instead, he remained sitting bolt upright in his seat much in the manner of the implacable naval captain he had played during the war in the film of In Which We Serve. 'Never in all my theatrical experience,' he recorded later in his diary, 'have I seen anything so appalling . . . Bad lyrics, dull music, idiotic, would-be-daring dialogue – interminable long-winded scenes about nothing, and above all the amateurishness and ineptitude, such bad taste that one wanted to hide one's head.'[23] Coward, who had seen and admired Look Back in Anger in New York, concluded that the Osborne comet, once blazing so brilliantly, had now fallen to the earth with an inglorious thud. The World of Paul Slickey revealed the so-called Angry Young Man to be 'no leader of thought or ideas' but instead 'a conceited, calculating young man blowing his own trumpet.'[24] Coward never-theless retained an actor's sympathy for the performers, the following morning dispatching a generous telegram to Dennis Lotis. 'Congratulations on a charm-ing performance', he wrote, 'in very trying circumstances.'[25]

Circumstances for Osborne, however, had become even more trying. Stand-ing in the wings during the curtain calls, he had reportedly burst into tears; the strain, it was assumed, was overwhelming. Someone warned him that a restive crowd of snarling ticket-holders was already massing at the stage door. When the offending dramatist emerged, it swooped upon him 'like a lynching mob', jostling and shouting.[26] Dodging through the scrum, Osborne sprinted up Charing Cross Road, the crowd in baying pursuit, until he managed to scramble into a luckily passing taxi and was safely carried away to Woodfall Street and home. The escapade later became one of his favourite anecdotes: 'I must be the only playwright this century to have been pursued up a London street by an angry mob,' he calculated proudly.[27] The following morning, he awoke to find the critics united in a Greek chorus of reproach. 'The ordeal lasts for three boring hours,' complained the Manchester Guardian. '. . . extraordinary dullness,' concurred The Times. Osborne has begun 'to slosh at everything he does not like,' related The Daily Telegraph, 'including a dragged-in tasteless jibe at religion (which earned him a loud burst of booing . . .)'. On Sunday, Harold Clurman in the Observer claimed that 'Osborne has been his own worst enemy . . . To satirise everything at once is futile as well as excessive.'[28]

At lunchtime on the day after the first night, the embattled playwright, 'a pale face above a red tie', appeared at the theatre, where Pelham had hastily arranged a retaliatory press conference. 'Smoking a thin, seven-inch cigar', from which the Daily Herald spotted that he had not removed the band ('pre-sumably one of his anti-Establishment attitudes'), Osborne proclaimed that the critical assault was exactly what he had expected from London theatre review-ers, 'none [of whom] has the intellectual equipment to judge my work.' First night audiences, he declared, 'bear no relation to real audiences . . . They are a bunch of professional assassins.'[29] Hovering beside him on the theatre steps, David Pelham promised: 'I still think [the production] can make money.'[30]

Within a couple of days, he had come up with a survival strategy based upon the principle of attack being more effective than defence. *The World of Paul Slickey* would be enlisted as a tool in the proletarian class struggle. All their hopes now lay with the Labour Party and the trade unions. If Tories and the middle classes jeered *Slickey*, he reasoned, then surely socialists and the working classes would cheer. In fact, they were already doing so. The evidence was in the *Daily Herald*, a newspaper supporting the Labour Party and in which Michael Foot was bathing *Slickey* in a rosy anti-capitalist glow. 'Osborne attacks the whole works,' he enthused, 'the whole caboodle, "the mechanics of success", the whole stuffy post-war attempt – assisted by the bright boys of Fleet Street – to restore a British society that is faded and done and drenched in hypocrisy and phoney values. Heavens above,' he exhorted, 'let them look at themselves, the pious men of Suez, the pinheaded champions of nuclear complacency, the immortal emasculators of freedom, the capital punishers with their saintly eyes fixed on the popularity polls and the whole apparatus of gossip column and television tomfoolery that helps to keep them in power. Yes, take a look through John Osborne's savage but compassionate eyes.'[31] And if more compelling evidence were needed, here was *Tribune*, the socialist weekly, also weighing in behind *Slickey* and lauding Osborne for giving 'the British ruling class . . . the theatrical trouncing of its life.' There had never been another production, declared Mervyn Jones, with 'a tenth of the originality, the punch, the sheer cleverness' of *The World of Paul Slickey*.[32]

This was extravagant, arguably preposterous praise, but with the alliance of the *Church of England Newspaper* and the socialists on their side, Pelham seized the day and plunged remorselessly onwards. 'I think we can win,' he cried.[33] Instead of being smothered, the dismal verdicts of the daily press were bruited abroad as the terrified cries of reactionaries in retreat. Appealing for the support of *Tribune* readers, Pelham unleashed a barrage of advertisements promising that: '"THEY" don't like it, but YOU will!'[34] *Tribune* rallied to the cause. '*Slickey: The Argument Rages*', blared its front page on 5 June, while its correspondence columns pulsed with views both for and against. 'We have needed a musical like this for a very long time, and the critical butchery visited upon it is probably the surest index of the rightness of Osborne's statement concerning the sickness of our society,' confirmed a reader from Leeds.[35] Yet the scriptwriter Ted Willis, who confessed himself 'pre-disposed in favour of *Slickey*', lamented that the writing was 'appalling' and an opportunity had been squandered. 'There is not one worthwhile human being in it,' he objected, and because of this, the production was both 'negative and destructive' when viewed from 'the socialist viewpoint'.[36] But 'Osborne's view is that of a large and growing number of people,' countered a second correspondent from Leeds. 'It's still a rotten world and it's rotten for exactly the same reason that we thought worth protesting about . . . twenty years ago.'[37] But with *Slickey* losing money daily, Pelham fired off a distress call in a further frantic attempt to lure audiences. An 'SOS to the Labour Party' was urgently transmitted from the Palace Theatre, in which tickets at embarrassingly reduced prices were offered to groups of trade unionists. '"Workers UNITE", cries an ailing Slickey', trumpeted the Daily Herald, almost hoarse with desperation. 'Roll up . . . all those transport workers. Forward the miners.'[38]

But Herald and Tribune readers remained at home, the transport workers failed to be transported and the miners stayed resolutely in the coalfields. Elsewhere in the West End, My Fair Lady was well on its way to making over £100,000 a year. But with audiences dwindling and weekly running costs of almost £4,000, The World of Paul Slickey, Osborne's first West End premiere, closed after only six weeks, the Battle of Cambridge Circus ending, like the ill-fated Saga, in the defeat of financial loss. And this time, there was no telephone call from David Merrick in New York, demanding Osborne's immediate presence on Broadway. The show has never been revived, and neither has the music, which the Telegraph thought 'nearly always pleasant', been recorded.[39] Dennis Lotis, though, emerged from the debris to resume a successful singing career with the Ted Heath Orchestra, surviving the musical innovations of the 1960s and several years later opening an antiques shop. As for Sean Connery, that is another story.

For Osborne, flight seemed the appropriate response. Hardly had the sounds of the first night denunciation subsided, hardly had the last bundle of unsold programmes been taken away to be pulped, than he turned gratefully to Jocelyn's embrace and escaped with her to France. He therefore missed the film premiere of Look Back in Anger, which opened at the Empire Cinema in Leicester Square on 28 May 1959 in the presence of Princess Margaret. Presumably, she had not been sufficiently offended by Osborne's jibes at the English obsession with the Royal Family, recorded in Declaration and widely publicised elsewhere, to forgo a night out at the pictures. The Royal response to the film is not recorded but in the weeks that followed, the anticipated audiences failed to materialise and it began to struggle at the box office. The capital was in the middle of an unaccustomed early heatwave that lasted a fortnight and Londoners, fearful that this might be only the summer weather they might get, decided to take advantage of it, preferring their gardens and the city parks to a dark and airless cinema. Moreover, the reviews were little more than respectful. After so many Angry Young Man stories in the press and so many touring and provincial productions of Look Back in Anger, Jimmy Porter had ceased to shock and had become instead an irksomely familiar figure. Saltzman, who flew to New York with a print of the film to show the elderly Jack Warner, reasoning that as his company had financed it, he would be interested in seeing the result, had an even less encouraging reception. At Warner's private cinema, the film was looped on to the projector, the lights dimmed and Richardson's jazz club opening flickered on to the screen. After a few moments, Warner shifted in his seat and asked which language the characters were speaking. 'English,' replied Saltzman, helpfully. 'This is America,' grunted Warner, and got up and left.[40]

Meanwhile, Osborne had already crossed the English Channel and was driving through the fields of France with Jocelyn at his side. He was not in the driver's seat of his Buick Sapphire, which remained safely garaged in London, but of another of his swaggering emblems of success: a green open-top Jaguar XK150.

CHAPTER 16

Betrayal

BY THE END OF the 1950s, critical interest in the Angry Young Men as a group had largely evaporated. The publication of Colin Wilson's third book, *The Age of Defeat*, was almost ignored and John Braine's second novel, *The Vodi*, appeared amid rumours that it was so inferior his publishers had been wary of committing it to print. Osborne's professional and private lives, however, seemingly plunging entertainingly into chaos, were commanding voracious press attention that would intensify over the coming years.

There was so much to write about, so many photo opportunities. His escape to France in the company of Jocelyn Rickards in the summer of 1959 proved to be the curtain-raiser to two years of flight in which, dodging from England to France and to Italy, and from London to Kent, first with one lover and then with another while simultaneously keeping a wife at bay, he was pursued by reporters avid for the latest events in the life of 'Britain's original Angry Young Man'.[1] His antics really were irresistible. There was his convoluted love life, the birth of a child, an apparently mad letter to a left-wing newspaper that caused a political sensation, his part in a sit-down demonstration in Trafalgar Square that resulted in a brief imprisonment and, the cherry on the cake, another clandestine flight, with, naturally, yet another lover, this time to a hideaway in the green and leafy English countryside.

*   *   *

Oblivious of the press already tracking their progress, Osborne and Jocelyn sped through France, the local cuisine marking the end of Osborne's *Egret*-assumed vegetarianism, driving past burgeoning vineyards, through secluded hamlets and fishing villages until, crossing the border into Italy, they stopped off at Rapallo, once the home of the novelist, critic and caricaturist Max Beerbohm. At the Inghilterra Hotel in Rome, they caught up on the news from England and from Stratford, where Mary was staunchly maintaining her dignity as one half of a happy marriage, explaining to inquisitive reporters that 'John is utterly exhausted. He's got the feeling, you know, when one simply has to get out of England.' And as far as Jocelyn was concerned: 'She is my oldest, dearest friend. She and John have known each other for years. She was going to Paris – so John said he could give her a lift.' It was just 'one of those theatrical holidays', she added, 'where one partner goes off on holiday – I'm afraid I can't join him – I'm up to my neck in it at Stratford.'² It was a generous but unconvincing gesture, and as reporters resumed the hunt for the elusive duo, the Daily Mail appealed to its readers to consider the strange morality of the modern show business marriage in which it seemed perfectly acceptable for one partner to swan off on holiday without the other. Supposing everyone did it? 'Supposing Osborne wasn't a successful playwright but a milkman? – And supposing his wife Mary wasn't a successful actress but a secretary?'³ Would it make any difference? Would readers write in with their views?

While in Rome, Osborne and Jocelyn were joined by her photographer friend Alec Murray, and together they travelled on to Anacapri and Il Rosaio, a small and sparsely furnished whitewashed villa belonging to Graham Greene, who a couple of years previously had written parts of Our Man in Havana there. But if they were hoping for seclusion, they were disappointed. One evening in the small, dusty piazza nearby, a stalking English press photographer caught them in his sights and snapped. Luckily, Murray was at Jocelyn's side and Osborne a few steps behind them in the potentially incriminating picture that appeared a few days later in several British newspapers. At the same time, thousands of American readers, through the syndicated column of the intrusive diarist Walter Winchell, were being kept up to date with the dramatist's affairs: 'Playwright John Osborne', he advised, 'tells his intimates he has an understanding with his mate not to be concerned about his dates with Jocelyn Rickards.'⁴

When Osborne returned to England in late June it was to discover that his flight from England with a woman who was not his wife was still of such absorbing interest that Woodfall Street was staked out with photographers poised to record his arrival. The accompanying reporters, though, hardly had the time to pull their notebooks from their pockets before he had quickly let himself into Number 15 and firmly closed the door. For the remainder of the summer, apart from a quick dash to Stratford with Nellie Beatrice to see Mary in Othello, he resumed his professional daily routine of devoting his mornings to reading and business matters and his afternoons to writing. By the end of the year he had completed A Subject of Scandal and Concern, his first play for television, based on the true story of George Holyoake. A schoolteacher and socialist lecturer, Holyoake had declared during a speech to the Cheltenham branch of the Social Missionary Society in 1842, that he did not believe in God, and consequently became one of the last men in England to be found guilty and imprisoned for blasphemy. The subject allowed Osborne to again denounce the culpability of the press, for Holyoake's prosecution was the result not of public objection to his atheism, but of a moralising campaign led by the local Cheltenham Herald.

Starring Richard Burton, the play was broadcast by the BBC over a year later on 6 November 1960, by which time Osborne was no longer in residence at Woodfall Street. There had also been a resolution on the Francine front, although as usual it was one that was thrust upon Osborne rather than one of his own making. Despite hosting a gargantuan dinner for various French dignitaries, Harry Saltzman had failed in his bid to have Look Back in Anger shown in competition at the Cannes Film Festival. Instead, the Acapulco Film Festival, 'a banana-republic fiesta with no cultural pretensions', had agreed to screen the film, and Osborne, Saltzman and Tony Richardson flew off for an expenses-paid week in the sun in November 1959.[5]

And it was there, at a beachside shanty-town near Acapulco Bay where they pitched up by tourist speedboat one day, that Osborne encountered Francine again. It was entirely unexpected, and he was astonished that she looked as fit as she did. When he was in New York for the opening of George Dillon, he had discovered that she was struggling against alcohol and drugs and rarely ventured far from her apartment. Once he returned to London, he had asked his accountant to send a substantial cheque, but had heard nothing in reply. And now, suddenly, here she was, looking much as she always had done, asking him to believe that she was married to the much younger man who drove the speedboat and who perhaps had alerted her to the presence of English visitors. What was more, the slovenly family who ran the tawdry beach café were her in-laws. It seemed bizarre, yet she insisted she was happy. They met a few times but there was no revival of their Montego Bay romance: 'We had intruded on her life and it had unsettled her.'[6] Osborne returned to England and never saw her again. Occasionally a report reached him; she had left her husband; she was in New York, or Geneva; but eventually the rumours faded into silence.

*   *   *

A few months later, at the end of February 1960, Mary left for Los Angeles to star opposite Vivien Leigh in Christopher Fry's Duel of Angels, a translation of Jean Giraudoux's Pour Lucrece. Her husband promptly snatched the opportunity to take alternative bed and board with Jocelyn at a house she had rented nearby at 29 Lower Belgrave Street. Moving to Belgravia, traditionally an area favoured by the aristocratic and the wealthy, presented him with only one immediate difficulty: that of finding a new secretary, Helen Henderson, his secretary of two years having taken the opportunity of her employer's defection from Mary to resign.

Osborne was sorry to see her go, but he was happier at Lower Belgrave Street than he had been since living on the Egret. He was now thirty, and for the first time he had relative peace in which to read and write. The house was spacious; there was an upper-floor room that he could use as a study and another adjacent to it in which he could install a new secretary. This was Joan Parker who, like Jocelyn, was an Australian, and who proved remarkably adept at bouncing the telephone enquiries from reporters firmly back into their own court. Osborne was content in his newfound domestic life. Tall and angular with prominent cheekbones, well dressed, his hair bushy and parted on the left side, he struck those who met him as good-natured, at ease and modest in his professional achievements. Occasionally, he and Jocelyn might see friends, but what time they had together would usually be spent reading or, in the evenings, sharing a meal and watching television. Down the road at the Royal Court, meanwhile, puffing apprehensively at his pipe, George Devine was wondering when Osborne might produce another play of the calibre of *The Entertainer*. On 11 March, the *Evening Standard* echoed his thoughts: 'John Osborne is being remarkably quiet just now. What is he up to?'[7]

In fact, he was secluded in his Belgravia study and deep into the first stages of a new play. The film of *The Entertainer*, shot mostly in the Lancashire seaside town of Morecambe with Richardson again directing Olivier, and Nigel Kneale again adapting Osborne's play, would open that summer to respectable reviews, but its author was already a long way from the world of Archie Rice and the seaside beauty contest that had been added to the script. Instead, he had immersed himself in theological complexities. When Osborne told Richardson that the subject of his new play was Martin Luther, the sixteenth-century German religious reformer and architect of Protestantism, the director looked dubious. Osborne had established his dramatic credentials as a chronicler of contemporary malaise; surely an historical epic was rather outside his range? But *Luther*, explained Osborne, was intended neither as historical epic nor biography, but a play about an intellectual rebel, a man who provoked and overcame crises both within himself and the church.

Divided into three acts and twelve scenes, the play follows Luther's career from his entering the Augustinian order of Emerites at Erfurt in 1506 when he was twenty-three, until his middle age twenty-four years later. It encompasses his defiance of the Dominican, Johann Tetzel, who sells indulgences in order to raise money for the Catholic Church, his devising a list of ninety-five theses questioning the authority of the Pope to forgive sins that he nails to the church door at Wittenberg; his refusal to retract; his quarrels with the Papal system and his proclamation at Worms that man will be saved, not by penance or the forgiveness of sins but by a simple, arduous faith in God. Luther is last seen, with his wife and baby son, at the Eremite Cloister at Wittenberg in 1530.

As Bamber Gascoigne later noted in the *Spectator*, the play offers little analysis of the causes either of the subsequent Reformation or Luther's personal magnetism, but instead concentrates upon 'one man's rebellion against the world into which he was born, and his search for a personal understanding of life.'[8] As such, Martin Luther is yet another icon of anguished defiance standing in a thematic line of development from Huw Prosser, Jimmy Porter, Archie Rice and George Holyoake, and which would reach its apotheosis in Bill Maitland in *Inadmissible Evidence* three years later. Osborne's Luther is a self-questioning iconoclast, a man whose uncompromising stand against authority – in his case the

Catholic hierarchy and Papal supremacy – symbolises both his deep faith and the stubborn resilience of the social upstart, the latter being a guise in which Osborne was fond of casting himself.

Yet there were other impulses that brought Osborne to Luther besides a search for a convenient rebel on which to base a play. As a child he had never been taken to church, but had observed the 'tapping feet and meticulous hymn singing' of his paternal grandmother and had 'assumed that being Welsh and believing in God was the darkest heart of religion.'[9] His introduction to the Bible had been in Scripture classes at Ewell School and his youthful conversations with Hugh Berrington, who had been reading *A Serious Call to a Devout and Holy Life* by the eighteenth century Church of England theologian, William Law. 'To my surprise,' remembered Berrington, 'he responded enthusiastically. The mockery element was not always uppermost with him.'[10] Several years later, and alone among critics, Harold Hobson had discerned a spiritual dimension underlying Osborne's writing, which would be sustained through later plays.

Both then and later, Osborne was intrigued if not by religion then by religious experience, and by the reassurance of a fixed moral system, the theological doctrines of faith, sin and redemption, and the discipline and mysticism of religious practice. He knew parts of the Bible well, enraptured, as in his admiration of Jacobean dramatists, by its language as much as anything else. In his writing, he had been careful to separate what he saw as the harsh demands of religious belief from its misinterpretations and abuses by what he saw as an inadequate and deluded clergy. In *Look Back in Anger* Jimmy Porter attacks the fictional Bishop of Bromley for supporting the development of the atomic bomb, as the Bishop of Winchester had done at the Convocation of Canterbury in 1954, declaring that 'it might be better to perish than submit to that parody of civilisation that seems to be the alternative presented from the other side of the Iron Curtain.'[11] In his *Declaration* article, Osborne had denounced elements of the clergy for failing to take 'a firm, unequivocal stand for simple social decency, let alone the Gospel.'[12] In *The World of Paul Slickey*, he had satirised those clergymen attempting to 'modernise' the church in the jiving figure of Father Evilgreene, and in *A Subject of Scandal and Concern*, he had touched on the themes of faith, conscience and action.

In *Luther* he developed this further, while at the same time groping for answers to the confusion of his private life. Luther's espousal of the sanctity of individual conscience and his conviction that salvation is achieved principally through faith rather than by incidental good works, appealed to Osborne's moral sense. Predestination, damnation and salvation were themes he found persuasive. Perhaps this was partly a whim from the Welsh valleys, but the Scots would have recognised a true Calvinist.

In the snugness of Lower Belgrave Street, he contentedly burrowed into Renaissance history and art, into Luther's writings, especially *The Bondage of the Will*, a book he kept on his shelves all his life, and into Erik H. Erikson's psychoanalytical study, *Young Man Luther*. In April 1960, he emerged to catch a train to Huddersfield, his first visit to Yorkshire since *Personal Enemy* was produced in Harrogate in 1955. This time his destination was Mirfield, the Yorkshire outpost of the Anglican Community of the Resurrection.

He was travelling at the recommendation of Father Trevor Huddleston, a former novice-master at Mirfield and now the Prior of the Community's London House in Holland Park. A tall, austere, radical and popular theologian, Huddleston was also a passionate campaigner against the nuclear bomb and the apartheid regime then in force in South Africa, a friend of George Devine and exactly the sort of man whom the latter liked to see settling expectantly into the stalls at the Royal Court. It was Devine who introduced Osborne to Huddleston, who quickly surmised that the dramatist was 'a very spiritual and religious young man' and on hearing of Osborne's interest in Luther, urged him to visit Yorkshire.[13] The former home of an ironmaster, a large, gloomy house of high ceilings and long corridors, Mirfield was home to a community of monks, the world of business and the foundry having been replaced by a life of silent contemplation alleviated by the therapeutic labour of gardening. Nothing intruded upon quiet meditation except the ringing of bells for the various daily offices. It offered Osborne a welcome retreat, but it was also instructive, for it gave him an insight not only into the monastic life, which, knowing he was there for only a week, he rather enjoyed, but also the monastic mind. At the same time, he discovered that Compline, the last of the canonical hours of prayer, provided a spiritually peaceful end to the day. The atmosphere, according to Huddleston, 'had an enormous influence both upon Osborne and upon Luther.'[14] At Mirfield too, he also discovered a resonant theatrical image, that of a monk at prayer.

*   *   *

In the beginning was the image; then came the word. This was the manner in which many of Osborne's plays began: first, a flickering image becoming stronger and more clearly defined; then the sound of voices becoming louder and more strident, and then the characters, pushing themselves forward, demanding his attention. The image of Victor Seaforth as Laughton's Quasimodo led to *The Entertainer*; that of a man isolated in the darkness of dislike would result in *Inadmissible Evidence*; the imagined sequence of a glittering drag ball would materialise into *A Patriot for Me*; and that of an elderly man tormented by his children and paralysed by terror would become Wyatt Gilman in *West of Suez*.

Osborne completed *Luther* at Lower Belgrave Street during the summer of 1960. He wrote, first with a fountain pen and then on a typewriter, for long, concentrated hours until he was satisfied that he had injected a vitality into history by juxtaposing intimate dialogue with passages of high rhetoric, and by creating a language both appropriate to the subject and resonant to the contemporary ear. From Erikson, he had discovered that Luther suffered chronically from constipation, and that Luther's revelation of being flooded by the Holy

Spirit took place not while he was at prayer, but seated upon a lavatory. In Hans, Luther's miner father, he created an outwardly boorish but inwardly good-natured figure perplexed by his son and his calling. Hans is a man whose love Luther both craves and values; perhaps significantly, it is his mother, whom he blames for flogging him ruthlessly, that Osborne's Luther loves less. The play ends on an image of domestic, father–child harmony as Luther, now married, cradles his child in his arms. It is a vision, perhaps, of what Osborne imagined marital happiness to be.

It was a momentous step forward in his writing, and Devine immediately scheduled production for the following year. This time, there was comparatively little opposition from the guardians of public morality at Stable Yard. Although St Vincent Troubridge, the Examiner who read *Luther*, despaired of the 'deplorable concern . . . with bodily functions and motions of the bowels', blue-pencilling several passages, he conceded that Osborne had drawn an appropriate correlation between 'Luther's physical constipation and a state of costiveness induced by the excesses of the R[oman] C[atholic] church.' He therefore permitted the use of such hazardous phrases as 'ripe stool' and the line: 'If I break wind at Wittenberg, they might smell it in Rome', which, he emphasised for the benefit of more doubtful readers of his report, was 'an alleged historical remark'. Luther's description of Henry VIII as 'a mandrill-arsed English baboon' might seem 'rather vivid', yet it was, Troubridge argued, 'justifiable in its context'. The Lord Chamberlain therefore found himself in the unlikely position of wholeheartedly endorsing a John Osborne play. 'During [Luther's] first celebration of Mass as a priest', he wrote, 'comes the uplifting glory of being in direct communion with God . . . with the feeling that all Christian souls should have the benefit of this. As a Protestant, I consider this a magnificent new conception of Luther.'[15]

*   *   *

With the script out of his hands, Osborne turned to the jangled emotional disorder of his marriage to Mary. There had been little communication between them since she had left for Los Angeles in February, but in July he decided to go to America in the hope of engineering some sort of solution to their marital impasse. There was a safeguard of sorts in that both George Devine and Tony Richardson were in town overseeing the American production of Shelagh Delaney's *A Taste of Honey*, a play that had opened at Stratford East in 1958, and which Osborne had very much admired. Osborne joined Mary, who was Richardson's guest at a house in Montana Street, Westwood, which he had rented from Eva Gabor, the Hungarian-born film actress, and which was almost entirely and ostentatiously decorated in shades of ivory and gold. Joan Plowright, who was starring in *A Taste of Honey*, was also a guest in what turned into a disconcertingly mismatched household. Each day, there were visits from local residents and expatriates including Christopher Isherwood, the English-born novelist, and Don Bachardy, his American artist partner. Vivien Leigh, Mary's co-star, from whom Laurence Olivier had requested a divorce in order to marry Plowright, arrived with her new companion, the actor Jack Merivale. Outside the house, silent Asian gardeners poked desultorily at the shrubbery and maintained a vigil over the swimming pool.

A friend of Richardson, the grey-haired, blue-eyed Isherwood recorded in his diary that Mary was 'one of the most loveable people I have met in a long time' and a far more beautiful woman than Marilyn Monroe, with whom she had frequently been compared.[16] On a visit to London, he had also met Jocelyn, who had informed him that 'Mary has "nothing to offer John"', implying, noted Isherwood, 'that she has'.[17] A fascinated observer of this uneasy triangle, Isherwood surmised that Mary's relationship with Osborne, whom he thought 'conceited', was 'undoubtedly masochistic'. 'He doesn't take the trouble to be nice to her,' he noted, 'but I suppose she likes it.'[18] A few days later, on 10 August, Isherwood overheard the Osbornes, both of whom had resorted to drinking too much, in the midst of 'a desperate quarrel'.[19] On the 15th, the warring couple were still growling at each other but: 'Mary luxuriates in scenes.'[20]

Osborne was eager to detach himself and return to London as soon as possible, while Mary, increasingly agitated by his presence, appeared dangerously volatile. One of their most spectacular disputes concluded a fraught evening when Osborne and Mary became increasingly drunk. Sometime after she had apparently retreated to bed, Osborne and Richardson, sitting drinking in the drawing-room, observed the startling apparition of 'a pink shadow' emerge from her room, glide out on to the terrace, 'throw itself into the pool and disappear.' As the sound of a splash subsided into ominous silence, it occurred to Richardson that 'Mary, naked, was trying to drown herself.'[21] In another instance of what his lawyer regretfully considered to be his client's capacity for cruelty, Osborne proclaimed indifference as to what might be happening. It was left to Richardson to dash outside, plunge into the water and haul a gasping, choking Mary out of the pool. A general fracas ensued between Mary and Joan Plowright, who had been awakened by the commotion, and Osborne and Richardson. Eventually, the women withdrew to their rooms and as the dawn light flared over Los Angeles, Osborne and Richardson opened another bottle of champagne.

*   *   *

By the time he flew home, Osborne and Mary had failed to agree either on reconciliation or separation. He briefly joined Jocelyn at Lower Belgrave Street before moving back to the marital home in Woodfall Street in readiness for his wife's homecoming after *Duel of Angels* ended its run. Within weeks of her arrival, however, the emotional deadlock between them was broken, not by any resolution on their part, but by 'the ingenuity of time': in this case, a house fire. During the early hours of 3 January 1961, an electrical fault caused a heater in the living-room to catch fire, causing suffocating smoke to weave through the ground floor of the house and up the narrow stairs. Roused from sleep by the insistent whining of Snoopy, Mary's pet dachshund, and realising that escape by the stairs was impossible, Osborne dragged his wife to a window and thrust her through it to balance precariously on a section of the sloping roof. Within minutes, Woodfall Street was filled with fire engines, their bells clanging, their flashing lights illuminating the houses around them. Scurrying firemen shouted instructions and unravelled hoses; figures hurried this way and that, while neighbours peered anxiously from their windows. A ladder swung upwards, nosing its way towards the roof, hands reached out and Mary and Osborne were lowered to safety. Later, they were reunited with the frightened Snoopy, whose picture appeared in newspapers the following day. While the press celebrated him as a canine hero, his owners discovered that their home, while not irretrievably damaged, was uninhabitable. This at least gave them a way out of their impasse: they would separate and find their own alternative accommodation. While Mary moved into a flat at 35 Cliveden Place, just off Sloane Square, Osborne retreated to the sanctuary of Lower Belgrave Street and a welcome from Jocelyn.

The mystery of why Mary appeared to tolerate her husband's affairs, first with Francine and then with Jocelyn, was resolved when she informed him that she was in the midst of an affair of her own with the actor Robert Shaw, whom she had met eighteen months previously and with whom she was now rehearsing in a revival of Middleton and Rowley's *The Changeling*, due to open at the Royal Court in February. A big man whose intimidating presence made him ideal casting as the villain in a succession of Hollywood films, Shaw was the son of a Scottish general practitioner and bi-polar alcoholic who had committed suicide when his son was eleven years old. Shaw was now thirty-seven and a vigorous drinker whose amiability when sober frequently descended to embarrassing coarseness when drunk. He was also married to Jennifer Bourke, a white Jamaican actress with whom he lived in Kilburn, north London, and by whom he had three young daughters. Now Mary revealed that she too was pregnant. Osborne's deception had been matched by hers. But this would be a year of betrayals, for within a few months, Osborne would deceive Jocelyn just as he had deceived Mary.

*   *   *

In 1956, *Vogue* magazine, the monthly journal of fashion and the fashionable, had decided to risk a flutter of glossy speculation on the events at the Royal Court Theatre. On 3 April, the day after the opening of *The Mulberry Bush*, Osborne and Richardson had walked into a nearby pub to keep an appointment to meet Penelope Gilliatt, one of the magazine's features journalists. Lively and fiercely ambitious, Penelope was strikingly good-looking, slightly built with red hair and cool, pale skin, high cheekbones and dark, shiningly playful eyes. The daughter of Cyril Conner, a prominent lawyer, and his wife Mary, she was born in London on 25 March 1932 and prestigiously educated at Queen's College in Harley Street and Bennington College, Vermont. That day at the pub, Penelope jotted down a few facts about the English Stage Company while Osborne and Richardson were photographed looking as if they were deep in earnest literary conference. The picture, with Penelope's paragraph beneath it, appeared in the 'People are talking about . . .' column in July.

Five years later, and a good many people were talking about Osborne and Penelope. She was now married to Dr Roger Gilliatt, a tall, saturnine neurologist who the previous year, 1960, had acquired a glamour of sorts by becoming the last-minute replacement as best man at Anthony Armstrong-Jones's wedding to Princess Margaret. A photographer, Armstrong-Jones had taken many of the production pictures at the Royal Court for display outside the theatre, including those of Laurence Olivier in The Entertainer. The Royal Court liked influential names. The substitution had been caused by Jeremy Fry, the original incumbent as best man, an architect and member of a family of chocolate manufacturers, being revealed to have been involved in a youthful homosexual scandal, the taint of which, it was decreed in official circles, might besmirch the wedding of the Queen's sister who, following the Peter Townsend saga, should be insulated from anything considered dubious. Roger Gilliatt was a safe alternative choice. He and Penelope lived on the other side of Belgravia from Osborne and Jocelyn, in an impressive, mid-nineteenth-century house in Lowndes Square.

Due to their tentacle-like contacts among a glossily metropolitan inner circle, invitations to the Gilliatts' cocktail parties were highly sought after. Journalists, film, theatre and literary critics, writers, artists and designers, the kind of people who would form fashion and fashionable opinion during the mid-1960s, all appeared at Lowndes Square, and during the first few months of 1961 it was not unlikely that they would bump into John Osborne. The more perceptive might have noticed that, although he was frequently accompanied by Jocelyn Rickards, he was becoming progressively enamoured of his hostess and she of him. 'Whenever he entered a room or spoke to her, she would light up like a one-armed bandit when someone hits the jackpot,' observed Rickards.[22] Osborne was intrigued by Penelope's vivacity and enthusiasm, two qualities he most valued. While 'not yet in love' he simultaneously found himself 'fearful of rejection' by this 'eternal redhead of my spellbound dreams.'[23] At the same time, like Pamela, Mary and Jocelyn before her, Penelope thought him enormously attractive, partly because he represented all that was invigorating and contemporary in the still rather sedate world of English culture.

Their behaviour, as they set about deceiving both the blameless Jocelyn and the irreproachable Roger Gilliatt, was, Osborne conceded later, 'probably grotesquely indefensible.'[24] Their affair was erotically highly charged and developed quickly as snatched meetings escalated into weekends and longer periods away from London. As Penelope had recently become film critic of the Observer, some of their encounters were under the pretext of Penelope's attendance at film festivals. The deception was only partially successful and soon Jocelyn issued an ultimatum. 'I have never loved anyone as profoundly and as deeply as I do you,' she told him, but if she and Osborne were to separate, then the decision must be his.[25] Osborne, as usual, prevaricated. A young man who might justifiably be accused of woeful emotional immaturity and, despite having written Luther, unable to face moral responsibility, Osborne disliked confrontation, hoping, as he again informed Creighton, that everything would somehow work itself out without his interference. The prospect of leaving Jocelyn was as daunting as that of abandoning Penelope and, like extricating himself from Mary, not something that could be done either quickly or easily. His private life was becoming absurd. Jocelyn and Penelope knew both about Mary and each other, while Mary knew about Jocelyn but possibly not yet about Penelope. Roger Gilliatt possibly suspected his wife and certainly knew about Mary and Jocelyn. As Osborne shuttled manically between them, avoiding the neurologist, it was as if a door-slamming French farce was being enacted within a few streets of the Royal Borough of Kensington and Chelsea.

*   *   *

Meanwhile, rehearsals for Luther had begun at the Royal Court at the end of May. Tony Richardson was once again directing, Albert Finney had been prised from the title role of Billy Liar in the West End to play Martin Luther, and George Devine was making his first appearance in a John Osborne stage play. The part of Staupitz, the wise and sympathetic Vicar-General of the Augustinian order of which Luther is a member, had been written with Devine in mind, Staupitz being a father-figure to Luther, as Devine was to Osborne. Their second act exchanges in which Staupitz observes that Luther admires authority but cannot submit to it, and demands a perfection that is unreachable, while Luther muses whether his rebelliousness derives as much from his personal conflicts as theological insight, reflects something of Osborne's view of the relationship between himself and Devine. Like Devine, Staupitz is both protective and encouraging; like Osborne, Luther is trusting but doubtful. Asking for Staupitz's love and blessing, Luther at the end of the play receives the assurances of both.

Having opened at the Theatre Royal in Nottingham on 26 June, the production travelled on to Paris, where it opened in July at the Sarah Bernhardt Theatre as part of the International Theatre Festival. Having taken Jocelyn to the Nottingham opening, Osborne left her in London in order to escort Penelope to Paris, from where the British critics dispatched enthusiastic reports of Luther's reception. It was, pronounced Tynan, 'the most eloquent piece of dramatic writing to have graced our theatre since Look Back in Anger.'[26] In The Sunday Times, Harold Hobson agreed that Luther was 'astonishing', while warning that: 'Christians are very poor hands at recognising Christianity in a drama.' Those 'shocked' by Osborne's physical depiction of Luther, 'a Reformer whose tongue is literally filthy with vomit', should consider 'how movingly, in an aside alive with emotion . . . the Papal Legate defends the unity of the Roman Church', 'the equally touching unemphatic phrases in which Staupitz . . . recalls the piety of many monks', 'the indefatigable and unattractive resolution with which Mr Osborne's Luther, racked with disease and tormented by his imagination, holds blindly and violently on to the path his broken feet have dedicated themselves to tread', and that at the end, the play 'leaves as the last thing in the audience's mind the words of Christ: "A little while and ye shall not see me, and again a little while and ye shall see me", finishing, actually finishing, with a tender and timid hope of immortality.'[27]

The production therefore arrived at the Royal Court on 27 July with all flags flying and all seats sold, a transfer to the Edinburgh Festival scheduled for August and a West End run confirmed at the Phoenix Theatre in Charing Cross Road on 5 September. By dint of Osborne and *Luther*, Devine's 1961 summer season at the Royal Court was financially secure, while the play also revived Osborne's critical fortunes, battered during the *Slickey* fiasco. While not all critics shared the enthusiasm of Tynan and Hobson, Michael Foot, now newly elected as the Labour MP for Ebbw Vale, took the opportunity in *Tribune* to look back in awe at Osborne's five-year career as a London dramatist. 'That a playwright should step with such assurance from his crowded bed-sitting rooms and sleazy music halls on to the stage of world history,' he wrote, 'that he should have the insight to see Luther as much a poet as a prophet; and that he should be able to interweave in the ancient drama his own modern strand of relentless astringency – these are further proofs of greatness, if any still were needed.'[28]

During that warm, dry summer of 1961, Osborne basked in the warmth of critical acclaim. Emotionally, he was as distracted as ever, living at Lower Belgrave Street but suspended between Jocelyn and Penelope, who had now left Roger Gilliatt and moved to a flat in Chesham Place, just off Belgrave Square. Mary, her pregnancy nearing full-term, was meanwhile living alone at Cliveden Place. With the popular press alert to his movements, and to those of Mary, Penelope and Jocelyn, it took little foresight to recognise that when Mary's baby was born, reporters and photographers would be descending upon Lower Belgrave Street. Deciding once more upon flight, Osborne and Jocelyn headed once more for France, Osborne this time driving an Alvis, another new acquisition and a car for which he had an almost unreasonable affection, its cobalt-blue exterior offset by a white leather interior. Their destination was La Beaumette, a stone farmhouse near Valbonne on the Cote d'Azur, which Tony Richardson had rented for the summer. Perched high in dusty hills, secluded among grape vines and lavender hedges, the house was reasonably isolated, its nearest neighbours being a nudist colony, which concealed itself deep within the woods. A few days later, George Devine arrived, teetering on the edge of a work-induced nervous breakdown, accompanied by Jocelyn Herbert. Oscar Beuselinck turned up to join the party, changing into challengingly bright swimming shorts in which to lie beneath the searing sun. On the terrace, playwright and director contemplated Woodfall's next project, a film adaptation of Henry Fielding's novel, Tom Jones, before Richardson headed back to London to supervise Luther's transfer to the West End.

Osborne's bucolic hideaway, however, proved no match for the persistence of Penelope and the determination of the local postman. In London, she wrote extravagantly in praise of Luther in Queen magazine: 'The most eloquent and rigorous play John Osborne has written', which an embarrassed Osborne instructed not to be splashed across the billboards outside the theatre, and each day dispatched a letter by express post that eventually appeared slipped beneath the gate of La Beaumette.[29] Within a few days, her letters arrived not from London but Venice, where she arrived in mid-August to report for the Observer on another film festival. Glittering with newfound love, Penelope's bulletins relayed her accounts of the pell-mell screenings and receptions, and glowed with her anticipation of the wonderful future that she and Osborne would soon share. 'I love you deeply & furiously & with total attention,' she wrote. 'I'm saturated with you & anyone who tried to pacify me would meet pretty stiff redheaded resistance.'[30]

Meanwhile. Osborne's despatches also included an open letter to Tribune, the journal that had supported his views, published his articles, praised his plays and rallied round in vainly attempting to create an audience for The World of Paul Slickey. Political protest that summer was mounting against the threat posed by the atom bomb, and Osborne's letter addressed to the British people, or at least those who read Tribune, consisted of a Porter-style tirade denouncing the government's atomic programme. The resulting explosive controversy would echo far beyond the house journal of the Labour Party and bounce the Angry Young Man once more into national controversy.

Politically, the Angry Young Man had not added up to much so far. And nowadays, at least domestically, there did not seem that much to be worked up about. Social surveys – and social surveys were becoming very popular – concluded that Britain was now a nation of optimists, with more people than ever believing their standard of living was improving, vastly outnumbering those who thought the opposite. Accordingly, in October 1959 the Conservative Party had cruised to its third successive General Election victory with a majority of 98 seats. Yet while the domestic political barometer seemed set on summer, wintry conditions loomed in a mainland Europe divided between a democratic West and a Communist East dominated by the Soviet Union, and where a Cold War of mutual suspicion and surveillance was being played out.

Britain's atomic programme had begun thirteen years earlier in May 1948, when the Labour government announced that in order to remain a prominent power in the post-war world, the country must develop its own hydrogen bomb, thereby maintaining pace with the United States in its race for atomic superiority against the Soviet Union. Britain, the United States and the Soviet Union each embarked upon a testing programme and, in the eyes of many, had recklessly begun a rivalry certain to end in cataclysm. Alarmed by such an appalling prospect, John Collins, Canon of St Paul's Cathedral, had founded the Campaign for Nuclear Disarmament, and at its launch in London on 17 February 1958, over five thousand people were addressed not only by Collins, but an array of worthies including the eighty-six-year-old philosopher Bertrand Russell, the novelist J. B. Priestley and Michael Foot. Here at last was a political question on which the Angry generation could agree. Having come of age during the Second World War and the years immediately afterwards, they now surveyed with quaking apprehension the spectacle of East and West stockpiling fearsome arsenals, and looked on in dismay at the failure of nations to limit, let alone ban, atomic testing. Perhaps there was just one good, brave cause left after all.

*   *   *

Amateurishly but enthusiastically run, CND attracted left- and right-wingers to its cause and quickly became the biggest mass protest movement since that opposing the imposition of the Corn Laws during the 1840s. At Easter 1958, over four thousand demonstrators took part in the first Aldermaston March, walking the forty-six miles from London to Aldermaston, Britain's atomic weapons research centre. It became an annual event, an outing in which a sense of crusade and the certainty of doing good intermingled with the ebullience of a carnival, a way of demonstrating a moral objection to the atomic bomb and having a good day out at the same time. Banners flew, jazz bands played, clowns juggled and protestors sang along to strumming guitars. There were earnest young men and benign young women, turtleneck sweaters and jeans, duffel coats and scarves, parents wheeling their children in pushchairs and delegations from here, there and everywhere, including the Royal Court Theatre, its banner held aloft by George Devine and the poet Christopher Logue. The cameras of Free Cinema circled and swooped and recorded, and the resulting film, March to Aldermaston, was widely shown later in the year.

A close inspection of the marchers, though, would have revealed a curious absence of official Angry interest. Osborne had declined to march, while Kingsley Amis was abroad, having been appointed a Fellow of Creative Writing for a year at Princeton University. Nevertheless, the historian A. J. P. Taylor identified the marchers with the spirit of Jim Dixon, averring in the sympathetic New Statesman that 'some thousands of Lucky Jims' had completed the hike.[31] Kenneth Tynan was technically among them, having appeared at the beginning of the demonstration at Trafalgar Square. Marching, though, was not Tynan's style, and he promptly vanished, only to reappear four days later from a taxi that deposited him at the head of the procession nearing Aldermaston in time to find an advantageous place at the celebratory picnic.

Three years later, the apprehension of many deepened with the building of the Berlin Wall on 13 August 1961. Isolated in Communist East Germany, Berlin, the fulcrum of the Cold War, had been divided since 1945 into four zones, three administered by Britain, the United States and France, and the fourth by the Soviet Union. Each examined the movements of the other through binoculars, long-range lenses and a bristling mass of clandestine observation techniques. As its citizens grimly struggled on under one of the most repressive of Soviet satellite regimes, the East German economy, sagging as a result of a chronic lack of investment, was nearing collapse, and by the beginning of the 1960s, over two thousand refugees a day were arriving in the city's western sector in the hope of a better standard of living. As almost half of the new arrivals were under the age of twenty-five and many had professions and trades useful to the West, East Germany was quickly being drained of its brightest and best young people. In an effort to stop the flow, security forces rapidly constructed a barrier of concrete and barbed wire across the city on the night of 13 August 1961, abruptly sealing off sixty-eight of the eighty crossing places between East and West.

After sixteen years of uneasy peace in Europe, it seemed to many that the inevitable outcome of the apparent intransigence of political leaders in both the East and the West, would again be war. These fears intensified when the United States called for more troops to be dispatched to West Berlin. As tension increased, the British government wavered. In Moscow, the Soviet Prime Minister, Nikita Khrushchev, waited. And at La Beaumette, sitting in the sun amid the lavender and the pine woods, John Osborne picked up pen and paper. Addressing both Conservative and Labour politicians, he fired off what he termed a letter of hate: the words 'hate' and 'hatred' cropping up thirteen times in a comparatively short piece. A deliberately inflammatory flight of hyperbole, written with an intensity reminiscent of that of an Old Testament prophet, he declared that: 'I fear death. I dread it daily. I cling wretchedly to life as I always have. I fear death, but I cannot hate it, as I hate you.' These were 'the men with manic fingers leading the sightless, feeble, betrayed body of my country to its death', and those of his countrymen 'who tolerate you . . . your condoning democratic constituents.' His loathing of the party leaders, Macmillan and Gaitskell, and 'those men of my country who have defiled it', had been roused to a righteous anger. 'You have instructed me in my hatred for thirty years,' he wrote. 'I only hope it will keep me going. I think it will . . . Till then, damn you, England. You're rotting now and quite soon you'll disappear. My hate will outrun you yet . . .' Having signed it, 'in sincere and utter hatred' he popped it in the post to the *Tribune*, where it was opened by Mervyn Jones.[32]

Although a trenchant admirer of Osborne's writing and sympathetic to his views, Jones was 'appalled' by this latest submission. It was, he thought, evidently sincerely felt but it was equally impulsive, ineptly argued and surely 'one of those letters about which you have second thoughts as soon as you've put it in the post.'[33] Passing it to his editor, Michael Foot, he advised that to print it would be detrimental both to the paper and to Osborne's reputation. Foot thought otherwise and published it on 18 August under the imposing heading of *A Letter to My Fellow Countrymen* and complete with Osborne's French address at the end. Daily newspaper journalists whose ears were pricked for the next John Osborne scandal immediately heard the astonished gasp of Tribune readers and realised that this was all good, incendiary stuff. Nothing could be more timely nor certain to incite a convulsion of moral disapproval than the spectacle of the Young Man whose Anger had made him wealthy sneering at his country from the south of France where life, according to the Daily Mail, was 'dedicated to the bikini rather than the H-bomb.'[34]

Suddenly, the Angry Young Man was everywhere again, both earning the nation's cheers and provoking its virulent hostility. What immediately became known as the 'Damn You, England' letter detonated thunderous salvoes of support and volleys of vociferous denunciation across newspaper columns for several days, prompting leaders from such eminent journalists as the Conservative columnist Peregrine Worsthorne, who suggested in the Daily Telegraph that behind 'the murderous language' Osborne's sentiments were 'shared, I believe, by a frightening number of his fellow countrymen', and that 'John Osborne speaks for far more people than we care to realise.'[35] Others, however, were quick to point out that if he did, then they were certainly not among their number. As it was only four months since Yuri Gagarin, the Russian cosmonaut, had become the first man to travel in space, a Telegraph reader suggested that the best way to dispose of the incessantly troublesome Osborne would be to blast him into the outer galaxies, while a Beefeater at the Tower of London proposed the more earthly and traditional remedy for traitors of incarceration in the Bloody Tower.

Newspaper reporters flew to the Riviera to reconnoitre La Beaumette. 'The most disconcerting feature of his hideaway is that one discovers it next to a nudist colony,' exclaimed one. 'Today, while Mr Osborne took his siesta, carloads of naked men and women went up to the camp . . .'[36] The Daily Mail published yet another article assessing Osborne's income, calculated as '£400 a week for a long time to come' from Luther alone, 'plus the success of his other operations.' Above it, a cartoon showed the cigar-smoking playwright sprawled on a sunlounger, a book, How to Cure Indigestion by Martin Luther, lying negligently at his side, as a middle-aged tourist exclaims to her companion: 'Look, dear, there's that poor Mr Osborne, clinging wretchedly to life as he always has done.'[37]

At home, cries of acclamation and condemnation tumbled over each other in newspapers from The Times to the Daily Mirror. Tribune exploited the furore to the full. Only two years previously, the journal's 'You're Telling Us' correspondence columns had been congested with Slickey letters; now, with the masthead altered to 'You're Telling Osborne', they were stuffed each week with the latest batch of correspondence, divided between support for Osborne's outspokenness, and indignation that he had assumed a socialist mantle while living in comparative luxury. 'Thank God for John Osborne!' cried a reader from Thetford. 'Damn You, Osborne!' came a rejoinder from Leicester. 'I am sorry,' wrote a correspondent reproachfully from Harrow. 'You were the articulate voice of frustrated youth screaming in protest against the bondage of imprisoned thoughts', but *A Letter to My Fellow Countrymen* was nothing but a 'a missile of futile despair . . .' 'You sit there in your contemptuous little villa,' admonished another. '. . . What the hell do you think you have contributed beside one miserable play [presumably *Look Back in Anger*] whose only attraction is that it is just short of pornography?' The secretary of the Eastern Regional Council of the Labour Party dismissed the letter as an 'abject and diabolical diatribe', while his counterpart from Portland urged that it be instantly reprinted as a leaflet and distributed to every household in the country. 'It is a letter that should be read by everyone.'[38]

Every day, every week, brought more letters and opinions. 'Every socialist should roar with approval at Osborne's letter,' exulted 'four navvies' from Dover. 'Your petty rages and puny spleen have added nothing to the life of this country you so despise,' raged a reader from London. A 'Christian and a Socialist' from Oxford mourned that in contrast to both creeds, *A Letter to My Fellow Countrymen* 'showed no hope, no understanding and worse still, no desire for understanding.' The Reverend Donald Soper, on the other hand, an eminent left-wing churchman and persuasive soapbox orator at the Tower of London, where the Beefeater who recommended Osborne's imprisonment might easily have heard him, suggested that Osborne had understood the political climate only too well. '. . . the ideas and projects which characterise the government of this country', he wrote, 'are not only (or in the first place) inept, specious and palsied – they are downright wicked . . . Self-interest, pride and violence are deadly sins however pleasantly they are wrapped up . . . John Osborne's letter ignores the wrapping and concentrates upon the actual contents of the parcel. For him it is a wicked parcel and he hates it . . . So do I.'[39]

Historians deliberated, authors adjudicated, politicians pronounced and commentators commented. Meanwhile, in Valbonne, the forces of reaction were already on the march. Major Colin de Vere Gordon-Maclean (Royal Artillery, retired), a thirty-three-year-old veteran of combat in the Malaysian jungle, had followed the hullabaloo in the press while on holiday and had decided to take decisive action on behalf of the nation. With the 'old scent of battle in his nostrils', he strode purposefully past the nudists and up the pathway towards La Beaumette, his rifle tucked under his arm, his benign troops, in the shape of Simla, his golden Labrador, panting at his side, his mission that of extracting from Osborne an apology to Britain which he would then bear with him triumphantly to London.

Entering through an unlocked door, the Major announced his presence to Jocelyn, established a strategic position in the study and sat down to wait for his quarry. Reluctant to engage the enemy, Osborne slipped a note under the door, claiming he was busy and asking the Major to leave. 'I wanted to discuss your outburst and have taken some pains to do so,' scribbled the Major in reply. A second note from Osborne slithered beneath the door, again signalling that the Major should leave. Disappointed, he 'retreated in good order' to a hotel in the nearby village, from where he launched Plan B, telephoning Osborne

who, somewhat surprisingly, answered. The Major informed him that he was
a disgrace to his country. At La Beaumette, the disgrace promptly replaced the
receiver. Outmanoeuvred, the Major abandoned operations and returned, chin
held high, to England. 'I would have liked to have got to close quarters with
him,' he regretfully told journalists expectantly awaiting his arrival. 'I felt I
ought to let him know what many people feel about his disgraceful outburst.'[40]

*   *   *

A Letter to My Fellow Countrymen might have been written 'with murder in my brain
and a knife in my heart', but Osborne's fears of global atomic catastrophe were
immediately superseded by the impending cataclysm in his emotional affairs.[41]
Before leaving London, he had arranged to join Penelope in Venice at the end of
August, an agreement he concealed from Jocelyn almost until the time he had
to leave. Suggesting that Jocelyn remain at La Beaumette until he returned – a
proposal to which, surprisingly, given the circumstances, she acquiesced – he
set off for Venice.

He and Penelope stayed at the Europa, a hotel on the Grand Canal. Between
film screenings, they walked in St Mark's Square, allowed gondolas to transport
them soothingly beneath the bridges on the canals, and ate meals in terrace
restaurants. The film press corps, far more absorbed by Alain Resnais's *L'Année
dernière à Marienbad* than in the latest turn of the Osborne saga, ignored them. It
was a relaxing interlude, a few days of comparative tranquillity. At the end of
the festival, Penelope took a flight home while Osborne returned to Valbonne
where Jocelyn was waiting for him. They stayed on until early September,
when they read reports in the British newspapers that a mass sit-down demonstration in favour of atomic disarmament would be held in Trafalgar Square on
the 17th. They agreed they must go back to London.

His return, however, would also mean that he could no longer avoid a
decision about his entangled relationships with Mary, Jocelyn and Penelope.
Leaving the car to be shipped back to England, he and Jocelyn took a flight from
Nice to London and from the airport took a taxi into the centre of town. By
chance, an escape hatch presented itself when the cab stopped at traffic lights
in Chesham Place, where Penelope was living. This was not an era in which
cab drivers locked the doors lest the passengers hop out without payment. It
was, therefore, the work of a second for Osborne to murmur: 'I'm sorry, my
darling, I'm going to behave rather badly again', open the door and jump out
in the few moments before the lights turned from red to green. It was a particularly heartless and cowardly act, he admitted, 'odiously expressed and odiously
executed'.[42] As the lights changed and the taxi drew away, he scurried up the
steps to Penelope's flat.

CHAPTER 17

Protest

HE HAD ARRIVED HOME to a press still reverberating with the controversy over *A Letter to My Fellow Countrymen*: 'A brilliant and much-needed attack', cried a supporter in the *Daily Mail*; 'The hysterical ravings of a psychopath', complained another; 'I want to say how much I and most mothers I know agree with it', ventured a third; 'What a pitiable state John Osborne is in', sympathised a fourth.[1]

The 1961 sit-down demonstration in Trafalgar Square for which he had returned to London was organised by the Committee of 100, an offshoot of CND and nominally led by Bertrand Russell, who was now dismissing the earnest, garden-party atmosphere of the Aldermaston marches as a 'yearly picnic'.[2] The atomic threat was so profound, he maintained, that it demanded more drastic methods of protest. As a result, he was colluding in a scheme masterminded by radicals designed to channel the mass support of CND into a campaign of civil disobedience. This involved forming a committee of a hundred prominent people prepared to undertake illegal protest and thereby risk high-profile imprisonment. Once behind bars, they would be replaced, wave upon wave, on the streets of London by others prepared to do the same until the sheer numbers of those confined burst prison walls and the government and arms manufacturers, shipwrecked by such a gargantuan tide of opinion, were obliged to reverse their policies. Summonses to this naïve enterprise were sent to an impressive array of names, including Osborne, Lindsay Anderson, Doris Lessing and Arnold Wesker, all of whom had attended the inaugural meeting of the Committee the previous year. The gathering debated a series of eye-catching acts of civil disturbance unheard of since the days of the suffragettes, including the disruption of the Trooping of the Colour, kidnapping the Chancellor of the Exchequer on Budget Day and even setting up a pirate radio station to bombard the airwaves with stridently propagandist messages. Osborne listened attentively, sincerely hoping that if any of these stunts actually came to pass he would not be delegated to take part. Wandering down Whitehall with a placard, as he had done with Mary Ure was, he thought, one thing; making off with the Chancellor of the Exchequer quite another and patently absurd. His credentials in the fields of ceremonial sabotage and unlicensed broadcasting remained untested, however, since none of these fantastic proposals came to fruition. Instead, and rather reluctantly for some, the Committee decided upon a more conventional sit-down demonstration in Trafalgar Square.

At the same time, Macmillan's government was busily making contingency plans both against external attack and internal dissent. Disarmament talks in Geneva had collapsed on 30 August, and both the Soviet Union and United States had resumed their atom bomb testing programmes. Consequently, London's civil defence forces revised their strategy to counter the threat from the skies, reassuring the Prime Minister that 'we have a complete scheme for dried milk for infants, if the iodine contamination from fall-out should become serious.'[3] On the home front, convinced that the Committee of 100 was a dangerously subversive organisation, the Home Secretary, R. A. Butler, declared a ban on processions, and several of the more prominent Committee members, including the snowy-haired Russell, appeared on 12 September at Marlborough Street Magistrates Courts to answer charges of inciting a breach of the peace. Refusing to be bound over to keep public order, Russell entertained the packed courtroom to a rousing defence of the merits of civil disobedience before being sentenced to two months detention at Brixton Prison, commuted on medical evidence to seven days.

The imprisoning of Russell, an eminent philosopher and Nobel laureate, or deluded old man, whichever way you looked at it, merely backfired, creating enormous publicity that made the government appear ludicrously heavy-handed. It also resulted in the Trafalgar Square protest going ahead without its leaders present. Thousands of protestors massed in the Square while hundreds more, including Osborne, crowded into the National Gallery on the north side of the Square, where they lurked in contemplation of Old Masters while the police outside closed the Square to pedestrians. Lindsay Anderson was there among the Titians and Tintorettos, as were William Gaskill, Arnold Wesker and his fellow Royal Court dramatist John Arden, and the actress Vanessa Redgrave, whom Tony Richardson would marry the following year. The jazz singer George Melly stood with Doris Lessing, who noticed that Osborne, who was not a natural mass demonstrator, was looking decidedly ill at ease. Oscar Beuselinck, who turned up to maintain a watchful eye on the fate of his various clients, noted that Osborne looked awkward and miserable.

As the demonstrators, Osborne among them, streamed out of the gallery and into the Square to join those already sitting there, they discovered that a force of four thousand police had been marshalled to contain almost fifteen thousand protestors. The idealists and peace-makers, 'misguided, but no doubt sincere', observed Macmillan, squatted and lay side-by-side, a display of civil protest resembling an act of mass religious homage.[4] Crackling through loudspeakers suspended above them, Russell's tape-recorded message evoked a grotesque apocalypse in which crazed world leaders would, on a whim, wipe out all art, knowledge and civilisation, leaving a ruined, lifeless planet to drift aimlessly around an incinerating sun. It seemed to incite passions as perhaps he had hoped it would, for soon afterwards, breakaway groups rose to their feet and attempted to force an illegal advance down Whitehall causing the police lines impeding their progress to buckle. Sir Joseph Simpson, the Commissioner of the Metropolitan Police, wearing a riding cape and a brown trilby hat, bawled directions this way and that from the vantage point of a Whitehall traffic island. Canon Collins, the CND advocate of constitutional order, appeared, 'going round, as it were, to see the troops . . . trying to keep them calm.'[5] But neither Simpson nor Collins had much effect. Protestors harangued the police, the police shouted at everyone, and reporters and photographers darted every-where, scribbling notes, snapping pictures and alert for the inevitable. 'At 5.20 the first demonstrator was arrested,' noted the *Daily Express*. 'Then the expected rumpus started.'[6]

There were shovings and scuffles as the more militant protestors repeatedly plunged forward, only to be forced back by police over more peaceful, still seated demonstrators. Splinter groups, making a dash for Whitehall and Parlia-ment Square, fought battles of their own. Protestors jostled this way and that and were hauled indiscriminately from the pavement by Simpson's men and thrust into police vans for distribution around London's police cells. Vanessa Redgrave was arrested, as was George Melly. Vigilantly noting police proce-dure, Beuselinck observed Osborne's arrest as he was prised from a relatively comfortable niche he had taken up beside one of the Landseer lions. As the afternoon wore on into evening and night, more and more protestors were bundled into police vans and driven away. If nothing else, the forces of law and order had achieved the largest mass arrest in British history. '1,140 Arrested Including John Osborne' cried the *Daily Express*.[7]

The next morning, at Bow Street police station, having spent an uncomfort-able night in prison in the cause of world peace, or at least for the Committee of 100, Osborne appeared at the Magistrate's Court, pleaded guilty to breaching the peace and was fined £1 by Mr Bertram Reece, the presiding magistrate. A small crowd of sympathisers cheered him as he hurried quickly away. Canon Collins, despite indignantly protesting that as a pacifist and representative of CND, he was in Trafalgar Square as an observer rather than a demonstrator, had also been arrested and fined. 'Jolly hard luck on the old boy,' murmured Ber-trand Russell, delightedly assuring journalists awaiting his release from Brixton Prison that he had been treated 'like an old lag.'[8] He had passed the time, he added, by catching up on his reading of detective novels and had enjoyed himself very much.

Osborne returned to Penelope and Chesham Place, and the confusion of his very public private life. Not that he had been able to put domestic matters to the back of his mind during the Siege of Trafalgar Square, for at its height he had heard an accusing voice sailing through the melee around him: 'Why don't you go back to your wife and baby and stop playing silly games like this?'⁹ *Wife and baby*. Osborne had no intention of returning to Mary, but the press and the awkward matter of his wife and her child had been pursuing him for over a fortnight, ever since the *Manchester Evening News* had bellowed its congratulations: 'John, you've got a son!'¹⁰

*   *   *

Just over a fortnight earlier, on 30 August, while Osborne was blundering between Jocelyn and Penelope and La Beaumette and Venice, Mary had given birth to a 7½lb baby boy at the private Welbeck Nursing Home in Welbeck Street in Marylebone. But with the new mother incommunicado at Welbeck Street and the apparent 'shy dad' in retreat in France, gossip columnists continued to contemplate 'the strange world of John Osborne.'¹¹ Speculation fizzed even fiercer once it was discovered that the provocative playwright who had abandoned his wife to travel abroad with Jocelyn was now being seen in London in the affectionate company of Penelope. With the popular press rampant, Oscar Beuselinck came to Osborne's aid by rustling up a discreet central London flat where his client and Penelope might temporarily escape the photographers' lenses and the reporters' questions. But in the end it seemed to Osborne that the only answer, once again, was flight. He would leave London altogether in the quest for another new start.

*   *   *

In fact, he had been contemplating this for several months. A house in the country, he reasoned, might offer both a haven from press harassment and domestic strife, and be a sanctuary in which to write. At first, he had contemplated moving to Wales, land of his fathers, and had reconnoitred property near Portmeirion, a peninsula village created by the architect Clough Williams-Ellis and surrounded by sub-tropical gardens. It all seemed extremely attractive until he calculated the hopelessly impractical length of time it would take to travel to London and back. Cancelling the Welsh option, he began searching within driving distance of London, eventually discovering The Old Water Mill at Hellingly, a village in Sussex. A two-storey, early seventeenth-century house with ivy clinging to the walls, where the current owners did a brisk trade in cream teas, it was just off the main road to Eastbourne and a ninety-minute drive from London, close enough for convenience but hopefully far enough away to deter anyone not specifically invited. Enclosed by two tributaries of the River Cuckmere, the property included several buildings in a few acres of overgrown but reclaimable garden. Besides the house, there was the now inactive water mill and a former granary suitable for conversion into a guest house or a study. Everything was in desperate need of modernisation, but otherwise it was ideal. A quick call to Beuselinck confirmed that it was within his grasp at

£10,000 and, by the time Osborne was squatting in Trafalgar Square registering his protest against the arms race, the contracts were signed.

Osborne and Penelope decided to leave London for Hellingly together, planning their escape as elaborately as a clandestine Cold War operation, innocently
overlooking the fact that his acquisition of The Old Water Mill had been
widely reported by Fleet Street. Nevertheless, they recruited Sonia McGuinness,
Osborne's new secretary, to negotiate the recovery of those of his possessions
that had found their way from Woodfall Street to Mary's home in Cliveden
Place. Anthony Creighton, who thought Penelope 'a very nice person', came
back into the picture, joining the conspiracy by hiring a small but serviceable
van and two removal men.[12] Then, on the evening of Friday, 22 September, a
week after Osborne's arrest in Trafalgar Square, they put their plan into operation. The van's first port of call was Lower Belgrave Street, from where Jocelyn
was tactfully absent and where Osborne and Sonia, assisted by Frank McGuinness, her husband, carried out his books and a small revolving bookcase, his
desk and leather desk chair, typewriters and *Harbinger Bird IV*, a bronze sculpture
by Elisabeth Frink. He had bought this alarming modernist piece, a sharp slab
atop two long legs, from a West End gallery a few months earlier. Evidently,
he was feeling more confident in matters of modern art these days, or, more
likely, Penelope was acting as his art advisor. They then moved on to the Gilliatt
household at Lowndes Square, where Roger Gilliatt was similarly diplomatically
absent, and where they struggled down the stairs with more boxes of books.
Then, with Frank and Sonia leading the way, followed by Creighton in the
van and lastly by Osborne and Penelope in her car, they set off under cover of
darkness for Hellingly.

Once they arrived, however, they discovered to their horror that their plans
had been blown. Their imagined secret getaway became one of the most extravagantly publicised of all Osborne's escapades that year: a journalistic frenzy,
lamented the *New Statesman*, 'unique even in the annals of popular slime.'[13] As
they turned into the lane leading to The Old Water Mill, the foliage suddenly
disgorged reporters and photographers brandishing notebooks, cameras and
flashlights. There was even a suggestion that one reporter emerged from the
boot of Penelope's car, where he had concealed himself 'at great personal
danger' in case the Hellingly destination proved to be a hoax.[14] Questions
rained down on them. What were 'Britain's bomb-squatting playwright' and
'the beautiful woman in a light coat' up to?[15] Where were John Osborne's wife
and Penelope Gilliatt's husband? Had not Mary Ure just given birth to a baby
boy? Was Osborne not the father? Jumping from the vehicles, the Osborne party
hopped over the low stone wall surrounding the house and dashed towards it,
as journalists scampered after them. By now, Osborne had devised a strategy
for dealing with reporters. 'Say nothing . . . Hang up [the telephone] . . . If you
are bigger than they are, push them out of the way . . . Buy a large dog – all
teeth and no scruples.'[16] Having, for the moment, no large dog, although he
would soon acquire one, he decided upon the first and third options, saying

nothing and pushing reporters aside, hustling Penelope, Sonia, Creighton and McGuinness into the house and slamming the door behind them. Stumbling from room to room, they searched for light switches as fists hammered at the door and enquiring faces appeared like voodoo dolls at the windows. Quickly, they made for the comparative safety of the upper floor.

The next day, shielded by Frank and Sonia from the gaggle of press camping on the lawns, Osborne and Penelope ventured out to go shopping for essential supplies. Returning to The Old Water Mill some hours later, vaguely hoping to find that the journalists had packed up and gone, they were appalled to discover what seemed to be a very lively press conference in full swing. Grateful for Creighton's early-morning provision of coffee, the reporters had found an off-licence and reciprocated with several bottles of probably expense-account wine and spirits, evidently believing that an alcohol-mellowed Creighton offered their best chance of an insight into the frolics of the Angry Young Man and the neurologist's wife. Overwhelmed by their apparent kindness, Creighton had invited them all into the house. 'I thought I was doing the best thing,' he recalled. 'I thought that if I took the press into my confidence, they might go away and leave us in peace.'[17] Incensed both by Creighton's gullibility and the invasion of his property, a furious Osborne plunged into the house and bundled his former collaborator outside. 'He went mad,' remembered Creighton. 'He was shouting at the top of his voice: "You're going. Get out and stay out. I don't ever want to see you again".' As they emerged grappling onto the pathway, Creighton fell. Hauling him to his feet, Osborne flung him across the bonnet of Penelope's car. 'It was terrible,' recalled Creighton. 'He was a big man, a strong man and his temper was terrifying. Absolutely terrifying.'[18] Shaken, Creighton watched as his friend turned back into the house. A few moments later, chastened reporters emerged one by one. Creighton got to his feet and limped off to the granary where he spent the night. The next morning, he took an early train to London.

The events of the weekend marked the end of the close friendship he had shared with Osborne since their Saga summer at Hayling Island eleven years earlier. They did not entirely part company, however, as Osborne would retain Creighton's name on the first-night guest list for his plays for a couple of years to come and Creighton would diligently send a good-luck telegram to 'me old mate' whenever a new production opened.[19] Osborne would continue to bail out Creighton financially, a plaintive appeal unfailingly prompting a gen-erous cheque. Their friendship puzzled several of Osborne's associates, who wondered exactly why the playwright appeared to be so loyal to a man who apparently had so little to offer. According to Sonia McGuinness, it was 'a somewhat curious friendship in which Creighton was remarkably sycophantic and John, although extremely tolerant and generous towards him, for the most part clearly found him something of a pain.'[20] Yet Osborne was not yet at the point – which he would later be – whereby he could peremptorily cut out of his life those who had offended him. Creighton was Osborne's oldest ally. He had been instrumental in Osborne's career as a fellow actor, a friend and a collaborator. He could not be entirely discarded yet.

*   *   *

At Hellingly, Osborne attempted to settle down to some writing but discovered over the next few days that the reporters camping outside were producing much more than he was. The Sunday papers gave widespread coverage to the story of his moonlit move, while on Monday, pictures were published of Osborne and Penelope 'strolling hand-in-hand along the seafront at Eastbourne' before disappearing into a cafe where 'they ate a meal of egg, bacon and chips.'[21] The *Daily Sketch* reported the arrival of Nellie Beatrice to inspect her son's new rural home, emerging from the recesses of 'a hired car' wearing 'a pale mauve costume' and 'bringing two dachshunds, a Siamese cat and a suitcase.'[22] The *Daily Telegraph* solicited an interview with Osborne, probably against his better judgment, and conveyed his admission that 'Mrs Gilliatt' was indeed 'staying there with him' although he 'politely but firmly' declined the paper's invitation to discuss either his marriage or hers. 'I really prefer not to go into that. I don't think she will want to either . . .' Had he been in touch with his wife? 'I do not want to discuss these matters either.' But what were his immediate plans? 'I cannot say.' How did he reconcile the acquisition of a country house with the hatred of England expressed in his open letter to *Tribune*? 'I don't think I want to comment on that,' replied Osborne. '. . . All I want is some peace and quiet.'[23]

There seemed little immediate prospect of this. Although most of the reporters left for London by Monday morning, the story ran for several more weeks. On Thursday 28 September, the *Daily Express* published adjacent photographs of three of the players in the Osborne Affair. 'A grey, grey London day, but there's nothing grey about it for Mary Ure', ran the caption beneath a picture of Mary emerging from a taxi at Cliveden Place after registering the birth of her son as Colin Murray Osborne, and naming John Osborne as the father on the birth certificate. 'A grey, grey London day,' read the caption of the neighbouring picture, 'but there's nothing grey about it for Mrs Penelope Gilliatt, wife of Dr Roger Gilliatt . . . as she crosses Waterloo Bridge with playwright John Osborne.'

That evening, however, there were further visitors at The Old Water Mill. Osborne's presence in Hellingly had not gone unnoticed by the villagers and, unfortunately for Britain's foremost Angry Young Man, they vigorously disapproved of demonstrating in Trafalgar Square and of chaps running off with other chaps' wives. Marshalled by 'the snuff-taking' Mr Fred Livingstone, Hellingly's answer to Major Colin de Vere Gordon-Maclean, twelve of the more elderly residents positioned themselves at Osborne's gate and, gravely bearing placards reading 'HELLINGLY'S ANGRY OLD MEN OBJECT', 'DAMN YOU, OSBORNE', and 'HELLINGLY WANTS MARY URE', began a silent vigil of disapproval. 'We were prepared to sit down . . . like Osborne did during the anti-nuclear demonstration,' asserted Livingstone, but with the evening's autumnal chill and the dampness of the grass threatening the onset of flu and a revival of rheumatism, so subversive a gesture was deemed unnecessarily melodramatic.[24] Instead, the delegation stood solemnly until the door of The Old Water Mill was opened and Sonia McGuinness emerged to explain that Osborne was disappointingly not at home. Like phantoms, The Hellingly Twelve departed as unobtrusively as they had come, for they were peaceful protestors, and the village slept undisturbed.

Press interest, though, deepened still further as the John Osborne–Mary Ure divorce proceedings began. As the events of the previous couple of years had provided fertile ground upon which his client could be further vilified by the more morally censorious newspapers, Beuselinck urged Osborne to make the first move by citing Mary's relationship with Robert Shaw. Portraying his estranged wife as adulterous might be ungentlemanly, agreed Beuselinck, but establishing himself as the betrayed rather than the betrayer might, after so turbulent a summer, earn him some much-needed public sympathy. Osborne, therefore, was first out of the gate, filing for divorce on 2 October 1961, on the grounds of Mary's adultery with Shaw. There was no response from Mary but a few days later, Jennifer, Shaw's wife, gave birth to his daughter and fourth child in London. Her husband, meanwhile, was appearing as Aston in Pinter's The Caretaker in New York. On 13 October, the William Hickey gossip column in the Daily Express reported the birth of Shaw's daughter and his being named in a divorce action by Osborne, alongside a reproduction of Penelope's change-of-address card, which she had sent to the Film Industry Publicity Circle, as evidence that her official residence was now, like Osborne's, The Old Water Mill. The next day, Mary left London on board a flight to the United States under the name of Mrs Fisher, baby Colin nestling in the arms of a nurse. After landing at Philadelphia, she sped away in a chauffeur-driven car to New York, where she joined Robert Shaw.

In November, Roger Gilliatt filed for divorce against Penelope, citing Osborne as co-respondent, and was duly granted a decree nisi the following February. On 2 December, Mary finally retaliated against Osborne. Laszlo Gombos, her Hungarian and impeccably besuited lawyer, announced that she would allege her husband's adultery with three women. Legal shadow-boxing continued for eleven months until 1 November 1962, when Mary instructed her lawyer to sue in the courts and melodramatically announced that she was now 'praying for divorce.'[25] The case came before the Divorce Courts on 14 November when, having admitted her own adultery, Mary 'spent forty minutes' claiming that her husband had committed adultery with 'Miss Jocelyn Rickards . . . in London, Miss Francine Brandt in Jamaica and elsewhere, and with Mrs Penelope Gilliatt at Hellingly . . .' before being granted a decree nisi and awarded custody of Colin. Osborne was ordered to pay the costs. 'I'm glad that's over,' she told waiting reporters.[26]

Several weeks later, Shaw and Mary emulated Osborne and Penelope by leaving London for the country, albeit in the opposite direction from Sussex.

Along with baby Colin, they moved into Porch House, an ill-proportioned, eight-bedroomed house in Amersham in Buckinghamshire. Having secured his own divorce from Jennifer, Shaw and Mary married in April 1963 at the local register office and two months later successfully applied to the county court to formally adopt Colin. There has, however, never been any doubt that it was Shaw and not Osborne who was the boy's father.[27] As Oscar Beuselinck later recalled, Osborne knew that the child was Shaw's and never contested it. The fact that Osborne's name appears on the birth certificate merely indicates, he added, that as Mary's husband, he was the child's legal father at the time of his birth and therefore the child was legally legitimate. It was still a severe social stigma to have been born out of wedlock, and had Mary entered her lover's name rather than her husband's on the certificate, she would have risked both her public reputation were Shaw revealed as the father during a subsequent divorce action, and perhaps jeopardised the rights of her child. Whether Osborne colluded in this protective action is not known, but he certainly did nothing to impede it.[28]

*   *   *

In November 1961, as Beuselinck and Gombos played the opening hands in the divorce proceedings and as builders began renovation work at The Old Water Mill, Osborne and Penelope flew to the Acapulco Film Festival, which she was covering for the Observer. The inevitable press posse that seemed permanently attached to Osborne was not far behind, grateful for another expenses-paid break in the sun. 'Far from wintry Britain,' perspired the man from the Daily Express, 'Acapulco Bay basks in hot sunshine, a glowing, golden coast protected by tall hills, with warm surf flowing over baking sands. Sinatra sings about it, Mexicans rave about it, tycoons flock to it.'[29] This time, there was no sign of Francine to complicate matters. Back home in England, Nellie Beatrice opened her newspaper upon an extensive picture-spread of her son and his latest lover; here they were, striding self-consciously in swimwear alongside the ocean; there he was, twisting in his chair to deliver a hostile rebuke to a lurking press photographer as they ate their meal at a restaurant.

The notorious runaways returned to spend Christmas at Hellingly and the consolation of Tribune, Osborne's old ally, joining the New Statesman in standing by him when all others were against him. 'It would be difficult to think of any more impertinent and disgraceful intrusion onto the private life of two individuals than the pursuit of these two people by certain gallant gentlemen of Fleet Street,' sympathised the paper.[30] Just to be on the safe side, Osborne took the precaution of having The Old Water Mill encircled by a six-foot high fence, which, reported the Evening News and Star, 'effectively barred the Mill from public view.'[31] In the New Year, while contractors resumed modernising work at the house, Osborne and Penelope moved temporarily back to London, renting a small flat on the top floor of 3 White Horse Street, a narrow turning between

Shepherd Market and Piccadilly. Each morning, she clattered down the stairs
to press screenings of films, leaving him to apply himself at long last to some
writing. On the table before him lay the beginnings of a screenplay for Tom
Jones for Tony Richardson, and a double-bill of short plays for the Royal Court.
They were lightweight, playful efforts and as such: 'No one will want them,'
he confided philosophically to his journal, 'but they'll be better than anything
else on offer.'[32]

CHAPTER 18

Other Englands

MOCKING AND SARDONIC, *Plays for England* were plays for the Sixties, spon–taneous, irreverent years, and for Osborne, years of extravagance, professional acclaim and personal turmoil. Culturally and socially, that much-mythologised decade had its origins in 1956, the year of *Look Back in Anger* and the Angry Young Man, *The Outsider*, Free Cinema, skiffle, teddy boys, 'Rock around the Clock' and rock-and-roll. Morally, according to Philip Larkin, it began much later, in 1963, between the lifting of the Chatterley ban and *Please Please Me*, The Beatles' first LP, released in March of that year. Politically it began in 1964, with the sea-changing election of the first Labour government for thirteen years.

Bowled along by increasing affluence, rising optimism and changing atti–tudes and expectations, the Sixties were years in which Britain became a more liberal and a more provisional place. In the arts and in the new enterprises, the pervasive influence of Oxbridge receded with the rise of a meritocracy based mainly in London. Distinctions of social class continued to be rigidly defined but were simultaneously more permeable. The young and increasingly prosper–ous products of the upper-working and middle classes, equipped with degrees from new universities and art schools, fortified by pop music and working in journalism and television, the theatre and the cinema, fashion, music and archi–tecture, set the tone of the times, celebrating a morality and cultural sensibility radically different from that of the immediate post-war years. For some, if the 1950s were in black-and-white, then the 1960s were vibrant with colour.

It was a decade jostling with fads and fancies and jangling with pop music as groups sprang from north and south, their records hurtling up and down the bestsellers' charts. The Beatles, who dominated those years, led the 'Mersey Beat' sound from Liverpool; The Hollies materialised from Manchester and The Animals from Newcastle, while The Rolling Stones, The Who, The Kinks and many more emerged from London and its suburbs. They amassed armies of rival fans, the scooter-riding Mods and motorcycling Rockers making excur–sions to seaside resorts on Bank Holiday weekends to fight pitched battles over the shingle. The Beatles, clean-cut and boyish, floppily fringed, their music innocent and melodic, appealed across the gender and generational divide; The Rolling Stones, pouting belligerence, their hair longer and their music anxious and sardonic, attracted the young and rebellious. London became the centre of the new record, fashion and design industries. Mary Quant, who had opened her first dress shop in Chelsea in 1955, expanded her business into Kensington while the designer Terence Conran launched the first Habitat store in 1964, introducing London to the wonders of flat-pack furniture, Japanese paper globe lampshades and French terracotta ovenware.

The theatre was changing as well. By the end of the 1950s, a new wave of politically and socially aware dramatists, many of whom were inspired by Osborne's achievement and who, like him, lacked upper-middle-class and Oxbridge credentials, were crowding through the door of opportunity that he and the Royal Court had flung open. These were the 'kitchen sink' playwrights who put all of domestic life on the stage. Arnold Wesker, a twenty-six-year-old former pastry cook, was living with his family in the Upper Clapton Road and working at his brother-in-law's furniture-making workshop when he saw a touring production of *Look Back in Anger* in Streatham. Convinced that 'not only was theatre an activity where important things were happening, but one which I could add to,' he immediately began writing *Chicken Soup With Barley*.[1]

The play opened at the Royal Court on 14 July 1958, directed by a friend of Osborne's from Derby days, the non-university educated John Dexter, whom Osborne had recommended to George Devine. Dexter also staged Wesker's following plays, *Roots* and *I'm Talking About Jerusalem*, completing a trilogy dealing with the emotional and political turbulence of the Kahn family during the twenty years from the mid-1930s. Osborne had uprooted domestic drama from drawing-rooms in Belgravia and the Home Counties and set it down in a provincial attic. In *Chicken Soup with Barley*, Wesker extended it into the basement of the Kahn family house in the East End of London, on the day of a British Union of Fascists march in 1936.

Alongside Arnold Wesker, there was John Arden. A twenty-eight-year-old Yorkshire-born architect, Arden was captivated by the stage, 'although it seemed', he recalled, 'that the theatre had lost touch with the fundamentals of English culture.' In *Look Back in Anger*, he discovered a voice he had not heard before. It was 'a plea for truth. Jimmy Porter pleads for personal integrity while everyone around him caves in to expedience.'[2] *Live Like Pigs*, in which the Sawneys, an anarchic travelling family, live side by side with more conventional neighbours on a housing estate, established Arden as a Royal Court dramatist, a reputation he consolidated in 1959 with *Serjeant Musgrave's Dance*. Yet Wesker saw himself and others like him not as Angry Young Men but as successors to them. 'How could we be angry?' he wondered. 'We were writing, our plays were being produced, we were successful and earning money.'[3]

But the most distinctive new voice in the theatre was that of Harold Pinter, the son of an East End tailor. Pinter, though, never became a Royal Court playwright and neither did Osborne influence his writing, although, like Osborne, he had been a repertory actor and had understudied Robert Stephens in *Epitaph for George Dillon*. Pinter's writing derived its impetus from Samuel Beckett and other continental European writers. *The Room*, his first play, was produced by the Bristol University Drama Department in 1958; *The Birthday Party*, his second and first full-length piece, at the Lyric, Hammersmith, later the same year; and *The Caretaker*, at the Arts Theatre in 1960. A dark account of a tramp intruding into the lives of two brothers, it subsequently transferred to a small West End theatre. Over the following five years, while Osborne's canvas became larger and his brushstrokes more sweeping, Pinter worked within a smaller frame to create plays at once realistic and elusive, sombre and sharply witty. In contrast to Osborne's linguistic expansiveness, Pinter created a precise but deceptive world of shifting alliances, blind alleys and sudden, unexpected revelations, in which nothing seems as it first appears and in which language is used sparingly as a weapon of domination, as evasion or as tactical negotiation.

Apart from Ann Jellicoe, whose *The Sport of My Mad Mother* was staged at the Royal Court in 1958, and Shelagh Delaney's *A Taste of Honey*, an account of a young working-class woman's sexual and social awakening, the theatre still remained very much a male preserve. Osborne admired both Jellicoe's and Delaney's plays, attended the premieres and was decisive in Woodfall producing the film version of *A Taste of Honey*. But although male writers continued to dominate the theatre, women's voices were among the most notable among the newer novelists. The essential Angry works, as Margaret Drabble has noted, were 'aggressively masculine and frequently misogynist. Womanising was a popular theme', whereas 'women's voices, in these post-war decades, were quiet and ladylike . . .'[4] Novelists such as Drabble, Lynne Reid Banks, Osborne's former fellow actor in The Saga Repertory Group, Edna O'Brien and Muriel Spark began charting the shifting and far from 'quiet and ladylike' sensibilities of women in such novels as *The Garrick Year*, *The L-Shaped Room*, *The Country Girls* and *The Prime of Miss Jean Brodie*.

Films were changing too, and while Lindsay Anderson's *This Sporting Life*, adapted from David Storey's novel about the trials of a young Rugby League player, continued the fascination with northern working-class realism, a crop of films appeared specifically to do with London and the kaleidoscopic new morality, which, while made by men, were told, sometimes hesitantly, from a woman's point of view. *The L-Shaped Room*, directed in 1962 by Bryan Forbes and based upon Lynne Reid Banks's novel, followed the fortunes of a young, pregnant actress who drifts to a dowdy lodging house in Fulham, while three years later Julie Christie won a Hollywood Oscar for her role in John Schlesinger's *Darling*, the story of an ambitious young model bedding her way into the company of the wealthy and well-connected.

Between the end of the 1950s and the mid-1960s, therefore, everything was changing, everything realigning, and after thirteen years in power, the Conservatives were looking as out of date as spindly-legged furniture. Yet the government's General Election defeat in 1964 was precipitated not so much by domestic mismanagement but by a sensationally sleazy scandal involving illicit sex, national security and the Cold War. The star players were John Profumo, balding, forty-eight years old and recently appointed Secretary of State for War, and Christine Keeler, a dark-haired showgirl less than half his age. Well liked and apparently happily married, Profumo had been among the audience at the first night of The World of Paul Slickey and should have been more informed of how relentlessly inquisitive the popular press could be. Revealed to be involved in an extra-marital entanglement with Keeler who, it transpired, was also no stranger to the bedroom of Oleg Ivanov, a naval attaché at the Soviet Embassy, he should have known better than to deny it. The story was intriguingly complicated by co-star Dr Stephen Ward, osteopath to the wealthy and a close friend of Keeler, who claimed to have been employed by the British security services to extract information from Ivanov about Soviet military activities; by Mandy Rice-Davies, a clubland friend of Keeler's; by peripheral gangsters and a surging tide of rumour and speculation about high-life hi-jinks and low-life villainy. Having initially proclaimed his innocence in the House of Commons, Profumo later admitted that he had lied, and resigned. In the misty Cold War atmosphere of conspiracy and deception, gossip and conjecture, nobody seemed to know quite whose side anyone was on: ours, theirs or both at once. Accused of living off the immoral earnings of Keeler and Rice Davies, Ward was prosecuted at the Old Bailey but the trial was never completed. Believing himself betrayed by the Establishment and sacrificed as a public scapegoat, he swallowed an overdose of sleeping tablets and died in August. Osborne, among others, sent a wreath to his funeral, bearing the legend that Ward had become 'a victim of hypocrisy.'

However, even though rumours had been current for some time, the Profumo revelations appeared to take the Prime Minister entirely by surprise. Sleaze pleased the popular press but fatally damaged Macmillan's administration. Despite his determination that the government would not be 'brought down by the action of two tarts', further allegations of executive sexual frivolities, such as a group of senior judges joining the participants of an orgy, left the government's reputation as low as the alleged judicial trousers.[5] 'At present the Conservative Party is in a shambles,' understated The Daily Telegraph.[6] But while his part in the negotiations leading to the Nuclear Test Ban Treaty in August 1963 restored much of Macmillan's personal standing, he was felled in the autumn neither by two tarts nor judges behaving badly, but by prostate trouble. And to the astonishment of many of his colleagues, he instructed that the Foreign Secretary should become his successor. Enter the fourteenth Earl Home, the elder brother of the West End playwright William Douglas-Home, a tweedy Scottish laird peering cautiously over half-moon glasses.

Having renounced his peerage to become Sir Alec Douglas-Home, the laird's stewardship lasted less than a year. At the October 1964 election, Harold Wilson's Labour Party scraped into office by a majority of four. It was an expected, if grudging victory but one that was culturally decisive. Douglas-Home's natural

territory was the Scottish moors rather than Downing Street, and as the historian Peter Hennessey has written, he 'treated the whole country as if it were
a great landed estate.'[7] Wilson, on the other hand, a shrewd political operator
who had become Party leader after the death of Gaitskell in 1963, strategically
presented himself as both a moderniser alert to changing times and the amazing
potential of technology, and as a down-to-earth, pipe-smoking northerner in a
Gannex raincoat. But all Wilson's talk of the 'white heat' of technology seemed
to Osborne profoundly soulless and nothing to do with socialism. There seemed
little difference, he objected, between the Conservative Party and Labour, and
when presented with the alternative of the devil and the deep blue sea it was
best to choose neither. He would, he said, withhold his vote.

Osborne may (or may not) have abstained from voting and while admitting
to socialist principles have only a sentimental idea of what they might be, but
in common with other writers, and despite his ignominious experience sitting
down in Trafalgar Square, he put his name to a fleet of liberal causes over the
following years. He imposed a ban upon his plays being performed in South
Africa as part of the cultural protest against the apartheid regime, and on 19 April
1961, he was one of fifteen signatories to a letter to The Times denouncing the
'Bay of Pigs' incident, in which a force of Cuban exiles and American mer-
cenaries invaded Cuba in a failed operation, planned by the American Central
Intelligence Agency, to overthrow the Communist regime of Fidel Castro.
During the same year, he supported Tony Benn, who had renounced his title of
Viscount Stansgate in order to be elected to the House of Commons as Labour
MP for Bristol South-East. Two years later, Osborne joined Kenneth Tynan,
Iris Murdoch and John Wain in publicising the plight of the Angolan poet, Dr
Agostinho Neto, imprisoned for opposing the Portuguese administration of his
country, and in 1967 he signed a petition addressed to the United Nations and
the Commission of Human Rights of the Council of Europe in protest at the
military regime that seized power after a coup in Greece.

*   *   *

Meanwhile, on 8 January 1962, a curious incident took place in Croydon,
south London. Cry for Love, a play billed as being by Robert Owen, opened at
the Pembroke Theatre for a fortnight's run. It was curious because it was a
lightly revised revival, under a different title, of The Devil Inside Him, a play that
had gathered dust ever since its Huddersfield outing in 1950. Produced by the
irrepressible Patrick Desmond, Osborne's name was not publicly connected
with the production and neither did he know of it in advance. Yet some of
the national critics, apparently unaware of its true authorship, took the trouble
to review it, The Times noting that it was 'a serious and ambitious work' if not
entirely original.[8]

Although the two short plays on which Osborne was currently working were
neither particularly serious nor ambitious, nor was one of them entirely origi-

nal, he completed the two short *Plays for England* under the respective working titles of *Listen, Comrade; Queens Cheer,* and *The Scoop,* later altered to *The Blood of the Bambergs* and *Under Plain Cover,* a few months later in April.

Like *The World of Paul Slickey,* both plays are satires on the press, *The Blood of the Bambergs* attacking what he saw as its sycophancy towards the Royal Family, and *Under Plain Cover* its readiness to harass private citizens for the sake of a sensational story. In the first, a pastiche of the press coverage of the wedding between Princess Margaret and Anthony Armstrong-Jones, and the substitution of Jeremy Fry by Roger Gilliatt, he swathed real events in the cloak of a plot pinched from Anthony Hope's 1894 romance, *The Prisoner of Zenda.* In the novel, when the future king of Ruritania is imprisoned at Zenda, Rudolf Rassendyll is crowned in his stead in order to thwart the treacherous ambitions of the pretender, Black Michael. As Rassendyll closely resembles the king, he is able to maintain the deception until the monarch is rescued and takes his rightful place on the throne. In Osborne's version, Prince Wilhelm Bamberg is killed in a car accident on the eve of his marriage to Princess Melanie, but the idea of substituting Prince Heinrich, his brother, as groom is rejected because, as a homosexual, Heinrich cannot be relied upon to father an heir. Wilhelm's place at the altar, therefore, is taken by Alan Russell, an Australian photographer. His vague similarity to the prince is later discovered to be due to his Bamberg blood: he is the result of one of Wilhelm's father's extra-marital affairs. Osborne therefore curiously blunted the sting of his play by sparing his Royal family the humiliation of marrying into common stock.

Under Plain Cover is a comedy of private innocence and public prurience. Tim and Jenny Turner appear to be a happily married couple leading a respectable suburban life. Their private pleasure is dressing in fantasy-wear and acting out their games of doctor and nurse, motorcyclist and Girl Guide, master and housemaid. Stanley Williams, a newspaper reporter eager for a front-page story, discovers that the couple are in fact brother and sister, something entirely unknown to Tim and Jenny, who were separated as infants and grew up in different parts of the country. Their unwitting incest is cruelly exposed and Jenny is remarried in a press-sponsored wedding to another man. Yet by the end of the play, she has deserted her new husband to live in seclusion with Tim while Stanley, drunk and miserable, bawls incoherent threats through their letterbox.

*   *   *

In 1960, Penguin Books challenged the 1959 Obscene Publications Act, which governed fiction as the Lord Chamberlain oversaw the theatre, by publishing the first unexpurgated edition of D. H. Lawrence's *Lady Chatterley's Lover,* a novel of adulterous passion between a Lady and a gamekeeper and first issued in a bowdlerised edition over thirty years previously, in 1928. The Act allowed for the publication of 'obscene' material if it could be 'justified as being for the public good on the ground that it is in the interests of science, literature, art or learning' and, after a much-publicised trial at the Old Bailey, Penguin won the case.

The *Chatterley* case was a breakthrough. Attention now turned to the laws governing the theatre, which Osborne, who had long opposed censorship, and several other dramatists now saw as additionally weakened and anachronistic. With their respective allusions to the Royal Family and to incest, *Plays for England* nudged at the boundaries of what was acceptable on the public stage and presented the Lord Chamberlain's Office with a quandary. 'Osborne may be seeing what he can get away with,' warned St Vincent Troubridge. But the 'devilish cleverness' of *The Blood of the Bambergs*, he reasoned, was that while it included 'horrid' attacks upon the monarchy, the refusal of a public performance licence could be represented as 'a ridiculous banning of the old *Prisoner of Zenda* story.'[9] In the event, Troubridge decided to risk being pilloried as a fool in Sloane Square and recommended that a licence be withheld. Maurice Coles, on the other hand, the Examiner who read *Under Plain Cover*, vacillated. Although the play was 'a study in sexual perversion', he conceded that 'it gains in force rather than loses from being largely suggestive.' Disconcerted by 'an inordinate number' of 'offensive' passages – Coles was especially alarmed by 'a lengthy discussion on the subject of women's knickers' – and, apprehensive as to what 'Osborne's bleery [sic] eyes will light on next', he decided neither to recommend the play for a licence nor suggest that it be refused, but instead submitted the script to the scrutiny of the Earl of Scarborough, the Lord Chamberlain himself.[10]

The seventy-six-year-old Earl had enjoyed a distinguished military career after Eton and Oxford, and served as a Governor of Bombay. Colonel Redfern and Billy Rice would have looked up to him. A pragmatic official, he recognised that after the *Chatterley* case, the continued imposition of a rigid code of stage censorship was failing to reflect changing public attitudes. Cautiously, he attempted a relaxation of the guidelines by proposing that the 'adults only' certificate applicable to films might be extended to include plays of dramatic merit that that might otherwise be refused a licence. However, R. A. Butler, the Home Secretary, advised caution. It would be 'unwise', he replied, 'to subject the censorship to Parliamentary discussion', as they might end up with something even more stringent than they had already.[11] Squaring his shoulders, Scarborough decided to ignore his Examiner's fears by demanding minor alterations and awarding performance licences to both *The Blood of the Bambergs* and *Under Plain Cover*. The latter was 'not an easy play to judge', he admitted to the Public Morality Council, whose President, the Lord Bishop of London, had written a peppery note questioning his decision, but it did not deserve to be prohibited.[12]

St Vincent Troubridge and Maurice Coles, however, were not the only ones dubious about *Plays for England*. Penelope thought them intellectually disappointing and came perilously close to Pamela Lane's dismissal of Osborne's early efforts as 'dull and boring', by coldly observing that he could do a lot better. George Devine was similarly bemused. Nevertheless, despite his misgivings, he gave *Blood of the Bambergs* to John Dexter and sent *Under Plain Cover* unannounced and under an appropriately plain cover to Jonathan Miller.

Never before had Osborne encountered directors so dissimilar as Dexter and Miller, twenty-eight years old and one of the writers and performers of the satirical revue, *Beyond the Fringe*. Osborne had long felt an affinity with the camp, abrasive and lower-middle-class Dexter, but was wary of Miller, suspicious of his sparkling intellect, boundless curiosity and a dazzling conversational agility that sprang from quotation to metaphor as nimbly as a tightrope performer. Devine, by contrast, never felt entirely at ease with Dexter, but Miller, middle class, hetero-sexual, a Cambridge-educated polymath and very much a wit, was the kind of person with whom he instinctively felt at home. Miller privately considered *The Blood of the Bambergs* second rate at best, a view subsequently widely shared. *Under Plain Cover*, he thought, had a schoolboyish charm which he assumed derived from the playfully flirtatious relationship between Osborne and Penelope, which he observed when they occasionally turned up at rehearsals in June 1962. His guess that Osborne's reputed socialism really concealed a deep conservatism was confirmed when the playwright offered him a lift after rehearsals one day in his Alvis. As they drove away from the theatre and down the King's Road, Miller settled in the soft leather upholstery and contemplated Osborne, his hands cradling the steering wheel as he negotiated the London traffic. This, Miller thought to himself, was a man not so much looking back in anger but forward to luxury.

Plays for England opened at the Royal Court on 19 July 1962. Neither critics nor audiences were enthusiastic, although Tynan and Hobson concurred that *Under Plain Cover* was the more substantial. It was, they agreed, a play about love. Tynan, whose sexual enthusiasms included spanking female bottoms, ludicrously applauded Osborne's portrayal of the Turners' 'sado-masochistic' relationship as 'perhaps the most audacious statement ever made on the English Stage.'[13] Although not writing from the same privately partisan viewpoint, Hobson favourably compared the play with Genet's *The Balcony*. Assuring his more sensitive readers that the Turners' fantasies had none of Genet's 'perverse delight', he insisted they were nevertheless wholly integral to the 'moral purpose' of the play. 'That purpose is tremendously fulfilled,' he declared, 'and the final figure of the newspaper reporter before the dark and silent house, self-loathing and abased, Judas before the clock strikes twelve, is an accusation as powerful in its way as was years ago Zola's.'[14] Mervyn Jones, on the other hand, one of the few who had thoroughly enjoyed *The Blood of the Bambergs* ('killingly funny in places'), cautiously saluted *Under Plain Cover* in *Tribune* as 'defiantly calculated to lose money', an assessment in which he was proved absolutely correct.[15] *Plays for England* not only lost money but joined *The World of Paul Slickey* in failing to transfer to another theatre. Unlike *Slickey*, however, they crossed the Atlantic to New York, where they were produced for a short season in 1964.

* * *

By the time that *Plays for England* opened, filming was well under way on Osborne's screenplay of *Tom Jones*. Henry Fielding's rollicking account of love, sex and dare-devilry among the squires, opportunists, hypocrites and misanthropes of the eighteenth century had first been published in 1749. It was Woodfall's sixth film in four years, *Look Back in Anger* and *The Entertainer* having been followed by *Saturday Night and Sunday Morning*, *A Taste of Honey* and *The Loneliness of the Long Distance Runner*. It also provided in the title role of the young man who revels in sexual conquest, loses his money, joins the army and is finally vindicated, a plum part for Albert Finney, fresh from his triumph with *Luther*.

Although he had written a play for television, Osborne had never attempted a feature film script, the screenplays for *Look Back in Anger* and *The Entertainer* largely being left to Nigel Kneale, and neither had he worked on an adaptation. Richardson quickly discovered that presenting him with a copy of the novel – long and dense with incident – and expecting him to produce a filmable screenplay from it was not going to work. Richardson therefore tried a second strategy, that of providing his Woodfall partner with a list of characters and scenes he thought would best transfer to the screen and waiting to see what happened. Eventually, Osborne produced a script that the director acknowledged as lively enough, but which he objected did not make a coherent narrative. Osborne bridled. Screenwriting, soothed Richardson, differed from writing for the stage in that film was primarily a director's medium and represented his vision above that of the author's. Although he succeeded in coaxing Osborne into producing several new pages of screenplay, they seemed to a disappointed Richardson 'more like pastiche Congreve than anything to do with movie narrative.'[16] For his part, Osborne regarded a script as complete when it left his desk and was beginning to take the view that those who commissioned anything from him should be grateful to be rewarded with the results. Hurt that Osborne appeared to have adopted an attitude of intransigence, but committed to begin shooting in the West Country on 25 June, Richardson continued to make cuts and changes while filming was in progress. Scenting treachery in the air, Osborne muttered darkly to Oscar Beuselinck, that as changes were being made without his being consulted, it seemed pointless that he had ever been employed on the project at all. This squib of disagreement would crackle dangerously, exploding later when Richardson came to film *The Charge of the Light Brigade*.

Yet *Tom Jones* was unlike any previous Woodfall film. It was in colour for a start, and by no stretch of the imagination could it be called Angry. It had no relation to the gritty northern landscapes of *Room at the Top* or the youthful realism of *Look Back in Anger* or *Saturday Night and Sunday Morning*. Instead, it was a boisterous romp in some of England's most beautiful landscapes, a lark, a costume drama filmed with a mid-Sixties, Carnaby Street lens. During the long, hot summer, Richardson filmed in Dorset and Somerset at some of England's most magnificent country houses, their gardens green and fragrant with flowers. Cerne Abbey, imposing itself over the village of Cerne Abbas, represented Squire Allworthy's house, while Steepleton House, near Blandford

Forum, stood in as Squire Western's mansion. Moving to Taunton, the crew and actors set out for Nettlecombe Court, near Williton, converted into a girls' school and, for the purposes of the film, reconverted for the bedroom scenes and the interior of Newgate Gaol.

Yet as Woodfall had secured barely a £500,000 budget from United Artists, there were fears that the money would run out before shooting was completed and the film might have to be abandoned. Richardson's spontaneous script changes made several scenes disconcertingly improvisational and his promises that all would be resolved by careful editing seemed less than convincing. By the early autumn, filming was complete but the high anticipation of the early summer had dissolved into disappointment. Conscious of 'all we hadn't achieved, all we had skimped', Richardson found himself miserably supervising the editing, 'cobbling the last bits together as best we could and realising how impoverished and threadbare our efforts were.'[17] Tom Jones the rough-cut resembled Tom Jones the novel in that it was a long and complex narrative and difficult to edit coherently. The head of British distribution for United Artists gloomily forecast that the film would be lucky to make £40,000 worldwide. United Artists, though, did not foresee that, like the original stage version of Look Back in Anger, Tom Jones, an evocation of a very different kind of England, would open in the exactly the right place at the right time.

CHAPTER 19

A Sixties Millionaire

'I THINK I'M JUST A compulsive marrier,' Osborne offhandedly told an interviewer from *Woman's Own* magazine in 1960. 'Perhaps I ought to do it every ten years or so.'[1] By 1963, however, and at thirty-four years old, he was already well ahead of his own game and keeping his lawyer busy by having divorced twice and married three times in the short space of twelve years.

On 25 May, fifteen months after Penelope's divorce, five months after Osborne and Mary Ure had divorced and six weeks after Mary married Robert Shaw, Osborne arrived at Hailsham Register Office in Sussex. An uncertain groom at his wedding to Mary, this time he was prepared and ready to go. A few moments later, Tony Richardson ostentatiously swerved to a stop in his red Thunderbird and out of the passenger door stepped the former Mrs Gilliatt, wearing a vivid lilac suit and an attention-grabbing straw hat. Having ignored the advice of her editor at the *Observer*, who, when she informed him whom she was going to marry had strenuously advised against, she was now only minutes away from becoming the third Mrs Osborne. It was swiftly done: the ceremony lasted ten minutes, Richardson playing the supporting role of best man as he had at Osborne's previous wedding, while Angela Conner, the bride's sister, appeared as a witness. Nellie Beatrice, George Devine and Jocelyn Herbert stood among the small clutch of guests. Eluding predatory reporters, the newlyweds nipped smartly out of a rear door and sped off in the back of the Thunderbird to a reception at The Old Water Mill.

Soon afterwards, they were flying to Venice, where two years earlier, they had enjoyed a semi-clandestine rendezvous during the Film Festival. As much as it was possible to do so, Penelope reconciled Osborne to his mother, as she now comes to the fore again. She liked Penelope, and Penelope liked Nellie Beatrice, who swiftly substituted the pictures of her son and Mary with those of the newlyweds and wrote excitedly to a relative that 'John and Penelope are so sweet and I really love them both.'[2] Her son and new daughter-in-law now arranged for her to join them in Venice for the remainder of their holiday. At the age of seventy, she was not only making her first excursion abroad and negotiating the hazardous adventure of foreign food, but one of her few forays outside of London. 'I shall always treasure my time in Venice,' she wrote later, 'your two lovely faces at the airport, my lovely room, complete with those beautiful flowers.'³ After Venice, they arrived in New York, where Nellie Beatrice squinted upwards at gleaming skyscrapers before the party moved on to Barbados, where she sweated beneath the punchingly hot sun and from where the travellers returned, Nellie Beatrice almost confused with gratitude.

They arrived home in time for the opening of Tom Jones at the Pavilion Cinema at Piccadilly Circus on 26 June 1963, almost a year to the day after filming began. It was three months after the release of The Beatles' first LP and the hedonism of the Sixties, in the eyes of Philip Larkin, had begun. That night, after a Beatles concert at the Majestic Ballroom in Newcastle, John Lennon and Paul McCartney wrote 'She Loves You', which would soon hit the top of the British bestselling record charts and become the group's biggest-selling record to date. Combining 'Lennon's downbeat cynicism and McCartney's get-up-and-go optimism', writes a Beatles historian, 'She Loves You' was 'an authentic distillation of the atmosphere of that time . . .'⁴ So was Tom Jones. 'Incomplete and botched' as it was in Richardson's eyes, its irreverent celebration of vice and virtue epitomised London's new-found youthful energy. During the following weeks, queues snaked around the cinema as Tom Jones broke the cinema's box-office records, taking £100,000 in six months and making Osborne, Richardson and Finney millionaires. Osborne insisted that George Devine, subsisting on his salary from the Royal Court, be given a share of the profits as well. Six years earlier, in New York and dizzy with acclaim, Osborne had jubilantly predicted he would be 'RICH'. Now, and with the additional worldwide royalties from his plays increasing each year, he actually was. What was more, the shelves at the Woodfall offices at Curzon Street were beginning to be laden with awards. The London film critics named Richardson as Best Director, while the Society of Film and Television Arts chose Tom Jones as the Best Film. Nominated along side Harold Pinter for The Servant, and David Storey for This Sporting Life, Osborne collected the Society award for Best Adapted Screenplay.

This entirely unexpected triumph was repeated in the United States, where Tom Jones was nominated for an astonishing ten Academy Awards including those for Best Picture, while Osborne was short-listed for Best Adapted Screen-play. However, as he and Penelope had already arranged to be on holiday in India at the time of the Oscars' award ceremony in Hollywood on 13 April 1964, Osborne was grateful that Penelope, whom he feared would jump at the chance of attending the Oscars, agreed that they need not alter their plans. Even though he very much liked being acknowledged and admired, the prospect of the ceremony filled him with dread. It would surely be an interminable nightmare of staggering insincerity and, worst of all, one could not be certain beforehand of winning anything. Why go all that way, he reasoned, only to smile while applauding someone else?

At the beginning of April, therefore, they arrived at Udaipur. These were years in which many of those troubled by the materialistic ethics of the West were discovering a respite in Eastern spirituality and cross-legged postures of peaceful contemplation. Young people in search of mystical enlightenment donned stout shoes, shouldered a rucksack and set off from London and provincial cities on the long trail to India. The Osbornes, however, were not of them, being wholly content with their inner selves and secure both in their materialism and their tastes, which were strictly luxurious. Arriving at the sumptuous Lake Palace Hotel, they began four weeks of heat and sightseeing, wandering through dusty markets admiring brilliantly coloured fabrics, peering into the cool interiors of glittering temples and retreating, in the evening, to their hotel and fine dining eased all the more by air-conditioning and five-star service. 'I keep looking at the picture of the castle where you're staying,' enthused Nellie Beatrice in reply to their postcard. 'It's all so exciting. I hope the sun does not make your head bad, the weather here is quite nice.'[5]

Their serenity was briefly disrupted when Osborne was attacked by wasps in a temple, an unnerving echo of being chased up Charing Cross Road by an irate audience, and, on 14 April, by surprising news from Los Angeles. Tom Jones had claimed four Oscars, including those for Best Picture (the first time a British film had won the award since Laurence Olivier's Hamlet in 1948), Best Director (Richardson) and Best Music (John Addison), while Osborne had won for Best Adapted Screenplay. 'Clever John Osborne, says I,' approved Nellie Beatrice.[6]

Yet nobody connected with the film had been in Los Angeles to collect its armful of statuettes. When Osborne's name was announced, therefore, it fell to Ivan Goff, the director of the 4-Star Television channel to receive his Oscar on his behalf, murmur a few words of gratitude and arrange for it to be conveyed to the playwright in London. When at last Osborne unwrapped 'replica number 1231 of the copyrighted statuette', he was surprised to find both how heavy it was and how ugly.[7] But it would, he told friends, make an admirable doorstop.

Oscar the doorstop duly took up his position not in Hellingly but at the Osbornes' new address in London. With renovations complete, Osborne and Penelope had settled in at The Old Water Mill, only for Penelope to decide that life there was really excruciatingly dull. The business of film criticism, she explained to her crestfallen husband, was not at all like play writing. It could not be done just anywhere and especially not in a village in the Sussex countryside. Commuting was irksome and conducting editorial conferences by telephone impossible. She itched to be back in the capital, close to the press screenings, the gossip and the Observer. She also desperately missed her social network and the stimulus of being a part of what she called 'London's intellectual life'.[8] Reluctantly, therefore, Osborne agreed to retain The Old Water Mill as an occasional retreat and buy somewhere in London as well. Tom Jones had ensured that he could afford it, and he became a double property owner by acquiring a large house at 31 Chester Square in Belgravia, just around the corner from Lower Belgrave Street, where Jocelyn Rickards still lived.

Part of a white-painted Georgian century terrace with elegant porticoes, on four floors and with a basement and attic, number 31 overlooked leafy central gardens. On the top floor, there was a nursery and two additional rooms, while the floor below included a bedroom and a large room which Osborne commandeered as his study, moving in his desk and chair, books, typewriter and a divan on which he could rest or read. On the first floor there was a substantial drawing-room and an office for Sonia McGuinness, while on the ground floor there was a dining-room and lobby. Outside the house stood another new acquisition: a green Bentley S3. Considered separately, the town and country houses were magnificent enough, but put together they represented a 1960s image of the hugely successful and the wealthy. Nellie Beatrice was enormously impressed by the luxury of it all as yet another emblem of her son's astounding accomplishments. He even employed domestic staff. In addition to the chauffeur at the wheel of the Bentley, a cook was installed in the kitchen while a vacuum-wielding housekeeper nestled in the basement. '. . . you said you had 11 bedrooms,' gasped Nellie Beatrice in wonderment. 'That's nice because you could have a different one every night.'⁹

Although the Square would acquire a touch of the bohemian in two years' time when the Rolling Stones singer Mick Jagger and his girlfriend Marianne Faithfull roosted briefly at number 62, at the time that Osborne and Penelope arrived it remained safely conservative. It had a tantalising history, Mary Shelley, the author of *Frankenstein*, having once lived a few doors away, while Terence Rattigan had inhabited number 16. But it was also sedate, and sedate was not Penelope's idea of an appropriate setting for the fulcrum of London's intellectual life. Number 31, she decreed, would be transformed into a home showcasing the very contemporary accomplishments of its occupants. Instigating a complete overhaul, her summons brought designers bearing swatches of fabrics, builders to knock at the walls and rap at the floorboards, and decorators to pin samples of wallpaper and colour test sheets to every available surface.

Everything was to be streamlined and made spectacularly up to date. Carpets were ripped up and thrown out, floorboards furiously sanded and soothingly varnished before pristine white rugs were haphazardly flung across them. Walls were painted white. *Harbinger Bird IV*, Osborne's bronze sculpture, was collected from Sussex and prominently displayed. A painting by Gwen John was hung in the master bedroom, where a large television set stared unblinkingly at the king-size bed, the headboard of which, cushioned in chocolate-brown fur, ran the entire width of the room. A chunk of amethyst, a stone traditionally believed to prevent intoxication but which in the event failed dismally, was artistically placed nearby on a low teak table. In the bathroom, the water pipes were re-routed to allow the bath to stand isolated in the centre of the room. A curtain teasingly fashioned from several dozen metal lavatory chains hung over the window, the effect intended to resemble that of chainmail. Downstairs, delivery men manoeuvred a huge antique refectory table into a white dining-room entered by newly installed sixteen-foot-high double doors finished in beaten copper. Instead of being hinged at the sides, they were pivoted, top and bottom, from the centre, so that they revolved as a pair. In the drawing-room, there were white leather and chrome chairs and more white rugs. Finally, Penelope declared she was satisfied. The Osborne stage set was now ready for the stars to take their place and shine, and their friends to express their admiration. This most stylish London house, she declared, symbolised their most stylish metropolitan marriage, for theirs was the grandest of passions and the 1960s would surely be their decade, the decade in which they would scale great heights.

Indeed, it all looked very promising. Osborne had returned from India reinvigorated and impatient to begin planning two ambitious new plays. 'I am already fired up into the future with *Inadmissible Evidence*, and, maybe, *A Patriot for Me*', he noted, adding as an afterthought: 'I am good at titles if nothing else.'[10] Financial independence, his marriage to Penelope, the sanctuary of Hellingly, the Chester Square house where Oscar had now been joined by a Tony award, the American production of *Luther* having won Best Play of 1964, had given him a sense of a new start and unleashed a surge of creative confidence. Culturally, he was a much admired figure, as was Penelope who, while passing judgments on new films each week in the *Observer*, had launched herself into writing fiction.

There was indeed much to celebrate, and a plentiful supply of champagne was stacked in the fridge to help push the boat out. And it began to be pushed out a lot; some weeks it was hardly in harbour. The grandson of publicans and the son of a barmaid, Osborne had never been disposed towards abstinence as far as alcohol was concerned. He enjoyed whisky and, fleetingly, during his Hayling Island and Bridgwater phase, he had flirted with pink gins. Nowadays, he preferred wine and especially champagne, and the best champagne that he could buy. 'He could drink champagne all day,' noted his lawyer.[11] Sometimes, Sonia McGuinness discovered that when she arrived for work in the morning, her employer would not yet have come downstairs or breakfasted, but would appear soon afterwards, a glass of champagne already in his hand.

In all outward appearances, Osborne appeared to share Penelope's assessment that theirs was a 'smashing life' and the Osbornes played their parts well.[12] They called each other 'Banks', a nickname possibly derived from his prodigious bank account, and lobbed outlandishly expensive presents at each other: a red MG sports car, gift-wrapped, for her; clothes by fashionable new designers for him; a Cartier watch for her on which, the first time she wound it up, she broke a fingernail. What fun! The champagne flowed and the rescue remedy of codeine tablets stuffed the bathroom cabinet. They entertained lavishly, their guests hoping that it would be the cook and not the hit-and-miss Penelope who was in charge of the catering. The Tynans and the Oliviers would be at their parties, as would actors and directors from the Royal Court, and from film and television; there were Spike Milligan and Peter Sellers and other comedians and satirists then very much in the public eye; there were the architects transforming London's skyline, and advertisers promoting what was new: names that appeared in the bright new colour sections of the Sunday newspapers. When Penelope bought a clavichord, the Osbornes instituted occasional musical evenings, which just might have reminded Osborne of Jim Dixon's despised gatherings at Professor Welch's home in Lucky Jim. Accounts were opened at Savile Row and Carnaby Street tailors, hairdressers and wine merchants. No expense was spared at Hellingly either, where another housekeeper was employed. They adopted rural pursuits, acquiring horses, Osborne's being a Welsh gray mare named Morag on which he took riding lessons, and stabling them at nearby Polegate. 'Osborne had to have these touches of luxury,' declared Oscar Beuselinck. 'I shook my head at it, really. He had an irrepressible urge to show people he'd made it, and he needed to keep on proving to himself and to the world that he'd got a bit of money.'[13]

As Osborne gravitated to Belgravia and as Kenneth Tynan to a large Victorian house in South Kensington, the vaguely-socialist credentials espoused by several of the Royal Court circle were beginning to some to look decidedly flimsy. Beuselinck, who remembered his harsh working-class upbringing and liked to take it with him wherever he went, looked on with ill-concealed distaste. 'A lot of them at the Royal Court pretended to claim affinity with the working class,' he declared, 'but none of them knew anything about it. Not one of them was working class, and many of them were anti-Semitic. They were a bunch of wine-drinking pinkoes peddling their social consciences, a set of bleeding hearts in beautiful drawing-rooms.'[14] It was a social circle that Osborne found both compelling and intimidating. 'Penelope introduced John Osborne to a strata of society he wanted to become a part of, but which he simultaneously loathed,' explained Beuselinck, 'partly because he felt he didn't fit in. She knew Ken Tynan as an equal, she knew [Princess Margaret's husband] Tony Snowden, she knew a lot of photographers, journalists and film-makers, but he could never see these people as she did. It was the same at the Royal Court. It was very difficult for him.' Osborne, noticed Beuselinck, seemed an 'awkward' host at Penelope's 'intellectual' gatherings, where she 'delighted at being at the centre of things.' While she was entirely at ease, laughing and talking, observed Beuselinck, Osborne 'remained anxiously detached'.[15]

Despite his professional achievements, Osborne's personal and social confidence remained fragile. He had never overcome his childhood sense of loss, of being somehow at a disadvantage, and in Penelope's company he was wary of being revealed as not quite up to standard. Moreover, the professional assurance that he presented to the world was beginning to be assailed by inner qualms of which she knew nothing. 'I am governed by fear every day of my life', he had confided to a journal in 1959. 'Sometimes it is the first sensation I have on waking . . .'[16] His remarkable eight-year record of achievement, from Look Back in Anger to Tom Jones, had successfully held his apprehensions in check, but now, after an Oscar-winning film and marriage to a highly ambitious, competitive woman, the enormous professional and personal expectations placed upon him

were suddenly apparent and etched in high relief. Penelope in particular anticipated great things. 'You've got it in you darling,' he recorded her as saying,
many times over.[17] But what exactly, he worried, *was* within him? And might it
all suddenly evaporate? If so, what might happen then? Would his health buckle?
His childhood had been accompanied by the fear of tuberculosis and then by
rheumatic fever; in his adolescence he had been susceptible to eczema and
skin rashes; now, an adult, he suffered from nauseous headaches and frequent
migraines. He was also prone to periods of deep despondency, especially in
January, the month of his father's death, and it all seemed to be getting worse.

Already, he was beginning to have misgivings in his marriage. He was
apprehensive of Penelope's steely determination, as he had been of Pamela's
and Mary's, although Penelope's was social as much as professional. Socially,
he saw, she was from a very different drawer. Whereas Osborne had worked
hard to acquire some sophistication in his manners and cultural awareness,
Penelope just seemed to have been born with them as part of her natural equipment. It was her heritage. Already he recognised that these were the things that
distinguished them and might well divide them. Perhaps he should have seen
it before. These unsettling thoughts and reflections he scribbled in the journals
into which he had begun to confide his misgivings and disquiet. 'Fear in love',
he wrote. 'Fear of being deserted, fear of being involved . . . It is fear and I
cannot rid myself of it. It numbs me, it sterilizes me, and I am empty, dumb,
ignorant and afraid.' [18]

These terrors, the fear of failure and the resulting self-loathing are woven
into both Inadmissible Evidence and A Patriot for Me, the plays on which he was now
working. They also draw upon themes eddying about Osborne's earlier work:
the sanctity of the human spirit, the nature of love, the question of whether
there are ideals worth fighting for and the value of individual struggle. Bleaker
and more darkly ominous than anything he had previously written, the vitality bounding through Look Back in Anger and the burning defiance of Luther are
choked in both Inadmissible Evidence and A Patriot for Me by the disillusionment first
glimpsed in The Entertainer. Charting the emotional disintegration of Bill Maitland, a London lawyer, Inadmissible Evidence is also a chilling herald of Osborne's
own imminent collapse. It was as if he foresaw his own life falling apart.
'Look Back in Anger is John's first personal statement and Inadmissible Evidence is his
second,' remarked Jocelyn Herbert, the designer of the original production.
'Bill Maitland is speaking in John's voice. It's a very bitter play, and full of
John's agonies, jealousies and sadness.'[19]

*   *   *

Until the beginning of the 1960s, Osborne followed dramatic convention by
writing in three acts. Inadmissible Evidence is his first full-length play written in the
contemporary manner of two acts. To Laurence Olivier, he remarked philosophically that there were no third acts in life any more, either. Originally, he had

entitled the play *Not in the Public Interest*, but altered it to *Inadmissible Evidence* as it had more of a legal ring to it. Initially, he had chosen the name of William Henry Crawford for his protagonist, an echo of his maternal grandfather, William Crawford Grove. But when Oscar Beuselinck warned him that, coincidentally, a solicitor of that name was alive and well and practising in Lime Street, Osborne hopped from one grandparent to another and altered the name to Prosser before settling on Maitland, an ironic echo of the teetotaller who appears briefly in *A Subject of Scandal and Concern*, questioning Holyoke on his attitude to God.

This time, the play was prompted not by a visual image but by a letter that Osborne read in a newspaper agony column in which a woman recounted her distress at watching her husband, a man she loved, becoming slowly isolated by the dislike and distrust he aroused in others. Oscar Beuselinck, though, liked to believe that Maitland was partly modelled upon himself, and there are superficial resemblances in that, like Beuselinck, Maitland lacks the Oxbridge background customary in the legal profession and since his teens has worked his way up eventually to succeed his employer. In Maitland's intrusive enquiries of his secretary, Osborne also appropriated Beuselinck's habit of greeting both male and female clients with sexually suggestive banter.

Beuselinck, however, was a conspicuously successful and effective lawyer, while Maitland is not. About to be investigated for malpractice by the Law Society, unable to cope with his staff and his hapless clients with their wretched tales of petty domestic betrayals, sexual misdemeanours and impending divorces, Maitland confesses that he has always expected to be exposed as an emotional and intellectual fraud. His secretary and managing clerk announce they intend to leave the practice, while Jane, his teenage daughter, and Liz, his lover, reject him. Only Maples, a shy, homosexual client, with his miserable account of marital compromise and furtive outdoor fumbling with men at night, elicits his momentary compassion. Like Archie Rice, Maitland is almost wholly obsessed with himself: harsh and harshly self-judging, emotionally bankrupt and blistering with self-disgust. Bitterness and spite make him insufferable, yet his capacity for recognising his own failure makes him human. The love he craves thwarted by his inability to love either himself or anyone else, the play ends as he telephones Anna, his wife, to tell her he cannot come home. He is left, as the curtain falls, frightened, disowned and alone. He stands four-square at the centre of the play and follows Jimmy Porter, Archie Rice and Martin Luther in a line of mightily resilient Osbornean protagonists, idealists overwhelmed, yet determined not to be defeated. Yet Maitland is far more battered than any of them, his torment more deeply ingrained, his redemption seemingly impossible.

A remarkable, if remarkably disturbing piece of writing, *Inadmissible Evidence* is almost a soliloquy of anguished self-searching. It is also richly evocative of many of Osborne's thoughts and feelings during and after its writing, and uncannily anticipates the anxieties and feelings and the eventual breakdown that would engulf him in the months to come. In undertaking the journey into the fears and vulnerabilities of Bill Maitland, he was also exploring the darkness within himself.

Maitland is thirty-nine, six years older than Osborne when he sat down in his study at The Old Water Mill in mid-1963 to begin the battle of composition. He continued the writing regime that he had established while working on *Luther* at Lower Belgrave Street, and which he would subsequently follow for *A Patriot for Me* and many of his later plays. If necessary, he would research background detail, making extensive notes, usually in black ink with a fountain pen. For *Inadmissible Evidence*, this involved legal technicalities and procedures. Once these notes were typed by his secretary, he would retreat with them into his study where he would write in feverish, gruelling bursts lasting several hours, frequently through the night, enveloped by loud classical and operatic music surging from his record player or the radio. For several weeks he would work like this, covering many sheets of paper. Having eventually arrived at a final draft, he would then transcribe a fair copy into one or more of his hardbound, green-backed reporter's notebooks from which his secretary would prepare a typed final copy. Alternatively, he would sometimes dictate to her. As his secretary discovered, it takes rather a knack to decipher Osborne's handwriting. It is well spaced but small and jagged, with the vowels sometimes squeezed and lost between the consonants. The cross-strokes of the 't's are sometimes detached from the stems while occasional words appear in capitals or are underlined, often for clarity rather than emphasis. Once the play had been typed, Osborne would not read it again until either rehearsals began or proofs were returned for his inspection from his publisher, and even then he might leave it to others to check for spelling and punctuation. 'He hated rereading,' recalled Sonia McGuinness, his longest-lasting secretary. 'He would rarely alter anything and would never allow any cuts to be made.'[20]

Inadmissible Evidence was exhausting to write and evolved over several months at Hellingly. Although very much based in the daily routine of a solicitor's office, Osborne attempted in Maitland's long speeches of self-examination to achieve a combination of the naturalistic and the metaphysical and thus attain what he had hoped to attain in *Look Back in Anger*: the quality of an operatic aria. It was 7 April before he pronounced that he was at last 'rid of Bill Maitland' and opened a bottle of champagne. 'I've done new language things for the first time,' he recorded in his notebook, before adding grimly: 'No one will notice.'[21] Finished copies were delivered to the Royal Court and to a new Lord Chamberlain. The previous year, the Earl of Scarborough had retired, to be succeeded by Lord Cobbold, a sixty-year-old Old Etonian and a former Governor of the Bank of England, who issued the expected list of alterations and deletions required before a performance licence could be issued. Among them was the word 'crumpet' meaning a sexually desirable woman, and the phrase 'that beautiful arse', which Cobbold agreed could be amended to 'that beautiful bottom'.[22] The homosexual character of Maples, however, survived.

This time, Anthony Page was leading the theatre's wearisome negotiations with Stable Yard. With Tony Richardson capitalising on *Tom Jones*'s Oscar haul by flying to Hollywood to film a star-laden production of Evelyn Waugh's *The Loved One*, Osborne had turned initially to George Devine to direct *Inadmissible Evidence*. But Devine had shaken his head and handed it on to Page, who thought it a 'masterpiece. Somehow in the eloquence and intensity with which it concentrates on a single threatened man,' he wrote, 'this play crosses English boundaries and joins writers like Kafka, Genet and O'Neill who made something universal out of exploring themselves unsparingly.'[23]

Devine had resisted directing the play not because he thought it inferior – quite the reverse – but because, at fifty-three, he felt that he no longer had the energy for so demanding a piece. He was becoming disenchanted with life at the Royal Court. On the one hand, the English Stage Company was now recognised and highly respected, but on the other, its very success was resulting in a dispersal of its talent. The attitudes and styles of production that he and Richardson had pioneered had become absorbed into the general currency of the theatre at large and the newly created, state subsidised national companies in particular. Peter Hall, the original director of *Waiting for Godot*, and who in 1960 had become the founder and director of the Royal Shakespeare Company at Stratford-upon-Avon, had lured William Gaskill and Jocelyn Herbert to Warwickshire to produce a revival of *Richard III*. Three years later, in 1963, the National Theatre was created at the Old Vic Theatre in Waterloo Road, and Laurence Olivier appointed as its first artistic director. When Kenneth Tynan proposed that he renounce both drama criticism and his post at the *Observer* to join him as Literary Manager and advise on the repertoire, Olivier quickly agreed: 'God – anything to get you off that *Observer*.'[24] With Tynan's defection, the English Stage Company lost one of their most eloquently supportive, though caustic, critics. The National also claimed Gaskill and John Dexter, who temporarily left Sloane Square in order to become directors at Waterloo Road. 'The birds are leaving the nest,' observed Devine despondently.[25]

The Royal Shakespeare Company and the National Theatre offered new opportunities to directors, designers, actors and writers. At its second home at the Aldwych Theatre in London, the RSC produced a succession of plays by Harold Pinter, while early productions at the National Theatre included the British premiere of *Play* by Samuel Beckett and *Armstrong's Last Goodnight* by John Arden, both of which might otherwise have been presented by the English Stage Company. The National was also discovering its own new dramatists, such as Peter Shaffer, whose *The Royal Hunt of the Sun*, an epic tragedy about the murder of the Aztec king Atahualpa, opened in 1964. At the same time, young commercial producers were staging the kind of drama that many of their predecessors would have summarily rejected, Michael Codron producing Joe Orton's *Entertaining Mr Sloane* in 1963, an outrageous comedy of sexual and social manners that both shocked and delighted audiences.

220   EXTRAVAGANCE

And yet 'We are supposed to be the spearhead,' lamented Devine, 'but how do you keep sharpening the spear?'[26] Even with the money that Osborne's plays had generated over the years, there seemed fewer spear-sharpening prospects now that the Royal Court found itself competing with well-subsidised national companies and a patchily more adventurous West End. Although the Arts Council increased its grant to the English Stage Company to £32,000 in 1965, the costs of producing new plays in so small a theatre as the Royal Court were escalating alarmingly. Devine found himself increasingly strapped for cash and dependent upon classical revivals and West End co-productions. Of the eight productions between *Inadmissible Evidence* in September 1964 and *A Patriot for Me* almost a year later, only three were of new plays and two of those were staged for one performance only, produced without decor on a Sunday evening.

While Osborne remained tenaciously loyal, he had noticed for some while the immense strain that sustaining the English Stage Company was imposing upon his mentor. Already in 1961, Devine had suffered a breakdown, and in the autumn of 1963, he was whisked into hospital for two days after suffering cardiac spasms. For the sake of his health, it was agreed that another director must oversee the 1964 season but as Richardson, the obvious heir-apparent, was one of those leaving the nest to pursue a film career, and as Gaskill and Dexter were at the National, Devine's mantle fell upon the shoulders of Anthony Page.

As far as Devine was concerned, Page, born in India, the son of a brigadier general and educated at Oxford, had exactly the right pedigree. Having arrived at Sloane Square as an assistant director in 1958, he was now twenty-nine, had recently returned to London after serving a year as artistic director of the Dundee Repertory Theatre in Scotland, and would go on to direct six of Osborne's plays for the Royal Court. While in wintry Dundee, city of jute and marmalade, Page had encountered Nicol Williamson, a young actor who had since appeared at both the Royal Court and at the Royal Shakespeare Company. The tall, red-haired and blue-eyed Williamson, declared Page, was absolutely the actor to play Maitland. Osborne, though, was sceptical. Apart from being unknown outside the profession, Williamson was a young-looking twenty-seven and Maitland supposedly prematurely middle-aged and eroded by bitterness. Besides, he had his own list of heavyweight contenders for the role whom he had invited to audition on 2 June 1964. Yet on the day, none of his prospective Maitlands turned out to be the one he was looking for and, at the end of a dispiriting afternoon, Page played his trump card of Williamson. That the actor had arrived wearing a suit that might pass for Maitland's own impressed Osborne immensely. He was of course far too young, but as soon as he began reading, Osborne was convinced. Williamson, he agreed, had the voice of Bill Maitland. All the rest would hopefully follow.

With Williamson surrounded by several Royal Court veterans, *Inadmissible Evidence* opened on 13 August at the Theatre Royal in Brighton, and on 9 September at the Royal Court, where it was greeted by Irving Wardle in *The Times* as 'a fine new play . . . which brings back Mr Osborne in embattled first person.'

Osborne, he added, 'seems alone among current British playwrights in being able to create heroes of our own times.'[27] At The Sunday Times, Harold Hobson exclaimed: 'I do not believe that any language could be too sumptuous to convey the pity and the pathos and the wit of Mr Osborne's work.'[28]

Yet while Hobson and other critics acclaimed both the play and Williamson's tour-de-force performance, some were left at the end of the evening in a despondency almost equal to that of Bill Maitland himself. Here was yet another Osborne play, they protested, in which the omnipresent protagonist, virtually unchallenged by any other character, held the stage firing invective at any convenient and increasingly incidental target, which this time happened to include the increasing proliferation of technology, the supporters of CND, the advocates of natural childbirth, the absence of imagination in young people, and suburban motorists, furry mascots dangling in the back windows of their small saloon cars, clogging the roads on Bank Holidays. Mary Holland, succeeding Tynan on the Observer, objected that the play was little more that the author's 'two-dimensional mouthpiece' and declared that the real, substantial 'anger' of only a few years previously had now dissipated.[29] Holland, though, was in a minority, and other writers were quick to acknowledge Osborne's achievement. Sandy Wilson, the dapper author of The Boyfriend, a long-running musical comedy of the anyone-for-tennis school Osborne had done much to render out of date, wrote to tell him that he was 'deeply moved and very excited' by the play.[30] Terence Rattigan, announcing himself as 'your most persistent fan' saluted it as 'not only your fullest and most moving work, but the best play of the century.'[31]

From now on, Rattigan became a regular correspondent and supporter. Noël Coward, having survived The World of Paul Slickey, condescended to an acquaintanceship, although wariness between 'The Master' and the former Angry Young Man never entirely evaporated. Inadmissible Evidence not only augmented Osborne's reputation as one of the leading dramatists of the day, but won him more admirers among the literary old guard. The seventy-two-year-old Edith Bagnold, the author of National Velvet and a woman whom Nancy Mitford, the novelist and former 'bright young thing' of the 1920s, likened to a 'fearfully nice gym mistress', informed him that his plays made others seem 'fuddy-duddy'.[32] Violet Bonham Carter, a daughter of Herbert Asquith, a former Prime Minister, and another septuagenarian, summoned him to tea so that he might elucidate the 'angry philosophy' for her.[33] Among the most important of Osborne's newer friendships, though, was with the poet John Betjeman. An amiable, even jolly man to his many admirers but also beleaguered by private bouts of depression, Betjeman declared that Inadmissible Evidence was 'tremendous . . . The best thing you – yes, even you – have ever written.' In watching Maitland's long journey into his soul, he had felt moments of deep recognition, and that 'increasingly the play was about me and that is what all the great playwrights and poets can do for their watchers and readers . . . Oh hell,' he concluded, 'what words are there to express myself? I feel as though I am writing to the elements.'[34]

*   *   *

Two apparently contrasting characters, Osborne had met Betjeman as a result of his sending the older man a 'fan letter'.[35] Born in north London in 1906, Betjeman had created in his poetry a suburban world of sporty girls and middle-aged, disappointed clerks, of open roads and depressing new towns, its nostalgia and lightness of touch often concealing an underlying melancholy, rather like Betjeman himself. He was a homely advocate of Victorian and Georgian architecture and a scourge of inept town planners, of the relentless march of electricity pylons and the proliferation of parking meters and concrete lamp standards, who had endeared himself to the nation during the war by giving cosy talks on soothing topics on the wireless. Indeed, Osborne may have listened to some of them. At first glance, the friendship between the jovial, avuncular poet and the former Angry Young Man seems ill-matched, but then a love of England, what it might have been and perhaps could be, and a rich seam of dissent was common to both. While both had a whimsical affection for a *Gem* and *Magnet* England, they also were simultaneously alert to the contemporary. Each found in the other a boundless curiosity, wit and energy, and they would talk for hours, reminiscing about the music hall, looking through old photographs and postcards (which Osborne had begun to collect, his speciality being theatrical cards), exchanging opinions about books and people and contentedly musing on the highways and byways of English etymology.

'There was always a lot of laughter,' recalled Betjeman's companion, Lady Elizabeth Cavendish. 'They loved each other's company. John adored JB and loved his humour, and JB admired Osborne's writing enormously. I think JB helped John become more confident. He made John feel serene.'[36] At Betjeman's tiny house at 43 Cloth Fair in the City of London, its living-room packed with books, lined with William Morris's red 'Bird and Anemone' wallpaper, presided over by Archie, Betjeman's childhood teddy bear, and its window overlooking the graveyard of St Bartholomew's Church, Osborne could relax away from the furious professional and social pace set by Penelope.

*   *   *

Meanwhile, *Inadmissible Evidence* had done much to restore the beleaguered fortunes of the Royal Court before the series of revivals that Anthony Page had scheduled for the winter and the spring. Costing just over £3,000 to produce, it had taken almost four times as much at the box office, its forty performances playing almost to capacity. But with Williamson already committed to the Royal Court for the remainder of the season, the play had to wait until 17 March 1965 before transferring to the Wyndham's Theatre in the West End, where Williamson once again played Maitland. One of the plays which followed *Inadmissible Evidence* at Sloane Square was *Cuckoo in the Nest*, 'the blessed Ben Travers masterpiece', thought Osborne, a 1925 farce in which a man and a woman, each married to someone else, are obliged while travelling to share a hotel bedroom.[37] Travers himself, aged almost eighty, was in the first night audience to see the creator of Bill Maitland appearing as Claude Hickett MP, one of the pursuing spouses. 'My word!' John Betjeman told Osborne. 'That was a good play and what immortal lines in it . . . You should have seen Ben Travers' shoulders heaving at his jokes.'[38]

CHAPTER 20

Of Mother, Money, Marriage and Manners

HE MAY HAVE ENJOYED relaxed and convivial interludes with John Betjeman, but otherwise Osborne's life had never been so hectic. Gossip columnists continued to monitor his movements, journalists still queued to canvas his thoughts and his doormat was swamped each morning by an increasingly voluminous mail. Film producers both in Britain and the United States attempted to coax him into writing screenplays, amateur playwrights appealed to him to comment upon their scripts, actors suggested themselves for his plays, theatregoers wrote letters quizzing him on his work while some testily demanded their money back, and correspondents of many nationalities and varying degrees of lucidity offered their suggestions on what he should write next.

The director of the Agricultural Aid Foundation in Los Angeles proposed that he write a play in which Martin Luther encountered Adolf Hitler. An admirer from Norway, requesting 'a dear souvenir and memory of one of the most eminent and famous authors of the world' was rewarded with a signed photograph.[1] A bundle of papers written in a compressed, jagged scrawl arrived for his commentary from Cambridge, its author advising him that while 'completely sane and in no way a crank or a killjoy . . . I am the adopted Son of God and Jesus Christ does inhabit my soul. Make no mistake about that.' Adding that he had gathered sufficient material for Osborne to write a play about 'the most extraordinary thing that has happened in human history', the correspondent promised that 'Jesus and myself would be pleased to talk to you at any time.'[2] An irate letter from Salisbury tersely informed him that 'you have kicked Britain to death.'[3] Osborne diligently answered his correspondence, responding promptly to those who had either appreciated or been disappointed by his plays, while those appealing for professional consultations were politely notified that he was already besieged by work, and the more dubious missives bundled away in a box marked LOONIES.

There was also the burdensome question of his wealth and how to control it. Although Osborne's attitude towards his money was recklessly cavalier, the sudden leap in his outgoings as revealed by the bills tumbling through his let-terbox was enough to cause occasional anxiety. 'I am in one of my periodic panics about money,' he signalled to his accountants, Bryce, Hammer and Isherwood, one day in 1962. His 'financially disastrous' divorce from Mary, he explained, had resulted in 'ruinous costs'. There was also the huge expenditure on renovations at Hellingly and Chester Square, where the house was heavily mortgaged and tradesmen and furnishing suppliers urgently required paying. 'I know this sounds slightly funny but I have got myself into a state of almost superstitious fear about the whole thing,' he confessed. Could his accountants explain exactly what his financial position was? After tax and other outgoings were paid, just how much of his income was he actually holding on to each month? Would they, he petitioned, consider 'all the possibilities, legal or other-wise, dodges, cheats, swindles, rackets etc., in order to preserve my income as intact as possible'?[4] Rigorously scrupulous, his accountants silently overlooked the invitation to bypass strict legal procedure and instead invited him to a full debriefing on his affairs and the best advice they could offer.

A generous man, Osborne had often anonymously assisted friends and asso-ciates who had not asked for his help. At the end of the 1950s, he had paid rent and electricity bills for a beleaguered John Dexter, and medical expenses for a stage manager injured in a car accident while working on The World of Paul Slickey. He had always given money where it was needed and deserving among those closest to him. But nowadays there seemed to be no shortage of sugges-tions as to the best way of parting him from his cash. Would he invest in this new play? Would he subscribe to this worthy cause? Would he come to the aid of the various Grove relatives who channelled their requests through Nellie Beatrice? At Christmas, he usually sent festive hampers to the further reaches of his family, although not all were easy to please. 'I feel I did not thank you sufficiently for your Xmas gift,' wrote Uncle Jack one year. 'A capon, Xmas pudding, a drink and a piece of roast beef . . . You see with those Harrods hampers you have sent us in the past, you get trivial things, such as mustard, peppers, sauces, we have some 3 years old. We even had two items missing. Do not think I am ungrateful . . .'[5]

And then there was Anthony Creighton, another perennial applicant for funds, whom Osborne had not seen since their falling out at The Old Water Mill. Since Epitaph for George Dillon Creighton's career had continued to be perilously haphaz-ard. He had collaborated with the American writer Bernard Miller on Tomorrow: With Pictures, in which Jasmine Adair, an American, arrives in London to found a new fashion magazine and encounters love and treachery all round. Premiered at the Lyric, Hammersmith in June 1960, it was frostily received by critics who consulted their watches at the end of what seemed an interminable evening and agreed that the authors had taken 'the best part of three hours to study a char-acter which even then they hardly succeeded in establishing.'[6]

Yet even though the acting roles he was offered in far-flung repertory com-panies were becoming thinner on the ground and writing did not seem to hold out much hope, even though he was obliged to fall back for temporary work at the debt collection agency, the telephone exchange and, once, at a meat pie factory, Creighton insisted that his future still lay in the theatre. Increasingly dejected, he resorted to the shallow coffers of Dillon Productions for sustenance. During 1962, calculated Osborne, Creighton had received £1,000 from the company, while he, Osborne, had paid Creighton's income tax, telephone bills and other expenses, making a total of £1,500. It was time, cried Osborne in alarm, to call a halt. He had subsidised Creighton for almost ten years, he told his accountants, but surely he could not be expected to support him indefinitely, even – a nightmare thought – into his old age. In a final act of charity designed to rid his feast of what he now saw as the wheedling spirit of Creighton, Osborne arranged to write off his £40 bank overdraft, pay him an allowance of £10 a week for six months, and that be an end of the matter. Yet Osborne would not yet shake him off entirely and remained unable to ignore his old friend's more plaintive appeals: 'No food. Please send 10/-', read one desperate telegram. Osborne responded with a cheque for £5.[7]

Among the multitude of financial entreaties was another, and in Osborne's eyes, far more deserving application for support. Early in February 1962, he told his accountant, he received 'a rather distraught telephone call' from Pamela Lane, his first wife. Since their divorce, she had not remarried, but had continued acting in repertory in York and Oxford and elsewhere, becoming a much admired and respected company member. Yet her career had faltered and she had covered bouts of unemployment by working for a market research company. Now living in London and having recently recovered from pneumonia, she had found herself in financial difficulties. 'She is not the sort of person to ask for help easily,' her former husband informed his accountant, 'so I know she must be under some considerable pressure.'[8] A cheque for £250 was promptly dispatched, with assurances that should she ever need more, then she must tell him. She did, and he responded immediately. Two years later, in 1964, he signed over a share in the profits of Inadmissible Evidence for her lifetime.

This marked the beginning of a reconciliation that would last, with interruptions, until his death. During the winter of 1964–65, Osborne began to feel increasingly detached from Penelope, socially diminished at Chester Square and absorbed by his own fears of professional failure and of his private life being somehow out of his control. It was then that he began to see Pamela regularly again, visiting her at her basement flat in Kilburn. He had never really resolved his feelings for her. When they had first met in Bridgwater, he had found himself mesmerised by her, and she was still something of a mystery to him. But Kilburn provided a safe haven from the uncertainties of Chester Square, and their surviving letters and the notes he made in his journal reveal that something of their old alliance had returned: 'Once again easy slide beneath the sheets,' he observed on 3 February 1965.[9] Her income from Inadmissible Evidence that year was about £200 a month: 'Thank you more than I can say for making

1965 so easy and comfortable for me,' she wrote to him in December; 'the income from *Inadmissible* has been welcome beyond words.'[10]

There was also the question of Nellie Beatrice. Osborne's relationship with his mother seemed so paradoxical, so convoluted, that it was difficult to fathom, both for those who knew him well and, frequently, for Osborne himself. On the one hand, he regularly professed an unrelenting hatred of her; on the other, he appeared a man of considerable filial loyalty and seemed to many a devoted son. Since his earliest years in repertory, he had regularly sent his mother money and had recently arranged a generous annual allowance, payable in weekly instalments. In 1963, after he and Penelope had whisked Nellie Beatrice off to Venice and elsewhere, he proposed that she leave her rented accommodation in Stoneleigh and that he buy her a flat. Nellie Beatrice flirted with the notion of somewhere by the sea, at Brighton perhaps, within view of the pier, but in the end she rejected the tang of the briny for central London and a flat in a recently built block in Pimlico. Moving in to No.1, Robin's Court in Lupus Street, she threw herself into frenzied housework, keeping the flat 'absolutely spotless' and extravagantly ornamenting her tables and window sills with photographs of her son.[11]

Yet in Nellie Beatrice, Osborne saw those aspects of his origins that he detested and had struggled all his life to overcome. 'My background', he wrote bitterly, 'drilled into me the discipline of low expectations,' something he had always fought against.[12] The spoor of his lower-middle-class roots, his sickly, impoverished childhood and 'the indoctrination of aggrieved lower-middle-class humility' were inhibitions he never stopped attempting to shake off as furiously as an animal shakes off water.[13] They were the ghosts by which he was constantly haunted and, in their corporeal form of Nellie Beatrice, always inescapably *there*, bound to him. Osborne's perception of his mother was associated with the deeply ingrained sense that she had been begrudging, even negligent in her care for Tom Godfrey, his beloved, idealised father, the shameful charity economics of his boyhood and the humiliation of social class. All his life he spoke as movingly of his father as he did disparagingly of his mother. 'Osborne had a father-fixation,' asserted Oscar Beuselinck. 'He thought his mother under-valued his father; he thought she was inferior to his father and he resented the fact that she was his father's wife and his mother. He hated her for it. It's as simple as that.'[14]

Perhaps it was with a sense of allegiance to his father rather than obligation towards his mother that Osborne registered her with a private doctor and paid all her medical bills. Perhaps he felt that he was similarly duty-bound to invite her to his opening nights, take her on holiday, provide her with private medical insurance, help her relatives and invite her for weekends at The Old Water Mill. Perhaps, somehow, he still sought declarations of her love. 'I call their home "Liberty Hall",' Nellie Beatrice exclaimed to a relative.[15] His generosity made her enormously happy and humbly grateful: 'Poor dear son of mine,' she reflected, 'he has had so little reward for all the money he has spent on me, the holiday alone in Nassau . . .'[16]

Nellie Beatrice was a looming symbol of what Osborne wanted to leave behind. The shortcomings he saw in her, he also recognised in himself. 'I was ashamed of her as part of myself because she seemed to represent part of the conflict within myself,' he wrote as early as 1955, 'because she was a disease I was suffering, and would go on suffering until one of us died.'[17] If mother and son craved a stable, loving relationship, their own inescapable inadequacies prevented their achieving it. It was scarred on his side by grudges, recrimination and resentment, and on hers by abject self-pity, a craven humility and often tearful admissions of her maternal failings.

Like her son, Nellie Beatrice found some release in writing and several of her letters survive. Like her son, she wrote as she spoke. Mostly, her correspondence relays the mundane ups and downs, the illnesses and misfortunes of relatives, but there are several occasions during the mid-1960s when Osborne's hostility results in her letters becoming desperate pleas for his affection and absolution. 'How right you were John when you said I was wicked,' she writes, 'but I was too much of a coward to admit it until this afternoon . . . It is beyond my Control to adjust myself . . .' 'I don't blame you for hating me so much from the hurt I have caused you,' she cries. 'I <u>hate</u> myself too . . . I beg of you to forgive me . . . <u>please</u> help me . . . Pleas [sic] John I beg of you to help me in my great distress' . . . 'how rotten can a mother feel,' she confesses. 'My Dear boy I feel so dreadful you will never know how cheap: selfish to know I treated you so cruelly . . . I did not mean to hurt you . . . I feel the most horrible creature alive cheap and low: now I am living in luxury by your brains and support, and in return you receive such cruel and unkind treatment it's unbearable . . .' 'The truth is,' she admits, 'I'm afraid: really *afraid*.' She awakes in the mornings, she says, to feelings of 'horrible guilt'. All she can do is 'beg' his 'forgiveness'.[18]

In *A Better Class of Person*, the first volume of his memoirs, published in 1981, Osborne unleashes a torrent of bitterness against Nellie Beatrice, recreating her as an absurdly monstrous figure, a pantomime gargoyle replete with dyed hair, cheap, badly applied make-up and a range of garish, ill-suited costumes; an embittered harridan stockpiling grievances and assaulting the world and most of the people in it with a scowl and a sharp retort. One of the great parental grotesques of autobiographical literature, she dominates both his memoirs and the television play he extracted from it. But when the American writer Gore Vidal congratulated him upon his 'particularly fine' portrait of 'an unrelenting monster' who was, 'like all great comic characters, never out of character', and enquired whether Osborne had kept a diary to which he referred while writing, Osborne replied: 'Good God, no. Actually I think I made it all up.'[19]

He may have been evading, but hard and fast facts were never Osborne's priority. Emotional candour was always what mattered most. And while some of the more reproving of her former suburban neighbours may have recognised Osborne's depiction, it jarred with the memories of many who knew her and who were appalled by Osborne's apparent malice. Hugh Berrington, Osborne's boyhood friend from Ewell, found his portrayal of her 'incomprehensible'. 'She was a pleasant person,' he remembered, 'devoted to John and always very encouraging to him. When he became famous, she was extremely proud. There is so much in his account of her that does not ring true. His treatment of her is extremely cruel.'[20] Anthony Porter, Osborne's cousin, similarly recalled 'Aunt Bob' as a benevolent presence.[21] According to Oscar Beuselinck it was yet another regrettable instance of his client's talent for cold-hearted cruelty. 'John grossly underestimated his mother and in those autobiographies did her a grave injustice.' Beuselinck liked Nellie Beatrice. 'She was a remarkable woman – a really cute, intelligent Cockney.'[22]

Yet when he and his mother were in company, Osborne would often be frozen with apprehension, petrified that at any moment Nellie Beatrice might embarrass him by some ill-timed gesture or inadvertently graceless remark. It was partly a matter of manners and partly that, although almost bursting with pride at her son's success, she could hardly comprehend it. The extraordinary world in which he had taken up residence was foreign to her, and, like Prospero's island, full of extraordinary apparitions. The money he earned! The houses he owned! The people he knew! Laurence Olivier, Terence Rattigan, Albert Finney, John Betjeman . . . Half of them had been in his plays and the other half wished they had written them! But when one met them, what on earth did one say? It was quickly noticed that Nellie Beatrice was desperately uneasy in such fabulously exotic social gatherings: 'She wasn't stylish, as he [Osborne] was,' a friend recollected. 'She didn't mix easily and she was terrified of letting him down socially.'[23]

Venturing forth with Nellie Beatrice was indeed a social minefield from which Osborne sometimes emerged smoke-blackened and shell-shocked with embarrassment. When he introduced his mother to Terence Rattigan, she happily talked to him for half an hour, having no idea of what it was that he did. John Betjeman, whom she encountered on several occasions, she habitually addressed as 'Mr Benjamin'.[24] Osborne was mortified, yet neither Rattigan nor Betjeman minded in the slightest. But the unsurpassable zenith of Nellie Beatrice's ham-fisted social career came one Christmas, when Olivier invited Osborne and Penelope to drinks at the home he shared with his wife Joan Plowright in Brighton. Fearing social calamity, Osborne declined, explaining that his mother was staying with them, but Olivier insisted. Of course they must come and, what was more, bring Mum along too. During drinks, Olivier served some particularly expensive, particularly oily, black Beluga caviar, presenting Nellie Beatrice with a generous portion. Within seconds, Osborne was watching in horror as the caviar slithered from Nellie Beatrice's plate and spattered on to the newly-laid carpet, whereupon, presumably hoping to disguise the freshness of the spillage, Nellie Beatrice ground it in with her heel. Osborne and Penelope were appalled; the Oliviers watched 'in well-mannered horror'.[25] It was a moment that Nellie Beatrice's son 'never allowed her to forget', recalled a friend. 'He could be quite nasty to her about it for a long time afterwards.'[26]

Osborne was ashamed of his mother. She was simply not the kind of mother that he would have chosen for himself. She stood at the centre of a conspiracy of childhood circumstances which, he believed, had denied him what he clearly felt to be his due: '. . . my sense of lost inheritance was as powerful as any downright deprivation.'[27] The deeply-etched belief that in the broadest sense he had been cheated out of an inheritance rightfully his was reinforced by all those who, in subsequent years, he felt withheld their loyalty and retracted their friendship or love. It led to the doubts and the fears that besieged him, and resulted in the recurring migraines, the nightmares and suffocating despondencies. An unusually sensitive man, whom some described as lacking a toughening layer of skin, he was discouraged and hurt easily. He seemed to take everything so *personally*. Yet one of the paradoxes of his character was, for so sensitive a man, he could be extraordinarily insensitive to others. But without all this, John Osborne might arguably never have had the drive, the passion, the 'anger' to become the writer he was.

Nellie Beatrice craved her son's affection, just as he craved the affection of others. The 'gift' of friendship was one that he valued highly and many of those who knew him thought of him as a modest, courteous, humorous man and exhilarating company. But the sense of loss, neglect and of his qualities not being recognised, at first inextricably associated with his mother, never left him, and no matter how much he attempted to subdue his feelings, they would volcanically erupt when he felt at his most vulnerable. 'I never hoped or wished for anything more than to have the good fortune of friendship and the love of women in particular,' observes Bill Maitland, before reflecting that in the first 'I hardly succeeded at all', and in the second 'I succeeded in inflicting, quite certainly inflicting more pain than pleasure.'[28]

Yet women in particular, argued Lady Elizabeth Cavendish, 'loved Osborne. He was very attractive in every sense. He had a great gift of love and laughter.'[29] 'Women loved him,' agreed Oscar Beuselinck, 'but he didn't like women very much. That was the important thing about him. He could never understand them.' With the exceptions of Pamela Lane, whom 'Osborne really did love', and of his fifth and last wife, Helen, with whom he was 'very contented', Osborne, according to Beuselinck, 'liked flirting, liked making love to women, but he didn't really *like* them. And the reason for his getting rid of them before they got rid of him, was unconscious revenge upon his mother.'[30] Given his marital history, and the changing social climate of the 1960s in which it was becoming more socially acceptable for a man and woman to live together without being married, some wondered why Osborne persisted in returning to the register office time and again. 'I asked him about it,' recalled Lady Elizabeth Cavendish. For many years, she had been John Betjeman's companion, he being married to the staunchly Catholic travel writer, Penelope Chetwode, an arrangement accepted by family and friends. 'I said to him, "Why marry these days? You could just live together." He said it was because he wanted the commitment. Marriage, he said, meant commitment.'[31]

Osborne, concluded Oscar Beuselinck, was 'a man who deep down never really believed in himself. He pretended to, but deep down, he didn't.' Once, when Osborne was staying at the Algonquin Hotel in New York, he had stepped into a lift to find it already occupied by the jazz singer Ella Fitzgerald, whom he admired hugely. 'But John said nothing. He was too shy to tell her how marvellous he thought she was. And *he* was famous at the time.'[32]

Harnessing the resolve of earlier Osbornes who had attempted 'a new start', Osborne had attempted to climb from what he imagined were lowly beginnings to a position whereby he might acknowledge Ella Fitzgerald. From the moment he entered the doors of the Gaycroft School of Music, Dancing, Speech, Elocution and Drama, he had thrown himself into purging his sensibilities of what he perceived as the coarse, make-do-and-mend sensibility embodied in the lower classes and epitomised by his barmaid mother. He had polished his vowels, clarified his consonants and worked hard to acquire a Belgravia sheen in his manners. Superficially at least, he succeeded brilliantly. He was a man, enthused an impressed interviewer, who appeared to have 'the innate ability to enjoy a good wine, a good cigar, Maria Callas in *Tosca*.'[33] But although to his friends he was considerate, attractive and courteous, a man of considerable achievement who was reaping the rewards – 'no more than he deserves', cried the same interviewer – he still felt that he never quite *belonged*.[34]

Increasingly, he was feeling that he did not belong in Penelope's social circle. The ease and the nuances of good taste which came so easily to Penelope often frustratingly eluded his grasp and highlighted the social division between them. The ferocity of Penelope's enthusiasms, her relentless devotion to her work and the dedication in extending her influence in London's 'intellectual society', profoundly unsettled him. Although widely read and a highly intelligent man, he was not, he knew, an intellectual in the spirit that Penelope understood the word. In the brutal chic of Chester Square, she had taken to calling him 'Muddle Headed Johnny', and it stung deeply. His homely lower-middle-class preferences for steak and kidney pudding, tomato ketchup with his fish, the underlying inadequacy he felt rather than the assurance she felt when confronted by an opera, and the music hall songs he loved but which could not possibly be played on a clavichord, were all simply out of place.

Some of his strategies for social acceptance were, on the face of it, ludicrous. A case in point was his velvet jacket. Now that he regularly accompanied Penelope to the Royal Opera House, Osborne was anxious to possess a velvet jacket similar to those worn by several other male members of the audience. His order was dispatched to the Savile Row tailor who held his measurements on file: 'chest: 40"; waist: 32½ . . .', with a specific request: that the jacket should not look new, but well-worn.[35] Osborne wanted to look as if he were accustomed to being at Covent Garden. Another instance was his purchase of the dark green Bentley. It was, he believed, a wonderfully elegant, sophisticated car, its coachwork and its leather interior proclaiming an owner with a gentlemanly sense of style and, incidentally, plenty of money as well. Initially, he kept its purchase a secret from Penelope in order to surprise her, and he keenly anticipated reaping the full harvest of her joyful appreciation. He was mystified therefore, when, her eyes wide in astonishment, she exclaimed that such a car was outrageously ostentatious. Osborne was mortified. That something was expensive and shone, it seemed, did not necessarily mean it was in good taste. It was a social blunder, cruelly exposed, and only explicable by background and class. As Bill Maitland observes in Inadmissible Evidence: 'I have always been afraid of being found out.'[36]

And yet during the mid-1960s John Osborne, contemporary and controversial, was in vogue and in Vogue. Photographed and interviewed for the magazine in 1964, the year of Inadmissible Evidence, he was awarded a double page spread and celebrated as 'inspired by love, driven by anger.' 'John Osborne is tall, lean and beautiful,' affirmed Polly Devlin. 'He looks almost tamed but a wildness lurks near the surface . . . Osborne stands flamboyantly alone in his fierce pride of England and his love for his country . . . He is a man of sharp intelligence and, what is rare, of wisdom, who is prepared to fight for what he thinks is right. He is a writer and a patriot, and with Osborne the two are inseparable . . .' The Angry Young Man had become the Chic Young Man. His 'brown silk suit narrowed to the lines of a sexy mobile body' might be cut in the European style and his cigarettes might be Black Russian, but nevertheless: 'John Osborne is unmistakably an Englishman.'[37]

Photographed, arms folded, standing before a Union Jack flag, he was presented as a patriot, which he was: 'I have a deep personal feeling for this country . . .' So much so that on his many visits abroad, and especially to the United States, he would sometimes reflect on what might happen if he suddenly died, whether his corpse would be consigned unceremoniously to some foreign soil or whether some kind spirit would bear his body back to rest in England. During his wealthiest years he rejected the suggestion that, like several prominent film actors of the late 1960s and early 1970s, he might live abroad in order to make tax savings. He was irrevocably English, he declared, and England was where he would stay. And it was Vogue that awarded him one of the accolades he most craved: 'John Osborne is a gentleman.'[38]

CHAPTER 21

❧

The Baron Who Went Too Far

ON 1 JANUARY 1965, George Devine announced that in September he would retire as artistic director of the English Stage Company. He was sixty-four and 'when a man begins to feel he is part of the fixtures and fittings, it is time he left.' William Gaskill would return from the National Theatre to succeed him. Under Devine's leadership, the Royal Court had produced 126 new plays in nine years, discovered several new playwrights of whom Osborne, Wesker and Arden were pre-eminent, encouraged new directors, given new opportunities to established actors and honed the talents of the new. The effort had almost broken Devine. 'I am deeply tired,' he admitted. 'I am getting out just in time.'[1]

Devine's notice of leave-taking coincided with a new arrival in Osborne's life. In July the previous year, Penelope had informed him that she was pregnant. In mid-February, she entered the Welbeck Street Nursing Home where, almost four years earlier, Mary had given birth to Robert Shaw's son and, after several hours of difficult labour, Nolan Kate Conner Osborne was born at five minutes past nine on the morning of 24 February 1965. The new addition to the family, noted Osborne, was 'quite pretty', which does not sound exactly enthusiastic.[2] Her arrival, however, was celebrated more exultantly at a Chester Square party where Nicol Williamson sang jazz songs, accompanying himself creatively on the clavichord. Since Osborne was researching the events of the Crimean War in preparation for writing the screenplay for Richardson's forthcoming film of *The Charge of the Light Brigade*, he and Penelope named their daughter after Captain Nolan, who had recklessly attempted to divert the fatal charge into the valley. A few years later, however, Osborne was astonished when Penelope informed him that this was not the case. Rather, she had been named after a figure in *The Day of the Rabblement*, an essay on the Irish Literary Theatre written by James Joyce in 1901. 'What an extraordinary, precious, mandarin lie,' Osborne fumed in his journal.[3] But then Penelope, he reasoned, would have known that he would be unaware of the essay and too intimidated by her display of intellect to dispute it.

Penelope had not enjoyed being pregnant and was wary of what lay ahead, complaining to friends that a child could too easily impede a career. The threat of a new film unseen or an *Observer* deadline missed made practical day-to-day motherhood a difficult terrain to negotiate. She would have the sleeping baby with her in her study while she wrote her weekly column, rocking her cot with a foot, but otherwise it seemed that having a child and all that entailed simply wrecked the day. It was not that Penelope was indifferent to a baby; rather that she wanted, in a phrase to be widely used in the future, to 'have it all' and found herself being pulled in one direction too many.

Therefore, a nanny was soon introduced into Chester Square. This was Christine Miller, a twenty-four-year-old professional with a liking for amateur dramatics who had answered an advertisement in *The Lady*, the glossy magazine in which 'society' advertised for its nannies, butlers, maids and gardeners. She was allotted a room next to the nursery on the top floor of Chester Square, well away from the Osbornes' room on another floor, while in Hellingly, she and Nolan shared a cottage in the grounds of The Old Water Mill. It sounds a rather nineteenth-century aristocratic arrangement, but it allowed the Osbornes to work at home without too much distraction. Osborne himself, though, would frequently look in to the nursery at breakfast time and administer Nolan's bottle. He adored his daughter, Miller noted, while simultaneously seeming rather overwhelmed by the practicality of having one. Then again, domestic family life was something Osborne was entirely unprepared for, having had little experience of it from his own childhood. At the same time, he was making his first excursion into directing after his debut with *The World of Paul Slickey*. This time, he was back at the Royal Court and the script he was clutching in his hands was *Meals on Wheels*, a surrealistic satire on provincial conservatism by Charles Wood. The reason he had been asked to direct it, he surmised, was that nobody else understood it. He could make neither head nor tail of it either, and as it turned out, the cast, the critics and the audiences were equally mystified.

Eight months after Nolan's birth, he left London for New York, where *Inadmissible Evidence* was opening at the Belasco Theater on 30 November, with Anthony Page once again directing Nicol Williamson. But eight years after *Look Back in Anger* had lit its October bonfire, Osborne discovered that a long and soul-searching play in which an English lawyer savours 'the stench of death in [his] nostrils', was to prove too daunting a prospect for audiences already intimidated by ticket prices rising as quickly as street crime, and further deterred by the difficulty of finding car parking space nearby.[4] These days, Broadway audiences preferred comedies and musicals, the more lavish the better, to what Arthur Miller would call 'a spiritual quest through theatre, the quest to discover what being human means in our time.'[5]

In an effort to keep the production going, David Merrick, who was once again producing, persuaded the actors to accept a reduction in salary while Osborne waived his royalties for two weeks over Christmas and the New Year, after which *Inadmissible Evidence* moved from the Belasco to the smaller Schubert Theatre. But even though the production won the New York Critics Circle award for Best Play, it was a disappointing experience. In common with many dramatists, he concluded that there seemed little point nowadays in bringing serious drama to Broadway. Returning to London, he dug himself in for what would become his most acrimonious tussle yet with the mandarins of state censorship, 'a battle of wills and wiles' waged between Osborne and the Royal Court on the one hand, and Stable Yard on the other, and going on to involve both Houses of Parliament and a House of Lords Committee and the Director of Public Prosecutions.[6]

*   *   *

Ever since *Personal Enemy* in 1955, Osborne had contemplated writing another play about homosexuality, still a hazardous subject considering that homosexual acts between consenting males remained illegal and would do until 1967. The 'abiding strength of homosexual strategy is to promote and encourage conspiracy', and that 'interests me', he informed the poet and journalist A. Alvarez.[7] It was something he had observed, he explained, from the moment he had begun his career in the theatre. Many might then have agreed with him. Binkie Beaumont, the most powerful producer in London in the years immediately following the war, was widely assumed to deliberately favour fellow homosexuals, most notably Noël Coward, Terence Rattigan and the actor John Gielgud. Some saw the Royal Court as a similarly closed circle, with social class being an alternative qualification of entry. 'The English Stage Company was run on a patrician basis by people who had come from public school and Oxford,' alleged Oscar Beuselinck 'but it also included a pronounced homosexual element.'[8]

But while Osborne derided what he termed homosexual 'conspiracy', he was by no means intolerant, in public at least, as many people were, of homosexuals. He was careful to make the distinction in 1959 when he wrote a piece for the *Daily Express* attacking an article condemning homosexuals in the previous day's paper. Commenting on the case of the choreographer John Cranko being fined at Marlborough Street Court for importuning men, the columnist John Deane claimed that an 'evil . . . secret brotherhood' practising 'this squalid unnatural behaviour' virtually controlled the London theatre. 'If your son wants to go on the stage,' he lamented, 'what will his future be? . . . Unless you are a member of an unpleasant freemasonry, your chances of success are often lessened.'[9] The theatre, Osborne agreed the following day, 'has indeed been dominated by highly-talented homosexuals', whose influence was damaging because 'homosexual art tends to be . . . over-traditional, conservative, narrow, provincial, self-congratulatory, narcissistic.' But, and bravely at the time, considering that the views of the Angry Young Man would inevitably be widely reported, Osborne defended homosexuality itself. It was, he declared, 'a factor of civilisation, in the same way as money or marriage . . . I challenge the morality of any man or newspaper that brands such men as "evil" . . . If any lout makes the pretence of charging at them with some blunted old barbaric lance of morality, I will defend their liberty to work and live as freely as that of my own friends.'[10]

He was speaking as one who had been the subject of rumour and suspicion himself. When he first moved to London, and despite his obviously energetic relationships with women, his demeanour, and that he was known to share the *Egret* with another actor, had led some to wonder whether he was as heterosexual as he appeared. For a time during the 1950s 'I became camp,' he told the broadcaster Melvyn Bragg in 1991. A camp manner – self-consciously artificial and teasing, and masking the seriousness of what one is doing – was widely used at the Court and elsewhere, and was in its curious way a social ploy. '. . . Being camp', Osborne explained, 'cut across all those boring things about class.'[11] To his female lovers and many of his associates, however, there was never any ambiguity about where Osborne's sexual interests lay. In private, though, and throughout his life, Osborne frequently spoke about homosexuality and Jewishness, and chided his homosexual or Jewish associates, in a manner that would later become unacceptable. Whether this was a particularly tiresome banter, whether he meant it, or whether it was yet another instance of his fondness for provocation, is a moot point. His friends seem to have given him the benefit of the doubt.

*　　　*　　　*

Written side by side with *Inadmissible Evidence*, Osborne's new play would counterpoint Bill Maitland's soul-searching with the extravagant sweep of an epic. *A Patriot for Me* would be operatic in scale and its theme that of passionate love. As with several of his plays, the germination was a single theatrical image as yet unrelated to a narrative. While he was holidaying at La Beaumette in the summer of 1961, Osborne had conceived an idea for a spectacularly operatic scene expressing the themes of deception and secret lives. Taking the form of a sumptuous reception attended by apparently female figures, only gradually would the audience realise the characters were male and that they were watching a drag ball. He outlined the idea to Christopher Isherwood, who reminded him that such entertainments, often clandestine, had been held in London during the Victorian era, and were still produced and attended by those in the know. In any case, Osborne was familiar with female (and male) impersonation from the Music Hall, where it was a staple and hugely popular part of the bill, and from pantomime, where cross-dressing is an integral part of the performance and caters to the peculiarly English love of dressing up as somebody else. Only that year, Betjeman had suggested they go to 'a panto – especially if there's one with [the female impersonator] Danny la Rue in it.'[12] Osborne enthusiastically agreed.

Ambiguity, deception and revelation would form one strand of *A Patriot for Me*, while from *Luther* he took the theme of the tension between public acts and private conscience. This was all very topical, as allegiance, patriotism and betrayal had become front page issues during the Cold War of the mid-1960s. The fear of treachery in high places was sharply brought back into public focus in 1963, both by the sensational revelations of the Profumo affair and by Kim Philby, a foreign correspondent for the *Observer* and a former director of the counter-espionage section of the British Intelligence Service, being unmasked as a Soviet spy and defecting to Moscow. There, he joined Guy Burgess and Donald Maclean, the 'disappearing diplomats' and his co-conspirators in the Cambridge Spy Ring, who had bolted twelve years earlier. At home, spy fiction and films were enjoying a renaissance, John le Carré's *The Spy Who Came In From the Cold* being published in 1963 and appearing as a film two years later. So did the film of *The Ipcress File*, Len Deighton's murky espionage thriller in which Michael Caine appeared as the downtrodden bespectacled British agent, Harry Palmer, an antidote to the ritzy world of James Bond. *Thunderball*, Bond's fourth cinematic outing starring the former *Paul Slickey* hopeful, Sean Connery, appeared in 1965, its exotic tropical locations contrasting vividly with the dowdy urban streets of le Carré and Deighton.

Yet while some critics would identify *A Patriot for Me* as an allegory of the Cold War, Osborne turned away from the contemporary world of surveillance, secret dropboxes and defecting diplomats. The history of the Habsburgs that Mr Prentiss had awarded him as an English prize at Belmont College was still on his shelves at Chester Square and, taking it down, he flipped through its pages. He foraged further, reading through more books on the subject, including Edward Crankshaw's *The Fall of the House of Habsburg*, A. J. P. Taylor's *The Habsburg Monarchy*, and Robert Asprey's *The Panther's Feast*. The more he read, the more he stumbled across the name of Alfred Redl. At the British Museum newspaper archives, he heaved bound files of ageing newspapers on to a desk, turning the dry, fading pages to uncover the case of Redl, a homosexual officer in the Austro-Hungarian Imperial Army blackmailed into spying for the Russians. This, he decided, would be the background and plot of the play.

He learned that during the nineteenth century, as a result of a series of ruthlessly negotiated marriages and bullying political treaties, the Habsburgs had created a vast European empire, an immense and polyglot society from which they demanded both unswerving allegiance to the Habsburg crown and unity against Tsarist Russia. In the Imperial Army, national patriotism, whether Austrian, Czech or Hungarian, was of no importance whatsoever; Czech troops might be serving in the Adige, Germans in the Hungarian borderlands, or Croats in Galicia, yet all were required to swear allegiance not to a country but to the Emperor Franz-Joseph, one of whose alleged remarks provided Osborne with his title. Presented with the credentials of an officer recommended for promotion, the Emperor scrutinised them while the candidate's sponsor assured him that the man was, naturally, a staunch patriot. The balding, impressively decorated Franz-Joseph looked up sharply, and from beneath his voluminous moustache, enquired: 'But is he a patriot for me?'[13]

Written at Chester Square and comprising twenty-three scenes in three acts, over eighty characters and set successively in Lemberg, Warsaw, Prague, Dresden and Vienna between 1890 and 1913, *A Patriot for Me* was the largest-scale and most technically complex play that Osborne had yet attempted. While *Inadmissible Evidence* is static and introspective, *A Patriot for Me* is fast-flowing and spacious, charting the rise of the vain and ambitious Redl from a lieutenant in the 7th Galician Infantry Regiment to the rank of colonel and head of the Prague Bureau of Counter-Espionage. Yet unlike Maitland, Redl has no great rhetorical speeches. As the play opens, he has joined the Staff College, an achievement he celebrates at a café where he finds himself attracted to Albrecht, a good-looking young waiter. Although he later becomes the lover of the Countess Sophia Delyanoff, Redl recognises that he is homosexual and by the end of the first act is deliberating why he had deceived himself for so long. Although betrayed, beaten and robbed, Redl makes no subsequent attempt to suppress his homosexuality. At the drag ball that opens the second act, he is accompanied by Lieutenant Stefan Kovacs, whom he eventually loses to the Countess. The act is completed by a coda in which Dr Julius Schoepfer, a Viennese Freudian neuro-pathologist, delivers a lecture denouncing homosexuality, and by a scene in a forest clearing outside Dresden, where Redl is confronted with evidence of his homosexual liaisons by Colonel Oblensky, the director of Russian Intelligence. Redl agrees to spy for the Russians but at the close of the third act, when his treachery is discovered, he shoots himself. The play ends with an epilogue set in Oblensky's office, in which the Russian is briefed about Schoepfer's past. Perhaps, it is suggested, and despite his teachings, he is also homosexual and will also be blackmailed into spying for Russia.

Osborne completed the play at the end of the summer of 1964 and handed the script to George Devine, who blanched when he read it. He was disturbed not by the play's homosexual theme, which would inevitably set the censor's blue pencil twitching, nor its unstable plot or the sketchiness of its character-isation, but by the staggering amount such an elaborate piece with a large cast would cost to produce, even if it was granted a performance licence. Theoretic-ally, even though homosexuality was still very much under cover, there was a slim chance of this as in 1958, a former Lord Chamberlain, Lord Scarborough, had conceded that plays that were 'sincere and serious' in their treatment of homosexuality might be publicly produced.[14] If nothing else, *A Patriot for Me* would constitute the 'first major test' of the Scarborough rules.[15] A copy of the script was duly dispatched to Lord Cobbold, the current Lord Chamberlain, who in mid-September replied that unless the play was entirely rewritten, no licence would be granted. The verdict was emphatic: not only was the play openly sympathetic to homosexuality, its production might also promote 'the vice' among the theatre-going public.[16]

*   *   *

Perusal of the Lord Chamberlain's bulky file of reports, memoranda and letters relating to Osborne's plays and now preserved as part of the Lord Chamberlain's Collection at the British Library, is vividly revealing of Establishment attitudes, the social codes of the time and the Examiners' apprehension in some cases, recognition in others, of the erosion of their powers at a time when cultural and political change was gathering momentum. But it was not merely the content of Osborne's plays that angered Charles Heriot, one of his most vehement adversaries among the ranks of Examiners, but the man himself: 'Mr Osborne's overweening conceit and blatant anti-authoritarianism causes him to write in a deliberately provocative way,' he complained. 'He almost never misses a chance to be offensive.'[17]

During his many tussles over the years with Stable Yard, Osborne had frequently expressed his exasperation with the Examiners. The 'behaviour of your office has been destructive, frivolous and irresponsible,' he had written as early as 1959. 'I am one of the few serious artists working in the English theatre, with a serious reputation in almost every civilised country in the world. And yet your office seems intent on treating me as if I were the producer of a third rate nude revue.' 'Which he is', one of Her Majesty's Examiners scrawled across his letter. When Osborne subsequently notified the Examiners that he had declined invitations from 'most of the national newspapers' to publish their correspondence, as this 'seemed to me an invitation to sensationalism which would obscure a serious subject', his letter was defaced by an Examiner's challenge: 'Print and be damned.'[18]

In 1966, after A Patriot for Me had been produced and during a debate on theatre censorship in the House of Lords, Lord Annan, who steadfastly defended homosexual rights, declared that: 'I cannot conceive of any play less sentimental towards homosexuality, more cold-eyed and ruthless in its exposure of life with a particular kind of homosexuality and less likely to induce anyone to go into this practice.'[19] But in 1964, as he read the script, Charles Heriot thought otherwise. 'The present text', he exclaimed, 'seems to be a perfect example of a piece which might corrupt, since it reveals nearly all the details of the homosexual life usually left blank even in newspapers.'[20] His colleague Ronald Hill agreed, pin-pointing the drag ball as especially degenerate. Apparently fearing that homosexuality, like influenza, was contagious, Hill warned that 'presenting homosexuals in their most attractive guise, dressed as pretty women, will to some degree cause the congregation of homosexuals and provide the means whereby the vice might be acquired.' Distastefully noting Scarborough's 1958 recommendation that the word 'pansy' to describe an effeminate homosexual might now be regarded as permissible on the stage, he sneered that A Patriot for Me 'looks to me like the Pansies' Charter of Freedom'.[21]

Lord Cobbold agreed that the best way of dealing with the play was to smother it entirely, and several pages of required deletions were fired back to the Royal Court in the hope perhaps of a swift and decisive victory. Anything to do with sexual 'inversion', he ordered, must be severely 'toned down', while four entire scenes, including the drag ball, must be instantly consigned to the refuse bin.[22] Glancing down the list, Osborne curtly announced that he rejected all the Lord Chamberlain's demands and that he would not be re-writing the play. Devine concurred. As adamant as Osborne that censorship must be abolished, Devine decided to evade the Lord Chamberlain's objections by turning the Royal Court into a private club in order to stage the play during the summer of 1965.

Although the creation of a private club was a ploy that had been used frequently in the past, this was not a tactic previously employed by Devine, who trenchantly believed that the Royal Court Theatre should be open to the general public. In practice, however, the establishment of a club, apart from abandoning a principle, merely meant that intending spectators paid an extra five shillings at the box office to register as members of the 'English Stage Society'. But the disadvantage was that there would be little hope of recouping the cost of staging A Patriot for Me by a West End transfer, as it was highly unlikely a commercial producer would consider taking an unlicensed play to Shaftesbury Avenue. Devine's decision to create a private club was therefore not only a reluctant last resort but an act of great loyalty to Osborne. In return, Osborne repaid his confidence by arranging to contribute half the estimated £12,500 production costs (four times the amount it cost to produce Inadmissible Evidence and twice as much as Luther) from his own pocket.

Rehearsals under Anthony Page's direction began on 20 May 1965. But even with Inadmissible Evidence a West End success and Osborne writing seemingly at full strength, casting had proved supremely difficult. Successive leading actors, when offered the role of Alfred Redl, hurriedly professed themselves unavailable. Even in 1965, playing a homosexual, especially under the furtive conditions of a private membership club, risked jeopardising a hard-earned professional reputation. The hunt moved to the continent and eventually ended when Maximilian Schell, a thirty-five-year-old Viennese actor who had appeared in several classical roles in Germany and New York, agreed to make his London debut. George Devine, for whom Osborne had written the role of Baron von Epp, the host of the drag ball, joined the cast, while the sole woman's role of Countess Sophia Delyanoff went to Jill Bennett, a woman who would become a cataclysmic influence in John Osborne's life.

'I don't want to create a scandal with this play,' Devine assured the press. 'I just want it to be seen.'[23] And so, with the club membership of the English Stage Society standing at 4,000 and most of the performances already sold out, the seven-week run of A Patriot for Me opened at the Royal Court on 30 June 1965, an occasion of considerable curiosity and high expectations with everything set, as Ronald Hill grimly predicted at the Lord Chamberlain's Office, for the creation of 'a cause célèbre.'[24] Among Osborne's first night guests were Nellie Beatrice, John Betjeman and Lady Elizabeth Cavendish, Michael Foot and Anthony Creighton. At the stage door lay the customary bundles of greetings telegrams from friends and well-wishers. 'Mario and all at the Caprice' in

St James, Osborne's favourite restaurant, wished both him and the play good fortune, while Terence Rattigan hailed him from the continent with 'every good wish for your biggest boffo yet.'[25] Thus braced, Osborne took his seat as the house lights dimmed, the curtain rose and the actors 'step[ped] into the unknown.'[26]

Until the first interval, all seemed thoroughly in keeping with a political thriller, an historical epic. Then, to the lyrical sound of a continuo played on the harpsichord, the second act curtain rose upon what the programme described as a ballroom in Vienna. Extravagantly costumed women, many of whom appeared to be in fancy dress – wasn't that a Marie Antoinette? A Lady Godiva? – encircled the stage and hovered in the shadows as a singer performed one of Susanna's arias from The Marriage of Figaro. When Figaro joined her, the couple sang a duet as the stage lights faded up to full, the orchestra struck up the melody and the dance was taken up by the guests. The audience's dawning suspicion that the 'soprano' and the guests were men, was confirmed by the appearance of Baron von Epp, most certainly a man but costumed as Queen Alexandra in a shimmering gown, sparkling coronet and elbow-length gloves. 'The effect of [Devine's] costume', observed his biographer Irving Wardle, 'was to throw maximum emphasis upon the face. And the face had . . . become a character mask suggesting an elated bird of prey . . . When he lifted his head and stretched his mouth into an avid ellipse, you expected some tremendous squawk.'[27]

At the end of the play, the curtain fell not to a squawk of protest but to the applause of a first night audience wishing an enterprise well. But there was also a distinct feeling that something momentous had been achieved. A decade previously, Anthony Creighton had predicted that Personal Enemy would be a theatrical breakthrough. He had been wrong, but with A Patriot for Me, whatever the merits of the play, and it would become and continue to be one of the most critically contested of Osborne's plays, official censorship had been challenged as being out of kilter both with serious theatre and the times. Osborne himself felt vindicated. 'My dear friend,' he told Anthony Page, 'you have revived my pleasure in the theatre.'[28] The only blot on the night was Creighton himself who, at the celebratory party after the performance, became drunk and tactlessly told Osborne that he thought the play inferior. It was not, Creighton later admitted, his moment of greatest wisdom. In a sudden spasm of rage, Osborne swung round and clenched his fist as if to hit him, as he had done four years previously when he and Penelope had moved to Hellingly. But he thought better of it, as perhaps he had during the incident that resulted in his expulsion from Belmont College. Instead, he had Creighton ejected onto the street before turning back to the party.

It was the last the former friends and collaborators would see of each other. No more invitations to Osborne's first nights arrived at Creighton's small flat in Belsize Park, and nor did he make further appeals for subsistence. Eminence, wealth, and a life in the theatre had eluded him. However, he managed to avoid returning to the debt collecting agency and the meat pie factory by puttering along instead teaching drama evening classes at a series of London adult education institutes. Over the years his kindness and encouragement were appreciated by his students, few of whom immediately recognised his name as having once appeared alongside one of the nation's great dramatists, or knew that he was privately fighting an addiction to alcohol, one battle at least in which Anthony Creighton was eventually successful.

*   *   *

Several critics turned out to be almost as admiring and supportive of *A Patriot for Me* as the first night audience. In *The Times*, Irving Wardle pronounced that 'the voraciousness of [Osborne's] talent is unequalled in the post-war theatre.'[29] Ronald Bryden in the *New Statesman* emphasised that the drag ball was 'the play's centre, its valediction . . . It is funny, compassionate, grotesque, humane and defiant.'[30] Yet others, while not disputing that the play should be produced, were uncertain as to whether it represented an attack upon homosexuality or a denunciation of social hypocrisy. What *exactly* was Osborne's point of view? It is a question that has orbited the play ever since its first production. In a full-page assessment of Osborne's output in the *Observer*, Mary McCarthy, the American critic and novelist, objected that 'reiteration' was 'the basic mode of the Osborne harangue and repetition the basic plot of the Osborne play.' His protagonists lacked self-will, his dialogue was no more than the terse semaphore of newspaper headlines and *A Patriot for Me* another 'tiresome and predictable work' in the same vein. 'Why did he write this?' she exclaimed. 'What does he mean to say?'[31]

This provoked a sharp response from Kenneth Tynan, for whom the play constituted a demand for both moral and social compassion. Its 'essential originality and audacity', he explained, was that 'not only does it repudiate loyalty to Freud and loyalty to country (the twin bastions of Western civilisation), its hero neither pities himself nor invites our pity . . . For the first time in Western drama, we are asked to identify with a queer not because he is charming or tragic or a genius but simply because he is queer.'[32] And in *The Sunday Times*, Harold Hobson, for nine years a champion of Osborne's work, remarked that Redl's fall was 'full of sadness, beauty and distress.'[33]

The Lord Chamberlain's Examiners, though, were not yet admitting defeat. At the same time as Rattigan was admiringly notifying Osborne that Redl was a finer and altogether more fully realised conception than Maitland, and the venerable Harold Hobson professing that there was no reason to ban the play and that 'if I didn't know it was untrue I should think that the Lord Chamberlain was mad' to attempt it, Cobbold's troops were devising a strategy whereby victory might still be snatched from the forces of liberalism.[34] If the Royal Court had announced its conversion into a private members' club for the purposes of producing the play but had failed to advertise membership regulations sufficiently clearly, it might, they argued, be claimed that the theatre was operating a 'subterfuge'.[35] If so, an application could then be made to Sir Norman Skelhorn, the Director of Public Prosecutions, to intervene.

In this they were encouraged by the testimony furnished by one D. V. G. Buchanan, who was not a member of the English Stage Society but had taken himself to the third performance of A Patriot for Me. 'I entered the theatre at approximately 7.05pm,' he noted stoically, 'showed my ticket to an attendant at the entrance to the dress circle, bought a programme for £1 and was shown to my seat, £10, in the back row.' During the first interval, he had treated himself to a light ale before venturing back into the auditorium for the second act, 'after which, thoroughly nauseated, I left.' Gulping the reviving air of Sloane Square, he recorded that 'At no time during the evening was I challenged to produce my membership card or asked whether I was a member of the theatre club. I cannot even remember having seen any notices to the effect that the performance was private and for members only.'[36]

But even armed with this seemingly persuasive evidence, Lord Cobbold wavered, reluctant to expose either himself or his office to possible public ridicule. A Patriot for Me was attracting considerable press attention and debate. Questions were being asked and statements made not only in the more serious newspapers but in the House of Commons. When, on 21 July, Captain Litchfield, the Conservative Member of Parliament for Chelsea, and in whose constituency the Royal Court stood, demanded that censorial restrictions be more stringently enforced, Harold Wilson, the Prime Minister, murmured ambiguously in reply that the law perhaps required attention. Evidently, Stable Yard could not look to a Labour government for robust support.

Meanwhile, the Royal Court took defensive measures in the mobilisation of Lord Goodman, one of the most powerful lawyers of the day and conveniently chairman of the Arts Council, who advised Cobbold that in his opinion that play was not in the least obscene. Faced with the dilemma that his office would look irrelevant if it did nothing but foolish if it pursued a prosecution that failed, Cobbold dithered. By the end of the month, the Department of Public Prosecutions informed him that while 'a prosecution would stand a good chance of success', it 'would be inexpedient' since the play 'has alerted a great deal of public interest and a good deal of support and . . . has been running for some time.'[37] And as no complaints about the play had been received either at the Lord Chamberlain's office or at the Department of Public Prosecutions, the Examiners reluctantly conceded defeat and abandoned their hopes of suppressing A Patriot for Me. The Evening Standard, however, presented Osborne with the Play of the Year Award for having written it.

* * *

The story, however, was not yet over. On the evening of Saturday 7 August, a few days before the play was due to close, George Devine came off stage at the end of the drag ball scene and began to climb the five flights of stairs to his dressing-room at the top of the building. It had been a long day. After a matinee performance he had dutifully hosted a reception for visiting members of the Berliner Ensemble. That night, having once again laced himself tightly into the Baron's corsets, he was more than usually tired, yet his performance was as commanding as ever. But suddenly, on the stairs backstage afterwards, he collapsed. He had suffered a heart attack.

An ambulance rushed him through the sultry night to St George's Hospital. Jocelyn Herbert arrived from the Flood Street house that she shared with Devine, only to discover that she could not see him because his wife, Sophie, had been named as next of kin. Osborne telephoned and, over the next few days, kept in touch with the hospital while at the theatre performances continued with Devine's understudy playing von Epp. Devine responded to treatment and within a week was sitting up, seeing visitors and writing letters. 'I really thought I'd had my chips that night,' he notified Osborne. '. . . Above all, John, your card meant the most. I can't help thinking I made a balls of it by collapsing.' The letter was signed 'From the Baron who went too far.'[38]

At the end of that week, on 14 August, as the curtain fell on the final performance of A Patriot for Me, Osborne stood on the stage at the Royal Court and told the audience that Devine was fighting back to full recovery. But a week later, a blood clot hit a motor nerve in Devine's brain, paralysing the left side of his body. Osborne, Penelope, Jocelyn and other friends maintained a round-the-clock vigil at the hospital, taking it in turns to sit on the steps outside his ward, occasionally peering in through the windows to glimpse the ashen, white-haired figure lying inside. A specialist advised Jocelyn about propranolol, a newly developed but hazardous drug; it might arrest the damage, he cautioned, but on the other hand its administration might prove lethal. She agreed to the treatment. The effects were beneficial and by mid-October, after two months in hospital, Devine was moved home to Flood Street. His speech had returned to near normal and his intellect was unimpaired, yet he remained paralysed on one side and was confined to a wheelchair. According to his biographer, he saw himself as a character that might have been dreamed up by his old friend Samuel Beckett, a fully functioning intelligence trapped within a useless body and tormented by observing the process of its own extinction. Osborne and Richardson paid a cheque into Jocelyn's bank account to enable Flood Street to be converted to accommodate his new requirements and in November she gave a party to celebrate his fifty-fifth birthday. Devine insisted upon learning to walk again and attempting to regain the use of his damaged left hand. He also suggested that he and Osborne take a holiday somewhere once he was well enough to do so.

But there were no convalescent trips for George Devine. And it seemed as if he knew there would not be. In January, Osborne presented him with one of the first copies of the published text of A Patriot for Me. 'I can't think of a better person to approach the grave with than Baron von Epp,' observed Devine.[39]

Three days later, on 20 January 1966, he buckled beneath a spasm of chest pain. The doctor was summoned as Jocelyn clamped an emergency oxygen mask over Devine's face, but 'suddenly it was as if all the blood seemed to zoom to his face and head. And he died.'[40]

Osborne, meanwhile, was in Newcastle upon Tyne, appearing as the narrator in John Cox's production of Stravinsky's The Soldier's Tale, in which Robert Stephens, an old friend from Epitaph for George Dillon, was playing the Devil and Derek Jacobi the Soldier. Their leisurely itinerary of four nights in the northeast, followed by a charity performance at the Royal Opera House in Covent Garden, was fractured by a telephone call from Penelope, relaying the news of Devine's death and an urgent request for an obituary from the Observer. Chilled by his loss, the depth of which he had not felt since the death of his father twenty-six years previously, Osborne sat down to write. His obituary was published three days after Devine's death, on 23 January. He paid tribute to the director's teaching, his vision, and his resilience in the face of criticism. Yet even Devine's tenacity, he reflected, had in the end not been enough. He had been slowly but irreversibly worn down by what Osborne perceived as the English malaise: indifference to spontaneity, imagination, effort and enthusiasm. Osborne recorded that he was also acutely aware that of the hundreds of actors, directors and writers inspired by or who owed their success to George Devine, it was he who had the greatest reason for gratitude. For the rest of his life Osborne would speak of him as devotedly as he did of his father, and liken Devine's influence upon the theatre to that of Diaghilev.

The funeral was held at Golders Green crematorium in north London. Rain fell relentlessly as the mourners arrived. Joining Osborne and Penelope were friends from the Royal Court and elsewhere, including Samuel Beckett, who was visiting London for a BBC television recording of his play, Eh Joe. They waited in a side-room until a door opened and a formally dressed figure that might have been an undertaker, beckoned them silently into the room where the ceremony would be held. 'It was Laurence Olivier,' observed William Gaskill. 'He always knew how to transform himself.'[41] There was some awkwardness as both Sophie, Devine's estranged wife, and Jocelyn, his partner, were present and mourners wondered whether where they sat would be interpreted as signifying a declaration of loyalty either to one or the other. Osborne and Penelope elected to sit near Jocelyn and in company with the congregation listened to a short reading and a passage, chosen by Penelope, from Britten's War Requiem. Afterwards, they filed out, the rain still falling, streaming from their umbrellas and soaking their coats. Within a few weeks, Sophie Devine was dead too, of cancer.

At the beginning of February, there was a memorial meeting at the Royal Court at which a band played jazz, Edith Evans recalled Devine at Oxford, Peggy Ashcroft remembered their acting together and read a speech by Dr Dorn, the country doctor in Chekhov's The Seagull. A man who responds to the new in art without quite realising why, Dorn was a role which Devine himself had played, by all accounts magnificently, eighteen months previously in Tony Richardson's production at the Queen's Theatre. In his own tribute, Osborne drew attention to the fact that he spoke French, a seemingly innocuous remark, reflected Richardson, but one that 'said everything' about Devine. It encapsulated his 'striving for a world and values outside his own . . . of his joy in all those sensual and visual pleasures – the wine, the food – with which, for anyone of his time, France was synonymous . . . Only John could have found that exact and spare eloquence.'[42]

But with Devine's passing, January for Osborne became a month marked by double loss. January had seen the deaths of Tom Godfrey and now George Devine, father and father-figure, within days of each other, albeit twenty-six years apart. January became a dark time of remembrance and mourning what might have been, a time when Osborne would be most vulnerable to the despondency that enshrouded him and the nameless fears that wrapped themselves around him most often during the long winter nights.

PART 3

Resilience

CHAPTER 22

Love and Loss

WITH THE DEATH OF Devine and the collapse soon afterwards of his marriage to Penelope Gilliatt, Osborne lost the two people closest to him who cared the most for his gifts and who encouraged and challenged him. Without them, he was bereft both of a professional compass and a safe harbour at home. During the following turbulent decade, after his divorce from Penelope and as his relationship with Jill Bennett, who became his fourth wife, descended into mutual spite and destroyed his fragile self-esteem, so his professional confidence, precarious at the best of times, disintegrated. As he submerged himself in alcohol, his health began breaking down and the recurring headaches and periods of self-searching gloom from which he had always suffered intensified. He began to see indifference and treachery all around him. It was a crisis from which he would never fully recover.

His plays began to reflect his distress and isolation. *The Hotel in Amsterdam* curdles with the rancour of a personal grudge; *A Sense of Detachment* mirrors the chaos of its creation and *Watch It Come Down* in 1976, the despair of loneliness, although each also reflects something of the political and social malaise of their times. Ensnared, it seemed helplessly, in a trap partly of his own making, Osborne searched desperately for a way out, in the process becoming increasingly self-destructive, recklessly throwing friendships aside, defending himself, he believed, against professional hostility and personal cruelty. Acting in the full knowledge of what he was doing but unable to stop, Osborne flailed onwards, re-enacting in real life the torments of Bill Maitland. Indeed, what is often astonishing about the decade following the ten years that had opened with *Look Back in Anger* and closed with *A Patriot for Me*, is not that his writing arguably declined or, as some suggested, that his audience began to desert him, but that he managed to complete any work at all.

From the mid-1960s onwards, Osborne's professional standing became increasingly questioned. This was not only the result of some critics pronouncing his plays inferior to his earlier work, but also simply a matter of changing

times. England, and more precisely London, had become a different place and
the Angry Young Man of the 1950s, who had appeared so refreshingly rebellious and culturally significant, was now seen, in the light of a new, more
politically radical and morally libertarian spirit, as having been not quite so
anti-Establishment after all. In 1965, Osborne was only thirty-five, but in a
decade preoccupied by pop music, fashion, liberal legislation and a new meritocracy, he already seemed much more to do with the past than the present, let
alone the future.

So for the moment did the Royal Court, as new performance styles and
new companies began cropping up in sometimes makeshift fringe theatres,
while subsidised theatres flourished, rediscovering the classics and fostering
new dramatists. The National Theatre produced *Rosencrantz and Guildenstern Are Dead*
in 1967, a quirky first play by Tom Stoppard, while at the Royal Shakespeare
Company Peter Hall directed bracing revivals of Shakespeare and new plays by
Harold Pinter. These, too, were years of political protest marches, against the
nuclear bomb, apartheid in South Africa, and the Vietnam War. At the RSC,
Peter Brook directed *US*, an anti-Vietnam war play that ended with the house
lights up and the actors staring accusingly at the audience. 'Excuse me,' loudly
enquired an indignant Kenneth Tynan from his seat in the stalls, 'but are we
keeping you waiting or are you keeping us waiting?'[1] In the commercial West
End, Michael Codron continued to produce Joe Orton's furious and farcical
comedies. Orton followed *Entertaining Mr Sloane* with *Loot*, a play energetically
making fun of the Catholic faith, bereavement and the police, and asserting that
homosexual relationships were acceptable. Orton set out to shock and lampoon
and by doing so was absolutely in tune with the irreverent tenor of the times.

Meanwhile, at the Royal Court, Edward Bond, the son of an East Anglian
labourer, wrote a series of socially critical, concertedly left-wing plays, the most
notorious of which came in the wake of *A Patriot for Me*. Set among uneducated,
chronically bored, urban young people prone to casual brutality, *Saved* is a *Look
Back in Anger* of the grimmer concrete council estates. But whereas Jimmy Porter
was alarmingly articulate, Len and Pam, the married protagonists of *Saved*, are
primevally incoherent. The scene in which a gang of thugs hurl stones at a baby
in a pram resulted in a scandalised Lord Chamberlain refusing a public performance licence and Gaskill's production opening in November 1965 at a Royal
Court once again retreating behind the defences of a private club.

Saved received savage reviews, its cruelty shocking and enraging critics and
audiences alike, although some reviewers, including Penelope Gilliatt, stridently
defended it. In the *Observer*, she insisted that the play was 'not brutish, it is about
brutishness', but for many, the new licence in morality, the media and the
theatre was becoming disturbingly out of hand.[2] In 1965, Harold Wilson, the
Prime Minister, nominated each of The Beatles for an MBE and in September,
there they were, being honoured by the Queen, a spectacle so affronting several
former recipients that they angrily returned their own awards. And there was
Kenneth Tynan making an exhibition of himself on a live, late-night television

programme declaring that 'I doubt if there are very many rational people to whom the word "fuck" is particularly diabolical or revolting or totally forbidden.'[3] As furious viewers and newspaper columnists objected that most people still found the expression all three, thank you, Tynan exulted in his new-found infamy as the dubious champion of artistic and sexual freedom.

Within weeks, Harold Wilson, still promoting himself as modernising man, decided the country would withstand its second General Election within eighteen months. The timing seemed perfect. The government was sufficiently ahead in the opinion polls to suggest that Labour would increase its hairsbreadth majority of four in the House of Commons, and Edward Heath, a bachelor with a love of sailing and Chopin and who had succeeded Sir Alec Douglas-Home as Conservative leader, had yet to exert his grip upon the opposition. Wilson's tactics paid off and on 31 March 1966, Labour was returned with a substantial majority of ninety-eight. The following day, magistrate Leo Gradwell passed judgement on what the newspapers had trumpeted as the 'THEATRE DEFIES THE CENSOR' case.[4] As if determined to avenge the defeat of A Patriot for Me, Lord Cobbold had pounced upon an infringement of the licensing laws at the Royal Court – someone had bought a ticket for a performance of Saved but had not been obliged to wait the twenty-four hours stipulated by club membership rules before seeing the play – and urged prosecution. William Gaskill, the English Stage Company secretary, and the Royal Court's licensee were charged with a violation of the creakingly elderly Theatres Act of 1843. In upholding the case and passing a sentence of a fifty-guinea fine and a conditional discharge for the defendants, Gradwell handed the prosecution a nominal victory. But it seemed as if his heart was not really in it. It was All Fools' Day, after all. Cobbold also recognised that victory was merely academic. 'I am tied to the rock of the law waiting for some Perseus to rescue me,' he sighed.[5]

He did not have to wait too long. The future of theatrical censorship was already being lengthily considered by a House of Lords committee at which Osborne, among others, gave encyclopaedic evidence. A few days earlier, on 8 March, Michael Foot, who as the editor of Tribune had published A Letter to My Fellow Countryman, moved a successful Bill in the House of Commons to abolish censorship. Declaring Osborne to be 'the greatest dramatist we have' he declared that 'Anyone who examines the history of the past few years will see the great liberalising effect which John Osborne has had on contemporary life.'[6] The following year, Roy Jenkins, the Home Secretary, a claret-loving bibliophile of Oxbridge erudition known as 'the father of the permissive society', advanced both to unleash the Lord Chamberlain from his rock and dispense with his services. On 27 September 1967, the Theatres Act became law, ending the Lord Chamberlain's powers of discrimination after 231 years. Reactionary, and often entirely unrepresentative of audiences, the censor had at various times succumbed to political persuasion, prevented discussion on the stage of issues debated with impunity elsewhere and had effectively controlled the repertoire for over two centuries. But henceforth, what was permissible on the stage would be a matter of negotiation between dramatists, directors, actors and audiences, and stage plays would be subject not to the Examiners of Stable Yard, but to the assorted Acts pertaining to obscenity, blasphemy and libel that governed publishing. In celebration, the evening after the abolition of censorship, *Hair*, an American 'tribal love-rock musical', a dramatically tedious if intermittently effervescent show featuring both male and female nudity – albeit murkily shadowed – opened at the Shaftesbury Theatre. Its hit song, 'This is the Dawning of the Age of Aquarius', captured a cultural hedonism and announced the beginning of another new era in the theatre.

Change – and to many, decay – was all around. A buoyant economy, pop music blaring from transistor radios tuned to Radio Caroline, a pirate station broadcasting from a ship anchored in the Irish Sea, and a spirit of liberalism made London a vibrant and, for many who were young at the time and lucky enough not to be living on the council estates of *Saved*, a hugely optimistic place to be in. These were the years of youth and money and a new sensibility in morals, music and fashion. Clothes burst into effervescent colours and swirling flower patterns. The A-line dress came and went, waistlines pinched and then relaxed, heels and hemlines rose. A military look flitted by. The Union Jack became a fashion accessory. Beads hung from young necks, bangles jangled on wrists, hair grew longer, trousers flared, and by 1968 the miniskirt had reached its height, both literally and in popularity. New styles generated a new journalism. Jimmy Porter's 'posh' Sunday newspapers arrived heavy with colour supplements avidly recording the developments in fashion, architecture, interior design and pop music, and the activities of film-makers, actors, musicians, photographers and models. An escalating number of glossy magazines breathlessly advised on what was 'in' and what was 'out'. It was exhausting just keeping up with it all.

It seemed as though to be alive and in London was to be a guest at a glorious party of possibilities. The old inhibitions, given voice in *Look Back in Anger* and elsewhere, were crumbling away, and in their place was a new and youthful metropolitan club for which the membership qualifications were based less upon social privilege and an Oxbridge degree than having the right face, a ruthless ambition and knowing the right people. Talent helped, and as many of the new stars, such as the actor Michael Caine and the photographer David Bailey discovered, having a 'working-class' background and accent was a distinct advantage. That everything was changing and anything was possible was confirmed when, on 15 April 1966, under the banner headline of 'London: the Swinging City', the American *Time* magazine reported that the British capital was now a city 'seized by change, liberated by affluence . . . It swings; it is the scene.' London was the 'City of the Decade', and had triumphantly thrust its way from its cocoon of austerity and become a fantastic multi-coloured festival of itself. The following year, youth raised its arms and swayed in time as The Beatles, the most inventive pop group of the era, sang the haphazardly delirious anthem, 'All You Need Is Love', and, momentarily at least, it seemed as though they might be right. This was 'the summer of love', in which the group produced a new long-playing record, *Sergeant Pepper's Lonely Hearts Club Band*, a 'shrewd fusion of Edwardian variety orchestra and contemporary "heavy rock".'[7] Hugely original, instantly successful, it was immediately and, some said, ludicrously, hailed by Kenneth Tynan as 'a decisive moment in the history of Western civilisation.'[8]

The ending of the Lord Chamberlain's dominion over the theatre was one of a fleet of good, brave causes to fight for these days. The battle to abolish the death penalty was finally won, the laws on abortion and divorce were overhauled and during the summer of love homosexual acts in private between consenting adults were decriminalised. The oral contraceptive pill for women, now obtainable by prescription through the National Health Service, theoretically made sex more a matter of recreation than procreation, and posters tacked onto student bed-sitting room walls urged their occupants, in eye-bruisingly vivid colours and 'psychedelic' lettering, to 'Make Love Not War'. The 'permissive society' was both celebrated and decried, its detractors worrying about where it would all lead. The summer of love was also the summer in which Brian Epstein, The Beatles' manager, was found dead of a drug overdose at his home in Belgravia; and at the flat they shared in Islington, Joe Orton, the Oscar Wilde of the Welfare State, was battered to death by his lover, the jealous, disaffected artist Kenneth Halliwell. Having murdered Orton, Halliwell committed suicide himself. Death occurred too in *Blow-Up*, one of the quintessential films of the decade in which the director Michelangelo Antonioni used Swinging London as the backdrop for a story in which a fashion photographer believes he has captured a murder in a park on film, only to find that his weightiest evidence, a corpse beneath a bush, has mysteriously disappeared overnight.

In the midst of all this whirling change, commentators once supportive of Osborne began issuing alarming weather warnings. 'John Osborne was a leader and became a lost leader,' pronounced Simon Trussler in 1969.[9] It would become a familiar verdict over the following years. Having once appeared rebellious and exhilarating, Osborne, it was said, was moving swiftly to the right and looking progressively old-fashioned and curmudgeonly. His audience was peeling away from him. And yet this was a response based partly upon a critical misapprehension. In celebrating Osborne, and Jimmy Porter, as speaking for a generation, many commentators had overlooked Osborne's intentions. He had made no claim to speak for a generation, or anyone other than himself. Indeed: 'The only life I can explore – or even begin to chart – is my own,' he wrote.[10] It was this that he continued to do, remarkably consistently. Underlying Osborne's and Jimmy Porter's disaffection is the conviction that an essential part of Englishness, its sensitivities, mellowness, kindness and capacity for dissent, is withering away, leaving only that part that is cruel, conformist and uncaring, and it is doing so almost without anyone noticing or even caring very much. This underpins all of Osborne's writing. During the years from 1965 and particularly from the mid-1970s, as England became, in his view and that of many others, an increasingly bland, unquestioning, brutal and brutalising place in which to live, this conviction was thrown into increasingly sharper relief.

*   *   *

Having begun as an adulterous passion, Osborne's relationship with Penelope had by 1965 survived for five years and their marriage for three. But with the birth of Nolan and the death of Devine, the alignments of Osborne's life irrevocably shifted. With Nolan equipped with a nanny, Penelope resumed a hectic professional life of film screenings and editorial meetings, and at home sandbagged herself into a fictional world, reading the proofs of One by One, her first novel, about a ménage à trois, which was published to approving reviews that year.

Socially, intellectually, ambitiously, her husband felt that he could neither be her equal nor sustain her pace. Competitive, highly achieving women unsettled him. As far as she was concerned, their marriage was as happy as ever, but like a small boat on an indifferent sea, he was drifting from her and in that summer of 1965, the year in which she had appeared in A Patriot for Me, a seemingly secure mooring presented itself in Jill Bennett.

At the time, Jill's disastrous three-year marriage to the playwright Willis Hall had careered into the buffers of divorce. She knew Penelope and, turning to the Osbornes for consolation, became a frequent visitor to Chester Square and an occasional weekend guest at The Old Water Mill. The growing affinity between Osborne and Jill was noted by Oscar Beuselinck who, calling at Chester Square one day, discovered her sitting with Penelope, tearfully lamenting the end of her marriage while Osborne 'hovered nearby in uneasy fascination.' Every few moments, recalled Beuselinck, Jill would look up and 'glance intently at Osborne, who steadily returned her gaze.'[11] Anthony Page later suggested that Osborne had been 'pursuing [Jill] vigorously' since their meeting at the Royal Court, but according to Jill, they had first met at a dinner party at which Osborne, sitting next to her, complimented her on her profile.[12] This had charmed her, as Jill, a woman of monumental vanity, was, she recalled, feeling 'particularly depressed' about the shape of her nose.[13] Whichever version is the more accurate, Osborne was entranced and was soon besieging her daily with enough red roses to stock a Kensington florist.

'There are only two classes in good society in England: the equestrian classes and the neurotic classes,' pronounces Lady Utterwood in Bernard Shaw's Heartbreak House.[14] If Osborne aspired to the equestrian class, many of her detractors would have agreed Jill's natural home to be the neurotic. Patrician, demanding, phobic, she was an immensely capricious woman who, by the time she encountered Osborne, had a history of cruel melodramatic histrionics. She had been known to alert friends and doctors, sometimes in the darkest hours of the night, that she had swallowed sleeping pills, but, having distractedly dashed to her assistance, they would be met by a delighted Jill opening her door with a glass of champagne in her hand, asking what all the fuss was about. On the other hand, her friends, while conceding that Jill could be enormously highly strung, argued that 'she was like a thoroughbred animal that could be very frisky, very gentle and very wild if it felt trapped. She was also a deeply and instinctively intelligent woman, who hated bullying and cant, which she was quick to challenge.'[15] Her unpredictability was all part of her natural actressy glamour.

Blonde and slight, Jill was not classically beautiful, although many thought her striking. Her features were sharp, with a high, broad forehead, deep-set eyes, a tip-tilted nose, and a wide mouth and jaw. Like several people in Osborne's circle, she was an only child. Born on 24 December 1929 (she was only twelve days younger than Osborne), in Penang in the then Federated Malay States, she was the daughter of James Randle Bennett and Nora, his spirited, gregarious wife. The owners of extensive rubber plantations, the Bennetts were accustomed to living in style among the English expatriates, yet the good life ended with the declaration of war when Jill was nine years old. While her father was dragged off to a prisoner-of-war camp, Jill and her mother managed to scramble aboard a ship bound for England. Like Osborne, she remembered a rootless wartime London childhood, led by her mother's hand from one temporary room to another. In their case, however, Nora having considerably more money than Nellie Beatrice, the rooms were not in suburban lodgings but those Rattiganesque harbours of the floating lonely, small private hotels. Even as an adult, Jill often felt more at ease in a hotel than in her own home. 'Going through my own front door is fine,' she wrote, 'but I always feel more at home in the Connaught.'[16]

Having made her acting debut at Stratford in 1949, she had played a series of supporting roles in London before appearing in A Patriot for Me, her performance convincing Osborne that she was a great actress whose gifts were underrated. That she also seemed a waif desperately in need of love and shelter and deserving of both, appealed to his romantic, protective instincts. For her part, Jill saw Osborne, much as Pamela, Mary, Jocelyn and Penelope had done, as a dynamically attractive and hugely talented figure. And she enjoyed flirting as much as he did, a game to be played for the sheer rakish, suspenseful pleasure of it. According to friends, he quickly became 'besotted with her', and increasingly dependent upon her embraces.[17]

At the beginning, and according to the evidence of their letters, a considerable sexual passion was accompanied by a genuine and happy-go-lucky sense of alliance. Creatures of instinct and passion, they shared a similarly romantic approach to the theatre, liking to think of themselves as vagabond players, sentiments recalling the theatre of a former age. Penelope, who had a critic's austerity and cool marksmanship, was able to shoot down the intellectually precarious at a hundred paces, an ability her husband found unnerving. Jill, on the other hand, appeared infinitely more relaxing and set a less hectic pace. He and Penelope had rejoiced in the private nicknames of 'Banks', but lately she

had taken to condescendingly calling him 'Muddle-Headed Johnny', a name
that made him writhe. He and Jill, on the other hand, liked to call each other
'Gypsy'. His avalanches of roses led rapidly to a vigorous clandestine affair conducted mostly at her flat at 33 Prince's Gate Mews in Kensington. Perhaps it was
guilt at his deceiving Penelope, or the sheer terror of making a moral decision
that prevented his admitting his duplicity to his wife. Instead, he blundered
on throughout the following spring of 1966, dodging here and darting there,
conducting an affair with Jill while maintaining a routine of commuting with
Penelope and Nolan, now just over one year old, between Chester Square and
Hellingly, resigning himself once more to his misplaced faith that 'the ingenuity of time or delayed inspiration' would come to his rescue.[18]

It did not take very long for Penelope to realise that something was up.
Certain that he was having an affair but initially unaware of with whom, her
anxiety and his guilt led to quarrels that often resulted in a panicking Osborne
scampering down the steps of Chester Square, a hastily-packed overnight bag
slung from his shoulder. Sometimes he went to ground at Hellingly, at others
to a rented house that Oscar Beuselinck had secured for him in Egerton Crescent
in Kensington. In these blustery domestic circumstances, Osborne continued to
grapple with his next play. Convinced that with Devine's death the curtain had
fallen on his days at the Royal Court, he had decided to take a tentative step into
the world beyond Sloane Square, and cautiously accepted a £250 commission
from Kenneth Tynan.

Having abandoned the *Observer* and regular theatre criticism, Tynan was now
installed as literary manager at the National Theatre, still housed at the Old Vic,
from where he promised great things. Turning to the dramatist whose career
he had championed, he commissioned an English version of *La fianza satisfecha*,
a blood-drenched, vengeance-with-honour tragedy by the Spanish playwright,
Lope de Vega. A contemporary of Shakespeare, Lope became a priest while
romping through innumerable love affairs and churning out a rapid succession
of plays, poems and pamphlets. Lope and Osborne was a strange pairing, but
Tynan was a man of sometimes eccentric enthusiasms who could mismatch
people and projects with the same imaginative dexterity as he could forge productive alliances. The play, noted Osborne, had 'an absurd plot', with 'some
ridiculous characters and some very heavy humour', but, working from a literal
translation, he began chopping, slicing and dicing, much as he had done for his
Hayling Island *Hamlet* all those years ago.[19] Hacking three unwieldy acts down to
one, he cooked up *A Bond Honoured*, in which Leonido, a man of horrific violence
and untroubled by moral scruples, blinds his father, seduces his sister, assaults
a priest and is finally crucified.

As the play went into rehearsal, Osborne joined Penelope in Positano, overlooking the Bay of Naples, where she had gone to work on her second novel,
A State of Change. Once he arrived back in London to look in on rehearsals, it
seems that Osborne may have had second thoughts about their marriage as his
letters to his wife were as effusive and as affectionate as ever. 'I can't get over all

you've done for me and my life,' he wrote. '. . . I love you with all my heart.'[20] On the other hand, he may not have been reconsidering to any great extent, as while he was writing he had virtually moved in with Jill at Prince's Gate Mews. Nolan and her nanny, meanwhile, remained at Chester Square, where Osborne quickly joined them as soon as Penelope announced her imminent return. It seems to be at this point that Penelope either discovered, or was informed, possibly by Osborne, of Jill's involvement. 'I understand nothing,' an anguished Penelope told her mother, 'we were flawlessly happy.'[21]

A Bond Honoured opened at the Old Vic on 6 June 1966, John Dexter directing the play in an austere style with Leonido, played by Robert Stephens, surrounded by a circle of actors who sat like a parliament of crows, shrouded in shadows, rising only to take part in the action. The violence was represented by mime, and blood by the actors drawing long red ribbons from the folds of their costumes. Osborne's lack of faith in the piece was echoed by the cast. Although he 'tried desperately hard to be Spanish and spouted away non-stop', Stephens recognised that he was on a losing wicket. Privately, he thought A Bond Honoured 'a wretched thing'; and indeed, not only is it arguably second-rate Osborne, but additionally impeded in that its wrathful, sixteenth-century Catholicism was simply out of kilter with the times.[22] Stephens's private verdict was publicly endorsed by most of the critics. Osborne had 'gone to work more in a spirit of self-indulgence than of re-interpretation,' judged Irving Wardle, resulting in a play that was merely 'delirious'.[23] In the Daily Mail, Bernard Levin dismissed it as 'pretentious bunkum'.[24]

But even though he conceded that the original play had shortcomings, Osborne had recognised some merit in its underlying theme of sin and Christian redemption, which he had gone to some lengths to highlight. 'Your final scene [of Leonido's crucifixion] emphasises the only thing about Christ's death that makes one quite sure he was Man,' John Betjeman confirmed. 'He thought everyone had deserted him including God who, he claimed, was his father . . .'[24] Yet the caustic critical response left Osborne both hurt and infuriated. This was his work, his livelihood that was being critically, publicly mauled. In what other profession but the arts, he wondered indignantly, would one be obliged to endure such open humiliation? Besides, he considered that by now he had established himself as a senior dramatist whose work should be accorded deference and critical respect. If this was not something that came naturally to reviewers, he told Robert Stephens, then perhaps a few retaliatory bricks through windows might do the trick. Although Stephens dissuaded him from actual criminal damage, Osborne flung a clove of garlic towards the critics in the form of a telegram that The Times published on 9 June. The gentleman's agreement, he announced, that existed between the playwright and the critic, whereby the former did not publicly dispute the pronouncements of the latter but preserved a dignified, tomb-like silence, would henceforth be consigned to the past. Instead, he declared a season of open reprisal in which no seemingly innocuous critical remark, no unapproved verdict would pass unchallenged. Irving Wardle, one of

the most conscientious and respected of theatre critics, good-naturedly emphasised the impartiality of his position. 'I think you're the best dramatist we've
got,' he notified him, 'but I feel no loyalty to you personally . . . [However] if
you fancy a gentlemanly British punch-up, I'm more than ready to oblige . . .'[25]

So was Osborne, but the fun of forming the First Battalion British Playwrights'
Mafia and inaugurating its campaign of issuing postcard threats and rebukes to
newspaper drama critics would have to wait. As soon as *A Bond Honoured* opened,
he began mugging up his lines for his next stage appearance, in an evening
at the Old Vic in memory of George Devine on 13 June. Comprising extracts
from Royal Court productions of the previous decade and reassembling many
of the original actors and directors, the evening would raise money towards the
establishment of an award in Devine's name for young playwrights. Kenneth
Haigh was returning as Jimmy Porter, Laurence Olivier as Archie Rice and
Robert Stephens as George Dillon. A cast of thirty would perform a scene from
The Kitchen, Arnold Wesker's rowdy, cutlery-clattering evocation of behind-the-
scenes life at a restaurant, prominent among them being Osborne in a white
tunic as a cook, Olivier as the head waiter, Vanessa Redgrave as a waitress and
Noël Coward as the restaurant owner. Most crucially, however, Osborne would
be appearing in a scene from *A Patriot for Me*, playing Redl opposite Jill Bennett's
Countess Dalyanoff. On the night, as the scene unfolded, it became undeniably
clear to Penelope and the more alert of Osborne's associates in the audience that
it was not merely the characters but the actors themselves who were embarking upon a sexually charged, reckless love affair. '. . . you're easily the most
beautiful . . . the most desirable woman I've ever . . .' falters Redl; '. . . please,
stay, stay with me,' urges the Countess, 'I'll look after you . . . I'll protect you,
protect you and . . . love you.'[26]

According to Stephens, Penelope was 'sloping around backstage' after the
performance and knocked on the door of Jill's dressing-room. It was opened
by Osborne. '"I've left you" he said brusquely. "I'm going away with Jill".'[27]
When Oscar Beuselinck heard the story, he remembered Osborne's snubbing of
Mary Ure in Bournemouth and sadly chalked up his client's summary rejection
of Penelope as yet another instance of his peculiar talent for cold-hearted cruelty.

Osborne and Jill retreated to Prince's Gate Mews, from where he confirmed to enquiring gossip columnists that they were now living together,
the news being relayed to readers of the popular press on 8 July. A few days
later, Osborne received a sympathetic note from his first wife. 'I hear you and
Penelope have separated . . .' Pamela wrote, '. . . if it was a bad time for
you which it must have been I'm terribly sorry . . .'[28] From Chester Square,
meanwhile, his third wife, distraught and embarrassed, launched a desperate
campaign to retrieve both her husband and her marriage.

Throughout July and August, husband and wife engaged in a surprisingly
sympathetic correspondence, their letters implying that both were bewildered
and saddened by the situation in which they found themselves, while having
different ideas of how to how to resolve it. Penelope urges that they start

again: 'I think of you constantly', she writes.[29] But for Osborne, everything has changed: 'I *was* happy with you,' he assures her, 'and yet I have gone through this hideous thing . . .'[30] Their letters are full of compassion for each other, yet Osborne's are also full of rueful self-examination and self-pity. 'All decisions, and I flail in front of them all,' he confesses. 'I fail you despicably. I fail Jill. I cannot succeed with myself. I see no way out.'[31] Penelope, however, maintains that she cannot imagine life without him: 'Our future could be reconstructed. I know it . . .'[32] 'I don't ask for forgiveness', he replies. 'There is a flaw and the flaw is me.'[33] Finally, Penelope concedes: if he is intent upon a divorce, then even though it is the last thing she wants, she will agree to his wishes. Her decision, he replies, 'rends my heart.' He repeats that he has failed everyone, including himself. He is suffering from migraine and acute anxiety, swallowing painkillers and tranquillisers, and sleeping at night only with the aid of a bottle of whisky. In a further effort to defeat insomnia, he invested in a 'Sleep Learning Pack' consisting of a series of theoretically sleep-inducing cassette tapes that he played to himself at night. They proved woefully ineffective, as did the French and German language tapes he bought at the same time. But: 'Please look after yourself,' he told Penelope. 'Hang on to Nolan. And above all hang on to yourself. You are an extraordinary girl.'[34] And yes, he will begin the proceedings for divorce. She responds that he must do as he wishes but confirms that her love for him is still as deep as ever. 'I have such a terror that I shall never see you again.'[35]

As these letters flew dismally back and forth, each with their appeals, concerns, doubts and reassurances, Sonia McGuinness, Osborne's secretary, discovered Penelope one morning in August slumped in the bathroom at Chester Square, tablets scattered across the floor. Rushed into hospital, she had her stomach pumped and recovered. Sonia was unable to decide whether Penelope was seriously attempting to end her life or whether her action was 'a cry for help'. The incident, however, although distressing, was never mentioned again. At the same time, increasingly befuddled by painkillers and alcohol, Osborne was himself retreating into a fog of indecision and self-recrimination. 'Oh Banks,' he wrote. 'I don't feel equipped. I *am* negligible. I am being so cruel to you both.' All he really wants to do, he declares, is take all his money out of the bank and 'DISAPPEAR'.[36]

Throughout this, Osborne was still in contact with Pamela Lane, and if he confided in anyone, it would probably have been her. She had known him longer than most and he trusted her more than anyone. Yet Pamela was evidently not entirely at ease herself this summer. 'For months I've felt – what is it? – oppressed, alone and I can't overcome it by myself, though I've tried,' she told him midway through July, only ten days after Osborne had moved in with Jill. 'I've found myself wanting to call on your strength, as I used to do, and I can't get this need out of my mind . . . All I want is to be assured that your love and friendship which you once offered me are still mine . . .'[37]

Osborne, however, had little strength left, either for himself or anyone else. The late summer dissolved into a 'cloud of events, scraps of a dream in illogical inconsequence', of which later he would remember very little.[38] Flight, as was often the case with the Osbornes, seemed the only answer, and one evening, without telling anyone and knowing the housekeeper in Sussex was away on holiday and the house deserted, he drove from London to Hellingly and let himself into The Old Water Mill. He drank steadily before finally sinking into a stupor and sleeping fitfully for many hours. At some point, he telephoned Jocelyn Rickards, who immediately drove down to Sussex with her new husband, the painter Leonard Rosoman. When they arrived, they found Osborne lying insensible on a bed. They alerted Penelope and the following day she arrived in Sussex and ferried her husband by car back to London, where she arranged for him to be admitted to the Regent's Park Nursing Home in St Edmund's Terrace, on the north side of the park. 'He was deeply troubled,' remembered Sheila McGuinness, 'both emotionally and with his writing. He couldn't see the way ahead and the events of the summer accumulated to the point where he just couldn't cope anymore. He was exhausted and simply broke down.'[39] His doctor, Patrick Woodcock, a theatre-loving private practitioner who, like Oscar Beuselinck, had acquired a predominantly show business clientele, diagnosed acute depression.

Osborne spent over a month in the clinic, submitting himself reluctantly to a programme of 'intensive psychiatric treatment'.[40] A psychiatrist, 'palpably madder than I could be in whatever clinical extremity', thought Osborne, appeared regularly to inspect him and 'pumped' him with Pentothal, a strong sedative.[41] Every so often, a 'very cheerful' nursing sister loomed up on him, 'giving me pills and urging not to drink too much water'.[42] The news of his breakdown, relayed to Oscar Beuselinck, Tony Richardson and a small circle of trusted friends, was otherwise kept as quiet as possible in the hope (successfully, as it turned out) of keeping his whereabouts and condition secret from the press. In reply to a letter from his Italian translator that ended, innocently, in the hope that Osborne was well, he volunteered that on the contrary, he was feeling ghastly. In the meantime, he coped with his doctors, psychiatrists and a battalion of visitors. Tony Richardson appeared with a copy of Donald Morris's *The Washing of the Spears*, 'the sort of book he thought might entertain a sickly blimp'; which it did, turning out to be 'a fascinating account of the Zulus' heroic resistance to the British army.'[43] Perhaps Richardson was hoping for a screenplay. Immobile, Osborne also found himself besieged by a regiment of anxious women. Sonia, Jocelyn, Penelope and Nellie Beatrice, who were supportive, arrived, as did Jill, who was also flippant, she and Penelope strategically timing their visits so that each avoided the other.

Advancing in her most maternal manner, Nellie Beatrice intervened in her son and daughter-in-law's marital difficulties: 'Chins up my Brave Ones,' she cried. 'John is going through such a terrible ordeal,' she counselled Penelope. '<u>He loves you so much</u> please don't let anything happen . . . no one deserves such a sweet wife only John Osborne my dear son, loyal, kind, sweet and understanding . . .'[44] While 'John's worried old mum' as she signed herself, fretted in Pimlico, her son was keeping track of his doubts and apprehensions in a journal. He observes that he feels threatened and isolated; he feels cramps around his heart but, alarmingly, nothing in the tips of his fingers: given coins to pick up, he cannot feel them; that Pamela has written and how kind she is; that his temperature seems out of control and that periodically he feels literally on fire, and that: 'Everything [is] gone but DREAD.'[45] Meanwhile, there were supportive letters from Penelope: 'I yearn for you to be well and yourself again, but ill and divided you are still the same, irreplaceable.'[46] 'WRITE YOUR PLAYS,' she urged. '. . . Take time to make yourself whole. You are JO. You are yourself. It will come back.'[47]

'FLIGHT', he instructed himself again, in capital letters.[48] His doctors concurred, recommending travel and recuperation. Emerging from the Nursing Home at the end of November, he flew to New York and then on to Jamaica, where he had holidayed with Francine eight years previously and where he now wrote a generous cheque payable to the Theatre Trust to establish a professional theatre on the island. 'Had an absolutely marvellous time,' he assured Margery Vosper on his return, 'and feel rested and relaxed.'[49] Yet he arrived back in London to confront the massing forces of litigation. Having already instructed Oscar Beuselinck to mobilise the troops for his third divorce, his lawyer advised him that the opening shots of a separate campaign were being fired from another direction. Harman Pictures, who had been threatening legal action over Osborne's screenplay of The Charge of the Light Brigade, were marching against both him and Woodfall Films. Both engagements would prove expensive, while the latter would result in a decisive breach between Osborne and Tony Richardson, collaborators for a decade.

CHAPTER 23

The Cavalry and the Law

TONY RICHARDSON HAD conceived the idea of recreating one of the bloodi-est, ludicrous, and most mythologized incidents of English military history soon after the completion of *Tom Jones*. Since being showered with Hollywood Oscars, Woodfall had produced four films in four years, none of them bearing much relation to the kind of work with which the company had made its name. Desmond Davis had directed *Girl with Green Eyes*, an adaptation by Edna O'Brien of her own novel, while Richardson had directed *Mademoiselle*, with a screenplay by Jean Genet, *The Sailor from Gibraltar*, adapted from the novel by Marguerite Duras, and *Red and Blue*, a bizarre, thirty-minute musical starring Vanessa Red-grave and a troupe of circus elephants.

The Charge of the Light Brigade, Woodfall's eleventh film, would be its most ambitious, an anti-war film for anti-war times, a reinterpretation of the fateful episode at the Battle of Balaclava on 25 October 1854 when, as a result of absurd tactical mismanagement and misunderstanding, an entire brigade of British cavalry charged into a valley to be cut down by enemy gunfire. The Crimean War, in which Britain stood in alliance with France and the Ottoman Empire against Russia, was, at least for the British forces, miserably misman-aged by an elderly, arrogant and outdated aristocracy. The blundering conceit of Field Marshal Lord Raglan, Lord Lucan, the officer commanding the cavalry of which the Light Brigade was part, and Lord Cardigan the Brigade com-mander, a charmless confederacy of 'whiskery, bottle-nosed old roués', threw men armed merely with swords into the face of modern, heavy artillery.[1] Young Captain Nolan, 'a hothead who had been talking very loud against the cavalry', was seen galloping alongside, vainly attempting to stop the charge.[2] Two-thirds of a brigade of just over six hundred men and horses were either killed or captured, with Nolan among the dead. Eager for another costume drama from the same stable as *Tom Jones*, United Artists had leapt forward with a substantial investment of 6.5 million dollars, thereby guaranteeing a galaxy of stars and a spectacular recreation of the massacre. There seemed no reason

why the film should not be a huge success, yet the project was almost unsad-
dled even before it had properly begun. As with the calamitous charge itself,
'someone had blunder'd.'[3]

On behalf of Woodfall, Richardson had approached Harman Pictures,
who held a film option on *The Reason Why*, a book by the historian Mrs Cecil
Woodham-Smith suggesting that antipathy between Cardigan and Lucan had
resulted in the disastrous charge. But when negotiations reached deadlock,
Richardson concluded that as his film would concentrate on Nolan, rather than
Cardigan and Lucan, it would be unnecessary to acquire the rights to a work in
which the emphasis would be on an entirely different aspect of a story already
in the public domain. Woodfall's would be an anti-war film and Osborne's
screenplay essentially a portrayal of the divisions between the British social
classes, reflected in the gulf between the champagne-swilling officers and the
cholera and hardship endured by the men under their command. The charge
would be represented not as a bid for glory but a gratuitous folly at the centre
of which Nolan would be presented as a figure-of-conscience, a Hamlet of the
Crimean battlefields. Accordingly, Richardson notified Harman that Woodfall
would not continue to seek the rights to Woodham-Smith's book, but press
ahead and announce their intention of making their own film.

Simultaneously working on *A Patriot for Me*, Osborne spent several weeks of
scrambling between the conspiracies of the Habsburg Empire and the miscalcu-
lations of the Crimean War. At Hellingly, he buried himself in a virtual dugout
of histories and accounts, Woodham-Smith being fortified by Alexander King-
lake's *The Invasion of the Crimea: Its Origin*, Christopher Hibbert's *The Destruction of
Lord Raglan*, and several others. The screenplay was completed at Chester Square
on 13 October 1965 and at Woodfall, a research department marshalled themselves to check the accuracy of period details. Meanwhile, at Harman Pictures,
Laurence Harvey was also interested in seeing a copy of Osborne's screenplay. A
tall, dark-haired actor with a face as thin as a knife and who had made his name
in the film of *Room at the Top*, Harvey was also a director of Harman. Alerted by
an announcement in *What's On* magazine on 10 December 1965 that Osborne
was adapting Woodham-Smith's book, Harvey overlooked a correction the following week that the screenplay was not an adaptation but an original work,
and 'obtained' a copy of Osborne's unpublished script.[4] Having read it, he
summoned his lawyer, with the upshot that Harman sued, alleging contravention of copyright.

Legal manoeuvring continued during the months that Osborne was otherwise
engaged by *A Bond Honoured*, juggling between Penelope and Jill, and confined at
the Regent's Park Nursing Home. At last, a judicial hearing in the case of *Harman
Pictures v. Osborne and Others*, the 'others' being Woodfall Productions and Woodfall
Film Presentations, mustered before Mr Justice Goff on 22 February 1967. Harman's legal army, commanded by Sir Andrew Clark, an urbane Queen's Council
of meticulous logic and a dry courtroom humour, ranged themselves against
Woodfall's defensive battalions under the leadership of John Arnold QC.

Clark's case rested upon four 'devastating' pages of closely typed evidence supplied by Harman Pictures and which listed alleged similarities in style and phrasing between The Reason Why and Osborne's screenplay.[5] With Osborne declining to appear in court, Arnold attempted to outflank Clark by producing a catalogue of a hundred and forty-six sources to which he announced his client had referred while writing the script. He also brandished an affidavit signed by Osborne, conceding that while he had read the book as part of his research, it was not the basis for the screenplay. Arnold concluded by claiming that, since verifiable historical events were a quarry common to all researchers, any similarity of chronology or phrasing between different accounts could not therefore constitute an infringement of copyright. Clark countered that historical events were entirely separate from their subsequent re-creation in literary form, and therefore it was untenable to argue that an author might compose a text that could be shown to be close in phrasing to an already published work while simultaneously claiming independence of it. After six days of legal jousting, Mr Justice Goff, claiming insufficient evidence from Osborne, awarded Harman Pictures an interim injunction pending a full trial, and preventing the use of copyright material. Confusingly, he decreed that work on Woodfall's film might proceed uninterrupted. Richardson therefore cautiously went ahead with casting and planning a shooting schedule.

However, the director found himself in a similar dilemma with Osborne's screenplay as he had with the script for Tom Jones, in that while it included some evocative passages, especially in its recreation of British society before the Crimean War, a good deal of work was required before filming could begin. Recognising that Osborne might be reluctant to redraft it, he turned instead to Charles Wood, the author of Meals on Wheels and several plays about the army as well as Help!, a film starring The Beatles, and an old friend of both himself and Osborne, to rework the screenplay. At the same time, Richardson held a series of frantic summit meetings with Harvey's lawyer, the formidable Lord Goodman, who had represented the Royal Court in its dealings with A Patriot for Me, to negotiate an out-of-court settlement with Harman Pictures. At last a deal was struck. Woodfall would formally acquire the rights to The Reason Why at £120,000, of which Osborne would be expected to pay £9,000. Richardson would also award Harvey a role in the film.

As he had already paid part of the production costs of A Patriot for Me, Osborne was not pleased to find himself presented almost two years later with another bill, especially when he disputed the central issue of infringement of copyright. In his view, artists throughout the ages had in one way or another used the works of others with impunity to create their own. Brecht, he complained to Oscar Beuselinck, had openly recycled John Gay's The Beggar's Opera in order to write The Threepenny Opera and had readily converted Shakespeare's Coriolanus into Koriolan. However, as his lawyer tactfully pointed out, in neither case were the original works subject to copyright restrictions. Osborne was further incensed when he discovered that Richardson had offered, and Harvey had accepted, the part of Prince Radziwill, a cavalry officer, in the film, a small but flashy role he had eagerly anticipated playing himself. Osborne had even proudly cultivated a handlebar moustache of Radziwillian splendour in order to appear authentically aristocratic and was looking forward to showing off his horsemanship, but as far as Richardson was concerned, their loss to the film was 'a small price to pay to avoid the threatened prosecution.'[6]

Osborne, however, whose response to anything he perceived as critical and professional provocation was to come out fighting, was furious that Richardson had seemingly used him as a bargaining chip to secure his own hand, and the disagreements and distrust that had begun to rankle on Tom Jones erupted again. For his part, Richardson was irked that Osborne apparently thought the cinema an inferior medium to the theatre and therefore had refused to devote the necessary time and energy to re-writing and re-shaping his screenplay. Ignoring the director's attempts to soothe him and white-knuckled with fury, Osborne composed a long and vehement letter to Richardson on 10 May 1967, accusing him of 'complete betrayal'. 'I am bitter,' he acknowledged, but: 'After all, I have known your character long enough to be unsurprised by the over familiar process of your deft exploitation of those unfortunates who regard themselves as your friends . . . I have been used and used calculatedly.' His old associate, he explained, was a Machiavellian figure, well known for ruthlessly manipulating others for his own ends while simultaneously requiring that his friends collude in his hypocrisy by maintaining the fiction that he was not a homosexual. Their ten-year partnership, he pronounced, was now at an end. 'We both have other things to do.'[7]

Osborne had a fearsome and impressively eloquent talent for personal abuse, and deployed in private correspondence it could be an alarming weapon. Shocked and deeply hurt, Richardson briefly considered suing his Woodfall partner for libel. Although some of those who had worked with him would have privately agreed with Osborne's allegations of his ruthlessness ('a conniving, manipulative but very brave man,' was Beuselinck's verdict; 'talented, courageous but not very likeable'), and many also speculated that he was either bisexual or homosexual, Richardson, who had by now divorced Vanessa Redgrave, preferred to keep his sexual inclinations private.[8] News that he was considering legal retaliation filtered back to Osborne and caused him a few days of panic, but in the event and preoccupied with filming, Richardson decided not to resort to his lawyers in the hope that the dispute might eventually blow over.

Yet the breach remained and they never worked together again. Richardson, who loathed as much as Osborne what he condemned as English snobbery and who had become a multi-millionaire through lucrative film contracts, decided to live abroad. He settled first at Le Nid du Duc, an old, tree-shielded farmhouse in the south of France where friends arrived to play cards and amateur theatricals and were soothed by the scent of log fires, fresh coffee, herbs and lavender. Eventually, he made his home in California, where he continued to make films and from where, many years later, recalling their 'old association, affection and real admiration', he and Osborne were eventually reconciled by telephone.[9]

But the filming of The Charge of the Light Brigade began beneath the shadow of hostility between the two former collaborators. Trevor Howard, John Gielgud and Harry Andrews were playing the Lords Cardigan, Raglan and Lucan; David Hemmings had been cast as Nolan, and Jill Bennett as Mrs Duberley, the pay-master's wife. Richardson had chosen Turkey as their main location, not only because its terrain, on the opposite side of the Black Sea to the Crimea, suited his purposes (a valley a few miles from Ankara proved an excellent location for the charge), but also because Turkey seemed to be the sole remaining country in Western Europe retaining a large number of serving cavalry who could be recruited as extras. The reason for this was that the Soviet Union was maintaining a similar cavalry presence on its own side of the Turkish border. It also fortuitously transpired that most of the Turkish cavalry horses were veterans of Hollywood westerns that had been shipped from the United States as part of an American aid package, and were therefore proficient at falling under cannon fire and dying before the cameras before getting up for another take.

As filming continued, Osborne and Jill spent a week together in Istanbul. After he returned to London, Jill joined the rest of the company at Ankara, from where she wrote almost every day, proclaiming her adoration of her new lover and passing on gossip from the set, where filming was frequently impeded by disputes between the British and Turkish factions and interventions by local mullahs. Everyone in the company, she informed him, knew of their affair and were delighted. Her hotel room was plastered with snapshots of him. She had never felt so loved in her life and, like a love-struck schoolgirl, she was counting the days until they were reunited. Like Mary's and Penelope's letters, Jill's correspondence is full of endearment, affection and plans for a shared future: they must immediately set up home together; they must marry; they would have a baby daughter and call her Daisy perhaps, or Abigail; he would write hugely successful plays and she would appear in them and they would live a wonderful life together into vigorous old age. Yet the difference between Penelope's letters and Jill's is perhaps indicative of the difference between the two women: Penelope writes as one to whom writing came naturally, and who has a distinctive sense of composition, style and wit; Jill's letters, on the other hand, are feisty but frequently sexually coarse, maudlin and agitated. Jill was a restless, frequently melancholic spirit.[10]

With Jill filming in Turkey and Osborne intent upon divorce in London, Penelope, still distressed by her husband's desertion but equally determined to maintain her career, scooped up the two-year-old Nolan and flew to the United States. Accompanied by Nolan's nanny, they went first to Los Angeles and then to New York, where Penelope began the first of several stints alternating with Pauline Kael as film critic of the New Yorker. Her work was absorbing, her writing admired and New York both welcoming and thrilling, but she missed Osborne deeply, and the 'smashing life' they had shared in London.[11] Only with the utmost reluctance, she repeated, could she contemplate the prospect of divorce from the man who had once been, and still was, her grand passion. 'I'm saturated with you,' she had written once.[12] She still was. Yet Osborne was insistent. Consequently, they applied themselves to the mechanics of separation, the division of the spoils of Chester Square and the dismal dismantling of a marriage. Osborne claimed a few pieces of furniture, the useless chunk of amethyst from the bedroom table, the portable television, his Elisabeth Frink sculpture and the Gwen John drawing, while Penelope put in bids for the pieces she wanted herself. Eventually, writing to wish her well at the *New Yorker*, he turned back to his typewriter and the new plays on which he had begun to work. So ended for Osborne the summer of love.

CHAPTER 24

Fearing the Future

HE WAS WORKING ON a projected trilogy under the general title of For the Meantime, of which the first two plays, Time Present and The Hotel in Amsterdam, both of which are dominated by unseen, offstage characters, were almost finished. 'The theme of both, if you like,' he told Sam Zolotow of the New York Times, 'is about living, or trying to live in the present.'[1] The third play would be a contemporary reworking of Shakespeare's Coriolanus, which, as Brecht had already proved and Oscar Beuselinck confirmed, was written sufficiently long ago not to land Osborne in the kind of copyright problems with which he had become ensnared with The Charge of the Light Brigade. As he wrote and revised, making fair copies in his green, hardbacked notebooks, Osborne infiltrated into each play his anxieties over the legacy of the past, his fears of an uncertain future and his restive musings on the nature of friendship and, more specifically, of love.

Written as a vehicle for Jill, Time Present features Pamela, Osborne's first female protagonist, a heavily-drinking actress in her thirties sharing a Pimlico apartment belonging to Constance, a pragmatic Labour Member of Parliament. Pamela's father, Sir Gideon Orme, seventy-two years old and a once-prominent actor, lies dying in hospital, and at the end of the first act a telephone call brings the news of his death. The second and final act takes place on the day of his memorial service. The Hotel in Amsterdam is similarly overshadowed by an unseen presence, in this case the tyrannical KL, a film producer. Set over a long weekend in the drawing-room of a first-class hotel, three couples congratulate each other that for once KL does not know where they are. Laurie, a screenwriter, and his pregnant wife, Margaret, are joined by Gus, a good-natured film editor, a hypochondriac and possible homosexual married to the perceptive Annie, and by Dan, a painter, and Amy, his wife, who is also KL's secretary. Other than recourse to the drinks table, there is little action in the play, which ends with the cheering news – to the characters – that KL has committed suicide.

Both Geoffrey Orme and KL have specific sources. Pamela's devotion to Orme echoes Jill's for Geoffrey Tearle, an actor whom Osborne might not have actually seen on stage but of whom he had heard a good deal from Jill. A large, imposing man who enjoyed his public image of the sprucely dressed gentleman-actor, he was frequently to be seen in the years immediately after the war striding along Piccadilly and the Strand in a capacious camelhair overcoat, a cornflower vibrant in his buttonhole. Conceivably, the young Osborne may have passed him one day on his way to work at Benn Brothers. Jill, however, had encountered him at the Shakespeare Memorial Theatre in Stratford in 1949, the year in which Osborne left Brighton to work as a stage manager for the Saxon Players in Leicester. Tearle was then sixty-five, a widower and, although far too elderly to be playing the title roles in *Othello* and *Macbeth*, enjoying belated recognition as a Shakespearean actor. Jill was nineteen and playing minor roles in the background. Tearle took her under his wing and a close relationship developed between them. Until his death in 1953, they took summer holidays together in Cornwall, and in London shared his Bentinck Street flat, where the retired sergeant-major whom he employed as a valet did not take kindly to Jill's elfin presence. Like Tearle, Orme and his theatre represent a vanished England, an Edwardian and between-the-wars England when West End theatres, lavish in red plush and gilt and warm in the glow of lamplight, were presided over by actor-managers guiding melodrama and light comedy smoothly across their stages. It was a world reclaimed only through old scrapbooks such as those perused in the play by Pamela, the programmes of dimly-remembered plays and the names of half-forgotten actors; names that both Colonel Redfern and Billy Rice would have recognised and for which Osborne was romantically nostalgic.

In *The Hotel in Amsterdam*, written as the debris fell from the fracas over *The Charge of the Light Brigade*, Osborne took 'malicious' revenge upon Tony Richardson by appropriating him as the model for the dictatorial film producer KL, a characterisation over which Richardson was subsequently 'furious'.[2] Osborne's representative in the play is the sceptical, scornful and self-pitying Laurie, and a speech in which Laurie vilifies KL is closely reminiscent of the letter that Osborne had sent to Richardson during his filming of *The Charge of the Light Brigade*, condemning 'your blackmailing, sneering, your callousness, your malingering, your emotional gun-slinging . . . You trade on the forbearance, kindliness and talent of your friends . . .'[3] As with Pamela in *Time Present* and many Osbornean heroes both before and since, Laurie spurts out a litany of his creator's loathing and anxieties, in this instance roaming restlessly across marriage, boredom, air hostesses, the contraceptive pill for women, grasping relatives and his fear of living alone. Becoming increasingly drunk, he finds himself alone with Annie, to whom with unexpected delicacy he declares his love and hesitantly asks for hers in return, a speech reflecting Osborne's affection for and dependence upon Jill Bennett: '. . . you have always been the most dashing . . . romantic . . . friendly . . . playful . . . loving . . . impetuous . . . larky . . . fearful . . . detached . . . constant . . . woman I have ever met . . . And I love you . . .'[4]

'I do indeed hope they [the two plays] are funny, but also full of the melancholy of the present time,' Osborne informed Margery Vosper.[5] Like Laurie, Osborne viewed the future with a good deal of unease. Uncertain of his standing with the new directorate at the Royal Court, he also continued to be worried about money. His forthcoming divorce from Penelope, he feared, would be expensive. Therefore he told his agent that he would rather the plays were produced commercially rather than by the English Stage Company although he would like the theatre to have 'an interest'.[6] The Royal Court, however, prevaricated. Margery Vosper sent the plays on to the National Theatre, where Kenneth Tynan read them and, having identified Richardson behind the figure of KL, promptly turned them down. 'The verbal slaughter of Tony Richardson is very funny,' he told Osborne, but a private feud, he asserted, had no place in the National's repertoire.[7] Disconcertingly, commercial managers also proved reluctant to come forward. As he had been a co-director of Oscar Lewenstein Productions for seven years, Osborne turned to Lewenstein, a co-founder of the English Stage Company and a Woodfall Films associate, who read the plays during the summer of 1967. As disturbed as Tynan by the 'cruel' allusions to Richardson and further deterred by his wife's assessment of both plays as 'frankly boring', he initially demurred, but eventually relented and agreed to produce them, ironically at the Royal Court, at the end of the following summer.[8]

A delay of a year was especially unwelcome financially, as Osborne's 'periodic panics about money' were becoming more frequent.[9] His homes, *The Charge of the Light Brigade*, the accounts with wine merchants, tailors, bookshops and garages, the stabling and maintaining of horses, the dogs, the cars, and chauffeur, a cook and housekeepers in London and Sussex: all of these were eating away at his earnings. The purchase of an expensive new house delivered a further substantial blow to a bank balance already throwing up its arms in submission in the face of relentless withdrawals. In September 1967, Osborne splashed out on a large terraced property for himself and Jill at 30 Chelsea Square, off the fashionable King's Road, comprising a substantial study where he could work, six bedrooms, two bathrooms, a double reception room and, after several thousand pounds' worth of renovation, the reckless addition of a Nordic solarium. 'My dearest love,' he jotted on a postcard to Jill. 'New house, new life. New everything. Thanks to you. Ever your <u>friend</u>.'[10] As he and Jill began moving in their belongings, word came from Oscar Beuselinck that Penelope had filed for divorce, citing her husband's adultery, and that the anticipated substantial demands on his bank account would inevitably result. There was also additional news, a rumour that Penelope was intending to marry the actor and director Mike Nichols, whose latest film, *The Graduate*, starring Dustin Hoffman, was one of the most successful of the year.

Penelope won her decree nisi on 4 December 1967, and as Osborne had feared, Beuselinck's financial predictions were correct. Osborne was presented with a bill for costs while Penelope was awarded principal custody of the two-and-a-half-year-old Nolan, her father being permitted to see her during specified

holiday weeks. The settlement also obliged Osborne to pay an annual maintenance of £1,000 after tax for his daughter, pay off the outstanding £15,000
mortgage at Chester Square and make the house, worth about £50,000, over to
his former wife (who had generously agreed not to claim any maintenance for
herself), for her to use in her lifetime and thereafter to be transferred to Nolan.
These arrangements were to be supervised by trustees agreed by both Osborne
and Penelope, which in itself turned out to be a tortuous and wearisome procedure taking several weeks of proposals, negotiation and compromise to resolve.
'I am very hard-pressed financially at the present as Penelope is putting the
screws on me in an alarming way,' he told Margery Vosper.[11]

Not only exhausted by the entire process, Osborne was also left feeling rather
cheated. He viewed the divorce court as a casino and each case a gaming table
at which the litigants, having placed their bets, either won or lost. Forever
fearful that the dice would roll against him and result in his paying a heavy
maintenance order or renouncing property, Osborne had until now managed
to escape both. Therefore, although it was he who had left Penelope for Jill, he
was nevertheless aggrieved by a settlement he regarded as being substantially
weighted in his former wife's favour, especially in the light of a suggestion that
she was about to marry a man who, by all accounts, was extremely rich. Jill
evidently connived in Osborne's view of things, the couple regarding Penelope and Nichols with a flinty hostility profoundly shocking to many who
knew them. These included Kenneth Tynan who, hearing of the contents of a
macabre package sent to Penelope 'with love from John and Jill', graded it high
on his list of 'the vilest thing[s] I have known one person do to another.' Since
childhood, as a reaction to a whooping cough vaccine, Nichols had been bald, a
condition he concealed by wearing a toupee, and the parcel from England contained one of Nolan's dolls 'so cruelly . . . mistreated' that at first Penelope did
not recognise it. 'Every hair', recorded Tynan, 'had been pulled from its head.'[12]
Penelope, he added, burst into tears every time she recalled the incident.

In the event, Penelope did not marry Nichols, with whom she remained on
good terms, but moved, with Nolan and her nanny, into an apartment on the
thirteenth floor at 275 Central Park West, from where she continued to write
profiles and film criticism for the New Yorker. Meanwhile, in London, The Charge of
the Light Brigade opened at the Odeon, Leicester Square, on 10 April 1968, where
it failed to repeat the critical and commercial success of Tom Jones, although
it is arguably the finer film and in hindsight, one of those best representing
the 1960s. The reviews were generally carping. It was one of those odd, in-
between films, according to John Russell Taylor in The Times, which was neither
as good as it should have been nor as bad as it might have been. Osborne, who
had demanded that his name be removed from the credits, did not attend the
premiere. As it had been infected by the rancour culminating in the break with
Richardson, the entire enterprise was something he regretted.

*   *   *

Throughout the travails of *A Patriot for Me*, *The Charge of the Light Brigade*, his separa-tion from Penelope, his taking up with Jill and his sojourn in the Nursing Home, Osborne had continued to meet Pamela Lane for long nostalgic lunches and after-noons at her 'very cosy Tiggywinkle Kilburn basement' flat.[13] They continued seeing each other until the spring of 1968, when Pamela, who knew Jill Bennett, advised her former husband against marrying her. In her view, they were cata-strophically mismatched. Osborne, who refused to listen but within a few years would very much wish he had, dismissed his first wife's concern for his welfare as an unwarranted intrusion into his private affairs. While continuing to assist her financially, the royalties of *Inadmissible Evidence* being supplemented by a cheque ferried through his accountants whenever it was needed, Osborne appears not to have seen much of Pamela for the next few years, although their relationship would resume later. On 19 April, therefore, at the age of thirty-eight and having preserved his Victorian-era cavalry moustache for the occasion, he accompanied Jill to Chelsea Register Office where, eleven years earlier, he had married Mary Ure, and where he was now married for the fourth time.

A few weeks later, *Time Present* and *The Hotel in Amsterdam* opened on 23 May and 3 July 1968 respectively, the former starring Jill as Pamela and the latter Paul Scofield as Laurie. Both were directed by Anthony Page. The reviewers, however, disagreed about their merits. Writing of *Time Present*, Philip Hope-Wallace complained in *The Guardian* that 'one comes away only with the memory of a monologue', although Ronald Bryden in the *Observer* suggested that Osborne had discovered 'a new theatrical craft and objectivity . . . unlike Jimmy Porter, [Pamela] refuses to pity herself – in this, if nothing else, *Time Present* is Osborne's most mature, least self-indulgent play.'[14] Commenting on *The Hotel in Amsterdam* in the *New Statesman*, Philip French (who had once warmly shaken Osborne by the hand after a performance of *Look Back in Anger*), grumbled that '. . . apart from Laurie's sad declaration of love for his best friend's wife – which consti-tutes one of the most affecting scenes in recent theatre – there are no moments of truth, no epiphanies . . . only lassitude.'[15] Yet Harold Hobson in *The Sunday Times* thought it the best contemporary play in London, while in the *Observer* Ronald Bryden added that with *Inadmissible Evidence*, the new plays 'add up to an impressive body of work, our most penetrating and truthful portrait gallery of the mean time we inhabit.'[16]

At the same time, a flurry of books and articles was appearing, picking over the phenomenon of the Angry Young Man and the ten years from *Look Back in Anger* to *A Patriot for Me*, and in doing so threatening to effectively close off and seal Osborne's achievement like the doorway to a tomb. A book-length collec-tion of articles on *Look Back in Anger* edited by John Russell Taylor was published in 1968 and a further four volumes appraising Osborne's work the follow-ing year. The critics Martin Banham and Alan Carter published one each and Simon Trussler two, one being a short study for the British Council. Kenneth Allsop and John Russell Taylor also published revised editions of their historical surveys, *The Angry Decade* and *Anger and After*, which had first appeared in 1958 and 1962 respectively. While all agreed that Osborne had dragged the English theatre into the late twentieth century and made it an essential component of cultural life, the cumulative effect of these publications was to convert the accolade of the Angry Young Man into a gallows from which his later work might dangle, unforgivingly exposed to the elements. More generously, though, Alan Carter wrote that 'Osborne's most original contribution to British drama may be summed up by the word "love". For Osborne the love between man and woman, and between man and society, creates situations worth exploring . . . When faced with the placid half-living of the masses, Osborne's emotional wobble becomes visible, and his love turns to anger, almost hate. Without love, we are nothing.'[17]

But Simon Trussler represented increasing numbers of critics in suggesting that Osborne had lost his position as an innovator, that his considerable eloquence had rarely been matched by technical proficiency and that while he was an instinctive artist, he was by no means a master craftsman. This would become a frequent criticism of Osborne's writing over the succeeding years, as would the suggestion that the potency of his earlier work had been exaggerated and its cultural influence misinterpreted. The Angry Young Man, many commentators concluded, had been something of a chimera. In fact, this had been continuing for some time. As early as 1957, Kenneth Tynan had warned that 'We made a big mistake over Mr Osborne.'[18] Watching The Entertainer, he concluded that Osborne's real subject was not, as many seemed to think, the decay of contemporary England, but his belief that it had been caused by the disastrous abandonment of the upright imperial values that had once bound society together. Osborne was therefore unmasked as a right-wing, and not a left-wing dramatist, and the true hero of Look Back in Anger was not Jimmy Porter but his father-in-law, Colonel Redfern. Looking back from the vantage point of the late 1960s, several commentators agreed that what, ten years earlier, had appeared to be a great rhetorical disparagement of the Establishment was in fact nothing of the sort. Jimmy Porter was certainly boiling with rage, not against the Establishment, as was first thought, but because he very much wanted to be a part of it. And so did his creator.

This impression was reinforced by critics and audiences who began pointing out that the targets of the protagonists' disenchantment in plays from Inadmissible Evidence onwards were becoming increasingly negligible. Reviewing Time Present, Ronald Bryden lamented that the play merely 'drifts from one inconsequent diatribe by Pamela to another.'[19] Moreover, having once virulently attacked the upper-middle class, Osborne, who had successfully negotiated the transition from lower-middle to upper-middle, was now becoming its apologist. Martin Esslin observed that while the younger Osborne had replaced the country house drawing-room with the Porters' seedy attic, he had now substituted this with a chic Pimlico living-room. The playwright whose stage invective twelve years ago had provoked astonished gasps of outrage and whose wit 'struck terror into the ranks of the philistines', was now fielding characters deriding youth and liberalism and complaining about the high rate of income tax. That the former Angry Young Man was now inviting the approval of the kind of audiences he had once vowed to blast out of their complacency, exclaimed Esslin, was the most extraordinary somersault. It was all extremely depressing. 'Thus do the angry young men of 1956', he concluded, 'turn into the Edwardian high Tories of 1968, the iconoclasts of yesterday into the satisfied upholders of established values of today.'[10]

It seemed a viewpoint to which Osborne himself appeared resigned. 'By 1968,' he reflected later, and at the age of thirty-nine, 'I was quite reformed and vilified by the priglets as a "Tory Squire" . . .'[21] His conviction, expressed in a *Vogue* magazine profile, that: 'I believe in the eighteenth-century idea of moral virtue, in the Calvinistic, certainly pre-Freudian idea, that some people are better than others, are born better', were sentiments that certainly did not sit easily with egalitarian ideals of the Sixties.[2] He was accused of being an elitist, to which he happily agreed, and of being a mass of prejudice. However, a single prejudice, he asserted buoyantly, was worth twenty principles, and he had a vast and battle-ready army of prejudices and opinions which he energetically deployed in occasional articles and letters to the press. These included an abhorrence of Europe and Britain's application to join the European Common Market ('a monumental swindle'); Independent Television ('the surplus-goods store of popular culture . . . irredeemably third-rate'); the Conservative Party ('always detestable and more so now with their adroit razor-sharp practice and thug success'); the Labour Party ('similarly despicable in its mean-witted shambling to keep up the same moral stride'), and all kinds of technological progress ('I'd like to see this whole, hideous, headlong rush into the twentieth century halted a bit').[23] In addition, he argued genially, his views had not changed at all over the years.

At least he was able to inform his accountants that the plays would be transferring to the West End, *Time Present* opening at the Duke of York's Theatre in St Martin's Lane on 11 July and *The Hotel in Amsterdam* at the nearby New Theatre on 6 September. A month later, a revival of *Look Back in Anger*, also directed by Anthony Page and produced by Oscar Lewenstein, opened at the Royal Court and transferred to the Criterion Theatre. By the end of the year, therefore, Osborne's reputation, and his bank balance, was bolstered by his having three plays running in the West End of London, something he had never achieved before. 'I had just moved my office from Curzon Street to Goodwin's Court just off St Martin's Lane,' remembered Lewenstein, 'and it was a great pleasure each time I stepped out of my office to see the whole of one side of St Martin's Lane occupied by John's plays.'[24] And at the *Evening Standard* drama awards the following January, the Osbornes and the plays were again applauded, Jill picking up the Best Actress Award for *Time Present* and Osborne the award for Best Play for *The Hotel in Amsterdam*. Again, like Penelope before her, Jill predicted great and glittering things ahead for them both.

*   *   *

And yet, even a superficial glance at the lists of his income and expenditure provided each month by his accountants caused the chill hand of panic to grasp at Osborne's heart. Although he was earning a considerable amount, revivals throughout the world of *Look Back in Anger* in particular providing a steady source of royalty payments, his wealth was proving alarmingly fluid. It was as if what he had apparently assumed to be a landlocked lake of unfathomable depth was in reality tidal. No sooner did money come in than it frustratingly went out again, leaving only a few stranded rockpools in its wake. In a quick sortie for funds he resorted to television acting. In December 1966, he and Jill had starred in *Brainscrew*, a play by Henry Livings in the BBC *Thirty Minute Theatre* series, and at the beginning of 1968 they appeared in *The Parachute*, a television play by David Mercer, Osborne looming up on the small screen as Werner von Ragen, a fastidious German aristocrat killed while testing a prototype parachute for the Nazi regime. 'John Osborne the actor is no threat to John Osborne the playwright,' commented the television critic of *The Times*.[25] A few months later, he starred opposite Jill in *It's Only Us*, a thirty-minute television play by Peter Draper about an affluent professional couple spending an afternoon in a seedy hotel.

But these money-making raids made little difference, and neither he nor Jill were the type to economise. The upkeep of Chelsea Square cost a small fortune, with its new leather furniture and shining steel floor-lamps, the chauffeur, the cook and the housekeeper. Then there was the Bentley in the garage and the champagne in the fridge, not to mention the dogs: his English sheepdog and Great Dane at Hellingly, and her yapping Pekingese and quivering, scampering Shih Tzus in London. In February 1969, Osborne endured another long and bewildering lunch with Walter Strach, his accountant, who spread such a fantastic array of figures and calculations, plans and permutations, alternatives and predictions before him that he was plunged into torment. The unpalatable news that he already owed £40,000 to his own production company and as much in unpaid income tax turned the food cold in his mouth. Although he owned £50,000 worth of shares, including some in Northern Songs, a company publishing the work of Lennon and McCartney, it appeared that he was seriously mismanaging his money.

Afterwards, he appealed to Oscar Beuselinck. Was the position really as bleak as it seemed? His lawyer sorrowfully confirmed that it was. For Osborne, this was mortifying. He was not yet middle-aged and hopefully had a fair future before him, but things he had hardly thought about a few years ago had now become constant anxieties. Supposing, he cried, he fell prey to 'writer's block' and became unable to work? Supposing his plays, including the hitherto reliable *Look Back in Anger*, fell from the fickle favours of directors? What would he do if the critics were right and his audience really was melting away? How would he survive? How might he provide for his old age, let alone anyone else's? Was he doomed to a treadmill of churning out plays, much as a cow converted grass into milk, just in an attempt to break even?

His advisers insisted that he ruthlessly cut his spending in order to pay his tax bills and urged more television and film work, which paid much more than stage plays. But, chastened by his experience with *The Charge of the Light Brigade*, Osborne recoiled. 'I don't want to write some film,' he cried. 'It's too boring,' he explained to his accountant. 'At my stage of reputation (of which you are clearly unaware) I should be able to devote my time to the theatre and things which interest me.'[26] He relented, though, on acting. Soon afterwards, there-fore, he hared off to Hungary to appear in *First Love*, a film adapted from the novel by Ivan Turgenev dealing with an adolescent boy's love for his father's mistress, and directed by Maximilian Schell from *A Patriot for Me*. Osborne played Maidenev, a poet, and was filmed sitting in a field wearing a large black coat and hat and reciting Elizabeth Barrett Browning's 'How Do I Love Thee?' It was a strange film, thought the critic Pauline Kael, in which the photography of Sven Nykvist, the distinguished Swedish cinematographer, was sabotaged by an editor who might more usefully be employed as a butcher's assistant. Return-ing to England, Osborne appeared the following year in *The Chairman's Wife*, a short television play by Gerry O'Hara, who also wrote episodes for *The Aveng-ers*, the popular television spy series. More substantially, he gave a splendidly laconic performance as Kinnear, the overlord of a north-eastern crime syndicate in Mike Hodge's malevolently atmospheric feature film thriller, *Get Carter*. Set mostly in Newcastle and starring Michael Caine as Jack, a London gangster hunting his brother's killer, the film, since acknowledged as a classic of its kind, provided 'sadism for the connoisseur' according to Kael, and marked the begin-ning of 'a new genre of virtuoso viciousness.'[27]

The brutality of *Get Carter* and the protagonist's remorseless zeal reflected something of the atmosphere of the time in that the pendulum of political and social change, having swung outwards towards liberalism, had begun to fall back towards and through the centre to something more reactionary. In the General Election campaign of 1970, Prime Minister Harold Wilson assidu-ously stumped up and down Britain, the people's man, pipe between his teeth, hoping to recreate the heady optimism of 1966. But something went wrong. Wilson had lost his appeal and disgruntled Labour voters stayed at home. On 18 June, the Tories celebrated an election victory with a majority of thirty-one, and Harold Wilson, a reforming Prime Minister who had attempted, perhaps too anxiously, to align himself with all that was new and youthful, left 10 Downing Street to Edward Heath, his grand piano and ambitions of European integration.

Heath's accession to power was only one of a litter of symbols of the soured spirit of the Sixties. The Beatles, in many ways the pre-eminent symbol of the decade but now divided by internal squabbles, went their separate ways, their last single, the elegiac 'Let It Be', bringing the decade of youth to its disillu-sioned close. Moreover, the England football team returned from the World Cup, having been overcome in the quarter-finals by Germany, the team they had defeated to win the tournament only four years previously. The Sixties had ended, the party was over and the debris lay waiting to be swept away.

CHAPTER 25

Detachment

KENNETH TYNAN'S REJECTION OF both *Time Present* and *The Hotel in Amsterdam* had wounded Osborne deeply. Scenting the odour of disloyalty he had detected in Richardson's rejection of his *Charge of the Light Brigade* screenplay, he decided to retaliate. At a New Year's Eve party at the Old Vic in 1970, Tynan and Olivier were astonished to be emphatically snubbed when they cornered Osborne and suggested that he might write a new play for the National Theatre. 'Help us to make history,' suggested Tynan. Osborne replied that he had already made history, thank you, and turned away.[1]

A few months later, on 19 March 1971, and settling into a new job as one of two literary consultants at the National Theatre, Tynan was horrified to discover that Osborne had inaugurated a 'furious attack' upon the National in an article in the *Evening Standard* in which he denounced the theatre's track record since its opening in 1963 as unremittingly mediocre.[2] John Dexter's production of *Othello*, in which Olivier had donned black make-up in order to play the title role, Osborne dismissed as akin to a 'black and white minstrel' show, while Ingmar Bergman's production of *Hedda Gabler* 'must have made poor old Ibsen turn in his Northern lights.'[3] And apart from Peter Nichols's *The National Health*, he added, there had hardly been a new play of any merit. Osborne, thought Tynan indignantly, was conveniently overlooking an impressive roll-call of new work, including Samuel Beckett's *Play*, John Arden's *Armstrong's Last Goodnight*, Peter Shaffer's *The Royal Hunt of the Sun* and Tom Stoppard's *Rosencrantz and Guildenstern are Dead*.

Having already excised Anthony Creighton and Tony Richardson from his life, Osborne now intensified his volleys against Kenneth Tynan. Three weeks later, in a letter to the satirical magazine *Private Eye*, he 'accused' the National directorate of 'mishandling' the talents of several actors, including Alec Guinness.[4] This was 'a curious charge' countered Tynan, considering that Sir Alec had never appeared at the National.[5] The episode confirmed Tynan's conviction that Osborne was becoming increasingly irrational and inclined to see betrayal in every shadow.

His estimation was, broadly speaking, correct. Although Time Present and The Hotel in Amsterdam had been successful, Osborne's apprehension of deception and treachery, never dormant for long, was exacerbated by his financial worries and professional doubts, mixing a cocktail of anxiety and suspicion that soured his relationship with Jill. After A Patriot for Me and Time Present, she stood poised to become the leading Osbornean actress, but his fear of being unable to live up to expectations and of his reputation being questioned plunged him over the succeeding months into periodic bouts of debilitating gloom that progressive amounts of alcohol and painkillers only exacerbated. Three years earlier, in 1968, when Tynan had asked him in a newspaper interview whether he considered himself 'paranoid', Osborne had admitted that he did. He seemed, he declared, hardly to have any close friends left nowadays. Yet one's enemies, he added conspiratorially, should never be forgiven, as 'they're probably the only thing you've got.'[6] At the time, this was possibly little more than mild bantering, but within a few years, as his struggles with his writing, the deterioration of his marriage, and his consumption of alcohol dramatically increased, it became a deep-seated bedrock belief.

*   *   *

'When I look back in the short years of my life,' Osborne reflected miserably in 1970, 'I can see all my personal relationships as an unbroken series of defeats, every one of them bitter and bloody.'[7] So it was in his marriage to Jill Bennett. The story of their relationship is complex and infused by a sustained campaign of what Anthony Page denounced as 'unreasoning hatred and abuse' that Osborne directed at Jill after their separation in 1976, and by the savagely dismembering 'obituary' which he wrote after her death in which he scorned her as 'an avaricious, talentless gorgon'.[8] 'To have been married to John Osborne,' observed Page, was 'like becoming a public wall on which accusations and crimes are scrawled.'[9]

Those sympathetic to Osborne, though, believed that at the outset of their relationship he had disastrously misread Jill's character. He had thought her high-spirited, light-hearted, endearingly vulnerable and in need of protection, all of which appealed to his sense of spontaneity and romance. He had also thought of her, after his breakdown in 1966, as a woman who would nurture, admire and divert him, and in the years immediately after A Patriot for Me, it seemed that this would be so. He had not realised until the door closed behind them at Chelsea Square there was an aspect of her that was emotionally brittle, and needing constant attention, reassurance and admiration. He failed to comprehend how accustomed Jill was to being at the centre of things and having her own way, how dependent she was upon praise and how draining of his energy, depleted after his breakdown, she would be. In a letter accepting his marriage proposal, written while she was filming The Charge of the Light Brigade, Jill had described herself as imaginative and passionate, but also warned him that she was depressive, abrasive, wilful and quick to anger. Osborne chose not to heed the signals.

At the outset of their affair and during the first two years of their marriage, they played the part of a glamorous show business couple. They were seen at the places to be seen, arriving by Osborne's chauffeur-driven Bentley for dinner at the Savoy Grill or the Caprice, where they were welcomed by Mario and his band of deferential waiters. They turned up as essential guests at parties or first nights, their various comings and goings recorded by ever-vigilant gossip columnists who requested their thoughts on this and that. But whereas her husband's instinctive response to a looming journalist was to turn and run, Jill, who liked to be thought of as radiantly dazzling, avidly courted the press. '. . . John loves me because he thinks I'm awfully glamorous in the right way,' she explained to the Daily Mail. '. . . he thinks I'm talented and funny . . . I've met my match at last'.[10] When they entertained at Chelsea Square, alcohol flowed like a river, but soon Osborne discovered that instead of the 'Muddle Headed Johnny' of Penelope days, he was now known among Jill's friends by the appalling sobriquet of 'Champagne Johnny'. It made him sound like a terrible music hall turn. Yet more or less anywhere you went these days, it was a matter of spot the Osbornes and you would have spotted the drinks, in their case, champagne. They referred to it as 'some': 'Let's have some,' they would say. It was an ever-present commodity at Chelsea Square, a fridge even being installed in the bedroom to save the Osbornes the nocturnal inconvenience of going as far as the kitchen for a freshly chilled bottle. It was also stacked with that very 1960s luxury: caviar. 'I'm always waking John up for a light snack and a jolly chat,' Jill brightly informed the Daily Mail.[11]

Between 1965 and 1976, Jill appeared in six of her husband's stage plays, two television plays and the film of Inadmissible Evidence, which Page directed in 1968, Nicol Williamson again playing Maitland. Even when their marriage was in its bleakest phases, she could be implacably supportive of Osborne's writing, while on each first night he sent her a card of fulsome praise and gratitude, pledging his love and often accompanied by a gift. These were times, when they stood before the jury of critics and their scratching pens, and before audiences having paid their hard-earned money, when they depended upon each other. Offstage, though, theirs was becoming a fearsome and mutually destructive misalliance, awash with champagne. For Osborne, worried about money and the apprehension that those claiming that his audience was deserting him was correct, Jill's self-centredness and, when angered, her vindictive disparaging of his professional reputation and personal qualities, amounted to an emotional battering with which he was unable to cope, other than resorting to drink. For her part, Jill was bewildered by her new husband's absence of belief in himself, his descent into despair and his increasing dependence upon alcohol.

Retreating into his study, he began to record the deterioration of his health and his marriage in his journal, which over the next few years became an astonishingly candid diary of his predicament, a logbook of collapse. He wrote in fretful, often staccato sentences, sometimes comprising a single word and linked in places by disconsolate trails of ellipses. Sometimes he dated an entry, sometimes not. Sometimes, there are consecutive entries for a few days; others, written in retrospect, cover a few days or a week, and even longer. That there was a gulf between Jill and himself became apparent in 'the first few weeks after our marriage', he wrote early in 1970. 'I was frightened and quite alone . . .'[12] It was already clear that he and Jill were entirely incompatible and that, rather than being another new start, his marriage was merely a continuation and a deepening of the crisis that had caused his breakdown four years earlier. 'I can see no future,' he confessed. 'There is no present . . . My wife dislikes and despises me.'[13]

The realisation that their marriage had been foolhardy at the least fuelled their drinking, which in turn stoked increasingly frequent and gruelling bouts of recrimination, during which not only insults would be thrown, but crockery and even the occasional item of furniture. Osborne quickly learned to duck. This new domestic battlefield must have reminded him of his final days at Woodfall Street, where Mary Ure would occasionally hurl the breakfast china at him. A drunken, enraged Jill so panicked him that he would summon Dr Woodcock even during the night to medically pacify her. Sonia McGuinness, Osborne's long-serving secretary and confidante, became accustomed to arriving at Chelsea Square in the morning to find her employer and his fourth wife exhausted by a night of arguing; a bedroom or living-room in disarray and plates, a vase, or sometimes one of the leather and chrome chairs lying broken on the floor where Jill had flung it. Occasionally, their quarrels became physically violent. Osborne claimed that Jill had once thrown a bottle at him, insisting years later that the scars on his forehead were still visible.

Drinking, disputes, hangovers, migraine and painkillers, amphetamine and codeine were becoming a daily sequence of events. As he had during his last weeks with Penelope, Osborne resorted once more to disappearing without informing anyone where he was going, sometimes escaping to Sussex, ostensibly to work. He visited John Betjeman. Did he visit Pamela? Yet if he left Chelsea Square without notifying Jill of his whereabouts, she would frequently become suspicious and distressed, angrily demanding on his return that she be kept informed of where he was going and who he was with. His disappearing acts proved hazardous for those who might find themselves on the receiving end of one of Jill's notorious rages. While questioning Sonia McGuinness one day upon her husband's whereabouts and furious that his secretary apparently did not know, Jill suddenly picked up a glass ashtray and hurled it at her. Sonia dodged to one side and it hit the wall behind her, leaving a noticeable mark. 'Hostility rampant,' noted Osborne distractedly in his journal. 'What to do? . . .' His health was causing him acute concern. '. . . feel ill . . .' he noted. 'Can't cry or eat. Such despair . . . Fear, always fear for my sanity, let alone anything else . . . I'm dying slowly of hatred.'[14]

The strain and hostility between them became increasingly evident to others beyond their immediate circle. Colin Clark, who had worked on the original production of The Entertainer, happened to see them one evening in a crowded theatre foyer when he was astonished to see the once self-confident Osborne looking 'panic-stricken and trapped as if he were being held in the talons of a great predatory bird.'[15] Proximity to the Osbornes began to risk being embarrassed and offended as they bickered loudly, sometimes drunkenly, at parties or in restaurants, their language, to the consternation of waiters and the dismay of other guests, often becoming gratuitously crude as they decried each other's character, reputation and sexual abilities.

Yet to some, Osborne appeared much like his old self. He was 'nothing like the angry, combative figure portrayed by the popular press,' thought Peter Meyer, who was delighted when his near neighbours agreed to take part in the recording of Marriage a la Feydeau, a series of one-act Feydeau farces he had translated for BBC radio. 'When Jill was at the theatre, we'd often dine together and he was a marvellous companion. He was gentle, courteous, we'd talk about the theatre and mutual friends. Conversation just flowed . . .'[16] Yet over the months, Osborne began to see 'betrayal, dislike everywhere . . .'[17] He began to be besieged by doubt. 'Who cares,' he wondered, 'and why should they . . . I've never been so inadequate, so frustrated, so irrelevant . . .'[18]

Increasingly alarmed by his plight and his drinking, Sonia McGuinness was astonished at the beginning of 1971 when Osborne asked her to leave his employment, claiming that her work was unacceptable, that she was frequently late and that she had upset his wife. There was no foundation in these allegations, yet Sonia's position at Chelsea Square was in any case becoming impossible. On several occasions, and despite Sonia being happily married and her relationship with Osborne strictly professional, Jill had quite falsely accused them of having an affair. But it appeared that having identified Sonia as an integral part of the Penelope set-up and an Osborne ally of long-standing, Jill was determined to stake out the territory of Chelsea Square as her own and had demanded Osborne dispense with her services. At first, Osborne refused. He and Sonia, he protested, had worked closely together for over a decade and he was unlikely to find another secretary as loyal and meticulous, or whom he could trust as implicitly. But Jill would not relent. The turning point came at Christmas 1970, when the Osbornes held a party at Chelsea Square attended by many of their friends. There was food, drink and dancing and Osborne danced with Sonia, as he had done at many similar parties over the years. But this time, their enjoyment infuriated Jill, who brought the party to a jolting, embarrassed standstill with a torrent of loud abuse. The following day, Sonia received a bouquet of flowers from Jill, with a note thanking her for her assistance at the party. Shortly afterwards, Osborne submitted to Jill's demands. Sonia, he agreed reluctantly, would leave. Yet, lacking the courage to inform her in person, he told her his decision in a letter that he instructed the chauffeur to deliver. Sonia threw it away. It was five years before they resumed their acquaintance.

Meanwhile, Maitland-like, Osborne spent more and more time alone in his study. 'I creep about . . . like a thief, trying to be unobtrusive. Trying to WORK . . .'[19] Sinking further into introspection and alcoholism, he was consuming a bottle, sometimes two, of wine a day, a bottle of vodka, copious champagne and various tablets for migraine and hangover. 'It gets worse,' he confessed to his journal.[20] It appears that he hoped, as he had many times before, that everything might somehow sort itself out, that somehow if he kept his head below the parapet, he may look up one day to find that once again he had muddled through. If so, it was a forlorn hope. On several occasions, when not befuddled by alcohol or almost immobile with migraine, he contemplated telephoning Pamela Lane, the one he could trust above all others. But each time he decided against it. How could he explain that: 'I feel such despair, desolation, hopelessness . . .'[21] The answer, he told himself, was somehow just to get on with his work.

Although he had not written for the small screen since *A Subject of Scandal and Concern* in 1960, he completed *The Right Prospectus*, a short television play in which a middle-aged couple enrol as pupils at a boys' public school, where neither staff nor pupils find their presence incongruous. James Newbold hopes to return to his schooldays for what the Osborne relatives would have recognised as 'a new start', but 'it went absolutely nowhere and had nothing to say at considerable length,' complained Stanley Price in *Plays and Players* after its broadcast on BBC Television on 22 December 1970.[22] Throwing the reviews aside, he sat down at his desk and fought on with a new stage play, impelled to write not only because of the need to earn money and to reaffirm his position in the theatre, but because he knew that without writing, he was nothing. 'I better get on with it,' he urged himself. 'I've got so damned much left.'[23]

*   *   *

A bitter elegy for times past and a disquieting vision of the future, *West of Suez* is an ambitious family play about culture and language and the frailty of both, and about the legacy of the past, the uncertainty of the present and the threat of a brutal, indifferent future. In this it reflects not only something of the unease that was consuming its author but also the discord beginning to spread throughout the country. A sense of confrontation was in the air as powerful trade unions began a series of strikes in pursuit of wage claims that threatened to undermine Ted Heath's fragile Conservative government. Already, in his first year of office, Heath had imposed two States of Emergency, the first after dock workers took industrial action and the second after the electricians' unions walked out. Osborne gloomily scanned the news and turned back to his typewriter. While writing the play, he noted his symptoms in his journal: 'Feelings of illness . . . nausea, stomach distended. Then head. Eyes always hurting . . . I see no future . . . only odd bits of work . . .'[24] Yet he fought on. In some ways, Osborne had considerable reserves of strength.

*   *   *

While not a direct re-working of Shaw's *Heartbreak House*, for Osborne had disliked Shaw since his earliest repertory days, *West of Suez* clearly echoes it in its
characterisation, its quasi-Chekhovian atmosphere of waste and inertia, and its
melancholic anticipation of the future. Osborne's Captain Shotover is Wyatt
Gillman and his domain his eldest daughter's villa on an unspecified sub-
tropical island and former British colony. Like Laurie in *The Hotel in Amsterdam*,
Gillman is a writer. He is, though, much older than Laurie, an ageing author
who has searched for excellence but never reached it and is now holding court
to an audience of four daughters, one of whom, Evangie, is in her turn an aspiring author. Evangie is single, while the others are married: Robin, a woman
resigned to not expect too much from life, to Patrick, a retired brigadier;
Frederica, an insomniac, to Edward, a pathologist; and Mary, in the process of
withdrawing from her husband and children, to Robert, a north-of-England
schoolteacher. Also present are Christopher, Gillman's secretary, and Owen
Lamb, a bestselling author. There are occasional glimpses of Jed, a truculent
American hippie, and a couple of puzzled American tourists who have stumbled
ashore midway through a holiday cruise.

Gillman is Osborne's spokesman, his catechism of loathing encompassing the
by now familiar Osbornean repertoire of social class; his – Gillman's – public
school and all who sailed in her and became the English Establishment of politicians and churchmen; literary critics and, naturally enough, considering the
presence of the Americans, tourists. Foreign tourists in London were one of
Osborne's new bugbears. They were, he declared, an unappealing sight: the
Americans, the Japanese and the Germans, a terrible human flotsam who, with
their cameras bouncing on their stomachs and waving their guidebooks, waylaid
the suspecting Londoner with perpetual requests for directions and information.

Like Osborne, Colonel Redfern and Billy Rice, Gillman prefers the sanctity of
a recollected past to the disarray of the present. Memories of his father's study
evoke for Gillman a gilded haven of imperial warmth and reassurance. Cluttered
with back issues of the *Times of Natal*, hung with dried python skins and dotted
with brass iguanas, the books smelling of curry powder and, most of all, the
sepia photographs of days long gone, the room is a kitbag of Empire and of a
life lived away from home. It represents a time when society must surely have
been more ordered and easeful. Nostalgia for an imagined past hangs like a mist
over the landscape of much of Osborne's writing. It is a past in which kindliness, sensitivity and loyalty, qualities which Osborne valued in others while
not always managing to practise himself, compensated for the harshness of life;
a past in which there was a pre-ordained, recognised social order to which
people uncomplainingly deferred. Reminiscent of the *Gem* and *Magnet* world of
his boyhood reading, it is part of Osborne's imagined lost Eden, an idealised
England which may have existed somewhere for somebody, one summer at the
turn of the century, perhaps, or between the World Wars.

Yet although there is a good deal of remembrance of the Empire in *West of
Suez*, it is less a lament to time past than a warning about the brutality of times

to come, a play, according to the *Guardian* critic Michael Billington, about 'the break-up of any civilisation that no longer puts its trust in reason, in respect for other people's values and, above all, in language.' A preoccupation with the nature and the power of words runs throughout. Osborne's point, wrote Billington, is that 'if you don't believe in language you are not only sacrificing something of your own essential selfhood but you are also destroying a bridge between human beings and hastening the day when the law of the jungle prevails.'[25] Gillman is an anachronism, at once the embodiment of the old social order and the reason for its passing, yet he and his kind will not be giving way to a fairer world, suggests Osborne, but to violence, intolerance and brutish indifference. Whereas Chekhov in *The Cherry Orchard* struck the baleful warning bell of impending change with the sound of a breaking wire in a mineshaft, and Shaw in *Heartbreak House* with the droning of approaching bombers, Osborne presents a savage onstage killing. At the end of the play, islanders invade the villa and shoot Gillman dead.

Once again, the play was 'an exhausting experience to write,' he told Margery Vosper and as soon as it was complete, the Osbornes went to Italy for a week's holiday.[26] They returned to the gratifying news that William Gaskill had scheduled the play for production at the Royal Court, with rehearsals under Anthony Page's direction beginning in July. Ralph Richardson, sixty-nine, merrily eccentric and one of the most English of actors, had agreed to play Gillman, while Jill Bennett was cast as Frederica. Richardson liked Osborne, 'a charming chap' he thought, and a man with whom he could talk happily about literature and drinks. 'It's a privilege to be in your play,' he told him.[27] After touring to Brighton and Oxford, the production opened at Sloane Square on 17 August 1971. While critics acclaimed Richardson's performance, once again many argued that Osborne had created a powerful central performance but little else. 'Nothing happens,' objected Benedict Nightingale in the *New Statesman*.[28] 'It merely irritates,' corroborated Simon Trussler in *Tribune*, the paper executing a swift about turn from its support in Osborne's earlier years. '. . . the play is a massive demonstration of its own failure, for it lingers nostalgically over the way of life it declares redundant.'[29] Osborne, Trussler added, had asked too many questions and failed to provide the answers. But the provision of answers, Osborne might have replied, was not his job.

After *Time Present* and *The Hotel in Amsterdam*, those of Osborne's critics suspecting that his political sympathies were gliding towards the right, spotted further evidence in *West of Suez*. 'Its basic tendency', explained Nightingale, 'is to idealise the supposed decency, dignity and warmth of the Imperial British. It is self-satisfied and more than a little chauvinistic.'[30] Yet Michael Billington hastened to redress the balance, protesting that the play had been 'chronically misinterpreted' by those of his colleagues who believed that Osborne had 'swung so far round to the Right as to be almost out of sight.' *West of Suez*, he insisted, was not 'a piece of Tory nostalgia but a cry of liberal despair.' Osborne's plays, he explained, continued to 'catch and interpret the mood of a time; and in *West of*

Suez he is (I believe) alerting us to the fact that there is a strong fascist instinct abroad . . . a spirit of fanatical intolerance.'[31]

And Harold Hobson, now sixty-seven and for many years faithful to Osborne's writing, saluted *West of Suez* as a 'powerful and troubling' play. Its final line, 'They've shot the fox', he asserted, was 'as reverberating a last line as you will hear in any theatre, a line that brings to a fitting conclusion one of his finest works.' The 'splendour of [Osborne's] despair cannot be denied.'[32] Reading his former great rival's review, however, Kenneth Tynan was moved to near apoplexy. He just could not understand it. Most critics seemed mad these days. *West of Suez*, he thought, was long, dreary and one of the most '*wasteful*' plays he could remember, 'illiberal, self-absorbed, self-indulgent', and it was astounding that Hobson hadn't recognised it. Osborne himself, thought Tynan, had become 'a friendless and mean-spirited man who feeds on hostility and only feels fully alive when he is hating or hated', and his plays 'more and more like extracts from an interior monologue of increasing bad temper and incoherence.'[33]

West of Suez, however, successfully negotiated critical rapids to transfer to the Cambridge Theatre in the West End, with Richardson still in the leading role. Like many of Osborne's leading actors, Richardson had agitated during rehearsals for lines to be cut. Reluctantly, Osborne deleted a few, yet in performance Richardson regularly did his own judicious pruning, forestalling the playwright's protests by assuming an expression of horrified remorse and exclaiming: 'Oh dear, old chap, you've got to forgive me. My memory's going.'[34] Richardson's blandishments delighted Osborne enormously. Jill also stayed with the play at the Cambridge and while Osborne duly sent her a card congratulating her on her performance, the atmosphere between them continued to be abrasive. Rumour and gossip circulated. After an expedition with Laurence Olivier and Joan Plowright to see the play, Kenneth Tynan recorded in his diary their subsequent conversation probing Osborne's 'general decline and specific *nastiness*'. Plowright, he noted, volunteered the information that Jill publicly complained that her husband now found it difficult to satisfy her sexually, while Olivier alleged that the Royal Court directorship disliked the play and were producing it merely from a sense of loyalty.[35]

And yet Osborne's West End prominence ensured that another crop of questions, demands, commendations and invitations continued to fall alongside the bills on to the doormat at Chelsea Square. The Royal College of Art invited him to receive an honorary degree, while a summons from the Lord Chamberlain referred not to their past squabbles but requested the pleasure of his company at a garden party at Buckingham Palace. Aspiring authors continued to petition him to read their work and advise on improvements, one specifying that he should write at least six pages of recommendations. And, recalling the hectic days of *The World of Paul Slickey*, self-styled play doctors wrote diagnosing what was wrong with his plotting, his dialogue and his characterisation, something especially galling when, for the first time in almost twenty years, Osborne was unable to find a producer for his new play.

This was *A Place Calling Itself Rome*, a contemporary reworking in two acts of Shakespeare's *Coriolanus*, and the third part, together with *Time Present* and *The Hotel in Amsterdam*, of the projected *For the Meantime* trilogy. Although its broad outline follows the original in that Caius Marcius, a former hero of Rome expelled by the people, defects to the Volscians and returns to sack the city, Osborne's Coriolanus is far less heroic, more arrogantly superior to Shakespeare's and his judgements markedly less liberal.

Osborne prefaces the main action with a scene in which Caius Marcius awakens from a troubled sleep and, taking a notebook, begins to record his jostling, agonised thoughts: his inability to concentrate or even think coherently, to perform well sexually, to remember how much he drank the previous day and his difficulties in eating properly; the legions of decisions he must make; the inordinate demands of women; his powerlessness in converting chaos into order; the conviction that he is entirely alone, and the resolution that he must keep going forward and do *something*. It is remarkably similar in style and substance to the entries Osborne was making in his journal. Everything he wrote he plundered for his plays. 'Concentration difficult,' murmurs Coriolanus. '. . . Things in flight on first waking . . . Decisions impossible . . . Mind racing but no engine . . . Eaten little. Four, no, what, five days.'[36] 'Concentration really difficult today,' wrote Osborne in his journal on 22 September 1971. 'Ideas in flight on first waking . . . Mind racing but no engine. Cannot think what to do. Not coherent. Speech suspiciously blurred. And not just by morning vodka . . . Not eaten for four days. Just throw it up . . . Head not too bad . . .'[37]

*   *   *

Completed in 1972, the script of *A Place Calling Itself Rome* bounced from one management to another for several months. The Royal Court declined it and Michael Codron turned it down in the West End. The National Theatre and the Royal Shakespeare Company returned the script with regrets. David Pelham, having survived *The World of Paul Slickey*, shied away from a modernised Roman epic. Throwing the rejection slips aside and brushing away managerial apologies, humiliated that his contemporaries appeared to command West End productions without too much trouble while he had to trudge, script in hand like a door to door salesman from one manager to the next, it seemed to Osborne that he was back at the very beginning of his career again, sending out stuff in the hope that someone, somewhere might like it. At her office in Shaftesbury Avenue, Margery Vosper sadly admitted defeat. *A Place Calling Itself Rome* became the first Osborne play since *Look Back in Anger* that failed to find a producer.

Deterred but unbowed, Osborne turned to the more straightforward process of writing a new English language version of a repertory stalwart. Ibsen's *Hedda Gabler*, written in 1890 and a study of boredom, envy and spite, was a play that had fascinated him ever since he had seen Peggy Ashcroft in the title role at Hammersmith in 1954. The impetus to write a new adaptation arose from the conviction the title role would provide a remarkably appropriate part for Jill. With her colonial background, her pretensions and her volatility, Osborne saw her as very much a Hedda-like character. Certainly he saw both women as having a sharp wit but little authentic humour, women who had been born bored. Hedda, he noted, is a snob but she also has the saving graces of energy, spontaneity and a loathing of hypocrisy, the qualities that on a good day he most admired in Jill. 'For my wife,' he had written, presenting her with a copy of Ibsen's *An Enemy of the People* at Christmas. 'An enemy of cant.'[38]

Osborne worked quickly from a literal translation, modernising the idiom, cutting Hedda's romantic notion of Eilert Lövborg, her former admirer, heading towards his self-inflicted death by wearing vine leaves in his hair, and replacing it with what he contended was the rather more ironic, more English sentiment of their imagining life as being 'all wine and roses.' He was cheered by William Gaskill's conciliatory signals that the Royal Court was anxious to produce it, yet rehearsals were arduous, and with Jill fearful she was unable to learn the lines, there was much anguished pacing of the drawing-room, many sleepless nights at Chelsea Square and much resorting to the fridge in the bedroom. Yet she did learn them and, according to Anthony Page, who again directed, once *Hedda Gabler* opened on 28 June 1972, 'she never stopped shaping the part with the humorous, down-to-earth persistence, intelligence and inspiration of the real artist that she could be.'[39] It was a performance to which Jill brought much of her colonial imperiousness and restlessness and one that Osborne and others greatly admired. 'Jill could be a rather mannered actress,' remembered Brian Cox, who played Lövborg. 'But she wasn't in this. She was very much General Gabler's daughter, very much a woman who knew how to hold horses.'[40]

Unfortunately, Osborne's own equestrian ability was rather more precarious. The previous summer he had been injured in a riding accident and conveyed to the private London Clinic in Devonshire Place just south of Regent's Park, from where he was discharged sporting a piratical black eye-patch. Other mishaps were to follow in what became a strange catalogue of unfortunate incidents. One night in September 1972, he opened the door at Chelsea Square to be confronted by a young scenery painter who, it seemed, bore a grudge against Osborne for some minor offence. An altercation ended with a terrified house-keeper calling the police. A few weeks later, on 26 November, there was a more publicly embarrassing episode in which the Mercedes Benz car that Osborne was driving through Battersea ran off the road and came to rest ignominiously in the middle of a roundabout. Breathalysed by police to ascertain the level of alcohol in his blood, he was subsequently deprived of his driving licence. Jill, meanwhile, who had been sitting in the front passenger seat and had cracked a bone in her foot during the impact, was carried off to St Thomas's Hospital. 'It's extremely painful,' she announced to curious reporters, but: 'I am being very brave.'[41] A few months later, Osborne discovered that he was one of the intended victims of a terrorist attack. When police raided the London home of Ilich Sanchez, better known as Carlos the Jackal and a member of the Popular

Front for the Liberation of Palestine, they found a list of names of people the Jackal had selected as targets for assassination, including Joseph Sieff, the chairman of Marks and Spencer's, several Jewish business figures and, bizarrely, John Osborne.

Meanwhile, at Chelsea Square, Osborne miserably deliberated upon a disheartening year. *Hedda Gabler* had failed to transfer to the West End, and neither *A Place Called Rome* nor *The Picture of Dorian Gray*, which he had adapted from the novel by Oscar Wilde, had found producers. Yet his mind fizzed with ideas. There were ideas for a play about Judas Iscariot ('What I don't know about treachery') and a play about the Third Reich ('Theatrical. The brutality of the age we're inheriting'), but he had little energy to begin writing.[42] Jill's disappointment and anxiety, often similarly soaked in alcohol, emerged in rancorous derision. 'In the morning she says (with scarcely any alcohol this time): I detest her career,' he wrote. 'I detest her as an actor; I am a phoney "genius"; third rate – agreed; unattractive – agreed; sexual non-starter: women were only flattering me. "You're not even a man . . ."'[43] Nowadays, he and Jill shared only an intermittent sexual relationship, and there was no more talk of their beginning a family.

His talent, she told him, was fraudulent, and his friends had never liked him very much. Writing in his journal, he wondered whether he should believe Jill, for at times she seemed to be right. He noted that he was eating far too little and that sometimes what he did eat he promptly vomited. His eyes and head seemed to be aching continually, while other, random pains, sometimes a sudden stabbing, at others an insistent throbbing, came and went almost daily. His skin itched. Strange rashes appeared. And still the bills landed on his doormat. 'I earn nothing except to pay servants I don't want . . . Nobody pays me . . . I owe £26,000 in surtax from seven years ago. My overdraft is £20,000 . . .'[44] Alone in his study, his mind began to drift. 'I thought of the immediate mechanism of suicide . . . It's a hole-in-the-.corner business. I know I don't have the strength or skill to use a knife . . . I just want to close it over my head. But how . . .' And yet: 'My best work is ahead of me . . . Even if no one wants it . . .'[45] There was nothing else for it, he confided to his journal, but to battle on with his work. He was, after all, still only forty-three.

CHAPTER 26

Despair

SEEMINGLY AGAINST THE ODDS, *A Sense of Detachment*, which had begun life as a short story in 1971 before being converted into a two-act play under the working title of *The Enemy Vintage*, gave Osborne some cause for buccaneering optimism. The play was 'a requiem for past and present', he told its director, Frank Dunlop, an ebullient man running the Young Vic in Waterloo Road, and required 'an almost blasting feeling of an icy landscape from the stage' to succeed.[1] It provoked the jeers of disapproval he had resigned himself to expect, but, rather to his surprise, it also elicited some refreshing support.

A Sense of Detachment is not so much a play as an anarchic cabaret, the names of the characters – the Chairman, Older Lady, Girl, Grandfather, Father and Chap – evoking the dramatic specialities of lower-rung Victorian actors. Sitting on bentwood chairs on a stage on which the only other furniture is a projection screen, a barrel organ and an upright piano, they reminisce, argue and blurt out Osborne's by now familiar indignant generalizations about the present state of England. Across the screen flicker images of crowded motorways and of blinded and gassed soldiers of the First World War; a Union Jack flutters as a rousing version of Blake's 'Jerusalem' blasts from a loudspeaker; the Older Lady recites the advertisements from a catalogue of pornographic books and films, the summaries of gropings and couplings on offer comprising 'the most explicitly-worded accounts' warned Frank Marcus in *The Sunday Telegraph*, 'yet uttered on the London stage.'[2] The Chap contributes a maudlin account of the women he has loved, some of whom echo those Osborne himself once knew: Jean, whom the Chap knew when he was nineteen, evokes Stella Linden, with whom Osborne had lived in Brighton. But then, the Chap adds gloomily, there were his wives, all of whom were 'dreary'.[3] Finally, each character steps into a pulpit to present a personal sermon, the Chap defending the miracle of falling in love, while others ruminate on Ireland, Women's Liberation, Britain's proposed membership of the Common Market, and the corruption of language.

The play is a dissident patriot's graffiti expressing Osborne's vision of an England befuddled and enfeebled by the liberalism of the Sixties and sliding into the unappealing brutishness he had anticipated in *West of Suez*. He had some justification in this: 1972 was a year in which the British Army in Northern Ireland shot twenty-six civilians taking part in a march against internment, an incident that became known as Bloody Sunday; a year in which the Provisional Irish Republican Army continued their campaign of bombing attacks in England in support of home rule; in which industrial unrest resulted in the government imposing two more States of Emergency; and in which unemployment rose above 1 million for the first time since the 1930s, the days of Osborne's childhood. Looking about him, Osborne saw a country drifting into squalor and indifference. To Arnold Wesker, he wrote gloomily that everything 'seems more frozen and uncharitable than ever.'[4]

At the same time, he felt increasingly alienated from contemporary theatre. In London, fringe theatres were flourishing and new small-scale companies emerging, many of them with left-wing sympathies, from the touring Portable Theatre and Joint Stock groups to the 'agit-prop' theatre of John McGrath's 7:84. The Royal Court was energetically producing plays by a fleet of dramatists who had emerged during the late 1960s and early 1970s, including David Hare, Christopher Hampton, Caryl Churchill and Howard Brenton. There were more new plays being produced, many of them exploiting what was now permissible on the stage. Although he had bullishly advocated an end to theatrical censorship, Osborne recognized that few things so conspicuously fail to shock as the gratuitous attempt to do so. The elderly woman in *A Sense of Detachment* reading from a pornographic book catalogue was there to prove his point. The ending of theatre censorship, commonly regarded as a 'breakthrough', was, he argued, in danger of becoming through its misuse no breakthrough at all. To the interviewers who still buttonholed him for his views, he lamented liberalism and 'permissiveness' in general. It was, he explained, unfeeling and largely distasteful, whereas he remained, his marital history notwithstanding, a genuine romantic and all for passion.

A Sense of Detachment opened at the Royal Court six months after *Hedda Gabler*, on 4 December 1972. 'We weren't a very good audience on the first night,' confessed Irving Wardle in *The Times*.[5] As it turned out, there were very few good audiences at all. The scripted heckling of three of the characters, a football fan installed in a stageside box and a 'planted interrupter' and his wife lurking in the stalls, were frequently and vigorously applauded by the audience. The spectacle of Rachel Kempson, otherwise Lady Redgrave, reading pornography in gentle, maternal tones proved especially provocative, 'her title', noted the playwright Alan Bennett, 'an important ingredient of the audience's resentment, their fury fuelled by a touch of class.'[6] The clatter of upturning seats during the performances as enraged audience members left and the applause at the final curtain bespattered by enthusiastic booing, recalled the days of *The World of Paul Slickey*. On several evenings, vegetables, and on one curious occasion, a pair of boots were hurled from the stalls and clattered on the stage at the feet of the hapless actors.

Osborne, though, claimed to find it all extremely invigorating. 'The audience responded – I couldn't believe it – exactly as I thought: outraged,' he recalled.[7] 'Booing', he added, was 'an odd, unforgettable sound when it's coming your way, exhilarating, like the tribute ringing in the ears of a wrestler in his corner.'[8] But as far as the critics were concerned, the evening was more sorrowful than outrageous. In The Times, Irving Wardle recorded his dejection at watching Osborne 'sinking into the bog of platitude at every step'; Frank Marcus wondered in The Sunday Telegraph whether Osborne would not have been wiser 'to hold his examination of the rudiments of his craft and stock-taking of his ideas in private rather than in public', while Kenneth Hurren in the Spectator reported that 'Osborne has not quite mastered the trick of writing about bores and boredom without being ineffably boring himself.'[9] Yet the Guardian's Michael Billington had had a wonderful time. A Sense of Detachment, he wrote, was 'a thinking-man's Hellzapoppin', a spiky, inconsequential collage, an attack on our own heartless, loveless, profiteering society . . . [and] a moving threnody for a dying civilization . . .'[10] But Billington, youthful, alert, and new to reviewing, was an exception. As if chiselling an epitaph, B. A. Young in the Financial Times solemnly pronounced that 'This must surely be his farewell to the theatre.'[11]

It was not, but to Osborne it certainly felt as if it was. More and more, he felt he was alone in a house in which he had once lived but had failed to move out of once new owners had taken possession and altered it entirely. Recognising how deeply he was hurt by adverse criticism, several friends and acquaintances hurried to tell him how much they had enjoyed the production. Arnold Wesker told him that it was 'a finely sustained and quiet work of pain and pity', while the novelist Angela Huth wrote 'simply out of some kind of inarticulate gratitude for having shaken me so, to laughter among other things.'[12] Terence Rattigan informed him that he had spent one of the most rewarding evenings in the theatre for many years and, having read the reviews, the sixty-one-year-old dramatist declared himself angry enough to stand naked outside the offices of The Times brandishing whatever placard Osborne might devise. David Nathan, a former critic, told him that he should have called the play The Story of Osborne, as 'what I thought I was seeing was the contents of your head laid out for inspection with a terrifying sense of detachment', adding that the play was 'surely about the resilience of the spirit, the refusal to submit in the face of apparently insuperable odds' and 'the unfailing rejuvenation of the capacity to go on loving.'[13] Osborne gratefully replied that Nathan had summarised his intention exactly.

Such friendly endorsement was well meant, but the conviction that his work was no longer wanted held Osborne firmly in its grip and although Nathan assured him that the play reflected his own resilience, he felt little of it. In the old days, he reflected, George Devine would have rung him occasionally to ask how he was and whether he might expect a new play. Nowadays, nobody rang from the Royal Court. Despite *West of Suez* and *Hedda Gabler* having been produced there, he felt detached from Sloane Square, and *A Sense of Detachment*, which closed, never to be revived, after its scheduled run of forty performances, proved to be the last play he wrote for the English Stage Company. But the fate of *A Place Called Rome* and *The Picture of Dorian Gray*, both still lying in his desk drawer, suggested that he had nowhere else to go. 'Silence and withdrawal all round,' he noted in his journal.[14]

At the same time, he strove to maintain some semblance of domestic harmony for Nolan's holiday visits from the United States. Since 1967, when she was two years old, Nolan had crossed the Atlantic for her annual six-weeks' reunion with her father, her travels chaperoned by her nanny, and sometimes also by Penelope and by Osborne himself. If her mother accompanied her, Nolan would stay with her at Chester Square, Penelope having preserved the house much as it was when she and Osborne lived there. Otherwise she would be billeted with her father and Jill at Chelsea Square. Nolan and Jill liked each other, while Osborne, who loved his daughter and was deeply concerned for her welfare, was irked by seeing her so little. Such sporadic contact, he fretted to Oscar Beuselinck, must surely hinder their being able to form the close relationship he wanted. Besides, it was 'a rotten arrangement', grumbled Osborne, 'which costs me about £600 a year'.[15] Neither was he happy with her living on the thirteenth floor of an apartment block in the middle of Manhattan, even if there was a view across Central Park. According to what he read in his newspaper and saw on television, New York was no longer the optimistic, exciting city of his youth but a bleak and battered urban hell where crime and violence raged virtually unchecked. Nolan, he blustered, should be brought home to the comparative peace of England and attend a private school, perhaps even as a boarder, for which he would volunteer to pay the fees. How he was going to afford this, he did not elucidate. But for the meantime, his hopes were unrewarded. Nolan stayed in New York, seeing her father only occasionally, until she was twelve years old.

*   *   *

And still the storm of financial catastrophe loomed over the horizon. During the months since he had endured the critical lunch with his accountants, Osborne had attended further desolate summit conferences at which his advisers begged him to avert financial collapse by writing for films, but Osborne prevaricated. He disliked and distrusted the film world, with its shifting allegiances, its American management, corporate takeovers and sudden reversals. No matter, persisted his accountants, writing screenplays was well paid, even if they were never turned into films. Reluctantly, he agreed. Yet the omens were not bright, considering that none of the film proposals with which he had been involved, apart from those under the Woodfall banner, had progressed much further than the first draft.

Fifteen years previously, at the end of the 1950s and confident with success, he had tentatively suggested adapting Evelyn Waugh's The Ordeal of Gilbert Pinfold for the screen, but Waugh would not hear of it. While working on Tom Jones, Osborne had sketched a screenplay for Daniel Defoe's Moll Flanders, transferring the saga of an orphan girl's seduction and the ensuing whirligig of love, crime and transportation to Virginia, from the early eighteenth century to the present day. But the initial enthusiasm expressed by Sophia Loren, the dark-eyed, glossy-haired Italian film star, and Carlo Ponti, her producer husband, had quickly evaporated. Later, in collaboration with Penelope, he had written an outline for Panic Stations, a comedy partly inspired by Blow-Up, a film that both Osborne and Penelope admired, in which an indolent young photographer encounters a young woman in a London park. Intended to follow their relationship as it descended from the high peaks of mutual rapture to the hazardous slopes of attempting to live together, it advanced no further than notebook jottings and became part of the debris of the collaborators' failed marriage.

After the fracas of The Charge of the Light Brigade, Osborne suggested to Sam Spiegel at Warner Brothers that he write a screenplay based on the life of Sir Charles Dilke. A radical politician and potential successor to William Gladstone as leader of the Liberal Party until his implication in a divorce case resulted in his downfall, Dilke was a hugely influential figure in Victorian society. It was a world, enthused Osborne, outwardly principled and strictly conventional, but in reality cruel and irrevocably divided by class and privilege, and just the sort of thing he wanted to write about. But despite Spiegel outlining various budgets and the possibility of Rex Harrison playing the leading role, the project was cancelled before it was even begun. In 1970, an idea of adapting The Hand-Reared Boy, a novel by the science-fiction writer Brian Aldiss, also fell by the wayside, as did a plan to film Brendan Behan's play, The Hostage, a tragi-comic account of IRA activities set in a down-at-heel brothel. Divorce His, Divorce Hers, mooted for Harlech Television in Wales, starring Richard Burton and Elizabeth Taylor as a couple reminiscing on their marriage, was eventually assigned to the writer John Hopkins and filmed in America.

But by the summer of 1973, however, things seemed to be looking up. Michael Holroyd's monumental biography of the critic and biographer Lytton Strachey provided Osborne with the Bloomsbury group as a suitable case for treatment. An intellectual, gossipy, cloistered world, moderately left-wing, agnostic and avant-garde, Bloomsbury represented what Bernard Shaw had called 'cultured, leisured Europe before the [First World] war.'[16] Holroyd's book introduced Osborne not only to Strachey and his relationship with Dora Carrington, a young painter, and their respective lovers, homosexual on his side, heterosexual on hers, but also to the writers Leonard and Virginia Woolf, the painters Duncan Grant and Vanessa Bell, their hangers-on and their various homes in Bloomsbury and in the country. Having finished the book, Osborne wrote to Holroyd broaching the subject of a screenplay. 'I'd like it myself of course,' the biographer signalled in return, 'since I believe you'd make the most interesting use of the dramatic possibilities in the material, and your analyses of England would be fascinating.'[17] Yet almost immediately, Laurence Harvey-like pitfalls loomed. A solicitor acting on behalf of Frances Partridge, one of the last surviving members of the group and the widow of Ralph Partridge (who had previously been married to Carrington), warned him that Carrington's diary was his client's copyright. Any unauthorised usage would therefore be subject to legal penalties. Alarmed at the prospect of once more negotiating a landscape mined by the complexities of copyright law, Osborne regretfully informed Holroyd that he had decided to beat a retreat. A film, Carrington, was eventually made in 1995, written by Christopher Hampton.

Ill-luck, the capriciousness of stars and executives and the possible intervention of lawyers conspired to scupper all his screenplay plans. Meanwhile, at Chelsea Square, his health, and his relationship with Jill, worsened even further. Sometimes he felt so ghastly on awakening he would consume a half-bottle of champagne before getting out of bed in the morning. In his study, he filled the hours with more champagne, supplemented by vodka and wine. During the summer of 1973, while nosing his way cautiously into the world of Lytton Strachey, he noted that 'I'm suddenly too old, ill and too weary even to run.'[18] Visiting his mother one day in Pimlico, he noticed that for the first time the cloth on her dining table, usually crisply clean, was soiled. Nellie Beatrice was now eighty and, watching her move with difficulty from one room to the next, he felt both pity and an overpowering dislike and, at the same time, a welling contempt for himself. Mortality loomed. 'Who'd be my literary executor?' he wondered. 'Who'd bother? Rightly. Power without steerage. Not eaten for four days. Just throw it up . . . Dread the bath. Water. Even toothpaste. Mustn't go on like this . . .'[19]

Everything, including himself, seemed to be falling to pieces. The more Osborne felt under siege, the more he laid siege to others, as Kenneth Tynan discovered when, on 4 November 1972, he opened the Sunday Times Magazine to find that the dramatist had resumed his 'eccentric provocations' against the National Theatre, claiming that it combined the worst aspects of a bureaucratic state institution with the profiteering instincts of the commercial theatre.[20] Extending his assault to include Laurence Olivier, Osborne declared him to be a woefully inadequate artistic director. Quite simply, Olivier's temperament was all wrong. On the one hand he craved be a pioneer, leading public taste like a Pied Piper, but on the other, he was far too cautious to be an innovator. Moreover, he was squirming under the 'disastrous' influence of Tynan, whose opinions and 'intellectual spivvery' he had disastrously mistaken for flair and insight.[21]

Arguably, Osborne's criticisms had a certain amount of truth. Olivier was both progressive and conservative and the National Theatre had not as yet attained a reputation as a home of new writing. Yet publicly attacking two people not only acting in good faith but who had been crucial to his own success was perceived as both ill-conceived and reckless. 'Some years have now passed since he [Osborne] first started to behave strangely,' Tynan protested in a retaliatory letter to *The Sunday Times*. Noting that during the past three years Osborne had written three plays, *West of Suez*, *Hedda Gabler* and *A Sense of Detachment*, each of which had suffered a bumpy ride, he diagnosed Osborne's outburst as the result of his having slumped into a professional 'bad patch', and that as his audience had diminished, his reservoir of bile had swelled. Contrary to Osborne's charges, asserted Tynan, the National Theatre had scored a higher percentage of critical and popular success over a ten-year period than any other British theatre company in history. Turning to his past association with Osborne, he reflected that 'I do not regret having done all I could, as a critic, to obtain for Mr Osborne in his early days the recognition that his gifts deserved . . . But nowadays I feel rather like a Good Samaritan who has crossed the road to be greeted by a kick in the face.' The Good Samaritan had had enough. From henceforth, he concluded, 'Mr Osborne will have to fend for himself.'[22] And with that, he pronounced the correspondence closed.

Osborne, however, was not finished yet, and turned his attention to a general spring-cleaning of his business affairs. Beginning with his accountants, he exchanged the prophesiers of doom, Bryce, Hamner and Isherwood, for Nyman Libson Associates, who turned out to be equally depressing in their assessments and similarly unyielding to his protests. Fishing for lucrative work in America, he appointed a manager, Barry Krost, who managed a list of actors and singers from offices in Hollywood. It was not destined to be a long association. Next, he turned to Marjory Vosper, his long-time agent, nestling in her cluttered office in Shaftesbury Avenue. With no work prospects, debts and a sizable mortgage to pay, he concluded the time had come for a change here as well: 'I have long needed another source of Blake's "divine energy",' he told her. 'Encouragement, enthusiasm and energy.'[23] He defected to Robin Dalton, a successful and well-connected agent at the International Famous Agency. Osborne also received unexpected support at Chelsea Square. Despite deriding her husband's talent to his face ('JB said I was written out. Disliked by all at the Court'), Jill was enormously supportive behind his back.[24] Anxious that his confidence be bolstered and his reputation restored, she discreetly encouraged Dalton in negotiating with Ewan Hooper, the director of the Greenwich Theatre in south-east London, to produce a season of Osborne's plays the following year.[25] Under Hooper, Greenwich was building a high reputation. Osborne, though, was nearing his lowest point: 'Liver swollen and puffy with alarming stabs and noises,' he noted on 6 June 1973. 'Too much drink . . . Back itchy and blotched . . . too much white wine . . . Gums bleeding.'[26]

*   *   *

While Osborne apprehensively waited for the season to begin, Jill went up to Yorkshire to film *Ms or Jill and Jack*, the first of two television plays her husband had written over the past few months. Breaking the cycle of rejection by actually being made, both were directed by Mike Newell, who twenty years later would direct the highly successful film, Four Weddings and a Funeral, and were broadcast within two weeks of each other, on 11 and 24 September 1974. In Ms or Jill and Jack, a play reversing the then conventional roles of businessman and girlfriend, Jill appeared as Jill, the high-achieving executive, opposite John Standing as Jack, 'the pouty bit of goods'. 'Its beauty', wrote Tom Stoppard in the Observer the following Sunday, 'lay in its masterly detail, the writing and the acting, which commented on the minutiae of a thousand television plays where Jack makes the running.'[27] The second play, The Gift of Friendship, is a more personal and melancholic piece in which Jocelyn Broome, an afflu- ent, elderly novelist and 'reasonably convincing . . . tormented Evelyn Waugh figure' played by Alec Guinness, appoints Bill Wakely, a fellow writer, whom he loathes, to be his literary executor. Osborne, averred Peter Lennon in The Sunday Times, had caught 'the ashen flavour' of writers fearful their talent had drained away from them, and whose wives, uncomprehending in Broome's case and resentful in Wakely's, 'reinforce the sense of defeat and decay that surround their men.'[28]

A similar sense engulfed Osborne himself. His marriage had become a tor- mented world of uncertainties, jagged edges, paradoxes and disjunctions. How and why, he wondered, did these things happen to him? Bewilderment and resentment that each was not what the other assumed, and the resulting bitter- ness aggravated and distorted by alcohol, had irreversibly infected the love that he and Jill had once shared. The truces between them were few and fragile. Jill's allies argue that she was appalled by his drinking. Others suggest that it was her drinking that repelled him, while her volatility confused and embar- rassed him. On at least one occasion, it seems, Jill had left the house at night while disoriented by drink and had been apprehended by police while cycling the wrong way along Fulham Road wearing only a nightdress. Complaining of her husband's impotence, Jill boasted to friends of taking lovers, naming names and dropping broad hints as to the identities of others. This may or may not have been a fiction. And yet at times they were extraordinarily protec- tive of each other. John Dexter once received a late-night telephone call from an enraged Osborne demanding to know why he had upset his wife. To his horror, Osborne discovered that Dexter had done no such thing and that Jill had manufactured the story knowing that he would confront his old friend and thereby be humiliated. 'They were both drunk, of course,' explained a friend of Dexter's.[29]

Osborne felt both plagued and trapped, by himself as much as by Jill. Sometimes, he would spend the day in his study, clad only in pyjamas and dressing gown, drinking and nursing bouts of pain. Noting each new develop- ment in his journal, he observes his hair coming away in his comb. His eyes are continually bloodshot. One day, after kneeling on his study floor, reading, he attempts to stand only to discover his legs 'paralysed up to the knee'.[30] His temperature is alarmingly unstable: he sweats and then he shivers, then sweats

again. Turning away from the mirror in which he inspected himself, he struggled to continue working. Much of the spring and summer of 1974, therefore,
he spent researching the background material for a screenplay about the Indian
Mutiny of 1857.

The Mutiny, he reasoned, would provide excellent background for a study of
nineteenth-century society and had tremendous potential for film. At the British
Museum, he rummaged through newspaper files, and from Chelsea Square
fired off requests to the Indian High Commission and the Pakistan Embassy for
background information for an idea he had for the story of Fleury, an English
romantic poet who travels to India in search of an understanding of Asian art
and thought, only to find himself behind the barricades with the British army
fighting the Sepoys. But once more, almost inevitably, everything fell apart.
Sadly setting the adventures of Fleury aside, he turned to a commission from
Yorkshire Television. This was an adaptation of Little Lord Fauntleroy, a once
hugely popular novel written in 1886 by Frances Hodgson Burnett, in which
a boy living in New York is discovered to be the heir to an aristocratic English
family. But this too came to nothing.

*   *   *

Meanwhile, risking a defiant last stand against the trades unions, Edward
Heath's three-year-old Tory government called a snap General Election on the
question of 'Who governs Britain?' The answer, when it came in February
1974, was the equivalent of a national 'Don't know'. The nation was hedging
its bets. Although Harold Wilson, a wily old survivor, took up residence once
again at Downing Street, it was to preside over a precarious minority government. In October, Wilson called another election in a bid to secure a workable
majority. 'I shall vote Labour once more, but with an even emptier heart than
usual,' announced Osborne. 'The shabbiness of Mr Heath and his supermarket
manager's vision of a cut-price future,' he asserted, 'has been one of the most
hideous spectacles of recent history', whereas 'the Labour Party has always been
bedevilled by its own rigid philistinism, aided by the unions, and has been
largely responsible for the moral slum and squalid climate we have created
since the heady days of 1945.' As for 'the Liberals, with their lack of substance
and tinkling squeaks of grandeur, [they] don't even represent an alternative to
the left-wing bully boys [of the trade union movement] . . . and the right-wing
bullies . . . [of reactionism].'[31] The nation echoed his lack of enthusiasm by
returning Labour to office but with a paltry overall majority of three.

Having begrudgingly cast his vote, Osborne set out from Chelsea Square for
Greenwich, where Ewan Hooper had agreed to produce the first London revival
of The Entertainer, a play of which Osborne was especially fond and which he
elected to direct himself, and two of the unperformed plays in his desk drawer:
The Picture of Dorian Gray and The End of Me Old Cigar. 'A turn' in his fortunes, wondered Osborne. 'Or no?'[32]

Although the accolade of an 'Osborne season', albeit at a theatre so far from the centre of town, patched his ragged self-esteem, it looked like doing little for his bank balance. Apart from his director's fee, he grumbled, the theatre was offering him only a meagre five per cent of the box-office royalties. Robin Dalton sympathised, but pointed out that neither the theatre nor any playwright stood fully protected against the bleak winds of a national economic recession. There simply was not the money about these days. His reputation, thought Osborne glumly, seemed to count for very little. Yet he signed his contracts as Dalton counselled and, having cast Max Wall, the sixty-five-year-old, blood-hound-featured variety artist as Archie Rice, got down to work.

For many of those who thought the original production had been imbalanced by Olivier's virtuoso performance, Wall's melancholic delivery restored the equilibrium of the play and made it a more satisfying experience. Olivier was very much the technically adroit conjuror; the lugubrious Wall, on the other hand, might well have passed for a disgruntled bookie. The role 'wraps itself around me,' he confirmed, as if he was shrugging on an old overcoat.[33] Critics agreed that it fitted snugly, his performance at the first night on 24 November 1974 being acclaimed despite an audience, thought the actor playing Billy Rice, 'like barbed wire.'[34]

The End of Me Old Cigar, however, the second play in the season, was a different proposition altogether. Superficially a modern-day School for Scandal, a bitter comedy of sexual manners, its title is derived from the mildly risqué music-hall song popularised by Harry Champion at the beginning of the First World War. Max Stafford-Clark's production opened on 16 January 1975 and starred Rachel Roberts, a biliously tempestuous actress formerly married to Rex Harrison, as Lady Regine Frimley, the madam of a house of pleasure for so-called Men Who Matter. Cynical, vulgar and conniving, Lady Regine leads a confederation of women plotting their clients' humiliation by exposing their corruption and sexual fetishes through a system of two-way mirrors, but whose plans are confounded when Isobel and Leonard, played by Jill Bennett and Keith Barron, discover a mutual and unexpected vision of love.

Although he had written the play surrounded by a wasteland of marital combat, Osborne nevertheless sent his wife a fulsome first-night card: 'With love and cuddles. And for yet again, making it work! John'.[35] While the play lacks much in the way of corresponding cheer or compassion, he retained enough sense of irony to mock (in a lengthy tirade by Lady Regine) masculinity and male sexuality, and had sufficient faith in things to offer at the end a glimpse of the redemptive power of love. Yet the final curtain falls, as one critic observed, with 'a haste that suggests lack of interest or a need to take his typewriter in for servicing', as if the resolution is one in which the author could not quite believe.[36] Harold Hobson, however, was entirely convinced by the play; it was, he professed, 'finely conceived' and moreover contained 'a gleam of hope', the possibility of salvation that he had discerned many years previously in Look Back in Anger and that he believed drama, at its most sophisticated, should deliver.[37] A horrified Kenneth Tynan, though, thought otherwise.

Eight years previously, when he read The Hotel in Amsterdam, Tynan had quickly detected that in the character of KL, the monstrous film producer, Osborne was exacting revenge upon Tony Richardson. Now, as he listened to Lady Regine denouncing a potential client as 'a famous ex-boy wonder from Oxford . . . who writes almost anything for anyone', who 'has been trying to cultivate style ever since he was seen wearing lilac knickers and a top hat on Magdelen Bridge' and who has a taste for spanking consenting young women, Tynan believed he recognized himself.[38] He had never been so appalled. This was nothing less than a public assassination, and he was even more mortified when he discovered from the programme note that Osborne had written the play the previous summer. Since then, Tynan considered, and against his better judgement, he had made concerted overtures to restore the friendship curdled by their public spat over the National Theatre. He and Kathleen, his wife, had even twice entertained Osborne and Jill to dinner. Now, sitting aghast in the audience at the Greenwich Theatre, it seemed to Tynan that if Osborne had any sense of honour, he should have done one of two things. He should either have declined their invitations to dinner or, having accepted, deleted the section in the play in which he had so extravagantly maligned his host. But to have eaten Tynan's food, drunk his wine, said nothing and presented the play as originally written was surely intolerable, an act so treacherous as to be worthy only of the underhand journalists Osborne had satirised fifteen years previously in The World of Paul Slickey.

Impervious to Tynan's indignation, Osborne turned his attention to The Picture of Dorian Gray, the third and final play of the Greenwich season. Having first read the novel as a schoolboy, he had returned to it as a result of his fascination with the themes of love, self-delusion and treachery. He may also have been attracted by its decadence, its vanity and covert homosexuality, and he might possibly have recognised something more than flippancy in Lord Henry Wootten's remark that: 'The one charm of marriage is that it makes a life of deception absolutely necessary for both parties.'[39] It was also, he thought, a story reflecting a world remarkably like the present: 'without a sense of sin but acutely aware of something vague but daily threatening which might even still be called evil . . .'[40] His 'great wheeze' of casting Mick Jagger, the thirty-one-year-old singer with The Rolling Stones and famed for his androgynous looks, in the title role, was, however, vetoed by the Greenwich management who favoured Michael Kitchen.[41] Rehearsals were uneasy and, by the time Clive Donner's production opened on 13 February 1975, Osborne had little confidence in its success, an assumption the reviews confirmed. When the play was televised eighteen months later, Martin Amis observed in the New Statesman that if Wilde had thought the idea dramatic, he would doubtless have been the first to write a play about it.[42]

Ending in March, the season bolstered Osborne's confidence as Jill and Robin Dalton had hoped it might, and by the spring he was feeling more optimistic than he had for several months. Partly this was the result of news from the United States. A film was being made of *Luther* starring Stacey Keach, which at least had the prospect of making him a little money, and The Robert Stigwood Organisation wanted to film *The Entertainer* for NBC Television, with Jack Lemon in the leading role, which was finally broadcast three years later in 1976. There were also encouraging signals being beamed from the National Theatre.

Two years earlier, in 1973, Olivier and Tynan had left the National, the former withdrawing to make films and the latter to give the nation the benefit of his views on things social and cultural in the 'Shouts and Murmurs' column of his old newspaper, the *Observer*. They were succeeded by Peter Hall, energetic and forthright, who left the Royal Shakespeare Company to become, at forty-three, the National's second artistic director, charged with leading the company from its base at the Old Vic to a new purpose-built theatre on the South Bank, scheduled to open in 1976. Anxious to smooth the feathers of England's most easily ruffled playwright, Hall wrote to Osborne on 7 August 1974, warmly assuring him that 'I would very much like you to consider the National Theatre as your house. This means very simply that anything you write will be performed by us.'[43] This was exactly the sort of letter that Osborne, in common with every other writer, liked to open over breakfast. It bucked him up enormously, and he immediately sent Hall a copy of *Watch It Come Down*, his new play.

CHAPTER 27

Desolation

OSBORNE HAD COMPLETED the play in July, its title deriving from an advertising slogan he had seen for a demolition company: 'We demolish it: You watch it come down'. It seemed an apt if dismal metaphor both for his domestic life and the country in general. *Watch It Come Down* is as much an autobiographical portrait of a marriage as *Look Back in Anger*, yet the zest and the optimism of the earlier play has given way to a rancid, agitated animosity, the relentless acrimony of Ben and Sally, the central characters, setting on the stage the daily feuding at Chelsea Square. *Watch It Come Down* also reflects the troubled political and social atmosphere of the time in which it was written. The theme of the play, he wrote, was 'the truth of the country. My country, My Truth.'[1] An unforgiving postscript to *West of Suez*, the play is Osborne's most abrasive, and his bleakest vision of England.

During the mid-1970s, Osborne was far from alone in believing that Britain, and particularly England, was in irreversible decline. Like millions of others, he scanned the front page of his newspaper each morning to be confronted with another episode in the troubles of a nation in deep economic recession and seemingly intent upon tearing itself apart. He read of continuing industrial unrest and strikes, intransigent trades unions submitting wildly excessive wage claims and getting them from a weakened, seemingly compliant government. He read of rising prices, spiraling unemployment and inflation soaring to 26 per cent, the millions of pounds accumulating in government borrowing, terrorist bomb attacks in the larger cities killing innocent civilians, and accounts of appalling crime, all of which Harold Wilson's government seemed unable to comprehend or remedy. Political and economic commentators both in Britain and the United States were even prophesying that England's fiscal collapse would not stop until it reached the level of a South American or Eastern European state. The flowering vibrancy and optimism of the Swinging London of only a few years previously had shrivelled into grim disenchantment. London's image had become grey and shoddy, the neon lights of Shaftesbury Avenue and the West End failing to conceal buildings now 'in the sort of condition', declared The Times, 'that in Birmingham or Manchester would qualify them for wholesale slum clearance.'[2] The Labour Party, the trades unions and even the teaching profession were widely thought to be infiltrated by Communists and militant radicals, while Wilson believed himself spied upon by malignant forces in British and foreign intelligence agencies. Rumours circulated of the possibility of left-wing insurrection. There was a sudden emergence of right-wing vigilante organisations, and in July 1974 The Times reported that if, or more likely when, Wilson's vacillating, demoralized government finally collapsed 'retired senior army officers and their business associates' were seeking volunteers in the event of 'a breakdown in law and order'.[3]

National decline dominated the newspapers. Playwrights dramatised it, novelists wrote fictions full of dark warnings, and diarists monitored it. Roy Strong, the flamboyant director of the Victoria and Albert Museum, where the main exhibition in 1974 was 'The Destruction of the Country House', took precautions against possible winter shortages of food and energy in the Hertfordshire village where he had his own country house, by stocking up on 'vast mounds of tinned and frozen foods, every sort of candle, matches, oil heater, oil lamp, Calor gas, the lot.'[4] In London, the iconoclastic Conservative MP Alan Clark, the elder brother of Colin, bemoaned a 'tatty, bad tempered, lazy' country.[5] And not only Conservative minds agreed with him. 'Britain is a miserable sight,' sadly noted Bernard Donoghue, the Head of Wilson's No. 10 Policy Unit. 'Meanness has replaced generosity. Envy has replaced endeavour. Malice is the most common motivation . . . Fascism could breed in this unhealthy climate.'[6] These were sentiments that largely matched Osborne's own and formed the background to Watch It Come Down.

A play about emotional and social bankruptcy, Watch It Come Down is set in an abandoned country railway station, its buildings converted into a large house inhabited by Ben Prosser (Osborne again borrowing his paternal grandmother's name), a film director, and Sally, his vulgar, brittle wife and the daughter of a colonial family. Middle-aged, bored, drinking a great deal and locked in a battle of mutual attrition, the Prossers are clearly portraits of the Osbornes. Ben has been to London, had lunch with his eleven-year-old daughter, whom he sees only about three times a year (a passing reference, perhaps, to Nolan, who would be eleven years old in 1976), and has slept with Marion, his first wife and his daughter's mother, a clever, perceptive woman who bears a glancing resemblance to Penelope and a woman of whom Sally is deeply jealous. In a room upstairs, Ben's unwanted, elderly mother, a Nellie Beatrice-figure, watches television and sometimes cries out for company and a cup of tea. In another room lies the ailing Glen, the author of waspish biographies, watched over by Jo, a capricious young painter, a relationship Osborne modelled upon that of Lytton Strachey and Dora Carrington. Like Carrington, Jo represents a Shavian life-force of love and hope, the affirmation that even from deepest desolation, the spring water of love can rise: 'It's hard to love, isn't it?' she muses. 'Release us from ourselves and give us each our other . . .'⁷

This was something to which Osborne had constantly returned: it is there in the ending of Look Back in Anger, in Archie Rice's evocation of the blues singer in The Entertainer, in Laurie's speech to Annie in The Hotel in Amsterdam, in the Chap's sermon at the end of A Sense of Detachment and in the encounter between Isobel and Leonard in The End of Me Old Cigar. Faith in the redemptive nature of love lay at the heart of Osborne's sensitivities and emerges as a recurring theme in his writing. Yet, like Carrington, Jo commits suicide and the ending of Watch It Come Down, like that of West of Suez, is violent. Vandals attack the station buildings, and as windows break there is the sound of gunfire. Ben is hit by a bullet and is either killed or rendered comatose and the curtain falls to a crashing hail of broken glass. As he wrote, ill and sleepless, Osborne recorded in his journal on 2 April, that 'The last two days and nights have been worse than anything. I just sat in the chair in my room all day, heart pounding, head almost as bad . . . Can't eat . . . During the night I was certain I was going to die . . . Trying to go on today but I don't think I can last much longer . . .'⁸

'I admire Watch It Come Down very much,' Peter Hall enthused to Osborne on 20 August.⁹ The first act, he thought, had 'a vigorous sardonic humour', while the second was 'one of the bleakest I have heard outside Strindberg.'¹⁰ With the theatre eager to press ahead, Robin Dalton negotiated a contract of £500 in advance with a ten per cent box-office royalty and rehearsals beginning on 16 January 1976. Great plans were laid: after opening at the Old Vic in February, Osborne would have the morale-boosting distinction of Watch It Come Down being the first new play to be performed when the company moved into Denys Lasdun's £16 million concrete-and-glass National Theatre building on the South Bank overlooking the Thames. After the opening production of Hamlet, starring Albert Finney, in the Lyttelton auditorium on 16 March, Watch It Come Down would open four days later, following Old Vic productions of Ibsen's John Gabriel Borkman and Beckett's Happy Days.

During the interval between his delivering the manuscript and rehearsals beginning, Osborne found himself once more encircled by collapsing projects in the film world. While Gross, a satire on pornography for Memorial Films, did not detain him long before he threw up his hands and protested he had nothing to say on the subject, an adaptation of Joseph Conrad's The Secret Agent for Paramount Pictures seized his imagination and seemed as though it might last the course. It was, he announced, 'one of the most exacting and difficult things I have done.'¹¹ Working at a frantic rate, he quickly completed a screenplay, chasing a financially appealing carrot of £11,000. But yet again, the project became bogged down in negotiations with the studio. Anxious for something along the lines of The Third Man, Paramount hoped that Osborne might transform Joseph Conrad into something more like Graham Greene. When Osborne failed to comply, Paramount called the whole thing off, Osborne emerging from the episode with not much over £100 for his efforts. And in the midst of this, while he continued to record in his journal the continuing battles with Jill and his various despondencies and maladies – he was now worried about gout – he opened his newspaper on the morning of 3 April 1975 to discover that Mary Ure had been found dead in a rented London flat. She was forty-two years old.

*   *   *

Like Osborne's marriage to Jill Bennett, Mary's relationship with Robert Shaw had reeled into one of mistrust and recrimination. Since her divorce from Osborne in 1962, she had devoted much of her time to making films and had appeared only rarely on the stage. But while her career had not prospered as she had hoped, Shaw continued to be sought after by both stage and film directors, and had recently completed work on Jaws, a spectacular yarn directed by Steven Spielberg in which he played a bounty hunter in combat with a man-eating shark, a performance which many were predicting would propel him to the ranks of actors able to name their own fees. Mary, it seems, became increasingly downcast by lagging, as she saw it, in her husband's wake. Their marriage souring, both took refuge in alcohol, and over the years barricaded themselves into 'a daily liturgy of drink'.[12] In New York, where Shaw was appearing in Harold Pinter's Old Times, they had spent much of their offstage time in bars, and at their new home in Ireland, Mary secreted bottles throughout the house so that alcohol was never much more than an arm's length away and on several occasions startled the housekeeper by her propensity when drunk to undress.

As Mary became progressively unreliable, her career suffered further. She took tablets to help her sleep, and became the victim of disturbing and seemingly random changes of mood and even blackouts, which her doctors diagnosed as the result of a 'salt deficiency' affecting her nervous system. Moreover, she suspected her husband of betraying her with other lovers, especially with Virginia de Witt Jansen, known as Miss Jay, who had become Shaw's secretary soon after his marriage to Mary. At the beginning of 1975, she was contracted to appear in The Exorcism at the Comedy Theatre, a 'Marxist ghost story' by Don Taylor, who, eighteen years previously, had directed the world premiere production of Epitaph for George Dillon in Oxford. Returning to London, she approached the play with trepidation born not of fear of the supernatural but simply of being on stage again. Renting a small and overheated flat at 56 Curzon Street near the Woodfall Films offices, she attempted to settle down to work and on the few occasions on which she emerged, she sheltered reclusively behind dark glasses. She was joined by her son, Colin, now thirteen years old, and her husband, who arrived in London not only to embark upon Diamonds, a 'caper' film about a jewel theft, but also intent upon procuring a divorce.

Partly as a result of nervousness, Mary's performance on the first night of The Exorcism on 2 April was hesitant and by the end of the evening her voice was exhibiting signs of strain. Nevertheless, she received respectful reviews the following morning, her 'unearthly eloquence' according to Irving Wardle in *The Times*, compensating for a play of tedious hokum.[13] After the curtain came down, she entertained her family, who had arrived from Scotland, at a restaurant in Leicester Square. When she returned to Curzon Street, Shaw and Colin were already asleep. Mary flopped down upon the sofa and took some tablets to induce sleep. The next morning, Shaw discovered her still lying on the sofa, apparently asleep. As a car was waiting to take him to film a scene for *Diamonds*, he left the flat to return a few hours later, when he was met by Colin who, despite several attempts, had been unable to awaken his mother. When Shaw looked at her, he saw that she was as pale as mist. At some point, she had vomited. She was cold to the touch.

An ambulance arrived, with the police and Shaw's lawyers not far behind. Mary's body was taken to St George's Hospital at Hyde Park Corner, and the flat sealed. Shaw booked himself into the Savoy Hotel, while the producers of *The Exorcism* announced that the show would go on and that Margo Mayne, Mary's understudy, would take over her role. The following day, Shaw retreated to Ireland. Later, at the inquest into Mary's death, it was ruled that she died from the effect of alcohol and barbiturates resulting in vomiting and asphyxiation.

Osborne did not attend the funeral in Guildford on 19 April. Mary left no will. Her money, such as it was, went mostly to Shaw who married Miss Jay the following summer. But three years later, he too was dead. Driving with his new wife on a country road near his home in Ireland, he suddenly clutched at his chest, managed to stop the vehicle and clamber out. Miss Jay flagged down a passing motorist who telephoned for an ambulance. By the time it arrived, Shaw had died of a heart attack at the roadside. He left nine children by three wives.

*   *   *

Equilibrium of sorts was restored in Osborne's life by Peter Hall and the National Theatre. In the autumn, Hall notified Osborne that Bill Bryden, its director, was 'mad about the play' and eagerly anticipating rehearsals.[14] At the first reading, on 16 January 1976, Osborne arrived, looking 'curiously pink and strained', noticed Hall, to meet Bryden and a cast including Frank Finlay as Ben and Jill Bennett as Sally.[15] The result of Hall's months of diplomacy was an Osborne glowing with self-assurance. The National Theatre, he declared, was such a marvellous place to be, and everyone was so welcoming that he promised to renounce his well-publicised gibes of the new South Bank building as looking like 'Colditz-on-Thames'. He was looking forward immensely to starting work.

CHAPTER 28

❧❧

Retrenching

'NEWS CAME FROM THE VIC about the reception of *Watch It Come Down* at tonight's preview,' recorded Peter Hall in his diary on 20 February 1976. 'There was a bit of a riot: boos and cheers and cries of rubbish and bravo. That's the stuff . . .'[1] Four days later, at the first night, the play was greeted by something closer to disappointment that *A Sense of Detachment* had not, after all, been Osborne's farewell to the theatre. 'Oh no, John,' lamented a headline in the *Daily Mail*, while Irving Wardle in *The Times* complained of 'the usual ambiguous treatment of homosexuality and the usual see-saw between sabre-toothed insult and exchanges of child-like affection.'[2] In the *Guardian*, Michael Billington pronounced that the play was 'an infuriating blend of the best and worst of Osborne . . . full of bilious wit' but 'intellectually muddled'.[3]

'Usual trouble and strife,' reported Osborne to Harold Pinter, 'but I think on the whole enjoyable, at least for those concerned.'[4] But knowing how hurt he would be by hostile reviews, friends hastily assured him, as they had after the reception of *A Sense of Detachment*, how much they admired the play. Edward Albee, the American dramatist and author of *Who's Afraid of Virginia Woolf?*, with which *Watch It Come Down* might justifiably be compared, wrote from Long Island, confessing himself so 'startled and intrigued by the general tone of hysteria and disdain in the press' that he had bought a copy of the published text. 'My God, it's a good play!' he wrote. 'Anger <u>and</u> disgust: hot and cold together . . . Mind you: you've been writing exciting plays for a long while.'[5] Osborne replied, thanking Albee for his kindness, adding that 'life here is quite bloody — almost literally' but: 'Onward — I suppose.'[6] But while Albee encouraged and, at the National Theatre, Hall took comfort from the Sunday newspaper notices ('Much better than I had feared'), many observers these days were wondering quite what to make of Osborne's plays.[7] The spirit of dissent that had once impelled his writing seemed to have turned into a blade of bitterness cutting ever deeper into whatever compassion he once might have had. The writer who once declared that his object was to give his audi-

306

ences 'lessons in feeling' now seemed to have little feelings for others himself.[8] 'Osborne', observed Benedict Nightingale in the *New Statesman*, 'no longer has the objectivity, empathy or insight to create anything resembling a rounded, or even half-rounded human being.'[9] *Watch It Come Down* 'wasn't one of his best', conceded the dramatist Alan Bennett, 'but, as always with Osborne, even when I disliked the play I found his tone sympathetic. I was in a minority.' At the performance he saw, the audience appeared mystified: 'Edward Heath was sitting in front, Alec Douglas-Home behind and the rest looked as if they'd come on reluctantly after the Lord Mayor's Banquet.'[9] From his own vantage point in the stalls, Bennett 'enjoyed the frozen embarrassment' of the audience as much as the play itself.[10]

Nevertheless, *Watch It Come Down* transferred to the newly opened Lyttelton Theatre on the South Bank and survived in repertory for twenty-nine performances before Hall, claiming falling box-office receipts, informed Osborne that the production would close. Probably audiences already downcast by the relentless news of economic and social doom were hoping for something more uplifting. *Watch It Come Down* is not one of Osborne's more successful plays, and certainly a pessimistic experience to watch, but he was incensed at Hall's decision to close it. Audiences had averaged a respectable seventy-seven per cent of capacity, he argued, and that even if ticket sales were falling, it was surely the National Theatre's duty to support serious plays that might not find a home elsewhere. Yet Hall was adamant and closed the production on 9 July, whereupon Osborne promptly transferred him from his private pantheon of the favoured to that of the great betrayers, where he joined Anthony Creighton, Tony Richardson and Kenneth Tynan. He took to calling him Fu Manchu, explaining that Hall's stocky build, narrow eyes, sleek black hair, moustache and goatee beard gave him an uncanny resemblance to the fictional criminal genius. In addition, Hall received a terse postcard on which Osborne announced that he was abandoning writing and taking up weaving instead. Yet only a week later, the director was invited to dinner at Chelsea Square, an occasion, he recorded in his diary, that 'passed very pleasantly, oiled by liberal quantities of alcohol.' His hosts, he noticed, conducted 'a constant banter of war, mocking each other, usually sexually', reminding him of the central characters in *Watch It Come Down*, 'except that tonight we were in comedy and not in tragedy.'[11]

Hall, though, was not the only recipient of a pithily expressed postcard from Osborne. He had long maintained that many critics were bumbling, even dishonourable figures who 'should be regularly exposed like corrupt constables or faulty sewage systems', and had threatened retaliatory strikes against critics who published what he considered malicious or ill-informed judgements upon his work.[12] These he now inaugurated, partly seriously, but partly in a spirit of mischievous fun. Reprisals took the form of a postcard campaign orchestrated by the fancifully entitled British Playwrights' Mafia, an organisation reminiscent of his schoolboy pranks with Mickey Wall. Awarding himself the title of President, with the militaristic name and rank of 'Osborne, J. (Fulham Welch)', he published a mock conference of war in the *Sunday Times Magazine* on 16 October 1977, in which he castigated critics as 'tipsters, form followers, Shaftesbury Avenue bookies' runners, tic-tac hacks who, without flair or talent, make a book on the real talent of other men.'[13] Several reviewers subsequently received humorous seaside postcards from Osborne on the Mafia's behalf, on the reverse of which were scribbled threats, perhaps of their safety being in danger unless they avoided certain areas of town. Mostly, these would be written on impulse as soon as Osborne had finished reading the review columns in the papers and posted without a second thought. In the country, where he bolted during the run of *Watch It Come Down*, more than one early morning dog walker glimpsed Osborne hurtling towards the post box clad in a dressing gown, Playwrights' Mafia postcard in hand.

Yet when he learned in 1976 that Harold Hobson was retiring from *The Sunday Times* after twenty-nine years, Osborne sent not a postcard but an affectionate note apologizing for having once sent him 'a rather churlish, ill-mannered letter. I have regretted having done so ever since. This is merely to say so and also that you will be sorely missed by many of us in this mad profession.'[14] Hobson had supported Osborne's writing from the outset. One of the most astute theatre critics of the second half of the twentieth century, he had discerned behind the rhetoric and the venom of Osborne's characters a spirituality and a will for redemption that had eluded many others. His verdict, however, on the question he had asked nineteen years previously, as to whether Osborne would become as outspoken a writer as his admired Anouilh, is not recorded. Yet while most of Osborne's recipients dismissed his postcards as a juvenile lark at the same time as hanging on to them as possible collector's items, a distinctly unamused Francis King, a novelist and critic for the *Daily Telegraph*, angrily responded to the receipt of 'your second obscene postcard' by urging Osborne to seek immediate medical advice.[15]

But Osborne had already decided that what he required was not medical advice but his frequent resort of flight, and to abandon both Jill and London for a new start in the country. As part of one of his frantic economy drives, The Old Water Mill at Hellingly had been sold to Nicol Williamson, but in a compensating spending splurge in 1975, Osborne had bought Christmas Place, a substantial and impressive Edwardian house at Marsh Green, near Edenbridge in Kent. Approached by a long drive and surrounded by twenty-two acres of grounds that included a three-acre lake, woods and a swimming pool, the house had a study, drawing-room, dining-room, a principal bedroom and dressing-room, five further bedrooms and three bathrooms. It was both a fitting residence for a man who nurtured aspirations of becoming a country gentleman and an appropriate sanctuary for a fugitive, and it was here that Osborne fled on 2 June 1976, tactlessly informing Jill by telephone that he was leaving her immediately before she was due to go on stage for a performance of *Watch It Come Down*.

In retrospect, many of their friends wondered why he and Jill had endured ten years together when many of them were so evidently and destructively miserable. Some suggested they were people who perversely derived their energy and sustenance from emotional combat; some that they had become trapped in a quagmire from which it was impossible for either of them to scramble with dignity intact, and others that in spite of everything, a bond of love still persisted between them. Besides, neither was the kind of person to admit defeat easily. Few, though, were surprised when Osborne left London for Kent, or when it transpired that he would not be alone in the country. He was joined at Christmas Place by Helen Dawson, a cultural journalist at the *Observer* who, during a short stint as the newspaper's theatre critic, had praised *West of Suez* and had written him a congratulatory letter after seeing *A Sense of Detachment*.

A small, slender, determined woman of thirty-six, Helen was ten years Osborne's junior. The daughter of a chartered accountant and his wife, her early years had been divided between home in Newcastle-upon-Tyne and a boarding school in Yorkshire. After reading History at Durham University, she had spent a year at Brown in the United States before joining the *Observer* and working as a programme compiler for the National Theatre, where she had edited the programme for *Watch It Come Down*. She and Osborne had known each other for some time and had gradually become close. Moreover, their political convictions and their views of the world dovetailed neatly. In later years they would describe themselves as compatible as a pair of old slippers.

Fanatically protective, Helen's belief in Osborne as a great playwright was, like all his former wives and lovers, absolute. But in contrast to Pamela, Mary, Jocelyn, Penelope and Jill, who were also devoted to their work, Helen voluntarily took second place. Having joined Osborne in Kent, she promptly gave up her job to minister to him, which arguably represented a full-time occupation in itself. He embarked upon a lengthy recuperation, beginning to eat properly again and during the autumn and winter gradually regaining some of the weight he had lost. With Helen's help, he managed to reduce his drinking, renouncing vodka and much of the wine, but he never relinquished champagne, which was a taste they very much shared. While recognizing that Osborne had been drinking to excess for a long time, Helen was not abstemious and the account with the wine merchant remained open. But even though he sometimes managed for several days, even a week or more, without alcohol, Osborne remained susceptible to random pains, migraines and bouts of introspection and gloom. Yet his friends agreed that the change in his demeanour over the following months was remarkably beneficial. Those living nearby were surprised, like many meeting him for the first time, to discover that contrary to what they had expected, he was courteous, quietly spoken, self-deprecating and apparently contented. 'He appeared neither particularly young nor angry,' recalled a near neighbour, Lady Patricia Barnes (the novelist Patricia Abercrombie). When she and her husband, Sir Denis, a former Permanent Secretary at the Department of Employment, invited Helen and Osborne to visit them, he 'sat cosily in the armchair, pink, bearded, and rather mild. We talked pleasantly, and he disagreed with no one.'[16]

However, arranging social occasions with Osborne and Helen were often
beset with unforeseen snags, requiring lengthy negotiation and a good deal
of patience to resolve. Invitations might result in apologetic last-minute telephone calls from Christmas Place, postponing and re-scheduling, with the
rather vague explanation that Osborne was unwell. This was taken to be a code
meaning that he was too despondent to go out (once he was so deeply plunged
in gloom that he had not spoken for thirty-six hours), or that he was suffering
from some minor injury, or that alcohol had played its part. Champagne was
always available. Whenever social gatherings, such as lunch at Christmas Place,
proceeded without any last-minute hitches, it was noted that Osborne served
lavish amounts of champagne before, during and after the meal. 'I once went
to Christmas Place to record a radio programme,' remembered Michael Billington. 'Everything was very ordered but at the same time relaxed. One arrived
at the station and there was Helen in the car ready to drive you to the house.
The car had a lot of the country about it; mud and a vague smell of animals.
And once you arrived at about eleven, the champagne would already be open.
Immediately, there was charm and warmth and hospitality. He was able to turn
a journalistic assignment into a social event.'[17]

There were further obstacles. Friends attempting to telephone Christmas Place
were frequently confounded by the Osbornes' ex-directory number proving to
be unattainable. Periodically changing his telephone number was part of the
elaborate defence system Osborne devised to evade Jill, who was pursuing her
husband with anguished calls, often in the early hours of the morning, and
bombarding him with letters, some written in disconcertingly uncertain handwriting, pleading that they meet to talk things over. Occasionally, she employed
more melodramatic tactics. One day, a blue shirt that Osborne had left in his
wardrobe at Chelsea Square arrived by post at Christmas Place with a curt note
from Jill demanding the instant return of its contents. On another occasion,
her mother intervened, pleading Jill's cause, declaring that she was lonely and
miserable and that only Osborne's immediate return to London might rescue
her. But Osborne had no intention of returning to London. In fact, he and
Helen put as much distance between London and themselves as they could, by
embarking for Australia.

Several months previously, Osborne had accepted an invitation to be a guest
at the 1977 Australian National Playwrights' Conference, a jamboree of discussions and performances taking place in Canberra. It came at an opportune
moment, and in early May, he and Helen flew first class (fares that Osborne
had ensured would be paid by his hosts) to Australia, where he emerged from
the aircraft to inform the local newspaper that 'I'm glad to be here, but I do
see the conference as a bit of a waste of time. I don't think I've got anything
to contribute.'[18] Understandably, this was not what the organizing committee
wanted to hear. The following few days confirmed to Osborne what he had
always known, that conferences were not his style, and that he had been wise to
avoid the earnest workshops in dramaturgy and character organised at the Royal

20.) *above left:* The press reports John Osborne and Mary Ure's romance.
21.) *above right:* John Osborne and Mary Ure in Times Square, New York, 1957.
22.) *left:* John Osborne in a quandary directing *The World of Paul Slickey*, 1959.

23.) *above*: Kenneth Macmillan, John Osborne, Dennis Lotis and Jocelyn Rickards in rehearsals for *The World of Paul Slickey*, 1959. 24.) *below*: John Osborne backstage with Albert Finney: the first night of *Luther* 1961.

Even a woodworm will turn, Mr. Osborne . . .

Workmen take over at the Old Mill to save it from the ravages of woodworm.

25.) *top left:* John Osborne and Mary Ure campaign for nuclear disarmament: Whitehall, London 1961.

26.) *top right:* Press coverage of renovations at The Old Water Mill, 1961.

27.) *bottom:* John Osborne, Vanessa Redgrave and Doris Lessing in Trafalgar Square, September 1961.

28.) *above left:* John Osborne at home in Belgravia, 1960s. 29.) *above right:* Penelope Gilliatt.
30.) *below:* John Osborne and Jill Bennett looking fashionable strolling in Chelsea Square, 1968.

31.) *above*: At their wedding, 1968. 32.) *below*: Looking pensive a year later.

33.) *above:* Michael Caine (right, as Jack) and John Osborne (left as Kinnear) in *Get Carter*, 1971.
34.) *below:* The Hurst, John Osborne's home in Shropshire.

35.) John Osborne and Helen Osborne at The Hurst, late 1980s.

36.) *above:* Peter Egan as JP in *Déjàvu*, London 1992.
37.) *below:* A country gentleman.

Court, insisting that analysis killed creativity and that drama should be written freely from the heart. He was relieved to board the flight home. After spending a few days exploring Bangkok and Singapore, where he and Helen lodged luxuriously at the Raffles Hotel, Osborne arrived back in England to provide readers of the *Guardian* with his opinion of Australia: 'the crunch of jackboots', he confided, 'is already there in that benighted land.'[19]

A more dignified and conciliatory message awaited them in Kent. '. . . we are better apart,' wrote Jill, appealing for an end to the bitterness between them. 'Let's have no more pain and think kindly towards each other.'[20] 'I agree with you entirely,' Osborne replied.[21] But this was easier said than done, and they were soon bickering over personal belongings that each claimed were in the other's possession. From London, Jill demanded the return of various items, including a fur coat, alleged to have been transferred to Christmas Place, while from Kent her husband insisted she relinquish various treasures he had left behind including, most importantly, the typewriter given to him by Pamela Lane and on which he had typed *Look Back in Anger*. Lawyers were rapidly marshalled on both sides, Osborne's protesting at Jill's hectoring messages and her refusal to return his possessions, while hers vociferously objected to Osborne addressing abusive letters to: 'Mrs Adolf Hitler, Pouffs Palace, 30 Chelsea Square', resulting in his asking in turn that she desist from referring to Christmas Place as 'The Abortion Clinic'. She alleged that he besieged her with drunken telephone calls so offensively threatening that she could hardly concentrate upon her role in a revival of Rattigan's *Separate Tables* at the Apollo Theatre. Her husband, she contended, had even heckled her from the stalls during a performance. This was entirely untrue, he countered. Not only was Rattigan a close friend, but at the theatre he scrupulously observed all the conventions of decency and decorum. But Jill persisted that she was living in a state of fear. Osborne, she said, was a powerful, volatile man who had assaulted her in the past. Apprehensive that he might appear at her door, Jill therefore sought, and obtained, an injunction preventing him from approaching Chelsea Square.

In his own submissions, ferried through Oscar Beuselinck, Osborne accepted the injunction but contested her other claims. Her contention that he had assaulted her and bruised her face was entirely untrue; the bruise was a result of her having fallen while drunk. Rather, it was she who, while drunk, had assaulted him, once with a bottle and once with a glass, cutting an ear. And in response to her assertion that he had destroyed one of her dogs at Christmas Place, Osborne countered that he had always loved dogs and had been advised by a veterinary surgeon that Luther, the dog in question, was dying of leukaemia and should be humanely put down. Jill, he maintained, was aware of this. And so the wrangling continued, channelled through lawyers, in letters and telephone calls. 'I am *not* an ex-playwright,' he wrote to her in July 1977, in a letter as vituperative and as bitter as that he had written to Tony Richardson eleven years earlier. Anticipating their divorce, he angrily challenged her to 'Get all the money I have sweated for since I was fifteen. Get the lot. You probably will. You've never *worked*. Not as I have, not as I *know*. I carry a knife for you and all your kind. The ones like you that are all crafty ruthlessness and unyielding ambition. Yes, there is an eighth deadly sin, and it is AMBITION. But most of all, there is CRUELTY. And you have that in abundance. But – and it's a good one – you cannot hurt *me*. I have taken too much from better ones even than you . . .'[22]

Citing Helen as co-respondent, Jill's action for divorce came to court on 10 August 1977. She chose not to pursue Osborne for money, electing neither to receive a maintenance allowance, nor claim a share of Christmas Place. Instead, and in return for these concessions, Osborne agreed not to 'make direct or indirect reference' to her in any interview, broadcast or publication without first consulting her and submitting a draft of any text he had written.[23] In effect, he was legally prohibited from publicly speaking or writing about their marriage. The house at Chelsea Square was sold and the proceeds divided, allowing Jill to buy a flat in Britten Street, off the King's Road. When Linda Drew, her secretary, helped her to move from Chelsea Square, they discovered a cache of empty bottles in the room that was once Osborne's study, where he had spent much of his time, writing, moping and avoiding the guests that she invited to the house. It was a melancholic ending to a viciously destructive marriage, as was *Almost a Vision*, an indifferent, thirty-minute television play that Osborne had completed at Chelsea Square and which was broadcast on Yorkshire Television on 1 September. A dialogue between a man and a woman (played by Keith Barron and Jill Bennett, who had appeared together in *The End of Me Old Cigar*), it is less a vision of love than a champagne-charged aria to sexual desire. It was also the last Osborne play in which Jill appeared.

*   *   *

At Christmas Place, Osborne arranged his new study and set his books on shelves that reached to the ceiling. Since childhood, he had been a voracious reader. The love of books and the will for self-education never left him. Each week, he scanned the review pages in the Sunday newspapers and ordered many of the new novels and biographies, as well as volumes of social and political history. He also kept himself well up on feminism, the subject of several books during the 1970s. His one blank spot was thrillers, which he studiously avoided. He was, therefore, not very well informed when he agreed to appear in a crime thriller for the cinema. Having checked his bank balance and blanched, he made another fund-raising foray into 'the old acting lark' and the world of film by playing a hotel owner in *Tomorrow Never Comes*, a plodding psychological drama starring Oliver Reed and Susan George, filmed in Canada and directed by Peter Collinson.[24] The film quickly disappeared and, having banked his fee, Osborne retreated back to the country and continued putting his house in order.

The indignant letters from the *Watch It Come Down* audience, one demanding that he personally refund his 'hard-earned' £2.40 ticket price, another informing him that she had endured the play only by fervently hoping the characters would soon shoot themselves, he stuffed into his collection of labelled box files containing his correspondence.[25] On uncovered walls, he hung drawings and paintings, framed posters from the premieres of his plays and an advertising photograph for the film of The Entertainer, showing Laurence Olivier as Archie Rice peering through a lifebelt. Setting out his desk and chair in his work room, he placed before him his dictionaries of quotations and of contemporary slang, and arranged his blotting pad, pens and ink, little trays of paper clips and pins, his hard-backed reporters' notebooks, and his tins of Sobranie Special Reserve pipe tobacco. He planned a peaceful, ordered, creative rural existence, 'a bourgeois existence', he asserted, of 'doing a thousand words before lunch, taking the [dogs] for a walk in the afternoon and in the evening redoing what I'd done in the morning.'[26]

He and Helen now visited London infrequently and on their occasional excursions to the capital went to the opera more often than theatre, from which they made their getaway during the interval if they agreed that life was too short to withstand the play they were watching. They seldom went to the Royal Court, where Max Stafford-Clark, the new artistic director, promised a regime of 'idealism tempered by compromise'.[27] According to Osborne, the Court had diminished irretrievably since the days of George Devine. It had lost all its spontaneity and sense of adventure and instead presented not plays but 'dramatized journalism about inadequacy or anorexia in high-rise flats or one-parent families in inner cities', evenings that were spiritually dowdy, emotionally dull and infected by spurious working-class worthiness. 'Whenever I think of going to see what they're doing,' he sighed, 'I find it's a play by someone called Les and directed by someone called Ron.'[28]

Instead, the man whom Kenneth Tynan had once described as 'the Fulham flame-thrower' devoted himself to more pastoral pursuits.[29] At Christmas Place, dogs bounded happily after him on his walks down the lanes and across the nearby fields. He became a recognized figure in the community, regularly popping into the Old Crown, the local pub, for a drink and a chat with villagers. He and Helen ate at a local tandoori restaurant and, billed as 'our special guest', he genially opened the church fête.[30] On good days, there were convivial lunches and dinners with the Barnes and other near-neighbours such as Lt Colonel Sir Simon Bland, a former private secretary to the Duke of Gloucester, and his wife, Lady Olivia. The Oliviers drove over from Brighton, and Pamela Lane came down from London, her friendship with her former husband, soured when she advised him not to marry Jill Bennett, now restored. Nellie Beatrice, whom Jill had thought socially embarrassing, also found herself returned to favour and arrived for festive weekends and large lunches of roast beef and Yorkshire pudding.

*   *   *

Osborne also became a regular member of the congregation at the local Angli-can Parish Church of St Peter and Paul. Before moving to Kent, he had not been a churchgoer, yet his interest in religious experience, nurtured during his researches for *Luther*, had been further fostered during his friendship with John Betjeman. A dedicated 'church-crawler', one of Betjeman's passions was inspecting churches from Penzance to Cape Wrath, and expounding upon their architectural and spiritual qualities. English churches, he wrote, were a guide in stone, wood and glass to the historical and spiritual heart of the nation. This was a sentiment to which Osborne responded, and during happier times with Jill, while they were staying with Betjeman and Lady Elizabeth Cavendish at the poet's house at Trebetherick in Cornwall, he had once asked if they might accompany their hosts to Sunday service at the local St Enodoc church. 'John and Jill sat in the pew behind us,' remembered Lady Elizabeth, 'although there was plenty of room beside us. I think neither of them was certain when to stand or sit or kneel, so they sat behind us so they could take their cue from us. I think he felt that if we couldn't see them, he wouldn't be embarrassed by sitting when he should have stood, or kneeling when he should have sat.'[31]

Noticing Osborne in the pews of St Peter and Paul, however, unsettled the vicar who, aware of the playwright's acerbic reputation, felt 'a little fearful'. Nevertheless, he braced himself and 'resolved to do things in the normal tra-ditional style.' But when he spoke to Osborne after the service, the Reverend Richard Mason was gratified to discover that traditionalism was exactly what his new parishioner wanted. Over the ensuing months, the two men became friends and enjoyed lengthy conversations at Christmas Place on matters spir-itual and ecclesiastical. Mason quickly recognized the other man to be 'a deeply conservative person in one aspect of his complex character' and 'his religion only partly to do with seeking spiritual solace.'[32] Osborne himself explained his religious belief as 'absolutely instinctive. It's not a question of seeking comfort. Religion for me is a rigour. Over the years I've come to believe more and more in the mystical side of religion and how it affects my work . . . my Christianity is not as many other people's. But it does sustain me.'[33]

His view was essentially Calvinist, he told Mason, in that he believed in the central concept of sin, the need to recognize it and the possibility of redemp-tion through the observance and celebration of the Book of Common Prayer. According to Osborne, the value of the King James Bible and the liturgy of the Church of England lay not only in their being religious texts, magnificent and mysterious in the architecture of their language, but that they were also, like the music of Vaughan Williams, of profound cultural significance, enshrining those elements of benevolence and severity fundamental to the English imagination.

The traditional religious services practised by the Church of England there-fore combined a fierce spiritual discipline with a majestic, pastoral quality reflecting the nation's island history and soul. Osborne's 'spirituality was quin-tessentially English', thought Mason. 'It was restrained, measured, and drew for its sustenance upon some of the great writings and prayers of the Christian tradition.' Osborne, he concluded, was a man 'to whom God was a reality, a Being who was drawing John's innermost self back to its home and its origin.'[34] When he had visited Mirfield, Osborne had drawn sustenance from Compline, the last of the daily services; now he favoured Evensong, partly, thought Mason, because it is non-sacramental. But it was also because in this service Mason used the 1662 Book of Common Prayer in preference to the modernised Alternative Service Book recently introduced into services and which Osborne wholeheartedly derided. This was a view with which Mason privately had considerable sympathy.

Over the previous twenty years, as the influence of the Anglican Church and its congregations had diminished, the ecclesiastical authorities had experimented with more modern forms of ministry and approved a revamped service of Holy Communion and an Alternative Service Book written in contemporary English. The latter, its Preface suggested, was intended not to supersede the Book of Common Prayer but to supplement it. This was an innovation upon which Osborne pounced, and the upholding of the Book of Common Prayer became the first of his crusades from the countryside. All his old energy flooded through him again and poured into newspaper correspondence columns and incidental articles.

Merely to countenance the idea of an Alternative Service Book, he cried, was nothing other than 'smarmy disingenuousness' on the part of 'glib populists'.[35] Meddle with the Book of Common Prayer, he argued, and one tampered not only with the very means by which the mystery of religious experience was communicated, perceived and understood, but a thing of innate beauty in itself, an evocation of that indefinable lost Eden that he believed to be the heart of Englishness. The Alternative Service Book represented a fumbled travesty upon something Osborne held sacred: the monumental cathedral of the English language, its infinite expressiveness and its depthless, immeasurable poetry. '. . . the language of the Alternative Services', he cried, 'is written in a style in which it is impossible to be religious.' More than that: 'It blasphemes against language itself in its banality and its fawning to please.'[36] The erosion of language and the diminution of meaning had, after all, been one of the themes of A Sense of Detachment, West of Suez and Watch It Come Down.

It was at St Peter and Paul Church that the Reverend Mason conducted a service for Osborne and Helen immediately after they were married at Tunbridge Wells Register Office on 2 June 1978, the vicar devising an improvised service from the Book of Common Prayer and the Authorised Version of the Bible. It was held in private, with only the three of them in the church. Afterwards, friends joined them for a celebratory lunch at Christmas Place. At forty-eight and married for the fifth time, Osborne was looking fitter and happier than he had done for years. Helen became the first of his wives to take his name.

Over the years, Christmas Place became one of the centres of village life, renowned for the sumptuous garden parties Osborne gave each summer, when the house and grounds would be open to scores of guests: writers, actors, directors and musicians who travelled down from London, and the neighbours and villagers who walked the short distance to the house. All clutched the amiably facetious invitation cards that Osborne issued for the *Cranmer's Summer Ball*, named after Archbishop Thomas Cranmer, who had established the liturgical structure of the reformed Church of England. Various spurious attractions beckoned guests onward. Music might be provided by 'The Rev. Len Bovver and the Trendy Skypilots'; there might be a 'Guardian Woman Rodeo' for Osborne emphasised that readers of the *Guardian*, a newspaper sympathetic to liberal and feminist causes, were especially welcome. Prizes were offered for the most elegantly dressed couple, including perhaps 'Life Membership of the Edenbridge Teetotallers' Association' or a 'tea-stained railway timetable', and the entire event, it was promised, would be held 'outside if wet'.[37]

By the time the great day came, a marquee had arisen on the Christmas Place lawns and a jazz band would be playing. 'The parties were splendid occasions,' remembered the vicar. 'John was lavishly generous in his hospitality and hugely benign to all his guests.' There was certainly no outward evidence of the host being tormented by debt. Food would be plentiful, drinks apparently endless and the swimming pool 'pressed into service' for impromptu dips. Expansively dressed in a striped blazer, cravat and open-necked shirt, his hair trimly cut, his beard flecked generously with grey and clutching a tankard of champagne, Osborne would stride across the gardens, welcoming all and enjoying himself immensely playing the part of lord of the manor. 'He did rather like that aspect of it,' observed Mason.[38]

Also present at the garden parties, from the summer of 1978, was a young girl whom guests identified as Nolan, Osborne's thirteen-year-old daughter, home from New York and now living with her father and his new wife. John Osborne had already reinvented himself several times: in his youth he had equipped himself with an approved accent and mastered the paso doble to become an actor; later, he had accepted the role of an Angry Young Man, and later still, assumed that of a fashionably metropolitan playwright and businessman. Now, at the same time as reinventing himself as a country gentleman, he was also attempting to re-model himself as a family man.

*   *   *

For several years, Osborne had believed New York an unsuitable place for a child to grow up in, but more recently, his concerns had been exacerbated by disturbing news of Penelope. She was as ambitious and accomplished as ever, contributing to the *New Yorker*, publishing fiction, and writing the script for *Sunday, Bloody Sunday*, a film starring Peter Finch and Glenda Jackson, and directed by John Schlesinger, and which had earned her an Oscar nomination for Best Screenplay. *Unholy Fools*, a compilation of her film criticism, had appeared in 1973. But as her work entailed regular socializing and irregular hours, she had found it increasingly difficult to cope with bringing up a young daughter. Much of the time, she had relied upon the support of Christine Miller, their English nanny, but after her return to Britain in 1975, the ten-year-old Nolan had frequently come home from school to spend evenings in the apartment alone. Penelope, who many thought had never fully recovered from Osborne's leaving her, was also drinking heavily, principally a mixture of vodka and orange juice, and becoming increasingly unpredictable. After the principal of Nolan's school wrote to Osborne expressing concern for his daughter's welfare, he seized the opportunity when she visited England a few weeks after he and Helen were married, to declare that she should not return to New York.

Penelope had no objection. Her difficulties with alcohol were beginning to overwhelm her. There were reports of her appearing drunk in public and at film screenings, and the following year, her career at the New Yorker ended after she submitted a profile of Graham Greene incorporating passages written two years earlier by another journalist, Michael Mewshaw, and published in The Nation. The New Yorker's fact checkers alerted Wallace Shawn, the editor, warning that to publish would leave the magazine, renowned for its impeccable professional standards, open to charges of plagiarism. But Shawn, who was aware of Penelope's personal struggles and fiercely supportive of her, decided to publish nevertheless, with the result that Mewshaw's lawyers advised their client to sue. Graciously, Mewshaw elected not to go to court but privately accept token damages, but Penelope's professional reputation in New York never recovered.

Meanwhile, in England, as they got to know one another, Osborne's newly assembled family appeared to bump along contentedly enough. Nolan seemed happy, travelling each day to St Michael's, a school in nearby Limpsfield, while Osborne took the train to London, where he was directing a revival of Inadmissible Evidence, with Nicol Williamson once again playing Maitland and which opened at the Royal Court on 12 August. His return to the play that so remarkably prophesied much of the despair which he had endured while living with Jill was his fourth excursion into directing. It also turned out to be his last and the most successful. 'All I can say is,' wrote Michael Billington in the Guardian, 'I found [the play] an overwhelming experience in which the sense of private pain, paranoia and anguish is deeply moving.'[39]

This was all very invigorating, and when on 29 December 1979 Osborne celebrated his fiftieth birthday, he did so in good spirits. During the worst of times with Jill, he had believed that he had few if any friends, yet fifty guests greeted him at a party held at the Garrick Club in Covent Garden. The Club, which includes 'many of the most distinguished actors and men of letters in England', and rigorous in its exclusion of anyone thought to be 'a terrible bore', had elected Osborne to their number in 1970.[40] Later, more than a hundred guests gathered for a shindig at Christmas Place. Fifty, Osborne asserted genially, was really a very young age indeed. He felt now exactly as he had when he was twenty-five and writing Look Back in Anger: bursting with energy and full of plans for the future.

In many ways, though, the younger Osborne would have been astounded by the older version; by his newly-discovered passion for ocean cruises, for instance, often on 'obscure Russian boats'.[41] Assuming charge of the organization and the itinerary, Helen would reveal their next destination to be Venice, perhaps, or Cape Town, Hong Kong, San Francisco or the Caribbean. Sometimes, there would be an arrangement that he give a 'lecture' on board for interested passengers, something that would have stopped the Osborne of even a few years previously dead in his tracks, either with indignation or terror. But life on the ocean blue, he maintained, was supremely congenial, and reclining on deck in the sun proved a remarkably conducive posture for writing. From this near-horizontal position, he quickly polished off three not especially distinguished television plays featuring bored, fractious women. In Try a Little Tenderness, Ted Shilling, a bohemian novelist burdened with an unhappy wife and her deaf, colonial mother, plans to disrupt a pop festival to be held in his village. Falling foul of the misfortunes that had dogged Osborne's screenwriting, it was never produced, but You're Not Watching Me, Mummy, in which an actress craving applause is plagued in her dressing-room by fawning admirers, was broadcast on ITV on 20 January 1980, although to a lukewarm reception. Very Like a Whale, in which a wealthy industrialist discovers that, having lost the respect of his wife and son, he cannot buy it back, was broadcast, again on ITV, three weeks later, on 13 February. 'The play is about money and success,' averred Joan Bakewell in The Times, 'the ambition to have them and the assumption they are life's crowning glory. These are false gods.'[42]

As far as Osborne was concerned, money was less of a false god than a necessary evil, and these outings briefly helped inflate his bank balance, as did another film appearance later in 1980. Mike Hodges, who had directed Get Carter, invited him to take part in his latest exercise, the wackily-costumed, extravagantly preposterous Flash Gordon, a film based upon the intergalactic adventures of the eponymous American comic book hero. Sam J. Jones, a former male model, gesticulated his way through the title role (his voice being deemed unsuitable and dubbed by another actor), while Osborne appeared in 'a loopily-loaded cameo scene', wrote the film critic of Empire magazine, as an Arborian priest initiating a novice, played by the presenter of a children's television programme, into an interstellar cult.[43] Behind them lurked Max von Sydow, the star of several gloomily introspective Ingmar Bergman films. The music, full of wailing guitars, crashing drums and hectic, near falsetto singing performed by the rock group, Queen, resulted in a film resembling 'a fairy tale set in a discotheque in the clouds', thought Pauline Kael.[44]

It was Osborne's last adventure in motion pictures. At Christmas Place, he sat down at his desk, flicked on the green shaded lamp over his blotter, and resumed writing, not a play this time, but a book. Looking back over his life and times, he was busy writing his memoirs.

*   *   *

'I took it on for a great deal of money,' he admitted. 'But at the beginning it was much worse than writing a play, because it took such a long time to establish the characters. The albatross that followed me was the fear that no one could possibly be interested in what I was putting down. I'd wonder who on earth would want to know what kind of make-up my mother wore in 1938 . . .'[45] By now, many of Osborne's relatives were no longer alive. Ada Grove, his last surviving grandparent, had died in 1974 aged 103. Nellie Beatrice, her daughter, although hearty, was not quite so hale these days, having endured several spells in Westminster Hospital and convalescing at a Romford nursing home, for which her son had footed the bills. Each time, she emerged triumphant and declaring herself once more fit and full of beans. Grove women were survivors. As Osborne began recreating her in his memoirs, Nellie Beatrice was eighty-seven and stooped, but she had weathered much: two world wars, hard work, domestic insecurity and early widowhood, her son becoming a figure of public controversy, his marriages, divorces and private life turned into a theatre by the popular press. She had also become accustomed to seeing her one grandchild only fleetingly. Yet while she remained enormously proud of her son while bewildered by his world, he, on the other hand, still viewed her with a combustible combination of dutiful concern and intense distaste. A generous amount of the latter he ladled into *A Better Class of Person*, in which he recounted the years until 1956 and his sending the typescript of *Look Back in Anger* to George Devine at the Royal Court.

Having taken three years to write, the longest he had spent on any project, the book was published at the end of 1981 to widespread and lengthy reviews, many of them admiring and many seemingly surprised at how admiring they were. The press coverage almost rivalled that awarded to Osborne during the days of *Look Back in Anger*, his scathing portrayal of Nellie Beatrice becoming, to borrow the title of an early television play, something of a subject of scandal and concern. Reviewers, newspaper commentators and correspondents in the letter columns all pitched in with their views. 'You seldom come across hatred as virulent as John Osborne's for his mother,' warned *The Sunday Times*.[46] 'It is immensely enjoyable, [and] is written with great gusto,' acknowledged Alan Bennett in *The London Review of Books*, which was not the kind of response Osborne was accustomed to these days.[47] *A Better Class of Person* sold well. 'People not only seem to like the book,' said Osborne incredulously, 'they seem to like me for myself.'[48] It was a refreshing sensation, and entirely unexpected.

Although he had produced no new stage play for five years, *A Better Class of Person* decisively restored Osborne's literary prominence. As a memoirist he was acclaimed the equal of the playwright who had written for the Royal Court, when, surely, he had been at his swaggering best. He was buoyantly in the news again, comprehensively profiled, interviewed and photographed. He reflected on his career on *Desert Island Discs*, the long-running weekly radio programme in which a guest 'castaway' is invited to choose eight pieces of music, a book and a luxury with which to be sustained on a desert island already thoughtfully provided with a Bible and the complete works of Shakespeare. Osborne's musical choices included Mozart, Elgar and Handel, and his favourite, Vaughan Williams's 'The Lark Ascending'. For his book, he selected Holy Living and Holy Dying, an edition of two volumes of Christian devotion by Jeremy Taylor, a seventeenth-century Church of England cleric who came to prominence during the Protectorate of Oliver Cromwell. As his luxury, he chose a piano and an instruction book. Interviewed by Melvyn Bragg for the prestigious television arts programme The South Bank Show, he appeared well groomed, relaxed and urbane, reminiscing on his suburban childhood and once again promising that he was full of plans for the future. His autobiography also brought a welcome crop of congratulatory letters, not only from friends but strangers. A correspondent from Chichester told him that that she was eighty-four, had seen Look Back in Anger in 1956 and had 'felt grateful' ever since. He must, she counselled, 'hold fast to that which is eternal – keep your enthusiasm and capacity for enjoyment and be true to your true self.'[49]

*   *   *

Osborne had the capacity for many things, enthusiasm and enjoyment being among them, but he was failing to discern them in his daughter or, rather, discern them in the way that he would have liked. The journalist Robert Cheshyre, arriving at Christmas Place to interview Osborne the family man for the Observer, noted that he was 'clearly very fond' of Nolan who appeared to be 'the epitome of the English middle-class girl'.[50] Osborne indeed loved his daughter, but he was dismayed to discover that her teenage world was not at all what he thought it should be.

He was disappointed and bewildered when he discovered that although Nolan lived in a house filled with books, she ignored those on his shelves for those of her own choosing. Neither did she like the opera that poured from his loudspeakers, preferring the rock music that blared from her room. Moreover, she appeared indifferent to the lustre of his literary and theatrical guests. He objected bitterly to some of her friends, with whom he thought she was wasting her time. Surely, he cried, he was providing her with a privileged life: he gave her what he imagined was generous pocket money, bought her a pony and arranged for riding lessons, yet she appeared to show little interest or gratitude. Her father could not understand it. Some of his guests would sometimes notice that Nolan appeared unusually reserved, even tense and strained. Yet this, they reflected, was perhaps not surprising. After all, as the daughter of divorced parents each with their own troubles and preoccupations, and living between two continents she had endured a traumatically disrupted childhood. And the teenage years inevitably brought their difficulties. But although Osborne recognized this, at least in theory, he was unable to comprehend it.

His own educational journey having been haphazard, he was concerned to secure his daughter's academic future, and in the summer of 1981, when she was sixteen, he decreed that she would leave St Michael's and go to D'Overbroeck's, a private tutorial college in Oxford. There, she would lodge with a local family, study intensively and hopefully achieve the qualifications to go on to university, as he had once hoped to do himself. Off she went, and at the end of her first term in December, she returned to Edenbridge for Christmas and the New Year. It was not a successful interlude. In her father's eyes, Nolan remained languid and remote. He found her presence unnerving, her behaviour inexplicable. There were disputes between them over small sums of money disappearing from the housekeeper's purse, disparaging remarks about him that he had discovered while leafing through her diary, and what he saw as her resistance to his attempts to communicate and form an enduring relationship between them. Sometimes, alone, Osborne wept in frustration. He could not elicit from her that which he most wanted, which was an open and unfettered declaration of her love. Later, Nolan in her turn would not remember her father ever telling her that he loved her.

Yet to others, she appeared cheerful and made friends easily, including with Sally Bennett, a girl of her own age and the daughter of the Reverend Guy Bennett, the Rector at nearby Oxted, and his wife, Judith. A man with a stage-struck enthusiasm for the theatre, Bennett had served as a theatre chaplain in the West End, where he had encountered Jill Bennett (to whom he was not related), while she was appearing in *West of Suez*. Through the friendship of their daughters, the Osbornes and the Bennetts became acquainted. Bennett speculated that Osborne's disappointment in Nolan – who, it seemed to him, behaved 'much like any other respectable teenager' – was rooted in 'his obsession with raising his own status. He wanted a son or a daughter who would complete the transformation from his lower-middle-class origins to something much grander, and in his eyes, Nolan was not doing this.'[51] She was not, in other words, someone whom her father believed might become a better class of person.

The situation between them, concluded Osborne, could not continue. During the first week of January 1982, Nolan returned to Oxford. On the fifth – Nellie Beatrice's eighty-ninth birthday – Osborne wrote his daughter an 'astonishing letter, full of vituperation', the ferocity of which surpassed even that which he had written to Tony Richardson or Jill Bennett.[52] 'I put it to you,' he began, 'that we dispense with the absurd charade that you regard this as your home.' He accused her of lassitude, deceit and deception, of lacking the will to enter into family life and of rejecting the overtures and accommodations that he and Helen had made for her. 'If you should ever bring yourself to read *King Lear* without coaxing, look up the very first act: "How sharper than a serpent's tooth it is to have a thankless child".' Therefore, he declared, he would not only refuse to continue paying the fees at D'Overbroeck's, but he would never open his door to her again. From now on, she must find her own way without his assistance. 'A life of banality, safety, mediocrity and meanness of spirit is what you are set on,' he predicted. 'Above all, don't underestimate my resolve or

anger.' His decision was irrevocable. 'This is where the long road really starts –
On Your Own.'[53]

When she received her father's letter, Nolan was shocked and deeply upset.
The news that Osborne had peremptorily disowned her quickly reached Guy
Bennett, who telephoned Penelope, who was then visiting London from New
York and staying at Chester Square. During a summit meeting with Nolan,
Penelope consented to her daughter's decision to accept Bennett's invitation to
stay indefinitely with his family at the Rectory. Osborne was informed of the
move, but no response from Christmas Place reached the Rectory. As Nolan
was sixteen years old and legally able to choose where she wished to live, there
were no official formalities required, and soon after her arrival at his home, the
Rector arranged with Osborne to collect her belongings from Christmas Place.

'I was prepared for him to punch me on the nose,' Bennett recalled. 'Instead,
he invited me in to the house and chatted extremely courteously over a drink.
From his demeanour, it was as if Nolan was merely joining us for a weekend
as she often did, rather than leaving for good. It was most curious.'[54] There
was, the Rector noticed, no sign of Helen. After some time, he murmured that
he was due to officiate at a funeral, whereupon Osborne indicated his daughter's possessions, thrust into large black plastic rubbish bags and waiting to be
loaded into the back of Bennett's car. Before he drove away, Osborne presented
him with a copy of his autobiography to give to Nolan. While writing it, he
had taken her to some of the places he had lived and pointed out where he had
spent different years of his childhood. The book had no inscription and neither
was it signed. It was a parting gift, a final gesture.

Yet while he appeared to Bennett disconcertingly gracious, Osborne was
privately greatly distressed. Although he looked back on his own peripatetic
childhood with little affection and recognized that Nolan had had an unusually
fraught upbringing, it was difficult, in the light of his new-found contentment
in the country, for him to understand the effect of such a chaotic childhood.
He had little practical experience of being a parent or a part of a loving family,
yet he had believed that his goodwill, the affection he felt for his daughter and
the alliance he shared with Helen would overcome everything. Apparently this
was not enough. In the end, he concluded, he had no option but to re-trench
and protect his own newly found happiness in another 'new start'.

CHAPTER 29

Defiance

'A YEAR IN WHICH my mother died can't be said to be all bad,' declared Osborne, summing up the events of 1983.[1] A year after he cast out his daughter, Nellie Beatrice died on 23 January of pneumonia at St Mary Abbot's Hospital in Kensington. She was eighty-nine. There were few mourners at the funeral service at Mortlake Crematorium, and her son was not among them. Osborne claimed that he felt no grief at her death. She was, he maintained, a dreadful woman. 'Her underestimation of my intelligence and sensitivity,' he noted in his journal shortly after she died. 'Also, of course, she discouraged ambition. She even denigrated me, especially physically, making me feel an ugly mess.'[2]

His mother's name joined the lengthening list of those including Anthony Creighton, Tony Richardson, Kenneth Tynan, Jill Bennett and Peter Hall, against whom Osborne had taken a biliously defiant, often public stand or, like Nolan, had cut out of his life altogether. Much of the vocabulary of denigration that he had previously directed at his mother he now transferred to his daughter. 'My mother wasn't very nice,' he told a national newspaper in 1986. 'She was disagreeable and rather immoral. She was just a cold, loveless woman.' A few moments later he added that 'I was unfortunate with my daughter, who's a very unpleasant girl . . . she's a cold creature.' On the surface at least, his attitude was uncompromising. 'It seems useless to pretend you like somebody if you don't,' he explained. 'You must be able to write people off. It seems cruel but if a relationship doesn't work you must cut it off like a limb.' His parting with his daughter had been painful but necessary: 'I don't think it will blight her life. It certainly won't blight mine.'[3]

Such peremptory casting out from favour was a routine that Oscar Beuselinck and many of those who encountered Osborne in his later years wearily recognised. It was, according to Beuselinck, emblematic of his central paradox, in that he was 'a man capable of great kindness and boundless hatred in equal measure. He treated me in exactly the same way. I used to get the most extraordinary letters from him; one would be full of gratitude, but the next would be a torrent of outrage. Then it would be back to civilised behaviour again as if nothing had happened.' Intrigued, bemused but seldom offended by Osborne, Beuselinck often reflected that his client would be 'a fascinating subject for a psychiatrist's couch.'[4] But professional therapy was not something to which Osborne or many men of his generation were inclined. Besides, he had already formed an implacable aversion to psychiatrists and distrusted doctors and the welfare profession generally. His writing provided sufficient soul-searching to be going on with. It was something mystical that he believed would be diminished and perhaps destroyed by attempts to analyse or rationalize. He explored his life in his plays.

Yet Osborne's behaviour towards Nolan may have been influenced by factors other than his conviction that they had failed each other. In June 1982, the summer after he barred his daughter from his home, he travelled to London and, as a member of the BUPA private medical scheme for which he paid regular premiums, submitted to an extensive medical examination at King's College Hospital. At the same time, he described the periodic numbness in his hands and feet against which a course of acupuncture had been unsuccessful, the dryness of his scalp and mouth, the curious blotches on his skin and the pains behind his eyes which lasted three or four days at a time. Subsequent cardiac tests revealed a heart murmur, possibly a legacy from his childhood rheumatic fever, but much more ominously: 'Your blood tests showed that you are drinking far too much alcohol,' observed Dr Kenneth Marsh in his report. Osborne's blood sugar, at 14.8 millimols per litre, was more than twice the upper limit of what was considered normal. Furthermore, there were disturbing traces of both sugar and red blood cells in his urine.

Marsh diagnosed type 2 diabetes. In fact, Osborne had been suffering the effects of high blood sugar levels for a considerable time. Perhaps he had not recognized it, but the symptoms he had recorded in his journals during the mid-1970s, of palpitations, sweating, a dry mouth, intense fatigue, nausea, sometimes blurred vision and numbness in the extremities of his hands and feet, are consistent with those of diabetes, while numbness is also a symptom of nerve degeneration and shortage of vitamin B12. Diabetes is sometimes precipitated, and certainly aggravated, by disproportionate stress, a deficient diet and an excessively high alcohol consumption, all of which had been part of Osborne's daily life for several years. Champagne is especially hazardous to the diabetic as it has a particularly high sugar content. Referred to a specialist, Osborne was recommended to control his diabetes by means of self-administered insulin injections and a nutritious diet, and immediately stop drinking alcohol and give up smoking. 'All this sounds thoroughly mean to a chap,' agreed Marsh, 'but . . . in the long run it will be worthwhile.'[5]

*   *   *

The death of Nellie Beatrice signalled that time was passing. Increasingly these days, Osborne learned of the deaths of those he had encountered in earlier days. In March 1973, Binkie Beaumont, once the most influential producer in London, had died, to be followed four days later by Noël Coward. Four years later, Terence Rattigan died in Bermuda. These deaths were followed by that of the self-styled war correspondent who, just over twenty years previously, had energetically packed them off into the wings. By the mid-1970s, however, Kenneth Tynan's stock was falling, not least with himself. He had made his name as a cultural agitator and found successive causes in Brecht, the Angry Young Men, sex and permissiveness, but his influence, which had once appeared so vital, had spectacularly diminished.

Tynan had left the National Theatre in 1973. He had created two unmemorable 'erotic revues', Oh! Calcutta! and Carte Blanche, both of which made money but the critical reception of which confirmed their creator's suspicion that Britain was quite the wrong place to champion a revolution, theatrical, social, sexual or otherwise. Dejected, he lost faith in his writing and in himself, and as financial troubles loomed alarmingly to the extent that his home telephone was briefly cut off, the strain became ever more difficult to conceal. At the end of 1976, disillusioned and suffering from chronic bronchial emphysema, he had abandoned Britain in search of a warmer and kinder climate. He docked in California, where his wife joined him and where the New Yorker offered $44,000 for a series of six profiles of entertainers. Yet Tynan thrived on performance and performers thrive on an audience. When he left journalism and the National Theatre he lost both, and in America he failed to regain a sense of either. Rootless, restless and without a cause, he died of emphysema in hospital at Santa Monica, California, in 1980. He was fifty-three. His wife brought his ashes back to England and buried them where he believed he had always been happiest, at Oxford, where he had invented the myth of the boy-wonder and from where the comet of his career had been launched.

*   *   *

Between his mourning of various deaths, or not in the case of his mother, and having embarked upon his regime of insulin injections, Osborne began making renewed forays into London. At the Garrick Club, he became a member of the 1400, a club-within-a-club consisting of members who met in the bar and proceeded to lunch at 2pm. Prominent among them was Kingsley Amis, who many years previously had shied away from being an Angry Young Man but who was now a testily impatient older one and a staunch supporter of the Conservative right. He and Osborne had little to say to each other. 'I don't think he likes me very much,' confided Osborne to Eric Shorter, a fellow luncher. 'One tried to reassure him that KA didn't like anyone much,' remembered Shorter, 'but it was sad that JO sensed it. Kingsley despised the theatre and most (but by no means all) actors. He was far more self-important in his last years than

JO would ever dare to be. Two of the most celebrated chaps of their time, each delightful as a companion yet nothing in common. Sad.'[6]

Now that he had disentangled himself from Jill, who following their divorce became increasingly dependent upon antidepressant tablets and alcohol, Osborne took the opportunity on his London excursions to resume seeing Pamela Lane. Both were now in their mid-fifties and by this time Pamela's acting career was flourishing once more. She was a valued and versatile member of the Haymarket Theatre company in Leicester, where she appeared in a variety of roles, including carrying a mop and bucket as Mrs Bird in a stage adaptation of *A Bear Called Paddington*, and being encased up to the neck in a mound of scorched earth as Winnie in Beckett's *Happy Days*. In Cardiff and Nottingham, she forged a productive collaboration with the prominent Shavian director Richard Digby Day, playing the title role in Shaw's *Candida*, and Queen Elizabeth in Schiller's *Mary Stuart*. She had also embarked upon a partnership with the director Angela Langfield, for whom she played an acclaimed Mary Tyrone in O'Neill's *Long Day's Journey into Night*. Angela became Pamela's companion from 1980 and joined her each summer to travel down to Kent as guests at Osborne's garden parties, and where Pamela's former husband was 'very charming'.[7]

Time, and the fluctuations of their respective fortunes, had cast their differences of thirty years previously in a rather different perspective, and their acknowledgement of their early failure and their own shortcomings created a similar intensity of reconciliation. There is a sense in their letters of time having been lost, and of love being reclaimed. 'I share your pleasure in (and amazement at?) our renewal of old but never forgotten feelings,' Pamela told Osborne on 26 August 1983. 'I was glad you'd kept some of the old letters . . .'[8] She too had retained his letters 'of thirty years and more', safely stored and 'lugubriously' marked, she assured him, 'for immediate destruction in the event of my death.'[9] She had also kept her original production programmes for *Look Back in Anger* and *Inadmissible Evidence*, and newspaper clippings of the reviews. By the following year, their relationship had deepened and she and Osborne were using their old nicknames of Bear and Squirrel again. 'Darling Bears,' she wrote, 'wonderful to see you and feel close to you once again (not just in bed) . . .'[10] '. . . my friendship and love for you is abiding,' Osborne assured her, repeating his promise later in the autumn.[11]

The 'renewal' of the love between Osborne and Pamela thrived through the spring of 1984. 'God bless our – to me astonishing reunion,' Pamela wrote in May; '– despite our respective constraints it feels more than ever firm and enduring: this is, I think, more than the pious and somewhat fragile hope that attends your average reunion, which, since it's taken thirty years, is as it should be.'[12] Letters darting back and forth led to a summer of meetings: 'I do love you my savage, benign bear,' cried Pamela, 'wherever we are in our separate necks of the forest, and to re-encounter you suddenly, briefly, is as literally breathtaking as ever . . . your lightest embrace whether of affection or passion revives the oldest memory I wish to keep – of deep familiarity, excitement, reassurance and of a trust now greater than before . . .'[13]

*   *   *

Meanwhile, Osborne was orchestrating another reshuffle on the business front. After his literary agent, Robin Dalton, moved to Fraser and Dunlop Scripts in order to pursue a successful career in film production, Osborne placed his affairs in the hands of Kenneth Ewing, the company's leading light, whose passions included piloting light aircraft and whose clients included Tom Stoppard. It was a propitious move, as welcome revivals tumbled over the horizon: Look Back in Anger and The Entertainer, this time starring Nicol Williamson, in New York, and a memorable production of A Patriot for Me, starring Alan Bates in the conservative confines of Chichester, and which transferred the following year to Los Angeles. 'Safer for your health to stay clear of downtown Chichester,' a pre-emptive British Playwrights' Mafia postcard warned Benedict Nightingale at The Times on the first night.[14] The play was also pressed into service as the basis for Colonel Redl, a Hungarian film released in 1985, for which Osborne was paid a much-needed courtesy fee of £20,000. He was therefore able to celebrate his fifty-fifth birthday in December 1984 in a mood of comparative confidence. Forty of his friends, including Pamela, rallied at the Garrick Club as they had done five years earlier, to drink his health in champagne and present him with a range of gifts ranging from a dictionary of music to a swordstick. Osborne appeared genuinely surprised to be held in such esteem. 'The presents are wonderful,' he announced. 'But you have given me something infinitely more valuable – the gift of your friendship.'[15]

The following year, two new television plays were aired. The first, God Rot Tunbridge Wells, is a pugnacious exploration of the life of George Frideric Handel, who died at his London home in 1759, shortly after (but not as a consequence of), a dreadful performance of The Messiah by the Tunbridge Wells Amateur Music Club. Although Osborne still continued the routine, established earlier in his career, of writing to the loud accompaniment of symphonic and operatic music, this was the first time he had tackled the life of a composer. It was 'such a pleasure,' he declared, as 'Handel is almost my favourite composer.'[16] With the seventy-two-year-old Trevor Howard playing the older Handel, the play was directed by Tony Palmer and transmitted on Channel 4 television on 6 April 1985 to a generally scathing critical reception. 'A vile travesty,' snorted Tom Sutcliffe, the music and opera critic of the Guardian, 'a reminder only of Osborne's maudlin egotism.'[17]

Having perused the 'quaintly peevish' reviews in the newspapers the following Sunday, Osborne promptly 'had a few more glasses of champagne and went into a prolonged coma.'[18] An ambulance, its siren blaring, whisked him from his Christmas Place guests to the Kent and Sussex Hospital, a bed in intensive care and a sudden swoop of doctors. At one point his condition was so critical it seemed that he might not survive and indeed he remained comatose for three days before reviving. 'I emerged', he wrote later, 'not cowed by the brush of the fearful angel's wing but angry and astonished at my determination not to go gentle into any good night . . .'[19] He regained consciousness as 'a young, pretty nurse' was 'beating me alive with her fists.' '"Do you know where you are?" "New York," I suggested. "No," she yelled . . . "No. You're in – Tunbridge Wells!"'[20] Was this what literary critics meant, he wondered, by 'a Kafkaesque experience?' He had over a fortnight to ponder this while being treated by specialists in diabetes and endocrinology, before being pronounced fit to leave hospital on 26 April. Osborne's private theory was that his collapse was attributable to his having ingested rat urine from the water in his swimming pool, rats having been observed ominously in the nearby stables. This evasive notion was given some sketchy credence by a blood test revealing traces of an infection linked, among much else, to rats. His doctors, though, insisted that the real cause of his coma was liver disease, mainly the result both of years of excessive and continuing alcohol consumption, and his failure to take his twice-daily insulin injections at the correct time.

Just over a couple of months later, on 1 July, Thames Television broadcast A Better Class of Person, Osborne's dramatization of part of his autobiography. Starring Alan Howard as Tom Godfrey, Eileen Atkins as Nellie Beatrice, and two actors as Young John and Older John, the play opens as war is declared in 1939 and closes as Nellie Beatrice and John stand at Tom Godfrey's grave. This time, the critical response was divided between the dismissive and the respectful. Byron Rogers in The Sunday Times, thought that 'it went wrong because everyone who appeared was increasingly more frightful . . . the unremitting bitterness deepened and it all went nowhere,' while Andrew Rissick in the New Statesman argued that it was 'one of the most complex, acute and moving' plays that Osborne had produced.[21]

*   *   *

After his return home from hospital and jovially dispatching a case of claret to Dr D. S. J. Maw, a consultant physician at Tunbridge Wells, in gratitude for saving his life, Osborne applied himself to taking his insulin at the prescribed times. At the same time, he attempted to renounce alcohol entirely, succeeding for almost six heroic months before resorting to a concession of two glasses of wine three times a week, inaugurated while on a recuperative holiday with Helen in the south of France. Later, when the shock of intensive care had receded, he reverted to his accustomed robust consumption of champagne. Other periods of abstinence would follow over the years, sometimes for up to a month at a time, only to be spectacularly broken. While playing her part in luring Osborne back from the furthest excesses of alcoholism, Helen, being a heavy smoker and able to maintain her husband's pace in terms of champagne consumption, was not the kind to enforce a domestic creed of harsh abstinence.

Osborne, moreover, treated his health in as careless a manner as he had treated his money. He was like a gambler who finds the most difficult time to leave the blackjack table is when the odds are most stacked against him. He continued, therefore, the near-constant champagne, and neither did he forgo his favourite brand of Turkish tobacco. Instead, he made the smoking of his weekly packet of Turkish cigarettes the subject of one of his bullish anti-European Union campaigns, which he had taken to pursuing in the correspondence columns of The Times. Vehemently protesting that 'a "European" diktat' had prevented his Jermyn Street tobacconist from importing further supplies, he wondered what might be the next target of a pleasure-draining European bureaucracy. Thankfully, he reported a month later, his was not a lone voice of protest against the 'outrages' of Brussels, as 'my front door mat has been buried beneath expressions of sympathy and shared despair.' To his surprise, many had been accompanied by 'huge parcels' of Turkish cigarettes, 'which will probably last me out.'[22]

*   *   *

Turkish cigarettes, champagne, rural living, a contented marriage, a renewed friendship with Pamela and his network of friendships in London and the country provided bulwarks both against a world that Osborne found to be out of joint, and his conviction, never dormant for long, that 'my days in the theatre are over.'[23] A National Theatre revival of The Entertainer, starring Alan Bates in 1985, seemed to prove the point, being scuppered even before rehearsals began, although it was also a case of Osborne appearing to be his own worst enemy. Not only might the production have garnished his resurgent professional reputation, but it would also have brought in some money, both of which Osborne needed very much. Advertised as forthcoming in the company's brochures, it was abandoned after Osborne vociferously objected to Joan Plowright playing Phoebe, Archie Rice's browbeaten wife. Even though the Oliviers and Osborne had been friends for many years, he had harboured a resentment of Plowright since her moral support of Mary Ure during the fraught, final stages of the latter's marriage to Osborne in the 1960s. To the National Theatre, however, he complained that he had not been consulted over the casting, although Peter Hall maintained that he had. The wrangling continued until Hall decided that in the face of Osborne's intransigence, there was no alternative but to cancel the production altogether. Hurt and angry, Osborne retreated, more than ever convinced that the London theatre was hostile territory.

*   *   *

God Rot Tunbridge Wells and A Better Class of Person were the last plays he would write at Christmas Place, for he and Helen were packing their belongings in anticipation of moving. Marsh Green and the surrounding villages were changing, reflecting the aggressive new wealth of London and the prosperous south-east. By the end of the 1970s, the Labour government led by James Callaghan, who had become Prime Minister after Harold Wilson's resignation in 1976, was struggling against a renewed onslaught of disputes and strikes, many of them punitively malicious, by industrial workers and public sector employees. It was even worse than 1974. Manufacturing output fell, while welfare services faltered and sometimes stopped altogether. Uncollected rubbish piled up in London's central squares and lined the streets of every city and town in the land. A road haulage strike resulted in food failing to be efficiently distributed and supermarkets and shops displaying notices listing items temporarily unavailable. Patients in need of treatment were sent home from hospitals, while in Liverpool, a gravediggers' strike resulted in coffins remaining briefly unburied. Unions seemed to exercise a tyrannical hold over their members, impervious to the growing sense of public shock and dismay their actions created. At the National Theatre, performances were abandoned as scene shifters struck. '. . . the tattiness of England now,' sighed an embattled Peter Hall. 'We seem to be presiding over the collapse of decency and integrity without the energy to realize what's happening . . . bully-boy, strong arm tactics rule.'[24] A crescendo of disruption and stoppages during 1978–9 resulted in those bleak and angry months becoming popularly known as 'the winter of discontent'. At Christmas Place, Osborne ruminated upon 'the awful brutishness of most of British life today' and shrank in horror.[25]

When Margaret Thatcher was elected leader of the Conservative Party in succession to Edward Heath 1975, she became not only the first woman to lead a political party in Britain, but one who promised radical and comprehensive economic reforms designed to revive an ailing nation. It was a message the electorate wanted to hear and at the General Election on 3 May 1979, the Conservatives were propelled into power with a comfortable majority of forty-three. People who had never considered voting Conservative before, did so this time. 'It wasn't at all difficult,' admitted Peter Hall. 'In fact it felt positively good: wanting change . . . and we have to change.'[26]

Mrs Thatcher would win two further elections, in 1983 and 1987. 'Thatcherism', a term minted by the journal, *Marxism Today*, dominated the 1980s and a good part of the 1990s. It was a potent creed of economic liberalism combined with an emotional appeal to patriotism and the invocation of 'Victorian values', vaguely defined as one of general self-help and the survival of the economically fittest. It appealed not only to the besieged middle classes but also, crucially, to the disaffected and materially ambitious working classes. Scorning the advocates of liberal consensus as a 'wet-pink orthodoxy' best suited to 'that sunset home of that third-rate decade, the 1960s', Thatcherism privatised national commodities, rooted out the unprofitable and the out of date, vigorously cut back public spending and de-regularised the stock exchange, which threw open its doors to young traders suddenly earning bewildering high salaries and bonuses.[27] But although Martin Esslin had claimed that *Time Present* in 1968 had revealed Osborne to be an 'Edwardian high Tory' committed to 'Victorian values', Osborne had no sympathy with neo-Victorianism or any political doctrine implying division by class and wealth. And in his eyes, Mrs Thatcher, whom he 'loathed', represented an unambiguous and dispiriting return to the meanness and selfishness for which he had condemned the Conservatives during the early 1950s.[28] According to Osborne, politics had long lacked moral convictions, honesty, compassion and any sense of style.

The free market frenzy that brought champagne to the City of London had marked effects in the Home Counties. In Osborne's small corner, a new breed of 'ghastly young exec[utives]', suddenly wealthy stockbrokers and financial advisers, attracted by green fields and good schools for the children, began snapping up cottages and converted oast houses and clogging once quiet, narrow country lanes with their high-performance cars.[29] The commuter belt, which during Osborne's childhood had been tightly buckled about London, loosened and flung itself across the peace of his late-middle years. At Christmas Place, he thrust a placard into the verge outside his gate indignantly protesting at the heavy lorries roaring past; turning his attention to the skies and convinced that pilots used his lake as a marker for beginning their descent into Gatwick Airport, he began obsessively counting the seconds between each flight, complaining that planes flew so low he could clearly see the whites of the pilots' eyes.

The longing for a mellow, more peaceful England drove the Osbornes to more remote surroundings and another new start. In the summer of 1986, Christmas Place was put on the market for £350,000. It was the thirtieth anniversary of Look Back in Anger that year, and on 8 May, Pamela sent Osborne a congratulatory note: 'My dear B[ear] – Happy Anniversary today . . . thinking of you. Much love S[quirrel].'[30] Six months later, on 24 November and with Christmas Place sold and leaving the new owners to dredge a silted lake where they discovered hundreds of empty champagne bottles, he and Helen moved to Shropshire, 'the heart of unchanging, timeless England' and the furthest Osborne had ever lived from London.[31] During Osborne's ownership, Christmas Place had had a curious history of harmony and discord. It had been a sanctuary for a fugitive, the setting for a failed attempt at family life, the stage for the lavish hospitality of a country gentleman, and a place of champagne, cigars and roast beef; of breakfast in bed, fireworks and garden parties.

They moved into The Hurst, from the outside at least an imposing stone-built mansion of twenty rooms built in 1812 near Clun, a village nestled in a valley not far from Ludlow. It was surrounded by extensive gardens dotted with trees and beds of potentially resplendent rhododendrons, beyond which rose rolling hills, 'those blue remembered hills', as the poet A. E. Housman had mused, 'the land of lost content'.[32] It is a landscape at once timeless, yet one in which time is measured in the changing skies and seasons, a place close to Osborne's imagined England, of what it might once have been and could be again. Like Anthony Creighton when he had bought the Egret, Osborne bought The Hurst as soon as he saw it, without bothering to commission a structural survey. He should have done: the house seemed to have been abandoned in a hurry and desperately needed extensive repairs. Chimneys were blocked and crumbling, plaster had fallen from ceilings, floors sagged alarmingly and the plumbing, masonry and woodwork all required urgent attention. The Osbornes arrived with their belongings, two horses and three dogs, took on a housekeeper and a gardener and began energetic renovations, which included installing a grand and expensive Aga stove in the kitchen. It became the centre of the house, a place of talk and dogs and where guests would meet. One of the first local visitors, the Revd Prebendary Richard Shaw, remembered champagne always being available. 'It did not seem to matter what time of day it was – generous hospitality was always on offer.'[33] Standing on his doorstep, Osborne would boast that 'I might be the poorest playwright in England, but I've got the best views.'[34]

Shropshire bolstered his image of himself as a country gentleman. Even though he was a Londoner and had lived in London or had had a London address for almost fifty years, and the central characters in his plays are urban people, Osborne was happiest in the country. For several years now he had adopted the appearance and dress of the wealthy rural property owner: half-moon glasses, a beard, casual jackets, bow ties, cravats and jaunty, multi-coloured kerchiefs, and in the colder months heavy outer coats with high collars and wide lapels to give added protection against the wind. Nowadays, as part of his health regime, he walked the lanes and the fields surrounding The Hurst with his dogs bounding before him, swinging his stick and sometimes thrusting a portable cassette player into his pocket and clamping headphones over his ears: 'The Dragoon Guards and the Highland Brigade get me up the lower slopes. Handel may lift me to the peak.'[35] Rural living suited him. Shropshire was essentially English and a place where he could indulge his conception of Englishness and English culture, in which, as Peter Ackroyd has written, 'the reverence of the past and natural affinity with the landscape join together in a mutual embrace.'[36]

On jaunts to London – sipping champagne on the train on the way – and even though he was strapped for cash, he and Helen would stay at the Cadogan Hotel in Sloane Street, notable as being where Oscar Wilde was arrested in 1895 and certainly not a place for the budget-conscious traveller. His bill and other outgoings were charged to his credit cards. Perhaps he thought of the Cadogan as the kind of place where a country gentleman might put up, his wardrobe for town now often consisting of three-piece suits, even a watch-chain, flowering, floppy bow ties and flowing overcoats ornamented with a variety of complicated flaps and overlays. A large red signet ring swelled over the third finger of his right hand. He looked rather like an Edwardian actor-manager.

The views on his walks and from his front door were certainly breathtaking, but then so were his debts. Concessions had been made: the cars, the Buick, the Alvis, the Jaguar and the Bentley, playthings of the metropolis, were long gone, there were no more garden parties where hundreds of guests had enjoyed lavish hospitality, and a holiday cottage in Cornwall, at 8b The Lugger, in the fishing village of Portscatho, a Betjemanesque whimsy that he had bought a few years previously, was quickly dispensed with. But far from emerging from the sale of both Christmas Place and the cottage with the profit for which he had planned, Osborne discovered that in The Hurst, he had taken on an even greater liability. Renovations were devouring money, while his new local accountants told sad tales of tax arrears amounting to almost £99,000 and a Barclays Bank overdraft nudging £100,000. Moreover, there were outstanding medical, dental and fuel bills, and Osborne's wine merchants were showing disturbing signs of anxiety. Although he could normally rely on an annual income of about £50,000 from the worldwide productions of his plays, a good deal of that coming from Look Back in Anger, which had faithfully paid the mortgage for years, Osborne's latest statements showed that his most recent earnings were half that. Money was leeching away much faster than he could earn it, and had been for a long time.

But once his books were on their shelves, his pictures on the walls, the champagne uncorked and with Don Giovanni bursting from the stereo, Osborne pronounced himself invigorated and inspired as never before. Great plays, he cried, were waiting to be written. A few years ago, he had an idea for a play about Judas Iscariot; surely he could return to that, and to his notes for a play about the Third Reich. 'But whatever it is, it will be large,' he promised an interviewer. 'I want a Titian-sized canvas: no more miniatures.'[37] He was even contemplating writing a television biography of Vivien Leigh incorporating excerpts from her films. By now, he had also equipped himself with another new agent. This was Gordon Dickerson, who was formerly Kenneth Ewing's assistant at Peters, Fraser and Dunlop. Following its acquisition by an American sports and events company, Ewing and several agents had found themselves unhappy witnesses to a company in a state of considerable turmoil. Deciding to jump ship and having persuaded Dickerson to set up on his own, Osborne promised to become his first client 'as a beacon to encourage others.' Several were. 'I think he was pleased and proud to have encouraged me on to the next stage of my career and life,' thought Dickerson.[38]

At least Osborne had the sustenance of journalism. The man whose relationship with journalists had been bitterly hostile for much of his career had always written occasional pieces on demand and fired grapeshot salvoes to the letters pages of various publications, but now he asserted himself rather more. The Observer, the New York Times and The New York Review of Books petitioned him for book reviews. It was an art to which he was well suited, providing him with a platform from which to demonstrate that he had lost none of his flair for a well-turned phrase in either admiration or condemnation. In his review of Timebends, Arthur Miller's autobiography, he saluted the enviable fact that, at seventy-two, Miller had lost neither his love of the theatre nor run out of things to say. Perusal of Noël Coward's Diaries and republished Autobiography gave him the opportunity to assert that Coward's achievement was to have been his own invention and to have written in Hay Fever, Private Lives and Blithe Spirit, three of the finest comedies in the English language. Artfully avenging himself upon

Peter Hall, he ridiculed the director's *Diaries* of the first years of his tenure at the National Theatre as a monumental exercise in vanity, 'a numbing record of banal ambition, official evasiveness and individual cupidity.'[39]

Hurling himself into renewed dissent, he upped his rate of letter-writing to the newspapers, developing a distinctive style of genial rural grumpiness. In the *Guardian*, he disputed Michael Billington's contention that Shaw was 'the greatest British dramatist since Shakespeare' by retorting that he was 'the most fraudulent, inept writer of Victorian melodrama ever to gull a timid critic', and that he 'wrote like a Pakistani who has learned English when he was twelve years old in order to become a chartered accountant.'[40] This 'friendly correspondence', he told *The Times*, had resulted in 'a lot of good-natured banter.'[41] Yet reviewing the first volume of Michael Holroyd's 'superb, Freud-free and moving biography' of Shaw a few months later gave him pause for thought: 'What always seemed to me examples of Shavian banalities and chilly posturing', he admitted, 'reveal themselves as weapons of a lifelong struggle against loneliness and imperfection, of heroic persistence and courage.'[42] Shaw, he was almost convinced, and to his great surprise, was a kindred spirit.

At the same time, he began writing a regular and vividly splenetic diary column for the *Spectator*, a weekly magazine supporting the Conservative interest and which paid a nominal £125 for each contribution, revealing a refreshingly humorous, gently self-mocking touch. 'Oddly enough,' he told Richard Eyre, who had succeeded Peter Hall as director of the National Theatre, 'only journalists, who have been my lifetime's adversaries, seem to have grasped that I STILL can write with more GRASP and FLIGHT than most people.'[43]

From his eyrie in the Shropshire hills, he defended the pastoral and the traditional and railed against the brash, the self-serving and the contemporary. He looked back in nostalgia to his days at the Royal Court, eulogising George Devine and those he, Osborne, admired: John Betjeman, Terence Rattigan, Noël Coward and Max Miller. He buoyantly kept his readers up to date with selected medical troubles. His morning muesli and other crunchy foods proving hazardous to his fragile teeth, he relayed news of his 'prolonged' encounters 'strapped down' by the 'British Dental Gestapo'.[44] Having experienced Intensive Care, he advised that instead of 'enduring hospital [lunch and dinner] menus', the patient should opt instead for three breakfasts a day. His own experience, he explained, was that a satisfying breakfast of poached eggs, bacon and wholemeal toast was the sole meal that could not be 'violated by bland dieticians and working-class cooking.'[45]

He enjoyed himself deriding the further extremes of the homosexual liberation and the feminist movements, scorned modern innovations in church liturgy and the efforts of 'trendy' vicars, and, like his old hero George Orwell before him, lamented the corruption of the English language. The invasion of 'peoplespeak' into public life, he declared, 'a *lingua franca* of joined-up recently minted clichés' was something to be rigorously exposed and denounced. Examples included 'a level playing field', 'targeted', 'taken on board', 'user-friendly', and the phrase 'No problem' used as a reply to an enquiry. 'Last week,' he recounted, 'on doctor's orders, I telephoned a pathology factory to organize a blood test. "No problem." How can they possibly know until I've had it? But I do hope they're right.'[46]

He also recorded the receipt of grim warnings from the Daughters of Eve, an extreme feminist organisation operating from Berkeley, California, who accused him of having perpetrated 'Fatal Damage' upon Jill Bennett. His British co-accused, he noted, were Harold Pinter ('Fatal Damage to his first wife, the actress Vivien Merchant') and, predictably, Ted Hughes ('Fatal Damage to Sylvia Plath'). The Daughters, who he depicted as pagan, witch-like figures, threatened him, in his absence, with a 'trial by the Daughters' jury'. The resulting transcript, he suggested, 'should make for a fruity evening at the Royal Court [Theatre] Upstairs.'[47]

During the summer of 1987, a severe abdominal pain alerted him to the fact that since their arrival in Shropshire, despite being diagnosed with diabetes and prescribed insulin, neither he nor Helen had registered him with a local doctor. Frantic telephoning secured him an appointment with Dr Jill Gray, a young local practitioner in her twenties whom Osborne decided he would trust and who immediately ordered him into the Nuffield private hospital in Shrewsbury for an operation on a hernia. Once discharged, he flew to Venice with Helen to recuperate at the Danieli, a luxury hotel overlooking the lagoons. The shock of his illness jolted him into giving up drinking for three weeks.

Antipathy towards Peter Hall did not, however, prevent Osborne from accepting a National Theatre commission to prepare a new translation of Strindberg's *The Father* for production in October 1988. Quickly reading the play in its first, eighty-year-old translation from the Swedish, he discovered that even in a version stilted with Edwardian cadences, it immediately fired his imagination. Its central character, the Captain, is a military man and amateur scientist whose purposeful wife, Laura, defies him by insisting that their daughter, Bertha, should become a painter. The Captain, claiming patriarchal authority, argues that she should become a teacher. A battle of wills ensues during which Laura implies that he might not actually be Bertha's biological father, a devastating blow that unhinges her husband entirely.

Strindberg seldom did anything by halves, and neither did Osborne, who discovered a personal resonance in the play's portrayal of a husband and wife at loggerheads and its dissection of discord between a father and daughter. He also felt an immediate and instinctive affinity with Strindberg himself who, during an enormously productive but emotionally hazardous life in which he married three times and suffered a mental breakdown, had found the time to write a pile of plays, novels, short stories and journalism, being alternately lauded as a sage and vilified as a scoundrel. 'I had never felt such proprietary instincts for the work of another playwright,' Osborne enthused as he settled down to work. 'If anyone was to carry the Strindberg torch into the arena, I knew I was destined to be undisputed front runner.'[48] Appointing himself 'Strindberg's Man in

England' and working from a literal translation into English that he spruced and modernised here and there, Osborne produced 'a feisty new version' approved Michael Billington later, entirely in keeping with Strindberg's 'wonderfully demented single-mindedness'.[49]

Because he recognised in Strindberg a fellow dissident, maligned and mis-understood, The Father is Osborne's most successful adaptation of another playwright's work. Directed by David Leveaux and starring Alun Armstrong as the Captain, the production opened at the Cottesloe Theatre on 26 October 1988, 'a surging, unstoppable nightmare', wrote Irving Wardle, 'backed by bursts of amplified music and double doors flying open.'[50] Other critics were equally appreciative, remarking that Strindberg and Osborne were particularly well suited. Yet Osborne did not attend the premiere. Having appeared once, rather drunk, during rehearsals, he developed a Strindbergian antipathy towards the production, informed the theatre that he disowned it and bolted back to Shropshire.

*   *   *

Osborne might have withdrawn to Housman's blue remembered hills, but as far as the popular press was concerned, he had not entirely disappeared. The Daily Mail especially liked to keep itself up-to-date with the relationship between the playwright and his daughter. The previous year, Nolan had turned twenty-two, although her father had not acknowledged her birthday other than informing the newspaper that he had no idea of where she was or what she was doing. In fact, she was preparing for her wedding, and on 13 June 1987, she married Stephen Parker, a financial consultant. Penelope was present, and Jill sent a cheque as a wedding present. Two years later, when a mutual acquaint-ance told Osborne that Nolan was expecting her first child, he replied tersely that he had no interest in becoming a grandfather. He was equally unmoved when a second grandchild was born two years later.

Between these unregarded births, there came news of more deaths. Laurence Olivier and Samuel Beckett died in 1989, the one in Brighton and the other in Paris. Osborne himself was sixty that year, although a birthday celebration at the Garrick Club was hurriedly cancelled when a few days beforehand he plunged into one of his recurring periods of despondency, always at their most malign during December and January, and professed himself unable to attend. At such times, insomnia held him in its grip and he would sit alone in his kitchen through the long dark hours, worrying over his debts or, when he felt at his most desperately unemployable, gazing at a late-night television programme advertising local job vacancies. In the spring of 1990, news filtered through that John Dexter, the part-model for Webster in Look Back in Anger, had died of a heart attack, aged sixty-four. And in the autumn, news of another death inspired one of his most venomous tirades.

*   *   *

On 5 October 1990, Jill Bennett, addicted to tablets and an alcoholic, committed suicide in London. Convinced that at sixty she was friendless and unloved, she had swallowed a lethal dose of barbiturates. Her body was discovered the following morning by her secretary and the funeral held at Putney Vale Crematorium six days later, when the Reverend Guy Bennett officiated. Osborne did not attend. Since their divorce, Jill had continued working in the theatre, appearing most notably as Gertrude in a production of *Hamlet* at the Royal Court in 1980. She was 'a great actress', said the Revd Bennett during his address, a woman 'vulnerable to life's traumas' who 'gave and attracted love in a way that only so sensitive a person could do.'[51]

Her former husband thought otherwise. Having read the tributes to Jill in the newspapers ('Who do we know with such gaiety?' asked Lindsay Anderson) and now liberated from his agreement that he would not write about or discuss his former wife without her consent, Osborne vengefully composed his own obituary.[52] For several years, he had vented his spleen by defacing photographs of Jill in his collection, adding Hitlerian moustaches and dollar signs in black marker pen. But now, flexing his fingers over his typewriter, he geared himself up to full throttle ignition and got down to 'this matter of Adolf', firing off an unremittingly caustic, five-page denunciation of what he derided as Jill's vanity, avarice and emotional tyranny. The manner of her death, he claimed, was a 'final, fumbled gesture, after a lifetime of glad-rags borrowings, theft and plagiarism', and 'must have been one of the few original or spontaneous gestures in her loveless life.'[53]

This vindictive tirade was published as 'Vale Nora Noel', a breathless, last-minute insertion into *Almost a Gentleman*, the long-awaited second volume of his autobiography, its title deriving from a remark by Cardinal Newman in his 1852 treatise, *The Idea of a University*: 'It is almost the definition of a gentleman to say he is one who never inflicts pain.' The book covers a further eleven years, from 1955 and the creation of the English Stage Company until 1966 and the death of George Devine. Osborne's response to Jill's death was added, despite the appeals to the contrary of his publisher, as the book went to press. 'How do I know that Adolf did not intend to kill herself?' he wrote. 'Very simple. Her body contained hardly a trace of alcohol. She was relying on someone "coming on her" sufficiently comatose for a good night's sleep but not enough to feel the brush of angels' wings.' Her death was therefore nothing other than 'a final common little deceit' perpetrated by 'a woman so demonically possessed by Avarice that she died of it', so ending a life in which 'everything' was 'a pernicious confection, a sham.'[54]

In passing, he noted that 'Adolf has left half a million to Battersea Dogs Home. She never bought a bar of soap in all the time she lived with me . . . She had no love in her heart for people and only a little more for dogs.'[55] In this, however, Osborne was unable to accurately gauge Jill's intentions. The bulk of her estate indeed went to the Dogs' Home, while the Theatrical Ladies' Guild of Charity and her secretary received a small legacy apiece. Jill's will had been drawn up some years earlier when she had barely £20,000 in the bank, yet when the subsequent death of her mother left her a comparatively rich woman, she had instructed her solicitor to draw up a new will in which her estate was to be redistributed. 'By a series of mistakes and legal entanglements worthy of Evelyn Waugh and Dickens', the procedure was incomplete at the time of her death and the original will was therefore judged to be still in effect.[56] Although Osborne was unaware of this, it would not have affected his opinion of the woman to whom he was married at the lowest period of his life.

Osborne had once imagined Jill to be a respite from the intellectual and social competitiveness of Penelope, which had left him floundering in its slipstream. One of his greatest vulnerabilities was his sense of his social background being inferior to that of many of the people he knew, and Penelope's natural social and professional confidence had exposed this all the more. Ironically, a similar sense of class difference, amongst other things, had separated him from Jill. 'One of the great differences between them,' observed Brian Cox, 'was that he was lower-middle class and she was upper-middle class. Their relationship took on a sense of grand-guignol and a lot of acrimony seeped through.'[57] 'I think what really hurt him was her patrician contempt,' surmised Richard Eyre.[58]

Like its predecessor, *Almost a Gentleman* was praised on its publication in the autumn of 1991 for the combative brio of its writing, and subsequently won the Ackerley Prize for Autobiography. Yet even those who had been entertained as much as shocked by his treatment of his mother in *A Better Class of Person*, were horrified at the cruelty with which he had written of Jill. Its inclusion in a book entitled *Almost a Gentleman* provided clear evidence for many of the considerable lengths he still had to go. A bemused John Carey, a professor of literature at Oxford, reviewing the book in *The Sunday Times*, suggested something was clearly wrong with its author. 'The weirdness of Osborne's dealing with women is the most obvious sign of his disturbed state,' he wrote. 'As he introduces us to each new partner, he scarcely pauses for breath before passing from admiration to blistering caricature.'[59] Anthony Page thundered into print, publishing a defence of Jill Bennett, 'my friend for thirty years', across two pages of the *Guardian* and complaining that 'I profoundly resent her being subject to this grubby memorial.' Appalled by 'John's habit of turning on his past wives and friends', he attributed Osborne's 'shifts of feeling' to 'his vehement lack of feeling in people and situations not directly relating to himself.'[60] Recording his reflections of the book in his diary, Richard Eyre noted that 'It's quite easy to understand him in the first half, in love with success . . . Then he becomes psychopathic – he appears to have no feelings and it becomes impossible to understand his actions or anything except for his bitter resentment at being cast out of paradise.'[61] Osborne, however, swept all carping aside. He had said what he wanted to at last. Besides, he was ready, against the odds, to climb combatively back into the ring with a new play.

Déjàvu, originally entitled *Déjàvu or, Everybody Wants you When You're Down and Out*, is a sequel of sorts to *Look Back in Anger*, which was revived in 1989 in a production directed by Judi Dench at the Lyric Theatre, Hammersmith. Kenneth

Branagh, highly acclaimed for a string of Shakespearean roles including Henry V and Hamlet, played Jimmy Porter, while Emma Thompson appeared as Alison. Osborne, however, was disconcerted to discover that the producers had scheduled a benefit performance at the Coliseum in aid of Friends of the Earth, for which 'they expected me to donate my royalty. I said: "Here am I, a penurious playwright; 10% of the Coliseum is not something I can afford to give up." You may be Friends of the Earth but what about the Friends of John Osborne?'[62]

Successfully placated and asked for his advice on the play, Osborne told the cast to 'remember the play is a comedy, not about some young man ranting and raving. Make it light.' 'I didn't expect them to take any notice' he gratefully remarked later, 'but they took it like tablets of stone.'[63] The result was that Branagh 'succeeded in taking the rant out of the part' and vindicated Osborne's perception of Jimmy Porter being a comic creation. That the production was played as an ensemble piece also revealed his original purpose in that it was Alison and not her husband 'who was the most deadly bully. Her silence and her obdurate withdrawal were impregnable.'[64]

He also directed the actors' attention to the language. 'The pursuit of vibrant language and patent honesty, which I always believed the theatre and the now abandoned liturgy of the Anglican church could accommodate, was my intention from the outset,' he added. Osborne frequently compared his writing to the precise notation of a musical score, and the longer speeches to operatic arias. Like the writing of Shakespeare, Pinter and Beckett, it was 'an intricate mechanism,' he insisted, meticulously constructed. 'The "ands" and the "buts" are the map-markings of syntax and truth, not the stammering infelicities of another's haphazard personal selection.'[65] In Déjàvu, he intended to pick up the same voice, thirty-six years on.

CHAPTER 30

Redemption

DÉJÀVU IS NOT A TRUE SEQUEL to Look Back in Anger but more of an improvisation upon it, both darting away from and winding itself back to the original. The exercise appealed to Osborne as a technical one as much as anything else, but the prospect of Jimmy Porter resurrected would, he thought, be bound to arouse commercial interest. There was also the additional advantage in that his old protagonist surely provided an ample megaphone for his thoughts on whatever subjects he decided to include. Taken together, Look Back in Anger and Déjàvu would form elegant bookends to a career spanning almost forty years of writing for the London stage.

He began writing on 9 December 1988, and continued as he fought a renewed onslaught of failing health and negotiations with creditors and tax officials: 'Inland Revenue disaster,' he noted gloomily in his journal in March of the following year.[1] By this time, 'health deteriorating alarmingly', he was 'struggling to finish' the last few pages, and by 10 April he had the play complete.[2] 'I might have done the best thing in my life,' he thought.[3]

This time, the curtain rises not upon the Porters' attic flat in Derby but the large kitchen of a country house, 'the kind sometimes advertised as "a minor gentleman's residence"', where Jimmy Porter (now known simply as JP and, like his creator, in his early sixties), lives alone. With a 'huge' Aga having replaced the gas cooker of the earlier play, it is much the same kind of kitchen in which Osborne ate his breakfast of muesli and whole-wheat toast each morning.[4] JP and Cliff, now a BBC producer and visiting from Twickenham, are once again reading the Sunday newspapers while a young woman wearing a t-shirt bearing the legend 'I AM SCUM' (a reference to Somerset Maugham's verdict on the state-aided university students to which Jimmy Porter belongs), is stationed at the ironing board. However, it transpires that the original Alison, Jimmy's wife in Look Back in Anger, left her husband several years ago, and the young woman now at the ironing board, also called Alison, is JP's daughter by a failed second marriage. A young woman called Helena reappears as Alison's friend, and later, as in the original, takes her place at the ironing board, her own t-shirt proclaiming that: 'JP IS SCUM – OK'.

Essentially a conversation piece, *Déjàvu* is disconcertingly inconsistent and meanders across vast stretches of waste ground. Yet there are also sections in which it seems that Osborne has recovered much of his old eloquence and combative bravado, adding a lightness of touch that had not always been apparent hitherto. As with many of his predecessors, the subjects of JP's loathing are those of his creator's and a catalogue familiar to the readers of his *Spectator* diary columns: the inertia and the limited horizons of youth; liberal education; politics; contemporary culture; the 'caring professions', the platitudes of bureaucrats and 'trendy' clergymen, and the vicissitudes of the contemporary world in general. After thirty-six years, JP is still 'a spokesman for no one but myself', still bilious, still melancholic, but he is also much more evidently a comic figure, harsh but arguably more charitable, and ostensibly more at ease.[5] By the end, he achieves a palpable sense of acceptance, even serenity, a spiritual coming to terms with himself, as if he has either overcome the obstacles before him or ceased to regard them as such. And, at last, in almost the final words he wrote for the stage, both Osborne and JP attempt to answer the question that had been snapping at their heels since 1956:

'"What's he angry *about*?" they used to ask. Anger is not *about* . . . It comes into the world in grief not grievance. It is mourning the unknown, the loss of what went before without you, it's the love that another time but not this might have sprung on you, and greatest loss of all, the deprivation of what, even as a child, seemed to be irrevocably your own, your country, your birthplace, that, at least, is as tangible as death.'[6]

There are moments of self-reflection, and moments too, of nostalgia, although the 'Edwardian Age' declares JP, the age shimmering in remembrance and imagination in the background of several of Osborne's plays, 'never existed. The *on dit* is that there never were long days in the sun, the slim volumes of verse . . . No, not only did we, did I at least, footlingly regret the passing of other people's worlds, they were ones we'd just confected for our vulgar comfort.'[7] Yet at the close of the play, JP stands alone, resurgent, triumphantly undefeated, arms aloft and beating time to the Champagne Aria from Mozart's *Don Giovanni*. He ends with 'a grand operatic flourish, the most upward theatrical inflexion he can muster and stands defiantly.'[8] This was also very much as Osborne would like to see himself: resilient and resurgent at the finish. In *Déjàvu* John Osborne had written his own valediction.

As in *Look Back in Anger*, there are several characters referred to but not seen. Alison, JP's first wife, is referred to in passing, while his unnamed second wife bears a passing resemblance to Penelope Gilliatt in that she has 'an obsession with what her sort of friends call "first-class minds".'[9] Hugh Tanner, Jimmy's old friend, has become a Tony Richardson figure, working on various film projects and living in California, a man to whom JP talks frequently, as Osborne

himself sometimes did to Richardson, late at night on the telephone. Colonel
Redfern is remembered affectionately as having given JP some money after his
separation from Alison. He was, observes JP, a kindly man who had the patrician quality of magnanimity, something that he and his creator had come to
admire. Jimmy, JP's son from his second marriage and young Alison's sister, on
the other hand, has few if any redeeming features and, having been charged by
the police with vandalizing a church war memorial, has been befriended by the
Reverend Ronald Peplow, the kind of community-minded, Alternative Service
Book vicar of whom Osborne was scathingly contemptuous. Peplow is probably very loosely modelled on the Reverend Guy Bennett, in that he provides
a home not only for Jimmy but also for Alison, who, dismissing her father
as both unloving and unlovable, leaves him to join the Peplow household, as
Nolan had joined the Bennetts.

*   *   *

On 25 June 1989, Osborne returned to the Nuffield Hospital, where he
underwent further surgery to his damaged hernia. At the same time, he was
preoccupied with guiding *Déjàvu* on what became a rancorously tempestuous
journey to production, made all the more difficult as by now Osborne was
ailing, suffering recurring bouts of nausea, migraine and insomnia, and requiring more than ever a peaceful and stringently regulated life. Although still
drinking far too much champagne, he made valiant attempts to regulate his
diabetes but frequently omitted to take his insulin injection at the prescribed
times, allowing his diabetes to become uncontrolled. Sometimes, this resulted
in distressing hypoglaecemic attacks during which he suffered a seizure and lost
consciousness. Once, he collapsed while out on a long walk in the hills, luckily
being revived after being discovered by a fellow rambler. On another occasion:
'I really thought it was d-e-a-t-h flapping its tiny wings against my upturned
face on the drawing room floor,' he wrote in his journal one cold early morning
in October 1989.[10] The list of his infirmities was lengthening alarmingly. The
numbness in his hands and feet was affecting him more regularly. His doctors
diagnosed peripheral neuropathy, a condition arising from his diabetes and
affecting the nervous system. Noticing his vision becoming more impaired, he
became distracted with the fear of losing his eyesight as his father had done,
and took to sheltering behind protective dark glasses. Staring into the mirror
and baring his teeth, he noticed his gums receding further. And the question of
how to pay his debts was gnawing at him continually. The Hurst was heavily
mortgaged and his credit must soon run out: what would he and Helen do, he
wondered, if the bank suddenly called a halt and demanded repayment? All his
hopes, personal, professional and financial, were pinned upon the new play.

At first, Osborne had cause for optimism. From his self-imposed exile in Los
Angeles, Tony Richardson volunteered to direct *Déjàvu*. He and Osborne had
not worked together for over twenty years and to collaborate on the staging

of a sequel to a play that had launched their careers would be a fitting reunion as well as a considerable commercial proposition. 'It's possibly the best play written this century,' Richardson told his old collaborator.[11] Yet Richardson was himself already ill and died of AIDS in the United States in November 1991, aged sixty-three. It was a crushing blow to Osborne, who wept when he heard the news. After their squabbles in the film world, neither man had quite managed to recapture his trust in the other, yet '. . . my love for him had grown into something taunting, mysterious and quite inexplicable,' Osborne wrote. 'The rewards are recorded in scars rather than stars, but I shall never regret one moment in his company . . .'[12] Meanwhile, with rumours circulating of a new stage play, commentators in the daily press began to speculate as to what might constitute Osborne's 'anger' this time round, while others questioned the advisability of resurrecting Jimmy Porter almost forty years on. A cartoon in The Independent shows a furtive, bearded figure in a graveyard at night, warily looking over his shoulder as he prepares to exhume a body beneath a headstone reading 'Youthful Success'.[13]

By this time, the directorship of Osborne's old home, the Royal Court, had rejected the play as outdated and uninteresting, so confirming, in Osborne's eyes, his disparaging views of the new artistic regime at Sloane Square. At the National Theatre, Richard Eyre read it and suggested that instead of their producing it, he, Osborne, should perform JP's speeches as a solo show prior to a performance of Look Back in Anger. This was a proposal, admitted Eyre, which he recognized would merely 'add insult to [the] injury' of rejection.[14] He was right. This was exactly in the spirit in which Osborne received it and he thrust Eyre's letter aside. He found himself reduced to bundling up the script and sending it out again and again, just as he had with Look Back in Anger all those years ago, only for it to bounce embarrassingly from one managerial desk to the next. The difference this time, though, was that the play's perambulations were avidly recorded by the press.

When the independent producer Robert Fox expressed interest, there followed speculation that Alan Bates, the original Cliff, an outstanding Redl in Chichester and a thwarted Archie Rice, might play JP, but negotiations stalled and the venture was called off. And still Osborne's accountants warned of rising debts. Twenty years earlier, in 1968, when he had been rich, had faith in the welfare state and anticipated the future with more equanimity, he acknowledged that the income tax system was 'still largely humane and decent' and added that 'I pay my crippling taxes sadly, as I don't wish to die poor and neglected.'[15] Now, in debt and in poor health and with the Inland Revenue beating at the door, he was contemplating the prospect both of the first and, professionally, the latter. 'I have a new tax inspector,' he morbidly notified Eric Shorter at the Garrick Club, 'a LADY, always the most vindictive – known locally as Lucrezia Borgia.'[16]

Eventually, he turned to Bill Kenwright, a former actor who owned the Liverpool Playhouse and the Thorndike Theatre at Leatherhead, and who had established himself as a leading West End producer. 'I don't suppose the follow-ing proposition will have much appeal,' wrote Osborne, '. . . but would you consider taking over the production?'[17] This time he struck lucky. Kenwright liked Déjàvu and directed it first to Liverpool, from where it was announced that the play would open, with Peter O'Toole, a former Jimmy Porter, in the leading role, on 13 November 1991 prior to a West End transfer. But in three acts and at more than four hours the play was far too long, protested O'Toole. Cuts must be made. Yet Osborne adamantly refused to make any revisions. He had never done so before, he retorted, and after forty years in the business, was not going to start now. Within a month, and before rehearsals began, the proposed production was abruptly cancelled. Following the difficulties at the National Theatre with The Entertainer and The Father, and his alcoholism being widely known in the profession, Osborne was quickly acquiring a reputation of being volatile and obstructive. 'Walkout in anger as Osborne play is scrapped', cried the press.[18] Where O'Toole had retreated, other leading actors advanced, but having read the play and stubbed their toes against Osborne's obdurate refusal to amend the text, hurriedly withdrew. 'Angry old men back out of new-look Osborne', chorused the papers.[19] The infuriated dramatist retaliated by writing to The Times, complaining bitterly of the 'lustreless discourtesy' of 'star' actors.[20]

Undeterred, Kenwright abandoned Liverpool for Leatherhead, a town in Surrey just beyond the furthest edge of the sprawl of Greater London. There were further convulsions before Osborne asked Tony Palmer, who had directed God Rot Tunbridge Wells and had many years of experience in music and opera but had never directed a play before, to take charge of the production. A cast was assembled including Peter Egan as JP and Gareth Thomas as Cliff. 'When I read the play I knew it wouldn't work, but I couldn't turn it down,' recalled Egan. 'Look Back in Anger had been one of the first plays I had seen as a student, and I remember the compelling energy of it. I knew Osborne deserved to be presented again – and that Déjàvu would be his last work. And there were passages in it in which he addresses England and Englishness that were remarkably resonant.'

After almost three weeks' rehearsal, the cast were invited to join Osborne at The Hurst for the day. 'I had never met him before and didn't know what to expect when we arrived,' Egan remembered 'There we were, in his magnifi-cent drawing-room, with a framed poster of Maximillian Schell as Redl on the wall, when the door opened and in wafted John, clutching a silver goblet of champagne. His presence was extraordinary. Everything one had heard about this raging, abrasive character, and that to all intents and purposes he was a very unpleasant man, was utterly dispelled. His manner was rather camp, which was partly his languid demeanour, and given that he began his career in the 1950s, one immediately thought of Binkie Beaumont, and that in his way, Osborne had become a rather Binkie Beaumont figure. He was very frail, and yet he still had a great energy of language.'

Egan was struck too, as many people were, by his charm and humility. 'From the moment I first met him, I was drawn to him, and we became great friends,' recalled Egan. 'John struck me as a man defying gravity. He was very vulnerable, and believed himself betrayed by the theatre and a great many people in it. But that day at The Hurst he was extremely generous, taking the time to talk to each member of the cast about ourselves and what we had done in the past. We walked in the gardens, Helen cooked a wonderful meal and there were of course great quantities of alcohol served as the day wore on. But what was interesting was that he and Helen seemed to have developed almost a private language; the more they drank, the more consonants they slurred, the more they drifted off into a strange ramble between themselves that nobody else could follow, but evidently they did. It was very curious.'[21]

Osborne even agreed to substantial cuts in the script, reducing the length by an hour and the original three acts to a more manageable two. He attended several rehearsals, the actors noticing that although he walked with the aid of a stick and quickly fatigued, when the work was progressing well something approaching the old energy would once again shine in his gaunt features. Osborne offered Egan the same advice as he had given Kenneth Branagh, that JP was 'a man of gentle susceptibilities, constantly goaded by brutal and coercive world' and 'best expressed by a mild delivery . . . Let the text surprise you,' he counselled, 'as if it took you off-balance, and lift you up even further into the battle of defeat and confusion. Take the words out of the air.'[22] 'At first, I just couldn't find a way into playing JP,' recollected Egan. 'Then I realised that of course John Osborne was JP, and that I had to play it as John Osborne.'[23]

Finally, Osborne pronounced himself satisfied with the result: Egan, he proclaimed, had 'triumphed'.[24] Déjàvu opened at the Thorndike Theatre in Leatherhead on 8 May 1992, just over four years since he had completed the script and on the thirty-sixth anniversary of the opening of Look Back in Anger. Changes to the script had continued almost until the curtain rose, with the result that 'I had to read the last scene,' remembered Egan, 'because I'd only had time to learn 90% of it.'[25] This time, Osborne attended the first night and when the theatre manager announced his presence to the audience and he was loudly applauded, expressed astonishment that he should be remembered, and apparently so benignly. A month later, on 10 June, the play transferred to the Comedy Theatre in the West End.

The arrival in London of Osborne's first original stage play for sixteen years was heralded by a flurry of critical speculation and journalistic comment, most of it more warmly welcoming than he might have expected. 'However much one would like to ignore John Osborne,' opined Claire Armistead in the Guardian, 'he has refused to pipe down.'[26] In The Times, the literary critic Philip Howard predicted that 'his works will last much longer than those of his imagined enemies and critics. It will infuriate him to read this, but he is a much-loved national treasure.'[27] The much-loved national treasure responded by declaring that he had never been on better form. He was also fully prepared for all critical eventualities. A recent visit to the dentist had not only equipped him with a pristine smile but also a new bite with which to confront marauding critics ready to 'crunch the bones of a life's work.'[28] 'I'm on red alert,' he assured Kenwright, with 'semtex in my handbag.'[29]

Yet the critical reception of *Déjàvu* was disappointingly circumspect and in some cases resentful, as if a much-anticipated dinner guest had turned out to be a crashing bore. Egan's marathon performance was highly praised but, as for the play itself, it was 'a coarse fiasco', protested Peter Kemp in the austere reaches of the *Times Literary Supplement*.[30] 'What is missing is much in the way of event, let alone plot,' agreed Benedict Nightingale in *The Times*. 'Where is the bile and bite?' he wondered.[31] In the *Daily Telegraph*, however, Charles Spencer opined that 'despite a bumpy and sometimes downright disagreeable ride, the play finally achieves an astonishing depth of emotion', while Paul Taylor in the *Independent* agreed that it was 'not a good play, but a fascinating phenomenon'.[32] In the *Guardian* Michael Billington confessed to being perplexed that Osborne should be 'so haunted by his own creation' as to write a sequel, but confirmed that his rhetoric 'still scorches the senses'.[33] On the BBCs *Late Show*, broadcast after the first-night curtain came down, John Lahr worried that both JP and Osborne had become increasingly isolated from the world around them: 'The voice is self-contained, he doesn't relate, he's locked into this sound, which just wants to broadcast the fact that it exists . . .'[34]

These days there was no Harold Hobson, Osborne's old ally on *The Sunday Times*, to support him even in an unofficial capacity, for Hobson had died a few months previously at a nursing home in Chichester. Yet once more the *Observer* rallied to Osborne's defence, its current critic, Michael Coveney, spirit-edly speaking up for the play on the *Late Show* and in his column the following Sunday. Osborne alone, he asserted, 'raises bilious invective to an art form and reminds us that good theatre is most powerful when it makes us want to shout back.' Recalling that thirty-six years ago Kenneth Tynan had declared *Look Back in Anger* to be the best young play of its decade, Coveney suggested that *Déjàvu* 'could well be the best old one of this'.[35]

Yet perhaps the play's worst enemy was not its battalion of critics but itself, in that it does not entirely stand alone but relies too much upon a thorough and appreciative knowledge of *Look Back in Anger*. It is forbiddingly uneven, while passion is arguably too often replaced by prejudice, and eloquence by coarse-ness. A heatwave did not help its fortunes either. It was a hot summer that year. In London the air was thick and still and even the most successful West End plays were lucky to find good audiences, despite theatres advertising the efficiency of their newly installed air conditioning. Very soon after opening, the *Déjàvu* company found themselves looking out from the stage to less than half-full houses. The theatre circle was roped off and ticket-holders directed to the stalls in an effort to fill the front seats, but to no avail and the play closed after seven weeks.

'I never thought to be treated with such contempt or assaulted by such battalions of mediocrity,' reflected Osborne sadly afterwards.[36] Deep in the Shropshire countryside, surrounded by unpaid bills, he was nursing a profound sense of not being wanted. 'I've half a dozen plays in front of me,' he cried to Jocelyn Rickards. 'But what's the point? No one wants them.'[37]

* * *

Jill Bennett's death in 1990 was followed by Penelope's three years later, on 9 May 1993. She was sixty-one. She had returned from New York to settle in London after an astonishingly successful career, having published several books on film, five novels and seven collections of short stories. She had also written a film screenplay, and the libretto for The Beach of Aurora, an opera commissioned (but not produced) by English National Opera and composed by Thomas East-wood, who had written the music for the original production of Look Back in Anger. Yet she had also continued to drink heavily and had descended into alcoholism. Although there had been other loves since Osborne, including a long and mutually happy relationship with the American theatre critic, Vincent Canby, it was believed by many of those who knew her that Osborne had been her great passion, their time together had been the time of her life and she had never recovered from their parting. She had diligently remembered his birthday each year, in 1976 mailing him the Oxford edition of Chekhov's short stories inscribed: 'For John on your birthday, from Nell with love always.'[38] Knowing of her deterioration, Osborne suspected that her death was imminent, but he was still shocked when he heard the news. They had shared some happy years, he told Eric Shorter. Invited to her cremation service in London, he pleaded instead a pressing and painful dental session. Nolan, though, was there, and later benefited from the sale of the house at Chester Square.

* * *

Déjàvu was Osborne's twenty-second stage play to be produced in his lifetime, and, as Peter Egan had suspected, it turned out to be his last work. It had done little for his reputation and less for his debts. 'Thank heavens for Look Back,' he would reflect frequently. 'It rarely brings in less than £15,000 a year.'[39] But it was not nearly enough. His bank overdraft stood at over £150,000, he still owed £175,000 in Income Tax arrears and his dental bills alone amounted to £18,000. On one appalling morning, as Osborne was 'chewing on some toast during the large breakfast I am obliged to consume, a £25,000 wall of dentistry collapsed as I could only have wished upon the Channel Tunnel.'[40] As his father had done before him many years ago, he was obliged to resort to charity. '. . . pensionless, toothless and maybe eyeless', he appealed for financial help to the Royal Literary Fund, an aid organization for impoverished authors, who responded with a cheque for £6,700, which paid for almost a third of his mouth.[41] Desperate, he sent out more begging letters. 'Apart from being unable to find the money, literally to eat,' he told Robert McCrum, his publisher at Faber, 'I can just about raise the train fare to London . . . I simply beg you to help me continue working without this burden of uncertainty and disruption.'[42] Yet a Faber-led rescue conference was curtly rebuffed. 'If Helen and I are to avoid the gutter,' he informed Gordon Dickerson, 'I must face the fact that I must simply take on ANY OLD WORK that I'm lucky enough to get . . . Whatever "creative" days I may have once assumed are clearly over.'[43] Frequently, he signed his letters as: John Osborne, ex-playwright. 'Every prospect seems gloomy,' he miserably notified Eric Shorter.[44] In his *Spectator* column he ruefully brought his readers up to date with the 'Zuni Curse' inflicted upon him by the Daughters of Eve after his 'trial', the effects of which would be 'peer mockery and artistic failure'.[45] 'Too true,' he admitted. 'Recent months have produced recurring waves of aftershock on the Osborne-Richter scale: loss of memory, eyesight and whirling artistic and financial declension. Stick with the old Zuni, girls.'[46]

Overwhelmed by the clamour for money, he decided to put his most valuable asset up for sale. An original handwritten manuscript of *Look Back in Anger* was therefore submitted for auction at Sotheby's in April 1993, but bids reached only half of the reserve price of £40,000, a sobering sign of the indifference in which his reputation was held. A month later, the Harry Ransom Humanities Research Center at the University of Texas in Austin swooped and gathered up the manuscript and several of Osborne's papers for $50,000. The money touched down briefly in his bank account before being immediately dispatched as part payment to the Inland Revenue.

He made fewer sorties from home these days. Since moving to Shropshire he had seen less of Pamela, and it appears their last surviving letters were exchanged in 1991. There were other intermittent excursions, including a pilgrimage in 1992 to Llandudno, across the border in Wales, to see Ken Dodd. The veteran and much-admired Liverpudlian comedian, pop-eyed and bucktoothed, arms flailing, black hair like an upturned feather duster, represented a last link to the music hall of Osborne's childhood. Dodd's shows, consisting of wild flights of surrealistic fantasy interspersed with songs and quick-fire one-liners, many using the traditional Aunt Sally figures of seaside postcards: 'I haven't spoken to my mother-in-law for eighteen months. I don't like to interrupt her', regularly lasted for several hours beyond their allotted time, Dodd gleefully goading the audience's compliant endurance: 'Do you give in?' Later that year, on 27 September, Osborne travelled to London to accept a Lifetime Achievement Award from the Writers' Guild of Great Britain. The President, the playwright Alan Plater, had met Osborne only occasionally, and remembered him as 'a rare spirit', 'unfailingly courteous, mischievous' and with a 'ready laughter'.[47] The evening, though, proved a catastrophe. Having forgotten to take his insulin injection at the correct time, and having drunk 'a couple of glasses of wine' at the Guild dinner, Osborne was unsteady on his feet as he rose to accept his award and clearly disorientated as he made his way to the podium to make his speech of thanks. Once he was there, he could only mumble a few incoherent words before being helped back to his chair where he was given lemonade to drink and wafers to eat. It appears that as well as being tired, he had begun

to suffer a hypoglaecemic attack, yet the 'press was there in force,' remembered
Plater, and the following day the newspaper coverage was unforgiving. Some
days later, however, Plater received 'a very sweet letter', in which Osborne told
him that 'his lifelong policy had been: never explain, never apologize.' He went
on to explain – about his illness – and apologise. 'I wrote back saying there was
nothing to apologize for.'[48]

The following year, 1993, Osborne travelled Stratford to see his old friend
Robert Stephens playing what would be his last role in the theatre, the title role
in King Lear for the Royal Shakespeare Company. Less happily, Osborne suffered
another chaotic episode at the National Theatre, where Di Trevis was directing
a revival of Inadmissible Evidence with Trevor Eve playing Bill Maitland. The day
on which Osborne attended a rehearsal, during which the cast was looking at a
scene for the first time, work was disrupted by the playwright angrily quarrel-
ling with the company's interpretation and scurrying back to the sanctuary of
the Cadogan Hotel. Again, the story reached the popular press, which seemed
to thrive these days on Osborne's unhappiness. He was later informed by the
theatre that it would not be beneficial if he attended further rehearsals. Humiliated and bitter, Osborne not only complied but did not attend the opening on
17 June either. The production received lukewarm reviews.

To Osborne, the incident once again confirmed his conviction that the
theatrical ground had shifted from beneath his feet. As a writer, his allegiances
and sympathies were primarily with other dramatists; as a former repertory
actor, he believed he also had an instinctive understanding of actors. He could
not comprehend a style of theatre which seemed to him to be in the ascendant
these days, in which the director or the designer appeared the most important
components of a production. He was intensely suspicious of what he perceived
as a directorial vision and judgment being imposed upon a play before rehearsals began, rather than the text being allowed to speak for itself. 'Don't think, by
the way,' George Devine had once warned Anthony Page, 'that your friend John
Osborne won't turn on you like a viper if he didn't think you were benefiting
his plays.'[49] The betrayal Osborne felt most deeply was by directors whom he
judged misinterpreted his work, and an Inadmissible Evidence that conceived of Bill
Maitland being largely defined as a misogynist, was a vivid instance of it. 'This
will certainly be the last production of my work in London during my lifetime,'
he told Richard Eyre sadly, 'and it is a melancholy way to say farewell to one's
profession . . .'[50]

*   *   *

In September 1993, his blood count having fallen alarmingly, Osborne was
taken to hospital suffering from anaemia and underwent an operation for a
duodenal ulcer. The following summer, he and Helen joined fellow members
of the Garrick Club on their annual excursion to the Derby at Epsom, during
which, having again omitted to take his insulin, Osborne disappeared, suffered

a hypoglaecemic attack and was discovered lying unconscious in a field. Setting these mortifications behind him, he published Damn You, England, a bracing, often insightful and richly peevish collection of his journalism from his earliest days to the present. '. . . the book attracted neither the contumely nor feigned indifference I had expected', he noted. In fact, 'It has all been reassuringly enjoyable. I have had telephone calls from old friends and whoopee letters from strangers.'[51] As it often had, and especially of late, recognition and appreciation astonished him and encouraged him in mapping out a new project.

This was England, My England, a lavish, two-hour play commissioned by Channel 4 Television as part of a season of programmes commemorating the tercentenary in 1995 of the death of the composer Henry Purcell. As with God Rot Tunbridge Wells, Osborne was less interested in the nuances of historical period than in expounding upon the relationship between the artist and the society in which he happens to find himself, and thereby providing a portrait of a nation, a celebration of its virtues and a diagnosis of its ills. Conveniently, perhaps, as far as the dramatist is concerned, much of Purcell's life is undocumented. He exists primarily in terms of his work: his operas, including Dido and Aeneas and The Fairy Queen; anthems and chamber music, songs and incidental music for the theatre, 'the soundtrack', in the words of the music critic, Michael White, 'to the lives and deaths of several monarchs, wars and revolutions.'[52] Osborne intended to counterpoint his narrative of Purcell during the reign of Charles II, with that of Charles, a dramatist, in the London of the 1960s researching play about the composer. This twentieth-century narrative would therefore, he imagined, become partly a quest for Purcell and partly – a by now familiar Osborne theme – a search for a lost England. 'It was [Osborne's] view that the reign of Charles II was the pinnacle of English life,' thought the actor Simon Callow, who starred in the film. 'Under a monarch of generosity, wit and imagination, fully aware of the sensuous pleasures and the need for balance and tolerance, English life reached its zenith.'[53]

Yet hardly had Osborne begun work on the play than he was obliged to admit that he was too ill to continue. The project was passed to Charles Wood who completed the play according to the outline Osborne had made. For several weeks Osborne had been failing quickly and visibly; he looked more gaunt than ever; his eyelids drooped, his hair and beard were thin, he walked slowly and with difficulty. He had begun suffering sudden and spectacular nosebleeds amidst his other aches and pains. His doctors diagnosed the onset of ascetis, a liver disease. During the autumn, the blood circulation in his legs became impeded to the extent that he could barely walk at all. Alarmed that his diabetes was out of control, and fearing that he may develop ulcers on the feet that might lead to gangrene and possible amputation, his doctors cajoled a reluctant patient into Intensive Care at the Nuffield Hospital for an operation on his right foot. It was 11 December, the day before his sixty-fifth birthday. He took with him a copy of Holy Living, the book he had elected to take to his desert island. Although the operation appeared to be successful, the extravagances and strains of earlier years and the heedlessness of his later years were flinging him remorselessly towards an untimely death. Unable to cope, his liver and kidneys finally collapsed. A few minutes after 10 o'clock on Christmas Eve, and with Helen at his side, he died. His last mumbled word was 'Sorry.'[54] His death was certified as being caused by a combination of liver failure and cirrhosis of the liver, the result of alcohol poisoning and diabetes. By a quirk of irony, and had she lived, that day would have been Jill Bennett's sixty-fifth birthday.

*   *   *

On 18 July 1984, while living at Christmas Place, Osborne had sat down at his desk and written a draft proposal for his funeral and memorial services complete with 'requests' for music and readings. Had either been performed as he imagined, it would have lasted for about five hours, but as he was now no longer able to object, judicious cuts and changes were made to both. The result was a simple funeral attended by Helen and a small group of friends at St George's Church at Clun on New Year's Day 1995. The National Theatre sent a wreath, but there was no tribute from the Royal Court, the theatre with which his name was indissolubly linked. Nolan had learned of her father's death from the car radio on Boxing Day, as she drove from her home in Sussex to visit the Bennetts at Oxted Rectory. She felt 'nothing', she told the Rector, 'absolutely nothing other than sympathy for the people who were fond of him that it happened at Christmas.'[55] Her father had not attended the funerals of three of his former wives nor that of his mother, and neither did his daughter attend his. Death failed to reunite his family.

Almost two hundred miles to the north, snow whipped and flurried through the bitingly chill air in the village churchyard. Osborne's coffin was carried from the church and lowered gently into its grave. A trumpeter sounded a lonely Last Post.

CHAPTER 31

Afterlife

THE FIRST FEW MONTHS of Osborne's afterlife were to prove as eventful and as turbulent as his mortal years. Within days of his death, newspapers were brimming with lengthy obituaries and tributes, appraisals of his career and generous reassessments of his achievement. He had, it was generally agreed, revitalised the English theatre, although several commentators suggested this had been done when he was twenty-five. Afterwards, his talent had slowly ebbed away and the anger with which he had galvanized the stage when younger had, as he aged, diminished into bitterness. In *The Independent on Sunday*, Irving Wardle mused on the 'tragedy' of John Osborne being that of a writer who had lost touch with his audience. After the death of George Devine, argued Wardle, 'the plays expired like beached fish', and what was once a 'voice of thunder' dwindled into 'one of peevish discontent'.[1]

Reflecting on Osborne's politics, the veteran socialist journalist Mervyn Jones, who had monitored his plays from the late 1950s, suggested that Osborne 'always had left- and right-wing attitudes. The latter became dominant in his later years, as the former had been earlier, but some of his more radical attitudes were never altogether renounced. I found the later plays pretty hollow and boring, but this was because he had nothing new to say – radical or conservative or whatever – so that one was more aware of their strictly literary faults.'[2]

Some commentators were rather more charitable. In his *Guardian* tribute, Michael Billington conceded that 'Osborne fell out of theatrical fashion' and was perceived as 'a rancorous theatrical Thersites', yet argued that his 'unique gift' was 'to create fiercely articulate dramatic heroes who embodied his own wounded and damaged spirit.' A good half-dozen of the plays, he estimated, would make 'a claim upon posterity' – an enviable amount for any dramatist. 'He was, to the very last, a man with a talent for dissent.'[3] John Arden, the Marxist dramatist and polemicist whose first plays had been produced at the Royal Court and who subsequently retreated to Ireland, agreed. Osborne, he

352

declared, was 'a man who stood for individual liberty. There's also something about the English character that delights in being downright awkward. And John Osborne was like this all his life, which meant that he attacked both the political and social left as well as, and as much as, the right. What he hated above all was hypocrisy.'[4] In what might have been an unusual experience, Arden found himself broadly in alignment with a *Times* editorial, grandly entitled 'A Patriot for Us'. Osborne was 'more than a great playwright', concluded the newspaper of record, but a man with 'a love of his country, its customs, music and liturgy . . .' He was 'that rare thing, a persistent rebel'.[5]

Yet it was not Osborne's capacity for dissent but his apparent duplicity that briefly preoccupied the press a few weeks later, at the end of January 1995. Anthony Creighton, then seventy-two, living alone with little money in a small flat in north London, emerged from years of obscurity with an astonishing tale to tell. He and Osborne, he claimed, had had a sporadic and intimate homosexual affair lasting from 1950 until 1961, the period during which Osborne was propelled from being a regional repertory actor to the most successful and talked-about playwright of the day. Creighton chose to make his allegations public in the London *Standard*, an evening newspaper. Talking to Nicholas de Jongh, the paper's theatre critic and author of *Not in Front of the Audience*, a book analysing the representation of homosexuality on the stage, Creighton described his former association with Osborne as 'a love affair, a good, happy, mutually supportive and enduring relationship.' Their physical intimacy, he declared, was a closely kept secret. 'One didn't discuss that sort of thing. It didn't even enter one's mind to talk about it.'[6]

Accompanied by a photograph of a downcast-looking Creighton, de Jongh's article appeared across two pages beneath the lurid headline of 'John Osborne's Secret Gay Love'. The historical background was quickly sketched in: in 1950, Osborne and Creighton were the helmsmen of The Saga Repertory Group at Hayling Island; they subsequently shared a houseboat on the Thames; by the early 1960s Osborne had written four critically acclaimed plays, been married twice – to Pamela Lane and Mary Ure – and divorced once. At the time at which Creighton alleged that their relationship ended, Osborne had left Mary Ure and was planning to live with Penelope Gilliatt, after which, as Osborne's career soared to even greater heights, Creighton's spectacularly plummeted.

Although his revelations provoked shock and fury among Osborne's friends, the nature of the relationship between the two men had provoked fleeting speculation among some of their associates at Hayling Island, Kidderminster and London. Yet conjecture had remained merely that; at Hayling Island and in Kidderminster the two men were liked both as individuals and as company members, while in the early days of the English Stage Company, Creighton was much less in evidence, appearing as a somewhat anonymous figure in Osborne's shadow. Speculation faded and was forgotten.

By chance, Gordon Dickerson had arranged to have lunch with Helen at a London restaurant on the day de Jongh's article appeared. Knowing that she would be late, Dickerson 'picked up the paper on my way into the restaurant and, hey presto, found the story.' It was his unenviable task to break the news to Osborne's widow. Helen 'broke down as soon as she read it', yet recovered to vehemently reject Creighton's claims.[7] Pamela Lane also quickly refuted the story, maintaining that the relationship between the two men when she knew them during the early 1950s, and when she and Osborne had lodged with Creighton in Hammersmith, was close and mutually supportive, but no more. If there was any truth in Creighton's claims, she insisted, then she would have been aware of it, or at least would have suspected it, at the time. Osborne, she contended, was a man unable to keep his allegiances and emotions hidden, and if he had a secret he was withholding from her, then she would have discovered it in Derby, where her husband would have tormented her with it during the storming arguments between them. But there was nothing. The story, she confirmed, was 'unbelievable . . . John and I maintained contact until quite shortly before his death and in all those years I think he would have told me because we were separated anyway.'[8] Sonia McGuinness, who had also known both men, similarly asserted there was 'no foundation whatsoever' to the allegations. Moreover, there was 'no rumour' of there being hidden aspects to Osborne's character within the theatrical profession, one not renowned for its aversion to gossip, 'even at the time of *A Patriot for Me*.'[9]

Creighton's account, as recorded in the *Standard*, was purportedly supported by extracts from letters Osborne had written from Bridgwater and Derby and which were still in Creighton's possession. And indeed, several include declarations of Osborne's affection and loyalty so effusively expressed that it is possible to conjecture whether the writer and recipient are intimately involved. Yet the fulsomeness of his youthful writing, argued Pamela Lane, reflects nothing more than his 'exuberant sense of friendship.'[10] Indeed, throughout his life, Osborne's effusiveness to those in favour equals his vindictiveness towards those who fell foul of him. Jocelyn Rickards, his companion during the late 1950s and early 1960s, also weighed in to denounce Creighton's 'wild flights of fantasy', while saluting, characteristically, Osborne's 'raging heterosexual desires.'[11]

Others also doubted Creighton's testimony. Hugh Berrington, who remembered Osborne as a young man in Ewell and had followed his career with interest, recalled him as being 'narcissistic, but resolutely heterosexual.'[12] And Osborne's lawyer, the pithy and perceptive Oscar Beuselinck who had known his client for almost forty years, agreed that Osborne had never been able to keep his true self hidden, sexual or otherwise. Far from being 'a practising homosexual', he was emphatically, recklessly the opposite. 'You couldn't trust him with women,' emphasised Beuselinck.[13]

Yet the publication of Creighton's interview raised other questions than his veracity. Why had he found it necessary to speak publicly, and why had he chosen to do so only after Osborne's death? Yet Creighton insisted that his motives were purely those of literary elucidation. Osborne, he alleged, had suppressed his homosexuality and loathed himself for it. This hitherto 'hidden aspect' of his personality, he claimed, had decisively influenced his writing to the extent that especially in his later journalism, Osborne had subjected homosexuals to 'derision, contempt and malice. And I think people should be able to appreciate', he added, 'that *A Patriot for Me*, which stigmatizes homosexuality, is a projection of his own self-hatred.'[14]

Creighton, however, admitted that he also considered himself a victim of his former collaborator's 'derision, contempt and malice.' He was, he declared, 'deeply hurt' that in *Almost a Gentleman* Osborne had publicly revealed his, Creighton's, homosexuality 'without my permission', and instead of giving a 'fair' account of their professional association had 'contemptuously' referred to him as a 'wheedling, homosexual drunk.' This, thought Creighton, was a calculated act of betrayal. 'I think', he concluded, 'John was a hypocrite.'[15]

Yet this raised further questions. The second volume of Osborne's memoirs had been published in 1991; if Creighton had been so offended by them, why had he waited over three years and until after Osborne's death to object? Moreover, within twenty-four hours of the publication of his allegations in the *Standard*, it was confirmed that Creighton had kept almost all of the letters Osborne had written to him and was 'seeking a publisher for the collection, to which he intends to add a commentary.'[16] Was the impecunious Creighton hoping that publicity might increase the financial value of the correspondence?

These and other questions remained unanswered. Under fierce attack and lacking corroboration, the story ran out of steam. And was it really of much consequence? In *The Times*, Benedict Nightingale, while agreeing that some of Osborne's writing, especially his later journalism, 'is full of homophobic rhetoric, some of it highly offensive even by his towering standards', contended that none of his plays were altered by Creighton's claims. Even Alfred Redl, the central and homosexual character in *A Patriot for Me*, was one of a long succession of Osbornean characters 'at odds with the pretensions and demands of their eras.' 'Osborne', he added, 'thought and felt his way into the mind of a man at war with his sexuality with a sensitivity and care seldom associated with him.' Rather than anything else, he concluded, 'it shows him to be a gentler man and a subtler dramatist than we usually suppose.'[17]

Creighton subsequently declined to repeat his allegations and later retracted them altogether. 'Yes, he [Osborne] was the most important person in my life,' he asserted, 'but we never had a sexual relationship.'[18] He had concocted a fabrication, he admitted, largely motivated by resentment, fearing that he would be remembered, if at all, as the grubbing figure portrayed by Osborne in his autobiography. And indeed, it might be argued that he had reason to feel slighted by Osborne's unreliable recollections in his two volumes of memoirs, books from which he omitted much, including, to many of those who believed they knew him well, the more considerate and generous aspects of his nature. Certainly, he omitted to acknowledge the depth of the companionship, trust and theatrical alliance that he and Creighton had shared during the 1950s, and the extent to which Creighton had encouraged his writing at a time when for

Osborne such support was invaluable. In drastically, almost mockingly, reducing Creighton's early importance and contribution, Osborne gave him little credit for anything. It was arguably a poor return.

*   *   *

Nicholas de Jongh, who had written the article, was promptly pencilled into Helen Osborne's lengthening list of those who were not to be forgiven, a list supplementing that of her husband's. On 2 June, four names from the Osbornes' inventory found themselves the members of a quartet banned from entering his memorial service at St Giles-in-the-Fields, not too far from the Palace Theatre, where The Entertainer and The World of Paul Slickey had been produced almost forty years previously. 'Look Back in Rancour', cried the Daily Express.[19] 'Osborne Hits Back in Anger from Beyond the Grave', announced The Times.[20] The evidence of this seemingly supernatural rage was a large, shabbily handwritten, glazed and framed notice propped at the church door to greet the assembling congregation of three hundred dramatists, actors, directors and friends.

MEMORIAL SERVICE for JOHN OSBORNE

it read, in thick black felt-tip marker pen.

The Undermentioned will NOT be admitted.
Their names are hereby posted at the gate:

FU MANCHU
NICHOLAS de JONGH
ALBERT FINNEY
the BARD OF HAY-ON-WYE

It transpired that the banished gang of four, none of whom had arrived for the service, had each incurred the incinerating wrath of either Osborne or the equally combative Helen. The notice itself was generally assumed to have been Helen's handiwork. Ever since Peter Hall had closed Watch It Come Down at the National Theatre, Osborne had nicknamed him Fu Manchu, while Nicholas de Jongh had earned his black mark in January. A dispute over royalties from Tom Jones had bubbled away between Osborne and Albert Finney, while Arnold Wesker, the still prolific dramatist and the so-called Bard of Hay-on-Wye, had provoked Helen's displeasure by publishing in the Guardian his reminiscences of a Buckingham Palace reception that he and the ailing Osborne had attended the previous year and in which he alleged that Osborne had been drunk.

The Reverend Gordon Taylor, the elderly rector of St Giles, learned of this 'remarkable' notice from his verger, who had 'found it with its glass broken on the pathway' after the conclusion of the service at which Taylor had officiated.

Taylor was appalled, and even more so when he read in his *Times* the following morning an allegation that it had been 'put outside the House of God apparently without any demur from the clergy.'[21] 'I am in my eightieth year,' he protested, 'and the fame or otherwise of my congregation is a matter of indifference to me but my principles are not.' He was ignorant of the existence of the offending notice, he asserted, but had he known of it: 'I would immediately have had it removed.'[22]

Inside the church, however, Osborne's memorial service was conducted with a decorum more befitting its eighteenth-century ecclesiastical atmosphere. The English Chamber Orchestra played Elgar's 'Chanson du Matin' and Handel's 'Let the Bright Seraphim'. Yvonne Kenny sang Purcell's 'Fairest Isle', and Michael Ball, who had appeared in *England, My England* and several West End musicals, sang 'If You Were the Only Girl in the World', 'one of the greatest songs ever written,' thought Osborne.[23] Peter Egan read extracts from *Look Back in Anger* and *Déjàvu*, and the voice of Laurence Olivier as Archie Rice crackled briefly from loudspeakers. The actor Richard Griffiths read from *Henry IV*, Sir Dirk Bogarde from *Holy Dying* and Dame Maggie Smith from *Pilgrim's Progress*. In his address, the playwright David Hare celebrated Osborne's decade of achievement at the Royal Court as years that had regenerated the British theatre. Of all the playwrights of the twentieth century, he declared, Osborne had been the most daring and had taken the most chances in his writing. As a result, he had frequently offered his audiences the most rewards.

*   *   *

Yet despite Osborne having secured a place in English cultural history, his attaining the gentlemanly trappings of an impressive Shropshire home and a flamboyant wardrobe, and even an aristocratic level of debt, there was one aspect of nobility he lacked. The country, in the form of the Queen or Prime Minister, had not sought to offer him any official recognition. Although Arnold Wesker had lobbied his local Member of Parliament to put forward Osborne's name for a knighthood, no proposal had materialized and therefore the dramatist who liked to describe himself as 'a radical who dislikes change' had not been placed in the invidious position of deciding whether to accept or decline.[24] What his decision might have been is debatable. However, an alternative, unofficial accolade, which he might have thought equally appropriate, had been bestowed only four days before his death. Anthony Astbury, a poet, memoirist and co-director with Harold Pinter of the Greville Press, which specializes in fine editions of poetry, notified Osborne that, in his view at least, 'since the death of [the idiosyncratic poet] George Barker a couple of years ago, you have taken over the mantle of the greatest living Englishman!'[25]

Meanwhile, a gravestone had been erected in Clun Churchyard, bearing the inscription of 'John Osborne Playwright Actor and Friend'. His adversaries and those he had swept to one side might have thought the last appellation to be stretching the truth until it snapped, but friendship, like loyalty, as Osborne defined it, was something he held in high importance. Besides, it rang a satisfyingly pastoral note and it had appealed to him ever since, while visiting Bath, he had seen a plaque commemorating John Christopher Smith, the amanuensis of Handel, which read: 'Handel's Friend and Secretary'. 'I thought that was marvellous,' he declared and decided to appropriate it for himself.[26]

Osborne's death also left his widow with eye-watering debts of £337,000 and an enormous house that required constant maintenance but which Osborne had urged her not to give up. Already some of the uninhabited rooms were falling into dilapidation. A solution was provided partly by the Harry Ransom Humanities Research Center which, for $200,000 acquired a further substantial batch of Osborne's play scripts, private journals, letters, business papers and assorted odds and ends. Any evidence on paper that might provide researchers with clues to the man and his work were carefully collected, docketed and ferried to Austin, Texas, where, once catalogued, they took their place in The John Osborne Archive, their repose meticulously monitored by humidity gauges and carefully calibrated air conditioning.

A further economic lifeline was thrown by 'Grey' Gowrie, otherwise the Earl of Gowrie, a former Conservative Arts Minister and then Chairman of the Arts Council of England, and a frequent guest of the Osbornes at The Hurst. Gowrie proposed that National Lottery Fund money be used to buy and refurbish the house as a centre for the Arvon Foundation, a highly respected organization providing courses and retreats for writers, and whose properties already included an eighteenth-century mill-owner's house in Yorkshire once owned by Ted Hughes. The Foundation duly acquired The Hurst in 1998. After a £2.3 million refurbishment programme, The John Osborne Centre, a building 'filled with inspiration . . . burning from the inside with light and laughter', and 'a place you can write, far away from daily distractions', opened to its first course participants in 2003.[27] Helen, meanwhile, remained living, rent free, in one wing of the house.

*   *   *

Within fifteen years of Osborne's death, the leading figures in his story had also died. Oscar Beuselinck, a 'randy, abusive and brilliant tyrant', and 'one of the great media lawyers of the century', died on 27 July 1997 aged 77.[28] 'To die on a walk before lunch on Folkestone beach only days after issuing his last writ, had flamboyance in keeping with his style,' observed the libel lawyer Harvey Kass in the Guardian. He also noted that, having been married and divorced three times, Beuselinck was a man for whom 'being a husband always proved difficult', yet during his last illness he was rewarded by his three former wives 'gathered at his bedside . . . at the same time.'[29]

Seven years later, on 12 January 2004, Helen Osborne, a woman like her husband with a decidedly 'short fuse', a chain smoker who could match his pace in emptying a champagne bottle and shared his frequently bilious view of the world, died of cancer at the age of sixty-four.[30] She was buried beside her husband at Clun. The following year, on 22 March at the age of eighty-two, Anthony Creighton died at the Royal Free Hospital in London, where he had been taken after collapsing at home. On 7 July, Jocelyn Rickards died at the age of eighty. Described 'with some admiration' by Oscar Lewenstein as 'the wickedest woman in the world' on account of her roll call of appreciative lovers, including A. J. Ayer, Graham Greene and Osborne, Jocelyn had designed costumes for some of the more notable British films of the 1960s and after, including the second James Bond outing, From Russia with Love, Antonioni's Blow Up, and Sunday, Bloody Sunday, written by Penelope Gilliatt.[31] Jocelyn later married the director Clive Donner. Five years after Jocelyn's death, and outlasting them all, Pamela Lane died on 28 October 2010, also at the age of eighty.

Pamela Lane had not become a nationally recognized name, yet she was an admired and popular actress at several regional theatres, was particularly encouraging to younger actors, and the directors with whom she had worked valued her talent highly. 'Her comic timing was brilliant and in tragedy she could be quite heartbreaking,' remembered her friend, Angela Langfield.[32] Richard Digby Day remarked that her professional dedication represented 'the heart and soul of our theatre.'[33] Among those with whom Osborne had remained on speaking terms, Pamela had known him the longest, for over forty years. As much as Anthony Creighton, she had determinedly supported his writing in his early years. Her faith in him, her encouragement and criticism were, like Creighton's, vital. After their divorce each had travelled a separate journey, yet had never forgotten the other. If Osborne spoke ill of her, it was during their marital difficulties and immediately after their separation, but never, it seems, since. Neither, after Look Back in Anger, is there any easily apparent allusion to her in any of his plays. She too remained discreet and reticent about their relationship. The sense of faith in love and redemption that Harold Hobson had detected in Look Back in Anger and noted in so many of his subsequent plays, is perhaps represented in Osborne's own life by his feelings for Pamela Lane. Each the other's oldest ally, each looked back with a romantic nostalgia and a certain regret. He thought of her often. 'I must stop mourning the past and what <u>didn't</u> happen between us,' he told her in the autumn of 1983.[34]

*　　　*　　　*

From the association between Osborne, Pamela and Creighton emerged Look Back in Anger, a play fated to define him as a dramatist and still performed somewhere in the world almost every night. Within weeks of its first production, it became a play that, like a traveller in the days of the Grand Tour, was destined to carry a great deal of very bulky looking baggage with it wherever it went. Look Back in Anger is 'at once a play and a myth,' noted Simon Trussler in 1969.[35] The date of its first production, 8 May 1956, has attained the resonance of a decisive military campaign and much of the writing about it has been in military terms. In his book, *Theatre in Britain*, Harold Hobson described the drama of the time as 'the great uprising', while for Kenneth Tynan, *Look Back in Anger* 'breached the dam', while the novelist Alan Sillitoe opined that 'John Osborne didn't contribute to British theatre; he set off a landmine called *Look Back in Anger* and blew most of it up.'[36]

Theirs was a generation, suggested Arnold Wesker, accustomed to the blast of bombs, who as children had experienced the effects of Europe at war, came of age in a 'debilitating, draining' era of austerity and doubt, and who strove 'to find a voice that surmounted and survived it.'[37] Both Osborne and Harold Pinter experienced wartime London and evacuation, remembering their provisional, precarious childhoods almost as a series of disjointed, black-and-white images. Samuel Beckett, almost fifteen years their senior, was living in France and covertly working with the resistance movement. Perhaps it is no coincidence that the three playwrights celebrated for reinvigorating the theatre of the second half of the twentieth century were preoccupied at the outset of their careers with broadly similar themes. *Look Back in Anger*, *Waiting for Godot* and *The Birthday Party*, first performed in London in 1955, 1956 and 1958, are partly plays about waiting, passing the time until something occurs, in which the leading characters position themselves against impending, sometimes unexplained, crisis. Perhaps this is partly a response to the war and its uncertain aftermath. 'It's a game in order to survive,' Beckett once observed about *Waiting for Godot*.[38] The same might be said about *Look Back in Anger* and *The Birthday Party*. The battle for survival, the registers of failure, the depth of absence and loss, and the deceptiveness of memory are common to Osborne, Beckett and Pinter.

By the end of the century, however, several historians were retreating from the rather apocalyptic view that the years preceding Osborne's debut at the Royal Court were something of a theatrical wasteland. Inter-war and immediate post-war culture was not as dismal as all that, was the cry, and indeed had qualities of its own. Besides, considered from the point of view of form and technique, *Look Back in Anger* was really a rather unremarkable piece. 'I think also that my generation heard more political revolution in it than was actually there, largely because we desperately needed to,' cautioned Peter Hall.[39]

Indeed, Osborne was never one of the great technical innovators, and neither was he particularly strong on narrative. Several of his later plays have virtually no narrative at all. Most of his characters do not develop in the traditional literary sense. They just *are*. They do not change the world but are buffeted by it and stand resiliently against it. But then, Osborne never set out to be innovative in anything other than language. Above all, the revival of the full expressive breadth and weight of English language was the form and fabric of his writing. He was interested in language as a way of expressing, as he saw it, emotional sensibility with truth, clarity and precision, and with the aesthetic intensity of poetry or of an aria. These were the qualities in the Jacobean and American playwrights that inspired and encouraged him as a young writer finding his

voice, and they continued to do so throughout his career. The rediscovery of
the power, virility and flexibility of language was the essential originality that
he brought to the English theatre.

A great writer is most clearly identified by his or her voice. It is unique and
lasting and transcends anything that is said or written about it. Read Osborne
on the page or hear his words in the theatre and the voice is immediately
recognizable. Seldom has an English writer revealed so much of his inner self
in his work, and in this sense Osborne's plays are his true autobiography; the
autobiography of the heart. At the same time, he managed to reflect public
troubles. As Peter Hall shrewdly noted: 'Osborne has an amazing ability to draw
into himself all the sicknesses of the moment and make plays which express
whatever our current mood is with great complexity.'[40] This is something in
which Osborne was remarkably consistent. The conventional assessment of
his writing is that it declined after the death of George Devine, and that in
comparison to the plays of the preceding decade, those following A Patriot for
Me are notable almost solely for their self-pity, their rancour, and the sense of
their author having become an embittered, isolated figure. Arguably, as vitality turned to despair, Osborne's later plays are not nearly as exhilarating as
theatrical experiences. And yet Osborne's writing is partly the art of defiance.
A conviction and a resilience remained, and rather than being dismissed, the
best of his later plays are more fittingly seen as a final flourish, an elegiac last
movement in a lifelong search for love and redemption in an increasingly brutal
and unforgiving world.

At its best Osborne's writing is compassionate, visceral, harsh, sentimental
and nostalgic; distinctive in its vocabulary, nuances and cadences, it is inescapably his. He stands alongside Pinter and Beckett as one of the greatest dramatic
stylists of his generation and arguably his century, and in his consuming passions of reverence and dissent vividly expressed, continued above all a tradition
arguably central to the English island imagination.

*   *   *

Meanwhile Osborne's theatrical afterlife flourishes. In fact, under the guidance
of Gordon Dickerson, who administers the John Osborne Estate on behalf of
the Arvon Foundation, he has never been better. Some of the most prominent
productions: in the year following Osborne's death A Patriot for Me appeared at
the Royal Shakespeare Company in London, while The Entertainer was staged in
New Haven. Four years later Look Back in Anger swooped down from Manchester
to the National Theatre, where Michael Sheen appeared as Jimmy Porter, while
in 2001, Luther was staged at the National in a production that, according to
Michael Billington, revealed the play as being 'close to a masterpiece'.[41] The Hotel
in Amsterdam appeared in London two years later, followed by the first revival
for many years of Epitaph for George Dillon. The same year Look Back in Anger opened
in Edinburgh, this time with David Tennant playing Jimmy Porter, and a 50th

anniversary production, starring Richard Coyle and directed by Peter Gill, was staged in Bath in 2006, while the following year, The Entertainer's 50th anniversary production, starring Robert Lindsay, appeared at the Old Vic.

Meanwhile, less familiar and even entirely unknown plays were dusted off and brought into the light. A Place Calling Itself Rome had its world premiere in the restrained form of a rehearsed reading at the King's Head pub theatre in Islington one Sunday night in 2008. The film screenplay of Tom Jones reappeared in a stage production by enterprising amateurs in Welwyn Garden City. The Devil Inside Him and Personal Enemy were published at last and revived for the first time since their premieres almost sixty years previously. Viewed through the prism of what was to follow, they were received far more enthusiastically than they had been originally. The Devil Inside Him surfaced in a production by the newly formed National Theatre of Wales in May 2010. It was 'an extraordinary discovery,' wrote Michael Billington in The Guardian, 'a combination of rep thriller and articulate cry of despair.'[42] Personal Enemy turned up a month later in a 'gripping' fringe production in London: '. . . a sensational revival', applauded Billington, 'that deserves wider exposure.'[43] It promptly flew across the Atlantic to New York, while Inadmissible Evidence, starring Douglas Hodge, was successfully revived at the Donmar in London.

At the same time, a continuing torrent of productions throughout Europe, the Americas and New Zealand: Look Back in Anger in New York, Riga, Buenos Aires, Lisbon, Prague, Istanbul, Naples, Milan and Dunedin . . . In Athens, Alison was played by an actress well into her middle years, looking back a quarter of a century to events earlier in her life . . . The Entertainer in Vienna, Amsterdam, Porto . . . and an updated version in Hamburg . . . The Devil Inside Him is translated into Polish and published, and performed in French in Paris . . . Back in England, A Patriot for Me is broadcast on BBC Radio Three in 2015 . . . The Picture of Dorian Gray turns up on the London fringe . . . A revival of Look Back in Anger in its home town of Derby is set to mark the 60th anniversary of the play in 2016, with an intrepid series of deconstructing lectures and readings taking place in the attic room once shared by Osborne and Pamela and which inspired the play's setting . . . The Entertainer, starring Kenneth Branagh, opens as part of the inaugural season of the Kenneth Branagh Theatre Company in the West End in August 2016 . . . 'And so it goes on,' reports Gordon Dickerson. 'And so it goes on . . .'[44]

Bibliography

THE HARRY RANSOM Research Center at the University of Texas at Austin holds the largest and most comprehensive archive of John Osborne's playscripts, personal and business letters, journals, notebooks and other assorted papers, while separate collections in the Center hold valuable material relating to the theatre of the time. There are also smaller but essential collections at the British Library, London, which also holds the Lord Chamberlain's Collection of playscripts submitted for production before the ending of state censorship in 1967. This collection also includes correspondence dealing with Osborne's plays between the Lord Chamberlain's office and the Royal Court Theatre and others. Some of Osborne's correspondence also remains in private hands.

Faber publish a three-volume collected edition of several of John Osborne's plays, while others are published by Oberon and still others remain as single editions. Among the many books dealing with the political and cultural events in Britain during the latter half of the twentieth century, Peter Hennessey's *Never Again* is a comprehensive overview of the years between 1945 and 1951, while Dominic Sandbrook's multi-volume history beginning in 1956 is the most comprehensive of the years since. Irving Wardle's biography of George Devine includes the most detailed account of the creation of the English Stage Company and Harry Ritchie's *Success Stories* is still the best overview of the Angry Young Man phenomenon. The archives of local newspapers are the main repositories of information about the activities of weekly repertory companies. I am grateful to those frequently anonymous critics in Leicester, Bridgwater, Kiddermister, Derby and other towns and cities who, many years ago, went along each Monday evening to their local rep to write their responses to productions that otherwise would have left no trace. Local libraries retain vital collections relating to the area they serve and these have been particularly invaluable in preparing the first part of this book. In an era when the continued existence of local libraries is threatened, a huge amount of local history is in danger of being lost.

The following are books I have found most useful. Unless otherwise stated, the place of publication is London.

By John Osborne

Plays

Apart from Look Back in Anger, which constantly reprints, collected editions of the plays are the most easily available. The following are published by Faber:

Look Back in Anger, Epitaph for George Dillon, The World of Paul Slickey and Déjàvu in Collected Plays Volume 1, 1996.
The Entertainer, The Hotel in Amsterdam, West of Suez and Time Present in Collected Plays Volume 2, 1998.
A Patriot for Me, Luther and Inadmissible Evidence in Collected Plays Volume 3, 1998.

Faber also publish:
A Subject of Scandal and Concern, 1961.
The Right Prospectus, 1970.
Very Like a Whale, 1971.
You're Not Watching Me, Mummy and Try a Little Tenderness, 1978.
The Gift of Friendship, 1982.
A Better Class of Person and God Rot Tunbridge Wells, 1985.
Hedda Gabler and The Father, 1989.

The following plays are published by Oberon:
The Devil Inside Him and Personal Enemy in Beyond Anger, 2009.
The Blood of the Bambergs, Under Plain Cover and Watch It Come Down in Plays For England, 1999.
A Sense of Detachment, The End of Me Old Cigar, Jill and Jack and A Place Calling Itself Rome in Four Plays, 2000.
A Bond Honoured in de Vega: Plays Two, 2002, and Tom Jones, 2011.

Non-Fiction

A Better Class of Person, Faber, 1981.
Almost a Gentleman, Faber, 1991.
The above are also available as a single volume paperback edition: Looking Back: Never Explain, Never Apologise, Faber, 2004.
Damn You, England: Collected Prose, Faber, 1994.

Other Publications

Allsop, Kenneth: The Angry Decade, Peter Owen, 1958.
Amis, Kingsley: Lucky Jim, Penguin, 2000 edn.

Anderson, Michael: *Anger and Detachment*, Pitman, 1976.

Banham, Martin: *John Osborne*, Oliver & Boyd, Edinburgh, 1969.

Banks, Lynne Reid: *The L-Shaped Room*, Penguin, 1962 edn.

Benn, Tony: *Years of Hope: Diaries, Letters and Papers 1940–1962*, Hutchinson, 1994.

Bennett, Jill: *Godfrey: A Special Time Remembered*, Hodder & Stoughton, 1983.

Billington, Michael: *The Life and Work of Harold Pinter*, Faber, 1996.

—— *One Night Stands: A Critic's View of British Theatre from 1971 to 1991*, Nick Hern Books, 1993.

—— *State of the Nation: British Theatre Since 1945*, Faber, 2007.

Bragg, Melvyn: *Rich: The Life of Richard Burton*, Hodder & Stoughton, 1988.

Braine, John: *Room at the Top*, Arrow, 1989 edn.

Browne, Terry: *Playwrights' Theatre: The English Stage Company at the Royal Court*, Pitman, 1975.

Campion, Sidney: *The World of Colin Wilson*, Muller, 1962.

Carter, Alan: *John Osborne*, Oliver & Boyd, Edinburgh, 1969.

Clark, Alan: *Diaries: Into Politics 1972–1982*, Orion, 2000.

Clark, Colin: *The Prince, The Showgirl and Me: The Colin Clark Diaries*, HarperCollins, 1995.

Clarke, Peter: *Hope and Glory: Britain 1900–2000*, Penguin, 2004.

Coward, Noël: *The Noël Coward Diaries*, eds Graham Payne and Sheridan Morley, Weidenfeld & Nicolson, 1982.

Crankshaw, Edward: *The Fall of the House of Hapsburg*, Penguin, 1983.

Dexter, John: *The Honourable Beast: A Posthumous Autobiography*, Nick Hern Books, 1993.

Duff, Charles: *The Lost Summer: The Heyday of the West End Theatre*, Nick Hern Books, 1995.

Eyre, Richard: *National Service: Diary of a Decade*, Bloomsbury, 2003.

Farrar, Harold: *John Osborne*, Colombia University Press, 1973.

Findlater, Richard (ed.): *At the Royal Court: 25 Years of the English Stage Company*, Amber Lane Press, 1981.

French, John: *Robert Shaw: The Price of Success*, Nick Hern Books, 1993.

Gaskill, William: *A Sense of Direction*, Faber, 1998.

Gilleman, Luc: *John Osborne: Vituperative Artist*, Routledge, 2002.

Goldstone, Herbert: *Coping With Vulnerability: The Achievement of John Osborne*, University Presses of America, Washington DC, 1982.

Hall, Peter: *Peter Hall's Diaries: The Story of a Dramatic Battle*, Hamish Hamilton, 1983.

Harewood, Lord: *The Tongs and the Bones: The Memoirs of Lord Harewood*, Weidenfeld & Nicolson, 1981.

Hayman, Ronald: *John Osborne*, Heinemann Educational, 1972.

Heilpern, John: *John Osborne: A Patriot for Us*, Chatto & Windus, 2006.

Henderson, Cathy and Oliphant, Dave: *Shouting in the Evening: British Theater 1956–1996*, Harry Ransom Humanities Research Center, University of Texas and Austin, 1996.

Hennessey, Peter: *Never Again: Britain 1945–1951*, Jonathan Cape, 1992.

—— Having It So Good: Britain in the Fifties, Allan Lane, 2006.

—— Muddling Through: Power, Politics and the Quality of Government in Post-War Britain, Weidenfeld and Nicolson, 2006.

Hewison, Robert: In Anger: Culture in the Cold War, Methuen, 1988.

—— Culture and Consensus: England, Art and Politics Since 1940, Methuen, 1995.

Hinchcliffe, Arnold: John Osborne, Twayne, Boston, 1984.

Hoare, Philip: Noël Coward, Sinclair-Stevenson, 1995.

Hobsbawn, Eric: An Age of Extremes: The Short Twentieth Century 1914–19, Abacus, 1995.

Hobson, Harold: Theatre in Britain: A Personal View, Phaidon, 1984.

Hoggart, Richard: The Uses of Literacy, Penguin, 2009 edn.

Holden, Anthony: Olivier, Weidenfeld & Nicolson, 1988.

Huggett, Richard: Binkie Beaumont: Eminence Grise of the West End Theatre 1933–1973, Hodder & Stoughton, 1989.

Isherwood, Christopher: Diaries Volume 1: 1939–60, Vintage, 2011.

Johnston, John: The Lord Chamberlain's Blue Pencil, Hodder & Stoughton, 1990.

Knowlson, James: Damned to Fame: The Life of Samuel Beckett, Bloomsbury, 1996.

Lewenstein, Oscar: Kicking Against the Pricks, Nick Hern Books, 1994.

Lycett Green, Candida (ed.): John Betjeman Letters Volume 2 1951–1984, Methuen, 1995.

MacDonald, Ian: Revolution in the Head: The Beatles' Records and the Sixties, Pimlico, 1995.

Macmillan, Harold: Pointing the Way: 1959–1961, Macmillan, 1972.

Marowitz, Charles (ed.): The Encore Reader: A Chronicle of the New Drama, Methuen, 1965.

Maschler, Tom (ed.): Declaration, MacGibbon & Kee, 1957.

Miller, Arthur: Timebends, Methuen, 1987.

Nicholson, Steve: The Censorship of British Drama 1900–68: Volume 3 The Fifties, Exeter University Press, 2011.

Olivier, Laurence: On Acting, Weidenfeld & Nicolson, 1986.

Porter, Roy: London: A Social History, Hamish Hamilton, 1984.

Rattigan, Terence: The Collected Plays of Terence Rattigan, Hamish Hamilton, four volumes, 1953 (first two), 1964, 1978.

Rebellato, Dan: 1956 and All That, Routledge, 1999.

Richardson, Tony: Long Distance Runner: A Memoir, Faber, 1993.

Rickards, Jocelyn: The Painted Banquet: My Life and Loves, Weidenfeld & Nicolson, 1987.

Ritchie, Harry: Success Stories: Literature and the Media in England 1950–1959, Faber, 1988.

Sandbrook, Dominic: Never Had It So Good: A History of Britain from Suez to The Beatles, Abacus, 2010.

—— White Heat: A History of Britain in the Swinging Sixties, Abacus, 2009.

—— State of Emergency: The Way We Were 1970–74, Penguin, 2011.

—— Seasons in the Sun: The Battle for Britain 1974–79, Penguin, 2013.

Stephens, Robert: *Knight Errant: Memoirs of a Vagabond Actor*, Hodder & Stoughton, 1995.

Taylor, John Russell: *Anger and After: A Guide to the New British Drama*, Methuen, 1962.

Tiratsoo, Nick (ed.): *From Blitz to Blair: A New History of Britain Since 1939*, Phoenix, 1998.

Trussler, Simon: *John Osborne*, Longmans Green for The British Council, 1969.

—— *The Plays of John Osborne*, Gollancz, 1969.

Tynan, Kathleen: *The Life of Kenneth Tynan*, Weidenfeld & Nicolson, 1987.

—— (ed.): *Kenneth Tynan: Letters*, Weidenfeld & Nicolson, 1994.

Tynan, Kenneth: *A View of the English Stage*, Methuen, 1984.

—— *Profiles*, Nick Hern Books, 1989.

Walker, Alexander: *Hollywood, England: The British Film Industry in the Sixties*, Michael Joseph, 1974.

Wansell, Geoffrey: *Terence Rattigan*, Fourth Estate, 1995.

Wardle, Irving: *The Theatres of George Devine*, Jonathan Cape, 1978.

Wilson, Colin: *The Outsider*: Weidenfeld & Nicholson paperback, 2001.

Wesker, Arnold: *As Much as I Dare*, Century, 1994.

Woodham-Smith, Cecil: *The Reason Why*, Constable, 1953.

Notes

IN THE SOURCE NOTES I have referred as much as possible to editions most easily available to readers. Several of John Osborne's plays, for example, have been published in a three-volume paperback edition by Faber, while a selection of his prose writing appears in *Damn You England*, also published by Faber. Several of Kenneth Tynan's reviews written for the *Observer* during the 1950s are collected in *A View of the English Stage*.

Abbreviations:

AAG: *Almost a Gentleman*: Volume 2 of autobiography, 1991.
BCP: *A Better Class of Person*: Volume 1 of autobiography, 1981.
BL: British Library.
CP: John Osborne: *Collected Plays* followed by volume number 1, 2, or 3.
DYE: John Osborne: *Damn You England*, Collected Prose, 1994.
HRHRC: Harry Ransom Humanities Research Center, University of Texas at Austin.
JO: John Osborne.
LCC: Lord Chamberlain's Collection of Playscripts.
NABS: National Advertising Benevolent Society.
nd: no date.
VES: Kenneth Tynan: *A View of the English Stage*.

Chapter 1: A New Start

1. *Daily Mail*, 14 November 1957.
2. Philip Larkin: *Annus Mirabilis*, 1967.
3. Richard Findlater: 'The Angry Young Man': *New York Times*, 29 September 1957.
4. Kenneth Allsop: *The Angry Decade*, p. 99.
5. *Times Literary Supplement*, 1956, quoted Harry Ritchie: *Success Stories*, p. 41.

6. JO: 'A Letter to My Fellow Countryman', *Tribune*, 18 August 1961; DYE, pp. 193–4.
7. *Sunday Pictorial*, 24 September 1961.
8. *Daily Telegraph*, 25 September 1961.
9. JO: journal, 1964, HRHRC.
10. Thomas Carlyle to Jane Carlyle, 16 August 1850. Carlyle Letters online.
11. Anthony Porter to author.
12. James Osborne, Newport newspaper advertisement, 1901.
13. Anthony Porter to author.
14. JO: BCP, p. 21.
15. JO: CP2, *The Hotel in Amsterdam*, pp. 127–8.
16. JO's astrological chart, nd, HRHRC.

Chapter 2: A Sense of Loss

1. Noël Coward: *Present Indicative*, p. 253.
2. Eric Hobsbawn: *The Age of Catastrophe*: the title of Part One of *Age of Extremes: The Short Twentieth Century*.
3. See John Heilpern: *John Osborne: A Patriot for Us*, pp. 475–83.
4. JO: notebook, 1985, HRHRC.
5. JO: journal for *Déjàvu*, Christmas 1988. The line is given to JP in the final text of the play: 'Anger is not hatred, which I see in all your faces. Anger is slow, gentle, not vindictive or full of spite', CP1, p. 314.
6. JO: BCP, p. 37.
7. JO: *AAG*, p. 130.
8. Alan A. Jackson: *Semi-Detached London: Suburban Development, Life and Transport*, Oxford, 1991, p. 228.
9. George Orwell: *Homage to Catalonia*, 1986 edition, pp. 186–7.
10. Stanley Baldwin: speech to the House of Commons, 1932, quoted in Nick Tiratsoo: *From Blitz to Blair*, p. 17.
11. George Orwell: *Boys' Weeklies*, 1939. *Collected Essays, Journalism and Letters of George Orwell*, vol. 1, p. 479.
12. JO: BCP, p. 85.
13. JO: CP1, *Look Back in Anger*, p. 13.

Chapter 3: Charity's Child

1. The NABS files record almost continuous payments made to the Osborne family between 1932 and 1949, including subsidies towards, and sometimes all, the rent and household bills, and all of Tom Godfrey's travel and medical expenses.
2. I am grateful to Hugh Berrington for his analysis of south London suburbs.
3. Nora Wood to author.
4. JO: BCP, p. 81.
5. Stanley Baldwin: newsreel broadcast, November 1935.
6. Neville Chamberlain: speech, 30 September 1938.

7. Angus Calder: *The People's War*, p. 25.

8. JO: journal, 1953. HRHRC.

9. JO: CP1, *Look Back in Anger*, p. 56.

10. Anthony Creighton to author.

11. JO to Melvyn Bragg: *The South Bank Show*, London Weekend Television, 2 December 1981.

12. Tom Godfrey Osborne to Annie Osborne, nd (Christmas 1939), HRHRC.

13. Hilda Banham to author.

14. Betty Hester to author.

15. JO: BCP, p. 107.

16. JO: BCP, p. 159.

17. NABS files: 25 January 1943.

18. Ibid.

19. Fay Pascoe to author.

20. Bob Hamnett to author.

21. Fay Pascoe to author.

22. Bob Hamnett to author.

Chapter 4: The Journalist

1. Tony Benn: *Years of Hope*, p. xii.

2. Labour Party: General Election Manifesto, 1945.

3. Winston Churchill: *After the War*, BBC radio broadcast, 21 March 1943.

4. Winston Churchill: BBC radio, General Election broadcast, 4 June 1945.

5. Tony Benn: *Years of Hope*, p. 91.

6. Mrs Landemare, quoted in Peter Hennessey: *Never Again*, p. 86.

7. Kingsley Amis: *I Spy Strangers*, short story in *My Enemy's Enemy*, Penguin, 1962 edn, p. 74.

8. JO: *Desert Island Discs*, BBC Radio 4, 5 March 1982.

9. NABS files: 14 May 1946.

10. Hugh Berrington to author.

11. JO: BCP, 171.

12. Hugh Berrington to author.

13. Robert Hewison: *In Anger: Culture in the Cold War*, p. 12.

14. Cyril Connolly: *Horizon*, April 1947.

15. JO: journal 1973, HRHRC.

16. John Moffatt to author.

17. JO: BCP, pp. 169, 171.

18. JO: BCP, p. 171.

19. Hilda Banham to author.

20. JO: BCP, pp. 83, 84.

21. JO: BCP, p. 82.

22. Hugh Berrington to author.

23. JO: BCP, p. 84.

24. Hugh Berrington to author.

25. Hilda Banham to author.
26. Hugh Berrington to author.
27. Ibid.

Chapter 5: The Actor

1. Anthony Hawtrey: Foreword, Embassy Successes 1918–62, Routledge, 1996.
2. Time Out Film Guide, 1997, p. 90.
3. The Scotsman, 11 May 1948.
4. Patrick Desmond: unpublished memoirs, quoted in Jamie Andrews, Introduction: Before Anger, p. 14.
5. June Ellis to author.
6. JO: BCP, p. 206.
7. JO: Tape transcriptions for A Better Class of Person, quoted Jamie Andrews: A Poor Jonah: John Osborne's Roads to Freedom, BL Journal, 2010.
8. Saxon Players, Leicester, programmes, nd (late 1940s) and Thelma Rogers to author.
9. Thelma Rogers to author.
10. The Stage, 13 November 1949, is a typical advertisement of the time that Osborne may have seen.
11. Anthony Creighton to author.
12. Ibid.
13. Lynne Reid Banks to author.
14. Anthony Creighton to author.
15. Rosemarie Croom-Johnson: John Osborne: Angry Man, Oxford Television/ Channel 4 Television, 25 December 2002.
16. Anthony Creighton to author.
17. Ibid.
18. Lynne Reid Banks to author.
19. Ibid.
20. Anthony Creighton to author.

Chapter 6: Bridgwater Bound

1. The Stage, 4 May 1950.
2. June Ellis to author.
3. Ibid.
4. Huddersfield Daily Examiner, 30 May 1950.
5. JO: Desert Island Discs, BBC Radio 4, 5 March 1982.
6. Stella Linden later divorced Patrick Desmond from Mexico and, apart from writing Shameless: The Story of a Bimbo, a semi-pornographic novel, in 1989, retreated into anonymity until her death in 2000. As for Reginald Barratt, he went on to a successful television career spanning thirty years.
7. Havant, Hayling Island and District Official Guide advertisement, 1950.
8. Anthony Creighton to author.
9. Ibid.

10. *The Stage*, 28 September 1950.
11. *Hamlet*, Act 1, Scene 2.
12. Pauline Berry to author.
13. Pamela Lane to author.
14. *The Stage*, 28 March 1951.
15. JO to Anthony Creighton Monday night, nd (1951), HRHRC.
16. Pamela Lane to author.
17. *Bridgwater Mercury*, 24 April 1951.
18. JO to Anthony Creighton, 1 May 1951, HRHRC.
19. Ibid, nd (1951), HRHRC.
20. Ibid, Wednesday, nd (1951), HRHRC.
21. Ibid, Tuesday (1951), HRHRC.
22. Ibid,Wednesday, nd (1951), HRHRC.
23. Ibid.
24. Ibid, Wednesday, nd (1951), HRHRC.
25. *Bridgwater Mercury*, 15 May 1951.
26. JO to Anthony Creighton, Tuesday, nd (1951), HRHRC.
27. Pamela Lane to author.
28. Pamela Lane to JO, nd (1951), HRHRC.
29. *Bridgwater Mercury*, 14 June 1951.

Chapter 7: Repertory
1. Anthony Creighton to author.
2. Herbert Morison, Labour Home Secretary, quoted in Peter Hennessey: *Never Again*, p. 425.
3. Winston Churchill: speech to the House of Commons, 6 November 1951.
4. Mavis Pugh to author.
5. Brenda Kaye to author.
6. *Kidderminster Shuttle*, undated clippings (1952), HRHRC.
7. Brenda Kaye to author.
8. Peter Nichols: Foreword, *Look Back at Frinton; Before Anger*, p. 7.
9. Violet Markham: *The Listener*, 28 May 1952, quoted in Nick Tiratsoo: *From Blitz to Blair*, p. 109.
10. Robert Hewison: *In Anger: Culture in the Cold War*, p. 74.
11. Oscar Hammerstein, quoted in Dominic Shellard: *British Theatre Since the War*, p. 23.
12. Michael Holroyd: *Bernard Shaw: The Search for Love*, p. 3.
13. Cyril Connolly: *Horizon*, December 1949–January 1950.
14. T. C. Worsley: *New Statesman*, 10 December 1949.
15. Evelyn Waugh: diary, 1946, quoted in Dominic Sandbrook: *Never Had It So Good*, p. 300.
16. Noel Coward: 'Relative Values', *Play Parade*, vol. 5, p. 371.
17. Terence Rattigan: *The Collected Plays of Terence Rattigan*, vol. 1, p. xi.
18. JO to Richard Findlater, 23 April 1953, HRHRC.

19. Thelma Rogers to author.
20. Pamela Lane to author. The 'd and b' contraction, appearing in a letter from JO to Anthony Creighton, quoting Pamela, Sunday, nd (1954), HRHRC, is often quoted by JO in his autobiographies and elsewhere.
21. Peter Ackroyd: Civil War, pp. 98, 100.
22. JO to Richard Findlater, 8 July 1953, HRHRC.
23. Kenneth Rose to JO, 21 March 1954, HRHRC.
24. Anthony Creighton to author.

Chapter 8: Doomed in Derby
1. Anthony Creighton to author.
2. Sylvia Plath: The Bell Jar, p. 1.
3. Anthony Creighton to author.
4. Pamela Lane to JO, nd, 1954, HRHRC.
5. Stella Jagg to author.
6. Ibid.
7. JO to Anthony Creighton, 16 March 1954, HRHRC.
8. Ibid, Tuesday, nd (1954), HRHRC.
9. Ibid, Sunday 5.30, nd (1954), HRHRC.
10. Ibid.
11. Stella Jagg to author.
12. Bette Jenkins to author.
13. JO to Anthony Creighton, nd (1954), HRHRC.
14. Ibid.
15. Anthony Creighton to author.
16. JO to Anthony Creighton, Sunday, nd (1954), HRHRC.
17. Ibid, Tuesday, nd (1954), HRHRC.
18. Anthony Creighton to author.
19. Ibid.
20. Derby Evening Telegraph, 25 January 1954.
21. JO to Anthony Creighton, Sunday, nd (1954), HRHRC.
22. Anthony Creighton to author.
23. JO to Anthony Creighton, Saturday night, nd (1954), HRHRC.
24. JO to Mary Allen, Nottingham Playhouse publicity department, 19 February 1963, HRHRC.
25. JO: BCP, p. 257.
26. JO: CP1, Epitaph for George Dillon, pp. 167, 168.
27. St Vincent Troubridge, reader's report on Personal Enemy, 24 February 1955, LCC BL.
28. Barry England to author.
29. Patrick Desmond, quoted by Jamie Andrews: Before Anger: Introduction, p. 24.
30. The Stage, 1 March 1955. Personal Enemy is also referred to as 'the sensational American drama' in The Yorkshire Post, 28 February 1955.

31. Revd Colin Cuttell: *Southwark Cathedral Magazine*, 1949, quoted in Shellard: *Kenneth Tynan*, p. 135.

32. Samantha Ellis: 'A View From the Bridge, October 1956': *The Guardian*, 16 July 2003.

33. Harold Hobson, quoted ibid.

Chapter 9: Creation

1. Jonathan Green, quoted in Dominic Sandbrook: *Never Had It So Good*, p. 446.

2. Jim Downer: Introduction to Ted Hughes and Jim Downer: *Timmy the Tug*, Thames and Hudson, 2009.

3. JO: CP1, *Look Back in Anger*, p. 40.

4. JO: journal, 1953, HRHRC.

5. Kingsley Amis: *Lucky Jim*, Penguin, 1992, p. 13.

6. JO: CP1, *Look Back in Anger*, p. 6.

7. Kenneth Tynan: *Observer*, 31 October 1954; *VES*, p. 147.

8. Ibid, *VES*, p. 11.

9. Kathleen Tynan: *The Life of Kenneth Tynan*, p. 3.

10. Kenneth Tynan: *Evening Standard*, 29 May 1953; *VES*, p. 123.

11. Kenneth Tynan: *Observer*, 31 October 1954; *VES*, p. 147.

12. Kenneth Tynan: *Observer*, 7 August 1955; *VES*, p. 161.

13. Kenneth Tynan: *Observer*, 31 October 1954; *VES*, p. 149.

14. Pamela Lane to author.

15. JO: CP1, *Look Back in Anger*, p. 55.

16. Ibid, p. 56.

17. Ibid, p. 43.

18. Ibid, p. 83.

19. JO: quoted in Dominic Sandbrook: *Never Had It So Good*, p. 479.

20. JO: CP1, *Look Back in Anger*, p. 57.

21. Ibid, p. 24.

22. Ibid, p. 66.

23. Ibid, p. 14.

24. Anthony Porter to author.

25. JO: CP1, *Look Back in Anger*, p. 71.

26. JO: CP1, Introduction to *Look Back in Anger*, p. viii; DYE, p. 45.

27. Anthony Creighton to author.

28. *The Stage*, 28 July 1955.

Chapter 10: Royal Court

1. Irving Wardle: *The Theatres of George Devine*, p. 149.

2. Ibid, p. 160.

3. Tony Richardson: *Long Distance Runner*, p. 24.

4. Irving Wardle: *The Theatres of George Devine*, p. 164.

5. Oscar Lewenstein: *Kicking Against the Pricks*, p. 27.

6. Irving Wardle: *The Theatres of George Devine*, p. 164.

7. Richard Findlater: *At the Royal Court*, p. 25.

8. Ibid, p. 16.

9. Oscar Lewenstein: *Kicking Against the Pricks*, p. 14.

10. Dan Rebellato: *1956 and All That*, p. 67.

11. George Devine, quoted in Irving Wardle: *The Theatres of George Devine*, p. 164.

12. *Theatre World*, May 1956.

13. Tony Richardson: *Long Distance Runner*, p. 74.

14. Anthony Creighton to author.

15. JO: *AAG*, p. 5.

16. Tony Richardson: *Long Distance Runner*, p. 78.

17. Ibid, p. 77.

18. T. C. Worsley: 'A Writers' Theatre', *New Statesman*, 24 March 1956.

19. Tony Richardson: *Long Distance Runner*, p. 77.

20. Ibid, p. 75.

21. Margaret Drabble: *Angus Wilson*, Secker & Warburg, 1995, pp. 210–11.

22. Ibid.

23. Kenneth Tynan: *Observer*, 8 April 1956; quoted Dominic Shellard: *Kenneth Tynan*, p. 153.

24. Tony Richardson: *Long Distance Runner*, p. 78.

25. Paul Nicholas to author.

26. Paul Scofield to author.

27. Charles Heriot: reader's report on *Look Back in Anger*, 1 March 1956, LCC, BL.

28. Charles Heriot: list of amendments to *Look Back in Anger*, 23 March 1956, LCC, BL.

29. Tony Richardson: *Long Distance Runner*, p. 78.

30. Kenneth Haigh to author.

31. Ibid.

32. Geoffrey Wansell: *Terence Rattigan*, p. 270.

33. Kenneth Tynan in *The South Bank Show*, ITV, 1991.

34. A selection of newspaper reviews of *Look Back in Anger* appears in John Russell Taylor: *Look Back in Anger: A Casebook*, pp. 35–56.

35. Ibid.

36. Ibid.

37. Hugh Berrington to author; Pamela Lane to author.

38. Angela John to author.

39. Pamela Lane to author.

40. Harold Hobson: *The Sunday Times*, 13 May 1956.

41. Ibid.

42. Kenneth Tynan: 'What Men Hate Most About Women', *Picture Post*, 4 September 1954; quoted in Kathleen Tynan: *The Life of Kenneth Tynan*, p. 120.

43. Kenneth Tynan: *Observer*, 13 May 1956; *VES*, p. 176.

44. Ibid.
45. Kathleen Tynan: *The Life of Kenneth Tynan*, p. 20.
46. Dominic Shellard: *Kenneth Tynan*, p. 149.
47. Ibid, p. 64.

Chapter 11: The Year of the Angry Young Man

1. JO: transcript of BBC Radio interview, 12 May 1956, HRHRC.
2. JO: *Panorama*, BBC Television, 9 July 1956.
3. Robert Muller: *Picture Post*, 23 June 1956.
4. Ibid.
5. Siriol Hugh Jones: *The Sunday Times*, 14 April 1957.
6. Robert Muller: *Picture Post*, 23 June 1956.
7. Nellie Beatrice Osborne, quoted in *Empire News*, 3 July 1959.
8. Robert Tee: *Daily Mirror*, 9 May 1956; Barbara Fearon to author.
9. Arnold Wesker: *As Much As I Dare*, p. 491.
10. Robert Muller: *Picture Post*, 23 June 1956; T. C. Worsley: *New Statesman*, 14 May 1956.
11. Harold Hobson: *The Sunday Times*, 24 June 1956.
12. Cyril Connolly in *The Sunday Times*, quoted in Harry Ritchie: *Success Stories*, p. 144. Ritchie writes a vividly entertaining summary of the Colin Wilson saga.
13. Philip Toynbee in the *Observer*, quoted ibid, p. 144.
14. V. S. Pritchett, Elizabeth Bowen and Kenneth Walker, quoted ibid, p. 145.
15. JO: quoted in *Daily Express*, 6 July 1956.
16. Daniel Farson: quoted in Harry Ritchie: *Success Stories*, p. 146.
17. Ibid.
18. *Daily Express*, 26 July 1956.
19. *Time*, 2 July 1956; *Life*, October 1956.
20. *Daily Express*, 26 July 1956.
21. *Daily Mail*, 18 July 1956.
22. *Daily Express*, 4 September 1956.
23. Daniel Farson: *Daily Mail*, 12 July 1956.
24. John Barber: *Daily Express*, 26 July 1956.
25. Colin Wilson, quoted in Sidney Campion: *The World of Colin Wilson*, p. 126.
26. JO, quoted in *Daily Mail*, 18 July 1956.
27. Lindsay Anderson: 'A Year of my Own', *The Colour Supplement*, BBC Radio 4, 23 September 1984, quoted in Harry Ritchie: *Success Stories*, pp. 205–6.
28. Lindsay Anderson: *Sight and Sound*, Autumn 1956.
29. Ibid.
30. Lindsay Anderson: *Get Out and Push: Declaration*, p. 155.
31. Anthony Howard, quoted in Dominic Sandbrook: *Never Had It So Good*, p. 59.

32. Fiona MacCarthy: *Last Curtsey*, p. 2.

33. Ibid, p. 13.

34. Ibid, p. 66.

35. *Daily Mail*, 5 September 1956.

36. JO: CP1, *Look Back in Anger*, p. 13.

37. Richard Hoggart: *The Uses of Literacy*, quoted in Dominic Sandbrook: *Never Had It So Good*, p. 183.

38. Ibid, p. 184.

39. JO, quoted in *The Sunday Times*, 14 April 1957.

40. Alan Lennox-Boyd, quoted in Peter Hennessey: *Muddling Through*, p. 130.

41. Irving Wardle: *The Theatres of George Devine*, p. 182.

42. Ronald Duncan, quoted ibid.

43. Kenneth Allsop: *The Angry Decade*, p. 140.

44. Irving Wardle: *The Theatres of George Devine*, p. 183.

45. Michael Halifax, quoted in Irving Wardle: *The Theatres of George Devine*, p. 185.

46. *Manchester Guardian*, 10 December 1956.

47. Philip French to author.

48. Michael Billington to author.

49. Fiona MacCarthy: *Last Curtsey*, p. 74.

50. JO: *Observer*, 20 January 1957: DYE, p. 66.

51. JO, quoted in Richard Findlater: 'The Angry Young Man', *New York Times*, 29 September 1957.

52. JO, quoted in *Daily Express*, 18 October 1956.

53. Ibid.

54. Ibid.

55. Anthony Creighton to author.

56. Harold Hobson: *The Sunday Times*, 3 February 1957.

57. Associated British-Pathé advertising campaign for *Yield to the Night*, a crime film starring Diana Dors, an actress widely promoted as Britain's answer to Marilyn Monroe, and released in the summer of 1956.

58. Derek Granger: *London Magazine*, December 1956.

59. *Daily Mail*, 13 December 1956.

Chapter 12: The King at the Court

1. Variety handbill, nd, London, 1950s.

2. JO: CP2, *Introduction*, p vii; *AAG*, p. 35.

3. JO: *Observer*, 20 April 1975; DYE, p. 122.

4. JO: CP2, *The Entertainer*, p. 28.

5. Peter Hennessey: *Muddling Through*, p. 149.

6. JO: CP2, *The Entertainer*, p. 54.

7. Ibid, p. 66.

8. JO to Richard Findlater, 28 May 1956, HRHRC.

9. JO to Anthony Creighton, nd (1957), HRHRC.

NOTES 379

10. Tony Richardson: *Long Distance Runner*, p. 86.
11. Anthony Holden: *Laurence Olivier*, p. 264.
12. Laurence Olivier: *On Acting*, p. 148.
13. Laurence Olivier, quoted in Arthur Miller: *Timebends*, p. 448.
14. Arthur Miller, quoted in *The Stage*, 22 November 1956.
15. Ibid.
16. Laurence Olivier: *On Acting*, pp. 151–2.
17. St Vincent Troubridge: reader's report on *The Entertainer*, 16 March 1957, LCC, BL.
18. Tony Richardson to St Vincent Troubridge, 1 April 1957, LCC, BL.
19. Undated photographs (1957) in *The Entertainer* files, LCC, BL Troubridge.
20. St Vincent Troubridge: reader's report on *The Entertainer*, 16 March 1957, LCC, BL.
21. Tony Richardson: *Long Distance Runner*, p. 86.
22. Ibid.
23. Laurence Olivier: *On Acting*, p. 152.
24. Stanley Meadows to author.
25. Ibid.
26. Colin Clark to author.
27. Ibid.
28. Stanley Meadows to author.
29. JO: *AAG*, p. 34.
30. JO's letter to the *Spectator* appeared on 12 April 1957. Evelyn Seymour's supportive letter appeared on the same date.
31. Hugh Berrington to author.
32. Oscar Beuselinck to author.
33. Ibid.
34. Ibid.
35. Ibid.
36. *Daily Mail*, 10 April 1957.
37. Ibid.
38. Ibid.
39. *Daily Mail*, 11 April 1957.
40. JO to ITN News, 10 April 1957.
41. W. A. Darlington: *Daily Telegraph*, 11 April 1957.
42. Kenneth Tynan: *Observer*, 14 April 1957; *VES*, pp. 202–3.
43. JO quoted in *The Sunday Time,s* 30 September 1956.
44. *Evening Standard*, 19 March 1957.
45. John Braine: *Room at the Top*, Arrow edn, p. 7.
46. Ibid, p. 29.
47. Joe Lampton has the unappealing habit in the novel of 'grading' women according to looks and financial prospects.
48. *Evening Standard*, 19 March 1957.
49. *Daily Express*, 23 March 1957.

50. *Daily Express*, 22 April 1957.
51. *Sunday Express*, 9 February 1958.
52. Tom Maschler: Introduction to *Declaration*, p. 7.
53. Ibid.
54. Kingsley Amis, quoted in Tom Maschler: Introduction to *Declaration*, pp. 8–9.
55. JO: 'They Call It Cricket', *Declaration*, p. 70.
56. Ibid, p. 76.
57. George Devine, quoted in *Daily Herald*, 15 October 1957.
58. Ibid.
59. Angus Wilson: *Observer*, 13 October 1957.
60. James Cameron: *News Chronicle*, quoted in Kenneth Allsop: *The Angry Decade*, p. 124.
61. *Daily Express*, 5 December 1956; Harry Ritchie: *Success Stories*, p. 149.
62. *Sunday Pictorial*, 16 December 1956; ibid, p. 150.
63. *Times Literary Supplement*, 14 December 1956; ibid, p. 155.
64. Sidney Campion: *The World of Colin Wilson*, p. 5.
65. Kenneth Allsop: *The Angry Decade*, p. 166.
66. Harry Ritchie: *Success Stories*, p. 150.
67. John Stewart, quoted ibid.
68. John Stewart, quoted in Kenneth Allsop: *The Angry Decade*, p. 167.
69. Colin Wilson, quoted ibid.
70. Colin Wilson: *Fame Is the Spur*, extracts from Wilson's diaries, *Daily Mail*, 23 February 1957, quoted extensively in Kenneth Allsop: *The Angry Decade*, p. 169.
71. Philip Toynbee, quoted ibid, p. 175.
72. *New Statesman*, quoted ibid, p. 173; *Daily Mail*, quoted ibid, p. 171.
73. *Time*, 18 November 1957.
74. Daniel Farson: *Books and Bookmen*, December 1957.
75. *News Chronicle*, 23 October 1957.

Chapter 13: Transatlantic
1. JO: *AAG*, p. 54
2. Ibid.
3. Ibid, p. 55.
4. *Daily Express*, 12 August 1957.
5. *Evening Standard*, 12 August 1957.
6. Hugh Berrington to author.
7. *Tass*, quoted in *The Times*, 5 August 1957.
8. David Dempsey: 'Most Angry Fella', *New York Times Magazine*, 20 October 1957.
9. Brooks Atkinson: *New York Times*, 2 October 1957.
10. *Daily Express*, 31 January 1958.
11. JO to Anthony Creighton: Thursday, nd (1958), HRHRC.

12. Ibid.

13. Ibid.

14. Oscar Beuselinck to author.

15. JO to Anthony Creighton: Thursday, nd (1958), HRHRC.

16. Ibid.

17. *Daily Express*, 31 January 1958.

18. *Daily Express*, 13 May 1957.

19. George Devine, quoted in JO: *AAG*, p. 7.

20. JO: *AAG*, p. 69.

21. JO to Anthony Creighton: Thursday, nd (1958), HRHRC.

22. Elaine Anderson, quoted in John Fass Morton: *Backstory in Blue: Ellington at Newport '56*, Rutgers University Press, 2008, p. 223.

23. JO to Anthony Creighton: 20 February (1959), HRHRC.

24. Kenneth Tynan: *Observer*, 16 February 1958, *VES*, p. 212.

25. Quoted in *Mary Ure – The Scottish Marilyn*, Helen's Heroes website.

26. Doris Lessing, quoted ibid.

27. David Dempsey: 'Most Angry Fella', *New York Times Magazine*, 20 October 1957.

Chapter 14: Black and White

1. *Evening News*, quoted in Ronald Harwood: *A Night at the Theatre*.

2. Unidentified American newspaper clipping (1957), HRHRC.

3. Lady Elizabeth Cavendish to author.

4. Valerie Eliot to author.

5. David Watt: *Encore* magazine, May 1958.

6. Kathleen Tynan: *The Life of Kenneth Tynan*, p. 140.

7. Free Cinema manifesto 1956, quoted in *Free Cinema*, 2006, BFI booklet accompanying a DVD selection of DVD Free Cinema films, 2006.

8. Lindsay Anderson: *Get Out and Push: Declaration*, p. 157.

9. Ibid.

10. Lindsay Anderson, quoted in *Free Cinema: Every Day Except Christmas*: BFI booklet, 2006.

11. Romulus Films advertising campaign for *Room at the Top*, 1959.

12. Ibid.

13. Alexander Walker: *Hollywood, England*, p. 45.

14. Ibid.

15. *The Times*, 26 January 1959.

16. *Evening Standard*, 22 January 1959, quoted in Harry Ritchie: *Success Stories*, p. 62.

17. Penelope Houston, quoted in Alexander Walker: *Hollywood, England*, p. 50.

18. *Saturday Review* (1959), quoted in Robert Hewison: *In Anger*, p. 154.

19. *Daily Mail*, 11 April 1959.

20. *The Guardian*: Jocelyn Rickards obituary, 14 July 2005.

Chapter 15: The Battle of Cambridge Circus
1. *Daily Mail*, 10 November 1958.
2. Tim Willis: *Nigel Dempster: Death of Discretion*, Short Books, 2010, p. 7; Penelope Gilliatt: *The Faceless Ones: Queen*, 13 April 1960.
3. Harold Macmillan: speech at Bedford, July 1957.
4. *Daily Mail*, 11 April 1959.
5. *Daily Mail*, 9 March 1959.
6. Ibid.
7. *Daily Mail*, 11 April 1959.
8. David Nathan: *Daily Herald*, 15 April 1959.
9. Correspondence between the Lord Chamberlain's office and JO on *The World of Paul Slickey* began with Charles Heriot's reader's report on an initial submission of the script on 26 September 1958, and continued until the opening night in Bournemouth in April 1959.
10. David Nathan: *Daily Herald*, 15 April 1959.
11. *Daily Sketch*, 15 April 1959.
12. *Dancing Times* (1959), quoted on Kenneth Macmillan.com.
13. *Bournemouth Times and Directory*, quoted in Ronald Harwood: *A Night at the Theatre*, Methuen, 1982; Harwood includes an entertaining overview of the *World of Paul Slickey*.
14. *Star*, 15 April 1959.
15. Oscar Beuselinck to author.
16. Estelle Maran to JO: 1 June 1959, HRHRC.
17. Kenneth Robinson: *Church of England Newspaper*, 15 May 1959.
18. Lawrence Kitchen to JO: 8 June 1959, HRHRC.
19. Letter to *Worthing Gazette*, 29 April 1959.
20. JO quoted in *Daily Herald*, 11 April 1959.
21. Milton Shulman: *Evening Standard*, 6 May 1959.
22. *Daily Mail*, 7 May 1959.
23. Noël Coward: *Diaries*, p. 409.
24. Ibid.
25. Dennis Lotis to author.
26. *Daily Mail*, 7 May 1969.
27. JO: *AAG*, p. 126.
28. Philip Hope Wallace: *Manchester Guardian*, 7 May 1959; Harold Clurman: *Observer*, 10 May 1959.
29. *Daily Herald*, 7 May 1959.
30. David Pelham, quoted in *Daily Telegraph*, 7 May 1959.
31. *Daily Herald*, 8 May 1959.
32. Mervyn Jones: *Tribune*, 17 June 1959.
33. *Tribune*, 5 June 1959.
34. Ibid, 15 May 1959.
34. Frederick May: *Tribune*, 22 May 1959.
36. Ted Willis: *Tribune*, 29 May 1959.

37. Kathleen Newman: Tribune, 12 June 1959.
38. Daily Herald, 12 May 1959.
39. Daily Telegraph, 7 May 1959.
40. Alexander Walker: Hollywood, England, p. 56.

Chapter 16: Betrayal

1. A phrase used consistently in the press and in books to describe JO, from 1956 onwards, including at the opening of Déjàvu, his last stage play, by Tracey MacDonald, The Late Show, BBC2, 2 June 1992.
2. Daily Express, 18 May 1959.
3. Daily Mail, 1 June 1959.
4. Walter Winchell: Lakeland Ledger and other newspapers, 10 July 1959.
5. JO: AAG, p. 139.
6. JO: AAG, p. 145.
7. Evening Standard, 11 March 1960.
8. Bamber Gascoigne: Spectator, 4 August 1961.
9. JO: BCP, p. 44.
10. Hugh Berrington to author.
11. Mervyn Haigh, Bishop of Winchester, quoted in Jonathan Gorry: Cold War Christians and the Spectre of Nuclear Deterrence, Macmillan, 2013, p. 84.
12. JO: They Call It Cricket: Declaration, p. 75.
13. Archbishop Trevor Huddleston to author.
14. Ibid.
15. St Vincent Troubridge, reader's report on Luther, 24 February 1961, LLC, BL.
16. Christopher Isherwood: Dairies Vol. 1, 1939–60, 17 July 1960, p. 883.
17. Christopher Isherwood to Don Bachardy: 12 February 1961, The Animals: love letters between Christopher Isherwood and Don Bachardy, p. 44.
18. Christopher Isherwood: Dairies Vol. 1, 1939–60, 6 August 1960, p. 891.
19. Ibid, 10 August 1860, p. 894.
20. Ibid, 22 August 1960, p 899.
21. Tony Richardson: Long Distance Runner, p. 119.
22. Jocelyn Rickards, quoted in JO: AAG, p. 195.
23. JO: AAG, p. 180.
24. Ibid.
25. Jocelyn Rickards to JO, 30 August 1960, HRHRC.
26. Kenneth Tynan: Observer, 9 July 1961; VES, p. 314.
27. Harold Hobson: The Sunday Times, 30 July 1961.
28. Michael Foot: Tribune, 4 August 1961.
29. Penelope Gilliatt: Queen, 2 August 1961.
30. Penelope Gilliatt to JO, nd (August 1961), HRHRC; quoted in New Yorker, 25 August 1997.
31. A. J. P. Taylor, quoted in Harry Ritchie: Success Stories, p. 78.

32. JO: 'A Letter to My Fellow Countrymen', *Tribune*, 18 August 1961; DYE, pp. 187–8.
33. Mervyn Jones to author.
34. *Daily Mail*, 19 August 1961.
35. Peregrine Worsthorne: *Sunday Telegraph*, 20 August 1961.
36. *Daily Mail*, 19 August 1961.
37. Ibid.
38. *Tribune*, 12 September 1961.
39. Ibid.
40. JO: *AAG*, pp. 204–6; *Daily Express*, 25 August 1961.
41. JO: 'A Letter to My Fellow Countrymen', *Tribune*, 18 August 1961; DYE, pp. 187–8.
42. JO: *AAG*, p. 215.

Chapter 17: Protest

1. All letters *Daily Mail*, 21 August 1961.
2. Bertrand Russell: *The Autobiography of Bertrand Russell*, Routledge, 2014, p. 597.
3. Harold Macmillan: *Pointing the Way*, p. 404.
4. Ibid, p. 401.
5. *Daily Express*, 18 September 1961.
6. Ibid.
7. *Daily Express*, 19 September 1961.
8. *Daily Telegraph*, 19 September 1961.
9. *Daily Express*, 18 September 1961.
10. *Manchester Evening Chronicle*, 31 August 1961.
11. *Daily Sketch*, 1 September 1961.
12. Anthony Creighton to author.
13. *New Statesman*, quoted by JO: *AAG*, p. 229.
14. *New Yorker*, 3 May 1976.
15. *Sunday Pictorial*, 24 September 1961; quoted in *AAG*, p. 226.
16. JO: *New Statesman*, 3 March 1961; DYE, p. 133.
17. Anthony Creighton to author.
18. Ibid.
19. Ibid.
20. Sonia McGuinness to author.
21. *Daily Mirror*, 26 September 1961.
22. *Daily Sketch*, 26 September 1961.
23. *Daily Telegraph*, 25 September 1961.
24. *Sussex Gazette*, 29 September 1961.
25. *The Times*, 2 November 1962.
26. Mary Ure, quoted in *Daily Mail*, 15 December 1962.
27. John French to author.
28. Oscar Beuselinck to author.
29. *Daily Express*, 30 November 1962.

30. Tribune, 8 December 1961.

31. Evening News and Star, 7 March 1962.

32. JO: diary, 17 February 1962: AAG, p. 241.

Chapter 18: Other Englands

1. Arnold Wesker to author.

2. John Arden to author.

3. Arnold Wesker to author.

4. Margaret Drabble: Angus Wilson, p. 219.

5. Julian Critchley, Conservative MP, quoted in From Blitz to Blair, p. 128.

6. Daily Telegraph, quoted in Richard Lamb: The Macmillan Years 1957–63: The Emerging Truth, John Murray, 1995, p. 219.

7. Peter Hennessey: Muddling Through, p. 242.

8. The Times, 9 January 1962.

9. St Vincent Troubridge: reader's report on The Blood of the Bambergs, 1 February 1962, LCC, BL.

10. Maurice Coles: reader's report on Under Plain Cover, 6 May 1962, LCC, BL.

11. R. A. Butler to Lord Scarborough, 11 August 1958, quoted in Steve Nicolson: The Censorship of British Drama, p. 108.

12. Lord Scarborough to George Tomlinson, General Secretary, Public Morality Council, 14 September 1962, LCC, BL.

13. Kenneth Tynan: Observer, 22 July 1962; VES, p. 240.

14. Harold Hobson: The Sunday Times, 22 July 1962.

15. Mervyn Jones in Tribune, 27 July 1962.

16. Tony Richardson: Long Distance Runner, p. 127.

17. Ibid, p. 135.

Chapter 19: A Sixties Millionaire

1. JO, quoted in Woman's Own, 20 February 1960.

2. Nellie Beatrice Osborne to Uncle Jack, nd (1963), HRHRC.

3. Nellie Beatrice Osborne to JO, nd (1963), HRHRC.

4. Ian MacDonald: Revolution in the Head, p. 74.

5. Nellie Beatrice Osborne to JO, nd (1965), HRHRC.

6. Ibid, nd (1964), HRHRC.

7. Undated Oscar certificate (1964), HRHRC.

8. Penelope Gilliatt, often quoted by JO: see for example AAG, p. 176.

9. Nellie Beatrice Osborne to JO, nd (1964), HRHRC.

10. JO: diary, 18 July 1962, quoted in AAG, p. 242.

11. Sonia McGuinness to author.

12. Penelope Gilliatt to JO, nd, note HRHRC.

13. Oscar Beuselinck to author.

14. Ibid.

15. Ibid.

16. JO: journal, 1959, HRHRC.

NOTES

17. Penelope Gilliatt, quoted by JO: diary, 17 July 1962, quoted in *AAG*, p. 241.
18. JO: journal, 1959, HRHRC.
19. Jocelyn Herbert to author.
20. Sonia McGuinness to author.
21. JO: journal, 7 April 1964; quoted in *AAG*, p. 244.
22. Maurice Coles: reader's report on *Inadmissible Evidence*, 13 June 1964, LCC, BL.
23. Anthony Page: 'Inadmissible Epitaph', *Weekend Guardian*, 6–7 June 1992.
24. Laurence Olivier to Kenneth Tynan, 27 August 1962, quoted in Kathleen Tynan: *The Life of Kenneth Tynan*, p. 217.
25. George Devine, quoted in William Gaskill: *A Sense of Direction*, p. 52.
26. Ibid.
27. Irving Wardle: *The Times*, 10 September 1964.
28. Harold Hobson: *The Sunday Times*, 13 September 1964.
29. Mary Holland: *Observer*, 13 September 1964.
30. Sandy Wilson to JO: 16 September 1964, HRHRC.
31. Terence Rattigan to JO: nd, October 1969, HRHRC.
32. Edith Bagnold to JO: 21 May 1968, HRHRC.
33. Violet Bonham Carter to JO: 29 May 1961, HRHRC.
34. John Betjeman to JO: John Betjeman, *Letters Vol.* 2, p. 280; *AAG*, pp. 245–6.
35. Lady Elizabeth Cavendish to author.
36. Ibid.
37. JO: journal, 22 October 1964, quoted in *AAG*, p. 247.
38. John Betjeman to JO: nd (October 1964), HRHRC.

Chapter 20: Of Money, Mother, Marriage and Manners

1. Tore Johansson to JO: Norway, 2 May 1959, HRHRC.
2. W. J. Turner to JO: nd, HRHRC.
3. M. Forsyth to JO: nd, HRHRC.
4. JO to Bryce, Hammer, Isherwood and Co., 4 April 1962, HRHRC.
5. Uncle Jack to JO, nd, quoted in JO: *AAG*, p. 33.
6. *The Times*, 2 June 1960.
7. Anthony Creighton to JO: 30 October 1962, HRHRC.
8. JO to Bryce, Hamner, Isherwood and Co., 5 February 1962, HRHRC.
9. JO: 3 February 1965, quoted in *AAG*, p. 249.
10. Pamela Lane to JO: 21 December 1965, HRHRC.
11. Hugh Berrington to author.
12. JO: *AAG*, p. 83.
13. Ibid, pp. 109–10.
14. Oscar Beuselinck to author.
15. Nellie Beatrice Osborne to Jack, nd, HRHRC.
16. Nellie Beatrice Osborne to JO, nd, HRHRC.

17. JO: journal, 1955, HRHRC.
18. Various letters from Nellie Beatrice Osborne to JO, nd (1964–65), HRHRC.
19. Gore Vidal: *Palimpsest*, Andre Deutsch, 1995, p. 99.
20. Hugh Berrington to author.
21. Anthony Porter to author.
22. Oscar Beuselinck to author.
23. Lady Elizabeth Cavendish to author.
24. Ibid.
25. JO: *AAG*, p. 229.
26. Lady Elizabeth Cavendish to author.
27. JO: *AAG*, p. 130.
28. JO: CP3, *Inadmissible Evidence*, p. 189.
29. Lady Elizabeth Cavendish to author.
30. Oscar Beuselinck to author.
31. Lady Elizabeth Cavendish to author.
32. Oscar Beuselinck to author.
33. Polly Devlin: 'John Osborne', *Vogue*, June 1964.
34. Ibid.
35. JO's tailoring measurements at HRHRC.
36. JO: CP3, *Inadmissible Evidence*, p. 189.
37. Polly Devlin: 'John Osborne', *Vogue*, June 1964.
38. JO, quoted ibid; Polly Devlin, ibid.

Chapter 21: The Baron Who Went Too Far
1. George Devine, quoted in Irving Wardle: *The Theatres of George Devine*, p. 263.
2. JO: diary, 24 February 1965, quoted in *AAG*, p. 250.
3. JO: journal, 1972, HRHRC.
4. Kenneth Tynan: *Profiles*, p. 255.
5. Arthur Miller: *Broadway: The Atlas of Literature*, ed. Malcolm Bradbury, de Agostini Editions, 1996, p. 247.
6. Nicholas de Jongh: *Politics, Prudery and Perversions*, p. 121.
7. JO, quoted in A. Alvarez: 'John Osborne and the Boys in the Band', *New York Times*, 28 September 1969.
8. Oscar Beuselinck to author.
9. John Deane: *Daily Express*, 9 April 1959.
10. JO: *Daily Express*, 10 April 1959.
11. JO to Melvyn Bragg, *The South Bank Show*, London Weekend Television, 1991.
12. John Betjeman to JO: 5 January 1965, HRHRC.
13. Programme note: *A Patriot for Me*, Royal Court Theatre, 1965.
14. Memo by Lord Scarborough, Lord Chamberlain, 31 October 1958, LCC, BL.
15. Nicholas de Jongh: *Politics, Prudery and Perversions*, p. 112.

16. Charles Heriot: reader's report on *A Patriot for Me*, August 1964, LCC, BL.
17. Ibid.
18. JO to Lord Chamberlain, 5 May 1959 and correspondence during the rehearsals for *The World of Paul Slickey*, LLC, BL.
19. Lord Annan: House of Lords, 17 February 1966.
20. Charles Heriot: reader's report on *A Patriot for Me*, August 1964, LCC, BL.
21. Ronald Hill: note to *A Patriot for Me*, papers, LCC, BL.
22. Listed deletions to *A Patriot for Me*, LCC, BL.
23. George Devine, quoted in Irving Wardle: *The Theatres of George Devine*, p. 275.
24. Ronald Hill: note to *A Patriot for Me*, papers, LCC, BL.
25. Terence Rattigan to JO: 30 June 1965, and other first night telegrams, HRHRC.
26. Helen Montagu, quoted in de Jongh: *Not in Front of the Audience*, p. 111.
27. Irving Wardle: *The Theatres of George Devine*, p. 276.
28. JO to Anthony Page, quoted in Anthony Page: 'Inadmissible Epitaph', *Weekend Guardian*, 6–7 June 1992.
29. Irving Wardle: *The Times*, 1 July 1965.
30. Ronald Bryden: *New Statesman*, 9 July 1965.
31. Mary McCarthy: *Observer*, 4 July 1965.
32. Kenneth Tynan: *Observer*, 18 July 1965.
33. Harold Hobson: *The Sunday Times*, 4 July 1965.
34. Ibid.
35. Internal memorandum to Examiners and Department of Public Prosecutions, Lord Chamberlain's office, urging 'further enquiries' to ascertain whether the creation of a members' club was a 'mere subterfuge', *A Patriot for Me*, papers, LCC, BL.
36. Letter from D. V. G Buchanan to Lord Chamberlain, with programme for 2 July 1965, LCC, BL.
37. Sir Norman Skelhorn, Director of Public Prosecutions, to Lord Chamberlain, 27 July 1965, LCC, BL.
38. George Devine to JO: nd (1965), quoted in *AAG*, p. 253.
39. George Devine to JO: 17 January 1965, HRHRC.
40. Jocelyn Herbert to author.
41. William Gaskill: *A Sense of Direction*, p. 72.
42. Tony Richardson: *Long Distance Runner*, p. 285.

Chapter 22: Love and Loss

1. Kenneth Tynan, quoted in Kathleen Tynan: *The Life of Kenneth Tynan*, p. 250.
2. Penelope Gilliatt: *Observer*, 7 November 1965.
3. Kenneth Tynan on BBC3, a late-night satire programme, 13 November 1965, quoted in Kathleen Tynan: *The Life of Kenneth Tynan*, p. 236.
4. *Evening Standard* headline, 26 February 1966.
5. Leo Caldwell, quoted in William Gaskill: *A Sense of Direction*, p. 69.

6. Michael Foot: theatre censorship debate in the House of Commons, 8 March 1966.

7. Ian Macdonald: *Revolution in the Head*, p. 184.

8. Ibid, p. 198.

9. Simon Trussler: *Observer*, 7 June 1969.

10. JO: journal, nd (1972), HRHRC.

11. Oscar Beuselinck to author.

12. Anthony Page: 'Inadmissible Epitaph', *Weekend Guardian*, 6–7 June 1992.

13. Jill Bennett, quoted in *The Sunday Times*, 10 October 1971.

14. Bernard Shaw: *Heartbreak House*, Act 3.

15. Anthony Page: 'Inadmissible Epitaph', *Weekend Guardian*, 6–7 June 1992.

16. Jill Bennett: *Godfrey: A Special Time Remembered*, p. 54.

17. Sonia McGuinness to author.

18. JO: *AAG*, p. 54.

19. JO: 'Author's Note' to *A Bond Honoured*, 1966.

20. JO to Penelope Gilliatt, nd (early summer 1961), HRHRC.

21. Penelope Gilliatt to Mrs Conner, nd (early summer 1961), HRHRC.

22. Robert Stephens: *Knight Errant*, pp. 90–1.

23. Irving Wardle: *The Times*, 7 June 1966.

24. Bernard Levin: *Daily Mail*, 7 June 1966.

25. John Betjeman to JO: 8 June 1966, HRHRC.

26. Irving Wardle to JO: 8 June 1966, HRHRC.

27. JO: CP3, *A Patriot for Me*, p. 122.

28. Robert Stephens: *Knight Errant*, p. 87.

29. Pamela Lane to JO: 18 July 1966, HRHRC.

30. Penelope Gilliatt to JO: nd (early summer 1961), HRHRC.

31. JO to Penelope Gilliatt: nd (early summer 1961), HRHRC.

32. Penelope Gilliatt to JO: nd (early summer 1961), HRHRC.

33. JO to Penelope Gilliatt: nd (early summer 1961), HRHRC

34. JO to Penelope Gilliatt: ibid, note 31.

35. Penelope Gilliatt to JO: nd (summer 1961), HRHRC.

36. JO to Penelope Gilliatt: ibid, note 31, HRHRC.

37. Pamela Lane to JO: 18 July 1966, HRHRC.

38. JO: *AAG*, p. 270.

39. Sonia McGuinness to author.

40. Oscar Beuselinck to author.

41. JO: *AAG*, p. 270.

42. Ibid.

43. Ibid, p. 271.

44. Nellie Beatrice Osborne to Penelope Gilliatt, nd (summer 1966), HRHRC.

45. JO: journal, nd (late summer 1961), HRHRC.

46. Penelope Gilliatt to JO: nd (late summer 1966), HRHRC.

47. Ibid.

48. JO: journal, nd (late summer 1966), HRHRC.
49. JO to Margery Vosper: 9 November 1966, HRHRC.

Chapter 23: The Cavalry and the Law
 1. A. N. Wilson: The Victorians, p. 180.
 2. Ibid, p. 182.
 3. Alfred Lord Tennyson: The Charge of the Light Brigade, 1850.
 4. The Times, 27 February 1967.
 5. Tony Richardson: Long Distance Runner, p. 194.
 6. Ibid, p. 195.
 7. JO to Tony Richardson, 10 May 1967, HRHRC.
 8. Oscar Beuselinck to author.
 9. Tony Richardson: Long Distance Runner, p. 195.
10. Several of Jill Bennett's letters are among the Osborne Archive at HRHRC.
11. Penelope Gilliatt to JO: nd (1963?), HRHRC.
12. Penelope Gilliatt to JO: nd (August 1961), HRHRC, quoted New Yorker, 25 August 1997.

Chapter 24: Fearing the Future
 1. JO to Sam Zolotow: The New York Times, 21 March 1968, HRHRC.
 2. Oscar Beuselinck to author.
 3. JO: CP2, The Hotel in Amsterdam, p. 119.
 4. Ibid, p. 141.
 5. JO to Margery Vosper: 4 August 1967, HRHRC.
 6. Ibid.
 7. Kenneth Tynan to JO: 5 October (1967), HRHRC.
 8. Oscar Lewenstein: Kicking Against the Pricks, p. 123.
 9. JO to Bryce, Hamner, Isherwood and Co., 4 April 1962, HRHRC.
10. JO postcard to Jill Bennett, quoted in Peter Charles: Admissible Evidence Plays and Players, 30 June 1973.
11. JO to Margery Vosper, 4 August 1967, HRHRC.
12. Kenneth Tynan: Diaries, 13 March 1971, p. 34.
13. JO: diary, 3 February 1965, quoted in AAG, p. 249.
14. Ronald Bryden: Observer, 26 May 1968.
15. Philip French: New Statesman, 12 July 1868.
16. Ronald Bryden: Observer, 26 May 1968.
17. Alan Carter: John Osborne, p. 181.
18. Kenneth Tynan: 'Dandy with a Machine Gun', Observer, 15 September 1957.
19. Ronald Bryden: Observer, 26 May 1968.
20. Martin Esslin: Anger Twelve Years On: Plays and Players, July 1968.
21. JO: AAG, p. 149.
22. JO, quoted in Polly Devlin: 'John Osborne', Vogue, June 1964.
23. JO: 'Market Swindlers', Tribune, 12 October 1967; DYE, p. 214; 'Middle

Class Poison', *The Sunday Times*, 11 April 1965; DYE, p. 231; 'The Socialist Once Angry', *Daily Herald* 16 March 1962; DYE, p. 195.
24. Oscar Lewenstein: *Kicking Against the Pricks*, p. 124.
25. *The Times*, 26 January 1968.
26. JO to Bryce, Hamner and Co., 12 February 1967, HRHRC.
27. Pauline Kael: *5001 Nights at the Movies*, p. 282.

Chapter 25: Detachment
 1. Kenneth Tynan and JO, quoted by JO: 'The Life of Kenneth Tynan', *New York Review of Books*, 3 December 1987; DYE, p. 141. See also Kenneth Tynan to *The Sunday Times*, 11 November 1973; *Letters*, p. 549.
 2. Kenneth Tynan: *Kenneth Tynan Letters*, ibid.
 3. JO: *Evening Standard*, 19 March 1971; DYE, pp. 23–4.
 4. JO: *Private Eye*, 4 April 1971.
 5. Kenneth Tynan to *The Sunday Times*, 11 November 1973; *Letters*, p. 549.
 6. JO, quoted by Kenneth Tynan, *Observer*, 7 July 1968.
 7. JO: journal, nd (1970), HRHRC.
 8. Anthony Page: 'Inadmissible Epitaph', *Weekend Guardian*, 6–7 June 1992.
 9. Ibid.
10. Jill Bennett, quoted in *Daily Mail*, 23 September 1967.
11. Jill Bennett, quoted in *Sunday Express*, 15 July 1973.
12. JO: journal, nd, HRHRC.
13. JO: journal, 30 October 1970, HRHRC.
14. JO: journal, nd (1970), HRHRC.
15. Colin Clark to author.
16. Peter Meyer to author.
17. JO: journal, nd (1970), HRHRC.
18. JO: journal, 30 October 1970, HRHRC.
19. JO: journal, 14 July 1972, HRHRC.
20. JO: journal, 28 January 1970, HRHRC.
21. JO: journal, 30 October 1970, HRHRC.
22. Stanley Price: *Plays and Players*, July 1970.
23. JO: journal, 11 July 1970, HRHRC.
24. JO: journal, nd (1970), HRHRC
25. Michael Billington: *Guardian*, 7 October 1971.
26. JO to Margery Vosper, 29 April 1971, HRHRC.
27. Ralph Richardson to JO, 8 October 1971, HRHRC.
28. Benedict Nightingale: *New Statesman*, 27 August 1971.
29. Simon Trussler: *Tribune*, 3 September 1971.
30. Benedict Nightingale: *New Statesman*, 27 August 1971
31. Michael Billington: *The Guardian*, 7 October 1971.
32. Harold Hobson: *The Sunday Times*, 10 October 1971.
33. Kenneth Tynan: *Diaries*, 13 August 1971, p. 59.
34. Oscar Beuselinck to author.

35. Kenneth Tynan: *Diaries*, 13 August 1971, p. 60.
36. JO: *A Place Calling Itself Rome*, Faber, p. 12.
37. JO: journal, 22 September 1971, HRHRC.
38. JO, quoted in Peter Charles: *Admissible Evidence Plays and Players*, 30 June 1973.
39. Anthony Page: 'Inadmissible Epitaph', *Weekend Guardian*, 6–7 June 1992.
40. Brian Cox to author.
41. Jill Bennett, quoted in *Daily Express*, 27 November 1972.
42. JO: journal, nd (1972?), HRHRC.
43. Ibid.
44. Ibid.
45. JO: journal, 8 October 1972, HRHRC.

Chapter 26: Despair
1. JO to Frank Dunlop, 9 November 1972, HRHRC.
2. Frank Marcus: *Sunday Telegraph*, 10 December 1972.
3. JO: *A Sense of Detachment*, Faber edition with *A Patriot for Me*, p. 136.
4. JO to Arnold Wesker, 2 January 1973, HRHRC.
5. Irving Wardle: *The Times*, 5 December 1972.
6. Alan Bennett: *Writing Home*, Faber, 2006, p. 490.
7. JO to Melvyn Bragg: *The South Bank Show*, London Weekend Television, 2 December 1981.
8. JO: *Spectator*, 3 August 1985; DYE, p. 113.
9. Kenneth Hurren: *The Spectator*, 9 December 1972.
10. Michael Billington: *The Guardian*, 5 December 1972; *One Night Stands*, pp. 21–2.
11. B. A. Young: *Financial Times*, 5 December 1972, quoted (often) by JO: e.g.: BCP, p. 276; DYE, p. 141.
12. Arnold Wesker to JO, 21 December 1972; Angela Huth to JO, 28 January 1973, HRHRC.
13. David Nathan to JO, 5 December 1972, HRHRC.
14. JO: journal, 13 October 1973, HRHRC.
15. JO to Barry Shaw (Oscar Beuselinck's legal partner), 27 May 1969, HRHRC.
16. Bernard Shaw: *Preface to Heartbreak House*, quoted in Michael Holroyd: *Bernard Shaw: The Lure of Fantasy*, p. 9.
17. Michael Holroyd to JO, 17 May 1974, HRHRC.
18. JO: journal, 16 June 1973, HRHRC.
19. JO: journal, nd (1971), HRHRC.
20. Ken Tynan to *The Sunday Times*, 11 November 1973; *Kenneth Tynan Letters*, p. 549.
21. JO: *The Sunday Times Magazine*, 4 November 1973.
22. Kenneth Tynan to *The Sunday Times*, 11 November 1973; *Kenneth Tynan Letters*, p. 549.
23. JO to Margery Vosper, 27 October 1973, HRHRC.

24. JO: journal, 24 June 1972, HRHRC.
25. Robin Dalton to author.
26. JO: journal, 6 June 1973, HRHRC.
27. Tom Stoppard: *Observer*, 15 September 1974.
28. Peter Lennon: *The Sunday Times*, 29 September 1974.
29. Riggs O'Hara to author.
30. JO: journal, 9 August 1973, HRHRC.
31. JO: *Observer*, 6 October 1974; DYE, pp. 197–8.
32. JO: journal, nd, September 1974, HRHRC.
33. Max Wall to JO, 11 December 1974, HRHRC.
34. John Kidd to JO, 3 December 1974, HRHRC.
35. JO to Jill Bennett: first night card quoted in Peter Charles: *Admissible Evidence Plays and Players*, 30 June 1973.
36. Ivan Howlett: *Plays and Players*, March 1975.
37. Harold Hobson: *The Sunday Times*, 19 January 1975.
38. JO: *The End of Me Old Cigar*, p. 33, Faber.
39. Oscar Wilde: *The Picture of Dorian Gray: Complete Works*, Collins, 1996, p. 20.
40. JO: Introduction to *The Picture of Dorian Gray*, DYE, p. 42.
41. Greenwich Theatre management letter to JO: 23 September 1974, HRHRC.
42. Martin Amis: *New Statesman*, 24 September 1976.
43. Peter Hall to JO: 7 August 1974, HRHRC.

Chapter 27: Desolation

1. JO: journal, 10 January 1976, HRHRC.
2. *The Times*, 16 October 1974, quoted in Dominic Sandbrook: *Seasons in the Sun*, pp. 77–8.
3. *The Times*, 29 July 1974, quoted ibid, p. 137.
4. Roy Strong: *Diaries*, quoted ibid, p. 179.
5. Alan Clark: *Diaries: Into Politics*, quoted ibid, p. 343.
6. Bernard Donoghue, quoted in Dominic Sandbrook: *Seasons in the Sun*, p. 344.
7. JO: *Watch It Come Down*, Faber, p. 39.
8. JO: journal, 4 April 1974, HRHRC.
9. Peter Hall to JO: 24 August 1974, HRHRC.
10. Peter Hall: *Diaries*, 16 January 1976, p. 206.
11. JO to Robin Dalton, 15 September 1975, HRHRC.
12. John French: *Robert Shaw*, p. 221.
13. Irving Wardle: *The Times*, 3 April 1975.
14. Peter Hall: *Diaries*, 16 January 1976, p. 206.
15. Ibid.

Chapter 28: Retrenching

1. Peter Hall: *Diaries*, 20 February 1976, p. 213.

2. *Daily Mail*, 25 February; Irving Wardle, *The Times*, 25 February 1976.
3. Michael Billington: *Guardian*, 25 February 1976.
4. JO to Harold Pinter: 27 February 1976, HRHRC.
5. Edward Albee to JO: 10 August 1976, HRHRC.
6. JO to Edward Albee: 22 August 1976, HRHRC.
7. Peter Hall: *Diaries*, 29 February 1976, p. 215.
8. JO: 'They Call It Cricket', *Declaration*, p. 65.
9. Benedict Nightingale: *New Statesman*, 5 March 1976.
10. Alan Bennett: 'What the National Theatre Means to Me', *Guardian*, 19 October 2013.
11. Peter Hall: *Diaries*, 27 May 1976, p. 236.
12. JO: *Sunday Telegraph*, 28 August 1966.
13. JO: 'The British Playwrights' Mafia', *Sunday Times Magazine*, 16 October 1977; DYE, pp. 135–48.
14. JO to Harold Hobson, 12 April 1976, HRHRC.
15. Francis King to JO, 15 October 1978, HRHRC.
16. Lady Patricia Barnes to author.
17. Michael Billington to author.
18. JO, quoted in *The Age* (Australia), 19 May 1877.
19. JO: *Guardian*, 14 July 1977.
20. Jill Bennett to JO, quoted in JO to Barry Shaw, 7 June 1977, HRHRC.
21. JO to Jill Bennett, quoted ibid.
22. JO to Jill Bennett, nd (July 1977), HRHRC.
23. JO and Jill Bennett divorce papers, HRHRC.
24. JO to Michael Medwin, 5 April 1976, HRHRC.
25. Ronnie Harris to JO: nd (1976), HRHRC.
26. JO: *Desert Island Discs*, BBC Radio 4, 5 March 1982.
27. Richard Findlater: *At the Royal Court*, p. 179.
28. JO, quoted in 'A Better Class of Osborne', *New Standard*, 6 March 1981.
29. Kenneth Tynan: *Observer*, 6 April 1968.
30. Newspaper clipping for Edenbridge Church summer fete, nd, HRHRC.
31. Lady Elizabeth Cavendish to author.
32. Canon Richard Mason to author.
33. JO, quoted in Philip Oakes: 'Osborne Looks Back', *Telegraph Sunday Magazine*, June 1985.
34. Canon Richard Mason to author.
35. JO: *The Oldie*, 11 December 1992; DYE, p. 233.
36. Ibid, p. 232.
37. Cranmer Summer Ball invitation card, HRHRC.
38. Canon Richard Mason to author.
39. Michael Billington: *Guardian*, 13 August 1978.
40. The Garrick Club website.
41. Valerie Grove: 'A Better Class of Osborne', *New Standard*, 9 March 1981.
42. Joan Bakewell: *The Times*, 14 February 1980.

43. Adam Smith: *Empire Essay: Flash Gordon*, Empireonline.com.
44. Pauline Kael: *5001 Nights at the Movies*, p. 250.
45. JO, quoted in Philip Oakes: 'Osborne Looks Back', *Telegraph Sunday Magazine*, June 1985.
46. *The Sunday Times*, 11 October 1981.
47. Alan Bennett: 'Bad John', *London Review of Books*, 3 December 1981.
48. JO, quoted in Philip Oakes: 'Osborne Looks Back', *Telegraph Sunday Magazine*, June 1985.
49. Mrs Marie Matthews to JO: nd (1981), HRHRC.
50. Robert Cheshyre: *Observer*, 16 November 1979.
51. Guy Bennett to author.
52. Ibid.
53. JO to Nolan Osborne, 5 January 1982, HRHRC.
54. Guy Bennett to author.

Chapter 29: Defiance
1. JO: rejected article for *The Sunday Times*, 1983, quoted Philip Oakes: 'Osborne Looks Back', *Telegraph Sunday Magazine*, June 1985.
2. JO: journal, 1983, HRHRC.
3. JO: *Daily Mail*, 19 June 1986.
4. Oscar Beuselinck to author.
5. Dr Kenneth Marsh to JO: 10 June 1982, HRHRC.
6. Eric Shorter to author.
7. Angela Langfield to author.
8. Pamela Lane to JO: 26 August 1983, HRHRC.
9. Ibid, 1 June 1984, HRHRC. In fact, although it appears that some of Osborne's letters to Pamela were subsequently lost, several survived and are now part of the British Library's collection of contemporary manuscripts and letters.
10. Ibid, 9 February 1984, HRHRC.
11. JO to Pamela Lane: nd, 1983, BL.
12. Ibid, 18 May 1984, HRHRC.
13. Ibid, 1 June 1984, HRHRC.
14. JO to Benedict Nightingale, quoted in 'Curtain Falls on Benedict Nightingale's Lifetime in the Theatre', *Guardian*, 29 January 2010.
15. JO, quoted in Philip Oakes: 'Osborne Looks Back', *Telegraph Sunday Magazine*, June 1985.
16. JO: ibid and *Desert Island Discs*, BBC Radio 4, 5 March 1982.
17. Tom Sutcliffe: *Guardian*, 8 April 1985.
18. JO: *AAG*, p. 269.
19. Ibid.
20. JO: *Spectator*, 13 July 1985; DYE, p. 32.
21. Andrew Rissick: *New Statesman*, 12 July 1985.
22. JO: *The Times*, 26 December 1991; DYE, pp. 220–1; 13 January 1992; DYE, p. 222.

23. JO: journal, 8 October 1972, and repeated several times since.

24. JO: journal, nd, 1993.

25. JO: 'Voting Pattern', *Observer*, 6 October 1974; DYE, p. 197.

26. Peter Hall: *Diaries*, 3 May 1979, p. 434.

27. Norman Tebbit, quoted in Peter Clarke: *Hope and Glory*, p. 379.

28. Sonia McGuinness to author.

29. JO, quoted in *The Sunday Times*, 30 July 1989.

30. Pamela Lane to JO, 8 May 1986.

31. Valerie Grove: 'No Mistake, the View is Still Unmellowed', *The Sunday Times*, 30 July 1989.

32. A..E. Housman: *A Shropshire Lad: XL: Into my Heart on Air That Kills*.

33. Prebendary Richard Shaw, quoted on The John Osborne Centre at The Hurst, Arvon Foundation website.

34. JO: quoted many times in various articles after the move to Shropshire and by Heilpern: *John Osborne: A Patriot for Us*, p. 438.

35. JO: *Spectator*, 6 June 1992; DYE, p. 161.

36. Peter Ackroyd: *Albion*, p. 449.

37. JO, quoted in Philip Oakes: 'Osborne Looks Back', *The Telegraph Magazine*, June 1985.

38. Gordon Dickerson to author.

39. JO: *The Sunday Times*, 5 September 1983; DYE, pp. 91–4.

40. JO to *Guardian*, 23 June 1977; DYE, p. 52.

41. JO to *The Times*, 22 July 1977; DYE, p. 53.

42. JO: *Spectator*, 24 September 1988; DYE, pp. 54–7.

43. JO to Richard Eyre: 26 December 1993, quoted in *National Service*, 31 December 1994, p. 277.

44. JO: *Spectator*, 30 June 1992 and others; DYE, p. 205.

45. JO: *Spectator*, 20 July 1985; DYE, p. 49.

46. JO: *Spectator*, 30 June 1992; DYE, pp. 205–6.

47. JO: *Spectator*, 17 April 1993; DYE, pp. 223–4.

48. JO: *Introduction The Father*, p xii, Faber; DYE, p. 38.

49. Michael Billington; *Guardian*, 28 October 1988.

50. Irving Wardle: *The Times*, 27 October 1988.

51. Guy Bennett's funeral address from Bennett to author.

52. Lindsay Anderson, quoted in Richard Eyre: *National Service*, 15 October 1990, p. 125.

53. JO, *AAG*, p. 259.

54. Ibid, p. 255.

55. JO: *AAG*, pp. 255–9.

56. Anthony Page: 'Inadmissible Epitaph', *Weekend Guardian*, 6–7 June 1992. Three years later, in 1995, a High Court settlement gave Jill Bennett's secretary and her hairdresser a total of £185,000.

57. Brian Cox to author.

58. Richard Eyre: *National Service*, 15 October 1990, p. 125.

59. John Carey: *The Sunday Times*, 3 November 1991.

60. Anthony Page: 'Inadmissible Epitaph', *Weekend Guardian*, 6–7 June 1992.

61. Richard Eyre: *National Service*, 6 April 1992, pp. 184–5.

62. JO, quoted in Valerie Grove: 'No Mistake, The View is Still Unmellowed', *The Sunday Times*, 30 July 1989.

63. Ibid.

64. JO: CP1, Introduction to *Look Back in Anger*, p. xii.

65. Ibid, pp. ix–x.

Chapter 30: Redemption

1. JO: journal, 20 March 1989, HRHRC.

2. Ibid.

3. JO to Tony Richardson, 7 October 1989, HRHRC.

4. JO: CP1, Déjàvu, p. 281.

5. Ibid, p. 367.

6. Ibid, p. 372.

7. Ibid, p. 311.

8. Ibid, p. 372.

9. Ibid, p. 316.

10. JO: journal, nd (October 1989), HRHRC.

11. JO: obituary of Tony Richardson, *Observer*, 17 November 1991; DYE, p. 110.

12. Ibid, p. 111.

13. *The Independent*, 14 November 1991.

14. Richard Eyre: *National Service*, 23 April 1989, p. 71.

15. JO to *The Times*, 2 September 1968; DYE, pp. 219–20.

16. JO to Eric Shorter: 19 August 1993, courtesy Eric Shorter.

17. JO to Bill Kenwright: 14 February 1992, HRHRC.

18. Among a montage presented by *The Late Show*, BBC2, 10 June 1992.

19. Ibid.

20. JO: *The Times*, 18 April 1991; DYE, p. 128.

21. Peter Egan: 'John Osborne was like a Wounded Animal', *Guardian*, 25 March 2014; and to author.

22. JO: CP1, Introduction to *Look Back in Anger*, p. xii.

23. Peter Egan to author.

24. JO: CP1, Introduction to *Look Back in Anger*, p. xii.

25. Peter Egan: 'John Osborne was like a Wounded Animal', *Guardian*, 25 March 2014; and to author.

26. Claire Armistead: 'Return of the Stylish Misogynist', *Guardian*, 11 June 1992.

27. Philip Howard: *The Times*, 10 June 1992.

28. JO: *Spectator*, 13 June 1992; DYE, p. 185.

29. JO to Bill Kenwright, 20 May 1992, HRHRC.

30. Peter Kemp: 'Tantrums and Teddy Bears', *Times Literary Supplement*, 19 June 1992.

31. Benedict Nightingale: *The Times*, 12 June 1992.
32. Paul Taylor: *Independent*, 3 June 1992.
33. Michael Billington: *Guardian*, 13 June 1992.
34. John Lahr: *The Late Show*, BBC 2, 10 June 1992.
35. Michael Coveney: *Observer*, 14 June 1992.
36. JO: *Spectator*, 4 December 1993; DYE, p. 263.
37. JO to Jocelyn Rickards: 2 September 1992, HRHRC.
38. Penelope Gilliatt to JO: inscribed copy of *The Oxford Chekhov, Vol. 5: Short stories 1889–91*, edited by Ronald Hingley, advertised for sale on the Abe Book UK website, June 2015.
39. JO, quoted in Philip Oakes: 'Osborne Looks Back', *Telegraph Sunday Magazine*, June 1985.
40. JO: *Spectator*, 14 May 1994.
41. JO to Fiona Clark, attached to the Royal Literary Fund reply, 10 December 1992, HRHRC.
42. JO to Robert McCrum: 10 October 1992, HRHRC.
43. JO to Eric Shorter: 19 August 1993, courtesy Eric Shorter.
44. JO to Gordon Dickerson: 3 September 1992, HRHRC.
45. JO: *Spectator*, 4 December 1993; DYE, p. 263.
46. Ibid.
47. Alan Plater to author.
48. Ibid.
49. Anthony Page: 'Inadmissible Epitaph', *Weekend Guardian*, 6–7 June 1992.
50. JO quoted in Richard Eyre: *National Service*, 7 June 1993, p. 221.
51. JO: *Spectator*, 7 May 1994.
52. Michael White: *Independent on Sunday*, 26 November 1995.
53. Simon Callow: *The Independent Weekend*, 6 January 1996.
54. John Heilpern: *John Osborne: A Patriot for Us*, p. 464.
55. Guy Bennett to author.

Chapter 31: Afterlife
1. Irving Wardle: *Independent on Sunday*, 1 January 1995.
2. Mervyn Jones to author.
3. Michael Billington: *Guardian*.
4. John Arden to author.
5. *The Times*, 27 December 1994.
6. Anthony Creighton, quoted in Nicholas de Jongh: 'The Secret Gay Love of John Osborne', *London Standard*, 24 January 1995.
7. Gordon Dickerson to author.
8. Pamela Lane: quoted in *The Daily Telegraph*, 25 January 1995.
9. Sonia McGuinness to author.
10. Pamela Lane to author.
11. Jocelyn Rickards to author.
12. Hugh Berrington to author. A close friend of the younger Osborne,

Berrington became a distinguished Professor of Politics at Newcastle
University, and died on 8 November 2010, aged 82.

13. Oscar Beuselinck to author.

14. Anthony Creighton: quoted in Nicholas de Jongh: 'The Secret Gay Love of
    John Osborne', *London Standard*, 24 January 1995.

15. Ibid.

16. *Guardian*, 25 January 1995.

17. Benedict Nightingale: *The Times*, 28 January 1995.

18. Anthony Creighton to John Heilpern, p. 149, and to author.

19. *Daily Express*, 3 June 1995.

20. *The Times*, 3 June 1995.

21. Reverend Gordon Taylor: *The Times*, 6 June 1995.

22. Ibid.

23. JO: *Observer*, 20 April 1975; DYE, p. 121.

24. JO, quoted in Philip Oakes: 'Osborne Looks Back', *Telegraph Sunday
    Magazine*, June 1985.

25. Anthony Astbury to JO: 20 December 1994, inserted with a
    presentation copy of *99 Poems in Translation*, advertised for sale on Abe
    Books UK website, May 2015.

26. JO: *Desert Island Discs*, 5 March 1982.

27. The John Osborne Centre at The Hurst, Arvon Foundation website.

28. Harvey Kass: *Guardian*, 30 July 1997.

29. Ibid.

30. Helen Osborne obituary: *The Daily Telegraph*, 14 January 2004.

31. Oscar Lewenstein, quoted in Jocelyn Rickards obituary, *The Daily Telegraph*,
    12 July 2005.

32. Angela Langfield to author.

33. Richard Digby Day, quoted in Pamela Lane obituary, *Guardian*,
    21 November 2010.

34. JO to Pamela Lane, autumn 1983, BL.

35. Simon Trussler: *The Plays of John Osborne*, 1969, p. 40.

36. Harold Hobson, *Theatre in Britain*; Kenneth Tynan, *VES*, p. 272; Alan
    Sillitoe, quoted in *Guardian*, 23 May 2003.

37. Arnold Wesker to author.

38. Samuel Beckett, quoted in *Damned to Fame*, p. 607.

39. Peter Hall, quoted in *Guardian*, 24 August 2005.

40. Peter Hall: *Diaries*, 18 February 1976, p. 213.

41. Michael Billington: *Guardian*, 7 October 2001.

42. Ibid, 12 May 2010.

43. Ibid, 29 June 2010.

44. Gordon Dickerson to author.

Acknowledgements

I OWE AN IMMENSE DEBT to Gordon Dickerson, John Osborne's literary agent and the administrator of his Estate on behalf of the Arvon Foundation. Through thick and thin, his faith in this book and his regular emails have been enormously encouraging and sustaining. He has also generously allowed me to quote freely from the published and unpublished writings of John Osborne that he administers for the Arvon Foundation, to whom I am also grateful.

At Oberon, I am equally indebted to a fine triumvirate of James Hogan, Andrew Walby, and my superlatively courteous and outstanding editor, George Spender. All have been wonderful to work with.

Any historian is indebted to the work of others in the same field and I am no exception. The books I have found particularly useful are listed in my bibliography. The theatre historian of this period is particularly fortunate to be able to turn to reviews written by Kenneth Tynan, Harold Hobson, Irving Wardle and Michael Billington, all of whom have left records of the first productions of Osborne's plays that combine critical insight, opinion and wit, with an extraordinary ability to capture the moment and magic of performance.

I began researching John Osborne's life and work several years ago, and some of those whom I interviewed and with whom I corresponded passed away during the lengthy journey from research to completion. I am grateful for the contributions of John Arden, Hugh Berrington, Oscar Beuselinck, Anthony Creighton, Thomas Eastwood, Valerie Eliot, Barry England, Christopher Fry, Giles Gordon, Jocelyn Herbert, Archbishop Trevor Huddleston, Pamela Lane, who also gave me permission to quote from her letters to Osborne, Canon Richard Mason, Jocelyn Rickards and Julian Slade.

I also thank Hilda Banham, Lynne Reid Banks, Lady Patricia Barnes, Guy Bennett, Pauline Berry, Michael Billington, Lady Elizabeth Cavendish, Mavis Chamberlain, Brian Cox, Peter Egan, June Ellis, Barbara Fearon, John French, Philip French, Peter Gill, John Greenwood, Geoff Hammerton, Betty Hester,

402 ACKNOWLEDGEMENTS

Stella Jagg, Angela John, John Johnson, Brenda Kaye, Barbara Keogh, Denise Larkin, Dennis Lotis, Samantha Rutherford Lörstad, Sonia McGuinness, Stanley Meadows, Peter Meyer, John Moffatt, Eileen Morgan, Riggs O'Hara, Anne Parmiter, Alan Plater, Anthony Porter, Mavis Pugh, Paul Scofield, Thelma Rogers, Eric Shorter, Irving Wardle, Arnold Wesker, Bunty Willard-Burrows, Nora Wood, Geoffrey Wright and B. A. Young. Some correspondents have chosen to remain private.

At the Harry Ransom Humanities Research Center at the University of Texas at Austin, I thank a fine research room librarian, Pat Fox. At the British Library I am indebted to Jamie Andrews, Head of Cultural Engagement and the author of a perceptive introduction to *Before Anger*, and of '*Poor Jonah: John Osborne's Roads to Freedom*', for the *British Library Journal*, and Helen Melody, Head Curator, Contemporary Literary and Creative Archives, Contemporary British Collections; both were especially kind and helpful. I also thank Linda Owen, Derby Local Studies library; C. M. Bayliss, Hammersmith and Fulham Archives Local History Centre; Michael Cudlipp, History of Advertising Trust; A. Kirby, Isle of Wight County Reference Library; Sarah Jones, Newport Library; J. Walsh, Surrey County Council Ewell Library, and Anne McQueen, Librarian, Yorkshire Post Newspapers.

Finally, I owe an immense debt to Eva, my wife, for her forbearance, belief, encouragement and critical insight.

Index

Abercrombie, Patricia 309; *see also* Barnes, Sir Denis and Lady Patricia
Ackroyd, Peter 70, 332
Aladdin 54
Albee, Edward 306
Albery, Donald 152, 164–5
Aldermaston marches 185, 190
Aldiss, Brian 293
Aldwych Theatre 219
Allan, Rae 55
Allen, Walter 85, 108
Allsop, Kenneth 119, 272–3
Almost a Gentleman 337–8, 355
Almost a Vision 312
Alternative Service Book 315
Alvarez, A. 235
American musicals 66–7
Americanization of culture 116–17
Amis, Kingsley 31, 83–5, 110–13, 137, 139, 159, 185, 325–6
Amis, Martin 299
Anderson, Elaine 151
Anderson, Lindsay 114, 139, 141, 157, 190–1, 202, 337
Andrews, Harry 266
Anglo-Saxon Attitudes 99
'Angry Young Man' phenomenon 4, 13, 44, 54, 108–14, 120–3, 139–43, 172, 187, 201, 250, 272–4, 316, 325, 363
Annan, Lord 239
Anouilh, Jean 86, 122, 308
Antonioni Michelangelo 253, 359
appeasement policy 20
Archer, William 97
Arden, John 98, 191, 201, 219, 233, 277, 352–3, 401
Armistead, Claire 345

Arms and the Man 65
Armstrong, Alun 336
Armstrong-Jones, Anthony 181, 205, 215
Arnold, John 263–4
Arnold, Matthew 101
Arts Council 69, 97–8, 220, 243, 358
Arvon Foundation 358, 361, 401
Ashcroft, Peggy 245, 286
Astbury, Anthony 357
Atkins, Eileen 328
Atkinson, Brooks 146
Attlee, Clement 30–1, 61–2, 115, 137–8
austerity 35, 66
Australia 310–11
Ayer, A. J. 111, 161, 359

Bachardy, Don 178–9
Bagnold, Enid 221
Bailey, David 252
Baker, Peter 163
Bakewell, Joan 318
Balcon, Michael 156
Baldwin, Stanley 15, 20
Ball, Michael 357
Banham, Hilda 401
Banham, Martin 272
Banks, Lynne Reid 49–50, 56, 60, 202, 401
Banzie, Brenda de 133
Barber, Chris 158, 160
Barber, John 105, 113
Bardot, Brigitte 151
Barker, George 357
Barker, Harley Granville 97
Barnes, Sir Denis and Lady Patricia 309, 313, 401
Barratt, Reginald 51–2

Barron, Keith   298, 312
Bates, Alan   101, 327, 329, 343
Battersea Dogs Home   337
Battle of Britain   26
'Bay of Pigs' incident (1961)   204
The Beach of Aurora   347
A Bear Called Paddington   326
The Beatles   200–1, 211, 250–3, 276
Beaton, Cecil   109, 168
Beaumont, Hugh ('Binkie')   43–4, 68, 80,
    101, 103, 158, 235, 325, 344
de Beauvoir, Simone   85
Beaverbrook, Lord   20
Beckett, Samuel   87, 100, 103, 202, 219,
    244–5, 277, 303, 326, 336, 339, 360–1
Bedford, Duke of   168–9
Beerbohm, Max   172
Behan, Brendan   293
Bell, Mary Hayley   49
Bell, Vanessa   293
Belmont College   27–9
Benchley, Robert   145–6
Benn, Tony   30–1, 67, 204
Benn Brothers (company)   33, 35, 29
Bennett, Alan   164, 290, 307, 319
Bennett, Billy   337
Bennett, Guy   321–2, 337, 342, 351, 401
Bennett, James Randle and Nora   255
Bennett, Jill   6, 240, 249–60, 266, 268–
    75, 278–81, 284–8, 292–9, 304–5,
    308–14, 317, 321, 323, 326, 335–8
Bennett, Judith   321
Bennett, Sally   321
Bergman, Ingmar   277, 318
Berlin Wall   185–6
Berliner Ensemble   137, 244
Berney, William   45
Bernstein, Leonard   164
Berrington, Hilda   38
Berrington, Hugh   32–3, 38, 57, 91, 145,
    176, 228–9, 354, 401
Berry, Pauline   401
Betjeman, John   221–4, 229–30, 236,
    240, 257, 280, 314, 334
A Better Class of Person   10, 22, 25, 228, 319,
    328–9, 338
Beuselinck, Oscar   135–6, 147, 155–6,
    167, 183, 191–3, 197–8, 208, 214–
    15, 217, 227–31, 235, 254–61, 264–
    5, 268, 270, 275, 292, 311, 323–4,
    354, 358, 401
Bevan, Aneurin   140, 168–9
Beyond the Fringe   164, 207
Billington, Michael   120, 283–5, 291,
    306, 310, 317, 334, 336, 346, 352,
    361–2, 401

Billy Bunter of Greyfriars School   92
The Birthday Party   202, 360
Blackwell, J. Edward   96
Bland, Sir Simon and Lady Olivia   313
Blond, Neville   96–7, 132
Bloody Sunday (1972)   290
Bloom, Claire   160
Bloomsbury group   293
Blow-Up   253, 293, 359
The Blue Angel   52
The Blue Lamp   157
Bogarde, Dirk   357
Bond, Edward   250
A Bond Honoured   256–8
Bonham Carter, Violet   221
Book of Common Prayer   314–15
Boulting Brothers   159
Bourke, Jennifer   180
Bournemouth   166–7
Bouverie Street   33
Bowen, Elizabeth   111
Bragg, Melvyn   236, 320
Braine, John   137–8, 159, 172
Brainscrew   275
Branagh, Kenneth   338–9, 345, 362
Brandt, Francine   151, 153, 161–2, 174,
    180, 197, 261
Braun, Eva   29
Brecht, Bertolt   96, 100, 137, 264, 268,
    325
Brenton, Howard   290
Brideshead Revisited   67
Bridgwater   56
Brighton   43
Brighton Rock   159
British Broadcasting Corporation (BBC)
    16, 119, 157, 160, 164, 174, 245,
    275, 281–2, 346, 362
British Institute of Fiction Writing Science
    27
British Library   363, 402
'British Playwrights' Mafia'   18, 307–8,
    327
Britten, Benjamin   96
Brook, Peter   45, 102, 250
Bruce, Edgar K.   52
Bryce, Hamner & Isherwood (accountants)
    155, 225, 295
Bryden, Bill   305
Bryden, Ronald   242, 272–3
Buchanan, D. V. G.   243
Burgess, Guy   237
Burnett, Frances Hodgson   297
Burton, Richard   121, 160, 174, 232, 293
Butler, R. A.   191, 206
Butlin, Billy   53

Cadogan Hotel 332, 349
Caine, Michael 237, 252, 276
Calder, Angus 20
Callaghan, James 330
Callow, Simon 350
Camberwell Place 61–3
Cameron, James 141
Campaign for Nuclear Disarmament (CND) 83, 185, 190
Campbell, Patrick 159
Canby, Vincent 347
Cardigan, Lord 262–3, 266
Cards of Identity 100, 119
The Caretaker 202
Carey, John 338
Carlos the Jackal 287–8
Carlyle, Thomas 6
Carmichael, Ian 159
Caron, Leslie 121
Carrington, Dora 293–4, 302–3
Carrington (film) 294
Carte Blanche 325
Carter, Alan 272–3
Cassady, Ruth 93–4
Casson, Hugh 165
Castro, Fidel 204
Cavendish, Lady Elizabeth 222, 230, 240, 314, 401
censorship 73, 80, 159, 251–2, 290; see also Lord Chamberlain's Office
The Chairman's Wife 276
Chamberlain, Mavis 401
Chamberlain, Neville 19–21, 25
Champion, Harry 298
The Charge of the Light Brigade 233, 261–6, 268, 271, 277
Charles II 350
Charley's Aunt 41, 63
Chekhov, Anton 139–40, 245–6, 284
Chelsea Palace variety theatre 127–8
The Cherry Orchard 284
Cheshyre, Robert 320
Chetwode, Penelope 230
Chevalier, Maurice 127
Chicken Soup With Barley 201
Christie, Julie 202
Christmas Place 308–20, 331
Church of England 314–16, 339
Churchill, Caryl 290
Churchill, Winston 25, 29–31, 62, 82, 115
cinema in Britain 156–61, 202, 292
cinema-going 69
Clark, Alan 302
Clark, Sir Andrew 263–4
Clark, Colin 281, 302

Clayton, Jack 159
Clayton Dulton, Michael 64
Clurman, Harold 169
Cobbold, Lord 218, 238–9, 242–3, 251
Cobham, Lady 167
Codron, Michael 219, 250, 286
Coles, Maurice 206
Collins, John 184–5, 192
Collinson, Peter 312
Colonel Redl 327
Committee of 100 190–2
Communist Party 19
Conner, Angela 210
Conner, Cyril 181
Connery, Sean 165, 171, 237
Connolly, Cyril 35, 67, 82, 85, 111
Conrad, Joseph 303
Conran, Terence 201
conscription 21, 38
consumer culture 116
Cook, Peter 164
copyright infringement 263–4, 294
Coriolanus 264, 286
Coronation Day (1953) 66
The Country Wife 100
Coveney, Michael 346
Coward, Noël 12, 43–4, 63, 68, 91, 131, 136, 168–9, 221, 235, 258, 325, 333–4
Cox, Brian 287, 338, 401
Cox, John 245
Coyle, Richard 361
Cranko, John 235
Cranmer, Thomas 316
Creighton, Anthony 5, 47–65, 71–81, 90–2, 99, 102, 122, 134, 136, 144, 148–9, 152, 155–6, 194–6, 225–6, 240–2, 277, 307, 323, 331, 353–6, 359, 401
Creighton, Elsie 47
cross-dressing 236
The Crucible 99, 101
The Cruel Sea 157
Cry for Love 204
Cuckoo in the Nest 222
Cuttell, Colin 80

Dahlberg, Gilda 166
Daily Express 20
Dalton, Robin 295, 298–9, 303, 327
Damn You, England (collected journalism) 350
Dark of the Moon 45
Darling 202
Darlington, W. A. 136
the Daughters of Eve 335

Davis, Desmond 262
Dawson, Helen 309–15; see also
    Osborne, Helen
Dean, James 110
Deane, John 235
Death of a Salesman 137
The Death of Satan 99, 119
debutantes 115
Declaration 140–3, 171, 176
The Deep Blue Sea 68, 92, 103
Defoe, Daniel 293
Deighton, Len 237
Déjàvu 338–47
de Jongh, Nicholas 353, 356
Deladier, Edouard 20
Delaney, Shelagh 178, 202
Dench, Judi 338
Dennis, Nigel 100, 119, 139
Department of Public Prosecutions 243
Derby Playhouse 74, 78
Desert Island Discs 319–20
Desmond, Patrick 42–6, 51–2, 58, 65,
    78–80, 92, 148, 204
The Devil Inside Him 44–6, 51–2, 69, 73,
    92, 152, 204, 361–2
Devine, Alexander 93
Devine, George 93–103, 107, 119, 131,
    140, 149, 152, 155–8, 164, 168,
    175–8, 182–5, 201, 206–7, 210–11,
    219–20, 233, 238–46, 254, 258, 291,
    334, 349, 363
Devine, Harriet 94–5
Devine, Sophie 244–5
Devlin, Polly 232
Dexter, John 76, 91, 201, 206–7, 219–
    20, 225, 257, 277, 296, 336
Diamonds 304
Dickerson, Gordon 333, 348, 353–4,
    361–2, 401
Digby Day, Richard 326, 359
Dilke, Sir Charles 293
Divorce His, Divorce Hers 293
divorce laws 134–5, 253
Dodd, Ken 348
Don Juan 99, 119
Donner, Clive 299, 359
Donoghue, Bernard 302
Don't Destroy Me 113
Dors, Diana 123
Dostoyevsky, Fyodor 44
Douglas-Home, Sir Alec 68, 203–4, 307
Douglas-Home, William 36, 53, 203
Downer, Jim 83–4
Drabble, Margaret 202
Dracula 65
Draper, Peter 275

Drew, Linda 312
The Duchess of Malfi 70, 91
Duel of Angels 174
Duet for Two Hands 49
Duff, Terence 41–3
du Maurier, Daphne 65
Duncan, Ronald 36, 96–100, 119
Dunlop, Frank 289
Duras, Marguerite 85, 262

Ealing Studios 156–7
Eastwood, Thomas 347, 401
Eden, Sir Anthony 82, 115, 118, 164
Edenborough, Betty 26
educational opportunities in Britain 84
Egan, Peter 344–6, 357, 401
Eliot, T. S. 53, 70, 98, 154–5
Eliot, Valerie 155, 401
Ellis, June 401
The End of Me Old Cigar 297–8, 303, 312
England, Barry 401
England, My England 350
English Stage Company 92, 95–105, 119–
    20, 130, 145, 157–8, 181, 219–20,
    233, 235, 251, 270, 292, 353, 363
    Council of 132, 140
English Stage Society 240, 243
Englishness 253, 314–15, 332, 344
The Entertainer 35, 128–33, 136–40, 147,
    150, 153, 175, 177, 181, 216, 273,
    297–300, 303, 313, 327, 329, 361–2
Entertaining Mr Sloane 219
Epitaph for George Dillon 78, 80, 91–2, 129,
    152–3, 155, 164, 168, 202, 304, 361
Epstein, Brian 253
Erikson, Erik H. 176–8
Esdaile, Alfred 97
Esslin, Martin 273–4, 330–1
'the Establishment' 98, 239, 273
Evans, Edith 245
Eve, Trevor 349
Every Day Except Christmas 158
Ewell 17
Ewing, Kenneth 327
existentialism 32–3, 85
The Exorcism 304–5
Experimental Theatre Club, Oxford 152
Expresso Bongo 164, 168
Eyre, Richard 334, 338, 343, 349

Faber & Faber (publishers) 154, 347–8,
    363
Faithful, Marianne 213
Farson, Daniel 112–13, 143
fascism 19–20
The Father 335–6

Fearon, Barbara 401
Fearon, George 109, 119
Festival of Britain 62, 66
Finch, Peter 316
Findlater, Richard 69, 71, 97
Finlay, Frank 305
Finney, Albert 84, 182, 208, 211, 229, 303, 356
First Love 276
Fitzgerald, Ella 231
Flare Path 49
Flash Gordon 318
Fleet Street 34
Foot, Michael 168, 170, 183–6, 240, 251
Forbes, Bryan 202
Fox, Robert 343
France 85–6
Frangcon-Davies, Gwen 99
Franz-Joseph, Emperor 237
'Free Cinema' 157–8, 185
Freedman, Harold 148, 154
French, John 401
French, Philip 120, 272, 401
Freud, Sigmund 242
Friends of the Earth 339
Frink, Elizabeth 194, 267
Frinton-on-Sea 65
Fry, Christopher 44, 53, 69–70, 98, 174, 401
Fry, Jeremy 181
Fulham 10

Gabor, Eva 178
Gagarin, Yuri 187
Gaitskell, Hugh 114–15, 186, 204
Gardner, Alan 163
Gardner, Jimmy 155
Garnett, Audrey and Betty 36–7, 39
Garrick Club 317, 325, 327, 336, 349
gas masks 20–1, 25
Gas World 33, 35
Gascoigne, Bamber 175
Gaskill, William 152, 191, 219–20, 233, 245, 250–1, 284, 287
Gaston, Robert 64
Gaycroft School of Music, Dancing, Speech Elocution and Drama 36–7, 39
The Gem 15–16, 222, 283
Genet, Jean 91, 207, 219, 262
George, Susan 312
Get Carter 276, 318
Gielgud, John 47–8, 72, 94, 235, 266
The Gift of Friendship 296
Giggles and Girls 41
Gill, Peter 361, 401
Gilliatt, Penelope 5, 57, 163, 180–4, 189,

192–9, 206–7, 210–16, 222, 226, 229–34, 244–5, 249–50, 254–61, 266–7, 270–1, 292–3, 316–17, 322, 336, 338, 341, 347, 359
Gilliatt, Roger 5, 81–3, 194–7, 205
Giraudoux, Jean 174
Girl with Green Eyes 262
God Rot Tunbridge Wells 327, 329, 350
Goff, Ivan 212
Goff, J. 263–4
Golding, William 84
Gollancz, Victor 111
Gombos, Laszlo 197–8
Gone with the Wind 131
The Good Woman of Setzuan 100, 119, 137
Goodman, Lord 243, 264
Goodwin, Michael 55–9, 61
Gowrie, Earl of 358
The Graduate 270
Gradwell, Leo 251
Granada Television 119
Granger, Derek 105, 123
Grant, Duncan 293
Gray, Jill 335
The Great Bear 70
Green, Jonathan 83
Greene, Graham 159, 161, 173, 317, 359
Greenwich Theatre 295–9
Greenwood, John 401
Griffiths, Richard 357
Gross 303
Grove, Nellie Beatrice 9–11, 13, 15, 18–29, 33, 36–8, 43, 46, 51, 54, 59, 63–5, 75–6, 102–5, 109, 129, 135, 144–5, 149, 156, 173, 196, 198, 210–13, 225–31, 240, 260–1, 294, 313, 319, 323, 325, 328, 331
Grove, William Crawford 9–10, 24, 129, 217
Grumpy 61
Guardian readers 316
Guinness, Alec 277, 296
Gunn, Thom 83
Guys and Dolls 67, 87

Habitat stores 201
Habsburg Empire 237, 263
Haigh, Kenneth 101–3, 145, 149, 258
Haley, Bill 116
Halifax, Michael 119
Hall, Peter 121, 219, 250, 300, 303, 305–7, 323, 329–30, 333–5, 356, 360–1
Hall, Willis 155, 254
Halliwell, Kenneth 253
Hamilton, Gerald 141–2

Hamilton, Michael 39
Hamilton, Richard 83
Hamilton, Sir William and Lady Emma 6
Hamlet 54, 70, 130, 337
Hammerton, Geoff 401
Hampton, Christopher 290, 294
Hancock, Robert 133–4
Handel, George Frideric 327, 332, 357–8
The Hand-Reared Boy 293
Hanson, Harry 63
Happy Birthday 44–5
Happy Days 326
The Happy Family 64
Hare, David 290, 357
Harewood, George, Earl of 96, 140
Harman Pictures 261, 263–4
Harris, Sophie 94–5
Harrison, Rex 293, 298
Harry Ransom Humanities Research Center 348, 358, 363, 402
Harvey, Laurence 159, 263–5
Hastings, Hugh 81
Hastings, Michael 112–13
Hayling Island 52–4
Heartbreak House 254, 283–4
Heath, Edward 251, 276, 282, 297, 307, 330
Hedda Gabler 99, 286–8, 292, 295
Heffer, Eric 28–9
Hellingly 3, 193, 196–8, 214, 256, 263, 275, 308
Hemmings, David 266
Henderson, Helen 155, 174
Hennessey, Peter 129, 204, 363
Henry V 130
Henry VIII 178
Hepner, Leon 165
Herbert, A. P. 95
Herbert, Jocelyn 95, 183, 210, 216, 219, 244–5, 401
Heriot, Charles 102, 239
Hester, Betty 401
Hewison, Robert 34
Higham, David 154
Hill, Ronald 239–40
Hitler, Adolf 15, 20, 29, 224
Hobsbawn, Eric 12
Hobson, Harold 80, 105–6, 109–11, 122, 146, 176, 182, 207, 221, 242, 272, 285, 298, 308, 346, 359–60, 401
Hodge, Douglas 362
Hodges, Mike 276, 318
Hoffman, Dustin 270
Hoggart, Richard 116–17, 158
holiday camps 53

Holland, Mary 221
Hollywood 147, 219, 266, 295
Holroyd, Michael 293–4, 334
Holroyd, Stuart 139
Holyoake, George 173
Home, Lord *see* Douglas-Home, Sir Alec
homosexuality 58–9, 63–4, 72–4, 83, 235–42, 250, 253, 265, 299, 306, 334, 353–5
Hooper, Ewan 295, 297
Hope, Anthony 205
Hope, Bob 147
Hope-Wallace, Philip 272
Hopkins, Bill 139
Hopkins, John 293
Horne, Kenneth 57
The Hostage 293
The Hotel in Amsterdam 10–11, 249, 268–74, 277–8, 283, 286, 299, 303, 361
Housman, A. E. 331, 336
Houston, Penelope 159
Howard, Alan 328
Howard, Anthony 115
Howard, Philip 345
Howard, Trevor 266, 327
Huddleston, Trevor 177, 401
Hughes, Helena 101
Hughes, Ted 83–4, 335, 358
Hungary 118–19
Hurren, Kenneth 291
Hurry On Down 84–5, 88, 138
The Hurst 331–3, 342, 357–8
Huth, Angela 291

Ibsen, Henrik 80, 286–7, 303
The Icpress File 237
The Importance of Being Earnest 74
Inadmissible Evidence 129, 175, 177, 214–22, 226–7, 232, 234–5, 238, 240, 272, 279, 317, 349, 362
Ionescu, Eugène 100
The Iron Petticoat 147
Isherwood, Christopher 141, 178–9, 236
Isle of Wight 21–2
Is Your Honeymoon Really Necessary? 59
It's A Boy 60
It's Only Us 275
Ivanov, Oleg 203
I Was A Drug Fiend 78–9

Jackson, Glenda 316
Jacobi, Derek 245
Jagg, Stella 402
Jagger, Mick 213, 299
Jaws 304

Jay, Miss 304–5
Jellicoe, Ann 202
Jenkins, Roy 251
John, Angela 402
John, Gwen 213, 267
John Osborne Archive and John Osborne
    Centre 358
Johnson, Bunk 129
Johnson, John 402
Jones, Mervyn 170, 186, 207, 352
Joyce, James 233

Kael, Pauline 266, 276, 318
Kafka, Franz 219
Kass, Harvey 358
Kaye, Brenda 64, 402
Kaye, Danny 131
Keach, Stacey 300
Keats, John 38, 57, 59, 70
Keeler, Christine 203
Kemp, Peter 346
Kempson, Rachel 290
Kenny, Yvonne 357
Kenwright, Bill 343–4
Keogh, Barbara 402
Khrushchev, Nikita 186
Kidderminster Playhouse 63–5
King, Francis 308
King, Philip 65
The King Is Dead 70–1
King Lear 321
Kipling, Rudyard 91
The Kitchen 258
Kitchen, Michael 299
'kitchen sink' playwrights 201
Kneale, Nigel 160, 175, 208
Krost, Barry 295

The Lady (magazine) 234
Lady Chatterley's Lover 205–6
A Lady Mislaid 57
The Lady's Not for Burning 69
Lahr, John 346
Lambert, J. W. (Jack) 109
Lane, Elizabeth 56, 58–60, 63, 81
Lane, Pamela 55–65, 70–1, 74–8, 81, 85,
    88, 91–2, 102–5, 133–6, 142, 144,
    149, 162, 181, 206, 216, 226–7, 230,
    258–61, 272, 282, 313, 326–31, 348,
    354, 359, 401
Lane, William 56, 58–61, 81, 90
Langfield, Angela 326, 359
Larkin, Denise 402
Larkin, Philip 3, 83–4, 200, 211
la Rue, Danny 236

Las Vegas 147
Laughton, Charles 127
The Lavender Hill Mob 156
Law, William 176
Lawrence, D. H. 32, 205
le Carré, John 237
Leigh, Vivien 80, 130–2, 174, 179, 333
Leighton, Margaret 103
Lemon, Jack 300
Lennon, John 211, 275
Lennon, Peter 296
Lessing, Doris 139, 141, 153, 190–1
A Letter to My Fellow Countrymen 187–90,
    196, 251
Leveaux, David 336
Levin, Bernard 257
Levitt, Cedric 165–6
Lewenstein, Oscar 96–8, 270, 274,
    359
Life magazine 112
Linden, Stella 41–6, 51–2, 56, 78, 91,
    289
Lindsay, Robert 361
Litchfield, Captain 243
Little Lord Fauntleroy 297
Live Like Pigs 201
Livings, Henry 275
Livingstone, Fred 196–7
Loesser, Frank 87
Logue, Christopher 185
Lohr, Marie 165
London, Bishop of 206
London blitz 25
Long Day's Journey into Night 137, 326
Look Back in Anger 4, 13–14, 23, 54, 59,
    75–7, 81, 87, 91–2, 98–106, 108–10,
    114–22, 129–30, 136, 143, 145–53,
    156, 160–1, 165, 169, 171, 174, 176,
    201, 216, 218, 272–5, 298, 301,
    303, 327, 333, 336–43, 346–8,
    359–62
Loot 250
Lope de Vega, Félix 256
Lord Chamberlains's Office (Stable Yard)
    73, 79–80, 102, 132, 166, 178, 206,
    218–19, 235, 238–43, 250–3, 285,
    363
Lord of the Flies 84
Loren, Sophia 293
Lotis, Dennis 165, 169, 171, 402
Lousada, Anthony 95
Love in a Myth 100, 162
The L-Shaped Room 50, 202
Lucan, Lord 262–3, 266
Lucky Jim 84–8, 138, 159

The Lugger, Portscatho 332–3
Luther 175–8, 182–4, 208, 214, 216,
    236–7, 240, 300, 361
Luther (Jill Bennett's dog) 311
Luther, Martin 224

MacCarthy, Fiona 115, 120
McCarthy, Joseph 72
McCarthy, Mary 242
McCartney, Paul 211, 275
McCrum, Robert 347
MacDonald, Ramsay 12
McGrath, John 290
McGregor Ure, Colin 101
McGuinness, Frank 194–5
McGuinness, Sonia 5, 194–7, 213–14,
    218, 259–60, 280–1, 354, 402
Maclean, Donald 237
Macmillan, Harold 164, 186, 191, 203
McMillan, Kenneth 165
The Magnet 15, 222, 283
The Makepeace Story 92
The Making of Moo 139
Mankowitz, Wolf 164
Marcus, Frank 289, 291
Margaret, Princess 115–16, 171, 181, 205
Markham, Violet 66
Marlowe, Christopher 70
Marriage à la Feydeau 281
Marsh, Kenneth 324
Maschler, Tom 139
Mason, Richard 314–16, 401
Maugham, Somerset 65
Maw, D. S. J. 328
Mayne, Margo 305
Meadows, Stanley 133, 402
Meals on Wheels 234
Melford, Austin 60
Melly, George 191–2
Mercer, David 275
Merchant, Vivien 335
Merivale, Jack 179
Merrick, David 146, 149, 152, 171, 234
Mewshaw, Michael 317
Meyer, Peter 281, 402
Of Mice and Men 64
The Miller (trade journal) 35
Miller, Arthur 55, 80, 87, 99, 105, 131,
    137, 234, 333
Miller, Bernard 225
Miller, Christine 234, 317
Miller, Jonathan 164, 206–7
Miller, Max 43, 128, 334
Milligan, Spike 214
Mirfield 177, 315
Mitford, Nancy 221

Moffatt, John 402
Moll Flanders 293
Momma Don't Allow 158
Monroe, Marilyn 80, 131, 179
Montagu, Lord 72–3
Moore, Dudley 164
Morgan, Eileen 402
Morris, Donald 260
Moscow 145
Mosley, Oswald 15, 19
Mother Courage 96
Ms or Jill and Jack 295–6
Muggeridge, Malcolm 108
The Mulberry Bush 99, 101
Muller, Robert 108–10, 113
Murdoch, Iris 84, 204
Murray, Alec 161, 173
music hall 128, 133, 236, 348
musicals 66–7, 164, 234
Mussolini, Benito 15, 20
My Fair Lady 164, 171
My Wife's Family 56

Nasser, Gamal 117–18
Nathan, David 166, 291
National Advertising Benevolent Society
    17–24, 27–8, 32–3
The National Health 277
National Health Service 61–2
National Lottery Fund 358
National Theatre 219, 250, 256, 270,
    277, 286, 294–5, 300, 303–9, 325,
    329–30, 333–6, 343, 349, 351,
    361
National Theatre of Wales 361–2
Naughty Girls of 1948 41
Nelson, Horatio 6
Neto, Agostinho 204
new writing for the theatre 69
New York 145–9, 211, 234–5, 261, 266,
    292, 316, 327
Newell, Mike 295–6
Nichols, Mike 270–1
Nichols, Peter 65, 277
Night Must Fall 48, 50, 53
Nightingale, Benedict 284, 307, 327,
    346, 355
Nolan, Captain 262–3, 266
No Orchids for Miss Blandish 41
No Room at the Inn 40–3
Northern Songs 275
Notley Abbey 130–1
Novello, Ivor 36–7
Nykvist, Steve 276
Nyman Libson Associates 295

O'Brien, Edna 202, 262
O Dreamland 158
O'Hara, Gerry 276
O'Hara, Riggs 402
Oh! Calcutta! 325
Oklahoma! 66–7
Old Times 304
The Old Vic 69, 87
The Old Water Mill 3, 5, 193–8, 210,
    212, 234, 254, 260, 308
Olivier, Laurence 80, 87, 130–3, 136,
    139, 142, 156, 175, 179, 181, 214,
    216, 219, 229, 245, 258, 277, 285,
    294, 298, 300, 313, 336, 357
Onassis, Aristotle 151
One by One 254
O'Neill, Eugene 137, 219, 326
The Ordeal of Gilbert Penfold 293
Orton, Joe 219, 250, 253
Orwell, George 14–16, 25, 35, 55, 67–8,
    91, 334
Osborne, Annie 15, 24
Osborne, Faith 11, 13
Osborne, Helen 230, 315–18, 321–2,
    325, 328–32, 335, 345, 349, 351,
    353–9; see also Dawson, Helen
Osborne, Jim 10, 15, 22, 24
Osborne, John
  acting work 28, 35, 38–9, 43–4, 49,
    52–7, 60–5, 74, 81, 92, 99, 119, 139,
    154, 162, 225, 245, 258, 275–6, 312,
    318, 349
  adolescence 24–5, 31
  ancestry 6–9
  appearance 57, 148–9, 154, 175, 231–
    2, 332, 350
  arrest 5, 192
  awards 122–3, 211–14, 243, 274, 285,
    338, 348
  backstage work in the theatre 40–53
  birth 11
  casual work 44, 65
  churchgoing and religious belief 314–
    15, 320
  cinema-going 36
  correspondence 224–7, 239, 255, 326,
    334–5, 354–5
  daughter see Osborne, Nolan
  death 351
  divorces 133–6, 162, 197, 210, 225,
    249, 259, 261, 266–7, 270–1,
    311–12
  drinking 214, 249, 259–60, 279–82,
    287, 294–6, 309–10, 324, 327–9,
    335, 342–5, 348, 351, 356
  earliest writing of any sort 18–19

  early work as a dramatist 42–4, 49, 51,
    69–71, 90
  elocution and dancing lessons 36–7
  evacuation when a child 21–2
  fondness for ocean cruises 318
  funeral 351
  generosity 155–6, 195, 225–7
  girlfriends when young 37, 51–2
  gravestone at Clun 357–8
  handwriting and writing method 218
  hatred of his mother 22–4, 227–30,
    294, 319, 323
  health problems 14, 19, 26–7, 33,
    37, 216–17, 230, 249, 259–61, 280,
    288, 294–6, 303–4, 310, 324, 327–9,
    334–5, 340, 342, 348–51
  horoscope 11
  income and wealth 4, 187, 211, 224–5,
    270, 274–6, 278, 288, 292, 298, 303–
    4, 318, 327, 329, 332–3, 342–3, 347–8
  interest in art 120–1, 194
  journal entries 216, 226, 233, 261,
    279–82, 286, 288, 292, 296, 303–4,
    323–4, 340
  journalism and letter-writing to
    newspapers 32–4, 68–9, 187–90,
    196, 251, 333–5, 350
  living as a country gentleman and family
    man 316, 320–2, 329, 332
  love of the theatre and music hall 10,
    16, 35–6, 127–8, 348
  marriages 60, 144, 210, 230, 249, 254,
    256, 272, 279–80, 296, 308–9, 312,
    315
  memoirs 6, 144, 228, 318–19, 337
  memorial service 356–7
  memories of childhood 14
  musical tastes 16, 55, 89, 120–1, 231,
    320, 327
  parents see Grove, Nellie Beatrice;
    Osborne, Tom Godfrey
  personality 32, 38, 56–7, 77, 130, 182,
    215, 227–31, 258–9, 265, 323, 344–5
  poetry writing 32
  political engagement 38, 55, 140, 184–
    92, 203, 274, 284, 297, 329, 331, 352
  press interest in 3–5, 108, 110, 121,
    136–7, 143–5, 162, 166, 172–3, 187,
    193–8, 224, 336, 349
  professional standing 249–50, 253,
    273–4, 285, 295, 306–7, 344, 352–3,
    357, 360–1
  prose style 32, 70, 87–8
  reading 15–16, 26–8, 37, 117, 120, 312
  recurrent sense of loss 13, 16, 23, 215,
    230

recurring themes in writing   129, 139–
    40, 175, 303
schooling   18–19, 22, 25–9
screenplay writing   208, 211–12, 224,
    233, 263–5, 276–7, 292–4, 303
seen as a symbol of change   4
self-confidence   130, 249, 215–16, 299,
    305
stage directing   164–5, 234, 297, 317
success and celebrity status   150, 154–6,
    171, 183, 212–15, 231–2
suspicions of homosexuality   58–9,
    63–4, 236, 353–5
vegetarianism   46, 121
views on the theatre   68–9
wives   see Bennett, Jill; Gilliatt,
    Penelope; Lane, Pamela; Osborne,
    Helen; Ure, Mary
Osborne, Nolan   233–4, 254–9, 270–1,
    292, 302, 316–17, 320–6, 342, 347,
    351
Osborne, Tom Godfrey   8–24, 227, 246,
    328
O'Toole, Peter   84, 344
Oughton, Hubert   21, 24, 27, 32–3
The Outsider   111–12
Owen, Robert   204

Page, Anthony   219–22, 234, 240–1, 254,
    272, 274, 278–9, 284, 287, 338, 349
Palmer, Tony   327, 344
Panic Stations   293
The Parachute   275
Parker, Dorothy   145–6
Parker, Joan   174–5
Parker, Stephen   336
Parmiter, Anne   402
Passport to Pimlico   156
Paterson, Neil   160
Patridge, Ralph and Frances   294
A Patriot for Me   28, 129, 177, 214–18,
    236–44, 255, 258, 327, 355, 361–2
Paul, Leslie Allen   109
Peacock, Peter   107
Pelham, David   165–70, 286
Percival, T. Wigney   61
Personal Enemy   71–5, 78–80, 102, 152
    241, 361–2
Philby, Kim   237
The Picture of Dorian Gray   288, 292, 297,
    299, 362
Pinero, Arthur Wing   42, 45, 75
Pinocchio   36
Pinter, Harold   201–2, 211, 219, 250,
    304, 306, 335, 339, 357, 360–1

A Place Calling Itself Rome   286, 288, 292, 361
Plater, Alan   348–9, 402
Plath, Sylvia   72, 335
Plays for England   200, 205–7
Plowright, Joan   178–9, 229, 285, 313,
    329
poetry   83–4
Poke, Greville   96
Ponti, Carlo   293
pop art   83
Porch House, Amersham   198
Porter family   15, 91, 229, 402
Portmeirion   193
Present Laughter   63
Presley, Elvis   116
Price, Stanley   282
Priestley, J. B.   36, 108, 185
The Prince and the Showgirl   131
The Prisoner of Zenda   205–6
Pritchett, V. S.   111
private club performances   240–3, 250–1
Private Eye   164, 277
Profumo, John   168, 203, 237
Pugh, Mavis   402
Purcell, Henry   350, 357
Pygmalion   79

Quant, Mary   201
The Quatermass Experiment   160
The Queen   140, 250
Queen (magazine)   163, 184
Queen (rock group)   318
Quitak, Oscar   65

Raglan, Lord   262, 266
Rain   65
Rattigan, Terence   36, 43–4, 48–9, 53,
    68, 75, 91–2, 94, 103–4, 131, 168,
    201, 213, 221, 229, 235, 241–2, 311,
    325, 334
Rebecca   65, 130
Red and Blue   262
Redgrave, Vanessa   191–2, 258, 262, 265
Redl, Alfred   237–42, 258, 355
Reece, Bertram   192
Reed, Oliver   312
Rees, John   76, 80, 136
Reisz, Karel   157
Relative Values   68
repertory theatres   45, 69
Resting Deep   42
Rice-Davies, Mandy   203
Richard III   130
Richardson, Howard   45
Richardson, Ralph   284–5

Richardson, Tony 95–104, 119, 130–5, 145, 150–2, 156–60, 164, 171, 174–5, 178–84, 191, 199, 208–12, 219–20, 233, 244, 246, 260–6, 269–71, 277, 299, 307, 323, 341–3

Rickards, Jocelyn 161–2, 165–7, 172–5, 179–83, 188–9, 193, 197, 212, 260, 347, 354, 359, 401

The Right Prospectus 29, 282

Rissick, Andrew 328

Ritchie, Harry 363

The Rivals 65

Roberts, Rachel 298

Robin Hood 92

Robinson, Kenneth 167

Roc Players 55–6

Rogers, Byron 328

Rogers, Thelma 402

The Rolling Stones 200–1, 299

The Room 202

Room at the Top 137–8, 159–60, 166, 263

Roots 201

Rose, Kenneth 71

Rosenberg, Julius and Ethel 72

Rosencrantz and Guildenstern Are Dead 250, 277

Rosoman, Leonard 260

Royal College of Art 285

Royal Court Theatre 92, 96–103, 109, 119–21, 131–2, 137–40, 152, 158, 175, 180–5, 199, 201–2, 214–15, 219–22, 233–6, 240–5, 250–1, 256, 258, 270, 274, 284–7, 290–2, 310–13, 317, 343, 351–2, 357

Royal Family 140, 171, 205–6

The Royal Hunt of the Sun 219, 277

Royal Literary Fund 347

Royal Opera House, Covent Garden 231, 245

Royal Shakespeare Company 219–20, 250, 286, 349

Russell, Bertrand 185, 190–2

Saga Repertory Group 47–50, 52–5, 58, 353, 361

St George, Clive 48, 52

Salzman, Harry 147–51, 156, 160, 171, 174

Sandbrook, Dominic 363

Sartre, Jean-Paul 85

satire 164–9, 176, 205, 303

Saved 250

Saxon Players 45–6, 69

Scarborough, Earl of 73, 206, 218, 238–9

Schell, Maximilian 240, 276, 344

Schiller, Heinrich 326

Schlesinger, John 316

Scofield, Paul 102, 272, 402

Seaforth, Victor 127–8, 177

Seagulls over Sorrento 81

The Second Mrs Tanqueray 42

Second World War 21, 24–6, 29–30

The Secret Agent 303

See How They Run 65

Sellers, Peter 214

A Sense of Detachment 249, 289–92, 295, 303, 309

Separate Tables 311

Sequence (magazine) 157

Serjeant Musgrave's Dance 201

Shaffer, Peter 219, 277

Shakespeare, William 69–70, 139–40, 264, 286, 339

Shaw, Bernard 65, 67, 77, 79–80, 91, 97, 113, 254, 283, 293, 326, 334

Shaw, Jennifer 197–8

Shaw, Richard 332

Shaw, Robert 180, 197–8, 210, 304–5

Shawn, Wallace 317

Sheen, Michael 361

Shelley, Mary 213

Sheridan, Richard Brinsley 65

Shinwell, Emmanuel 33

Shippard, Renee 37

Shorter, Eric 325–6, 343, 347–8, 402

Shulman, Milton 168

Signoret, Simone 159–60

Sillitoe, Alan 360

Simpson, Sir Joseph 192

The Sixties 200, 211, 214, 252–3, 274, 276, 290

Skelhorn, Sir Norman 243

Slade, Julian 401

Smith, John Christopher 358

Smith, Maggie 357

Snowden, Lord see Armstrong-Jones, Anthony

social reforms 83

The Soldier's Tale 245

Soper, Donald 188

The South Bank Show 320

Soviet Union 31

Spanish Civil War 14–15

Spark, Muriel 202

The Spectator 334

Spencer, Charles 346

Spiegel, Sam 293

Spielberg, Steven 304

The Sport of My Mad Mother 202

The Spy Who Came In From the Cold 237

Stafford-Clark, Max 298, 313

The Stage (newspaper)   46–9, 53–5, 65, 69,
    92, 98
Standing, John   296
A State of Change   256–7
Steinbeck, John   64
Stephens, Robert   152, 202, 245, 257–8,
    349
Stephenson, Margaret   45–6
Stephenson, Richard   45, 69
Stewart, Joy   141–2
Stoker, Bram   65
Stoneleigh   14, 17, 24–5, 29, 38
Stoppard, Tom   250, 277, 296, 327
Storey, David   158, 202, 211
Storme, Peter   46
Strach, Walter   275
Strachey, Lytton   37–8, 293, 302
A Streetcar Named Desire   64, 80
Strindberg, August   335–6
Strong, Adele   46
Strong, Roy   302
A Subject of Scandal and Concern   173–6
Suez crisis (1956)   117–18, 129
Sunday, Bloody Sunday   316
Sutcliffe, Tom   327
von Sydow, Max   318

Table by the Window   103–4
Talking About Jerusalem   201
A Taste of Honey   178, 202
Taw and Torridge Festival   96
Taylor, A. J. P.   185, 237
Taylor, D. J.   68
Taylor, Don   152, 304
Taylor, Elizabeth   293
Taylor, Gordon   356–7
Taylor, Jeremy   320
Taylor, John Russell   271–3
Taylor, Paul   346
Tearle, Geoffrey   268
teddy boys   83, 110
Tee, Robert   109
television   66, 119
Temple, Joan   40
Tennant, David   361
That Uncertain Feeling   110
Thatcher, Margaret (and Thatcherism)
    330–1
Theatre World   98
Theatrical Ladies' Guild of Charity   337
They Call It Cricket   139
'This is the Dawning of the Age of
    Aquarius'   252
This Sporting Life   202
Thomas, Dylan   40
Thomas, Gareth   344

Thompson, Emma   339
Thorndike, Sybil   71
The Threepenny Opera   264
Thunderball   237
Tidmarsh, E. D.   59
Time magazine   112, 142, 252
Time Present   268–74, 277–8, 286, 330–1
Tom Jones   184, 199, 208–9, 211–12, 356
Tomorrow Never Comes   312
Tomorrow With Pictures   225
Toulouse-Lautrec, Henri   127
Townsend, Peter   115–16
Toynbee, Philip   111, 142
Travers, Ben   222–3
Trevis, Di   349
Trewin, J. C.   104
Tribune   170–1, 183–7, 198, 251
Troubridge, St Vincent   79, 132, 178, 206
Trussler, Simon   253, 272–3, 284, 359
Try a Little Tenderness   318
Twelfth Night   65
Twelvetrees, Leslie   74, 92
Tynan, Kathleen   299
Tynan, Kenneth   86–7, 100–7, 109, 111,
    114, 130, 135–41, 146, 152, 156,
    182, 185, 204, 207, 214–15, 219,
    242, 250–3, 256, 270–3, 277–8, 285,
    294–5, 299–300, 307, 313, 323, 325,
    346, 360, 401
Tynan, Letitia Rose   107

Udaipur, India   212
Under the Net   84
Under Thirty Group   65
Unholy Fools   316
United Nations   118
United States   31–4, 62, 66–7, 72,
    116–18
Ure, Mary   4–5, 101–2, 121–2, 133–6,
    144–5, 148–55, 160, 162, 167, 172–
    4, 178–83, 189–98, 210, 216, 225,
    258, 280, 304–5, 329
  son (Colin)   196, 198, 233, 304–5
US   250

Vadim, Roger   151
Vaughan Williams, Ralph   17, 55, 314,
    320
de Vere Gordon-Maclean, Colin   188–9
verse drama   44–5, 53, 69–71, 96–100,
    119
Very Like a Whale   318
Vidal, Gore   228
A View from the Bridge   80
Virol   15
The Vodi   172

Vogue (magazine)   180, 232, 274
The Vortex   92
Vosper, Frank   100
Vosper, Margery   100, 147, 154, 164,
   261, 270–1, 284, 286, 295

Wain, John   84–5, 110–13, 139, 204
Waiting for Godot   87, 105, 121, 219,
   360
Walker, Alexander   159
Walker, Kenneth   111
Wall, Max   298
Wall, Mickey   18, 26, 33, 38
Wanamaker, Sam   74–5
Ward, Stephen   203
Wardle, Irving   94–5, 119, 220–1, 241–2,
   257–8, 290–1, 305–6, 336, 352, 363,
   401, 402
Warner, Jack   171
The Washing of the Spears   260
The Waste Land   70, 91
Watch It Come Down   44, 17, 249, 300–3,
   306–9, 312–13
Waterhouse, Keith   155
Waugh, Evelyn   67–8, 219, 293
We are the Lambeth Boys   158
Webb, Beatrice   99
Webster, John   70–1
Welchman, Harry   165
welfare state   32
Welsh, John   101
Wesker, Arnold   98, 190–1, 201, 233,
   258, 290–1, 356–7, 360, 402
West Side Story   164
West of Suez   117, 129, 177, 282–5, 290,
   292, 295, 303, 309
Whelan, Christopher   164
White, Michael   350
Who's Afraid of Virginia Woolf?   206
Wilde, Oscar   91, 288, 299, 332
Wildeblood, Peter   72–3
Willard-Burrows, Bunty   402

Williams, Emlyn   48, 53, 100, 121
Williams, Raymond   111
Williams, Tennessee   55, 64, 80, 87, 105,
   120, 166
Williams-Ellis, Clough   193
Williamson, Nicol   220–2, 233–4, 279,
   308, 317, 327
Willis, Ted   170
Wilson, Angus   99–101, 141
Wilson, Cecil   104
Wilson, Colin   110–13, 138–42, 172
Wilson, Harold   203–4, 243, 250–1, 276,
   297, 301–2, 330
Wilson, Sandy   221
Winchell, Walter   173
Winchester, Bishop of   176
'winter of discontent' (1978–9)   330
Wolfenden Committee   83
Wood, Charles   234, 264, 350
Wood, Nora   402
Woodcock, Patrick   260
Woodham-Smith, Cecil   263
Woolf, Leonard   293
Woolf, Virginia   67, 293
The World of Paul Slickey   162–71, 176, 184,
   203–7, 221
Worsley, T. C.   43–4, 67, 85, 100, 103–5,
   110
Worsthorne, Peregrine   187
Wraight, Robert   104
Wright, Geoffrey,   402
Writers' Guild of Great Britain   348
Wuthering Heights   130
Wycherley, William   100

You Never Can Tell   77
Young, B. A.   291, 402
You're Not Watching Me, Mummy   318
youth culture   83, 110

Zola, Émile   207
Zolotow, Sam   268